1970

y be kept

STUDIES IN HISPANIC AMERICAN AFFAIRS

Edited by

A. CURTIS WILGUS

Volume V

SOUTH AMERICAN DICTATORS

South American Dictators

During the First Century of Independence

EDITED BY

A. CURTIS WILGUS, PH.D.

NEW YORK

RUSSELL & RUSSELL · INC

reissued, 1963, by russell & russell, inc.

by arrangement with george washington university

l. c. catalog card no: 63—8375

(Printed in the United States of America)

PREFACE

THIS is the fifth and final volume in the series of "Studies in Hispanic American Affairs," which the undersigned has had the privilege of editing. Like the previous books, this is a symposium embracing lectures given before the Fifth Seminar Conference on Hispanic American Affairs held during the summer session of 1936 at The George Washington University. Like previous courses of this nature it covers a historical unit of time and space. Editorial effort has been largely confined to achieving some uniformity of presentation, while at the same time maintaining each author's literary style and manner of treatment. As in the past, Mr. Henry William Herzog has been responsible for guiding the book through the press. The editor has been greatly assisted in proof reading by several of the authors and by Dr. Raul d'Eça, who has also compiled the index. To them he is exceedingly grateful.

A. Curtis Wilgus.

TABLE OF CONTENTS

I. INTRODUCTION

CHAPTER ONE

THE HISPANIC AMERICAN DICTATOR

By A. Curtis Wilgus

SHORTLY before taking his own life, President Balmaceda of Chile penned a letter to his good friend José de Uriburu, defending and justifying his actions. One sentence in this pessimistic note is of interest here. Balmaceda wrote: "I have lost all hope that a government that is arbitrary in form will work with justice."[1] An elaboration of this succinct observation would be superfluous. It states a truism that many have come to realize more completely since the lines were written. But axioms in politics are easily forgotten by the people of some countries, while certain individuals in those countries, attempting to establish and maintain dictatorships, find it expedient not to remember them. There is an ill-concealed feeling on the part of many persons and on the part of certain groups of the human family as well, based chiefly on ignorance of past history or upon a superb self-confidence, that conditions of the past will not repeat and that things that have resulted from certain actions will not again result from similar causes. Hence the political cycle completed by dictatorship may be expected to continue in a more or less regular fashion extending from democracy to oligarchy to dictatorship and back again to democracy.

There is a Spanish proverb which in substance says: "The man who at eighteen is not a revolutionist has no heart, while a man who at forty-five is not a conservative has no head." How true to these standards have been many Hispanic Americans. In fact, one can predict with a fair degree of certainty what the political life history of a rising Hispanic American leader will be, barring, of course, acts of God or assassination.

During the past century there has been what might be considered a periodicity in Hispanic American dictatorships, with major peaks about the years 1835, 1850, 1865, 1890, 1910, and 1935. Generally speaking, the earlier dictators were bloody, vicious, brutal, and overbearing, like *Facundo* described by Sarmiento. They were less polished socially and they accomplished their aims with violence. As Francisco García Cal-

[1] For the complete letter see N. A. N. Cleven, *Readings in Hispanic American History* (New York, 1927), 505-506. This letter is dated September 19, 1891, the day of Balmaceda's death.

derón says, they sprang from barbarism and periodic anarchy.[2] But some later dictators have become etiquette conscious and have mixed suavity with their actions and decrees. And while they have been supported by the army, they have with few exceptions attempted to give a semblance of legality to their actions and have by argument persuaded their followers to see the advantages of their rule.[3]

I

The bases on which Hispanic American dictatorship rests are to be found in past history, in racial inheritance, and in the geographical and cultural environments.

The first invaders of the Iberian Peninsula developed a one-man rule which was to become traditional and habitual for centuries.[4] This fact made the various attempts to establish democratic institutions in Spain and Portugal almost impossible and so contrary to history and tradition as to appear exotic. The kingship gained prestige rapidly in the struggle with the Moors and it gradually consolidated its gains within family limits. Because the Reconquest was a religious crusade and because the popes supported the Iberian kings, their prestige was not only increased but recognized. Eventually the king could do no wrong.

On the discovery of America the natives were found to be under the one-man rule of *caciques,* or chiefs, and organized into tribes for social and political reasons. This fact enabled the Spanish Crown rapidly to incorporate the Indan tribes into the Spanish Empire by methods of conquest and persuasion, much in the same way as the political and geographical divisions of the Peninsula had been united for political purposes. Intermarriage between Spaniards and natives, a natural result of the shock of impact of the two races, resulted in furthering this political unity, but at the same time it failed to produce any greater democratic feeling in the offspring of this miscegenation than had existed in either race.

---

[2] Francisco García Calderón, *Latin America: its rise and progress* (New York, 1917), 16. No better book exists in English covering the general topics of Hispanic American dictators and the political make-up of the people of Hispanic America. See also Alcides Arguedas, *Los caudillos bárbaros* (Barcelona, 1929).

[3] For a discussion of Hispanic American dictatorship in general and this point in particular see Charles E. Chapman, "The age of the Caudillos: a chapter in Hispanic American history" in the *Hispanic American Historical Review,* August, 1932, 281-300.

[4] A good discussion of political backgrounds and precedents may be found in the thought-provoking book by Cecil Jane entitled *Liberty and despotism in Spanish America* (Oxford, 1929). Chapters 3 and 4 are especially valuable.

Throughout the colonial era, a period of about ten generations, the king's person, power, and prestige were represented in the colonies by the viceroy, who exercised his functions in so paternalistic a manner as to discourage constructive thinking, individual initiative, and collective coöperation. Thus the one-man tradition of rule was naturally perpetuated in America with little opposition, and even the elements of democracy existing in the municipalities in the sixteenth century disappeared before the overwhelming preponderance of historical factors and traditions.[5] No matter how far back the Hispanic Americans looked, they saw a vast panorama of rulers extending from the Roman Emperors through Germanic Chieftains, Moorish Caliphs, Spanish Kings, Indian Chiefs, and Colonial Viceroys. What worse preparation for democracy could they have had than this; and what excellent precedents were established for the justification of dictatorships!

The blood that flows through Hispanic American veins is as varied as that coursing through the bodies of any group of people on earth. A man's race may not be easily identified, but the traits which he has inherited may give him a variation in character from his fellow men that is traceable in the dim past to one of his numerous progenitors associated with one of the racial groups providing his inheritance. When such a variant occurs he usually stands out from his contemporaries who recognize, if the traits are aggressive, an individual of unusual ability. When such characteristics assume a political nature, that man is *ipso facto* a potential leader. These individual character mutations based upon some racial traits are often sufficient to account for the rise of a dictator in Hispanic America.

In the Hispanic American character itself there are many contradictions which tend to make the masses tolerant of dictators. Blanco Fombona has expressed this clearly:

> "As a people they are essentially democratic and at the same time eminently despotic. . . . They are of indomitable personal independence but as a nation submit to the most personal absolutism. . . . The Spaniard and the Spanish American do not tolerate abuses from servility, but from excess of individualism, through lack of social cohesion, and through failure to exercise their rights."[6]

[5] Dr. E. Gil-Borges has presented a summary discussion of colonial, and especially municipal, democracy in Hispanic America in the chapter entitled "Historcial backgrounds of constitutional organization in Hispanic America" in *The Caribbean area* edited by A. Curtis Wilgus (Washington, 1934), 522-553.

[6] R. Blanco Fombona, *El conquistador español* (Madrid, 1922), 169. For a pertinent discussion of dictatorship and its background see this author's *La evolución política y social de Hispano-América* (Madrid, 1911).

When the popular conditions are propitious there is always a leader to take advantage of opportunities. Gil Fortoul has stated the same idea by saying that in the people of Venezuela—and it is true everywhere in Hispanic America—there is the initiative to govern rather than to follow.[7]

The factor of environment, of course, has been recognized as of great importance in the rise of Hispanic American dictators. Mountains, deserts, plains, and jungles have all played a part in making not only the people of Hispanic America but the states of Hispanic America what they are today. Vast distances, or great elevations, or impassable terrain have tended to isolate peoples and to give them a feeling of self-importance and self-dependence which they might not otherwise have. A remote seat of government authority encourages unrest and sectionalizes a state into individualistic communities which are easily led by local power-aspiring persons. Had it not been for the vast *pampa* of Argentina, Rosas might never have appeared; or had the altitude been lower in Peru and Bolivia, Santa Cruz might never have achieved his political pinnacle; or had the climate been less tropical, Francia might never have played the despot *par excellence* for so many years. Moreover, the prevalence of numerous diseases and the oppressive and steady moist tropical heat make for weak wills, little self-restraint, and lack of ambition on the part of the masses. An individual who can rise above such handicaps contains potential material for the making of a dictator.[8]

II

Perhaps no truer words were ever spoken in fiction than those put into the mouth of Dr. Francia of Paraguay by Edward Lucas White in his incomparable novel entitled *El Supremo*.[9] Francia is made to say that a dictator is "a ruler who endeavors to make his people happy by giving them what he considers good for them, instead of what they want, and then wonders why they are not pleased." No doubt there are as many definitions of the term dictator as there are dictators, for each has his own opinion on the subject of his aims and ideals. Each considers himself a savior of his country and usually speaks of himself as "Protector of the Constitution," "Restorer of the Laws," "Pacificator," and

[7] José Gil Fortoul, *Filosofía constitucional* (Paris, 1890), iii. For further discussion of Spanish American political feelings see chapter 2 in José Vasconcelos and Manuel Gamio, *Aspects of Mexican civilization* (Chicago, 1926).

[8] Cf. J. Fred Rippy, "Dictatorship in Spanish America" in *Dictatorship in the modern world* edited by Guy Stanton Ford (Minneapolis, 1935), chapter 4.

[9] Edward Lucas White, *El supremo* (New York, 1926 edition), 242.

"Liberator"; or he may use any other appellation calculated to lead his people into a blind support of his policies.[10]

Dictators have been first of all individuals and first and last ardent believers in the one-man tradition of control. Hence the concepts of *personalismo, caciquismo,* and *caudillismo* have been introduced into the Hispanic American political parlance. Not only are such men as good as their neighbors, but they are better. There is a Spanish phrase, *Del rey abajo ninguno,* which Professor Chapman renders as "No person below the King is any better than I am."[11] This very individualistic feeling among all Hispanic Americans has been the undoing of many a dictator, for his enemies consider themselves as good as or better than he—and then the political cycle is turned to the next step by revolution.

A dictator may be illiterate or well educated, but often he is instinctive in his actions or reactions, frequently fanatical, usually impressionable, and in many respects unstable in character.[12] García Calderón has said that in character the dictator displays "heroic audacity" and a "perpetual and virile unrest."[13] He rules "by virtue of personal valour and repute. . . ." He resembles the democracies by which he is deified.[14] His religious training gives him no conception of tolerance, and he aims to achieve victory by exterminating his enemies.[15] He is an ardent idealist and any means are justified if his ideal can be attained. Quite often the dictator lacks a sense of humor, for how else can his Quixotic acts be explained? In any case, a dictator is a do-it-now man where, in a land in which *mañana* is the busiest day of the week, he is by contrast with his fellow humans an exceedingly superior individual. Usually a dictator is a hero-worshipper and he has in mind a brilliant example of individual accomplishment on the part of some past leader. Probably he has a Greek or a Roman example before him. But if not a Cæsar or a Themistocles, an Alexander or a Hercules, he may condescend to emulate a Napoleon and rarely a George Washington. In no better place can one study the psychology of conceit than in the thoughts and actions of a Hispanic American dictator.

---

10 See Chapman in article already cited, 294.

11 *Ibid,* 287.

12 Cf. the writer's comments in *Modern Hispanic America* (Washington, 1933), 593.

13 García Calderón, 96.

14 *Ibid,* 99.

15 *Ibid,* 369.

III

But unquestionably the dictators have played preëminent rôles in the progress made by the Hispanic American states. Although they have been "adventurers in politics," as Cecil Jane calls them,[16] they have helped their countries survive great struggles and acute crises just as surely as they have brought to their countries numerous catastrophes and international embarrassments.

Dictators have taken advantage of the political inexperience of their people, and by appealing to their fanatical patriotism they have climbed into office over the dead bodies of their personal enemies. With the use of political trickery and military force, dictators have paved the way for their own rapid collapse. For, with the use of force to enter office, dictators have found that they have to continue the use of force to remain in office. Thus despotism has been inescapable. But too much despotism is a cure for dictatorship, as many peoples have discovered, and the political cycle continues—with a revolution.[17]

In Hispanic America the armies have always been oversupplied with generals and each is likely to be a dictator on a small scale. When once the generals feel themselves slighted or double-crossed by the general whom they and the army have helped into office, they begin to jostle each other for an advantageous position from which one of their number may spring into the presidential chair and push the offending executive into exile. Only the presidency is on a higher plane and affords greater privileges than the position of general, for in this high office a brilliant uniform is mandatory, a dashing charger with brilliant trappings may be ridden through the streets, or in modern times a limousine of the latest pattern (often bulletproof) may be sent dashing about the capital.

Another ego-inflating satisfaction derived from dictatorship is the right to be supported in a fitting fashion by the state. Even the wealthiest of dictators may thus live in a style and ostentation beyond their fondest dreams. For example, the constitution of Paraguay provided certain honorary marks of distinction which appealed to the inordinate self-love of the dictator Francisco Solano López:

> "1. The President of the Republic shall wear the uniform of Captain-General, and underneath the uniform a tricolored ribbon from right to left, from which shall be pendent over his breast a national emblem or jewel of honour, both being at the cost of the Treasury of the Republic.

---

[16] Jane, 5.

[17] See the very thought-provoking volume by Laureano Vallenilla Lanz, *Cesarismo democrático* (Caracas, 1919).

> "2. The jewel of honour shall be a star of gold set in diamonds, in the center of which may be read on one side, 'Executive Power,' and on the other, 'Republic of Paraguay.'
>
> "3. The President of the Republic shall have the attributes and prerogatives of the Captain-General, and be entitled to form a guard of honour for the safety of his person. The guard shall not exceed the number of 75.
>
> "4. He shall have besides, two or three aides-de-camp in waiting in the Palace, who shall perform their duties in turn; as also a warden and such domestic servants as may be required, the salaries of the same to be paid by the National Treasury."[18]

When in office, dictators seldom tinker with the public debt, but they invariably doctor the constitutions into untimely deaths, or amend them into the limbo of impracticable and unworkable ideas. Such activity on the part of dictators indicates a common weakness. Of necessity their governments must have constitutions, for national policies demand them and international opinion requires them, but their predecessors' constitutions are "outgrown," "past history," or "incompatible with the public good"; and besides, to the Hispanic American, change means progress. So new political instruments are necessary to meet new needs, and a "New Deal" is planned by each new dictator. Constitutions in Hispanic America are panaceas and they everywhere give evidence that practical politics in certain quarters hardly exists. Even when a benevolent dictator extends the franchise, he frequently finds that his people prefer bullets to ballots as being much more exciting and often more profitable.

The executive under the constitution, while patterned generally after that of the United States, is in reality only what the dictator conceives his functions to be. And with the delightful constitutional expedient of giving the chief executive the right to suspend constitutional guarantees in times of crisis, the president, whether or not he is a dictator at heart, is sorely tempted to test such a power if only to prove that it works. When once tried this process becomes habit-forming, and the political cycle is soon likely to turn again—by revolution.

Often political parties, like constitutions, are as but clay in the hands of dictators. When a faction places its leader in office the members do so often from personal motives, hoping to get their share of the public treasury. An unusually honest dictator may be repudiated by his followers unless he can deliver to them the right to spend national funds; or if he is unusually dishonest he may be deposed for stealing too much for himself. In any case, a revolution is likely to result sooner or later

[18] *British and Foreign State Papers*, XXXIII (1844-45), 751

within the party, if the enemies of the dictator belonging to the other factions do not combine and stir up a revolution first. Dictatorship and factional jealousies invite and sanction revolution, making it appear a divine right of the people to overthrow anyone not looking after their individual or collective welfare. In some countries, therefore, the system of political factions maintained by the people is only a pseudo-legal means of accomplishing a political end. In such cases politics becomes a fetish.

Most dictators are little concerned with educational improvement, for the illiteracy of the people is a convenient excuse for the establishment and maintenance of a strong government controlled by a will which knows better what the people need than do the people themselves. Generally speaking, the higher the percentage of illiteracy in a country, the greater number of dictators that country is likely to have.

Internal improvements often are concerns of the dictator, for the people can be put to work and their general living conditions can be so improved that they reward the government with their support because of the visible evidence of its activities in their behalf. Moreover, good railroads and highways enable the dictator to move troops rapidly to points of unrest or opposition. Besides, it is to the advantage of the dictator to perpetuate his all-too-fleeting fame in the form of public buildings, bridges, and other edifices which may bear his name in a conspicuous place or record his deeds sealed in corner stones. One of the characteristic weaknesses of a dictator is to show a much too vulgar haste in perpetuating his name in marble, bronze, or brass.

In their dealings with foreign nations dictators are likely to reach the pinnacle of diplomatic absurdities in seeking recognition, not so much of their state as of themselves, so that they may win the much coveted decorations necessary to convince many of their followers of their place in the society of great statesmen. Even the slightest provocation is sufficient for a dictator to display on the front of his uniform or on the bosom of his dress shirt the ribbons, sunbursts, medallions, and crests of numerous awards from abroad. When such foreign recognition is not forthcoming, a convenient substitute is to be found in the erection of monuments or statues or in the naming of streets, cities, theaters, and babies after the gracious benefactor of the country. Dictators are much like small boys who have never grown up.

But the crowning crime of dictators is, too frequently, corruption. There are too many demands from insistent henchmen for the dictator to resist his friends. And since his enemies accuse him anyway of the peculation of public funds, it benefits him nothing to be honest. How often have Hispanic American governments been overthrown for the simple reason that an irresponsible individual wished to get his fists into the public treasury! And in some cases the fist was immediately withdrawn and the booty taken abroad. Most prodigal dictators have expressed a secret desire to die in Paris. And why not, for this is much preferable to dying before a bullet-pocked wall or in a dungeon of one's own creation!

One example may suffice to indicate how vividly the enemies of a dictator may describe him. Of Christophe in Haiti it was said that his person was a rude, indigested mass of matter; his laugh, the grimace of a tiger; and when he opened his mouth in rage it extended from ear to ear, disclosing a double row of long, pointed, cannibal teeth.

> "He was without honor, without faith, without law and without religion—in obscenities surpassing all the sacrilegious and filthy horrors with which Sardanapalus and Nebuchadnezzar were formerly reproached—a slave to his passions, an enemy of justice, cruel, arbitrary, avaricious, proud, selfish, blood-thirsty, incapable of the least sentiment of gratitude. Such, and much more so, is the fallen Henry described by those who have succeeded to his power, and who say that to give a detail of his vices would require volumes, and that no language could furnish expressions sufficiently strong to give an adequate idea of the excesses of his barbarity or of the horror it ought to inspire in the human heart."[19]

But though much evil has been said of Hispanic American dictators in particular and of all in general, some good may be said of each one. No blanket condemnation is entirely justifiable. Among the general run of dictators are men with some rare ability which sets their personalities at a tangent from the average type. Francia benefited the Paraguayan masses, Díaz for a brief period made Mexico in the eyes of Europeans greater than the United States, while Gómez freed Venezuela from international debt and developed the national resources to the highest point in history. But even successful dictators such as these have made innumerable enemies for themselves and eventual strife for their countries. Today dictatorship still remains in Hispanic America, and no man can say to what depths it may yet go, or what heights it may yet attain in the development of national interest.

---

[19] The *New York Advertiser,* February 5, 1821.

CHAPTER TWO

MONARCHY OR REPUBLIC?

By J. Fred Rippy

I

IN 1782, as the end of the war for independence in English America drew near, a number of Washington's military subordinates suggested that he should become a king, but he sternly refused to consider the proposal. The idea of establishing a monarchy seems to have been considered again during the Philadelphia Convention of 1787, the second son of George III and Prince Henry of Prussia being suggested as possible candidates. Not only do the records of that convention reveal frank expressions of sentiment in favor of a limited monarchy as the best form of government, but approximately a third of its delegates are said to have been in favor of a king for the United States. It is not likely, however, that this notion was seriously entertained. Provision was made instead for a president with ample powers; and the thirteen former colonies of England moved steadily and almost unhesitatingly toward a democratic republic.[1]

The liberated colonies of Spain, on the contrary, acted with less steadiness and assurance. There was much doubt, hesitation, and vacillation among the leaders of this region before the final decision was made in favor of a political system based, in theory at least, upon the principles of freedom and popular rule. If they had followed the signposts of custom and tradition, as well as the apparent trend of the age, it is probable that they would have established monarchical and not republican institutions.

At the dawn of last century the trend of the Occidental World hardly appeared to be toward democracy. In 1816, just as the Spanish American movement for independence was passing the futile stage and entering the period of substantial achievement, the Western World contained only one republic, and that republic was not in Europe. It was in America.[2]

---

[1] Louis Martin Sears, *George Washington* (New York, 1932), 331-332; Bernard Fäy, *George Washington, republican aristocrat* (New York, 1931), 217-220; Max Farrand, *The framing of the constitution* (New Haven, 1913), 77, 88, 162, 173-174.

[2] In Europe there was the Swiss Confederation, but it was suffering from serious internal disorders as well as because of pressure by France and the Holy Alliance.

In Europe a reaction had swept away the institutions set up by men inspired by the English philosophers of the seventeenth century and the French philosophers of the eighteenth. Absolute monarchs sat upon their thrones almost everywhere save in England, where the king's power was limited by a parliament by no means democratic. Spain, the mother of practically all of the nations of southern America, had known, with the exception of one brief period (1812-1814), no other type of government than absolutism since the days of Ferdinand and the Hapsburgs; and Portugal, the mother of Brazil, had been governed for more than three centuries by autocratic rulers.

Even in America the generous appreciation of the philosophers for the innate wisdom and goodness of the common people had been rejected in part in the Philadelphia Constitution and in the various fundamental charters of the states. Jefferson and his followers had led a protest in 1800—a protest which had not greatly expanded the basis of political power; but while the Virginia dynasty, aided by a few men of democratic convictions in the several states, were carrying out modest Jeffersonian reforms, John Marshall was erecting the Supreme Court into a bulwark against the common mass. The people would be given not precisely what they desired, but what elderly gentlemen of the bench considered it proper and expedient to give them.

All the exuberant faith of the English and French philosophers in the plain people had gone no farther! Not even the leaders of their first-born republic would fully trust the masses! If the people were white and had sufficient property, they might choose their executives and legislators, the most exalted of these indirectly; but these agents of the populace would be held in check by the Supreme Court. Congressmen in caucus would choose the presidential candidates; state legislatures composed of men of property would select the senators and the governors; and aged savants in judicial robes would restrain them all.

It was evident that many political leaders in the United States did not fully trust the masses. Hamilton thought the people were "a great beast"; John Adams panted for an aristocracy; even Jefferson confided only in the wisdom of small farmers of the Caucasian race, distrusting the urban proletariat of Europe and doubting the political capacity of the mixed and primitive population of Spain's former colonies.

It was into such a world that the nations of Hispanic America were born. The climate of opinion was apparently not favorable to democratic republics when the leaders of a dozen new nations to the south confronted the problem of ascertaining the proper form of government for their constituencies. Their attitude and immediate course was determined by the political literature which they read, by their estimate of the political capacity of the people of Hispanic America, by what they supposed these people would demand, and in part no doubt by the prospect of maintaining special privileges for themselves.

Once freed from the intellectual fetters of the colonial period, their minds became active and politico-centric. Some of them at least were not unacquainted with the political thought and practices of ancient Greece, but they appear to have taken few lessons from the Greeks. Some of them were not without knowledge of the history of Rome, but they were to be impressed mainly by its censors, triumvirs, consuls, and dictators. In the main, they concentrated their attention upon the men who had supplied the dynamic ideas of their heroic struggle for independence; upon the French Encyclopedists, Thomas Jefferson, Thomas Paine, and the framers of the Philadelphia Constitution.

The advice which they received from these authoritative sources was not unreservedly and unanimously in favor of the democratic republic. The Founding Fathers of the United States rejected monarchy, but were divided, as already observed, with reference to the political capacity and reliability of average men. The French *philosophes,* while insisting on liberty, natural rights, equality before the law, and the ultimate sovereignty of the people, were not all flaming evangels of democracy. Montesquieu even idealized the British form of government.

If advice from this source gave rise to doubts, careful observation of their constituency caused further perplexity. The nations with whose political destiny they were so deeply concerned were inhabited for the most part by mixed and primitive peoples with traditions of paternalism, oppression, and servilism, and with no experience in freedom and self-government. They lacked homogeneity in race, culture, and ideals. Some forty-five per cent of the people of Spanish America were pure Indians, thirty-one per cent were *mestizos,* perhaps less than nineteen per cent were whites, and the rest negroes and mulattoes. In Brazil the negroes and mulattoes outnumbered the whites three to one, and there were several hundred thousand *mestiços* and Indians besides, although the problem of government was rendered temporarily less difficult by the fact that most of the Africans and mulattoes were slaves. Everywhere the primitive and mixed inhabitants were largely untutored, and many of the whites themselves were illiterate. Moreover, the long and bloody struggle for independence had left the people impoverished and turbulent. The Spanish yoke had been cast off, but the constructive elements required for a democratic régime were almost totally lacking.

One is not surprised, therefore, to find among the leaders of these incipient nations a sharp division of opinion with reference to the kind of political institutions that should be established. In all of the leading centers of population there were civilian political theorists who were advocates of monarchies as well as republics. It is probable that most men of wealth and social position dreaded the social and economic consequences of placing political power in the hands of the plebeians, and were, therefore, monarchists. The outstanding warriors, with the possible exception of José Artigas, Francisco de Paula Santander, and Simón Bolívar (during his early career), were opposed to republics, at least to democratic republics. José de San Martín, Manuel Belgrano, Marcelo T. Alvear, Agustín Iturbide, Rafael Urdaneta, and many others were frankly in favor of monarchs. Bolívar later advocated life senators and presidents; José Antonio Sucre accepted in part the conservative ideas of his great chief; Iturbide grasped the imperial scepter; Bernardo O'Higgins became the autocrat of Chile; José Antono Páez offered Bolívar a crown; the negroes of Haiti became kings and emperors.[3]

However, all monarchial plans eventually failed to be realized in Spanish America; the royalties of Europe and the monarchists of America had difficulty in reaching an agreement, the United States was opposed to American kings, the princes were difficult to find, and the people were not disposed to tolerate them. The emperors of Haiti were soon assassinated or deposed; Iturbide was driven from Mexico in 1823; and the ephemeral Maximilian was shot by the Mexicans in 1867. Moreover, Portuguese Brazil, with its republican sentiment before 1800 and its republican uprising in 1817, finally unseated its monarch in 1889. All Hispanic America was destined to be a land of ostensible democratic republics and of actual anarchy alternating with dictatorships. Plato had predicted centuries before that democracies composed of masses of inexperienced and unenlightened men would end in tyranny.

II

In this vast region there has been an almost perpetual and complete contradiction between practice and theory, between the actual and nominal systems of government. On the one hand their constitutional con-

[3] For the political views of the period, see Carlos A. Villanueva, *La monarquía en América* (4 vols., Paris, no date), and Bernard Moses, *The intellectual background of the revolution in South America* (New York, 1926).

ventions have everywhere declared that the foundations of state organization should be those conceptions of individual and collective freedom which inspired the political theorists of the French Revolution or received practical recognition and application in England and the United States. The doctrine of popular sovereignty has been explicitly proclaimed; the right of the citizens to change their form of government at any time that has suited them has been expressly admitted. The constitutions have contained practically all of those guaranties which customarily have been accorded to the members of a democratic state: freedom of speech, freedom of the press, freedom of association for all legitimate purposes, freedom to move from place to place at will and to engage in any lawful occupation, equality before the law, the right to a speedy trial, and even a large amount of religious toleration. Everywhere, in brief, the most complete liberty compatible with social security and the continued existence of the state has been assured, so far as this result could be attained through the medium of written constitutions. On the other hand a very different régime has existed in actual practice. Chief executives have frequently invoked the emergency clause, contained in all, or nearly all, of the constitutions, permitting the head of the state to assume discretionary powers in times of crisis, while they have disregarded the provision which limited the use of such powers strictly to the duration of the crisis. And with equal frequency individuals have openly seized the government and ruled with despotic authority in patent disregard of fundamental charters. Every nation to the south of the United States has had such rulers, including even the young republics of Brazil, Cuba, and Panama. Dictators have been so numerous that the history of most of these countries is to a large extent the biography of these imperious personalities. For a time it appeared that some of the states had passed through the Caudillo Age into an epoch of orderly democracy; but more recently the trend has been reversed. Autocrats now hold sway in the majority of the nations south of the Río Grande.

It is likely that this trend of events may be explained by physical setting, colonial heritage, and racial composition, which are alike unfavorable to the proper functioning of democracy. Most of the region is characterized by lofty mountains and tropical jungle, and the centers of population, native as well as Spanish, were, and are, located mainly in the highlands of the interior or in coastal areas made comfortable by the cooling breezes. The settlements were, therefore, widely scattered and, owing to Spain's failure to build good roads or to establish an adequate system of fluvial and coastal transportation, were so difficult to reach from the seat of government that insurgency could not be suppressed in its incipient stages. The privileged groups—the clergy, the planters, and the owners of the mines—who wished to preserve their favorable status by establishing a monarchy now refused to submit themselves to the leveling processes of democracy. Racial animosities existed; the various ethnic groups did not understand one another; there was no community of ideals or interests. The untutored inhabitants lacked habits of self-restraint and self-direction. The whites and mixbloods had been accustomed to the absolutism of viceroys, captains-general, and governors; the Indians had been subjected indirectly to these Spanish officials and directly to their own chiefs, who had been allowed to survive as instruments of social control, or to the local Spanish administrators and clergy. Participation of the colonials in government had been confined largely to the whites and almost exclusively to the town councils; and the activities which centered around these councils tended to exaggerate local loyalties.

The long and expensive struggle for independence did not tend to promote democracy and freedom. Spaniards born and reared in the Peninsula, the men who constituted almost the only group with any experience in government, were expelled, and the shackles of militarism were riveted upon the people. The generals refused to accept the obscurity of private life under civilian rule; the common soldiers, accustomed to plunder and adventure, were loath to exchange the camp for the field and the shop; the illiterate masses could not resist the appeal of the brilliant uniform and the seductive slogans of the mounted adventurer. Individualism, always strong among the Spaniards and the Indian chiefs, experienced a renaissance at a period when treasuries were empty and administrative ability extremely scarce.

In short, the new nations confronted a domestic crisis.

> "It was the crisis of anarchy, the anarchy of atomic, imperious wills operating in a medium where the strong man was admired for his virility and liberty worshipped as a fetish. In brief hours of ecstasy fledgling political philosophers had written into virgin constitutions all the idealism of their time, but it was as if they had attached wings to lead."

The very perfection of these documents caused their violation and thus called for new struggles and new fundamental charters; for ambitious militarists or aspiring reformers could point to the yawning chasm between the utopias described and the exasperating realities which were plainly evident around them.

> "The constitutions served as a mighty stimulus to individualism, but they were without power to impose restraints. They urged loyalty to the nation, but the constituency knew only loyalty to a locality or a leader. They held up the ideal of the general welfare as the goal of the state, but this ideal was too impersonal for simple men accustomed to following headstrong individuals. To such men, and to their chiefs as well, the government was not an instrument to be employed for the benefit of the whole nation, but rather a trophy to be captured and used in the interest of the leader and his followers. The fundamental laws offered the ballot as a means of selecting statesmen and determining policies, but why should mere pieces of paper be endowed with such virtue and power . . . ? Government by the counting of ballots at the polls and in legislative assemblies appeared inane and absurd. It was far more heroic to hew one's way to power by saber and *machete* and to determine policies with the musket and the pistol. . . .
>
> "In addition to domestic crisis, the new nations were exposed from time to time to external danger—the menace of foreign invasion and conquest. A score of boundaries were unmarked and uncertain; no definite and reliable agreements designated the number of nations that should be set up in the late Spanish Empire; ambitious leaders threatened almost constantly to extend their dominions at the expense of their neighbors or to impose their political programmes on other countries at the point of the sword; and the United States as well as European nations sometimes threatened the security and integrity of the infant states."[4]

Whatever their origin, crises tend to produce strong governments, and in democracies they often produce dictators. In Spanish America, at any rate, this is what occurred. The restraints of custom, conscience, and a community of ideals were not sufficient to preserve order. Coercion by the armed force of the supreme *caudillo* often appeared to be the only bulwark against anarchy or the only method of achieving social change. And yet it must be admitted that the soaring ambition and intense selfishness of the leaders often drove them to exaggerate the crisis in order to justify their appearance as men of the hour or their retention of the reins of government.

Whether sincere or deliberately deceptive, the documents of the period always employed expressions suggesting a crisis: liberator, restorer, regenerator, vindicator, deliverer, savior of the country, and so on.

---

[4] J. Fred Rippy, in *Dictatorship in the modern world* (Minneapolis, 1935), edited by Guy Stanton Ford, 55-57.

Somebody was constantly having to "save" these countries, although it was not always clear from what calamity they were to be rescued or what benefits their alleged salvation brought. The language of the time was the language of messianic hope and hyperbole.

III

The national history of Hispanic America is filled with stark tragedy: poverty, suffering, repression, corruption, sycophancy, nostalgic exile, torture, assassination, and death on the field of battle. Yet the historian will hardly censure the leaders of the area for choosing the democratic republic. For, aside from the fact that monarchies would have been most difficult to establish and maintain, it may be doubted whether they would have been better for the majority of the people of these countries than turbulent republics characterized by the alternation of revolutionary chaos and strong men on horseback. The monarchical régime would have meant a hierarchy of churchmen, landlords, mine owners, and wealthy merchants, with a following of lawyers, physicians, army officers, and the like. It probably would not have resulted in appreciable benefits for the people, and it is likely that such a system would have closed the doors of opportunity to many a talented son of the masses.

Waldo Frank, in a half fanciful description of the famous interview between Bolívar and San Martín at Guayaquil, Ecuador, in 1822, presents the situation in all of its tragic relief.

> *San Martín:* "Ideals can be dangerous. . . . An ideal form of government cannot be successfully willed upon a people. . . .
>
> "Yes, the republic is the ideal form. . . . It rises organically from the will of a close-knit, tranquil nation. Its technique of action is the peaceful creating and spreading of public opinion by a ruling class in accord with all other classes. A common language, a common religion, economic mutuality, literacy, accessibility of [all its territory], the sense of common enterprise, and a strong middle class in control of the economic life and in contact with the masses—are the prerequisites of the republic. Some of the cities of Greece possessed them, the homogeneous United States of North America possesses them. . . . We have none of them. Absolutely none."
>
> *Bolívar:* "I know it."
>
> *San Martín:* "Of course you know it. . . . Our countries are vast wildernesses, it takes weeks and months to traverse them. In some parts live Indians with their own deep-rooted cultures, in other parts live creoles, [in others, negroes, mulattoes, and *mestizos*]. There are no possible means of communication between

these alien cultures; there is no common enterprise to communicate. Our ruling group is not a middle class, it is feudal. It has recognized only two loyalties in the past, a Court and a Church. It cannot suddenly change its nature. Only a Court, founded on the common Catholic religion, can bind this ruling class together and keep it in its place and serve to spread loyalty and control throughout the masses."

Bolívar: "Why have we freed America?"

San Martín: "Surely not to plunge it into chaos! A liberal monarchy under the support of the ruling classes would bring order, dispel personal ambitions, preserve the hierarchies, encourage economic growth and the arts. . . . I propose monarchies, liberal and constitutional, fashioned after that of England, with North American laws."

Bolívar: "We are not North America, we are not England. Monarchy in our nations, as you have said, would be feudal. It would rely on a feudal caste, it would make feudal serfs of the Indian and the Negro. It would change nothing. American kings instead of a Spaniard—is that what we have fought for?"

San Martín: "Then you have fought for chaos?"

Bolívar: "Yes. Have it so. I have fought, perhaps, for chaos."

San Martín: "The name of a king frightens you, though it bring order. The name of a republic soothes you, though it bring anarchy."

Bolívar: "There is much in a name. A name is an ideal. A name calls our vision close; and, as we repeat it, holds it ever present. All growth is in a name, all that is human. . . ."

San Martín: "Chaos and anarchy—these will be the facts you so splendidly name republics."

Bolívar: "The name will outlast the anarchy and chaos. The reality of the name (being the true will of the people) will rise from the disorder. . . . The *form* of the republic alone is possible for us. But this form will be the threshold to a human freedom and a human potentiality which no republic as yet has ever dared approach. You are wrong, General. The name of the republic does not soothe me, it frightens me. I know our America, and love it. I see the nameless things—bloodshed, tyranny, treason—which the name of the republic will call out from the depths. The nameless things! We must go through this dread passage to find our future. The republic is only the opening door. Do you not see? What we go toward, through the republic, is also nameless—it is unborn America."

San Martín: "I see, General, our duty as guardians of an infant people."

Bolívar: "Let them be infants! Could the child mature, if he were prevented from living the child's life, and if he were not made constantly aware that his heritage is manhood? A people under a monarchy may be well nursed—and perpetually condemned to childhood. . . .

"We shall not see, nor the generation after us, the America we are founding. This world we are in is not even a child, it is a chrysalis. There will be a metamorphosis of the *physical* life; there will come finally a recasting of all the races, which will result in the unity of the people. . . .

"Such a metamorphosis must be preceded by transition. And transition is agony. Perhaps a hundred years of chaos are before us. We shall go down in it, my friend; have no doubt of that. The monarchic order you would impose might save us. It might protect America from chaos—the chaos of birth."[5]

The two great soldiers separated forever. San Martín soon left for Europe, lonely exile, and death in a foreign land. Bolívar finished the work of liberation and then undertook the task of governing the turbulent people whom he had freed from the Spanish yoke. He confronted the most difficult problem of his life. He had embarked upon a stormy sea, and he could not turn back. Perhaps he did not wish to turn back. Let us follow him in his labors and his agony.

---

[5] Waldo Frank, *America Hispana* (New York, 1931), 297ff. No one seems to know exactly what occurred at the Guayaquil interview. The political philosophy which Frank represents Bolívar as expressing was evidently suggested to Frank by Tomás de Mosquera's report of the interview, but there is some doubt regarding Mosquera's presence during the conference between the two great military leaders. See Vicente Lecuna, *Cartas del Libertador* (10 vols., Caracas, 1929), III, 58-63; Villanueva, I, 235-251; C. Parra-Pérez, *Bolívar* (Paris, 1928), 113-115; J. M. Goenaga, *La entravista de Guayaquil* (Rome, 1915). San Martín may not have been as liberal a monarchist as Frank represents him to be.

CHAPTER THREE

THE ANGUISH OF BOLÍVAR

By J. Fred Rippy

I

FOR fifteen years Simón Bolívar stood out supreme in northern South America. His career possesses the irresistible attraction of a romance. Born (1783) rich, he died (1830) poor, having spent his fortune in the struggle for South American independence. Of pure Spanish blood and noble descent, at the age of three he was left an orphan in care of his uncle. Among his teachers were an errant philosopher, Simón Rodríguez, and a poet named Andrés Bello. He was not yet sixteen when sent abroad to complete his education in Europe. He visited Mexico and Cuba on his way to France and Spain. In Madrid he associated with the nobility and saw the corruption of the Spanish Court. Before the end of 1802 he fell deeply in love and married. He returned to his vast Venezuelan estates to settle down; but in less than a year an epidemic carried away his wife, and he returned to the Continent in an attempt to assuage his grief. In Paris he witnessed the brilliant coronation of Napoleon I. He also met his old, austere teacher, Rodríguez, and confessed to him his patriotic yearnings. A new Hannibal now, on the Sacred Mountain in Rome he took an oath to redeem his oppressed America. He returned to Venezuela again in 1807, stopping on the way long enough to visit the battlefields of the United States. Shortly afterward he joined the revolutionary movement in northern South America. Within three years he was its recognized leader. He marched with marvelous speed across tropical jungles and snow-clad mountains, thrilling men by his eloquence, organizing military campaigns and governments, drafting plans of operation and constitutions, creating nations. Difficulties intensified his will; defeat rendered him more terrible than victory. By 1819 the tide had definitely turned in his favor. By 1825 the royalist armies had been driven out of the vast area which stretched from the Orinoco to Lake Titicaca and beyond, a region embracing two million square miles and containing a population of more than five million. Always the grand cavalier, he freed a thousand slaves by the stroke of his pen, renounced pensions, thought of committing suicide because of his poverty, refused to accept a crown.[1]

In Spanish America he was the wisest and most versatile man of his time. He possessed an ardent and soaring imagination, and was both an industrious reader and a profound thinker. He read history diligently and discussed literature with the poets. He knew the Greek and Latin classics, Condillac and Buffon, Mably and Montesquieu, Locke and all the Encyclopedists.[2] He had a clear conception of his environment and his epoch, and predicted the future of Spanish America so accurately that its future appears to have obeyed his encantation. Yet he became predominantly a man of action at the early age of twenty-seven, and most of his political ideas were expressed while he was in motion or in the midst of anarchy.

During the long war of liberation dictatorial powers were repeatedly conferred upon him by such civil authorities as existed. Except for brief periods of enforced exile in the West Indies, there was hardly a day between 1814 and 1825 when he did not possess full discretionary authority within the sphere of his military operations. Such authority, considered necessary for the effective conduct of hostilities against the Spaniards, inculcated in him habits of absolute command; but during this period he showed great respect for the civil authorities, or seemed to do so at least.

He was always deeply concerned with political institutions, and this problem became for him a primary and fundamental consideration as the struggle for independence terminated. Although his political ideas may be found in numerous letters and proclamations,[3] most of them

---

[1] It would be pedantic to cite the many biographies of Bolívar. The best in the English language are: F. Loraine Petre, *Simón Bolívar, "The Liberator"* (New York and London, 1910); Hildegarde Angell, *Simón Bolívar, South American liberator* (New York, 1930); T. R. Ybarra, *Bolívar, the passionate warrior* (New York, 1929).

[2] On Bolívar's reading, see Lecuna, *Cartas*, IV, 338, VII, 155-156.

[3] One of the earliest formal expressions of Bolívar's political ideas is contained in his "Memorial to the Citizens of New Granada," written from Cartagena on December 15, 1812. In this document he attributes the recent failure of the independence movement in Venezuela to Utopian liberalism, federalism, and the political incapacity of the Venezuelans. "We had philosophers for governors," he said, "philanthrophy for legislation, dialectics for tactics, and sophists for soldiers." The theorists were loath to apply restraints and coercion. Every province and every village must govern itself; and the state should not take a man's life even for the crime of high treason. Each conspiracy was followed by a pardon, which was followed by another conspiracy and another pardon. The result was division, dissension, and anarchy, followed by resubjugation by Spain. The Venezuelans lacked the virtues required to operate such a system of government, for these

are contained in his famous Letter from Jamaica, in his Discourse at Angostura, in the constitution which he drew up for Bolivia, and in his message recommending this document to the constitutional convention of that new state.

II

The political ideas set forth in his letter of September 6, 1815, written while he was in exile in Jamaica, are brilliant and significant. "The position of the inhabitants of the American hemisphere," he said, "has been for centuries purely passive: their political existence was null. We were on a plane still lower than that of servitude, and for that reason it will be all the more difficult to raise ourselves to the level where we may enjoy liberty." America was not only deprived of its liberty, he continued, but it was also deprived of the privilege of actively participating in the tyranny which dominated it. The Americans were in worse condition than the subjects of the despotism of Persia, Turkey, and China, because the subjects of these countries were oppressed by their own rulers, who were the agents of the despots, while the residents of his America were oppressed by satraps sent over from Spain. They were reduced to the status of mere laborers and consumers. They were people abstracted, "absent from the universe in all that related to the science of government and the administration of the state." They were seldom permitted to be viceroys, governors, archbishops, or bishops; they were never allowed to be diplomats; and they took part in military affairs only as subordinates.

The Spanish Americans had, therefore, arisen suddenly from their low status, "without previous training; and, what is worse, without practice in public affairs, to represent on the world's stage the lofty dignities of legislators, magistrates, fiscal administrators, diplomats, generals, and all the other supreme and subordinate authorities which form the hierarchy of a regularly organized state." And recent events in Venezuela and New Granada had demonstrated that "perfectly representative institutions" were not adapted to the character, customs, and enlightenment

virtues were not acquired under an absolute monarchy where the rights and duties of citizens were unknown. In particular were the people of Venezuela incapable of a prudent and orderly exercise of the right of suffrage. The "rustics of the field" were so ignorant that they voted mechanically; the "intriguing inhabitants of the cities" were so ambitious and passionate that they converted everything into faction and tumult. A free and fair election was never seen, and the government was placed in the hands of "disloyal, inept, or immoral men." This failure of the electoral function, this violently partisan spirit, disorganized and disrupted the state. "Our division and not the arms of Spain returned us to slavery." (Lecuna, *Cartas,* I, 35-41.)

of the people. In both countries democratic societies and assemblies, popular elections, a passionate partisan spirit, and extreme federalism had frustrated the independence movements and returned the inhabitants to slavery. "Until our compatriots acquire the political talents and virtues which distinguish our brothers of the North, entirely popular systems, far from being beneficial, will, I very much fear, come to be our ruin."

Montesquieu had said that it was more difficult to deliver a people from servitude than to subjugate a free people, and the history of all times had proved the truthfulness of the assertion. Yet the people of South America, moved by a blind instinct which causes all men to seek the greatest possible happiness, had manifested a desire to secure liberal and even perfect institutions. Mankind's maximum happiness would certainly be attained in societies established upon the foundations of justice, freedom, and equality; but "are we capable of maintaining in its true equilibrium the difficult burden of a republic? Is it conceivable that a people but recently freed from its chains can ascend into the sphere of liberty without melting its wings like Icarus and plunging into the abyss? Such a marvel is inconceivable; it has never been seen."

Would it be advisable, then, to set up monarchies? Such a system would neither be useful nor possible. Kings would be interested in augmenting their wealth, possessions, and power, and the pursuit of these ends would lead to wars of conquest. Existing abuses would not be reformed and the regeneration of Spanish America would be indefinitely postponed. The people preferred peace and the opportunity to develop commerce, agriculture, and the sciences and arts. They desired republics rather than kingdoms. Perhaps some system might be found which would represent a compromise between the two. "The states of America need the kindly guardianship of paternal governments which will cure the sores and wounds of despotism and war." They should avoid the anarchy of demagogues on the one hand and the tyranny of monocrats on the other.[4]

III

Such in substance were the political ideas expressed by Bolívar in 1815. Less than four years later, when a constituent assembly met at Angostura to frame a fundamental charter for Venezuela, he announced his views in greater detail.

[4] Lecuna, *Cartas,* I, 181-205.

He began by an examination of the character of the people and their heritage from Spain. The people of his America were neither Indians nor Europeans. Indeed it was difficult to determine the family to which they belonged. The European element had mixed with the American and with the African, and the latter had mixed with the Indian and the European. Moreover, none of the groups had any knowledge of or experience in government. Bound by the triple yoke of ignorance, tyranny, and vice, these inhabitants had been unable to acquire either wisdom or virtue or power. "Slavery is the child of darkness; an ignorant people is the blind instrument of its own destruction." Intrigue and ambition would take advantage of credulity and lack of experience. The masses would mistake illusions for realities: "license for liberty, treachery for patriotism, vengeance for justice." It would be difficult to persuade them that happiness consists in the practice of virtue, that they must obey the law, that the exercise of justice is the exercise of liberty. Rousseau had said that liberty was a nourishing food, but that it was difficult to digest; and the weak citizens of Spanish America would have to add much strength to their spirit before they would be able to digest the salutary nourishment of freedom.

Only democracy, in his concept, was capable of furnishing absolute liberty. But what democratic government had been able to attain at the same time not only power and prosperity, but permanence as well? Had not all republics been ephemeral, and were not all the great and enduring states of history monarchies and aristocracies?

Venezuela had already declared itself a republic, proscribed kings and all the titles, distinctions, and special privileges that accompanied the royal system, and pronounced itself in favor of the rights of man and freedom to work, think, speak, and write. He admired the noble aspirations which prompted this course; but he was compelled to confess that Venezuela's federal constitution was entirely impracticable. It was true that such a system was in operation in the United States; but the people of North America were unique in their political virtues and moral enlightenment, and the survival of even that nation under such a system was nothing less than a miracle. The Spanish Americans and the English Americans were not even remotely similar, and this model should not be followed in Venezuela. Had not Montesquieu said that all laws should be adapted to the people for whom they were made?

Bolívar urged the members of the convention to be modest in their aspirations. Unbridled liberty and absolute democracy were the reefs upon which all republican hopes had been shattered. Social perfection and perfect systems of government were noble ideals, but the legislators were dealing with men and not angels. A steady nerve and a firm hand would be necessary to prevent this heterogeneous multitude of diverse racial origins and culture from plunging into anarchy. The executive power should be made very strong, and the senators should serve for life. The citizens should be divided into two groups, the active and the passive. Qualifications for active participation in government should be carefully weighed. Elections should not consist in the assemblage of mobs of turbulent, blind, and blundering people. Voting should be safeguarded. The liberties of the nation would depend upon the wise exercise of this important function.

Moreover, Bolívar suggested that a fourth power be added to the legislative, the executive, and the judicial. After carefully considering the methods of effectively regenerating a people debased by tyranny, he proposed a Moral Power which he found described in the laws designed to maintain virtue among the Greeks and Romans, and recovered from the obscure depths of antiquity. "Let us take from Athens its Areopagus," he exhorted, "let us take from Rome its censors and domestic tribunals; and making a holy alliance of these moral institutions, let us revive in the world the idea of a people which is not content with being free and strong, but which desires to be virtuous as well. Let us take from Sparta its austere establishments, and having formed of these three streams a fountain of virtue, let us give to our republic a fourth power." The Areopagus would have dominion over the education of the children and the youth, over the heart of the adults, over customs, public spirit, and republican morality. It would have its books of virtue and vice, in which would be registered its proceedings, its lists of moral principles, its judgments passed on the acts of citizens and officials under its jurisdiction. This Moral Power was fully described in the draft constitution which he submitted to the assembly.[5]

Although this phase of his plan was rejected, the legislators in general followed Bolívar's advice. But the constitution was framed for a nation not yet free from Spanish bondage, and was never put into operation. Two years later another fundamental law was drawn up for New Granada and Ecuador as well as Venezuela. On that occasion the Liberator was too busy with military operations to exert any direct influence on the deliberations of the assembly. A few years afterward he was to complain of the defects of this constitution; but for the moment he made

[5] The Discourse and the Constitution of Angostura may be found in José Gil Fortoul, *Historia constitucional de Venezuela* (3 vols., Caracas, 1930), II, 480-550.

no comment. Elected president under the régime which it provided, he took the oath of office and soon departed with full discretionary powers for Ecuador, leaving Santander in charge as vice-president at Bogotá. These extraordinary powers were confined to the field of military operations, and were conferred in accordance with a provision in the new constitution itself (Art. 128).

IV

Five years afterward, having driven the last of the royalists from a region two-thirds as large as present-day United States, he was called upon for advice in providing a constitution for Bolivia. The response which he made on May 25, 1826, shows that his fundamental conceptions regarding political institutions had not changed. He attempted to draft a model constitution for all of northern South America, perhaps even for all Spanish America. For almost three years he had been dictator of Peru.

The constitution which he proposed was quite conservative. Designed as a compromise between a monarchy and a republic, the government which it provided was virtually a monarchy in disguise. The government was vested in executive, legislative, judicial, and "electoral" powers. The chief executive bore the title of president, but his term was for life and he was to choose the vice-president. The legislature was composed of three houses: tribunes, senators, and censors, with the latter likewise serving for life. In fact the censors were another version of his Areopagus of 1819. They were to supervise education, the press, and the conduct of public officials; and they were to promote the arts, the sciences, and public morality. Officials subject to election were few, and the power of the electorate was limited. A literacy test was required for voting.

The message which accompanied his draft constitution revealed clearly his distrust of the people. He remarked that tyranny and anarchy formed an immense ocean of oppression which surrounded a small island of liberty perpetually lashed by furious waves and hurricanes. He said that elections were the great scourge of republics, since they tended to produce anarchy, the most immediate and most terrible danger of popular governments. Yet the personal guarantees which he provided were fairly ample, religious liberty being included among them.

Forseeing that his constitution might arouse apprehension among the democrats, he sought to reassure them by pointing out that the powers of the president were greatly curtailed. In this connection he also remarked that Spanish America contained neither great wealth nor powerful ecclesiastics, nor an ambitious clergy, nor great nobles. Without these supports tyrants could not be permanent, and any who aspired to become kings or emperors would be deterred by the fate of Dessalines, Christophe, and Iturbide. No power was more difficult to maintain than that of a new prince; the fall of Napoleon I was convincing evidence of that fact. Men need have no fear that monarchs would be established in America. Thrones would turn out to be royal scaffolds; crowns would be but so many Swords of Damocles suspended above their heads. Already it was evident that the Liberator was giving considerable thought to the question of monarchy.[6]

His grand plan for the political future of Spanish America was now taking full shape. He wished to consolidate Bolivia, Peru, Ecuador, New Granada, and Venezuela into one vast state under his conservative constitution. This large entity would then become the dominant unit in a sort of league of Spanish American nations, and the whole area would be given stability and prestige under the patronage of Great Britain. The congress soon to assemble at Panama was designed to form the new league. Perhaps he might become the life president of the states of northern South America.

V

Whether the Liberator exaggerated the dangers which threatened Spanish America is a question difficult to answer. There could have been only two motives for exaggeration: a desire to frighten the people into the adoption of stronger governments, or an eagerness for supreme power. His private correspondence does not tend to convict him of harboring extreme personal ambitions. It rather suggests that he was anxious to retire, but continued at the head of the government in the hope of giving stable institutions to the inhabitants whom he had liberated. As he surveyed the new nations from the lofty peaks of the Andes, the scene which presented itself to his keen vision was alarming enough. Chaos was reigning in Chile and the Río de la Plata; anarchy was beginning to threaten Mexico and Central America; a tyrant was reigning in Paraguay; the Island of Haiti was oscillating between license and despotism; and during the next four years conditions not only tended to become worse in most of these states, but anarchy threatened to sweep over the vast region which he had freed from Spain. More-

[6] The Constitution and the Discourse may be found in Gil Fortoul, II, 587-623, or in Villanueva, IV, 339-374.

over, his anxiety was heightened by fear of the Spanish Bourbons and the neo-Holy Alliance.

Reluctantly, perhaps, he undertook to remedy the evils which he observed. He warned the political leaders and the people against the federal system and the excesses of democracy. He urged the adoption of his model constitution. He appealed to England for help. He rushed to Quito and Guayaquil to calm the disorders caused in part by his own imprudent agents. He proceeded to Bogotá where he was vested with extraordinary powers to settle difficulties which were threatening a bloody civil war in Venezuela. He advocated another convention and waited impatiently for the assembly which met in Ocaña in 1828 to give *La Gran Colombia* a more conservative and vigorous constitution. When the convention ended in a tumult he resumed his dictatorship in the hope of resisting the tide of anarchy. In 1829 he hurried south to deal with disorders in Ecuador and Peru.

But the waning strength of his declining years was not equal to the burden which he took upon his frail shoulders. The task of liberating half a continent had depleted his energies. He would not be able to construct the great state of his dreams; much less was he able to bring into existence a Spanish American league of nations. The very nature and scope of his enterprise defeated him. The magnificence of his undertaking and his frank warnings and confessions aroused the fears and jealousies of those who called themselves democrats and liberals, many of whom were, like Santander, men of power and determination. He promoted anarchy by his attempts to banish it. Men declared that he was ambitious, that he would become a tyrant. Crowns offered by ardent friends in good faith and ambitious enemies in bad faith tended to defeat his efforts. Friends who sought refuge in a monarchy headed by a European prince involved him in grave embarrassments. In order to avoid offense to the kings of Europe, in order not to provoke intervention by reactionary governments across the sea, he must either keep silent or resort to evasive or vague language. Even in private letters he could merely point out the difficulties which would attend such a transformation. Moreover, he shrank from the use of force because this would give plausibility to the arguments of those who said he was an aspiring tyrant, and perhaps also because he was at heart a liberal. He was too lenient with the insurgency of Páez; and although he put down other revolts and conspiracies with a sterner hand, he would not resort to the policy of blood and iron in erecting his ideal state. In the main, he confined himself to moral suasion.

His last years were filled with anguish. Shortly after he finished the arduous work of driving out the Spaniards, a note of pessimism began to appear in his letters and interviews. All is bad and becoming worse was almost a constant refrain. The specter of a race war in which the inhabitants of European descent would be destroyed sometimes haunted him, and he talked of an *albocracy*—a government by the whites. He was losing his popularity among the liberals of Spanish America and the whole world. He wished to give his people a stable government as well as independence from Spain, but he feared his glory might be tarnished in the process. He was exasperated by critics and perplexed by doubts. Hannibal was becoming Hamlet. The great liberals of Europe expressed anxiety regarding his ambitions; Jacksonian democrats in the United States criticized him; many newspapers in Europe and America questioned his motives; ambitious captains revolted against his régime; conspirators planned to depose or assassinate him; partisans and opponents aroused the people; and seething mobs surged along the streets of a hundred towns and villages shouting their views pro and con. No help came from England, and little effective aid was to be had from any source. Bolívar stood alone confronting the terror.

As the year 1830 approached, all Spanish America, save Paraguay, seemed to be a raging sea of anarchy, and stark despair seized the Liberator's soul. "There is no faith in America," he said, "between either men or nations. Treaties are papers; constitutions, books; elections, combats; liberty, anarchy; and life, a torment."[7] In April he resigned his dictatorship and left Bogotá. Spanish America was ungovernable, he declared. In trying to give freedom to these people he had merely "ploughed the sea." The region was rapidly falling into the hands of frenzied mobs. Soon it would become the prey of petty tyrants of every race and color. It would be devoured by crime and extinguished by ferocity. If it were possible for any portion of the world to return to primeval chaos, this would be the final doom of Spanish America.[8] Already the shadow of death was closing in upon him. He spent his last days at a country place near Santa Marta. Into his feeble hands, as the end drew near, an attendant, a Spaniard, placed a book. Its title was *Don Quijote;* and as he glanced through the old classic again, he was

[7] Quoted from his *Mirada sobre América española,* a pamphlet published at Quito in 1829.

[8] Letter to Juan José Flores, Nov. 9, 1830, in Lecuna, IX, 376.

reminded of Jesus Christ, and of himself—broken and frustrated idealists.[9]

---

[9] Raúl Carrancá y Trujillo, *La evolución política de Iberoamérica* (Madrid, 1925), 107-108. A vivid impression of the anguish of the last four years of Bolívar's life may be obtained from reading his letters of the period, published in Lecuna, VI-IX. The best discussion of Bolívar as statesman and political philosopher will be found in C. Parra-Pérez, *Bolívar: contribución al estudio de sus ideas políticas* (Paris, 1928). Consult also Villanueva, and the present writer's *Rivalry of the United States and Great Britain over Latin America* (Baltimore, 1929), 152-216. The legislation of the period, including Bolívar's decrees as dictator, will be found in República de Colombia, *Codificación nacional* (23 vols., Bogotá, 1924-1933), I-IV.

II. THE DICTATORS OF ARGENTINA, PARAGUAY, URUGUAY, AND CHILE

By LEWIS W. BEALER

CHAPTER FOUR

ARTIGAS, FATHER OF FEDERALISM IN LA PLATA[1]

THE countries of southern South America—Chile, and the three Plata republics of Argentina, Paraguay, and Uruguay—have, in common with their sister Hispanic American republics to the north of them, problems of a similar nature arising out of their common Hispanic heritage. But, like those sister republics, they have had other problems peculiar to themselves individually or as a group, problems arising out of geography, out of past experience, and out of differences in racial makeup. Thus, set apart by desert and high mountain ranges, Chile is the product of geographic isolation, and even in colonial times was a distinct and individual area, virilized by a long struggle with the warlike Araucanian Indians—whose descendants have been assimilated only within the past half century—and internally unified by the sea, which provides ready communication from one part of the country to another. Chile's problems have been national in character; her political struggles have never been along regional lines of cleavage.

In the Plata basin, there was, on the other hand, a variety of conditions, and, although in Spanish times the country was politically a unit in theory, its several parts were possessed of distinct and conflicting interests and individual historical backgrounds. Until late in the Spanish colonial period, the Plata provinces were governed at long range from Peru. In 1776 there was organized the Viceroyalty of the Río de la

---

[1] The most comprehensive and authoritative writings on Artigas are those of Eduardo Acevedo, *José Artigas, jefe de los orientales . . .*, (3 vols., Montevideo, 1909-1910); Hugo Barbagelata, *Artigas y la revolución americana* (2nd ed., Paris, 1930); Pereda, *Artigas . . .* (4 vols., Montevideo, 1930); and Juan Zorilla de San Martín, *La epopeya de Artigas* (2nd ed., Montevideo, 1916). De-María, *Historia . . . del Uruguay* (6 vols., Montevideo, 1893-1895) contributes heavily to the economic aspects and Alberto Zum Felde, *Proceso histórico del Uruguay* (Montevideo, 1920) to the sociological. The Fregeiro collection of Artigas documentos, *Artigas, estudio histórico. Documentos justificativos,* edited by Clemente L. Fregeiro (Montevideo, 1886)—cited as Fregeiro (ed.)—is an invaluable contribution to the history of the earlier period of Artigas' wars of independence career. The present discussion of Artigas is a condensation of the writer's unpublished "Artigas and the beginnings of Uruguay, 1810-1820," written in partial fulfillment of requirements for the M.A. degree in history at the University of California in 1930. For further bibliographical references on the Artigas period, cf. Lewis Winkler Bealer, "Contribution to a bibliography on Artigas and the beginnings of Uruguay, 1810-1820," in *Hispanic American historical review,* XI (1931), 108-134.

Plata, or Buenos Aires, with the viceregal capital at the chief port of the region, Buenos Aires. This new viceroyalty embraced a huge area, including Charcas (roughly the modern Bolivia), Tucumán and the provinces of the interior, Paraguay, the provinces of the Littoral—Santa Fe, Entre Ríos, and Corrientes—and the *Banda Oriental* (the modern Uruguay), lying across the Plata estuary from the city and province of Buenos Aires. These widely separated provinces resented the domination of the *Porteños,* or people of the port (as the inhabitants of Buenos Aires are called). Particularly was this true of Paraguay and the *Banda Oriental.*

Paraguay looked upon herself as the elder sister among all the Plata provinces. Isolated, she had always maintained an independence of spirit and, on several occasions, had asserted herself to the point of expelling unpopular governors. Subtropical, with a large Indian population, she was distinct from her sister provinces. Too, her situation on the rim of the Spanish empire and therefore close to the Portuguese possessions had brought her into sharp conflict with the Portuguese, most notably as the victim of raids on the Jesuit missions.

Sharing with Paraguay the Portuguese danger of the frontier, but lacking her isolation, was the *Banda Oriental,* the Eastern Shore of the Uruguay River. Far more than Paraguay, the *Banda Oriental,* or Uruguay, as it is called today, had been a Spanish borderland, a debatable land, contended for by Spain and Portugal since the intruding Portuguese had founded Colonia in 1682. Countering this, the Spanish had founded Montevideo in 1724, and the eighteenth century saw the province the scene of bitter rivalry and almost constant friction, even after the Portuguese had been expelled in 1777. Under these circumstances, the people of the *Banda* became self-reliant and developed a strong local patriotism, which was enhanced by Montevideo's jealousy of the larger and more favored port and capital across the estuary—Buenos Aires.

Thus, when separation from Spain came in 1810, the immediate question was that of government.[2] Buenos Aires, the old viceregal capital, had taken the lead. She had dominated the viceroyalty, and she presumed a continuation of that domination under the new government. The provinces, resentful of her, took a different stand and wanted as great a regional autonomy as possible. Consequently, there arose two basic political ideas: unitarism and federalism, centralized and decentral-

[2] The discussion of the bases of the federalist-unitarist struggle has been based upon Mario Falcão Espalter, *Formación histórica del Uruguay* . . . (Madrid, 1929), ch. 1, *passim.*

ized government. This question, in various forms, while complicated and modified by personalities and local rivalries, was the fundamental issue in Plata politics for a half century after 1810, and even down to 1880.

In the struggle, which is paralleled to a varying degree elsewhere in Hispanic America, it may be said broadly that the unitarists were the inhabitants of the old capitals, men of distinction—judges, lawyers, high functionaries of one sort or another, and members of the mercantile classes, whose economic interests were best furthered by a strong central government. The federalists were of the provinces, wealthy *hacendados,* landowners, members of old provincial families, some of whom became political leaders in their provinces, and the masses within each province, who were imbued with strong feelings of local patriotism and acutely resented the outsider.

Throughout South America, at least, the revolution had its beginnings in the capitals of the old viceroyalties and captaincies-general. In the Plata provinces it was inaugurated at Buenos Aires; its initial leaders were of that city or associated with it; its foreign contacts were there; its finances were handled there and rested largely on the commerce which passed through that city. Thus, the unitarists started off with an initial advantage. Their leadership was accepted by the provinces of the Littoral and of the interior. With the exception of Paraguay, where Belgrano's "army of liberation" was repulsed, and of the *Banda Oriental,* where the royalists still held sway from their stronghold of Montevideo, and Charcas, which never actively associated itself with the movement for independence in the Plata, the provinces generally accepted the leadership of Buenos Aires. Nowhere did federalism rear its head in 1810. Sentiment existed, but a leader was lacking. And Artigas of Uruguay furnished that leadership. Under his direction and his influence, the spark of federalism was developed, nourished, and sustained, and the absolute domination of the Plata from Buenos Aires was prevented.

I

To write or to speak of Artigas and to understand him, it is essential to have a clear view of the immediate stage upon which he was so prominent a figure. Any discussion of Artigas, whatever it may be, is complicated by the controversial nature of its subject. As one English writer has aptly expressed it, "Perhaps never did the memory of man meet with more honor in his own country and with less favor outside of it."[3] In all Hispanic American history there have been few, if any, concerning whom there is so great and so sharp a divergence of opinion. To the Argentine historians, with rare exception, and to those who have followed in their footsteps, Artigas was a semi-barbarian, motivated solely by self-interest. At the opposite pole stand the vast majority of the historians of Uruguay, to whom he is a veritable demigod, at the least comparable only to Washington. Indeed, one of the more extreme of them has modestly claimed for his country's hero a combination of "the austerity of Cato, the purity of Aristides, the temperament of the Gracchi, the nobility of Camillus, the generosity of Fabricius, which virtues, allied to heroism and determination, have been found united in the breasts of none but Artigas."[4]

This man Artigas, then, was the champion of federalism; but why? What were his qualifications? What fitted him to be the leader? To answer such questions one must look, albeit briefly, at Uruguay of the eighteenth century. For centuries Uruguay had been a bone of contention between Spain and Portugal. Not until 1777 was Spain able definitely to expel the Portuguese and to occupy the entire region. Even then, the uncertain and ill-defined frontier made border raids and skirmishes chronic. Smuggling was rampant. Indian troubles with the wild Charrúas were frequent. In short, it was a frontier country and its people self-reliant and independent of spirit, accustomed to act and to act quickly.

José Gervasio Artigas, born in Montevideo in 1764, grew up in this atmosphere. He came of one of the leading families of the *Banda Oriental,* of "*Mayflower* lineage," as it were, for his grandfather had been among the original settlers of Montevideo, while his father had made a name for himself in the warfare against the Portuguese. José Gervasio himself was at one time destined for the church and received the best education which Montevideo could offer—at the Franciscan academy of San Francisco. But the life of the *campaña,* the rural *pampa* region, attracted him instead, so that he devoted his time to the varied business of his father's *estancia,* or great ranch, at Cásupa. From there, he, too, engaged in the eternal struggle against the Portuguese and Charrúa raiders and against the smuggler, although unsupported tradition has it that he was also a smuggler at times. There, in the "wide open spaces," he developed, achieving an enviable reputation as a leader of prowess and ability. In 1797 he entered the *Blandengues,* a corps of mounted

[3] W. H. Koebel, *Uruguay* (London, 1911), 61.
[4] *Ibid.,* preface. The quotation is from Múñoz Ximénez.

border guards, and served as an officer in Spanish service until the patriot rising in 1811. As an *estanciero* and as a soldier, he came to know the *gauchos* of the *pampas;* knowing them and being one with them, he gained their admiration and undying loyalty. At the same time he stood in a peculiarly favorable position to obtain the united support of the *Orientales*—the people of the *Banda Oriental*—when the time came. And that time came in 1811.

May of 1810 saw Buenos Aires separate from Spain, rejecting the Regency of Cádiz and proclaiming loyalty to the captive King Ferdinand VII, who, as Napoleon's prisoner, was indeed a harmless ruler. This move, as has been seen, was generally adhered to by the other provinces, except Paraguay and the *Banda Oriental.* The former made its own arrangements; the latter, because of its distrust of *Porteño* leadership and because of the presence of a strong Spanish garrison in Montevideo, remained aloof; nevertheless, an undercover movement of considerable scope was secretly organized, with Artigas one of its mainstays.

Obviously, the presence of rival governments on either side of the Plata, each claiming to represent the Spanish Crown, could not long continue without a clash. Therefore, when Francisco Elío, recently captain-general, returned to Montevideo from Spain in January 1811, with a viceroy's commission from the Regency of Cádiz, it was clear that the rupture was near. Upon the Buenos Aires *junta's* refusal to accept his viceregal authority, Elío prepared to reduce the recalcitrant rebels to obedience and issued a formal declaration against the *junta* on February 13, 1811.

Artigas was at this time an officer in the *Blandengues* stationed at Colonia. When word of Elío's pronunciamento reached him, he took French leave of the royal service and fled by land to Buenos Aires, spreading the word as he went.[5]

At Buenos Aires an expedition against Montevideo was already in preparation. Artigas was given a commission and two companies of patriot troops to serve as a nucleus for the Oriental army he was expected to raise. This small force went by water as an advance guard for a much larger body which marched by land.

Meanwhile, events had moved with rapidity in the *Banda.* Within two weeks of Artigas' separation from Spanish service, the first call to arms had been raised at Asencio in the western *Banda*—the outgrowth

---

[5] Cf, especially, Acevedo, I, 39.

of orders issued by Artigas in his flight.[6] Starting in the west, the flame of revolt had swept eastward, so that within a month of Artigas' return, all but Montevideo and its immediate district was in patriot hands.

Accepted as leader by the *Orientales,* Artigas moved against Montevideo, his force serving as an advance guard for the main Buenos Aires army under Rondeau which followed. By the end of May, Montevideo was in state of siege, and soon the royalists were in panic. Elío, seeing no prospect of aid from Spain, turned to Rio de Janeiro, where the Portuguese court had been established since 1808, and appealed to the Princess Regent Carlota Joaquina, Ferdinand VII's sister, to retrieve her brother's lost dominions for him, or at least for the house of Bourbon. The Portuguese needed no second invitation, and in July, Portuguese troops poured across the border.

Now it was the patriots' turn to become alarmed, and in October, an armistice, the so-called "October Treaty," was signed with Elío. Essentially, it called for the *status quo ante,* leaving the *Banda* to the tender mercies of the vengeful viceroy. Uruguayan historians are prone to criticize bitterly this abandonment of the *Orientales* by Buenos Aires, but actually the *Porteño* government had little alternative.[7]

The October Treaty was, at best, a makeshift. Neither side was inclined to scrupulous observance; each felt it a poor bargain for itself, but the best way out of a muddle. Failing even to achieve the evacuation of the province by the Portuguese, its only positive result was the raising of the siege—and within a year that was resumed!

With the consummation of the October Treaty, a new and difficult task faced Artigas. It had been absurdly simple to move the Buenos Aires troops, who had neither homes nor families in the *Banda,* and their evacuation by way of Colonia was accomplished within a few days. Artigas, in literal fulfillment of the treaty, began to retreat toward the Uruguay River at the farther end of the province. In this way began the famous "Exodus to Ayuí," a mass movement of an entire people scarcely paralleled in modern history. Faced with the prospect of being left defenseless in their homes, already harassed by the Portuguese bands, both regular and irregular, who now infested the country, the rural population almost to a man began to follow Artigas. As one writer has graphically described it:

[6] Zorrilla de San Martín, I, 219. Cf., also, *Gaceta de Buenos Aires* (1810-1821), edición facsimilar (6 vols., Buenos Aires, 1910), March 8, 1811.

[7] The "October Treaty" in full is given in Luís Varela, *Historia constitucional de la república argentina* (4 vols., La Plata, 1910), and in Araújo, *Resúmen de la historia del Uruguay* (3rd ed., Montevideo, 1904), 425, note.

"Meanwhile Artigas crossed the Banda to the river Uruguay, followed not only by his troops, but by thirteen thousand men, women, and children. Escorted by three thousand soldiers, the march of the families began. Carts filled with women and children, herds of cattle, troops of horses, companies of pack mules, to say nothing of the riders themselves . . . the tragic procession toiled its way northwards through the summer dust clouds. . . . Mingled with the slowly advancing ranks and lending still greater variety to the whole went four hundred faithful Charrúa Indians, armed with bolas and spears."[8]

So complete was the exodus that the Portuguese commander, Souza, related that six months later the town of Paysandú was entirely deserted except for two aged Indians.[9]

The great trek finally terminated as the exiles settled themselves on the western, or Entre Ríos, shore of the Uruguay River and along the Ayuí, a small tributary. For several leagues, the whole shore of the Uruguay was populated with families from the *Banda,* "some living under carts, others beneath the trees, and all exposed to the inclemency of the weather, but with such conformity and pleasure as to cause admiration and to set an example."[10] From this base, parties of men raided the *Banda* seeking supplies and combating the Portuguese.

II

Ayuí marks the definite beginning of a break between Artigas and Buenos Aires. One may see now five periods of his career: his coöperation with the new, or second, siege of Montevideo, during which he fought valiantly for the acceptance of his principles of federalism and local autonomy; his withdrawal from the siege and a period of temporary eclipse; then, the collapse of the unitarist group controlling Buenos Aires and the partial federalization of the provinces, with Artigas at the height of his power; the growing Portuguese menace from the north, culminating in actual invasion in 1816 and a bitter four-year struggle of Artigas against the Lusitanian invader, with his final collapse in 1820; and, as an epilogue, his thirty years of exile in Paraguay.

Artigas remained at Ayuí for several months, as meanwhile roving bands of Portuguese ravaged the *Banda.* During this period, he was in regular correspondence with Paraguay, seeking not only Paraguayan

---

[8] Koebel, 62-63.

[9] Diego da Souza to Count das Galvaes, June 13, 1812. In "Documentos relativos a historia do Rio Grande do Sul," *Revista trimensal do Instituto histórico e geographico brasileiro* (XLI, part 1, 379).

[10] Laguardia to the *junta* of Paraguay, March 1, 1812, in Fregeiro (ed.), 84.

military aid, but likewise a definite understanding with a view to the formation of a federalized state. Paraguayan response to his overtures was, however, noncommittal, although some aid in supplies was given; even at this early period Paraguay was following a defensive, isolationist policy, as will be seen later.[11]

Early in 1812 the royalists at Montevideo and the patriots at Buenos Aires broke once more, and the October Treaty was swept entirely into the discard. A short while later, the Portuguese reluctantly withdrew after very strong pressure from the British minister at Rio de Janeiro. This was the signal for a renewal of the campaign against Montevideo, and, in June 1812, Manuel de Sarratea was appointed by the Buenos Aires *junta* to be "general-in-chief of the army operating in the *Banda Oriental*."[12]

En route to the *Banda,* Sarratea and a part of his command camped alongside Artigas. When Sarratea pursued a studied policy of enticing Artigas' supporters from him, there developed a bitter and long drawn-out dispute between the two commanders, the crux of which was the question of the status of Artigas and the force under him. Sarratea looked upon Artigas and the *Orientales* as a component part of the troops of the United Provinces under whose authority he himself acted, while Artigas considered himself commander of an army allied with that of Buenos Aires, but in no sense subordinate. Even when both armies set forth to join the now renewed siege of Montevideo, bickerings and almost interminable recriminatory correspondence continued, until by February of 1813 a crisis was reached, and Artigas cut the Gordian knot. He demanded Sarratea's personal retirement entirely, and, when Sarratea stalled, raided his camp and drove off his horses. Then it was that Rondeau and other officers under Sarratea intervened and compelled him to depart.[13] Command of the Buenos Aires forces at the siege now devolved upon Rondeau.

The whole episode smacks strongly of comic opera, yet it was not without significance and lasting effects. Not only did it definitely widen the breach between Artigas and Buenos Aires, but it caused the latter to distrust and dislike Artigas himself. Consequently, new friction soon developed, this time hinging directly on the form of government. In October 1812 a general constituent assembly of the United Provinces

[11] Cf. Fregeiro (ed.), *passim.*
[12] *Gaceta de Buenos Aires,* May 1, 1812.
[13] Cf. Fregeiro (ed.), 124 ff. and *passim;* Acevedo, II, 313-407.

had been called, and, just as the Artigas-Sarratea duel was reaching its finale, that assembly met on January 31, 1813.

Despite the fact that no deputies from the *Banda Oriental* had been invited, due primarily to the unsettled state of the province, the assembly demanded that the *Banda* formally recognize its authority and instructed Rondeau to convoke a provincial assembly for that purpose. Artigas' response was to call an assembly of his own early in April, one rather informally chosen due to the disturbed condition of the province.[14] Under Artigas' direction, this assembly chose six deputies to represent it at Buenos Aires and issued to them a set of instructions for their guidance at the constituent assembly, now famed in Uruguayan history as the "Instructions of the Year XIII." The Instructions show clearly the influence of the North American constitution, while they themselves, in their turn, were to be a strong influence on the basic Argentine Constitution of 1853.[15] Among their more salient points were: a demand for absolute independence; "no other system of government than confederation"; division of governmental powers among three distinct branches—legislative, executive, and judicial; full civil and religious liberty; the capital of the confederation to be *away* from Buenos Aires (a cardinal point of federalist demands in later years); and republican form of government.

These provisions, the very essence of federalism, clearly sought to decentralize the governmental system of the United Provinces, and to minimize the economic and political influence of Buenos Aires. The actual authorship of the Instructions is unknown, but Artigas' responsibility for them cannot be questioned. The same assembly named Artigas as military governor and president of the province.

But, when the deputies reached Buenos Aires, they were summarily rejected on technicalities based upon the irregular manner of their election. Technically, the election had been faulty, to be sure, but whose had not! Obviously, this was but a subterfuge; the true cause was the Instructions. Artigas, champion of federalism, had thrown down the gauntlet; the assembly, protagonist of unitarism and defender of the rights and prerogatives of its bulwark, Buenos Aires, answered the challenge.

---

[14] For an exhaustive treatise, cf. Héctor Miranda, *Las instrucciones del año XIII* (Montevideo, 1911; later ed., 1935). Ravignani, *Historia constitucional de la república argentina* (3 vols., Buenos Aires, 1926) gives extensive treatment.

[15] *Ibid.*, I, 215 ff.

Artigas now determined that if this first assembly and its deputies were unacceptable, he would convene a new one. In this, however, he was outmaneuvered, and in December 1813, the so-called Congress of Capilla Maciel met under the presidency of Rondeau and the domination of Buenos Aires bayonets, with the additional and potent threat that Rondeau would give up the siege if the congress were interfered with.[16] Even at that, Artigas himself stubbornly refused to accord recognition, thereby committing a serious tactical blunder, to say the least. Instead, on the night of January 20, 1814, he silently withdrew his entire command from the siege! On this action has been based most of the vilification subsequently heaped upon Artigas. The best and most favorable explanation of Artigas' attitude is that offered by one of his great biographers, Eduardo Acevedo. Acevedo's view is that Artigas, forced to a decision of some sort, had three courses of action open to him: he might submit to the domination of Buenos Aires and permanently sacrifice all that he had struggled for; he might throw down the gauntlet and force out-and-out combat; or he might withdraw from the siege and thus permit a very heated situation to cool off, thereby facilitating satisfactory settlement of the questions at issue.[17] Of these three, he chose the last, with the result that he found himself embarked upon a course which widened more and more the breach which had been present since Ayuí.

There followed a period of three-cornered warfare, with Spaniard, *Oriental,* and *Porteño,* each pitted against the other, until the successful conclusion of the siege of Montevideo brought about the elimination of the Spanish—and the Buenos Aires occupation of Montevideo. For over seven months the *Porteño* occupation of Montevideo continued. The star of unitarism was high, and Artigas' troops, reduced almost entirely to guerrilla warfare, were definitely on the defensive. Then, in January 1815, at the Battle of Guayabos, the *Porteño* forces under Dorrego suffered a stunning defeat at the hands of Artigas' chief lieutenant, Fructuoso Rivera, a man destined later to leave his mark on Uruguayan history. At one blow the backbone of Buenos Aires control was broken. From being on the run, the *Orientales* suddenly took the offensive, and, shortly, Montevideo was occupied.

Earlier, the constituent assembly had revised the executive branch of the government at Buenos Aires, substituting a single "supreme director" for the plural *junta* and naming Gervasio de Posadas to the post.

---

[16] Acevedo, II, 358; Francisco Bauzá, *Historia de la dominación española en el Uruguay* (2nd ed., 3 vols., Montevideo, 1892), III, 430-431.

[17] Acevedo, II, 381.

Guayabos and disaffection in the army of the Andes had sealed the fate of Posadas, whose fall came in January, but the assembly merely reorganized the personnel and named Carlos de Alvear, a strong unitarist, to be supreme director. The choice was unhappy. Proud and ambitious, disdainful and contemptuous of those beyond his own sphere, the young general was personally unpopular and, unless by his own military brilliance he could forestall it, his downfall was inevitable.

Federalism, sponsored by Artigas, was in the rise. After Guayabos, Artigas' influence in the provinces of the Littoral increased by leaps and bounds. Corrientes declared for him, as did Entre Ríos; and Santa Fe was ripe for revolt. Even distant Córdoba, where the federalists had recently seized the reins of government, hailed Artigas and presented him with a sword.[18]

"The new director [Alvear]," says a contemporary, "saw the cloud which was forming about his head" and sought an understanding with Artigas.[19] But these efforts came too late, and, when negotiations failed, he moved to save the province of Santa Fe, the key to control of the United Provinces. But his campaign collapsed, and his own commander, Ignacio Alvarez Thomás, turned sharply against him in the famous "Mutiny of Fontezuelas." This mutiny, actively encouraged by Artigas, was the signal for a headlong and wholesale desertion of Alvear by his former supporters, and he himself was soon in flight from the country. Alvarez Thomás, thereupon, became provisional supreme dictator.

On the surface, the new group in power was at least mildly federalist in its sentiments, but already personalities were playing their part in clouding the basic issue. Not only was Artigas' federalism of a stronger brand, but past antagonisms with members of the new government made friendly relations difficult. A policy of rigorous proscription was adopted by Alvarez toward the Alvear men: an orgy of banishment, punctuated by at least one execution. And, with the idea of placating Artigas, seven of his personal enemies were sent to him in chains as a present! If his object was to have Artigas wreak vengeance on the seven and thus discredit himself, Alvarez had certainly misjudged his man, for Artigas, upon receiving the present, forthwith returned the prisoners with the message: *"El general Artigas no es un verdugo"* (General Artigas is no hangman).[20]

[18] Ignacio Garzón, *Crónica de Córdoba* (3 vols., Córdoba, 1898-1902), I, 222 ff.

[19] Gregorio Funes, *Ensayo de la historia civil de Buenos Aires, Tucumán, y Paraguay* (2nd ed., 2 vols., Buenos Aires, 1856), II, 395.

[20] Acevedo, I, 230.

The Fontezuelas revolt put Artigas on top. Momentarily, the outlook for internal peace appeared bright. But fundamental differences yet existed, as Artigas stood adamant in demands that the autonomy of the *Banda Oriental* be definitely recognized. When no agreement could be reached, he convoked a congress of the provinces which looked to him for protection, "the first federal congress which functioned in South America."[21] This congress, meeting at Paysandú, attempted to iron out the differences with Buenos Aires. Instead, disputes developed, arising particularly out of factional strife in Santa Fe. Within short order actual fighting broke out once more, and in the campaign which followed, the cause of federalism as represented by Artigas triumphed, and Santa Fe continued under the protection of Artigas.

III

The Santa Fe campaign might well be considered Artigas' high watermark. Placing him at the very height of his power, it at the same time engendered such feeling on the part of Buenos Aires that from that time forth the government there was his bitter enemy. With the decline of *Porteño* influence, Artigas was definitely at his zenith. He was protector over an area of some 350,000 square miles. From Córdoba to the sea he was looked to as leader, while his influence was manifested even in the northwest. In the *Banda* he was "chief of the *Orientales,*" and directly responsible for a program of internal rehabilitation and development. By means of a loose federal league, he was in control over the provinces of Santa Fe, Entre Ríos, and Corrientes, and of the Misiones territory, under the title of "Protector of the free peoples." Paraguay was in accord with him; Córdoba was loosely allied to him; and even in Salta the ideals of federalism which had been promulgated in his famous Instructions a scant two years previously had been emulated by Güemes, who staunchly took up the cudgel for federalism and local autonomy and paved the way for other federalist leaders there in subsequent decades.

At the base of all was the fundamental divergence of the agricultural and pastoral interests of the rural districts from those of the commercial areas. The *gauchos,* inherently democratic and suspicious of the motives of the proponents of centralism, were strong for localism and gave ready support to Artigas, a man who was one with them.

Such a man was Artigas, simple in his habits, yet withal possessing a poise and a polish which permitted him to mix with the most cultured

---

[21] *Ibid.,* I, 233.

classes. Father Larrañaga, the distinguished presbyter of Montevideo, as a result of one of his visits to the protector, has left a lengthy description of the man and of life at his camp.

> "In no way did he appear a general [the good priest wrote in his diary]. His clothing was that of a civilian and very simple; his pantaloons and a blue jacket with neither lapel nor cuffs, shoes and white stockings, and a cape made of very heavy cloth, these were his best, and even they were poor and threadbare. He is a robust man of regular stature, of light complexion, of very good appearance, with an aquiline nose, black hair with few grey hairs; he appears to be forty-eight years of age;[22] his conversation is attractive; he speaks quietly and deliberately. It is not easy to confound him with long reasonings, for he reduces the difficulty to a few words, and, full of many experiences, has foresight and an extraordinary ability to hit the mark; he knows the human heart very well, especially that of our countrymen, and therefore there is no one who can equal him in the art of controlling them. All surround him and all follow him with love, even though they live naked and full of misery at his side, not through lack of resources, but rather in order not to oppress the people with contributions; he would prefer giving up the command to seeing that his orders were not carried out in this region. . . .
>
> "Our sessions lasted until suppertime. This meal was in keeping with the tone and manner of our general: a bit of roasted beef, soup, stewed meat, plain bread, and wine served in a cup for lack of glasses; four plated iron spoons, with no knives or forks save those each man brought with him; two or three porcelain plates, a pewter platter whose borders were loose; three chairs and a chest served as seats, the rest remained on their feet. Thus may be seen of what our table service consisted, with tablecloths of Misiones cotton, but without napkins and even, as I have learned, much of this was borrowed. After finishing dinner, we went to sleep, and the general gave me not only his leather cot, but also his room, and he himself retired to a ranch. He would not listen to my excuses, but strongly pooh-poohing me, would not give in.
>
> "Very early . . . we had the general in the house; he surprised us while we were yet in bed; we rose immediately; I said mass; then came breakfast, but this had neither tea nor coffee nor milk nor eggs. Nor was there *maté,* but a *gloriado,* which is a sort of punch, very hot, with two beaten eggs which they had found with difficulty. . . . There was nothing else to do but accustom ourselves to this Spartanism."[23]

---

[22] At the time Larrañaga wrote (June 12, 1815), Artigas was just completing his fifty-first year.

[23] "Fragmentos del diario de Padre Larrañaga. . . ." In *Contribución documental para la historia del Río de la Plata* (5 vols., Buenos Aires, 1913), III, 277.

For Artigas there were two major aims: the safeguarding of his protected provinces in accord with the principles enunciated in the Instructions, and the rehabilitation of his own province. The former led inevitably to conflict with Buenos Aires; the latter concerned the economic and cultural betterment of the *Banda,* but the effects of the first prevented more than a scant beginning being made.

In order to maintain his control over the protected provinces and to direct their affairs, Artigas spent most of his time in the western *Banda* and beyond the Uruguay. Montevideo as a capital was impossible, as much because of jealousy of the city as from its distant location. Too, from a point of view of strategy, it was badly located.

At first, in true *gaucho* fashion, Artigas and his government had been largely on horseback. Later, he located a concentration camp for Peninsular Spaniards at Hervidero, close to the Uruguay River and the western border of the province. At Hervidero, or Purificación, as it came to be known, the more dangerous of the royalist sympathizers were interned. And, because of its central location and ready defense, Hervidero became Artigas' actual seat of government. There occurred, or were supposed to have occurred, many of the violent deeds of which Artigas has been accused, although the wild stories of conditions there, which were once told so freely, are nowadays fairly well discredited. At Purificación, in simple style quite in keeping with his *gaucho* democracy, Artigas held court, as it were.

The English trader John Parish Robertson has given a vivid picture of Artigas at Hervidero.

> "I came to the Protector's headquarters at the so-called town of Purificación. And there (I pray you do not turn skeptic on my hands) what do you think I saw? Why, the most excellent Protector of half the New World (!), seated on a bullock's skull, at a fire kindled on the mud floor of his hut, eating beef off a spit, and drinking gin out of a cow horn! He was surrounded by a dozen officers in weather-beaten attire, in similar positions, and similarly occupied, with their chief. All were smoking, all gabbling. The Protector was dictating to two secretaries, who occupied at one deal table, the only two dilapidated rush-bottom chairs in the hovel. To complete the singular incongruity of the scene, the floor of the one apartment of the mud hut (to be sure, it was a pretty large one) in which the general, his staff, and secretaries, were assembled, was strewn with pompous envelopes from all the Provinces (some of them distant some 1,500 miles from the center of operations) addressed to 'His Excellency the Protector.' At the door stood the reeking horses of couriers arriving every half hour, and the fresh

ones of those departing as often. Soldiers, aides-de-camp, scouts, came galloping in from all quarters, all was referred to 'His Excellency the Protector'; and his excellency the protector, seated on his bullock's skull, smoking, eating, drinking, talking, dispatched in rapid succession the various matters brought under his notice, with that calm, or deliberate, but intermitted nonchalance, which brought most practically home to me the truth of the axiom, 'Stop a little that we may get on the faster.' . . . He received me, not only with cordiality, but with what surprised me more, comparatively gentlemanlike manners, and really good breeding. . . . The Protector's business was prolonged from morning till evening, and so were his meals; for, as one courier arrived another was dispatched, and as one officer rose up from the fire at which the meat was spitted another took his place."

Robertson, who had come, with much trepidation, to ask reparation for damages he had suffered in Corrientes, likewise gives an interesting insight into Artigas' financial difficulties and the state of his treasury. When he had submitted his claims, Artigas, far from being outraged as the Britisher had expected, merely smiled.

> " 'You see,' said the general with great candour and nonchalance, 'how we live here; and it is as much as we can do, in these hard times, to compass beef, aguardiente, and cigars. To pay you 6,000 dollars just now is as much beyond my power, as it would be to pay you 60,000 or 600,000.' 'Look here,' said he; and, so saying, he lifted up the lid of an old military chest, and pointed to a canvas bag at the bottom of it. 'There,' he continued, 'is my whole stock of cash; it amounts to 300 dollars; and where the next supply is to come from I am as little aware as you are.' "

Thereupon, Robertson tells us, the protector granted him trade concessions which in short order more than retrieved his entire loss![24]

In this manner, Artigas directed affairs of his provinces from Hervidero, though all the while absorbed by military or diplomatic struggles with Buenos Aires. These former involved many and varied subjects, ranging from subjugation of Indians who menaced the *Banda* from the north to the institution of a library and the regulation of ecclesiastical affairs. Once the *Banda* was cleared of hostile troops, Artigas' first move had been for the restoration of law and order. Montevideo, after one serious disturbance, was quickly put in good order, but the rural districts, still the habitat of irresponsible bands, were more difficult to handle, and for that reason severe and summary punishment was meted out to offenders.

---

[24] J. P. Robertson and W. P. Robertson, *Letters on Paraguay* . . . (3 vols., London, 1838-1839), I, 111-113, 118-119, *passim.*

In furtherance of his idealistic desires, Artigas, at the instigation of the esteemed Father Larrañaga, ordered the establishment of a public library at Montevideo; likewise, "The Theater" was reëstablished. A determined effort to establish a newspaper was made, but the embryonic *Periódico oriental* died aborning. Education, too, was given recognition and attention with the establishment of a school at Montevideo in May 1816, just before the storm broke.

In the *campaña,* Artigas' policy was to encourage the development of agriculture and of the pastoral industry. On September 11, 1815, he issued a *reglamento,* or regulation, "for the development of the *campaña* and the security of the *estancieros."* Twenty-nine articles made provision for various and sundry matters in connection with the land problem. A policy of repopulation of deserted regions was provided and a commission set up to handle the several needs of the *campaña.*[25]

The importance of this *reglamento* lies not in its actual results, for they were scant, due to the annihilating warfare which soon returned to plague all the *Banda Oriental.* Rather, the project is of significance as concrete evidence of the constructive aims of Artigas' policies.

Administrative reorganization of the province for judicial and political purposes, and the settlement of ecclesiastical disputes topped off the list. These internal adjustments and projects were in the main but ephemeral, for the period of tranquillity was too short. But, had it been possible to preserve peace, great things could have come from these beginnings.

Too, given peace, Artigas might have evolved a federalized state out of his loose federal league. With time to consolidate its position, the league might well have stood the test. Unfortunately, the essential breathing spell was not forthcoming; hence, once Artigas' control was seriously challenged, decline set in. This decline and the ensuing collapse came about as a direct result of the Portuguese invasion initiated in 1816.

IV

The year 1815 saw Artigas at the height of his power. Then, early in 1816, came two developments which were destined to mark the beginning of his decline and eventual fall—the Congress of Tucumán and, above all, the Portuguese invasion of the *Banda Oriental.*

The famous constituent assembly of 1813 had failed to achieve definite results for the United Provinces. Since its fall there had been renewed demand for a national congress of all the provinces of the old viceroyalty.

[25] De-María, III, 32 ff.

Definite plans were made in 1815, and in March 1816 there was convened at Tucumán in the interior what was designed to be a general congress of the provinces. All the provinces were invited to send deputies, but actually only a scant two-thirds were represented. Of the Artigas provinces, Córdoba alone sent deputies. Paraguay, too, was absent. Artigas himself demanded as a prerequisite to his adherence, the formal and public ratification of the recent treaty affirming the integrity of Santa Fe and other guarantees for federalism. But, dominated by unitarists, the congress refused. Another strong factor, aside from the generally unsatisfactory state of Artigas' relations with Buenos Aires, was the growing inclination of the unitarists toward monarchism as the salvation of the Plata. The monarchial agitation achieved considerable *sub rosa* attention at the congress, but the movement failed. Greatest of the acts of the Congress of Tucumán was, of course, the declaration of independence proclaimed July 9, 1816. By that date, however, other developments had taken place, and the Portuguese were already invading the *Banda Oriental.*

V

Portuguese activity at this time was motivated by three factors whose relative importance has been the subject of no little controversy. Ostensibly, it was for the purpose of pacifying the *Banda Oriental,* "to annihilate the forces of anarchy there." The Portuguese dominions could not be in security so long as Artigas oppressed the inhabitants of the *Banda,* declared General Lecor, who commanded the invading horde. Such was the avowed object of the invasion, with its basis the occurrence of raids across the disputed and uncertain border. According to the Portuguese, Artigas "had incited southern Brazil to revolution and anarchy." But all this was merely subterfuge, as was later admitted by Lecor himself.[26]

Of far greater importance was the centuries-old aspiration of Portugal for control of the northern shores of the Plata. She had been expelled in 1777; her return had been frustrated by the British in 1812, but the ambition still lived on. Now, the close of the Napoleonic Wars found Portugal in a more favorable position for the achievement of this ambition than for a generation or more. In 1815 she sent fifteen thousand Peninsular War veterans to Brazil, partly to overawe any Brazilian attempt at revolution, but as much with an eye to the south.

The time, then, was auspicious for an invasion of her southern neighbor, and towards the favorable situation which had arisen, the Portu-

---

[26] Proclamation of the Portuguese commander-in-chief (Lecor), November 1, 1816. In *British and Foreign State Papers* (London, 1818), IV, 982.

guese court at Rio de Janeiro took an attitude well epitomized by its general, Lecor, who declared:

> "The king my master has resolved to send his troops to recover what in other times he possessed with a just title dating from the conquest, and which the crown of Castile wrested from him by violence. Moreover, he cannot, with indifference, see the tranquillity and security of the peoples under his rule menaced by the bad example of the Banda Oriental, the ambition of Artigas, and his hatred of the Portuguese." [27]

But not merely the ostensible cause, the disorder and unrest in the *Banda,* nor yet the imperialism of the Portuguese may be given the entire responsibility. A third factor needs to be noted, the most controversial of all: the extent of Buenos Aires' influence, direct and indirect, upon Portuguese policy.

Ever since Alvear's time, the confidential commissioner of the Buenos Aires government, Manuel José García, had been negotiating at Rio de Janeiro. As the best escape from Spain, he proposed the delivery of the entire United Provinces to the Portuguese Crown. Such a scheme was extensively discussed at Tucumán. The new supreme director, Pueyrredón, a staunch unitarist and a capable leader, destined to remain in power for some three years, seems to have seriously feared the menace of Portuguese arms for the entire United Provinces. Motivated by a desire to protect them from invasion, he eventually made what was at least a tacit agreement with the Portuguese, whereby the latter were given a free hand in the *Banda* in exchange for immunity of the rest of the United Provinces from invasion. Such, at least, is one interpretation. According to some Uruguayan historians, the very invasion itself was at the invitation and suggestion of the *Porteño* in order that Artigas' influence in the provinces of the Littoral might be destroyed. At the other extreme, Argentine historians assert that the Buenos Aires government was helpless, that Artigas' intractability made Buenos Aires' aid impossible. Whatever the motives, certainly the policy of Buenos Aires was vacillating at the outset and lent encouragement to the projected invasion.[28]

The early months of 1816 were a time of anxiety and uncertainty on both sides of the Plata. Portuguese troops were being massed on the

---

[27] Mitre, *historia de Belgrano* . . . (6th ed., 4 vols., Buenos Aires, 1913), III, 243; Acevedo, III, 40.

[28] Cf. E. Acevedo, *Historia del Uruguay* (9 vols., Montevideo, 1916-1932), I, 291-292, for a clear-cut presentation of Buenos Aires relations with the Portuguese court.

border, and their ultimate destination was uncertain. As early as June 1816 the *Cabildo* of Montevideo called the people to arms against the coming invasion. The actual invasion began in August as two main columns of invaders, supported by irregulars, moved into Misiones and into the *Banda.* In preparation for defense, Artigas drew up plans which, according to the great Argentine military leader and statesman, Mitre, "theoretically considered, would do honor to any general."[29]

Weakened by five years of all but constant strife, the *Orientales* were no match for the well-equipped and seasoned Portuguese veterans. Consequently, a series of defeats occurred. Pueyrredón's diplomatic representations to Lecor were met by defiance, tempered with promises to restrict operations to the *Banda.* Upon the appeal of the *Cabildo* of Montevideo, Pueyrredón did, indeed, offer aid, but only upon terms involving an absolute surrender to the authority of the United Provinces.

For three years the unequal struggle continued, as under Artigas' leadership the *Orientales* fought a bitter, but steadily losing, struggle. In February 1817, Montevideo capitulated to the Portuguese, only to be subjected almost immediately to an informal, but thoroughgoing, land siege by guerrilla bands.

Despite the loss of Montevideo and the defection of many of his followers, Artigas still received external recognition. Indeed, on the high seas and abroad, he met with more success than at home! In August 1817, six months and more after Montevideo had been lost, he concluded his first foreign treaty, a commercial convention with Commodore Bowles, British naval commander in South American waters.[30] Of greater international significance was the privateering carried on under the *Oriental* flag.

Since 1815 Buenos Aires had made effective use of privateering, chiefly through commissions sold in the United States to former War of 1812 privateersmen. So, too, had other patriot governments. In common with them, Artigas likewise began to issue commissions, with the additional advantage that, being at war with Portugal, he could authorize action against Portuguese shipping as well as that of Spain. Several privateersmen, previously prominent in Buenos Aires, took out commissions under him and inflicted tremendous damages upon Portuguese

[29] Mitre, III, 233. This is indeed strong praise when the source is considered, for Mitre himself ranks among Argentina's great military men. Moreover, as a historian, he was scarcely pro-Artigas.

[30] Convention between the chief of the Orientales and the commander of H. B. M.'s naval forces in South American waters, August 8, 1817, in De-María, 36-37.

commerce. Prizes were actually taken within sight of Lisbon. So great and widespread was their activity and, with the lack of supervision and control by Artigas, so extensive were the damages and depredations inflicted that they became a serious international problem. It is decidedly questionable, however, that the *Oriental* exchequer profited financially from these operations. Rather, the benefits lay in the losses inflicted upon the Portuguese and, perhaps, in the advertising value, for to the North American and European public in general the privateer was their first introduction to the name of Artigas, which many took to be that of a province rather than of a man.[31]

However, despite the successes of his privateers, Artigas was slowly weakening at home. The eventual collapse was coming nearer and nearer. Occasional spectacular victory scarcely offset the steady but slow decline. One by one, his lieutenants were captured or killed, or else deserted. Colonia was lost in January 1818, and with it, the chief port of entry for supplies and munitions. By the end of the year 1818, Artigas and Rivera had the only *Oriental* forces of consequence left in the *Banda;* the Portuguese definitely had the upper hand; *Oriental* morale was low. Aid from the protected provinces was impossible, as there the friends and allies of Artigas were engaged in local struggles with rivals, or else directly with forces representing Buenos Aires.

In December 1819 Artigas desperately undertook an invasion of Brazil. Initial success embraced him, but it was no more than the last flicker of a star about to die. Faced by overwhelmingly superior forces, he retired upon *Oriental* territory and with two thousand men took up a position at the *arroyo* of Tacuarembó, January 22, 1820. There he made his last stand against the Portuguese. After a desperately fought and thoroughly bloody battle, Artigas, beaten, fled the field with a scant three hundred men, leaving eight hundred dead and fifteen wounded, behind![32]

From Tacuarembó, Artigas fled to the Uruguay River and, leaving his native soil for the last time, crossed into Corrientes. From there he sent instructions to the greater and lesser *caudillos* of Entre Ríos,

---

[31] The privateering under commission of Artigas has yet to be studied and presented in its proper relation both as to privateering under other patriot flags and to the wars of independence as a whole. *Niles' weekly register* (Baltimore), *The Times* (London), *Le moniteur universel* (Paris), and other contemporary newspapers have frequent references to various activities of Artigas provinces. Cf., also, Zorrilla de San Martín, II, 160-163.

[32] Acevedo, I, 354. These figures come directly from the report of the Portuguese commander, Figueira. Araújo adds that 490 prisoners were taken. Cf. Araújo, 517.

Misiones, and Corrientes, as well as to Rivera, ordering that they concentrate all possible resources.

VI

All the world loves a successful man, but few will follow a failure. Artigas, once the generous protector of a third of a million square miles, now felt the touch of man's ingratitude. Some of those circularized hearkened to the call, but Ramírez, long loyal to the chief who had made him, was now himself the successful *caudillo* of Entre Ríos. He had just achieved the rout of Buenos Aires troops at Cepeda. Pueyrredón had fallen the year before, and kaleidoscopic changes were in order in Buenos Aires and the Plata in that "Year of Anarchy" 1820. Among the new allies of Ramírez were Sarratea and other old-time enemies of Artigas. Following what seemed to be rising stars, Ramírez repudiated Artigas, and was soon at open warfare with him.

Artigas now made his last stand, and for some months maintained a bitter, though hopeless, struggle against Ramírez. Almost none of his former adherents remained with him, now, and even Rivera, still in the *Banda,* capitulated to the Portuguese and took service under them. For Artigas, defeat followed defeat. The Indian Siti, one of the very last of his lieutenants, deserted and, joining Ramírez, actively pursued him.

Yet, even now, Artigas was possessed of marvelous recuperative powers; only by constant, dogged pursuit could he be crushed. It is related that, defeated by Ramírez and Siti in one engagement, he fled the field with no more than a dozen followers, managing to shake off Ramírez, who meanwhile searched in all directions for him. A week passed before the Entre Ríos *caudillo* located Artigas—at the head of nine hundred men, vigorously besieging Siti in the town of Camby! Only the timely arrival of Ramírez saved his Guaraní Indian ally.[33]

One by one, the remaining few were dropping away. Harassed on all sides, lacking resources with which to continue the war, deserted by his lieutenants, Artigas and a handful of men fled northward along the Paraná, closely pursued by the enemy. But even in flight, he was honored.

> "So great was the prestige of this man, [wrote one of Ramírez' officers], that despite his continued defeats, during his flight through Corrientes and Misiones the Indians came out to ask him his bene-

[33] Zorrilla de San Martín, II, 397. The story is from one of Ramírez' officers (Cáceres). For detail on this period, see the excellent work of Hernán Félix Gómez, *Historia de la provincia de Corrientes* (3 vols., Corrientes, 1929-1934), I, 290, ff.

diction, and followed with their families after him, abandoning their homes."[34]

Approaching the Paraguayan borders, he wrote Francia, the great dictator of Paraguay, asking asylum. Previously the United States consul at Montevideo had offered him, in the name of his government, asylum in the United States along with "a pension in keeping with his rank." But that generous offer, actually the consul's own inspiration, was refused, and he directed himself to Paraguay.[35]

A hunted man, his following all but dispersed, Artigas and a handful of adherents, crossed the Paraná on September 23, 1820, and sought the hospitality of the great dictator of Paraguay, Francia the Supreme One. Francia seems to have suspected trickery, collusion between Artigas and Ramírez, and at first imprisoned Artigas, distributing his few remaining officers and men throughout Paraguay. Soon, however, he determined to intern him in the village of Curuguatí, eighty-five leagues northeast of Asunción, and therefore well away from the borders. There Artigas was assigned a house and given a monthly pension of thirty-two *pesos* to cover his subsistence.[36]

So thoroughly was Artigas submerged in the forests of Paraguay, that for a long time few outside that country knew whether he was alive or dead. Indeed, a definite rumor of his death in 1826 was circulated, and many nineteenth-century writers give that year as his last.[37] The death of Francia opened Paraguay to the outside world, so that no longer was the venerable protector, now nearly eighty, left in the unholy quiet of isolation and oblivion which had been his lot for two decades. Rivera, at the moment president of the Uruguayan republic, soon sent an envoy to persuade his old chief to return, but Artigas' sole answer in response was a request to be left alone.

This was the era of Rosas in Argentina, and in these, Artigas' last years, he was visited by the unitarist exile, General Paz. In 1846 Beaurepaire Rohan, a prominent Brazilian engineer, visited him. And in that same year, Artigas' son, José María, now a colonel under Rivera, came to pay his respects to his illustrious father. To him, the aged protector gave a verbal account of his life in Paraguay which was subsequently published in Montevideo.

---

[34] Cáceres, *Memoria.* Quoted in Zorrilla de San Martín, II, 397.

[35] This interesting bit of information is derived from Artigas' own verbal account given to his son in 1846 and is otherwise unsubstantiated. Cf. Acevedo, I, 381-382.

[36] For detail on Artigas' stay in Paraguay, see especially the work of Lamy Dupuy, *Artigas en el cautiverio . . .* (Montevideo, 1913).

[37] Cf. *Le grande encyclopedie,* IV (Paris, 1886), article on Artigas.

Four years more passed; then, on September 23, 1850, thirty years to the day from his entry into Paraguay, José Gervasio Artigas died at Asunción, at the age of eighty-six. There in Paraguay, he was buried in simple fashion. His death passed almost unnoticed in Uruguay, which was at the time torn by strife with Rosas; but, six years later, his remains were brought to Montevideo and solemnly interred there.

VII

This man Artigas, what then is his importance in South American history? As military leader, *caudillo* of Uruguay, he led the struggle against the Spaniards, against the *Porteños* of Buenos Aires, and against the Portuguese. A political idealist, he was ceaseless in his fight for the principles which he set forth in his Instructions in 1813, and, though he was himself downed, his work lived on.

By his stubborn fight for federalism and for the elimination of Buenos Aires as the dominating factor in the Río de la Plata, Artigas gave the people of the Plata provinces a rallying point and crystallized the already existing resentment of *Porteño* control into active opposition. His opposition deprived unitarism of its great opportunity, and, thus, he paved the way for the creation of the Argentine Republic on a federal basis.

A creole aristocrat by birth, he was nevertheless a man of the people; he recognized no class distinctions; he was one with the highest as well as the lowest. A true democrat, he furthered the cause of the masses.

A sincere republican, Artigas early pronounced himself for absolute independence of Spain and for a republican form of government. Leading the opposition to the creation of a monarchy, he played his part in preventing the selection of a European prince as a ruler.

Ironically enough, the achievement of Artigas which even his detractors concede him—the foundation of an independent state—was one which he did not desire and which was, in fact, repugnant to him. He struggled for federalism, but in so doing he developed a national consciousness on the part of his people. They, embittered by a long warfare, believing Buenos Aires had left them to the tender mercies of Portugal, developed the tradition of their own individuality and were ripe for separatism and nationalism. From the national foundations laid by Artigas, there arose the Republic of Uruguay, which today acclaims as her founder José Artigas. And, as founder of Uruguay and father of federalism in the Plata, Artigas stands out, if not preëminent, at least in the front rank in Plata history of his period.

CHAPTER FIVE

FRANCIA, SUPREME DICTATOR OF PARAGUAY[1]

PARAGUAY, an interior country, yet the oldest white settlement in the Plata basin, is, with the possible exception of Uruguay, historically the most nearly unique, the most individual and distinctive country in all South America. For practically sixty years from her initial assertion of independence, Paraguay was ruled successively and almost without a break by three great dictators, each of whom was thoroughly distinctive and scarcely paralleled elsewhere in Hispanic America.

When the *Cabildo* of Buenos Aires renounced the Regency of Cádiz in May 1810 and, in effect, separated from Spain, Paraguay was under the governorship of the popular Bernardo de Velasco. News of Buenos Aires' action reached Paraguay in June through the medium of emissaries of the new government, who came with a demand that the province give recognition to its authority. Immediately Governor Valasco called the *Cabildo* of Asunción into consultation, and upon its advice an assembly of some two hundred-odd notables of the province was convened in July. Among the more prominent of the members of this assembly was Dr. José Gaspar Rodríguez de Francia, *síndico procurador,* or attorney-

[1] The career of Francia is well surveyed by Cecilio Báez in his *Ensayo sobre el doctor Francia y la dictadura en Sud-América* (Asunción, 1910). The value of Báez' work, which has been generally followed in the present treatment, is considerably enhanced by a critical bibliography. The best detailed account is in the factual and uncritical work of Enrique Wisner, *El dictator del Paraguay, doctor José Gaspar Rodríguez de Francia,* ed. by J. Boglich, (Concordia, Argentina, 1923), brought together in 1862 by order of the younger López, but unpublished until 1923. Anti-Francia accounts include J. M. Estrada, "Ensayo sobre la revolución de los comuneros del Paraguay . . . seguido de un apéndice sobre la decadencia del Paraguay y la guerra de 1865," in his *Obras completas* (Buenos Aires, 1899), I; Juan Andrés Gelly, *El Paraguay: lo que fué, lo que es, y lo que será* (Asunción, 1926); and Charles A. Washburn, *History of Paraguay* (2 vols., Boston, 1871). Contemporary accounts of great value include those of the brothers Robertson (J. P. Robertson and W. P. Robertson), *Letters on Paraguay . . .* (3 vols., London, 1838-1839), and J. Rengger and I. Longchamp, *Essai sur la révolution du Paraguay . . .* (Paris, 1827). The Spanish translation of the latter, edited by the Argentine historian Mariano A. Pelliza, *Ensayo histórico sobre la revolución del Paraguay . . . precedida de una biografía del tirano Francia, y continuada con algunos documentos y observaciones históricas* (Buenos Aires, 1883), has been used in the following pages. The greater part of information on the earlier years of Francia's reign of rigor comes from these two accounts and from Wisner. Wisner is the only work covering the entire period. Carlyle gives much pertinent criticism of the two first-named books. Cf. Thomas Carlyle, "Doctor Francia," in his *Critical and miscellaneous essays* (London, 1872) VII.

general, of the province, a man fated to exercise a tremendous influence upon the destinies of Paraguay.

Rodríguez de Francia, or Dr. Francia, as he preferred to be known, is one of the most fascinating figures of all history, yet at one and the same time one of the least known. Habitually he has been represented as a "grim and somber potentate," a Borgia reincarnate, a cruel despot without redeeming features. But as the great Argentinian Alberdi declared, "America does not know the story of that land [Paraguay] save as it is related by its rivals. The silence of isolation has left calumny victorious."[2] So much legend has grown up about him that it is often difficult if not impossible to distinguish truth from fancy. Three main works, those of the Swiss surgeons, Rengger and Longchamp, and the brothers Robertson, residents of Paraguay during part of the early period of Francia, and the recently published work of Wisner, originally compiled by order of the younger López, are the main sources of information.[3] That he is a fruitful subject for fiction has been ably demonstrated in one of the greatest historical novels, Edward Lucas White's *El supremo.*[4] Much of the detail of the man's life is but vaguely known. His earlier career in particular is much disputed as the result of conflicting accounts based on legend and oral tradition. But, since the personal character of Francia so thoroughly influenced his actions, and since Francia was Paraguay and Paraguay was Francia, it is necessary to pay more than ordinary attention to the man and his life.

I

José Gaspar Rodríguez de Francia was born in Asunción, January 6, 1766.[5] His father, García Rodríguez de Francia, was a native of Rio de Janeiro and had come to Paraguay as a tobacco expert during the attempted regeneration under the Bourbons. His mother was daughter of a one-time governor of the province. Francia himself was wont, however, to claim French ancestry in lieu of the rather despised *Carioca* lineage.

[2] Juan Bautista Alberdi, *Las disenciones de las repúblicas del Plata y las maquinaciones del Brasil* (Paris, 1865), 184.

[3] Cf. note 1, *supra.*

[4] Edward Lucas White, *El Supremo. A romance of the great dictator of Paraguay* (New York, 1916).

[5] The *Cabildo* of Asunción, in naming Francia a deputy to the *Cortes* of *Cádiz* in 1809 gave his age as forty-three. Cf. Wisner, 18. Wisner's own account and those of others give the year of birth as 1758. Wisner also gives a varied version of his parentage and his early life. Cf. *Ibid.,* 10.

Young Francia was educated in the academy at Asunción and destined for the priesthood. With the holy calling in mind he was sent at the age of fourteen to the University of Córdoba, where five years of study brought him the degree of master of philosophy and doctor of sacred theology in 1785. Even in his youth at Córdoba he had a reputation among his fellows as a misanthropic individual prone to heavy study and deep ponderous thought. But that he was not entirely unlike the modern university student is well demonstrated by the earliest letter of his on record. In this, writing to his father after his graduation from Córdoba, he asks for money to get home on and complains of the high cost of living in a university town.[6]

When Francia returned to Asunción in 1786, he was already showing some of the characteristics which influenced his later history. As a doctor of theology, said to have been one of but two "doctors" in all Paraguay in that era, he was looked up to as a man of great learning—after all, Paraguay was quite provincial in its attitude and ideas. Moreover, he spoke what was supposed to be a fluent French, an achievement of which he was inordinately proud; and who else in Paraguay spoke more than Spanish and the native Guaraní?

Disliking the idea of an ecclesiastical career, the youth looked for some position suitable to one of his learning and talents. But, since in this period most of the choicer governmental posts were filled by native-born Spaniards, the youth encountered serious difficulties. Thus it was that a thorough dislike of the favored Peninsular Spaniard was inculcated in him. Nevertheless, the young erudite did secure a position for himself, although he held it for some months without pay. This was the chair of Latin at the *Colegio Real de San Carlos* (the Royal College of San Carlos). Soon, however, his liberal ideas, based largely on Rousseau, brought him into conflict with the vicar of the college and he was dismissed. From this time dates his pronounced antipathy to the church and the clergy.

Several stories are told of José Gaspar's youth which tend to throw light upon his character. One, varying in its detail in different accounts, is that of the hatred between him and his father. Immediately upon his return from Córdoba, they quarreled over his mother's estate and over the youth's refusal to follow the church career set out for him. "Giving his father two months to turn over the property . . . he retired to live in a little place at a distance from the paternal home, where he followed a

[6] Rengger, (introduction), 21.

solitary life, without friends, having relations with no one, and with no companions other than his books." Eventually the father surrendered the legacy, but young José Gaspar never forgave him.

Years later, when the father lay on his death bed, he sent for his son, who flatly refused to come. Robertson tells the story as it was current in Asunción in his time.

> "The old man's illness was increased by the obduracy of his son, and indeed he showed a horror of quitting the world without mutual forgiveness taking place. He conceived his soul to be endangered by remaining at enmity with his first-born. Again, a few hours before he breathed his last, he got some of Francia's relatives to go to him, and implore him to receive the dying benediction of his father. He refused: they told him his father believed his soul could not reach heaven unless it departed in peace with his son. . . . 'Then tell my father that I care not if his soul descend to hell.' The old man died almost raving, and calling for his son José Gaspar."[7]

Such was Francia, unrelenting and unforgiving when an injury, or fancied injury, was done him.

Following Francia's dismissal from the *colegio,* he turned to the law. While strictly speaking he was not a lawyer, for indeed there were no lawyers in Paraguay, his Córdoba training was an invaluable aid to him in drawing up legal papers and in presenting arguments before the local courts. He was steadily the friend of the underdog, of the wronged man; most particularly he seems to have befriended the native Guaraní Indians, in whose eyes he ever after stood as a veritable demigod. In this calling he acquired a wide reputation for honesty, integrity, and ability. A story often told of him is that on one occasion a friend of his, one Rodríguez, came to ask him to draw up some documents showing Rodríguez' title to a piece of land. The title was manifestly a fraud, and the whole case a plot to take advantage of one Machaín, a bitter enemy of the future dictator, all the more so, it is said, because he had wooed and won the only young lady Francia had ever loved!

> "Francia saw at once that his friend's pretentions were founded in fraud and injustice; and he not only refused to act as his counsel, but plainly told him that much as he hated his antagonist Machaín, yet if he [Rodríguez] persisted in his iniquitous suit, that antagonist should have his [Francia's] most zealous support."[8]

And when Rodríguez did persist, Francia fulfilled his threat. Literally forcing himself into the house of Machaín, he volunteered his services,

---

[7] Robertson, II, 297-298.

[8] *Ibid.,* II, 29-32. The account is frequently quoted or cited, but Robertson appears to be the published source.

insisted upon rendering them, and despite venality of the court, won his case! But this did not in anywise mean a reconciliation; Francia and Machaín continued enemies, and years later, under Francia's dictatorship, Machaín faced the firing squad.

Possibly Francia's failure to win the hand of the future Señora de Machaín was a factor in making his character what it was, and well before the revolution came he was known as an austere and loveless, but not necessarily ascetic, individual. For his time, he was unusually well read and possessed "the largest library in Paraguay," some two hundred and fifty to three hundred volumes. These included writings of Rousseau, Rollin, Voltaire, and others, and, apparently, some works on Roman history. Likewise, he had some acquaintance with astronomy and mathematics. To the average Paraguayan this erudition served to enhance the man's prestige and to weave about him a sombre cloak of awe and mystery.

II

Shortly before the wars of independence broke out, Francia became *síndico curador* (attorney-general) of the Province of Paraguay. In 1809 when the *Cabildo* of Asunción, in common with other *cabildos* throughout the Spanish Empire, was called upon to send a deputy to the Spanish *Cortes,* Francia was chosen to represent Asunción, although he never served.

Then came 1810, that momentous year in Hispanic American history, and Paraguay was forced to make a decision between Spain or separation. Governor Velasco called the *cabildo,* as has been pointed out, and then upon its recommendation the assembly of notables. Among them was Francia, whose legislative ruling in accord with Rousseau's doctrine of Social Contract was that the Spanish authority had indeed ceased with the king's abdication and that sovereignty had reverted to the people of Paraguay. But, with deliberate intent to avoid conflict with either Spaniard or *Porteño,* the assembly declared for fidelity to the Regency of Cádiz, for the maintenance of good relations with Buenos Aires, and for the speedy formation of a *junta* for the defense of the province.

The new government at Buenos Aires considered the attitude of Paraguay to indicate separatism, that is from the old viceroyalty, and promptly made preparations to force the adherence of the recalcitrant province. But the Buenos Aires army, commanded by General Manuel Belgrano, met two successive defeats at Paraguayan hands early in 1811, and was compelled to capitulate and obtain the *junta's* permission to withdraw.

On the face of it, Belgrano's defeat had been a royalist victory. Actually, however, Creole sentiment in Paraguay was as thoroughly separatist as that down the river. The difference lay in Paraguay's determination not to be dominated by the metropolis, and, indeed, here may be seen one of the earliest manifestations of federalism in the Plata. Once the *Porteño* danger had been overcome, the Creoles of Paraguay changed front. As a concession to form and as a precaution against defeat, Governor Velasco had not only been permitted to continue in his old office, but had been a member of the *junta.* However, when he was discovered to be in communication with royalist agents in the west, a *coup d'état* was effected in May 1811, the governor was deposed, a new *junta* set up, and independence from Spain proclaimed. This revolution was directed by Francia, who from being secretary of the old *junta,* now became a member of the new. From this time, with the exception of one period of nearly a year, Francia was "in the saddle." First as a member of the *junta,* later, successively as "consul," "temporary dictator," and finally as "perpetual dictator," he guided the destinies of Paraguay for the next twenty-nine years, a period longer than that of any other Hispanic American dictator with the single exception of Díaz of Mexico. This era is generally designated as "Francia's reign of terror," although it is more properly a "reign of rigour," as Thomas Carlyle remarked. Francia was the guiding force of the new state from its beginning, but his rise to absolutism was more gradual. At first, more subtle methods were used.

The *coup d'état* occurred in mid-May, and one of the earliest acts of the new *junta* was to convoke a national assembly of a thousand members, the greater part of them from the rural districts where Francia's popularity was greatest. In June when the assembly met, Francia dominated it. One writer, by no means friendly to Francia, has claimed that the large number was sent in order that poorer men, friends of Francia, might conveniently be included and, above all, that since these deputies were poor, the congress would be anxious to adjourn and avoid the excessive costs of the city.[9] Be that as it may, the congress was at least roughly representative, however much it may have been unduly influenced.

The new *junta* was confirmed in short order, and the congress adjourned. Under the *junta,* friendly relations with Buenos Aires were established; two commissioners, Belgrano and Echevarría, visited Para-

[9] *Ibid.,* II, 22-24.

guay in hopes of gaining the province over, but the best they could do was to arrange a treaty on October 11, 1811, by which the independence of Paraguay was recognized, and a mutual federal pact, rather vague in its nature, undertaken[10]

Not long after the treaty, and possibly because of it, Francia withdrew from the *junta* complaining that the military dominated it. For nearly a year he remained in seclusion in his house in Asunción, although continuing "a mysterious influence." But, late in 1812, after much pressure, he returned to his position in the *junta.* Perhaps, as Carlyle would have it, his real objective was to show how indispensable he was to the government.[11]

III

Now indeed Francia was Paraguay; never again until his death did he let go the reins of power. In 1813, as difficulties with Buenos Aires over river navigation developed, a new commissioner, Nicolás de Herrera, came from Buenos Aires, only to be so isolated by Francia that he had no opportunity to confer with other members of the *junta,* or even with a new assembly which had been convened. This assembly, or rather Francia through it, formally confirmed Paraguayan independence, definitely renounced the Treaty of 1811, and, suppressing the *junta,* set up the "Republic of Paraguay."

Francia, a student of Roman history and government, proposed that, in lieu of the *junta,* two consuls be named, to serve alternate terms of four months. Readily acquiescing, the assembly appointed Francia and Fulgencio Yegros as First and Second Consuls. Yegros, a popular creole *estanciero* who had been a member of the last *junta,* although he possessed some military experience and prestige, was nevertheless an ignorant sort of fellow, of whom William Parish Robertson tells an amusing and illustrative story.

> "We had received letters from Buenos Aires, [Robertson relates], and were giving the Consuls the latest news from Europe. We mentioned among other things that the Emperor Alexander had joined the general alliance against Napoleon, and that several vessels laden with arms and munitions of war had been despatched from England to Russia. 'Malhaya,' said Yegros, after considering awhile, 'Malhaya, soplara un viento sur, largo y recio, que traxese todos estos buques aguas arriba.' 'I wish to goodness a long and strong south wind would blow, and force these vessels up the river.'

---

[10] Báez, 60.

[11] Carlyle, VII, 34.

> Yegros fancied [so Robertson explains] that if the south wind blew long enough, it would force every vessel bound for the Baltic up the Paraguay, and into the port of Assumption [Asunción]."[12]

Francia was Cæsar and Yegros Pompey under the consulate, and in actual practice, the Paraguayan Cæsar ruled for over a year until the country had become more accustomed to him. In this time he so shifted the military commands as to eliminate all unfriendly officers. Likewise under the consulate there was passed the famous edict forbidding any Spaniards to marry either within their own group or with creoles. No Spaniard could contract marriage except it be with a *mestizo* or an Indian.

The consulate endured a little more than a year. Then, in 1814, still another congress was convened, and the consulate in its turn suppressed. In its place Francia was named dictator for the period of three years, but before that period had elapsed, the last of the Paraguayan congresses of the era met on June 1, 1816, and, "considering the full confidence which the citizen José Gaspar de Francia has merited of the people, it declared and established him as perpetual dictator of the republic, for life." A salary of seven thousand *pesos* was allotted him, but this Francia, ever indifferent to money itself, rejected.[13]

For over a quarter of a century José Gaspar Rodríguez de Francia, now accorded the title of "El Supremo" (The Supreme One) ruled Paraguay as absolute dictator. The ideas of government as shown were derived largely from Rousseau's *Social Contract,* with old Roman forms. He is said, likewise, to have been a strong admirer of Napoleon, whom he desired to emulate.[14] But, he himself declared that Benjamin Franklin was his great model. "That man is the first democrat of the world, and he is the model whom we must imitate," he told Belgrano and Echevarría as he presented the latter with a picture of Franklin. But, he added, and herein is shown the practical political leader, "within forty years, it may be that these countries will have men like him, and only then shall we enjoy the liberty for which we are not prepared today."[15]

IV

The policies of Francia, before and after his dictatorship, were clearcut. Upon his foreign, or external, policy and its outcome hinged the

[12] Robertson, II, 304-305.

[13] Báez, 68.

[14] *Ibid.*, 66.

[15] Bartolomé Mitre, *Historia de Belgrano y de la independencia argentina* (6th ed., 4 vols., Buenos Aires, 1913), II, 25.

internal developments. Premised upon a fear and distrust of Paraguay's neighbors, especially of those provinces which today constitute the Argentine Republic, and upon a determination to prevent Paraguay from becoming the prey of the disorder and civil strife which so rent those neighbors, the "external policy of the dictatorship was one of peace and amity with all nations and of no intervention in the neighboring provinces."

After Belgrano's defeat, when Governor Velasco was still in at least partial control, he had ordered the occupation of Corrientes, the province bordering Paraguay to the south. Within two weeks of the overthrow of Velasco, Francia and the new *junta* ordered evacuation. Paraguay "desires nothing more than that her liberty be respected . . . she does not meddle and will never meddle in the internal affairs of other provinces," Francia declared in explanation.[16] Even when, in 1830, the Brazilian government interested itself in a scheme for the monarchization of the Plata and the erection of Corrientes and Entre Ríos into an independent state under Brazilian domination, Francia limited himself to a statement of objection and disapproval. Two years later, however, when the governor of Corrientes, the intrepid *caudillo* Ferré, took exception to the presence of Paraguayan troops in the Misiones region, which Corrientes claimed, Francia obdurately stood his ground, maintaining Paraguayan sovereignty there. Thereupon, the Corrientes government backed down. The dispute continued an open one for two years, amid a popular demand in Corrientes for the use of force.[17] After Francia's time, under the elder López, Paraguay altered her policy and entered into an alliance with Corrientes which dragged her into the civil wars, while still later, the younger López's policy in regard to Uruguay precipitated the great Paraguayan War and the near annihilation of Paraguay. But, under Francia, Paraguay asserted herself solely to the extent of defending her own boundaries.

Primarily it was the Argentine provinces which encountered the ire of Francia. Even in the early days of his preëminence, Francia was determined against entanglements there, but he felt differently toward other states. Thus we have the story given by Robertson of Francia's desire to effect a trade agreement if not an alliance with Great Britain. One day in the period of the consulate, Francia sent for John Parish Robertson, the elder of the brothers, who was then preparing to return to Europe. Greeting Robertson cordially, he commenced a long oration.

[16] Báez, 98.
[17] Pedro Ferré, *Memoria del general . . . Ferré* (Buenos Aires, 1921), 210.

> " 'You know what my policy has been with respect to Paraguay; that I have kept it on a system of non-intercourse with the other provinces of South America, and from contamination by that foul and restless spirit of anarchy and revolution which has more or less desolated and disgraced them all. Paraguay is in a more flourishing state now, than any of the countries around it; and while all here is order, subordination, and tranquillity, the moment you pass its boundary, the sound of the cannon, and the din of civil discord salute your ears. As may naturally be anticipated, these internal broils paralyze industry, and chase prosperity from the land. Now, whence arises all this? Why, from the fact that there is not a man in South America but myself, who understands the character of the people, or is able to govern them. The outcry is for free institutions; but personal aggrandizement and public spoliation are the objects alone sought. The natives of Buenos Aires are the most fickle, vain, volatile, and profligate of the whole of Spain's late dominions in this hemisphere; and therefore I am resolved to have nothing to do with the Porteños. My wish is to promote an intercourse with England direct. . . . The ships of Great Britain, triumphantly sweeping the Atlantic, will penetrate to Paraguay; and, in union with our flotillas, will bid defiance to all interruption of commerce, from the mouth of the Plate to the lake Xarayes. . . .' "

Thus clearly and succinctly, Francia expressed his own policy and its foundation, as well as his attitude toward the haughty *Porteños*. Then, continuing with an expression of admiration for Great Britain and British institutions, he called his sentinel and desired him to order in the sergeant of the guard. Robertson describes what followed.

> "On the appearance of this person the Doctor gave him a significant and peremptory look, and told him emphatically to bring '*that*.' The serjeant withdrew, and in less than three minutes returned with four grenadiers at his back, bearing, to my astonishment, among them, a large hide package of tobacco of two hundred weight, a bale of Paraguay tea of similar dimensions and exterior, a demijohn of Paraguay spirits, a large loaf of sugar, and several bundles of cigars, tied and ornamented with variegated fillets. Last of all, came an old negress with some beautiful specimens of embroidered cloth made from Paraguay cotton, and used there by the luxurious as hand towels and shaving cloths."

At first the Scot thought that Francia meant to make him a parting gift, but he was soon disillusioned as the dictator continued.

> " 'Señor Don Juan, . . . you are now going to England; you know what a country this is, and what a man I am. . . . Now, I desire that as soon as you get to London, you will present yourself to the House of Commons, take with you these samples of the productions of Paraguay; request an audience at the bar; and inform

> the assembly that you are deputed by Don Gaspar Rodriguez de Francia, Consul of the Republic of Paraguay, to lay before it these specimens of the rich productions of that country. Tell them I have authorized you to say that I invite England to a political and commercial intercourse with me; and that I am ready and anxious to receive in my capital, and with all the deference due to diplomatic intercourse between civilized states, a minister from the Court of St James's; I will also appoint to that Court an envoy of my own. . . .
>
> "'Present yourself,' continued he, 'at the bar of the house, and there deliver my message, as of old the ambassadors of independent states delivered theirs to the senate of Rome. . . .'"[18]

Ludicrous as Francia's instructions were in their detail, they nonetheless reveal Francia's own interest in foreign trade during the era of the consulate. More, they show how thoroughly his ideas and conceptions were influenced by ancient Rome. To him the House of Commons, the ruling body of Great Britain, was the old Roman Senate reincarnate.

Foreign intercourse was not to be, for Paraguay, landlocked and accessible to the sea only by way of the Paraná, found herself subject to the whim of restriction of the lower provinces, and, above all, of Buenos Aires. The civil wars of the provinces and, indeed, the studied policy of the Buenos Aires government, especially in the time of Rosas, prevented direct intercourse with the outside. "It was not Francia who isolated Paraguay, but the Argentine civil wars and Rosas—not López [Carlos Antonio] who lifted the isolation, but Urquiza."[19]

Even before Rosas, Buenos Aires was imposing discriminatory tariffs on Paraguayan goods. In 1817 she formally prohibited the importation of tobacco from Paraguay until "the incorporation of that province with the remaining provinces of the nation." By this act Paraguay lost what had once been an extensive market for her tobocco.[20]

This sort of restriction upon Paraguayan commerce and the general interference of various warring factions during the civil wars was not only not to Francia's liking but he would not tolerate it. Consequently, after the abortive revolutionary plot of 1820, the borders of Paraguay were sealed to commerce, whether incoming or outgoing. Only at Itapúa, or Encarnación, was trade permitted. In 1822 when Brazil declared her independence, Francia sought to open diplomatic and commercial relations with her, and for that purpose opened the port of Itapúa

---

[18] Robertson, II, 279 ff.
[19] Báez, 100.
[20] *Ibid.*, 101.

to commerce, although with fastidious restrictions and formalities. In a series of decrees, restrictions were laid down. Foreigners could enter Itapúa, but might not go more than a league beyond. A certificate was required, showing that the person trading was the actual owner of the goods and that he was "a good servant of the motherland and addicted to the sacred cause of liberty." Upon the filing of such a certificate, a license would be issued, but never one to European Spaniards. Later, a decree of 1825 restricted commerce to barter and prohibited the exportation of precious metals by foreigners. Paraguayans might export coin only for the purchase of arms and munitions.[21]

The creation of the special port of entry and its continuance at Itapúa was the result of efforts on the part of a Brazilian consular agent, Antonio Manuel Corrêa da Camara, accredited to Asunción in 1824. Two years later Corrêa da Camara was promoted to be chargé d'affaires.

So close did Paraguay and Brazil appear to be in this era that it was feared in Argentina that Paraguay would join with Brazil in the Argentine-Brazilian war of 1825 to 1828. This diplomatic relationship between Brazil and Paraguay was summarily terminated and Corrêa expelled when, in 1828, Brazilian troops infringed on Paraguayan territory. Simultaneously, Itapúa was closed.[22]

Primarily, the friendliness with Brazil had been the result of the ever-present distrust of the United Provinces, the contagion of whose disorders was feared by Paraguay. Not merely did Francia fear the contagion of Argentine disorders; his distrust went to the point of suspecting the entire motives of Buenos Aires, even her sincerity for the cause of independence. In his mind this last was borne out by the celebration of an armistice between Spain and Buenos Aires in 1823. When Rivadavia, then foreign minister of the latter state, sought to have the various independent governments of South America adhere to this armistice and sent Francia a note to that effect, the Paraguayan dictator refused even to receive Rivadavia's emissary, and returned his letter unopened.

If Francia's isolationist policy be criticized and condemned, as it has been by so many, it must at least be admitted that, in contrast to her sister states, Paraguay maintained internal peace and order. As one great Paraguayan of recent days has expressed it:

> "Foreign dangers never intimidated the Paraguayan dictator. The governments at Rio de Janeiro and Buenos Aires always found in

[21] *Ibid.*, 92.
[22] *Ibid.*, 102; Wisner.

him an arrogant chief of state and a jealous guardian of the territorial rights of the Republic. The latter's frontiers were always guarded by a considerable force which prevented the Brazilians from annexing new territories and the caudillos of the neighboring provinces from throwing her into political convulsions.

"Contrast this attitude with that of Rivadavia, Belgrano, Posadas, Alvear, García, Pueyrredón, and other political leaders of the Río de la Plata, who, indulging in imaginary dangers, committed many errors and humiliating acts."[23]

Not only was Francia adamant toward the efforts of his Plata neighbors to bring him into the struggle for independence and its aftermath, but into trade relations also. He followed a similar policy toward other South American states. Early in 1829 the governor of Santa Cruz de la Sierra, the Bolivian territory adjacent to Paraguay, wrote a letter to the great dictator seeking to open commercial relations. On this very same letter, which the dictator returned, he placed the following: "Reasons of state preclude the government of Paraguay taking into consideration this proposal. Asunción, February 15, 1829, [signed] Francia." The envelope itself was endorsed by Francia's secretary, "Received at eleven a. m., and returned at two p. m."[24]

Bolívar, through the famous Dean Funes of Córdoba, who acted as his deputy at Buenos Aires, made attempts on more than one occasion to shake the Paraguayan hermit loose from his isolation. On the well-known occasion of Francia's sensational kidnapping of the great naturalist Bonpland, Bolívar added his voice to those protesting, only to have his communication returned to him. In 1825, however, he received somewhat more courtesy, even if no greater satisfaction. An officer in Bolívar's service, one Captain Rúiz, was sent as bearer of a letter requesting that Paraguay join in Bolívar's proposed union of all South America. Rúiz was coldly received, permitted communication with no one, and on the afternoon of the very day of his arrival given the following letter for the Liberator:

" . . . The Portuguese, the *Porteños,* the Chilians, the Brazilians, and the Peruvians have all manifested to this government desires the same as your own, with no other result than the confirmation of the principle which has guided the happy régime which has freed this province from the rapine and other evils and which it will follow steadily until there has been restored to the new world the tranquillity it enjoyed before there appeared revolutionary apostles, who covered with the olive branch the perfidious dagger which ruled

[23] Báez, 103.
[24] Wisner, 143.

with blood. . . . But Paraguay knows them and as a result will not abandon her system, at least not while I am at the head of her government. . . ."[25]

Francia's external policy, then, was absolute isolation from her neighbors until such time as those neighbors had settled down to peace and order. The abandonment of this policy by his successors, while it resulted favorably for a time, did eventually bring ruin upon Paraguay.

V

The internal policies of Francia were premised upon a most complete absolutism, with all authority and power centered in himself. "Jealous of his own authority to the point of exaggeration, he had no confidantes."[26] None could count themselves his intimate friends. To the Swiss surgeon and naturalist Rengger, he declared, "If the Holy Father himself should come to Paraguay, I would do him no other honor than to make him my chaplain."

Robertson describes him as a man of striking and dignified appearance, of dark complexion, with penetrating black eyes and jet-black hair, which he combed back from his forehead, and which hung in natural ringlets over his shoulders. He wore a suit of black, with a large scarlet cloak thrown over his shoulders, and golden buckles on his shoes and at the knees of his breeches. His manner was quiet and unostentatious, and there was nothing in his behavior or conversation to suggest the dogmatic or capricious dictator of later years. Vanity was a ruling feature; he was evidently pleased in his knowledge of French and his acquaintance with the writings of Voltaire, Rousseau, and others.[27]

Personal profit meant nothing to him. Avaricious on behalf of the state, he was generous in his personal expenditures. When the assembly, naming him to be dictator, prescribed a salary of seven thousand *pesos,* he promptly cut it to a third of that figure. Under no circumstances would he accept a gift.

Francia derived his ideas from his readings on Napoleon, on the French Revolution, and on ancient Rome, and from Franklin, so he claimed, and the encyclopedists of the eighteenth century, particularly Rousseau. In defense of his absolutism he declared, quoting Rousseau, "When the motherland was in danger, even Sparta let her laws lie dor-

---

[25] *Ibid.,* 134-135.

[26] Báez, 69.

[27] W. H. Koebel, *Romance of the river Plate* (2 vols., London, 1914), II, 390. Cf., also, Richard F. Burton, *Letters from the battlefields of Paraguay* (London, 1870), "Introductory essay," *passim.*

mant. But only the greatest dangers can compensate for altering public order, and never should the sacred power of the law be suspended unless it is for the well-being of the country. . . . Then may be named a supreme chief who may silence all laws."[28]

And, when the assembly of 1816 made him "Perpetual Dictator of Paraguay," Francia did indeed silence such laws as conflicted, in his opinion, with the best interests of the state. Probably most of his acts can be readily justified, but, like dictators before him and dictators since him, he went to extremes. The "reign of terror" or, more accurately, the "reign of rigor" which he inaugurated came after the abortive revolutionary plots of 1820. In that year, the year of Artigas' fall, Ramírez, the *caudillo* of Entre Ríos, entered into a conspiracy with some of the leading Creoles and Old Spaniards of Paraguay. Unfortunately for the conspirators, a communication from Ramírez was intercepted late in that year, and early in January began a series of arrests and trials. The erstwhile consul Yegros was executed. Caballero, hero of the defense against Belgrano, committed suicide in prison. From forty to sixty-eight persons were executed. Others were subjected to the lash and imprisonment. This sweeping vengeance did indeed terrorize the country, but only in its suddenness and intensity does it differ from the practices followed elsewhere in the Plata from the very beginning of the revolution.

One consequence of the conspiracy was an edict ordering the imprisonment of all Spaniards resident in Asunción. Some three hundred were thus affected, including old Governor Velasco, who died in prison; eventually most of these prisoners were released after paying forced contributions to the state.

Thus began twenty years of the most complete absolutism and isolation, broken at first by the trade through Itapúa and by the occasional visits, voluntary and involuntary, of several foreigners. In general it may be said that once a foreigner entered the country he stayed there until it suited Francia's pleasure that he be permitted to depart. This pleasure he exercised in the case of a number of British subjects after the Battle of Ayacucho, the Yorktown of South America, in recognition of the aid individual Britons had given the cause of independence.[29]

The brothers Robertson, perhaps the best known of the visitors to Paraguay in Francia's day, had already left before the conspiracy. Their trade with Paraguay, welcomed at first, had later run into difficulties,

---

[28] Báez, 81.

[29] *Ibid.*, 96. Wisner, generally strong on detail, makes no mention of this in his chapter on the years 1824-1825. Cf. Wisner, 125-132.

and in 1818 they made a rather hurried departure. In 1819 came two more foreigners who were later to impress the world with their opinions of Paraguay, the Swiss surgeon-naturalists Rengger and Longschamp. Their purpose was to study the rich flora of the country, but once they were in Paraguay, Francia would not permit them to leave, although he treated them well, telling them: "Do as you wish; profess whatever religion most suits you, no one will molest you; but do not mix yourselves in affairs which concern my government." Finally, in 1825, they were permitted to leave. On their return to Europe Rengger published his famous *Essai sur le Paraguay,* which was eagerly read and translated into English and Spanish. Despite its generally favorable tone toward Francia and his dictatorship, when a copy reached his hands it was immediately banned by him in a great outburst of invective.[30]

Artigas, once the great protector of Uruguay and of the provinces of the Littoral, fled, as already noted, to Paraguay for asylum in 1820. His arrival shortly preceded the discovery of the great Creole conspiracy, already suspected by Francia, and he was imprisoned for some months. Later he was granted a small pension and a house at Curuguatí in the interior. There, after thirty years in quiet exile, he peacefully ended his days.

Most famous of all the visitors to Paraguay was the great French naturalist Bonpland, who had been a companion and colleague to the immortal Humboldt during the latter's visit to South America in the first decade of the century. In 1821 Bonpland was engaged in a scientific study of the flora of Corrientes, close to the borders of Paraguay. Perhaps he had even inadvertently crossed the border when, on orders from Francia, he was kidnapped and brought to Asunción. For nine years he was kept a prisoner, permitted to move at will within the country, but forbidden to leave. Meanwhile, protests from all Europe failed to move Francia. By 1830 Bonpland had become so much enamoured of his "prison" that when Francia released him as a reward for medical aid he had given him he left the country almost by force. Later, he returned to Corrientes, where he made his home until his death in 1858.

Among the internal improvements and changes were those affecting agriculture, public works, the church and education, and the army. These were effected ordinarily under the personal direction of the dictator, who trusted none so well as himself. Dissatisfied with the translation rendered him of an English trade document he is said to have

[30] Wisner, 150-157.

taken an English grammar, absorbed its rudiments, and then personally translated the document to see for himself what it contained! If cloth were of too loose a weave he would impose a fine and tell the offender that he might consider himself lucky. When, in checking state accounts, he found a shortage of twelve hides, he forthwith imposed a sentence at hard labor.[31]

Under Francia's assiduous care Paraguay became self-sufficient in agriculture. The formerly profitable tobacco export to Buenos Aires had been lost. Instead, he developed cotton-raising and produced cotton for the cloth formerly imported. Yerba mate (Paraguay tea) was developed. The cattle industry was aided and improved. On two occasions he took radical measures to combat an epidemic which was killing off cattle. Any herds containing even a single infected animal were slaughtered by the dictator's orders.

When, in October 1827, a plague of locusts swarmed over Paraguay and destroyed the season's crops, the country faced starvation. But Francia, who well knew his country's potentialities, forthwith decreed that a second crop be planted. As a result the country was not only saved from famine, but thereafter the Paraguayans regularly and profitably planted two crops instead of one.

The streets of Asunción were widened and straightened. This was done arbitrarily under direction of Francia, who himself performed the surveys. Owners of houses encroaching on the new streets were compelled to tear them down and to rebuild.

Francia's policy toward the church was founded upon the idea of subordination of all to his authority. Processions were forbidden. The bishop of Paraguay, an old man, was removed on grounds of senile decay, and a new provisional bishop named in his stead. To destroy the social and political influence of the Old Spaniards, they were forbidden to marry within their own circle, or yet among the Creoles. Monasteries and seminaries were suppressed, and no outside influence was permitted to come in. Public instruction was all but done away with, but private schooling was encouraged.

The army came in for a great deal of Francia's attention. Although he had absolutely no military training himself, he personally drilled his soldiers and laid the basis for the well trained army of later régimes. A standing army of 5,000 men, with a reserve of 20,000, was quite sufficient to render the boundaries of the country inviolable. Yet its func-

[31] *Ibid.,* 133.

tion was purely defensive, and militarism had no place. Part of his defense measures included the building of extensive forts against the Indians of the Chaco and along the frontiers. Lest his officers think too highly of themselves, none was given rank above that of captain. Even the commander of a fort was distinguished only by the title of "commandant of a detachment."

As the Reign of Rigor continued, Paraguay prospered. Absolutism continued, although somewhat mellowed at times. Annually, on the 6th of January, the people celebrated the birthday of El Supremo, whom they blindly obeyed and of whom they stood in great dread.

The crops of 1833 were so bountiful that his minister of *hacienda* dared even to propose an exportation of the surplus. But Francia, although recognizing the advantages which might accrue, declared that isolation must continue until the neighbors of Paraguay had become peaceful.

VI

Francia himself during all this time lived methodically, with vigorous care and scrupulousness, in the old house of the governors of Paraguay, rarely leaving the city or the immediately surrounding country. Four servants completed his household.

Every day, winter or summer, he arose at sunrise and had breakfast, a bit of mate, and wandered about the spacious corridors of the house until his barber came to shave him and to trim his hair. But little work indeed did this barber have to do, for he had few hairs on his face.

Then he resumed rambling about the house, where he received those persons who wished to speak with him. This was the occasion when he received petitions and appeals. At first these had been made in person, but both by reason of their volume and because of the danger of assassination, he altered the system so that his secretary, Patiño, was charged with the preliminary handling of petitions and with eliminating those not in proper form. Every petition had to be exact. On one occasion Patiño is said to have refused one written in green ink, whereupon the petitioner rewrote it in the same color of ink used by the secretary, only to have it rejected again![32]

To combat disaffection and to ferret out plots, Francia employed an extensive spy system. In addition, there were spies whose duties were to check on the activities of their fellows. This very efficient system prevented a repetition of the extended plot of 1820.

[32] *Ibid.*, 153; Gelly, 50.

After lunch the dictator regularly took his siesta, then went for a ride about the city and surrounding country. Four horses, always used in order, were regularly kept for his use. Fifty paces ahead of him rode an escort of soldiery. On these rides he carefully watched all that went on, visited public works, and supervised any project that was in progress.

After sunset he read until supper time when he consumed a frugal supper of a bit of meat and a small glass of wine. His daily personal expenses, it is said, did not run over two *pesos*.[33]

Francia had no cronies. Of his several living brothers and sisters, only his sister Petrona received any sort of special consideration, a small estate outside the city. His brother Pedro was for a time in charge of one of the state *estancias,* but when he failed to show efficiency, Francia promptly removed him from office.

The pillars of the dictatorship were his secretary Patiño and four military commandants. In addition, he had various chiefs of departments. The treasury itself he did not touch. Instead, the actual funds of government were left in the care of two functionaries or custodians, each with one key, so that only together could they open the strongroom.

For twenty-nine years Francia ruled Paraguay, imposing his arbitrary but enlightened will upon his people. Not power for power's sake, but the benefit of his country as he saw it was his objective. A dictator of the first rank, he was more arbitrary than others only because he was more nearly absolute. "A man such as Francia," says the Paraguayan scholar and statesman, Cecilio Báez, "does not love power except to dominate disorder or to realize an end. . . . He did not convoke congresses to resign, feigningly [as did Bolívar], for he was no comedian. Nor did he indulge in frivolous pleasures, nor yet make himself happy by adulation and flattery."[34] Like Rivadavia in Buenos Aires, and others elsewhere, Doctor Francia believed himself the Man of Providence in Paraguay, and he acted accordingly.[35]

Perhaps his greatest mistake was committed just prior to his death. In declining health, and realizing death was not far off, he systematically destroyed his papers, documents which had they been saved might well have preserved the record of his achievements for posterity. Three months later, on the 20th of September, 1840, Francia breathed his last. Even then, so thoroughly had he inculcated discipline that, according to

[33] Wisner, 151-161, *passim.*
[34] Báez, 117.
[35] *Ibid.,* 122.

one story, probably apochryphal but nonetheless illustrative, just before the end,

> "Francia, when consulting a doctor, fell into a fit. The doctor . . . called in the sergeant of the guard, but was met with a refusal to enter without an order from the Dictator. 'But he can't speak,' explained the doctor. 'No matter,' replied the man, 'if he comes to, he will punish me for disobedience.' "[36]

Within a few hours he was dead.

[36] Koebel, II, 408.

CHAPTER SIX

BERNARDINO RIVADAVIA, ARGENTINE DICTATOR AND INSTITUTION BUILDER[1]

THE year 1820 was marked by strong disintegrating tendencies throughout the Plata basin, which Argentine historians customarily denominate "the anarchy of the year Twenty." The once strong government of Pueyrredón, which had ruled from 1816, had weakened and then fallen late in 1819. Rondeau, ever a compromise choice, had succeeded to ephemeral power, but his government, too, collapsed, as the provinces began to assert themselves under petty rulers such as Ramírez of Entre Ríos—he who gave the *coup de grace* to Artigas and whose machinations with the anti-Francia elements of Paraguay contributed so largely to the development of Francia's policy of isolation. Rivalling or aiding Ramírez as the exigencies of the moment demanded were the greater Estanislao López of Santa Fe, Bustos of Córdoba, Ocampo of La Rioja, and a dozen other provincial *caudillos,* each a virtual overlord in his own province. Ramírez and López it was who overturned Rondeau's government at the crucial Battle of Cepeda early in 1820. Following that event the Province of Buenos Aires and the three Littoral provinces (Santa Fe, Entre Ríos, and Corrientes) came together in a loose inter-provincial accord, the Treaty of Pilar, but more as allies than as parts of a whole.

Disunity was the keynote of the 1820's; nevertheless, through Buenos Aires may be traced the main threads of Plata history in that decade, particularly through Bernardino Rivadavia, who, first as chief minister of the Province of Buenos Aires and later as president of the Argentine Republic, dominated in Buenos Aires and contributed heavily to internal development and progress. Coincident with Rivadavia, however, there arose several federalist leaders in the provinces. Ramírez had gone the way of the usual man of violence, but Estanislao López and Juan Facundo Quiroga, "the tiger of the *pampas,*" lord of La Rioja and neighboring provinces, held sway in the interior along with Bustos of

[1] In the present study the factual presentation of Mariano Vedia y Mitre, *De Rivadavia a Rosas* (Buenos Aires, 1930) has been followed. In addition, the manuscript work of Dr. Philip Coolidge Brooks "Bernardino Rivadavia, Argentina's statesman among warriors," written as an M.A. thesis at the University of California in 1930 has been extensively utilized for its valuable references.

Córdoba and other lesser figures. Union with Buenos Aires was at times accepted and at times repudiated, as, meanwhile, that province developed in a more orderly fashion under the ægis of Rivadavia, "Argentina's statesman among warriors," as he has been aptly called.[2]

The Battle of Cepeda had been the triumph of provincial autonomy over unitarism, whose strength centered in Buenos Aires, a triumph, too, as one of the great Argentine historians of the present day, Levene, points out, of the democratic masses over the cultured but oligarchic aristocracy of the capital.[3] Left alone as the result of quarrels between López and Ramírez, Buenos Aires pulled herself together and set up a government, in which the unitarist elements were soon able to assert themselves and then to predominate, although, ironically, the organization was made possible by the two great federalist leaders of later years, Dorrego and Rosas. An election of a provincial legislature was held, and then Martín Rodríguez, one of the early leaders in the separation from Spain, was chosen governor of the province. Rodríguez himself was greater as a military than as a political leader. Under him in theory, but nevertheless outshining him, was his minister of government and foreign relations, Bernardino Rivadavia.

I

Like Rodríguez, Rivadavia had been long in the public service, and, indeed, his record was the more distinguished and outstanding. At this time he was forty-one years of age, having been born in Buenos Aires in 1780. A stumpy person of slightly more than medium height, he fairly exuded dignity: his head was ever erect, with prominent chin, thick lips, heavy eyebrows, and a nose made prominent by a well-developed bridge.[4] His appearance, as shown in portraits, well bears out his personal reputation. Something of a dandy, he had a high conception of himself and his ability, as has been amply testified to by many foreigners whom he met.[5]

It has been stated by at least one Argentine author, a writer of popular

[2] Cf. Brooks, MS cited in footnote 1.

[3] Ricardo Levene, *Lecciones de historia argentina* (1933 ed., 2 vols., Buenos Aires, 1933), II, 231.

[4] Cf. Francisco García Calderón, *Latin America: its rise and progress* (New York, 1913), 138; Clemente L. Fregeiro, *Lecciones de historia argentina* (2 vols., Buenos Aires, 1886), II, 176.

[5] Ricardo Sáenz Hayes, "Rivadavia íntimo," in his *La politica de Alberdi con Sarmiento* (Buenos Aires, 1926), 94.

history, that Rivadavia was a mulatto.[6] The charge is, however, founded on nothing more than superficial points of his facial features, especially his unusually thick lips. Actually he was of direct Gallego extraction, son of Benito González y Rivadavia, a native of Galicia, by his first wife and cousin, Doña María Josefa, a first-generation Creole. The elder Rivadavia, a Spanish official in the colonial period, held various important posts at different points in the viceroyalty. Later, these two, Spanish father and Creole son, were pitted against each other in the wars of independence.[7]

Young Bernardino was educated in the *colegio,* or secondary school, in Buenos Aires, although he never completed the entire course of studies. At the time of the British invasions in 1806 and 1807 he was an officer of the defending troops, but can scarcely be said to have been an outstanding soldier. In 1809 he married Juana del Pino y Vera, a daughter of the late Viceroy Joaquín del Pino.[8] Almost coincident with this he became active in the troubled politics of the viceroyalty, and, when within the year the famous *cabildo abierto* of May 1810 met, he was one of the leading spirits. The following year, 1811, he was secretary to the governing *junta,* and from that time until 1827 he was almost constantly associated with the government. "No matter what position he occupied, whether secretary of the government, a minister in it, or a diplomatic agent," he made his influence felt.[9] In 1812 he became a member of the triumvirate *junta;* when that government fell from power in October of the same year, Rivadavia was sent to Europe as diplomatic agent for the United Provinces. Thus, he became "the Franklin of the Argentinian revolution," as the great Mitre, historian and unitarist, expressed it.

Rivadavia's diplomatic career, lasting eight years, was not always crowned with success, but it did give him valuable contacts and experience. At different times he was agent in Great Britain and in France and even in Spain itself, where he sought to arrange with the Spanish government some *modus vivendi* for the termination of the war and settlement of its issues. His journey to Spain in 1816 was made possible

---

[6] "It is certain that he was a mulatto, and this stain constituted a stigma in Buenos Aires, the city of all America least degenerated by mixing of castes. Rivadavia was the prototype of what is called in Havana a 'negro catedrático,' a man of bearing, solemn, if impressive appearance, and of severe tone." Ciro Bayo, *Examen de próceres americanos* (Madrid, 1916), 284.

[7] Vedia y Mitre, 18.

[8] Viceroy of the Río de la Plata from 1801 to 1804.

[9] Vedia y Mitre, 29.

by a guarantee of safe conduct from the British government. At Madrid, in interviews with Ferdinand's minister Ceballos, Rivadavia flatly asked for the erection of the United Provinces into an independent state under British protection, but with a Spanish prince as monarch.[10] In France he was active in the negotiations which looked toward the establishment of a monarchy in the Plata, with some European prince at its head, a Bourbon if possible.[11] In no way was Rivadavia anti-monarchial, nor was he yet a dyed-in-the-wool monarchist. Rather, the issue was the practical one of getting European support for the newborn nation which he represented.

Rivadavia's career in Europe, coming as it did at the height of the restoration period, inclined him all the more toward a centralized government. Perhaps, too, since it isolated him from his own country, it prevented him getting a thorough grasp of the problems involved in interprovincial relations and, above all, an understanding of the provinces' point of view. Consequently, when he returned to Buenos Aires in 1821 he was not only definitely and thoroughly a unitarist in sentiment, but was possessed of a disdain for the less cultured provincials, whose resistance to centralization of authority received no sympathy from him.

Rivadavia's return followed closely on the establishment of the Rodríguez government. Rodríguez promptly availed himself of Rivadavia's talents and appointed him to be minister of government and of foreign relations. In this latter capacity, he was, under the system of government then prevailing, not only representative of the Province of Buenos Aires, but *encargado de negocios extranjeros* for the loosely-knit government of the United Provinces.[12]

III

When Rivadavia assumed office there was already underway a project for still another congress, to meet at Córdoba, where, it was hoped, a definite plan for the organization of a general government might be evolved. Rivadavia's opposition, however, put an end to the negotiations which were being carried on. In his opinion the time was not ripe and, in view of the strong federalist sentiment of the provinces, "it would be futile to seek a new congress." As a result the Plata provinces achieved a federalism in fact, tempered only by the very loose union of

---

[10] Vicente Fidel López, *La revolución argentina* (4 vols., Buenos Aires, 1891), I, 393-394.

[11] Cf. Carlos Correa Luna, *Rivadavia y la simulación monárquica* . . . (Buenos Aires, 1915), *passim.*

[12] *Ibid.*

the Quadrilateral Treaty in the following year.[13] Rivadavia never accepted this provincial isolation as more than a provisional régime; never did he resign himself to the loose federal status as more than a temporary, fleeting condition. Yet, he was willing to bide his time.[14]

Instead of making fruitless gestures toward union, Rivadavia set himself the task of internal development of the Province of Buenos Aires and the settlement of burning international issues, principally that of recognition of independence. As a founder of institutions and as a foreign minister, he was definitely outstanding in the period which followed.

> "If the title of 'founder' can be given anyone it is to Rivadavia, [declares Vedia y Mitre]. He founded everything: from responsible democratic government to the institutions of social aid; from the most complete liberty of the press even to the literary movement of which the press was both tribune and bulwark; from the publicity of governmental acts to the public discussion of those acts before the Parliament [of the province]; from institutions of education to the regulation of their studies; from woman's education to the elevation of her social function.
>
> "And above all," [this author insists], "it must be said, because it is true, that he was founder of the provincial governments, since thanks to his forces and his action, the Province of Buenos Aires existed for the first time as a government entity and, as has been said, served as an example to the others. . . ."[15]

Extreme as the foregoing quotations may be in some respects, it must nevertheless be admitted that, broadly, they are correct, even though the influence of Rivadavia on the provinces was indeed indirect.

Rivadavia had been greatly impressed by Old World events and conditions, and his policies show clearly that influence. Under him were inaugurated political, economic, ecclesiastical, educational, social, municipal, and military reforms.

Parliamentary government as practiced in Europe had appealed greatly to Rivadavia and, consequently, under his influence the *Junta de Representantes* of the province became a parliamentary body. As minister, Rivadavia frequently engaged in its debates and pushed his own ideas. An electoral law was enacted; the suffrage was broadened. The old *Cabildo* of Buenos Aires was suppressed as incompatible with the new government.

---

[13] *Registro oficial de la república argentina* . . . (50 vols., Buenos Aires, 1879-1880), II, 4.

[14] Vedia y Mitre, 42-43.

[15] *Ibid.,* 43.

One of the earliest enactments was the *Ley de Olvido,* or Law of Oblivion. Under it a full amnesty was granted to all who had been involved in the fratricidal struggles of the past and various edicts of banishment were declared "forgotten" and cast into oblivion. "To enjoy most completely the fruits of such painful sacrifices, it is necessary to forget, it is necessary to do away with, if it be possible, the ingratitudes, the errors, the weaknesses which have degraded men and have afflicted the people in that great enterprise, the war of emancipation," asserted Rivadavia.[16]

Several measures of economic significance were attempted under Rivadavia. Perhaps the most outstanding and certainly the most discussed in its time was the "Law of Emphytheusis," pertaining to the agrarian scheme. Under this law, subsequently repealed, no public land could be completely alienated; rather, the "owner" was to pay perpetual rent, somewhat in the manner later developed in Australia and New Zealand. Essentially Rivadavia advocated what was in effect the Single Tax Theory of which Henry George was the great exponent in later years, so that "single-tax" advocates have pointed back to him as a precursor of George.[17] His interest in the development of the rural regions was further shown by his activity in promoting immigration, especially to Patagonia, while he was personally responsible for the introduction of the merino sheep into Argentina.[18]

Under the auspices of Rivadavia and at his initiative an official "commercial exchange," or *Bolsa de Comercio,* was put into operation in 1822—not entirely the first of its kind in the country, for there already existed a small British mercantile organization. Similarly, a Bank of Discounts was organized, although that institution was primarily the creation of Rivadavia's colleague García. In addition there was arranged an important loan authorized by the provincial legislature in 1822 for building a port, providing running water for the City of Buenos Aires, and establishing towns on the frontier and on the seacoast of the province.[19]

Declaring that ways of communication and security of mail delivery should exemplify the efficiency of a government, the minister, by decree of August 1821, appointed a commission and had funds set aside for the

16 *Ibid.,* 48.
17 Cf. Emilio Coni, *La verdad sobre la enfiteusis de Rivadavia* (Buenos Aires, 1927).
18 Vedia y Mitre, 75-76; Bartolomé Mitre, *Ensayos historicos* (Buenos Aires, 1918), 246.
19 *Registro oficial . . .,* II, 20.

payment of officials who were to arrange for road improvement, protection of travel, and facilitating of mails.[20] Other similar measures were taken to expedite communications within the province and with other provinces.

One of the most important and controversial of all the reforms under the ministerial dictatorship of Rivadavia was in regard to the church. He himself proposed that the supremacy of the state over the church be clearly established and, furthermore, that the convents and monasteries be suppressed.[21] The former was, indeed, effected in its entirety, although achievement was only partial in the latter. In the face of intense opposition and after angry and violent debates in the legislature, Rivadavia put through a church reform measure on December 1, 1822, which abolished the exemptions of the clergy, did away with tithes, secularized monasteries and cemeteries, and laid down stringent rules for the conduct of devotion and for life in the monasteries.[22]

This church policy served strongly to prejudice public opinion in the provinces against him. Thus in La Rioja, for example, Quiroga used "defense of religion" as a rallying cry against the central government.[23] Within Buenos Aires itself rioting close by akin to organized revolt broke out shortly after the enactment of the law, but the incipient uprising was promptly suppressed.[24]

Most outstanding of all was the aid Rivadavia gave to education. "There is no liberty or prosperity without learning," was his dictum.[25] "Education is the secret of the greatness and prosperity of the nation."[26] In 1810 there had been less than fifty schools within the limits of the entire viceroyalty and these had, one and all, been conducted along antiquated lines, with religious instruction their principal if not sole function. Rivadavia was responsible for the establishment of the Lancastrian system of education in Argentina, for which purpose he brought James Thompson, a member of the Lancaster Society, from England. Under this reform the beginnings of a more modern school system were made in the City of Buenos Aires, even though it remained for Sarmiento to develop and extend it a third of a century later.

---

20 *Ibid.,* I, 584.

21 Vedia y Mitre, 51-52.

22 Levene, II, 226.

23 *Ibid.,* ch. 4.

24 Adolfo Saldías, *Historia de la confederación argentina . . .* (5 vols., Buenos Aires, 1892), I, 156.

25 Andrés Lamas, *Rivadavia. Su obra política y cultural* (Buenos Aires, 1882), 40.

26 Saldías, I, 132.

One of the projects in which Rivadavia was most deeply interested, and one perhaps with the most lasting and valuable results, was the establishment of the University of Buenos Aires. Under the old viceroyalty there had been strong advocacy of a university to be located in Buenos Aires, but the project had never been carried to fruition. Now, however, under Rivadavia, the University of Buenos Aires was founded and stands today as the leading university of all Hispanic America. Later Rivadavia arranged to bring a number of foreign scholars to teach in the university. The first of these was Dr. Carta Molina, an Italian who came from England in 1824 to found a department of physics.[27]

Social reform was another problem attacked by Rivadavia. A foundling's home and an orphan asylum, an asylum for the insane, and a woman's hospital were among the institutions given formal establishment in his time. The *Sociedad de Beneficiencia,* or Public Welfare Society, another creation, gave particular attention to the elementary education of women, and assumed general charge of the several charitable institutions.[28]

Municipal administration of the City of Buenos Aires was given a good share of Rivadavia's attention. After suppressing the old *cabildo* in 1821, he was able to gain control of the city and thus to carry out a program of civic development. The port was improved and running water provided by means of the British loan which he had obtained; the cathedral was completed in accord with plans he himself had brought from Paris; public cemeteries were established; and the city itself was redistricted for better administration.[29]

Other accomplishments for which Rivadavia is given credit were the inauguration of the *Registro oficial,* the establishment of the *Archivo general,* founding of a museum of natural history, and the development of the public library. In addition to the *Registro oficial,* which was no more than an official register of governmental acts, several newspapers were in existence at this time.[30]

Finally there should be noted the question of military organization and reform. No striking changes were effected in the army, but the military system was nevertheless overhauled. A celebrated set of regulations for the army included as its salient features provision for retire-

[27] Juan María Gutiérrez, *Origen y desarrollo de la ensenanza pública superior en Buenos Aires* (Buenos Aires, 1868), 318.

[28] Vedia y Mitre, 60.

[29] Cf. Ismael Bucich Escobar, *Buenos Aires ciudad* (Buenos Aires, 1921), 80-82.

[30] R. Melgar, *Rivadavia* (Buenos Aires, 1908), 58-65. Cf., also Saldías, I, 135.

ment and for pensions, allowing the replacement of old soldiers.[31] Later, when troubles across the estuary threatened, "The Army of Observation" was created to "observe" conditions along the Uruguay River.[32]

Nor was Rivadavia, in his capacity as minister, concerned only with internal improvement and organization. Not merely was he minister of government, but of foreign relations, as well. In the former capacity he served only the Province of Buenos Aires, but under the Treaty of Pilar of 1820, the governor of Buenos Aires was empowered to act in foreign relations on behalf of all the provinces. This constituted one of the very few links which, technically speaking, held the provinces together. The arrangement, continued under the Quadrilateral Treaty of January 1822, permitted Rivadavia to carry on negotiations with foreign powers, notably the United States and Great Britain, seeking recognition of the independence from Spain, and even with Spain herself. Too, there were handled the intricate relations with Brazil over the *Banda Oriental,* which had been conquered by the Portuguese in Artigas' time.

Later in 1821, upon the insistence of the United States agent at Buenos Aires, Forbes, the government promulgated a decree ordering the complete cessation of the privateering operations which were still being carried on against Spain.[33] Portugal had already acknowledged the independence of the Plata, just before Rivadavia's arrival in 1821. The following year Brazil and the United States both accorded recognition of independence to the United Provinces, as did Great Britain in de facto form in 1823. Recognition would have come regardless of Rivadavia, but undoubtedly the stability and the progressive measures undertaken at Buenos Aires served to hasten it. Rivadavia himself, however, cannot be given entire credit, for indeed most of the preliminaries to recognition were carried on abroad, away from Buenos Aires itself.

In 1824 when the term of Governor Rodríguez expired he was succeeded by Gregorio de las Heras. Rivadavia, however, continued to serve as minister until late in the same year, when he resigned to go abroad on a diplomatic mission to Great Britain, there to negotiate for the formal recognition of independence and incidentally to obtain British diplomatic aid in averting the crisis which was threatening with Brazil.[34]

[31] *Registro oficial,* II, 6.

[32] Vedia y Mitre, 67-68.

[33] *Diplomatic correspondence of the United States concerning the independence of the Latin American nations,* ed. by William Ray Manning (3 vols., New York, 1925), I, 579-591, *passim.; Registro oficial,* I, 591.

[34] *Registro oficial,* II, 75.

IV

Portugal, it will be remembered, had invaded the *Banda Oriental,* or Uruguay, in 1816 and, after the long struggle with Artigas, had conquered the province. In 1821 Uruguay had been formally annexed to the Portuguese domain as the "Cisplatine Province," although the United Provinces officially claimed it as part of the old Viceroyalty of La Plata and refused to recognize the annexation. After Brazil, and Uruguay along with her, had separated from Portugal in 1822, the situation in Uruguay had grown more and more acute, and the Buenos Aires government sought to secure the return to her of the "lost province." At London Rivadavia invoked the old British understanding of 1812 whereby British diplomacy had compelled Portuguese evacuation of the province. His efforts, however, were to no avail, even though he did achieve the long sought recognition. Indeed, his persistence at London seems rather to have antagonized the British. As Canning, then foreign secretary, commented in a private memorandum: "I have come to realize that Mr. Rivadavia is one of those men accustomed to demand as a right that which he can ask only as a favor." Perhaps in that comment of Canning's is the key to the cause of Rivadavia's eventual fall.[35]

By the time Rivadavia returned to Buenos Aires in October 1825, the country was, in fact if not in name, actually at war with Brazil. In May a group of thirty-three exiles from Uruguay, who have gone down in Uruguayan history as the "Immortal Thirty-three," landed in Uruguay and began a revolution into which Buenos Aires was soon drawn. These were headed by Juan Lavalleja, a one-time lieutenant of Artigas who now sought to revolutionize the province and bring it back into union with the other provinces. As the movement met with continued success it was given support, private as well as secret government assistance, from across the estuary. A congress proclaimed separation from Brazil in August, and two months later the recently organized general constituent congress of the provinces approved annexation.

This new congress, a national body, was the result of long agitation. Three years before, the proposed meeting at Córdoba had been prevented by Rivadavia as premature. Agitation had continued, nevertheless, and, hastened perhaps by national recognition of the acuteness of the situation in Uruguay, the congress was convened at Buenos Aires in December 1824, shortely after Rivadavia's departure. There it continued to function for three years.

[35] *Vedia y Mitre,* 58.

One of the first steps taken by the congress was the enactment of the so-called Fundamental Law, which declared for a national government distinct from those of the provinces and obtained general consent from the provinces for a constitution, provided that the document be submitted to the provinces for their approval. It then proceeded to debate the question of the extent of the provinces' rights.

When the Uruguayan storm broke, however, the congress tacitly made itself into a legislative body and took steps to carry on war if necessary. Governor Las Heras himself added an additional complicating element by presenting to the congress his resignation, not as governor of his province, but as *encargado de relaciones exteriores,* thus focusing attention once more upon the need for a definite national organization, with a distinct and separate chief of state.

Such was the situation when Rivadavia returned to Buenos Aires in October 1825: a congress functioning provisionally; the country at war, practically speaking. Already, too, dissatisfaction with the congress' actions was being expressed in the interior, although, for the moment at least, the country was unified.

Forced by Las Heras' insistence upon resignation and impelled by war obligations, the congress determined definitely upon a national government to be headed by a "permanent president" with full powers. After long debate the Presidential Law was enacted in January 1826. The congress, so it is claimed, had withheld acceptance of Las Heras' resignation and the enactment of the law until Rivadavia's return. Now it proceeded almost immediately and well-nigh unanimously to elect Rivadavia as the first president of the Argentine Republic.[36]

V

From February 1826 to July 1827 Bernardino Rivadavia served as president. But already his greatest work as an executive and practical dictator had been achieved. He had reached the height of his accomplishments before assuming office as president; even as he entered upon his new and exalted position, the end was already in sight. Since the country was at war and since the political form was still uncertain, Rivadavia's chief activities were of necessity military and political. He did, nevertheless, grant some mining concessions, notably in La Rioja,

[36] Ismael Bucich Escobar, *Historia de los presidentes argentinos* (Buenos Aires, 1918) 70.

which he had arranged while still in Great Britain.[37] Even these became a cause of serious resentment in the provinces affected.[38] Some of the reforms inaugurated during his ministry were brought to completion or extended.

Rivadavia named Julián Segundo de Agüero for his own former post, General Alvear as minister of war, and Del Carril for finance. In furtherance of the president's own policies, Agüero continued the development of public instruction, especially in regard to rural schools, and established the first medical school in the country, as part of the university.

But as the constitutional question continued an issue, the old federalist-unitarist struggle was resumed, with lines much more clearly drawn. For the *caudillos* of the provinces a government which nationalized the customhouses of the country, as did Rivadavia's minister of finance, Del Carril, and which authorized a national bank to issue paper money, and which, at the same time, prohibited the provinces from chartering banks or companies without national legislative approval, could only be an enemy.[39] Meanwhile, acrimonious debate over the new constitution continued. Federalist opposition, led by Manuel Dorrego, was insufficient within the congress to prevent passage of the strongly unitarist constitution in December 1826; but in the provinces the constitutional efforts were rebuffed, and a general renewal of domestic warfare was postponed only by the external danger.

War had been formally declared in January 1826, and throughout that year and into the next Argentine arms met with success as General Alvear pressed into Brazil, defeating the Brazilians at the famous Battle of Ituzaingó. But, with the increasingly threatening internal situation, Rivadavia, rather than lose power himself, took advantage of proffered British mediation to undertake a peace settlement. For this purpose he sent Manuel José García to Rio de Janeiro as a peace commissioner.

García's activities were, unfortunately for Rivadavia, in the nature of a boomerang and materially hastened the downfall of Rivadavia. García, a man very friendly with Brazil in the past, violated or at least misinterpreted his instructions and signed a treaty whereby Argentina would have relinquished Uruguay to Brazil.[40] Even though Rivadavia promptly repudiated the treaty, public resentment focused upon him. García's

[37] Vedia y Mitre, 75.
[38] *Ibid.*, ch. 4.
[39] *Ibid.*, 91-92.
[40] *Ibid.*, 113-116.

treaty was the last straw, and amid a wave of public indignation Rivadavia was compelled to resign early in July 1827.

VI

Rivadavia's public career was at an end. He remained in Buenos Aires only long enough to see the entire governmental organization which he had headed follow him out of office. Disheartened, he left on his third trip to Europe. After spending some time in the Old World, chiefly in Paris, he attempted to return to his native land during the régime of Viamonte, in the era of Rosas, only to be denied entry and forced to depart. For a brief period he lived in Uruguay; then followed a sojourn of some years at Rio de Janeiro. It is of this period that Avellaneda tells the story of two young students from Buenos Aires who tried to see their country's exiled former president, only to receive the answer: "For the Argentinians, Bernardino Rivadavia lives no more."[41]

From Rio de Janeiro the "celebrated wanderer" at length took his last journey to Europe. During his last years, spent at Cádiz, he completed his sole literary work, the translation back into Spanish of the work of Azara, a work whose original has been lost. The book was published in Montevideo in 1850, but five years earlier Rivadavia, "statesman among warriors," egotistic first president of the Argentine Republic, had died in Cádiz on September 2, 1845.

As a member of the government, as a diplomat, as minister and virtual dictator, and finally as president, Rivadavia had served his country well. His institutional developments, above all, were of lasting value and influence. But the man was cold and dogmatic and regarded himself, as the Paraguayan Báez has expressed it, as "the chosen instrument of providence." He was never personally popular. Foreign diplomats commented upon his haughtiness and his excessive dignity, while his insistence upon taking as a right, that which he is entitled to only as a privilege, as Canning expressed it, served to injure the cause which he represented.[42] Not only did outsiders resent his presumptions to glory, but so, too, did the people, who found him rather ludicrous. The tale is told that "the presidential pomp was repulsive to the sentiments of the people and they would lie in wait for the presidential retinue in

[41] Nicolás Avellaneda, *Escritos literarios* (Buenos Aires, 1915), 37.
[42] *Ibid.*

order to burst out laughing when it passed."[43] He was foreign and unsympathetic to the people of Buenos Aires and, above all, to the uncultured *gaucho* of the rural districts, for whom he had neither sympathy nor understanding.

With Rivadavia's fall came a reaction and the short federalist régime of Dorrego. His death in 1829 marks the rise of Juan Manuel de Rosas, who, as a federalist, for more than two decades ruled the Plata from Buenos Aires. Rosas' policies brought him into the long, drawn out conflict in Uruguay—acknowledged independent by the final treaty of peace with Brazil—against Rivera, whose dictatorship there he challenged. Too, Rosas' own brand of federalism, altered and modified by circumstances, came to be less and less acceptable to the provinces until finally in 1851 his chief lieutenant, Urquiza of Entre Ríos, made common cause with his enemies, the unitarists, and with Rivera. Aided by Brazil and Paraguay, Urquiza led a movement against Rosas, overthrowing him at Caseros.

[43] Melgar, 97.

CHAPTER SEVEN

JUAN FACUNDO QUIROGA, "THE TYPICAL CAUDILLO OF THE ARGENTINE PROVINCES"[1]

EVEN before the advent of Rivadavia to the presidency a none too latent federalist sentiment had existed in the provinces. The unitarist Constitution of 1826 and the attempt to effect a definitely unitarist state aroused that sentiment; as a result Rivadavia's government fell. Sectionalism became rampant and, in the course of the reaction, "took the form of violent opposition to any central authority, no matter how democratic such central authority might be. This refractoriness to authority inaugurated the so-called 'period of anarchy,' during which the country was divided—as in 1820 and 1821—into a great number of local jurisdictions, republican in name, but tyrannical in fact."[2]

Chief exemplars of this regional autonomy were Dorrego and his successor Rosas in the Province of Buenos Aires, and the provincial *caudillos* Estanislao López of Santa Fe and Juan Facundo Quiroga in the region of Cuyo. After the death of Dorrego and the ephemerally successful unitarist period which followed it, Rosas, López, and Quiroga were the dominant personalities in their own provinces or regions, united in little else but opposition to *"los unitarios salvajes,"* the "savage unitarists," as those who sought to restore centralism were denominated. Gradually eliminating his rivals, Rosas rose to supremacy. But meanwhile, these several *caudillos* and other lesser ones ruled, each in his own sphere, maintaining governments which were "republican in name but tyrannical in fact."

I

Second only to Rosas, although equalled perhaps by López, was Juan Facundo Quiroga, "the tiger of the *pampas,"* in whose personality and career was epitomized so much of the provincial *caudillo*. The story of

[1] The chief source of information on the life and career of Juan Facundo Quiroga is the great work of Domingo Faustino Sarmiento, *Facundo: ó civilización y barbarie en la república argentina* (1st ed., Santiago, 1845). The English translation of *Facundo* by Mrs. Horace Mann *(Life in the Argentine Republic in the days of the tyrants,* New York, 1862) has been followed herein. Ramón J. Cárcano's recent biography of Quiroga, *Juan Facundo Quiroga: simulación, infidencia, tragedia* (3rd ed., Buenos Aires, 1931), has also been used. For the evaluation of fundamental factors and movements in the period, the great work of Ernesto Quesada, *La época de Rosas* (Buenos Aires, 1898) has been followed.

[2] Leo S. Rowe, *The federal system of Argentina* (Washington, 1921), 32.

Quiroga's rise to power, of his dictatorship in the provinces, and of his eventual downfall is well worth extended consideration, not only because of his own importance, but as that of a typical regional dictator of the period.

This "tiger of the *pampas,*" aptly described as "the typical provincial *caudillo,*" has attained to great fame. Domingo Sarmiento, "educator-president of Argentina" as well as one of his country's greatest intellectualists, has presented him as the central figure in his famed work *Facundo ó civilización y barbarie,* rated by critics in the front rank of Hispanic American literary achievement. From this work, which was translated into English by Mrs. Horace Mann in the 1860's, has come much of the present-day knowledge of Facundo.[3]

Rivadavia's time had not been one of entire internal peace. Unitarist and federalist had not always walked side by side. More often, rather, they had stood face to face. But, as one great Argentinian historian, Quesada, has expressed it,

> "for an instant the national war against Brazil seemed to give triumph to unitarist doctrinarianism, whose famed congress was an academic tourney: the fleeting presidency of Rivadavia quieted internal passions in the face of external danger. But once this had ceased, thanks to the victory of Ituzaingó, passions broke loose anew and more fiercely than before. Nevertheless, the country did return to calmness upon the ascension to the governorship of Buenos Aires of a federalist such as Dorrego, a man who had respect for provincial autonomy."[4]

But, unfortunately, to follow Quesada's interpretation, the tenacious struggle between provincials and *Porteños,* between local autonomies and metropolitan centralism, had reduced the country to a state of well-nigh absolute prostration, dragging it from the pathways of its normal existence, creating habits of vagabond life, and giving origin to *caudillos* who governed despotically within their own local spheres.[5]

All the indiscipline and defiance of established law and order was not, however, confined to the federalists. Indeed, it was the unitarists who plunged the country once more into the chaos from which the Dorrego régime was extricating it. The Brazilian war had been largely a *Porteño*-unitarist undertaking, and, as the army returned from the war, two of its generals led unitarist mutinies. At the head of a body of returning troops, Lavalle violently seized Buenos Aires, while Dorrego

---

[3] Cf. footnote 1, above.
[4] Quesada, 45.
[5] *Ibid.,* 45-46.

withdrew into the Province of Buenos Aires to reorganize his troops. There he joined with Rosas, one of his principal lieutenants in the interior of the province, a man fated to exercise a tremendous influence over the destinies of the Plata basin. Dorrego himself, however, was betrayed, treacherously captured, and turned over to Lavalle. The unitarist *caudillo* had him executed forthwith, "for the good of the country." Meanwhile, another unitarist, the great general José María Paz, upon returning from the wars, entrenched himself in Córdoba, which he made the center of his operations.

To quote once more from Quesada:

> "These generals, subverting discipline and making the national army serve their own partisan plans or personal desires, seem to be the resurrection of the Italian condottieri. . . . There is in them the reflection of that unhappy epoch of the Thirty Years' War, which prostrated the German countries, obliging all to be Roman Catholic or Protestant at the will of a Wallenstein or a Gustav Adolph. . . . It explains then the profound indignation of the Argentine provinces, and the cry of vengeance which echoed from one end of the land to the other in the presence of such an unwarranted proceeding as the killing of Dorrego. It was the effort of an oligarchy which, convinced of its own unpopularity, wished to regenerate the nation by force."[6]

The entire country rose to its feet: Quiroga in Cuyo, López in Santa Fe, Rosas in Buenos Aires; each put himself at the head of his people, and across gulfs of blood these "regenerators by force" were thrown, one by one. As one knocks over a castle of cards, so Quesada expressed it, Rosas overthrew Lavalle, López captured Paz, Quiroga destroyed La Madrid.[7]

Thus the country came to be governed by *caudillos,* "the genuine fruit of the anarchy of the year 1820."[8] The provinces were constituted a confederation, each preserving to itself a quasi-sovereignty, yet delegating by provincial pact all foreign representation to the government at Buenos Aires. Federalism became supreme, but under the multiple, feudal governments of petty *caudillos,* who quarreled among themselves, first one and then another were eliminated by Rosas. Of Rosas himself more will be said later. For the present one may look rather at this

[6] *Ibid.,* 46-47.
[7] *Ibid.,* 48.
[8] *Ibid.,* 49.

period of disunity and supremacy of petty caudillism and in particular at Juan Facundo Quiroga, in whom is epitomized the *caudillo* of the provinces.

II

Little can be said of the early life of Quiroga—or Facundo, as he is as often known—that is, little which can be shown with absolute certainty. But much that falls only a bit short of being absolutely verified truth is known, and, however much it may have been exaggerated or otherwise altered in its detail, it does express the man Quiroga.

Juan Facundo Quiroga, son of an *estanciero* of La Rioja, was born on his father's *estancia* about 1788 or 1790. There, amid the *gauchos,* he grew to manhood. While still young the future *caudillo* demonstrated the *gaucho* temperament and training. His father sent him to school in La Rioja. Quick with the lasso, headstrong and courageous, but well-nigh uncontrollable, he became the terror of his classmates at school and the despair of his teachers. When he was only eleven years of age, it is related, one of his teachers attempted to punish him for failure to master a lesson. But Facundo, ever defiant of discipline, knocked the teacher out of his chair and, fleeing from school, lay in hiding for three days before he was found. No one was able to influence Juan Facundo Quiroga; even the suggestion of authority was odious to him; finally his own family was compelled to disown him.[9]

As he approached manhood, young Quiroga became yet more imperious and ungovernable. He developed into an inveterate gambler. Often, it is said, he took cattle from his father's *estancia* and drove them into San Juan or to Mendoza, selling them there to get money to pay his gambling debts or else for further stakes at the gambling table.

He was indeed a true *gaucho,* hardriding, independent, the very personification of individualism, a *gaucho* of the type the Argentine historian López has described so well.

> "His [the typical gaucho's] conduct was elegant, his manner serious, and even though he seemed gentle, his actions were fitting and incomprehensible at the same time. Sometimes he was fiery and impetuous, giving rein to his passions; at other times he was gentlemanly and generous. But he was always queer and difficult to understand. . . .
>
> "In general the Argentinian gaucho was amicable and hospitable in his own cabin; outside it he was suspicious and quick to take offense. Always he kept his word; never did he fail to help those who claimed his protection, even though they were enemies. He

[9] Sarmiento, 78.

> spoke slowly and with a low voice that would seem sweet if one did not know that his words were always sparing, ambiguous, or cunning. . . . His anger was not expressed by shouts or gestures as is that of the Italian, and when in danger or dominated by wrath, he was always cool, holding an appearance of moderation that was so amazing because of its very laconism."[10]

Quiroga was, indeed, typical of the gaucho whom López has described. He himself was picturesque in appearance. Sarmiento describes him as

> "a stoutly built man of low stature, whose short neck and broad shoulder supported a well-shaped head, covered with a profusion of black and closely curling hair. His somewhat oval face was half-buried in this mass of hair and an equally thick black, curly beard, rising to his cheek bones, which by their prominence evinced a firm and tenacious will. His black and fiery eyes, shadowed by thick eyebrows, occasioned an involuntary sense of terror in those on whom they chanced to fall, for Facundo's glance was never direct, whether from habit or intention. With the design of making himself always formidable, he would keep his head bent low, to look at one from under his eyebrows. . . . To conclude, his features were regular, and the pale olive of his complexion harmonized well with the dense shadows which surrounded it."[11]

When the revolution broke out in 1810, Quiroga, who was scarcely out of his teens, responded whole-heartedly. Enlisting under Corvalán, a minor commander in the Mendoza region, he quickly caught the attention of his chief through his attitude of aloofness toward his fellow soldiers. His refusal to sit at the same table with them especially struck Corvalán, and the latter took him into his personal service. Family pressure, particularly from his father, however, induced Corvalán to send the young Facundo back to La Rioja. Soon, however, he was once more in the field, this time under Ocampo, one of the leaders in his Province of La Rioja.[12]

Little is known of Quiroga's career over the next few years, but in 1819 there occurred an incident which was to bring him a certain fame throughout the *pampas*. He had become involved with an outlaw group in San Luís Province when he was wounded and taken as a prisoner to San Luís. In the same prison with him were a number of Spaniards who had been captured at Maipú and Chacabuco, the battles which had

---

[10] Vicente Fidel López, *Historia de la república argentina* (10 vols., Buenos Aires, 1926), III, 109-110.

[11] Sarmiento, 76-77.

[12] Antonio Zinny, *Historia de los gobernadores de las provincias argentinas* (3 vols., Buenos Aires, 1879), III, 378-379.

liberated Chile. These were well treated at San Luís and, since escape was not considered possible, the officers were allowed to live away from the prison itself in homes within the city.

For a number of months the Spaniards had been talking means of escape and plans to overcome the small garrison. Early in the morning of February 8, 1819, one Spaniard, a Captain Carretoro, having secured knives and sticks, armed as many as possible of his fellows and sent parties to different points. One party was ordered to release the prisoners in the prison, expecting that they would join. Once released, however, these prisoners, led by Quiroga, turned upon the Spaniards and killed all but one. Quiroga himself boasted of having slain fourteen men with the iron bar of his fetters. As a result of Quiroga's action and the unexpected diversion it caused, the rising was suppressed. Quiroga was released as a reward for his action and soon returned to La Rioja with new honors and with something to add to the terror of his name.[13]

III

Such was the background upon which this prestigious *caudillo* rested his fame. His own public career began in his native province in that fateful year 1820, when Governor Ocampo made him "sargeant-major of the *llanos.*" Soon he achieved such prestige that, of necessity, Ocampo was compelled to consider him more as an ally than a lieutenant and looked for means of getting rid of him. The following year, under Ocampo's orders, he led a force against those of another petty chieftain, Aldao, brother of the later famous friar-*caudillo*. When the conflict was indecisive, Aldao and Ocampo made peace. Quiroga was then sent to escort the erstwhile enemy over the difficult road to San Luís.

This was the era of petty *caudillos,* of rude local chieftains who struggled for local leadership, and amidst this atmosphere Quiroga got his start. The contact with Aldao developed into an alliance. Aided by a hundred trained Aldao soldiers, Quiroga turned back upon La Rioja. Seizing the city by a *coup d'état,* he overthrew his erstwhile chief, Ocampo. Before long he had at his back a force of some four hundred men, sufficient to control the entire province. Although he now held La Rioja, Quiroga wisely refused to make himself titular governor, perhaps because he realized his own limitations and lack of administrative ability, perhaps, as Sarmiento puts it, because he did not care to be bothered

---

[13] Bartolomé Mitre, *Historia de San Martín y de la emancipación sudamericana* (2nd ed., 3 vols., Buenos Aires, 1890), II, 350-357.

by annoying details of government,[14] or perhaps even because he was still too weak. Whatever the motive, his procedure was to set up as puppet governor Nicolás Dávila, member of a powerful family of the province which had long been in opposition to Ocampo. For two years all went well, but eventually the Dávila family broke with Quiroga and was entirely ousted from control.

Quiroga's method of financing and equipping his army is of interest. The old system of farming out revenues had prevailed in La Rioja before his time, with the tithes of the province bringing an annual return of 10,000 *pesos;* but when the time came, Quiroga bid 2,000 *pesos* and, overawing all potential competition, obtained the bid. Thus, in addition to the normal profits, he had 8,000 *pesos.* Likewise, using a method typical of cattle barons everywhere, be they Hispanic American, Anglo-American, or what not, he laid claim to ownership of all stray animals as well as all who were unbranded. Within ten years' time half the cattle of the province were his. Then, to dispose of his cattle to best advantage, he monopolized the meat supply of the province and forced the butchers of La Rioja to buy only from him—at his own prices.[15]

Still another means of profit presented itself as a group of Englishmen became interested in mines in the province. Quiroga permitted them to mine without hindrance, but withheld title. Then, as the property was developed, he threw such obstacles in their way that they were compelled to abandon operations. As government property, the mines were then operated by Quiroga.[16]

In all this period Quiroga had not lost his proclivity for gambling, and played both to amuse himself and to increase his income. The steadiness with which he won gave rise to assertions by his enemies that he cheated. Actually there seems to be little truth in such charges, for, whatever else he might be, Quiroga was always thoroughly honest in his gambling. Rather, it was that his companions feared his anger too much to allow him to lose heavily.

IV

Meanwhile, as Quiroga had been gradually building up his local power, Rivadavia was making his supreme effort to give the country a unitary government. Popular opposition and resistance was promptly forthcoming, and Bustos of Córdoba formed a league with Governor Ibarra

[14] Sarmiento, 98.
[15] *Ibid.*, 103-104.
[16] Cf. John Anthony King, *Twenty-four years in the Argentine Republic* . . . (New York, 1846), 157-162.

of Santiago del Estero and Quiroga, the better to resist the encroachments of the metropolis. To this triple alliance was soon added the already powerful figure of Estanislao López. In this manner was Quiroga inducted into national politics on a large scale.

Efforts were made by Rivadavia's government to conciliate Quiroga. A letter was sent him offering him a commission and an important command in the army then fighting Brazil, but Quiroga returned the communication unopened, declaring that he did not care "to surrender himself to the chains which would bind him to the pompous chariot of despotism."[17]

As a provincial leader, resentful of outside authority, Quiroga was thoroughly in sympathy with federalism. Now, in the interests of the movement, he undertook a campaign against the unitarist governor of Catamarca, Gutiérrez, whom he harried and pursued into Tucumán. There, Gutiérrez was joined by the unitarist Aráoz de la Madrid, better known as La Madrid. The combined unitarist forces met Quiroga in the Battle of Tala, but Quiroga emerged triumphant again and occupied Tucumán. He forthwith imposed a heavy indemnity on the City of Tucumán and forcibly enrolled the province in the ranks of federalism. Only when a new and larger unitarist force under Arenales of Salta moved against him did he withdraw toward his base and home Province of La Rioja.

At La Rioja he took full advantage of the recent religious toleration edicts of Rivadavia, and when the question shortly became acute in the sister Province of San Luís, Quiroga moved upon that province (January 1827), flaunting a banner bearing the motto *"Religión ó Muerte"* ("Religion or Death").[18] The government of San Luís, at the time in sympathy with Rivadavia, was overthrown without a blow, as the governor and many principal families took flight to Mendoza. Quiroga now organized a league of the provinces which had constituted Cuyo. Once his rear was protected by friendly forces in Cuyo, Quiroga joined with Ibarra who proclaimed "war to the death" against the unitarist provinces of Tucumán and Catamarca, where La Madrid was again active. Once again he defeated La Madrid, this time at the Battle of Rincón.

Federalism was now supreme in the north and in the interior in general. Rivadavia had fallen from power and Dorrego was seemingly firmly entrenched in Buenos Aires, when suddenly Lavalle and Paz re-

---

[17] Andrés Lamas, *Rivadavia: su obra política y cultural* (Buenos Aires, 1915), 333.

[18] F. A. Kirkpatrick, *History of the Argentine Republic* (Cambridge, 1931), 139.

turned from the Brazilian war. As Paz and one unitarist force went into Córdoba, Lavalle, with another army, seized Buenos Aires and shortly sealed his success with the unnecessary shooting of Dorrego.

A bomb thrown into the federalist camp could have caused no more excitement than did Lavelle's summary execution of Dorrego. Everywhere men began arming, the unitarists to defend Buenos Aires and to conquer the federalist provinces, the federalists to avenge Dorrego.

From this year 1829 dates the rise of Rosas, and, to a large degree, Quiroga's campaigns merge into the general activity of the Rosas period. As Rosas, triumphant against Lavalle, entrenched himself in the metropolis of Buenos Aires, Quiroga bore the brunt of a less successful campaign against Lavalle's associate, Paz.

> "General Paz, a one-armed veteran of many wars, a scientific tactician, occupied Códoba, thrice routed the onslaught of Quiroga's gauchos and for two years (1829-1831) maintained a unitarist league, first of five and then of nine provinces. A cultivated man, of sober, studious and humorous countenance, author of valuable historical memoirs, the very opposite of the headlong Facundo, he aimed at opposing urban civility to rustic *caudillaje,* but, like Rivadavia, failed to give due weight to regional sentiment and to gaucho individualism, forces which were to be recognized and regulated before national organization should be possible."[19]

Three successive times Quiroga led his army against Paz. Each time, even though beaten back, he continued his fight as long as he could muster men about him. After the Battle of Tablada, his second reverse at Paz's hands, Quiroga returned to La Rioja. There he found the people celebrating his defeat. On the night of his arrival, the citizens were congregated in the plaza, singing national songs and dancing in the public square, which was decorated with inscriptions reading, "Long live the great triumph of Tablada," "Death to Quiroga," "Freedom through Paz," and the like. Quickly the scene changed, as Quiroga arrived. Furious at the celebrations, the *caudillo* executed twenty-nine persons and ordered all the inhabitants, regardless of sex, to take their belongings and leave the city for the *llanos* within three days, threatening death to all who disobeyed.[20] When, shortly, the pursuing unitarist troops arrived at La Rioja they found the city in silence and desolation.[21]

Quiroga had learned at Tablada that he could not succeed against Paz with an undisciplined force, no matter how large, and early in 1830 set-

[19] *Ibid.,* 144.
[20] Zinny, III, 393.
[21] *Ibid.,* III, 396.

tled down to give intensive training to a newly gathered army. Four months passed before Quiroga, with a smaller but better organized force than he had commanded at Tablada, was ready. Once again he moved against Paz, but once again he was defeated, at the Battle of Oncativo. His baggage was lost, twenty pieces of artillery were captured, and Quiroga was again in flight, this time to the protection of Rosas at Buenos Aires.

When word of Quiroga's approach with a handful of fellow fugitives was given Rosas, the latter issued a proclamation announcing that Paz had been defeated by the "brave General Quiroga," who was approaching to make his triumphant announcement in person! General Pedro Ferré, later governor of Corrientes, who was in Buenos Aires at the time, gives an interesting description of Quiroga's arrival. The reception, he says, "was more of a burlesque and a joke than homage and demonstration of appreciation." Rosas went to the outskirts of the city to receive his distinguished guest and fellow federalist. Then began a bacchanalian celebration which continued all night, with the chief of police leading the music.

Already the city was decorated for the occasion. Flags waved everywhere; the road through which Quiroga was to pass was strewn with flowers and lined with thousands of people. Soon, amid the drunken clamor and celebration, mobs began to tear down doors and to break windows. "There were all sorts of disorders," says General Ferré. They violated respectable houses and insulted families, and not until the following morning did the city calm down.

Later Ferré was visiting Rosas when Quiroga was announced. From Ferré's account it would appear that Quiroga had already developed a great bitterness toward Rosas, in whose presence he declared "I no longer have confidence in the present governor of Buenos Aires" and threatened Rosas to his face. Subsequently, however, Quiroga was at least partially reconciled to the dictator, with whose aid he soon organized a new force.[22]

Paz had meanwhile been captured by López; now La Madrid was commander of the unitarists in the interior, and against him Quiroga directed his attention. In a series of campaigns, marked by bitterness and cruel retaliation on both sides, Quiroga drove La Madrid into flight and exile, and for a time the unitarist movement was prostrate. The

---

[22] Pedro Ferré, *Memoria del brigadier general Pedro Ferré. Contribución a la historia de la provincia de Corrientes* (Buenos Aires, 1921), 46. Cf. King, 212.

provinces began to enjoy a period of tranquillity such as had not existed for a decade.

Quiroga himself retired to his *estancia* in San Juan province and rejected all efforts to bring him back into political or military activity. After three years of quiet and inaction he tired of the *estancia* and determined to move to Buenos Aires, in order, it is said, that his children might be given an education. Early in 1834 he quietly and unostentatiously entered Buenos Aires. Soon he located himself on a rich farm near the city and abandoned himself to a life of leisurely pleasure.

One can almost forget now that he was ever the "terrible tiger of the *pampas*." Leading a rather desultory life, he divided his time between his family and friends, enjoying the admiration and praises of the people. Only one of his old desires remained—that for gambling. To satisfy his craving for the gaming table he entered society.

During this all too brief period Quiroga seems to have developed a sympathy for the unitarists and to have shown a definite preference for the company of persons of unitarist leanings. Indeed, some assert that he was actively working on behalf of a new unitarist movement. On the occasion of Rivadavia's return to Buenos Aires in 1834 and his unsuccessful attempt to obtain permission to land, Quiroga is said to have sent him a message in which he expressed his regret for having rejected Rivadavia's unitarist Constitution of 1826. Whether this attitude represented a real conversion to the unitarist cause, which had the support of the wealthy class in which Quiroga was now numbered, or whether it arose from personal opposition to Rosas, is a matter of opinion.[23]

V

The calm and peaceful existence of the now tamed tiger was of short duration. Late in 1834 factional disturbances broke out in Salta, and, much against his own desires, Quiroga was persuaded by Rosas to undertake a mission of mediation there. In December 1834 he set forth on what was to be his last journey on earth.

On his way to fulfill his mission Facundo Quiroga heard again and again rumors of a plot against his life. His own speedy progress, however, carried him safely to his destination. Salta had calmed down meanwhile, but before turning toward Buenos Aires, Quiroga went on to Santiago del Estero, where he conferred with leaders in an effort to bring about more satisfactory conditions. Steadily he was beset with

[23] Cf. Adolfo Saldías, *Historia de la confederación argentina* (5 vols., Buenos Aires, 1892), II, 234; Sarmiento, 217; Lamas, 28.

reports that his assassination had been ordered. The route to Buenos Aires ran through the Province of Córdoba, which was under the control of the sinister Reinafé family, who had ruled the province as their feudal barony since the capture of Paz. Now the reports took a more definite form and it became clear that the Reinafé were aiming at his murder. But Quiroga, still believing that his name had the power to instil fear and terror in the hearts of his enemies, decided to risk the passage through Córdoba. Suddenly, at a place called Barranca Yaco, his small party was attacked by a band of some thirty men, headed by one Santos Pérez. Quiroga was shot in the head as he looked out from his carriage, and died instantly. With him perished his entire party. Thus was eliminated from the Argentine political scene "the typical provincial *caudillo,*" Juan Facundo Quiroga.

Responsibility for Quiroga's death has ever since been a strongly debated question. The Reinafé were unquestionably involved as was Estanislao López, in all probability. Rosas himself has likewise been charged with directly conniving to send Quiroga to his death. Be that as it may, and evidence is none too conclusive, Rosas did indeed hunt down the murderers and compelled them to pay the supreme penalty.[24]

That Rosas benefited from Quiroga's death is incontrovertible. With Quiroga dead and López definitely on the downgrade, Rosas dominated in the Argentine provinces more than ever before.

---

[24] For discussion of Quiroga's assassination and the events leading to it, see Saldías, II, 229-246, and Sarmiento, 230-233.

CHAPTER EIGHT

JUAN MANUEL DE ROSAS, GREATEST OF ARGENTINE DICTATORS[1]

GREATEST among the *caudillo* dictators, provincial or national, of Argentina is the figure of Juan Manuel de Rosas, who dominated the Argentine Confederation from 1829 to 1852. Rosas, who had been the chief lieutenant of Dorrego in the Province of Buenos Aires, stepped into the place of his murdered chief and gave to the federalist movement and the federalist party a vigorous leadership. At first he was little more than the senior partner in a quasi-alliance with federalist *caudillos* of the Littoral and the interior provinces: López of Santa Fe, Quiroga, and Bustos, not to mention secondary and tertiary kinglets and would-be kinglets, who stood out as a bulwark against the attempted unitarist restoration. But, one by one, his chief allies were overtaken by death or other disaster, and Rosas became well-nigh supreme in the Plata.

With the exception of a two to three year period, when he was in control only by indirection, Rosas served continuously for almost twenty-nine years. His period of rule is marked by contradictions: a federalist, he centers all authority in himself and the government at Buenos Aires, while amid a steady stream of persecutions of his enemies, he develops his country. During his long reign, he was almost constantly beset by strife with one set of opponents or another. Thus, early in the period, he and his two *compañeros,* López and Quiroga, wage a long but eventually successful warfare against the unitarists of Lavalle, Paz, and La Madrid. Once comparative peace was attained by 1833, he engaged

[1] A vast literature exists on the subject of Rosas and his period in Argentine history. Among the best earlier accounts are those of the two Chilean exiles, Santiago Arcos, *La Plata: étude historique* (Paris, 1865) and Manuel Bilbao, *Historia de Rosas* (1919 ed., Buenos Aires, 1919); Adolfo Saldías, *Historia de la confederación argentina* (5 vols., Buenos Aires, 1892), and Rosas' nephew Lucio V. Mansilla, *Rozas: ensayo histórico-psicológico* (Paris, 1899). For its interpretations and analogies Ernesto Quesada's *La época de Rosas . . .* (Buenos Aires, 1898) is unsurpassed, if indeed it is equalled. The most recent biography is that by Carlos Ibargurén, *Juan Manuel de Rosas: su vida, su tiempo, su drama* (2nd ed., Buenos Aires, 1930). The present paper has followed Saldías and Mansilla for the general factual presentation, utilizing Mariano Vedia y Mitre, *De Rivadavia á Rosas* (Buenos Aires, 1930) for the immediate political background to the Rosas period and J. F. Cady, *Foreign intervention in the Río de la Plata, 1830-50* (Philadelphia, 1929) for the external relations of the era. For good characterization of Rosas in English see *Argentina, Brazil and Chile* (Washington, 1935), 82-101, 417-433.

with the hostile Indians to the south, reducing them to subjection; then, in the late 1830's he waged war against the dictator Santa Cruz of Bolivia, fought Lavalle and a unitarist rising, resisted a French blockade, involved himself in Uruguay, broke with his ally Estanislao López and the latter's successor Cullen, and suppressed a rising in the southern part of Buenos Aires Province. By 1842 he was once more supreme, but soon met with opposition from Corrientes and Paraguay while he intervened actively in Uruguay, and once again felt the effects of a blockade by the French, with whom the British were now associated. Throughout most of the decade of the 1840's he maintained his power on land, but the Anglo-French blockade so sapped his economic resources that his star began to decline; his chief lieutenant, Urquiza of Entre Ríos, broke away from him, and in 1851 a general alliance of Brazil, the unitarists, Urquiza, the *Colorados* of Uruguay, and Paraguay was formed against him. Overwhelmed by superior force, defeated at the great Battle of Caseros, and deserted on all sides, Rosas fled the country in 1852, passing the remaining quarter century of his life in England. Such, in brief, is the career of Juan Manuel de Rosas.

Rosas, like so many other figures of Plata history, has had the misfortune to be presented to posterity mainly through the writings of his enemies. Consequently, the man has held the villain's rôle in the English language histories covering his epoch. Yet, not all historians of his own country can be said to be inimical to him, and modern writers are coming to admit that, despite the persecutions and vengeances which marked his rule, Rosas did definitely contribute to the development of his country, that the evils of his reign were the product of the time, rather than of the man.

I

Juan Manuel de Rosas, or Rozas, to follow the family rendition of the name, was born in Buenos Aires March 30, 1793, the son of a prominent family of landholders in the southern part of the Province of Buenos Aires. His father's family traced its lineage back for some centuries, yet according to his mother, her husband was a mere plebeian, for she claimed descent from even more ancient lines. It was from his mother that Juan Manuel seems to have derived his strong will and his more outstanding characteristics. Doña Agustina it was who ran the Rosas family and its affairs and who thoroughly dominated her husband. Strong willed and assertive she would not be intimidated. It is related of her that on one occasion during the temporary ascendancy of Lavalle, at a time when she was the sole occupant of the family mansion in Buenos Aires, she was ordered to supply horses from her stables to the officers of the unitarist army. She refused in no uncertain terms and locked the stable doors. Soon a party of soldiers came to take the horses by force, but upon breaking down the stable door they found every horse inside with its throat cut! Thereupon, not satisfied with having deprived Lavalle's men of the anticipated horses, the imperious lady demanded that they remove the dead bodies, as their presence was distasteful to her.[2]

Young Rosas seems to have inherited his full portion of his mother's strong will and stubborn determination. Mansilla, a nephew of the dictator, is authority for an interesting as well as valuable illustration of Rosas' independence of spirit and determination to be beholden to no one. Rosas, it seems, found himself in trouble at school for insulting one of his teachers and for refusing to perform some of the menial work which was part of the discipline of the school. In consequence, he was sent home to his mother. Upon her son's continued refusal to make amends, so Mansilla tells the story,

> "Dona Agustina did not hesitate; she took him by the ear and led him to his room, where she locked him up, with this warning, 'Here you shall stay and have only bread and water until you obey me.'
>
> "Juan Manuel said nothing. A day passed with only bread and water. . . . Then, as the household slept, he broke open the blinds, wrote a few words on a piece of paper, undressed himself and, almost as Adam himself was, descended to the street and thence to the house of his cousins the Anchorenas. . . .
>
> "The following day . . . they found the note, which read as follows: 'I leave all that which is not mine—Juan Manuel de Rosas.' "

Thereafter, indeed, Juan Manuel ceased to spell the family name with a "z," and entirely dropped his mother's name.[3]

With this event a new life began for the youth. He gave up his schooling and life in the city, and after a brief apprenticeship was given a position on one of the *estancias* of his kinsmen the Anchorenas. Instead of the pursuits of the classroom, he devoted himself whole-heartedly to the life of a *gaucho*. As such he acquired popularity and fame in his district; there he was always the leader.[4]

At the age of eighteen young Rosas married Doña María de la Encarnación Escurra, a lady who was to be a staunch helpmeet and aid to

---

[2] Mansilla, 10-11.
[3] *Ibid.*, 25.
[4] Bilbao, 116.

him in later years. By this time he had acquired an *estancia* of his own, Los Cerrillos. In this period, too, he seems to have devoted much of his spare time to study under the instruction of Manuel Vicente Maza, who taught him mathematics and writing. Later, Maza was one of his principal advisers, but eventually was a victim of the persecutions inaugurated in 1842.

Rosa's military career began in 1820. In that "terrible year," upon the recommendation of the Anchorenas, he was given the military leadership of his district. His participation in politics began, when at the head of his *gaucho* following he came to the aid of Rodríguez at the time that governor was experiencing difficulties just at the beginning of his term. Through the era of Rivadavia, Rosas continued at Los Cerrillos, where he gradually gathered around him a group of loyal followers. "Any man who could break and back a horse, use the lasso, the *bolas,* and the lance, was sure of pay and provender if he would fight for Juan."[5]

Rosas was a close friend and associate of Dorrego, and when the latter came to power, promptly gave him full support. Upon the execution of Dorrego, he immediately put himself at the head of the opposition to Lavalle. Unable to take Buenos Aires by force of arms, he nevertheless systematically cut off the food supply of the city, or at least that portion which came from the interior of the province, so that, for lack of food, Lavalle and his army were compelled to evacuate the city. In the campaign which followed, Rosas routed the unitarist *caudillo* at Puente de Marquez and, destroying his army, drove him into exile.

II

In November 1829, Rosas was named to be governor of the Province of Buenos Aires for a three-year term, replacing General Viamont, another federalist, who had been serving *ad interim.* Thus formally installed in office, Rosas began a dictatorship which was to last till 1852.

> "Two significant acts opened the government of Rosas [declares his most recent biographer]: the exaggerated honors and homage given to the 'Restorer of Laws' as he was officially denominated—a title which he accepted after having refused it once—and the explosion of hatred against his adversaries, which was manifested through an auto de fe ordering 'that there be burned by the hangman in the doorways of the Hall of Justice' all papers published be-

[5] David Hannay, "Argentine love drama," in *Blackwood's magazine* (Edinburgh, 1911), CLXXXIX, 63.

tween December 1, 1828 and the convention of June 24, 1829 which attacked Dorrego, Rosas, or other federalist governors."[6]

The color red was officially approved as the emblem of the Federalist Party. Soon, too, he was to ban the use of blue as unpatriotic, for it was the color symbolizing "the savage unitarists."[7]

Laws for the furtherance of education were enacted. But children "must be educated according to the desires and policy of the state," and it was ordered that each wear a red sash.

Other important steps were taken. Rivadavia had opposed the church. Rosas embraced a policy friendly to it and throughout his régime maintained close relations with it, benefiting greatly from its support.[8]

Rosas entered likewise into agreements with López, Quiroga, and other leaders in the interior, albeit with the studied policy of diminishing their influence at the same time. Thus, he received Quiroga after his defeat at Oncativo, giving him a refuge as well as aid for new campaigns; yet simultaneously he permitted him to be held up to ridicule.

To combat Paz and his league of nine provinces, Rosas inaugurated the "Federal Pact of 1831," one of the pillars of the Argentine Confederation. Under this agreement, made with the three Littoral provinces of Santa Fe, Entre Ríos, and Corrientes, a defensive league was established "to resist aggression or preparations for aggression." Foreign affairs were placed in the hands of the governor of Buenos Aires, that is, Rosas, who was to be *Encargado de Negocios Exteriores.* Free trade was established between the pacting provinces. Other provisions aimed at unified action in the face of outside danger.[9]

In accordance with the policies of this pact, Rosas gave aid to Estanislao López against Paz and to Quiroga against La Madrid. When fianally Paz was captured by López, he was turned over to Rosas, whose prisoner he remained for seven years.

Under the vigorous policies inaugurated by Rosas, many persons of unitaristic sympathies and connections emigrated from the country, chiefly to Montevideo. There they formed the nucleus of future opposition to Rosas.

By 1832, when Rosas' term had expired, practically the entire country was tranquil. The unitarists had been defeated in all attempts at resist-

---

[6] Ibargurén, 219.

[7] *Ibid.*, 222.

[8] For an extensive treatment of Rosas' relations with the church, cf. Almon R. Wright, in appendix of this volume.

[9] Frederick A. Kirkpatrick, *History of the Argentine Republic* (Cambridge, 1931), 144. For further discussion on this point, cf. Quesada, 66.

ance, and Rosas categorically refused to accept a continuation of his term.

Instead, he effected the election of Juan Ramón Balcarce, a rather weak man, as his successor. He himself prepared to lead a great expedition against the Indians to the south. In this he was motivated by the desire to punish and subject the Indians, who during the disturbed recent years had become troublesome. The expedition would also give him an opportunity to absent himself from the country and yet at the same time to maintain a large armed force at his command.[10]

Rosas' Indian campaigns occupied a year. Though he was not entirely successful he did explore a little-known region and push back the Indian frontier.

Meanwhile, during his absence, Doña Encarnación, his wife, had been the power behind the throne at Buenos Aires. Balcarce himself had become so unpopular that he was compelled to resign, as was his successor, Viamont; and Maza, the former tutor of Rosas, acted temporarily as governor. Then, in April 1835, Rosas accepted from the legislature a five-year term as governor. Thereafter, until his overthrow in 1852, he was regularly reëlected.

III

During this time Rosas built himself a magnificent home at Palermo, on the outskirts of Buenos Aires. There he lived with Doña Encarnación (until her death in 1838), and with their daughter Manuelita. There, too, he would receive distinguished guests. It was at Palermo that Darwin, when on his famous voyage of the *Beagle,* visited Rosas.[11]

Rosas spent many days at Palermo in uninterrupted labor, seeking further education, and trying himself to perform all the more important duties of government. It is said that he ate but a single meal a day, and often spent the entire night at his desk.

Rosas was not, however, without his lighter side, and he was possessed of a keen sense of humor, as may be well illustrated by his famous practical joke on the British Minister.

> "In a jocular mood the despot wagered with the British Minister —at a period, moreover, when relations between the two countries

[10] Ibargurén gives an extended treatment of Rosas' campaigns against the Indians. Ibargurén, 251-276. Cf., also, Antonio Zinny, *Historia de los gobernadores de las provincias argentinas* (3 vols., Buenos Aires, 1879), I, 149 ff.

[11] For Darwin's own description of Rosas, cf. his *Voyage of the Beagle . . .* (New York, 1896), 71-141, *passim,* and *Readings in Hispanic American history,* ed. by N. Andrew N. Cleven (New York, 1927), 479-483.

> were strained—that the latter would soon be performing menial labor in his [Rosas'] house. The Minister laughingly accepted the wager and thought no more about it. A little later he had to visit Palermo on business. There, in the courtyard, was the charming Doña Manuelita weeping soft tears, and pounding maize. . . . The Minister, shocked, hastened forward, took the implements from the distressed lady and, just as he had begun to pound . . . Rosas and his friends, laughing heartily, appeared upon the scene, and the Dictator demanded the payment of his wager."[12]

Like most dictators, Rosas maintained himself by force, and, when force alone did not suffice, by terrorism. The chief instrument of the latter was the notorious secret society, The People's Society, generally known as the *Mazorca,* so-called because its members clung together like the kernels on an ear of corn; Rosas' enemies, however, were prone to claim that "mas horca" (more gallows) was the proper rendition of the name. The functions of this group included the spying out of any disloyalty and the infliction of punishment through secret terroristic measures. Many and varied stories of its activities are told, most of them, quite probably, with no little exaggeration. That it existed and that it functioned effectively, and often through barbarous measures, is generally admitted. But that the means adopted were no worse than the tactics of many unitarist leaders from Lavalle on must likewise be conceded.

Not all of Rosas' acts were based upon terror, as the writings of his enemies would lead us to believe. One of his greatest achievements was in the orderly methods he introduced into public administration. "It is well known," declares Dr. Rowe, "that he would not tolerate inefficiency in the conduct of public business and punished with almost brutal severity the slightest laxity in public accounts."[13]

Quesada, one of the most thorough students of the history of Argentina, calls Rosas "the Creole Louis XI." The great French monarch who organized the French monarchy, he says, could not be soft or scrupulous in his methods. Nor could Rosas. Rosas had to deal with *caudillos* who, like the feudal nobility of France, impeded the organization of the state. They and the semi-savage masses understood only terror and, of necessity, terror had to be used. Estanislao López was reduced to but a shadow of his former prestige before death destroyed his power entirely in 1838. Rosas, who had been protected by López

[12] William H. Koebel, *Romance of the river Plate* (2 vols., London, 1914), II, 476.

[13] Leo S. Rowe, *The federal system of Argentina* (Washington, 1921), 36-37.

at an earlier time, eventually undermined him as did Louis XI his earlier protector, the Duke of Burgundy. "Louis XI," Quesada declares, quoting an unnamed historian of the past, "was equally celebrated for his vices and for his virtues, and placing all in the balance the result was—a king." So, too, Rosas was a man of both vices and virtues and so, too, the result was a dictator.[14]

Quesada also sees in Rosas some interesting parallels with Philip II of Spain. Each kept an eye on everything which went on. Each was possessed of a rare ability to master detail, to ignore nothing, to see all. "Both made war constantly, yet without being pugnacious and aggressive and without mounting a horse." And, finally, to complete the parallel, "Rosas, like Philip, governed too long." His last years of rule were marked by failure and his work failed to show itself as his own achievement.[15]

IV

Rosas had pacified the country in the early 1830's, but late in the same decade came a new series of disturbances—from within and without. In 1837 he engaged in a successful yet costly war with the dictator Santa Cruz of Bolivia, terminated only by the fall of that famed leader. A revolutionary outbreak in the southern part of the Province of Buenos Aires in 1839 required great attention from Rosas. In 1838, France, then under Louis Philippe and his arrogant imperial policies, took umbrage at fancied insults given the French vice-consul. As a consequence, the French instituted a blockade of Buenos Aires and of the Paraná. Lavalle and a considerable force of unitarists, aided by the French and transported by French vessels, began an invasion which was suppressed only with difficulty. When Rivera, the great *Colorado caudillo* of Uruguay, gave asylum to unitarist refugees, Rosas espoused the cause of Rivera's rival, the *Blanco* leader Oribe, and thus inaugurated a policy of intervention in Uruguay, which he continued later to his great cost.

By 1842 these several foreign embroilments had been more or less successfully liquidated: the French had made a settlement with Rosas in the celebrated Mackau Agreement,[16] the civil strife had been suppressed, and even the Uruguayan troubles had momentarily died down. In the reaction which followed the successful emergence from these multifarious conflicts, the reign of terror came to Buenos Aires. Flushed

[14] Quesada, 69-78.
[15] *Ibid.*, 79-90.
[16] Cady, 87-88.

with victory over the "savage unitarists," upon whose heads he laid most of the responsibility for the wars, whether foreign or domestic, Rosas ordered general and widespread confiscation of unitarist properties. In Rosas' absence from Buenos Aires, his minister Arana, acting as governor, instituted a reign of terror and bloodshed. Throughout the months of April and May 1842, the *Mazorca* was active, and if reports of contemporaries are to be given credit, the streets of the capital city were washed in blood.[17]

The next year, Oribe, aided by Rosas, defeated Rivera and began the famous siege of Montevideo, "the new siege of Troy," which was to continue for nine years. From that time until the end, Rosas was constantly at war. The death of Francia in Paraguay had not only opened that country to commerce again, but it had placed in power there a new and aggressive dictator, Carlos Antonio López. When Corrientes revolted against Rosas, Paraguay intervened and gave aid to her next door neighbor. But, thanks to the military genius of the rising leader Urquiza, who was governor of Entre Ríos under Rosas, Corrientes was restored to loyalty.

In 1845, however, new troubles with France as well as with Great Britain broke out, and those two powers instituted a blockade of the ports of the Argentine Confederation and gave aid to the besieged City of Montevideo. The blockade, while failing in its objectives, nevertheless dealt Rosas' dictatorship a blow from which it never recovered. For sixteen years Rosas had been able to continue control as a result of the plentiful revenues coming from customs duties on imports. With the blockade these were reduced to a mere trickle. The treasury was his great phalanx; through it he had given aid to the provinces and brought them under his suzerainty. Rigid, suicidal economies were now necessary and the government could ill bear the strain. Too, as the blockade cut off commerce from the Paraná, the provinces of the Littoral were stirred against Rosas. And by 1851 Urquiza, after growing steadily colder toward Rosas, broke with him. Forming a general coalition with the unitarist exiles, with Rivera and the *Colorados* of Uruguay, with Brazil, and with Paraguay, Urquiza marched upon Buenos Aires. Rosas, at the head of his own troops, met him at Caseros, but was routed and forced to flee aboard a British vessel to England, leaving Urquiza in control.

[17] Koebel, II, 469-470. For a justification of Rosas, cf. Mansilla, 178-189, *passim.*

V

All but penniless, Rosas and his daughter Manuelita reached England. Manuelita herself married within a few months of their arrival. Rosas, left alone, resided for twelve years in a hotel in Southampton, where he spent his time assiduously studying the English language. Meanwhile, the provincial government of Buenos Aires confiscated all his property there. Urquiza, however, made advances to him, at first on behalf of the government, later, apparently from his own pocket.

In 1864, after twelve years of hotel life, Rosas purchased a small farm not far from Southampton, and there he sought to make that little bit of old England seem like Argentina.[18] Attired as a *gaucho* he tended his small farm and received occasional visitors. Finally, in his eighty-fourth year he died of pneumonia on March 13, 1877.[19]

---

[18] Cf. Paul Groussac, "Notas biográficas del doctor don Diego Alcorta," in *Anales de la Biblioteca* (4 vols., Buenos Aires, 1901-1905),II. Zinny gives an interesting description of Rosas' personal appearance during his final years. Zinny, I, 234-241. Cf., also, Ibargurén, 439-468.

[19] Zinny asserts that Rosas died of indigestion "at the age of 84." Zinny, I, 213.

CHAPTER NINE

FRUCTUOSO RIVERA, COLORADO CAUDILLO OF URUGUAY[1]

WHEN Artigas fled from the *Banda Oriental* early in 1820 and crossed the Uruguay River into Entre Ríos, never to return, there was left behind only a single small force of Uruguayans to continue the struggle against the Portuguese—some four hundred men under command of Fructuoso Rivera. Rivera had been Artigas' principal lieutenant; with the elimination of Artigas he was the strongest leader in Uruguay, and for thirty-four years he continued to be a power to be reckoned with in his native land. Rivera, *gaucho,* patriot, warrior, thrice president of Uruguay, and founder of the *Colorado* Party, left more of an impression upon his country than any other Uruguayan of the nineteenth century, save only Artigas.

I

Fructuoso Rivera, son of wealthy, landowning Creole parents, was born in Peñarol, near Montevideo, in 1788.[2] Like Artigas, Quiroga, and Rosas he spent his early life in the *campaña,* living the rigorous life of the *gauchos.* When the revolution of May 1810 broke out in Buenos Aires, it is said that Rivera's father sought to send him along with some other young *Orientales* who were going to Europe in order that they might complete their education away from the American revolutionary atmosphere. Young Fructuoso's trip had to be cancelled, however, when he fell ill on the very eve of departure. But, once the trip was given up, comments a prominent Uruguayan historian, "health and calm returned to the future illustrious warrior,"[3] and in the following year,

---

[1] The present chapter has followed the factual presentation of José Salgado, *Historia del Uruguay* (7 vols., Montevideo, 1905-1931) and Telmo Manacorda, *Fructuoso Rivera, defensor perpetual de la República Oriental del Uruguay* (Madrid, 1933). For the general Uruguayan background Salgado and Acevedo, *Historia del Uruguay* (9 vols., Montevideo, 1915-1932) and the two monumental works of Isidoro De-María, *Anales de la defensa de Montevideo* (4 vols., Montevideo, 1883-1887), and *Compendio de la historia de la República Oriental del Uruguay* (6 vols., Montevideo, 1893-1902) have been utilized. Briefer than the preceding, but of incalculable value for their clear-cut presentation are Mariano Falcão Espalter, *Formación histórica del Uruguay* (Madrid, 1929) and Alberto Zum Felde's great social history, *Proceso histórico del Uruguay* (Montevideo, 1919).

[2] Salgado, I, 20; Manacorda, 7.

[3] Salgado, I, 21.

1811, when the *Banda Oriental* rose under Artigas, young Rivera, now twenty-three years of age, headed one of the first groups to raise the standard of revolt.

Over the entire period of Artigas' leadership in the *Banda Oriental,* Rivera was found steadily loyal to the great protector. From being commander of a small irregular company he advanced rapidly. He served with Artigas at Ayuí; a few months later he took a conspicuously prominent part in the dispute between his chief and Sarratea; after Artigas' withdrawal from the siege of Montevideo in 1814 Rivera continued steadfast in his support of the protector, and it was he who commanded at the Battle of Guayabos in January 1815, which crushed the *Porteño* army of occupation of the *Banda Oriental* and forced Buenos Aires to abandon control. Thenceforth, he was indeed Artigas' right hand man.

Guayabos made Rivera a leader second only to Artigas. A man of no mean military ability, he was at the same time courteous, carefree, and easy-going. "A good personal appearance, round face, big modest eyes," and courtesy of expression were the points one contemporary, Father Larrañaga, noted in him.[4] A later writer, the poet-sculptor Zorilla de San Martín, describes him more fully:

> "He was courteous, had very expressive black eyes, a Caucasian profile, was jovial, fluent and witty in speech, and extravagant. They say he was given to games of chance, and I don't judge it unlikely; to him money did not have the least importance; it came and went like a lodger who takes leave without grief and is received without affection. He spoke easily and even eloquently; he was fond of speeches, of sparkling toasts during banquets . . . and of scriptural phrases. . . .
>
> "Nobody possessed more than Fructuoso Rivera, not even Artigas himself, the secret of winning the goodwill of the people. The soldiers believed him to be an amulet; the masses treated him with familiarity; they called him Don Frutos or plain Frutos. The little corporal of the Napoleonic legend, visible everywhere, was in him a reality. . . ."[5]

A hail-fellow-well-met, then, a good mixer, a fine soldier and leader, but not necessarily a good administrator—such was Rivera.

II

The prestige of Guayabos was further enhanced by a period as military governor of Montevideo, where a mixture of courtesy and firmness

[4] Juan Zorilla de San Martín, *La epopeya de Artigas* (2nd ed., 2 vols., Montevideo, 1916), I, 528-529.

[5] *Ibid.,* I, 529.

served to pacify and calm that city after a period of disorders. During his tenure there, he married a young lady of Montevideo, Doña Bernardina Fragosa, to whom he was devoted ever after. She and his country, says his biographer, the historian Manacorda, were his two great and only loves.[6]

Throughout the period of the Portuguese invasion Rivera continued to be an all-important factor. Under Artigas' general command he maintained a steady and vigorous guerilla warfare against the invader, practically besieging him in Montevideo on occasions. When, finally, after the defeat of Tacuarembó, Artigas retired into Entre Ríos, he sent word to Rivera to join him there, but Rivera was not a pursuer of lost causes; rather, he realized that "he who fights and runs away may live to fight another day." The country was exhausted; why prolong the fight till death came? "The revolution promises us a paradise and gives us a hell," he declared to his troops, and rather than permit the *Banda Oriental* to continue in its inferno, he exacted from the Portuguese good and favorable terms for himself and his men, an act which Artigas never forgave him.[7]

Rivera surrendered to the Portuguese, but in so doing permitted the restoration of his country to peace. He himself was rewarded, given a brigadier-general's commission, and even granted a patent of nobility by his new monarch as the Baron of Tacuarembó.[8] Soon he was in command of the militia of the Cisplatine Province, as the Portuguese had renamed the *Banda Oriental*. When Brazil separated from Portugal in 1822, after a brief and almost bloodless war, Rivera's allegiance was transferred to the newly created Empire of Brazil. Nevertheless, he continued at heart a patriot and merely bided his time. Before Lavalleja made his famous "expedition of the Thirty-Three," Rivera, brigadier-general of the Brazilian Empire and Commandant of the *campaña,* was visited secretly by Colonel Juan Manuel de Rosas, as yet an almost unknown figure.[9] Rivera promised Rosas that upon the proper occasion he would put himself in accord with Lavalleja. Thus, when the Thirty-Three landed and initiated the war for independence from Brazil, Rivera hastened to the scene, ostensibly to suppress the rising, but actually to join it.[10]

[6] Manacorda, 177.
[7] *Ibid.,* 64. Cf., also, Acevedo, I, 355, and Zum Felde, 91.
[8] Manacorda, 80.
[9] *Ibid.,* 82.
[10] Cf. De-María, *Compendio,* V, 68-69, and Zum Felde, 95.

Immediately, however, the rivalry between Rivera, future *Colorado,* and Lavalleja, the later *Blanco,* began to manifest itself. Almost from the start two factions existed; one, under Lavalleja, favoring adherence to the United Provinces, and another under Rivera, inclining toward independence as an objective. During the course of the war, the friction between Rivera and the Argentinians, with whom Lavalleja affiliated, became so strong that Rivera was for a time proscribed and almost steadily operated independently. His campaigns in the Misiones region in the closing period of the war conflicted seriously with Argentine policies for a time. Eventually in 1828 his separationist movement strongly influenced the final treaty, when, through British mediation, there was effected a peace treaty which erected Uruguay into a supposedly independent buffer state to stand between Argentina and Brazil as the República Oriental del Uruguay, "the Republic east of the Uruguay." "After having been until 1828 the apple of discord—at first between Portuguese and Spanish, later between Brazilians and Argentinians—the Republic of Uruguay was to be in the future the necessary basis for the international equilibrium of the Plata."[11] Thus, the ensuing decades saw Uruguay still the bone of contention between its great neighbors, with actual control through its supposedly independent government the objective. Plata history for the next forty years was to revolve more and more about that struggle, with Rivera a principal member of the cast for more than half the period.

III

Owing to the already sharp rivalry between Rivera and Lavalleja, the two outstanding figures of the country, neither was acceptable as governor of the new state pending the organization of a permanent government. Therefore, General José Rondeau, perpetual compromise choice, twice supreme director of the United Provinces, was now selected to fill the post—"an honorable man," so Lavalleja described him, "but a poor devil."[12] When Rondeau promptly appointed Rivera as chief of staff he thereby immediately precipitated a crisis. An incipient revolt headed by Lavalleja was ended only by a forced reconciliation between him and Rivera. Late in the same year Rondeau named Rivera minister of war, Now,

> "a vertigo of activity, a dissipation of organizing energy settled on the new minister. Enslaved by them he absorbed the other minis-

[11] Zum Felde, 107.
[12] Manacorda, 145.

> tries and even the functions of the governor himself to convert himself into a general minister. In December and January he created a commission of hygiene, the registry of statistics, the first girls' school, the archives of the state. . . ."[13]

The following year, 1830, however, when the assembly met, it deposed Rondeau and named Lavalleja in his stead. The new governor promptly removed Rivera from office, and now it was the latter's turn to organize for revolt. But like Lavalleja before him, Rivera desisted at the last moment, "being unwilling to be the assassin of the country."[14] By virtue of a compromise he recognized Lavalleja as governor and was himself permitted to continue in command of the army.

A month later the new republic rejoiced as a permanent constitution was put into effect by the general assembly—destined to continue as the organic law of the nation until 1919—and preparations were made for the election of the first legislative body in which was vested the right to elect a president.[15] Rivera's earlier compromise had been a wise one; as commander of the army he was not without influence, and when the new assembly met in October he was overwhelmingly elected first constitutional president of the republic. "The popularity of the conqueror of the Misiones" still prevailed.[16] So, too, did the power of the commander of the army.

IV

On the 6th of November 1830, the new executive was formally inducted into office for a four-year term. In his inaugural address he declared: "Let us begin by recognizing that the past exists no longer except as a useful reminder for the bettering of the future. The *Oriental* people and their constitution: let that be our motto; with it we shall be strong; with it we shall be invincible."[17] Brave, heartening words, but ironic indeed in the light of the following four years.

With a new burst of energy, Rivera began reforms. His nephew Bernabé Rivera was sent to suppress the turbulent Charrúa Indians along the frontiers. The country appeared to be on the eve of prosperity, especially as unitarist émigrés from across the Plata, fleeing from the wrath of Rosas, began to settle at Montevideo. Commerce improved.

---

[13] *Ibid.*, 145.

[14] *Ibid.*, 146.

[15] Zum Felde gives an excellent analysis and interpretation of the Constitution of 1833 and its significance. Zum Felde, 108-131.

[16] Salgado, I, 19.

[17] Manacorda, 147.

"A democrat by sentiment and thought, strongly republican, more a caudillo than a general . . . the President of the Republic was soon seen wandering the streets of Montevideo alone or with friends, talking with all the world, praising the humble, joking with the soldiers, affectionately greeting the old veterans of the revolution. One morning he entered the shop of his tailor. 'Compadre,' he said to the proprietor, 'I wish to provide uniforms for my escort and as you are my friend I have come to have you do it for me.' 'Very good, compadre, but pardon the question, who will pay me?' 'Why I, the president of the republic.' The tailor, somewhat disturbed, grew excited and replied, 'None of that, compadre; if you don't give me a better guarantee than that of the President of the Republic I cannot fill your order, for even now I have some troubles from that chosen of God, my compadre.' 'Am I not sufficient guarantee for you?' 'The thing is clear, Mr. President. I do not trust you for a single thread; you must give me cash or else a guaranty.' "[18]

Rivera walked out laughing heartily, and the next day he gave him the guaranty and thereafter favored him more than ever.

The year 1831 passed peacefully, but by its close the old Lavalleja quarrel was resumed, as Lavalleja's friends began to foment disorder. Rivera gathered about him strong advisers, but discontent developed all over the country. Then in June 1832 a carefully planned revolt was launched. The first step was an attempted assassination of Rivera, when a party of his enemies penetrated by night into the president's bedroom; but given warning by shouts from his overpowered guards, Rivera defended himself and repelled the attackers.[19] Assassination failed, but for two months a revolution captained by the friends of Lavalleja, whose restoration they demanded, was rife; but in August it was finally suppressed.

Throughout, the first term of Rivera was a failure.

"The suppression of Brazilian money, whose copper coins had formerly circulated; slavery existing despite the law; international troubles; insecurity of agricultural and pastoral industry; conflicts between owners of land and actual holders; alienation of public land; slowness in payments; bankruptcy of the national credit; the collection of import duties; fiscal difficulties in general, woven, and tangled together, these things complicated the situation."[20]

---

[18] *Ibid.*, 148. "It is true that he had no idea of money," remarks Manacorda, 161.
[19] *Ibid.*, 151-152.
[20] *Ibid.*, 155.

Still further internal disturbances from Lavalleja and his followers continued to upset the country until Rivera in person took the field and pursued his rival to the borders of the country. When at last the four-year period was at an end and Rivera was ready to retire, he was able to say, despite the misfortunes of the country under his rule, in a Farewell Address:

> "During my long career my conscience has never accused me of having infringed upon the laws of my country. . . . During my rule and outside of it, it is necessary that the Oriental state know that I am nothing more than a soldier quick to sacrifice my life to maintain her liberty and her institutions."[21]

Then, voluntarily, he stepped down from the chief magistracy. Despite the unsatisfactory condition of the country, Rivera was still acclaimed by his *gaucho* following. "Merely to mention his name was enough to electrify the *gauchaje* of Uruguay."[22]

V

Succeeding Rivera as president was Manuel Oribe, who appears to have been quite acceptable to him at the time, despite some Lavallejista leanings he had already manifested. Upon his election, Rivera went in person to the capital to congratulate Oribe. Apparently the two had agreed upon a procedure for alternating in office. "You and I can direct the country, if we go together," declared Rivera, "you take the capital; we have no enemies to fear."[23] Between them they could govern the country, so Rivera indicated.

But once Oribe was in office, he broke forth into strong attacks upon Rivera. The new administration was responsible for a commission to investigate the affairs of its predecessor. Particularly the financial accounts of Rivera's régime were scrutinized. Then, the commandant-generalship of the *campaña* and a sword of honor previously given Rivera were taken away from him.

Infuriated at the turn events had taken, Rivera broke with Oribe and on the 17th of July 1836 initiated a new revolution. In the course of taking measures to put down his rival, Oribe followed recent examples from Rosas and issued a decree creating for the army and for public employees a white emblem which was to bear the theme *"Defensores de las leyes"* ("Defenders of the laws"). From the white color of this

[21] *Ibid.*, 157.
[22] *Ibid.*, 159.
[23] *Ibid.*, 161.

came the name *Blanco* popularly given to the party of Oribe. The adherents of Rivera, on their part, felt obliged to adopt a distinctive color of their own. The first color used was the pale blue of the heavens, taken from the national coat of arms, which incidentally was the color of the unitarists of Argentina. But weather conditions and the quick fading of the dye used caused this to turn white or near-white and the party color was changed to red or *colorado*. That color, more lasting and more striking, was already commonly used among the *gauchos* of Rivera's following. Too, "it had the virtue of appealing to the psychology of the gaucho and of being, better, an incentive, a magnet, a symbol of the primitive sentiments."[24] From this time dates the creation of the two great parties, *Colorados* and *Blancos,* which have now endured a century. "For all time," so one great present-day Uruguayan declares, "even beyond the hundredth generation, the masses will continue being *Colorados* and *Blancos.*"[25]

Behind these symbols stand fundamental distinctions in the groups. They had their origin in the rivalry of two great *caudillos,* but supporting the two were different elements, elements which from the start of the wars of independence had been in opposition to each other. Oribe's following was, broadly, that which had been with him and Lavalleja at various previous times of crisis. "There were," says Zum Felde, "affinities and antagonisms of character among these elements which grouped or separated them as interest demanded." These were "not differences of ideals, but of actions." "The leaders could readily agree on a general principle and declare: Nothing must separate us. And promptly they would be separated."[26] Rivera and the *Colorados* represented more democracy, the *Blancos* an aristocracy. The one is liberal and progressive, the other conservative and authoritarian; as time develops, the one looks toward Brazil for support, the other turns to Argentina and her dictator Rosas, and is therefore friendly with the federalists of that country; Rivera and the *Colorados* give aid and asylum to the unitarists and, in the future, are closely linked with that group.[27] Out of this arise some of the more significant alignments in the great political maneuvering which precedes the Paraguayan War.

[24] *Ibid.,* 162-163.
[25] Zum Felde, 150-151.
[26] *Ibid.,* 143-144.
[27] For an excellent discussion of the fundamental bases of party differences, see Zum Felde, 132-156, *passim.*

VI

Behind Rivera's connections with Brazil lay not only his former close associations, but the outcome of this very rising of 1836. Crushed in the Battle of Carpintería, his revolution collapsed and he himself fled to Brazil for refuge; in Brazil he became involved with some of the revolutionary movements even then sweeping the southern Brazilian province of Rio Grande do Sul, but despite that, he was permitted to remain and even aided in his plans. Men were recruited, supplies were obtained, and once more Rivera swept into Uruguay at the head of an army. Even then he sought peaceful adjustment with Oribe. "In this unfortunate struggle one of us will win out," but meanwhile Uruguayan blood would be shed, Rivera wrote his rival.[28] But Oribe, ignoring Rivera's letter, moved his troops against those of his rival, and, indeed, one did triumph, but this time it was Rivera, and it was now Oribe's turn to flee. As Rivera established himself a second time as president, his rival turned to Rosas at Buenos Aires for support. The refuge which Rivera had earlier given to unitarist exiles from Argentina had already angered Rosas and he readily gave aid to Oribe. Now the struggle became one in which Rosas backed the *Blanco* leader, while the unitarists and France and Great Britain, enemies of Rosas, gave aid and comfort to Rivera.

In the long run, however, that aid was insufficient, and in 1834 Oribe swept his rival's forces before him and inaugurated by land the famous seige of Montevideo, which was to last nearly nine years. Thus began the *guerra grande,* or "Great War," of Uruguayan history, which was finally terminated only by the fall of Rosas. Rivera himself, meanwhile, was seeking troops and resources for a new campaign against his *Blanco* enemies. Finally, in March 1845, reinforced and aided from Brazil, he met the troops of Oribe and Rosas under the general command of Urquiza in the great Battle of India Muerta. In that crucial engagement Rivera's army was so crushed and routed that the *Colorado caudillo* was put to precipitate flight across the Brazilian border.

VII

Now, indeed, did Rivera lose prestige, as the Brazilian government, entangled in a diplomatic web with Rosas, ordered the arrest of Rivera on the pretext that he had been connected with the earlier revolution in Rio Grande do Sul. Meanwhile, within the ranks of his own *Colorado*

[28] Manacorda, 165.

Party in Montevideo, there had arisen opposition to his leadership, and by decree of his own *Colorado* government he was formally deprived of his command and forbidden to return to the republic without the express permission of the minister of war. Thus did the *Colorado* government turn upon and banish the great *Colorado* leader.[29]

Soon, however, as the diplomatic checkerboard changed its appearance, the Brazilian government released Rivera and granted him permission to leave Brazil, provided he did not set foot within the boundaries of Uruguay. Early in 1846 he took ship from Brazil for Paraguay, going of necessity by way of Montevideo. As his vessel lay in the harbor of the Uruguayan capital, which the *Blancos* still besieged by land, there broke out a revolution in Rivera's favor and against the war minister, Pacheco y Obes, author of the edict of banishment. The situation would have been humorous if it had not been so deplorable. Here was a *Colorado* leader returning from a banishment decreed by a *Colorado* government. A revolution is started by a group of *Colorados* against other *Colorados,* while around the city is a besieging army of *Blancos!* The rising itself was immediately successful, and Pacheco y Obes was obliged to leave Montevideo. Thereupon, Rivera entered the city to resume his post at the head of the army and to direct again the operations against Oribe. But fortune refused to turn in his favor.

After an ill-fated campaign in which he lost an army, Rivera found himself in the City of Maldonado with a small force, closely besieged by the victorious *Blancos.* In that difficult situation he conceived the idea of entering into negotiations with Oribe. Although he did not go far in his effort, the government of the defense learned of his action and moved quickly. For the second time it removed Rivera from his post and in October 1847 decreed his banishment to Brazil.

VIII

For four years Rivera lived in exile at Rio de Janeiro. More than once he suffered the persecutions of the Brazilian police. In February 1851, at the behest of the Uruguayan legation, the imperial government imprisoned him in the Fortress of Santa Cruz. There he remained even when Brazil allied herself with the *Colorados,* the unitarist exiles, Paraguay, and Urquiza in the final effort against Rosas and his ally, Oribe. The *Blanco* was quickly crushed and compelled to surrender, but it was not until February 1852, coincident with Rosas' overthrow,

[29] Cf. Leogardo Miguel Torterolo, *Vida de Melchor Pacheco y Obes* (Montevideo, 1920), 119.

that Rivera was released. Even then he continued to live in Brazil until 1854, when he was once more called to serve in the government of his country.

In Uruguay, meanwhile, continued political instability prevailed. A brief *Colorado* régime was followed by the *Blanco* government of Giro, which in its turn fell before the new *Colorado* leader, Venancio Flores, and Rivera's former enemy within the party, Pacheco y Obes. Those two convoked a convention of the leading citizens of the country to determine upon a satisfactory government. That convention agreed upon a triumvirate, to consist of Flores and the two old antagonists, Rivera and Lavalleja, and called the old warrior from Rio de Janeiro to assume his new post. But the grim reaper intervened in a most decisive manner. On his way to Montevideo, Rivera was overtaken by death on January 13, 1854; even then Lavalleja had preceded him by nearly three months; only Flores remained.[30]

The renowned general and ex-president was accorded magnificent funeral rites by the government. On his tomb was inscribed: "The Oriental People to its Perpetual Defender. He served 43 years, he gained many battles, he consecrated all his life to the motherland, and he died leaving no fortune. . . ."[31]

Rivera had indeed been loyal to the soil from which he had sprung: under Spain and under Buenos Aires, then successively under Artigas, Portugal, and Brazil, and finally under the colors of independent Uruguay, he had always remained the "Perpetual Defender" of his native land. A *caudillo* he was, and a dictator. "The Government, it is I; Montevideo, it is I," he told Sarmiento. He was not a superman. "General Rivera has not been, to be sure, a Washington. He belongs to the family of the caudillos—the product of the backwardness of civilization in Spanish America," a contemporary wrote. A *caudillo,* ruling by force, it is true, "but the annals of General Rivera are unmarked by blood except that shed in battle."[32]

[30] Acevedo, III, 580.
[31] Manacorda, 255.
[32] Melchor Pacheco y Obes, *Notas sobre los partidos del estado oriental y sobre el general Rivera,* quoted in Manacorda, 243.

CHAPTER TEN

JUSTO JOSÉ DE URQUIZA, DICTATOR, STATESMAN, AND PATRIOT[1]

THE defeat of Rosas at Caseros in February 1852 brought to the fore Justo José de Urquiza as head of the Argentine Confederation. For nearly a decade he had been the overlord of Entre Ríos, in alliance with Rosas, whose right-hand man he had come to be. For almost another decade he was the dominant figure in the Plata provinces, during his own presidency and that of his successor, Derquí. Even after Derquí's defeat at the crucial Battle of Pavón in 1861 and the resultant ascendancy of Buenos Aires, Urquiza continued to be a factor definitely to be reckoned with.

I

Justo José de Urquiza was born on October 18, 1801, in the Province of Entre Ríos of a prominent provincial landowning family. In his early days he was a merchant and as such amassed a fair fortune, the nucleus of a larger one which he developed as a landowner in his native province in later years.[2] When the civil wars broke out in the 1820's he promptly espoused the cause of federalism and became a soldier, rising to a position of local prominence under Governor Echagüe, one of the lesser *caudillos* of the Littoral. By 1842 he had attained to the command of the pro-Rosas forces in the Paraná provinces and was governor of Entre Ríos. It was he who by his superior military prowess broke the resistance of Corrientes, routing the unitarist General Paz and forcing the hasty withdrawal of the Paraguayan troops from Corrientes in 1845. In the same year he invaded Uruguay and crushed Rivera's *Colorado* army at the Battle of India Muerta. This victory for the Rosas-*Blanco* coalition paved the way for an extended control over most of Uruguay; not until Urquiza himself broke with Rosas was the latter's grip on his trans-Platine neighbor broken.

Gradually over the ensuing six years Urquiza and his chief drifted apart. Fundamentally the split came as a result of divergent and con-

---

[1] There is no adequate biography of Urquiza, although several valuable works on him exist. The present account has depended for its factual information on Julio Victorica, *Urquiza y Mitre. Contribución al estudio de la organización nacional* (Buenos Aires, 1818). The collection of monographs entitled *Urquiza. Su vida, su personalidad, y su obra* (Buenos Aires, 1911) and Martiniano Leguizamón, *Rasgos de la vida de Urquiza* (Buenos Aires, 1920) are also helpful.

[2] Leguizamón, 11-24.

flicting interests of Buenos Aires and the river provinces, although ambition, too, no doubt, had its influence on the *gaucho* general of Entre Ríos. Urquiza was not only a practical man, but being possessed of large landholdings in the province, he was acutely aware of the injuries wreaked upon Entre Ríos by Rosas' interference with river navigation. This was the prime factor in the increasing coolness which developed between the two and culminated in Urquiza's renunciation of Rosas in 1851.

Urquiza it was who definitely turned the tide against Rosas and brought about his defeat at Caseros. It was not merely the strategic position of Entre Ríos which made the defection of Urquiza so important. Of greater significance was Urquiza's own personal prestige and influence, as well as his military ability. He himself headed the allied armies against Rosas and routed him at Caseros on February 3, 1852. That date marks the end of an epoch in Argentine history. Rosas had fallen; Urquiza now rose to fame and honor.

II

So much for the earlier career of Urquiza. Once he achieved the elimination of Rosas he turned toward the unification of the Argentine provinces—the Argentine Confederation. At that moment he dominated Buenos Aires as well as the other provinces, but the unitarists, with whose aims he was scarcely in sympathy, proceeded promptly to take up a policy which was in effect that of Rosas in later years: Buenos Aires leadership over all and discrimination in favor of the great port.

Those interests within the metropolis which had upheld Rosas now supported the returning unitarist groups. Very soon the breach had been reopened. While it would have been possible for Urquiza to maintain control by force of arms, such was not his aim or desire; instead he permitted the organization of a new provincial government containing elements which were distinctly unfriendly toward him. His task was a difficult one: to allay the apprehensions of the *Porteños* and at the same time to construct a national system for a confederation "which still had no cohesion, no Constitution, and no Government except the despotism of provincial caudillos."[3] Force was of no permanent value; the country must be organized and, above all, a constitutional system must be evolved.

---

[3] William H. Koebel, *Romance of the river Plate,* (2 vols., London, 1914), II, 162.

Two months after Caseros, Urquiza convoked a congress of provincial governors at the village of San Nicolás in the Province of Buenos Aires, out of which came the *Acuerdo,* or agreement. of San Nicolás.[4] A constitutional convention was called to meet at Santa Fe, and a program was outlined for its guidance. Meanwhile, the old federal pact of 1831 was reaffirmed; interprovincial customs duties were abolished; and the land and naval forces of the confederation were placed at the disposal of Urquiza, who was likewise to act as "director of foreign affairs" *(encargado de relaciones exteriores),* in reality provisional president, until the constitutional convention should meet. The *Acuerdo* of San Nicolás was promptly submitted to the several provinces, by whom it was soon ratified.

Although the government of Buenos Aires had ratified the *Acuerdo,* the strong powers vested in Urquiza immediately provoked serious opposition in that province, and its Urquiza-appointed governor was forced from office. Urquiza, thereupon, dissolved the provincial legislature and appointed a new governor. But Urquiza's own departure for the convention of Santa Fe was the signal for a series of conspiracies in the capital, and finally revolution broke out in September 1852. After a brief struggle with the confederation, during which the navy mutinied and went over to Buenos Aires, Buenos Aires established herself as an independent province and refused to send deputies to Santa Fe.

Prominent in the new *Porteño* government were Valentín Alsina and Bartolomé Mitre, strong unitarists of long standing. Mitre it was who was now destined to be Urquiza's great rival. In the two was embodied the conflict which was to continue in pronounced form for another nine years. The Paraguayan historian O'Leary epitomizes the struggle between the two.

> "Two men personify the two tendencies in the new act of the great tragedy of Argentinian life: Urquiza and Mitre.
>
> "Mitre was the localist spirit of Buenos Aires.
>
> "Urquiza represented the provincial longings, the vehement desires of communities tired of an interminable vassalage.
>
> "Mitre was the colonial monopoly, which fought to perpetuate its dominion.
>
> "Urquiza was the reaction, which came out of the depths of history, of all those oppressed by a long economic dictatorship, of the inhabitants of the Littoral subjected to the caprices of the old viceregal capital.

[4] Victorica, 44.

> "Urquiza was the 'barbarism'[5] which aspired to create a nation for the benefit of all, putting all Argentinians on the same plane.
>
> "Mitre was the 'civilization' of the frock coats, beneath whose stuffed shirts throbbed a most reactionary egoism, an egoism capable of compromising the national integrity to satisfy its appetites."[6]

Though he made some effort to reduce Buenos Aires by force, Urquiza concentrated his attention upon the constitutional convention which met at Santa Fe on November 20, 1852. The outlook for its success was dark, for Buenos Aires flatly refused to send delegates.

> "The prospect of forming a vigorous federation without Buenos Aires was not encouraging. With less than a third of the population and about one-fourth the wealth of the country, the thirteen provinces were certain to cut a sorry figure in their isolation. The most serious factor in the situation was that the central government had always depended upon the customs duties for its support. Inasmuch as Buenos Aires was practically the only port of entry this was a vital factor."[7]

Obviously the absence of Buenos Aires meant the beginning of a new struggle between the provinces and the indispensable port, and the convention was willing to force the adherence of the recalcitrant province. Urquiza himself declared:

> "The absence of Buenos Aires does not mean permanent separation; it is more in the nature of a passing accident. Geographical conditions, historical traditions, and a series of treaties and agreements bind Buenos Aires to the nation. She can no more continue indefinitely without her sister provinces than her sister provinces can continue indefinitely without her. In the Argentine flag there is room for more than fourteen stars, but it is not possible to eliminate any one of them."[8]

Considerable sentiment existed for postponement of the convention until Buenos Aires should be persuaded to join, but Urquiza felt that the primary need of the country, with or without Buenos Aires, was a constitutional basis. At his insistence the convention was continued.

The *Acuerdo* of San Nicolás facilitated the proceedings of the convention, for it had laid down definite agenda. Therefore, with its work outlined for it, the convention did not, as had many of its predecessors,

---

[5] The reference is to Sarmiento's "Civilization and Barbarism," by which he sought to characterize unitarism and federalism.

[6] Juan E. O'Leary, *El Paraguay en la unificación argentina* (Asunción, 1924), 15.

[7] Leo S. Rowe, *The federal system of Argentina* (Washington, 1921), 41.

[8] *Ibid.*, 42.

exhaust itself in fruitless discussion of the propriety of including or excluding controversial subjects. For this achievement Urquiza was responsible, and under his determined insistence the convention continued until it brought forth the definite constitution which has endured, with some major changes, until the present.

Urquiza is entitled to credit for the constitution to the extent that his was the driving force which brought the convention's effort to fruition. The general lines of the constitution, too, were in keeping with his principles, although he shared those principles with many others. The details of the document, however, were not his creation or even his inspiration. They were the work of Juan Bautista Alberdi, whose previously drawn plans, as enunciated in his *Bases* for a constitution, were extensively used and provided for the fundamental structure of the new government. Beyond Alberdi was his model, the Constitution of the United States, which he had adapted to Argentine needs as he saw them.[9]

Two further acts were passed by the convention. By the "Law of Capitalization" it was decided that the City of Buenos Aires should be the national capital, but as a federalist district separate from the province and under federal control. But Buenos Aires rejected both the constitution and the "Law of Capitalization." The second act provided for the financial reorganization of the country.[10]

On May 1, 1853, the new constitution received final approval, and on the 25th of May, the national holiday, General Urquiza, as provisional director of the Argentine Confederation, proclaimed it in effect. Three months later, as the first congress met under the new constitution, Urquiza was named president. Pending the return of the prodigal sister province to the fold, the City of Paraná in Entre Ríos was declared temporary capital. That city was conveniently located with respect to the outside and to the other provinces; of like importance was its closeness to Urquiza's vast estate and palatial manor of San José. San José, located some six leagues from the town of Concepción in Entre Ríos, was Urquiza's true seat of government and center of operations; more, it was home. There, more than anywhere, he was the supreme ruler.

> "The road from Concepción to San José was planted like an avenue, with Paraíso trees. Woe to the man who touched them. . . .
>
> "All the length of the eighteen miles the deer and ostriches were

---

9 "The draft of the committee has been cast in the mold of the Constitution of the United States, the only model now existing for a real federation." "Proceedings of the constitutional committee, session April 20, 1853," as quoted in Rowe, 43.

10 Rowe, 43.

as tame as barnyard fowls. No one was allowed to chase or harm them, and if a gaucho, coming out of town with half a bottle of Geneva . . . beneath his belt, should have been impelled to raise his hand and touch his pingo with spurs, yell, and throw his boleadoras at any of them, and chance to be found out, he had to expiate his misdemeanor by being staked out for the night, his hands and feet stretched to their utmost limit, or pass a year as a foot soldier. No punishment was more dreaded by the centaurs of the plains than to be sent into the infantry.

"Urquiza's flocks and herds were on a patriarchal scale. His cattle numbered half a million head. His herds of horses and of mares some twenty thousand. For leagues, riding through Entre Ríos, only one brand was to be seen upon the animals. It was the 'marca de la flor,' simple and easy enough to alter or disfigure with a hot iron, but as the saying runs, 'Fear guards the vines and not the fence.'

"The palace was a low building in the colonial style, with two tall towers, fifty to sixty feet in height, called Miradores. A sentinel kept guard in one of them, as they commanded a wide view of the country.

"A line of hitching posts stood under the shade of some Ombús, and fastened to them, nodding in the sun, the horses of the peons and the guards were tied."[11]

III

Urquiza was a man of contrasts, a man who even now is not understood: at times cruel even to the point of barbarism, he was a gay miser, a soldier of no mean ability, a thorough patriot, devoted above all to the interests of his own province, an organizer and builder of institutions.

Lieutenant Page, who had extensive dealings with him in 1852 and 1853, appears to have thought more highly of him than he did of any other Hispanic American leader with whom he came in contact. Urquiza's "quick and decisive manner of transacting business" and his great temperance in eating and drinking, traits none too common with his contemporaries, appealed to Page, who has left a not uncomplimentary description of his personal appearance and characteristics.

"[He is] . . . a stout well formed person of medium height, with fine piercing eyes and frank countenance. His dignified but highly courteous manners at once impressed me favorably. If he is 'without education' and 'a mere gaucho,' as I was told by many, he has a native intelligence and bold capacity which will enable him to

[11] R. B. Cunninghame Graham, *José Antonio Páez* (New York, 1931), 304-305. The description is from Páez' own writings.

administer with ability the responsible duties imposed upon him by the people of the Argentine Confederation.

"Our minister was unbounded in his expressions of admiration for this 'man of the times,' an opinion which impressed me favorably, knowing his familiarity with the political events which have brought Urquiza into so distinguished a position before the world."[12]

Urquiza was a great lover of music. In his earlier, bloodier days, after the Battle of India Muerta, he ordered prisoners taken to be beheaded in time with music. Similar bloody executions marred his career after the Battle of Caseros, although without the orchestral accompaniment. But once the man had come to a position of power and responsibility over the entire country, he changed and broke entirely with the ruthlessness of the past.

He is described as "being very partial to dancing, especially the cotillon, attentive to the ladies, courteous, and perhaps a flatterer. He had fame as a lover." He danced with "ceremonious elegance." Dancing was almost a nightly pastime with him, and to its influence one contemporary, writing long after, ascribes the softening of his character.[13]

Even in the field he dressed with great care and correctness, yet he was by no means a mere dandy and was quite ready to dare death.

As a general he ranked with the best the Plata countries have produced. Sarmiento asserted that he was greater than Paz, whose knowledge of military tactics was proverbial. General Alvear, who, to be sure, was wont to deprecate San Martín's ability, went so far as to declare that, as a military leader, Urquiza was superior to the great liberator of southern South America.[14]

Urquiza was a true *gaucho,* but nevertheless as well educated as were most political and military figures of his day, having spent some years at the *Colegio* of San Carlos in Buenos Aires. Education of his people was one of his greatest interests, and he furthered it wherever possible. As governor of Entre Ríos he founded the *Colegio* at Concepción, which was supposedly maintained at provincial expense, but actually ran regularly into a deficit which was covered out of the governor's own pocket.[15]

Urquiza's extraordinary memory was the marvel of those who knew him. His interest in education carried him so far that he regularly

---

12 Thomas J. Page, *La Plata, the Argentine Confederation, and Paraguay* (New York, 1859), 40.

13 *Urquiza. Su vida . . .*, 17-18.

14 Alfredo de Urquiza, *Campañas de Urquiza . . .* (Buenos Aires, 1924), 75 ff.

15 Leguizamón, 161 ff.; *Urquiza. Su vida . . .*, 34.

scrutinized the reports from the school examinations held throughout the province. On one occasion as he was traveling he saw a youth not far away who excited his curiosity.

> "He sent an aide to call him, made him climb into the carriage, and asked him who he was. Upon his response, he said to him, 'Then, you are the son of N. and I know that you led your school this year, when you completed your primary studies and, Why hasn't your father sent you to the *colegio?*' 'He is unable to, sir, because of all the chores at home.'"

The general immediately accompanied the lad to his father's house and insisted that the boy be sent to the *colegio.* "This young man was one of the best students in the *Colegio del Uruguay* and came to occupy with brilliance high posts in the administration of the province."[16]

The generosity of Urquiza, too, was famed. He saw to it that Rosas was granted a generous pension by the national government under him and when, later, the pension was stopped by the Mitre government, paid it from his own pocket. San José, located as it was not far from the Uruguay River, became the place of refuge for exiles from the civil wars which swept the neighboring Republic of Uruguay. Whether *Blanco* or *Colorado,* the refugee was given asylum at San José.[17]

Urquiza was the prince of landowners in the entire province and because of his vast interests, he appreciated the need for development of communications. Railways were given their first impetus in Argentina during his presidency, and under him William Wheelwright, the great steamship entrepreneur, was granted a charter for his activities in development of steam transportation, although the actual beginning was made after Urquiza's retirement from the presidency.

IV

The presidential administration of Urquiza was marked by bitter disputes between the confederation and Buenos Aires. Even while the convention had been in progress, Urquiza had attempted to bring Buenos Aires into line by force. From December 1852 to July 1853, a federalist-*gaucho* insurrection in the Province of Buenos Aires under Lagos had besieged the city by land. Urquiza lent national aid to Lagos, sending the squadron of the confederation to blockade by water, but its commander, Coe, sold out to the *Porteño* government and surrendered his vessels to it. On this occasion Urquiza, who was directing operations

---

[16] *Urquiza. Su vida,* 34-35.
[17] *Ibid.,* 36-37.

by land, was compelled to flee aboard the United States ship *Water Witch* and the attempted coercion failed.[18]

The next few years saw a long intermittent struggle between the confederation and Buenos Aires, complicated and made bitter by the tariff situation, for independent Buenos Aires was still the entrepôt and levied duties on goods imported from abroad, reshipping them to the provinces. In 1856 the confederation retaliated by imposing discriminatory duties, hoping in that way to force Buenos Aires into the union, but with little effect. Foreign trade directly with the provinces of the confederation was encouraged and treaties of navigation and commerce, which recognized the rights of foreign vessels to enter the Paraná and its tributaries, were made with Great Britain, the United States, and France. In general it may be said that foreign states, whose ministers resided at Paraná even when they were also accredited to Buenos Aires, tended to favor Urquiza in the struggle. In 1857 the United States Minister Yaney attempted mediation between the two contestants, but failed when Buenos Aires demanded as a *sine qua non* that Urquiza "retire entirely from public life" or at least for the "space of six years," that is, the duration of a presidential term.[19]

The national struggle finally culminated in open warfare. "Seeing that the resistance was from the government, while the majority of the citizens was not in agreement with the isolation in which Buenos Aires maintained herself," Urquiza prepared to use force. Mediation by the United States minister again failed, and the forces of the confederation, under Urquiza's command, moved against Buenos Aires. Arrayed against them was the army of Buenos Aires, under General Mitre, superior in numbers, but not in generalship. The two contestants met at Cepeda, scene of the great battle between Buenos Aires and the forces of federalism under Estanislao López and Ramírez nearly forty years before. Again the federal cause was triumphant and Urquiza moved rapidly on Buenos Aires. Faced with the possibility of conquest, the provincial government accepted the mediation of Francisco Solano López, son of the dictator of Paraguay, and signed the Pact of San José de Flores. Under its terms Buenos Aires agreed to enter the confederation and was granted certain concessions in return: her former allotment of representation in the national congress was doubled and a promise of further amendments to the constitution was made, which

[18] Page, 43-44.

[19] *Diplomatic relations of the United States: Inter-American affairs,* ed. by William Ray Manning (7 vols., New York, 1932-1936), I, 728.

were agreed to at a new national convention. Actually, the Unitarist leaders of Buenos Aires were resolved that the settlement "should be but a breathing space for them to reorganize their forces. For them the issue was supremacy or independence. If they could not rule the confederation, they were determined the confederation should not rule them."[20]

V

Buenos Aires was back in the fold; her deputies were admitted to the national congress, which still met temporarily at Paraná. Then, with the expiration of Urquiza's term of office, Santiago Derquí was chosen as president. Derquí, although a federalist, was not on good terms with Urquiza; nor was he in any respect as capable a man as Urquiza, who now became governor of Entre Ríos and retired from the national scene.

Soon the excuse for which Mitre seems to have been waiting came. Buenos Aires deputies to the congress were rejected on technicalities of doubtful validity, and Buenos Aires seized the occasion to secede. Under the leadership of Mitre, who had been elected as governor of Buenos Aires in 1860, a Buenos Aires army moved against the national forces, at whose head was Urquiza once more, called back from his retirement. The fortunes of war now shifted. Urquiza and Derquí were unable to agree as to policies and tactics; indeed Urquiza's heart was scarcely in the fray. Aided by the friction in the enemy camp, Mitre and the *Porteños* triumphed in the great Battle of Pavón on September 17, 1861; Derquí was compelled to relinquish the presidency, and shortly Mitre was chosen to take his place at the head of the Argentine Confederation, whose capital was placed definitely at Buenos Aires.

VI

Urquiza himself retired to San José, exercising from there the functions of governor of Entre Ríos. In 1863 and 1864 Urquiza played an important rôle in the diplomatic conflicts which precipitated the Paraguayan War. The dictator Francisco Solano López of Paraguay counted at first upon his aid in the event of intervention on behalf of the *Blanco* government of Uruguay, which traditionally was the friend and supporter of the Federalist Party in Argentina. But López' intransigent policy and, above all, his invasion of Argentine soil precluded any co-

[20] Pelham H. Box, *Origins of the Paraguayan war* (Urbana, Illinois, 1927), 81. The following discussion of Urquiza's relationship to the Paraguayan War is based on Box.

öperation or even neutrality on the part of Urquiza. Urquiza was willing that López be permitted to cross the sparsely populated Misiones region with his armies, but not Corrientes. Thereupon, López ceased to depend upon Urquiza.

López, nevertheless, did have the backing, or at least the close sympathy, of many of the old federalists, some of whom felt extremely bitter toward Urquiza on account of his support of the national war, conducted by the arch-enemy of federalism, Mitre. Among these was Ricardo López Jordán, a petty *caudillo* of Entre Ríos, and it was he who raised the standard of revolt early in 1870, and with a party of some sixty men raided San José in April 1870. Urquiza, who no longer kept at hand the great armed force of earlier days, was seized by López Jordán and shot down and killed in cold blood. The brutal murder was eventually avenged by the national government, but the great paradox of Argentinian history, José Justo de Urquiza, patriarch of Entre Ríos and constitution-giver of the Argentine Republic, was dead.

Conqueror of Rosas, initiator through the *Acuerdo* of San Nicolás of the constituent congress of Santa Fe which gave to Argentina the constitution best adaptable to her needs, president of his country, patriot, builder of institutions—Urquiza had not lived in vain.

CHAPTER ELEVEN

CARLOS ANTONIO LÓPEZ, ORGANIZER AND DICTATOR OF THE PARAGUAYAN REPUBLIC[1]

BEFORE Francia died, it was generally expected that his death would bring about a more or less violent reaction from his repressive, absolutist measures. It was predicted by his enemies that the people "would rise like Lazarus at the voice of his Redeemer."[2] Instead, they remained docile as before. At most, the conditions which momentarily existed at his death were incomparably more orderly than those which have followed the death or overthrow of the vast majority of dictators. And this when there had been absolutely no provision made for a successor! Strong indeed was the awesome hold which the great dictator had over his people.

Francia died September 20, 1840, without naming or leaving any indication as to his choice of a successor. Promptly, his secretary, Patiño, called together a *junta* to govern the country. He himself is said to have had ambitions to be the new *Supremo,* but of that, proof is lacking, for he soon followed his late master. For a few days he was secretary to the new *junta,* a post into which he had pushed himself; but within short order the *junta* threw him into prison, and there, possibly fearsome of the vengeance which might be wreaked upon him, he hanged himself.

The *junta* served for less than six months, giving way in an orderly fashion to the choice of a new national congress which it called into being. This congress, meeting in March 1841, determined to follow the precedent of 1813 and established anew the consulate. As consuls were appointed Mariano Roque Alonso, commander of the army at the time of Francia's death, and Carlos Antonio López. These consuls were to hold office for three years.

---

[1] The best brief account of the elder López' reign is that given by Captain Richard F. Burton, *Letters from the battlefields of Paraguay* (London, 1870) in his rather lengthy "introductory essay." For factual information Burton has been followed. The only account dealing at any length with López is that of Andrés Gelly, López' minister at Rio de Janeiro, *El Paraguay; lo que fué, lo que es, y lo que será* (Paris, 1926). Although a near-panegyric, it presents valuable material on developments to 1848. Washburn, *History of Paraguay . . .* (2 vols., Boston, 1871), the product of the United States minister to Paraguay in the era of the younger López, is woefully unreliable and biased except where direct quotation is made.

[2] Burton, 54.

The congress likewise declared Paraguayan ports open to general trade once more and concluded a treaty of friendship with the neighboring Province of Corrientes, then at war with Buenos Aires. At the same time an amnesty, embracing most of the political prisoners left from Francia's reign of rigor, was ordered. Thereupon, it adjourned.

López it was who dominated the consulate; Alonso was merely his Yegros. Three years later, a new congress established a presidential régime and elected López to fill the office for a five-year term. For eighteen years thereafter, until his death in 1862, he was reëlected at regular intervals.

I

Francia was the founder of independent Paraguay; Carlos Antonio López was the organizer. As one not unfriendly English writer puts it, Francia was the Joseph Smith, López the Brigham Young of Paraguay.[3] Under his régime many internal improvements and changes were made, but, except for foreign relations and the prevalence of a cancerous nepotism, the policies of López were those of Francia, modified to a degree, it is true, and certainly accomplished with more regard for public opinion.

The new dictator was as essentially absolutist in his policies as Francia, however much these policies contributed to the development of the country. On occasions he was quite capable of being thoroughly arbitrary. Yet, with his family, the dictator was far from absolute. The family ruled him, and nepotism held sway. They and his foreign policy between them eventually brought Paraguay to ruin.

In his foreign relations López quarrelled over river navigation with Corrientes and with the Argentine dictator, Rosas. He was constantly involved with Brazil, either as an ally or as an opponent, with Brazilian imperialism at times making a complete tool of him. Among the nations outside South America, the United States in particular was at odds with him, as was Great Britain only to a lesser degree—in both cases as a result of López' dictatorial absolutism. The wounds of all these quarrels and, as far as Brazil and Argentina were concerned, the actual matters in dispute were bequeathed by him to his son and successor, Francisco Solano López, at his death in 1862.

Carlos Antonio López was, yet, for all his failures, a capable man, and, considering his lack of training in government, he did well. At the time of Francia's death he was about forty-four years of age, al-

---

[3] *Ibid.*, 57.

though the age is variously rendered. He was born in the 1790's, of mixed parentage, son of a Creole father and part-Indian mother. Indeed, the self-styled historian Washburn asserts that his mother was part negro. But Washburn, who was United States minister to Paraguay in the time of the younger López, must be taken with caution even concerning those events of which he was an eyewitness.[4] The novelist, Edward Lucas White, author of the great historical novel of Francia, would have him a relative of *El Supremo,* but of that there is no proof.

López, despite his rather lowly origin, was educated at the *colegio* in Asunción. Later, he taught courses in philosophy and in theology there, but like Francia, he gravitated toward the law. After following the legal calling for a time, he retired to an *estancia* some forty leagues from Asunción which had come to him as part of his wife's dowry. There he is said to have interspersed considerable reading with his agricultural pursuits. "Although he had never left his native land, he was looked upon as an enlightened man, and he had acquired, in comparatively early life, a general reputation for patriotism, special knowledge, and administrative aptitude."[5] Under Francia for the most part he stayed in retirement and out of sight, although at one period he was an accountant in the employ of the state. Some two years before the death of Francia, he incurred the dictator's displeasure and was exiled to his *estancia* at Rosario.

Quite unlike the lean and wiry Francia, Carlos Antonio López was a fat individual of unpleasing appearance, so fat indeed that it is claimed he was unable to ride a horse during the last few years of his life. Several foreigners who visited him have preserved and published sketches of him, and, on the basis of them, one later writer, Burton, gives the following description of him:

> "Page and Mansfield make him hideous, burly, and thick-set as Dictator Francia was thin and lean. With chops flapping over his cravat, his face wears, like the late George IV, a porcine appearance, which, however, . . . is not incompatible with high intellect. On the other hand [Burton continues], Colonel du Graty [a French visitor of his time] presents a stout but respectable looking citizen. He generally received visitors sitting in an armchair, probably to conceal the fact that one leg was shorter than the other, and he wore, *honoris causa,* his hat, which was a little cocked on one side. At times he would astonish visitors by his courtesy in asking them to sit down in the presence."[6]

[4] Washburn, I, 338-339.

[5] Burton, 56-57.

[6] *Ibid.,* 57.

His wife, from whose dowry his initial start was gained, was almost as fat as he. They had five children, three sons and two daughters. The eldest son, the future dictator Francisco Solano López, according to Washburn, was an illegitimate child, the product of cuckoldry. Washburn, however, hated the younger López in as thoroughgoing a manner as any one could hate, and was probably quite willing to lend an ear to derogatory gossip. All five of the children, pampered and spoiled from childhood, played a part in the Paraguayan history of their time.

Save only with his children, Carlos Antonio López was despotic and arbitrary to an extreme. He is recorded as having exiled a Frenchman resident in Paraguay for having engaged in mesmerism without permission, and the story is told that a sergeant was executed for the sole offense of having, in his ignorance, torn up some stamped paper belonging to the treasury.[7] He was a stickler for ceremony, demanding respect and deference to a degree. More than once his determined insistence upon the Paraguayan custom of sitting, his hat on his head, to receive visitors while they stood, brought trouble, especially with foreigners. Perhaps this variation of the kowtow might be excused as a means of upholding the dignity of a rather undignified-looking personage, but his demand that he alone be called "Excellency" or "Most Excellent One," while his ministers could be designated only as "you," is rather indicative of excessive vanity.

Masterman tells a story illustrative of this.

> "When Mr. Doria, Her Majesty's Charge d'Affaires, went to Paraguay . . . he addressed an official letter to the Minister for Foreign Affairs. 'A S. Excelencia, Señor Don Francisco Sánchez,' etc., as is usual. The next day the minister called upon him privately, and told him in some trepidation that he must not give him the title of Excellency, lest it should offend the President. Mr. Doria said that it was the usual way of addressing men in his position, and he could not see how 'El Excelentisimo' could be offended by it. Señor Sánchez replied that he could not accept it, and asked him to mention the subject to the President the next time he saw him. He did so, and López gruffly answered, 'Call him what you please, he will remain but a blockhead still.' "[8]

At the beginning of his long reign López welcomed foreigners with arms open and catered to their every desire. Subsequent events tended rather to justify Francia's determined and unyielding policy toward the

[7] *Ibid.*, 60.

[8] George Frederick Masterman, *Seven eventful years in Paraguay* (2nd ed., London, 1870).

outsider, and after a long series of conflicts with representatives of other governments, as well as with their nationals, López turned sharply against the foreigner and came to distrust him.

II

When López came into actual power in 1841 he had several tasks to face, tasks requiring the use of considerable judgment and tact, and, at least in so far as internal questions were concerned, he faced them well. "It was necessary to create, for Francia's system had died with him," explained Gelly, one of his chief underlings.[9] At any rate, it was necessary to adjust to the new, and, above all, it was necessary to conciliate. Those who had suffered under Francia must be appeased; those who by reason of their activities on behalf of Francia had gained popular hatred must be protected and the people reconciled to them.

Consequently, a policy of moderation was followed. Since the death of Francia, arrests and executions had ceased, but political prisoners to the number of some six hundred were still incarcerated. Therefore, at López' behest, the very congress which named him consul granted a general amnesty. Wherever it could be done without injuring subsequent beneficiaries, property confiscated under Francia was restored. Where restoration was not feasible, indemnities were granted out of the coffers of the state. In this manner López consolidated his position and gained support, so that when the consulate came to an end in 1844 the new congress willingly let him dominate and granted him the sole executive power.

The Congress of 1844 gave to Paraguay its first constitution, an ideal dictator's constitution. Loudly it decried monarchy and declared that the Republic of Paraguay should "never be the patrimony of one person or family." Then it set up an executive in whom was vested almost a totality of power, with the one and only obligation of preserving and defending the independence and integrity of the state. This chief of state was an autocrat at once legislative, judicial, and executive. Ministers of state were mere clerks. The church was entirely subordinated and subjected to the state.

Much can be said in defense of such a constitution. At least it was a frank and open admission of what has all too frequently been the practice, but not the letter, under constitutions theoretically liberal. As weaknesses, of course, it had all the drawbacks that afflict and encumber

[9] Gelly, 73.

any dictatorship, any form of government where the people are unable to express their will.[10]

López may well be designated the organizer of the Paraguayan republic. His job of creating was begun immediately under the consulate. He had little difficulty in internal government, for the people had been well trained in obedience to authority under Francia and under the Jesuits of a century and more before. "His office," says the English surgeon Masterman, who served under him, "was looked upon with such reverential awe, that his decrees, however harsh, were obeyed with timorous submission. He made but little difference in the severe laws of Francia," Masterman continues, "but he administered them more mildly."[11] The essential change was that, although the executive power was as strongly centered in him as it had been in Francia, the administration was left to others. He organized and put into motion an administrative machine to carry out his will. A system of police and a judiciary were set up. The church and education were regulated. The army was reorganized, and internal improvements in keeping with the new day were effected. Although he did not give every department of government the personal attention Francia was wont to give, his ministers and other subordinates were administrators and nothing more.

Francia's secret spy system was modified and changed, but the new police regulations were severe. Particular pains were taken to prevent the gathering of large groups. "For instance, if one wished to give a ball or an evening party it was necessary to get a license from the chief of police to do so; and when the time arrived a row of lanterns was hung up in front of the house to notify the fact; and the doors and window shutters were left open in order that the guests might remain under observation."[12] Foreigners were subjected to the same regulation, but in a modified and less onerous degree. Whether from popular satisfaction with his régime or from the thoroughness of his control, cannot be said, but only one revolutionary attempt, or asserted attempt, occurred in his period.[13]

The judiciary was organized with the dictator as the supreme court. Local judges of no particular training were appointed for terms of one

[10] Gelly presents an interesting discussion of this need for strong government. Gelly, 104-106.

[11] Masterman, 50-51.

[12] *Ibid.*, 51.

[13] For references to the Canstatt affair and its accompanying events, see note 31 below.

year, subject to removal even then. They carried on their offices while still engaged in whatever other occupation they might have—something of a parallel to our own justices of the peace. An interesting innovation was evolved for criminal cases, however, for with each judge would be associated a sort of jury of two, chosen entirely by lot.

The church and education were relieved of some of the discriminations formerly applied against them. The *colegio* was reopened and education resumed under two Jesuits who came to the country, although these last were expelled in 1846. A school system of a sort, if indeed it may be called a system at all, was inaugurated. In this, Paraguay labored under great difficulties, for education had to be organized from rock bottom. Thus, many rather amusingly minute regulations were imposed. The duties of professors of the "Literary academy" were prescribed in minute detail by the law itself, even the very hours of classes. Thus:

> "Latin shall be taught from seven o'clock in the morning until nine; afterwards a half hour of recreation. At half past two in the winter and at two forty-five in the summer shall begin the teaching of Latin for two continuous hours. On Saturday mornings, lessons will be given on the elements of the Christian religion for one hour after the ordinary task, instead of recreation."[14]

Rules for the conduct and deportment of the students themselves were given in great length. Parents were commanded to see to it that their children came to school well washed and combed—and dressed. "Then there was incorporated into the law rules of study and deportment to be committed to memory."[15] Little indeed was left to the discretion of the teacher. But, be that as it may, education was encouraged.

The church itself was thoroughly subjected to the state. The dictator, unable even here to restrain his inclination to nepotism, appointed his brother, Basilio López, a member of the Franciscan order, to be bishop, and secured his confirmation. Basilio was a man "not well spoken of," according to one fairly reliable commentator.[16]

Church buildings and cemeteries were constructed. The old cathedral of Asunción, dating from 1557, was torn down in 1842, and a new cathedral built.[17] Cemeteries were established, and their administration and regulation prescribed in minute detail. Thus, the precise compen-

---

[14] Washburn, I, 346. For a more favorable interpretation and description, cf. Gelly, 114.

[15] Washburn, I, 347.

[16] Burton, 61.

[17] Gelly, 83.

sation of undertakers and gravediggers was set at five Paraguayan dollars a month. The hearse driver was to be paid the same figure, while the muleteer was to receive a fifth as much. "No person shall ride in the dead-carts except the corpse that is carried," the law declared, "and, therefore, no person shall get up and ride behind." Even the exact dimensions of the grave and the method of lowering the body into it were set forth.[18]

A printing press was set up and a newspaper established. This latter, the *Semanario,* edited by López himself, was really more of an official bulletin than a dispenser of news.

Slavery, never extensive in Paraguay, was abolished to the extent that all children born to slaves were declared free. Thus, the initial Brazilian step of three decades later was anticipated.

Under the régime of Carlos Antonio López the army and the navy came in for extensive development and organization. Under Francia, many soldiers had seen as much as fifteen years of service at frontier posts without being relieved. Now a definite term of enlistment was established, and as rapidly as possible Francia's soldiers were released to their homes. The superannuated were granted pensions. Out of gratitude for their release from the isolation of the frontier, they became loyal supporters of the new ruler, yet at the same time, collectively they constituted a strong reserve force. Eventually a system of conscription was established. From each district a quota of youths between eighteen and thirty was chosen by lot under direction of the local magistrate.

The military position of the republic was further strengthened by the building of new forts, especially along the river Apa, to the north, and in the Gran Chaco. An arsenal was established, and a factory for the manufacture of arms and munitions built. Likewise, a foundry was built, at which various needs, not only of the military, but of the civil branch of the government were satisfied.

Various measures were taken to encourage general commerce. Definite patent laws were enacted, and special rights and privileges accorded to inventors.[19] Before the end of Carlos Antonio's reign, a regular biweekly steamer service from Asunción to the coast had been established. This, of necessity of course, had to await the pacification of the lower

---

[18] Washburn, I, 347.

[19] These and other similar laws are given *in extenso* in Hadfield and Thompson: William Hadfield, *Brazil, the river Plate, and the Falkland islands* . . . (London, 1854), 333-336, and George Thompson, *The war in Paraguay* . . . (London, 1869), 5-8.

provinces. A railroad from Asunción to Paraguarí, one of the first in South America, was begun in 1859 and finished in 1862, the year of the elder López' death. Apart from its value for tapping the resources of the agricultural interior, the railroad was of value for strategic purposes. Communications were likewise facilitated through the building of new roads and the widening of old ones, through the erection of bridges, and, where bridges were not practicable, by establishment of ferries.

Agriculture was aided. The yerba mate, a state monopoly, came in for especial attention. Canals were cut, one for the better drainage of the Villa Rica district, others for conservation of water in the arid Villa del Rosario and San Estanislao regions, where serious cattle losses had occurred in time of drought. The Rosario district, it may be noted, was the location of López' original *estancia.*

In the earlier part of his reign López encouraged foreigners to come to the country, and in 1845 issued a formal decree setting forth the rights and privileges to be accorded them. Some discriminations were permitted, as for example, requiring licenses to transact business or to contract marriage with Paraguayans; but these were not onerous. Later, López came to distrust the foreigner and to hold him in check as much as possible. A number of foreigners, Europeans and North Americans, took service under López in the army, such as Masterman, who was chief surgeon, and Colonel Thompson, who was in his engineering corps.[20] Others engaged in trade on their own behalf.

Trade with the outside was encouraged from the beginning. Duties on imports and exports, which were very high at first, were moderated, although even then much foreign complaint existed. The greatest deterrent to foreign trade, however, came, not from excessive duties, but from the restraints and hardships placed on river traffic by the neighbors of Paraguay—Corrientes at first, and later Buenos Aires. Out of them came difficulties which Francia, foreseeing, had averted.

III

The neighboring Province of Corrientes had been in revolt, or at civil war, depending upon the point of view, against Rosas since 1839. Seeing the non-intervention policy of Francia, Rosas had been content to leave Paraguay alone and had even ordered a public eulogy of Francia

[20] Both Masterman and Thompson wrote accounts of their experiences which are of tremendous value for the period.

at his death.[21] But within three months of the creation of the consulate, López, in the first flush of Paraguay's new freedom from commercial and political isolation signed a treaty with Governor Ferré of Corrientes. This "treaty of friendship, commerce, and navigation," along with a a simultaneous agreement on a provisional boundary, was the origin of Rosas' antagonism to Paraguay: it fortified him in his determination to refuse to recognize Paraguay as an independent state, as López formally requested in 1842. Two years later, in 1844, López, now president, again raised the question of recognition, which Rosas refused, although, in a conciliatory mood, he offered to sell Paraguay arms and munitions.

López, distrustful of Rosas, now signed a new treaty with Corrientes, which, at least by implication, recognized Corrientes as a sovereign state.[22] To this, Rosas' answer was a formal proscription of all trade with Corrientes and Paraguay. At the same time he protested Brazilian recognition of Paraguayan independence. His Uruguayan ally, the *Blanco caudillo* Oribe, was likewise induced to join in this "continental system," and Paraguay was effectively blockaded, with commerce cut to the veriest trickle.

Meanwhile, a Brazilian envoy had reached Asunción and had negotiated a treaty with Paraguay. By its terms the opening of the Paraná and the Paraguay, vital to Brazilian economic development in the interior, was accorded, while Brazil on her part engaged to secure a general recognition of Paraguay's status as an independent state. Likewise, arrangements were made for a boundary settlement. By this treaty, the first step in a series of events which for a time made Paraguay the cat's paw of the capable Brazilian diplomacy, Brazil managed to align Paraguay against Rosas. As the blockade began to be felt, López concluded a general offensive and defensive alliance with Corrientes, by which he engaged to aid the anti-Rosas government of that province with an army of ten thousand men, and even proposed that Entre Ríos and Corrientes should formally proclaim themselves independent of the Argentine Confederation—a main cog in the Brazilian diplomacy which sought to break up the Plata provinces into several separate states.

[21] Enrique Wisner, *El dictador del Paraguay* . . . (Concordia, Arg., 1923), 167-168.

[22] The account given by Box has been followed in discussion of relations of Paraguay with Argentine provinces and with Brazil. Pelham Horton Box, *Origins of the Paraguayan war* (Urbana, Ill., 1927), chs. I-III. This work is without question the best on the international relations preceding the Paraguayan War.

The Corrientes campaign was short and decisive. The *Correntinos,* acting as vanguard for the Paraguayan force, went down to inglorious defeat before Urquiza, the great *caudillo* of Entre Ríos, then allied with Rosas. The valiant army of Paraguay, with the dictator's nineteen-year-old son Francisco Solano at its head, recrossed the Paraná without firing a shot! Thus was Corrientes occupied by the pro-Rosas forces and a "federalist" government enthroned.

Rosas, prevented by international complications with France and Great Britain from completing his victory in Corrientes, did not send Urquiza across the Paraná.

> "He felt it would be better on the whole to keep Paraguay on hand as a mild permanent crisis, [so a modern British scholar interprets it]. The great Dictator . . . contented himself [instead] with making Carlos Antonio López' flesh creep from time to time, though there is no evidence that he even made serious preparations for the invasion of Paraguay."[23]

López, however, fearing invasion, instructed his minister at Rio de Janeiro, Gelly, to seek a defensive-offensive alliance with Brazil and at the same time a settlement of boundaries. But Brazil was uninterested, for at the moment she had great hopes that Rosas' fate would be sealed by the Anglo-French intervention in the Plata which had already reached the stage of blockade.

To such lengths did Brazilian complacency go that when in 1849 Señor Gelly requested the Brazilian minister of foreign affairs to grant a passport to his compatriot, Colonel Bernardino Báez, the minister refused it under pressure from Rosas' own minister at Rio de Janeiro, who asserted that Báez was an Argentine citizen because Paraguay was an Argentine province! Thereupon Gelly demanded his passports and left the Brazilian court.

The turn Brazilian relations had taken compelled López to do an about face and seek an agreement with Rosas. The latter, who was almost out of his difficulties with France and Great Britain, made answer to López' olive branch by having his own subservient congress authorize an unlimited use of the treasury to effect the "reincorporation" of Paraguay into the Argentine Confederation.[24]

López himself, unable to come to an agreement with his neighbors, seems now to have determined upon an independent policy in his foreign

---

[23] Box, 22.

[24] Cecilio Báez, *El doctor Francia y la dictadura en Sud-América* (Asunción, 1910); Box, 24.

relations. Failing to eliminate a Brazilian garrison in the disputed frontier region by diplomacy, he forcibly ejected the offending garrisons. Thus he saved his face and somewhat restored his prestige. Brazil swallowed her resentment only because the termination of the Anglo-French intervention had once more left Rosas a figure to be reckoned with, wherefore Paraguay was a potential weapon with which to combat him. Indeed, on Christmas Day, 1850, Brazil and Paraguay signed a treaty of alliance against Rosas. This treaty was but a step in the general alliance then being made to overthrow the dictator of Buenos Aires and was quickly followed by a break between Rosas and his great ally Urquiza in 1851. By this move Rosas' own fate was sealed, and his power broken at the Battle of Caseros in 1852.

To the final movement against Rosas Paraguay lent moral support, but did not participate in the actual fighting. Nevertheless, the victory was hers, for as payment of her support, she was able to obtain general recognition of her independence.

IV

One of the cardinal points of López' foreign policy had been attained. There still, however, remained two other main objectives, settlement of troublesome boundary disputes with the Argentine Confederation and Brazil, and adjustment of the problem of free navigation of the Paraná. Eventually these were to loom as vital factors in Paraguay. Meanwhile, other foreign embroilments hinged on the capricious absolutism in which the dictatorship indulged. Chief among these were the so-called Hopkins and *Water Witch* affairs and the resulting crisis with the United States, and the Canstatt case involving Great Britain.

The Hopkins affair had as its origin the arrival of Edward Augustus Hopkins at Asunción in 1845. Hopkins came as the United States "confidential agent to Paraguay for the purpose of obtaining information concerning the political condition and commercial resources of that country, with a view to the acknowledgment of its independence."[25] At least he was so described by the United States Department of State, although his actions belied the word "confidential"!

Hopkins soon ingratiated himself with the dictator, whom he assured that the United States would definitely recognize Paraguay's independ-

[25] Secretary of State Buchanan to Chargé d'affaires Harris, March 30, 1846. In *Diplomatic correspondence of the United States. Inter-American affairs,* ed. by William Ray Manning (Washington, 1932), I, 29-32. Cf., also, Washburn, I, 361-388.

ence. Likewise, he offered, on behalf of the United States, to mediate López' difficulties with Rosas. All this was done despite the fact that he was not officially accredited and "had no power whatever to negotiate or to act in a diplomatic character."

Having got himself into the good graces of the dictator, Hopkins looked next at the commercial possibilities which Paraguay offered and obtained valuable concessions from López. As soon as the United States government learned of his activities, he was summarily recalled.[26] Instead of informing López of the actual facts, however, he represented to him that he was merely going back to the United States on business connected with his concession and would return.

In the United States Hopkins organized a company, "The United States and Paraguay Navigation Company," backed chiefly by Rhode Island capitalists, among whom was one United States senator. The company equipped a ship, loaded it with machinery and goods, and sent it to Paraguay, only to have it wrecked on the Brazilian coast. Despite this loss, Hopkins was able to return to Paraguay, chiefly to exploit the concessions of the company. At the same time, probably through political connections, he had obtained appointment as United States consul at Asunción. Inasmuch as there was no minister resident in Paraguay, Consul Hopkins became the official representative of the United States.

Meanwhile, disappointed and disillusioned through the failure of Hopkins' glowing promises of recognition to materialize, López turned against him, and the company found itself operating under difficulties. And taking their cue from the dictator, the populace likewise changed its attitude toward the North Americans. Then came an incident, small in itself, but large in its consequences. The brother of Hopkins, while riding with the wife of the French consul, inadvertently disturbed and almost stampeded a herd of cattle which was being driven by a Paraguayan. In fury the latter rode up to Hopkins and, taking his sword, beat the consul's brother over the head and shoulders.

When Consul Hopkins heard of the assault he was highly indignant and hurried to López. Appearing before him in unceremonious fashion, he demanded that the offender be punished. Despite the domineering attitude of the United States consul, López acquiesced, only to be met with a further demand that the fact of punishment be published in the official newspaper. López drew the line at this and let his resentment be plainly shown, not only in his speech, but in subsequent actions. The

[26] Secretary of State Buchanan to Argentine Minister Alvear, August 14, 1846, in Manning, *Inter-American affairs,* I, 35.

company and its property were subjected to a variety of studied annoyances, and, finally, the concession itself was cancelled.

At this point there happened to arrive on the scene the United States ship *Water Witch,* commanded by Lieutenant Thomas Jefferson Page.[27] Page, a capable and scholarly officer, was at the time engaged in an extensive official government survey of the waters of the Plata and its tributaries. At an earlier date he had been well received by López, who, however, instructed him that, in his explorations of the upper Paraguay, he should not go beyond Paraguayan waters. Instead, however, having permission from the Brazilian and Bolivian governments, he had gone well above the Paraguayan limits. In consequence, López had taken strong exception, alleging that Paraguay was put in a difficult position in its relations with Brazil, inasmuch as similar permission had been denied the latter country. As there was little that could be done to remedy that particular dispute, it had been smoothed over, and Page had continued his explorations at other points on the river. At the time of Hopkins' dispute, the *Water Witch* was just returning to Asunción once more.

Now it was Page's turn to assert himself. As commander of a United States vessel of war, he supported his consul to the best of his ability. Hopkins and the entire personnel of the company were taken on board, but only after great difficulty and long continued recriminatory debate with the government. One obstacle after another was interposed by the government of Paraguay. First, there was trouble in getting permission to reship the company's machinery and other property, upon which López attempted to impose an export duty. Following that came a formal demand for a return of the company's deeds and other documents attesting its rights. Both of these demands were capricious and unjustified on the part of López. They were, however, at least partially offset by a serious breach of etiquette on the part of Page, who wrote his communications to López in English and flatly refused the government the courtesy of a translation, alleging that López could read English and that, therefore, a translation was unnecessary.[28]

When finally the dispute was settled, albeit to the satisfaction of neither side, the *Water Witch* sailed down the Paraguay and up the

[27] Page, in language unusually restrained for a naval officer, gives extensive discussion of his own actions. His account has been used in the description of the *Water Witch* affair. Thomas Jefferson Page, *La Plata, the Argentine confederation, and Paraguay* . . . (New York, 1859), *passim.*

[28] Page, 281-283. This seems to be the sole instance in which Page conducted himself in an unseemly fashion.

Paraná to continue its survey in that portion of Paraguayan waters. There, capping the entire affair, occurred a serious incident when a Paraguayan fort opened fire on the United States vessel and killed one sailor.

Page's explorations were put to an end, and he himself made formal report back to his government. As an aftermath of the entire dispute, a United States squadron under Commodore Bowlin was sent to the Plata and reparation or arbitration demanded from López. Amid the turmoil immediately preceding the North American civil war, the eventual arbitration, however, came to naught, and the United States claims were disallowed.[29] Whether the United States fleet could have successfully forced the river to Asunción if López had not compromised is a moot question. The experience of Brazil in a similar effort would rather indicate otherwise.

In 1855 the long drawn-out unsettled boundary dispute between Paraguay and the Brazilian Empire flared up once more, as Brazil erected a post on territory claimed by Paraguay. López promptly expelled the intruders, while Brazil prepared openly for war. A squadron of ten vessels under the Brazilian Admiral Ferreira de Oliveira was, therefore, sent up the Paraná, but was stopped by the strong Paraguayan fortifications at Humaitá, which commanded the route to Asunción. The admiral, recognizing the futility of attempting force, accepted a parley instead, and, with the permission of López, took a single vessel to Asunsión. There a partial compromise, in which Paraguay had the best of the bargain, was effected.[30]

Paraguay, with her inland location, was almost impregnable before a naval attack, as the failure of Admiral Ferreira's coercive expedition and subsequent events in the Paraguayan War demonstrated. The Paraguayan absolutist could, therefore, act with little fear of successful foreign intervention; his whim could be indulged almost with impunity. Only when retaliation or reprisal could be made beyond the limits of Paraguayan waters could it be effective without great cost. Such a situation developed in the course of a dispute with Great Britain in the Canstatt case.

In 1859 there occurred the only instance under Carlos Antonio López of an attempt at revolt—or alleged attempt. Shortly after Commodore Bowlin's abortive effort at indemnity for the treatment of Hopkins and

[29] For diplomatic correspondence on the affair, see Manning, *Inter-American affairs,* I, *passim.*

[30] Box, 33-36.

the *Water Witch,* a number of Paraguayans were arrested at Asunción. They were charged with conspiring against the government, although it is asserted that the actual basis was personal enmity on the part of López and that the accusations were false; certainly no conclusive proof of guilt was offered. After the prisoners had been arrested and were awaiting trial, it developed that one of their number, one James Canstatt, was a British subject, although he was born in Montevideo. The British consul, Henderson, therefore made representations to the dictator and demanded that a fair trial be accorded and that Canstatt should have the right of counsel and be confronted with his accusers. When this was refused, Henderson closed his consulate and left the country.

Canstatt had meanwhile been tried along with the other accused, found guilty, and sentenced to be shot. López, however, delayed the execution, pending further British action; perhaps, as one commentator has expressed it, he hoped Canstatt would "conveniently die in prison." British action came in a peculiar and unexpected fashion. Upon reaching the Plata estuary, Consul Henderson had informed the British admiral stationed there of the whole affair. Thereupon, the admiral took matters into his own hands. As it happened, the Paraguayan war vessel *Tacuarí* was then in the harbor of Buenos Aires, preparing to take young Francisco Solano López (who had just returned from Europe) back to Paraguay. As the *Tacuarí* started to leave the harbor of Buenos Aires, two British vessels attempted to stop her while she was yet in Buenos Aires waters. Although she managed to get back into port, young López was compelled to travel overland, while the British blockaded the *Tacuarí,* holding her as hostage for Canstatt until Carlos Antonio released his prisoner.[31]

V

Especially during the last years of Carlos Antonio López' life, his children exerted a tremendous influence on the affairs of Paraguay. Particularly was this true of his three sons, Francisco Solano, Venancio, and Benigno, each of whom held important posts under their father.

One and all, they were profligates, proverbial "spoiled children" of the great. From early childhood the three sons, and the two daughters as well, were left to their own devices and desires almost entirely. Venancio especially was "something of a licensed ravisher," as one writer has described him. Francisco Solano was guarded in his conduct and "paid considerable outward respect to appearances," but

[31] Burton, 64-65. For a version of the plot story itself, see Masterman, 52-55.

> "Venancio, who was of a coarser and more stolid character, was the terror of those families that, not belonging to the upper classes, had yet some regard for the reputation of their daughters. The lot of many of these dwellers in Asunción was no happy one. Whatever one of the young López' might do, there was no remedy for the wronged and injured."[32]

Señora de López and her daughters were very much addicted to fine clothes, and as a result brought the latest styles from Paris. In order to take care of the costs of fine living and fine dressing, which could scarcely be covered by the modest presidential salary of four thousand dollars, the family was reputed to have resorted regularly to various grafts, petty and great.

Page, the chief officer of the *Water Witch,* who was, despite his conflicts with Don Carlos Antonio, quite restrained in his judgments and in his acceptance of rumor and legend, describes the advantages which accrued from the yerba monopoly, whose yield was re-sold by the dictator at a profit of some six hundred per cent.[33] The children of the president, so it is frequently averred, habitually engaged in commercial transactions, acting as middlemen and, taking advantage of their position, bought at prices below the market and sold above it. Meanwhile, others carefully refrained from entering into competition with them.

Francisco Solano was appointed to the command of the entire army of Paraguay at the age of nineteen and was early slated to be his father's successor, in patent disregard for the provision of the Constitution of 1844 that "the Republic of Paraguay should never be the patrimony of one person or family." Similarly, Venancio and Benigno were given similar exalted positions. In 1854 Francisco was sent on a mission to Europe, during which he toured the continent while acting as Paraguay's diplomatic representative. In Paris he met the famous Madame Lynch, an Anglo-Irishwoman of doubtful past, who was to exert almost unlimited influence on him and through him on Paraguay during the ensuing years.

The supine congress of Paraguay had, at Carlos Antonio's request, authorized the president to make provision for a successor in the event of his own death. Thus, in 1862, when he was already suffering greatly from the ailment which was soon to bring his death, the elder López signed a secret decree, often referred to as his will, by which his eldest

[32] William Henry Koebel, *Romance of the river Plate* (2 vols., London, 1914), II, 520.

[33] Page, 136-137.

son, Francisco Solano, was to be provisional president upon his father's death.

Within a month Carlos Antonio López was dead. For twenty-one years he had been the actual ruler of Paraguay. He had organized the country; he had developed its resources; he had opened it to foreign trade and commerce. To his son and successor he left an economically prosperous land.

CHAPTER TWELVE

FRANCISCO SOLANO LÓPEZ, "A DICTATOR RUN AMUCK"[1]

CARLOS ANTONIO LÓPEZ, dictator-organizer of Paraguay, died in September 1862. Only a short while before his death he had added his signature to a document often referred to as his will by which, in accordance with authority granted him by the Paraguayan congress, he named as his successor his son Francisco Solano López, who was to serve as provisional president until a general congress could elect a new executive.

The selection was a foregone conclusion, for in his later years Carlos Antonio had come more and more to rely upon his son, whose advice and opinions had weighed heavily with him. Francisco himself had rather effectively consolidated his own position and, consequently, no opposition at the general congress was anticipated. Nevertheless, a month later, when the congress met, an abortive attempt was made so to revise the constitution that the executive's powers would be curbed. Some sentiment, too, appears to have existed in favor of his youngest brother, Benigno López, generally regarded as the most capable of the three sons of the deceased Carlos Antonio.[2] Benigno, however, made no open attempt to obtain consideration.

Francisco Solano López was destined, or doomed, to rule but eight years, a far shorter period than either of his great predecessors. But, in that period was to occur the Paraguayan War, which brought death to him and near annihilation to his country. Indeed, the story of the Paraguayan War is, to a large degree, the story of the second López, and he is commonly judged solely by that controversial conflict. Rare indeed is the historian or writer on the Paraguayan War who has succeeded in preserving a freedom of bias on the subject.

---

[1] There is perhaps no dictator in all Hispanic American history concerning whose life and times there has been such voluminous and at the same time such contradictory writing as Francisco Solano López. Dr. Pelham H. Box, the most thorough scholar treating the subject, in his *Origins of the Paraguayan war* (Urbana, 1927), includes twenty-seven pages of bibliography. Box's account, invaluable for its clear-cut presentation of Paraguay's foreign relations which led to the Paraguayan War, and that of the contemporary Sir Richard F. Burton *(Letters from the battlefields of Paraguay,* London, 1870) are outstanding for their lack of bias, as is, in some respects, the work of Thompson, *The war in Paraguay* . . . (London, 1869), who was a colonel of engineers under López. The interpretations of the two former have been closely followed herein.

[2] Box, 182. Burton considers this an "idle tale." Cf. Burton, 67.

It would be easy to say with the Argentine historians and with those of Brazil that "López was a maniac who to satisfy his ego plunged his country into a war which was literally almost suicidal"; or with the Paraguayon O'Leary and the great Uruguayan *Blanco* statesman and historian, Luís Alberto de Herrera, that López was but the unfortunate and innocent victim of the greed of his more powerful neighbors.[3] All seem woefully to confuse two separate and distinct aspects: the personality of López and the causes which underlay the war itself. Actually, the younger López sought in general to continue the policies of his father, except that in his foreign relations he exerted a much more vigorous diplomacy. He was neither a demi-god or even a genius, nor yet Satan come to earth.

I

Francisco Solano López, eldest son of his predecessor, was born on his father's *estancia* on July 24, 1826. Almost from the beginning of his father's reign he was treated as the crown prince of the dynasty. In accordance with the dominant nepotism he was regularly on the pay roll of the state. At the age of nineteen he was commander of the Paraguayan expeditionary force to Corientes which returned so ingloriously. Four years later he was again in command of a foreign expedition, this time to Misiones during the troubles with Rosas.[4]

Always he was the spoiled child; in common with his brothers and sisters he could do no wrong. Through this idea there was developed the egotism and cocksuredness, the blind determination to continue on a policy once embraced, regardless of consequences, the traits which were to bring his downfall. When he was scarcely twenty-three, he had already developed a high opinion of his own Napoleonic military genius. "The military art has no secrets for me," he declared. "General Paz cannot teach me, nor have I anything to learn of his science." "He who spoke was still a boy of twenty-three," comments the English scholar Box, "and had never seen a battle. The one-armed General Paz in his

[3] Carlos Pereyra, *Francisco Solano López y la querra del Paraguay* (Madrid, 1919); Luís Alberto de Herrera, *La diplomacia oriental en el Paraguay . . .* (5 vols., Montevideo, 1908-1930); Juan Emiliano O'Leary, *Nuestra epopeya (Guerra del Paraguay, 1864-1870)* (Asunción, 1919), and his *El Paraguay en la unificación argentina* (Asunción, 1924). An inadequate and rather error-filled reply to Pereyra's work is that of the Brazilian Lemos Britto, *Solano López e a guerra do Paraguay. Replica ao livro de . . . Pereyra* (Rio de Janeiro, 1927).

[4] See chapter 11, *supra.*

day was regarded as one of the best tacticians and military organizers in Latin America."[5]

The younger López' personal conduct was scarcely above reproach even in his father's time, although it must be admitted that, like other sons of the great, he and his activities received more than ordinary attention from the public. Several stories of his and his brothers' sensual adventures have often been told.[6]

In 1853 he went to Europe as the representative of his father.[7] In the course of two years' travel there, he paid especial attention to the purchase of arms, munitions, and other supplies for the Paraguayan government and was responsible for the hiring of a number of foreign experts. As the son of his father he was given great attention and lionized at various courts. His stay in Europe made him a great admirer of Napoleon III, whose influence he felt; it likewise gave him a superficial acquaintance with diplomatic practices of the continent. It was at this time, too, that he met the attractive Elisa Lynch, whom he brough back to Paraguay with him. Upon her has been laid much of the blame for some of his later caprices.[8]

Francisco's first opportunity to make use of his skill and ability as a diplomat and mediator came after the Battle of Cepeda in 1859. Then it was that he headed a fairly successful mediation between Buenos Aires and the Argentine Confederation. As a result of the compromise terms he obtained, Buenos Aires gave him credit for having rescued her, and hailed him as the saviour of Buenos Aires. "Perhaps General López is destined by Providence to preside over a great nation composed of all the river provinces of the Paraná, Paraguay, and Uruguay and guarding the equilibrium with the empire of Brazil," declared *El Nacional* of Buenos Aires, as it exuded praise for López.[9] Ironical, indeed, that half a decade later, as López did seek to guard that equilibrium, his *Porteño* panegyrists of 1859 should lead in the movement against him!

As minister of war and marine, Francisco Solano occupied a prominent place under his father's government. He is credited with being the guiding influence behind Carlos Antonio's enlargement of the Para-

---

[5] Box, 180.

[6] See, especially, the works of Washburn *(History of Paraguay . . ., 2 vols., Boston, 1871)*, Masterman *(Seven eventful years in Paraguay,* London, 1869), and Koebel *(Romance of the River Plate,* 2 vols., London, 1914).

[7] See Box, 179-182, for a summary of López' European travels.

[8] See Burton, 74-75. For an extended account of this interesting lady, see Héctor Varela ("Orión," pseud.), *Elisa Lynch* (Buenos Aires, 1870).

[9] O'Leary, 97.

guayan naval and military establishment.[10] Undoubtedly, he did influence the new policy of the elder López, but credit must be given primarily to the generally unsatisfactory foreign relations of Paraguay in the 1850's. Altercations with Brazil, the United States, and Great Britain called attention to the defense needs of the country.

II

When Francisco Solano López came to power he continued his father's policies of internal developments, and, above all, communications. His chief concern was the contribution which the improvement of the transportation and communications made to the better defense of the country. Railroad building, designed particularly for strategical purposes, received his attention. Steamer connections were improved. During the all too brief period of peace with which his rule began, he established the first telegraph line in South America. All these contributed to the better defense of the country, and with the same objective in mind he improved Humaitá, the semi-impregnable fortress which guarded the Paraguay River against attack from below.[11] But where his father had been concerned solely with military developments as a defense, Francisco Solano López saw in it a possible offensive weapon. He dreamed of Paraguay as the great arbiter of South America or at least of the Plata, whose political equilibrium would be maintained by Paraguay by force if necessary.

Like his predecessors, Francisco Solano López was a strong exponent of personal power, authoritarianism, and absolutism, and in Paraguay he was indeed the law. More than that, he conceived of each other nation being similarly situated, so that public acts of its citizens were of necessity indicative of governmental attitude. In Paraguay he was the press, and when, in 1860, the newspapers of Buenos Aires began to poke fun at him and at Elisa Lynch, he took it as a personal affront emanating not merely from the editors but from the government itself.

"Liberty" was as incomprehensible to him as to many of the economic dictators of the present day. It was merely a liberty for those in authority.

These factors, accentuated by the Buenos Aires government's willingness to tolerate a "Junta of Liberal Paraguayans" within its gates, served as strong irritants and impediments in any development of truly friendly

[10] See Box, 179-182.

[11] Luís Alberto de Herrera, *La diplomacia oriental en el Paraguay: el mariscal Francisco Solano López* (Montevideo, 1912), 18.

relations between Buenos Airs and Paraguay. When the great conflict broke, López' own personality and his arbitrary procedure served to weld together an opposition which might easily have been divided and to detach from him and Paraguay the potential ally available in the river provinces. The great Paraguayan War, which might well have been limited to a conflict with Brazil or Buenos Aires, came to be an alignment not only of those two but of Uruguay and the Argentine provinces as well.[12]

III

The situation of Brazil and, above all, the policies of the Empire had made it almost a foregone conclusion that she would sooner or later resort to force. Her policy was one of imperialism and territorial aggrandizement. Boundary disputes between Paraguay and Brazil, having their roots in the colonial period, had come to a head in the elder López' time. He had managed to delay any showdowns, but the issue remained a critical one which might be resurrected at any moment. The boundary question, therefore, forced Paraguay into diplomatic opposition to Brazil.

From the Brazilian point of view, however, the Uruguayan problem was far more pressing than that of Paraguay. Indeed, it was the Empire's policy in regard to her small neighbor to the south which precipitated actual hostilities. Officially, Brazil had renounced her claim to Uruguay in 1828; nevertheless, throughout the epoch of Rosas she had steadily given aid to the *Colorado* Party. This concern over affairs in Uruguay was not, indeed, without its justification for that country had become the mecca of fugitive slaves from Brazil, and the contagion of its disorders had reacted upon the Brazilian border province of Rio Grande do Sul, ever a turbulent region. After Caseros, when disturbances in Uruguay continued with rapid shifts of control, the question in the minds of Brazilian statesmen was: If intervention is refused, can rebellion in Rio Grande do Sul be averted?

The potential leader of such a revolt was the Rio Grande cattle magnate and separatist, General Felipe Netto, who had made a huge fortune through supplying Oribe with cattle during the great nine-year siege of Montevideo. Now, as *Colorado* opposition to the *Blanco* government continued, Netto, who had his own grievances against the *Blancos,* stood silently inactive, but he watched developments with an intense interest. When Argentina under Mitre aided the rebel *Colorados* of Flores, Bra-

---

[12] The following discussions of Paraguay's relations with her neighbors are based upon Box's account.

zil became alarmed at the disturbed situation; fearing especially that Netto and other separatists would be influenced to disorder if the revolution were to continue, the imperial government sent José Antonio Saraiva on a special mission to Uruguay to obtain reparation for injuries suffered by Brazilian subjects. Under Saraiva's able direction, the mission became, too, one of pacification, and notable results seemed probable for a time. The revolution of Flores in Uruguay was fomented and encouraged by Mitre and the government at Buenos Aires; only later did Brazilian intervention come—and following it the outbreak of hostilities between Paraguay and Brazil.

The fall of Rosas had made no fundamental changes in the political chaos of Uruguay. Civil war had now become endemic, with the *Blancos* more often in power. Such was the situation in 1863, when the exiled *Colorado* leader Venancio Flores prepared a new revolution in furtherance of which he received aid from his old companion-in-arms, Mitre, and the unitarists, whom he had rendered signal aid at Pavón. The Argentinian federalists, traditionally allies of the *Blancos,* had cooled toward them due to the *Blanco* failure to join them at Pavón—a studied and praiseworthy attempt on Uruguay's part to disentangle herself from the Argentinian internecine struggles.[13]

Mitre's aid to Flores was the principal cause of the continuation of the civil strife. Without it the *Colorado* rising would have failed in short order; with it the movement became a serious threat. Brazil, ever suspicious of all Buenos Aires inspired activity, was at first opposed to Flores, but as the *Blanco* government fell under control of the more extreme diehard element of the party, Brazil became more and more intransigeant, and finally, ignoring threats and warnings from Asunción, the imperial government bowed to the demands of its own domestic situation and ordered the invasion of Uruguay—without a declaration of war.

The Brazilian forces and the *Colorados* of Flores promptly united, and thenceforth the *Blancos* were on the defensive. There followed the bitter siege of Paysandú, marked by *Blanco* heroism and Brazilian bad faith. Before the siege was at length terminated by the surrender of Leandro Gómez and his *Blancos* and the subsequent treacherous murder of Gómez, "the most passionate indignation" had been aroused in the neighboring Argentinian provinces.

[13] Box, 84.

> "Feeling in Entre Ríos against the Brazilians ran high, and Urquiza had the greatest difficulty in preventing a general rising on behalf of the neighboring republic. The spectacle of Leandro Gómez with his handful of defenders beating off 10,000 besiegers and the Brazilian fleet roused the gauchos like a trumpet. The ancient national antipathies for Brazil; the close ties, political and economic, between the lands on either side of the Río Uruguay; the profound suspicions of Brazil's designs on the independence of her little neighbor; republican and idealistic suspicion of the Brazilian monarchy and her 'peculiar institution' of negro slavery, voiced in the volcanic polemics of the great Alberdi—all these factors rallied Argentine opinion as a whole to the support of Uruguay, and feeling mounted higher with every day of Leandro Gómez' resistance and culminated with the news of his atrocious murder."[14]

Meanwhile, López had maintained an intense interest in the situation which had developed. Had he been a statesman of first or even second rank and ability, had he shown good faith toward the *Blancos* of Uruguay and lived up to promises made or implied to them, and had he been truly the capable diplomat he thought himself to be, he might easily have so maneuvered that the course of events would have been radically different. Instead, he betrayed bad faith toward the *Blanco* government which looked to him for assistance; he refused to put himself into any sincere accord with Urquiza and the anti-Mitre, pro-*Blanco* federalists of Argentina, and when the Brazilian invasion actually began he stalled and procrastinated; when, he did unleash his war machine, he directed it at first, not toward Uruguay, but northward into the Brazilian Province of Matto Grosso; when at length he belatedly moved to the aid of Uruguay, his opportunity had vanished for the *Blanco* government had fallen. Then, to cap it all, he deliberately provoked Argentina by attacking Corrientes, and uniting the discordant elements of the country made it possible for Mitre to join in as the ally of Brazil and of Uruguay, which by now had come under Flores' control!

The impending crisis in Uruguay had brought López into diplomatic negotiations with the *Blanco* government at Montevideo and with Brazil. His incompetent handling of these relationships helped further the development of the critical situation which ultimately grew into the Paraguayan War.

IV

Carlos Antonio López' unsatisfactory relations with Rosas and with Brazil had served to inculcate in Paraguayan diplomats a strong sus-

---

[14] *Ibid.*, 222.

picion and distrust of the motives of Paraguay's two great neighbors, a feeling which the Uruguayans shared. The younger López, fresh from his contacts with European diplomacy, its chicaneries, and its system of alliances, saw the solution of Paraguay's difficulties in the creation of a strong alliance of Paraguay and Uruguay, supplemented by the Littoral provinces, whose dual objective would be the control of the river system, Paraguay's vital commercial artery, and the protection of the smaller provinces and states along it against the aggressions of their two great neighbors. Such a project might indeed have been feasible had López not permitted his own ego and vainglorious ambition to get the better of him.

Early in 1862, some months before the elder López' death, an Uruguayan mission had visited Asunción. The following year Octavio Lápido was sent by the Uruguayan government to further close relations between Paraguay and Uruguay, whose policies should be "directed to the establishment of a balance of power, . . . for the system of balance of power preserves peace."[15] Once Brazil and Argentina realized that an attack on either Paraguay or Uruguay meant war with both, they would hesitate to precipitate war. Out of the Lápido mission and its influence upon López came López' "abandonment of the policy of isolation that was rapidly to draw Paraguay into the cockpit of the Río de la Plata."[16]

López did indeed embrace the proposed policy, whose basic thought was by no means new to him. Coöperation was an idea entirely foreign to López; however, Paraguay as personified by its dictator must be the leader. Soon, without consulting Uruguay, López sent copies of confidential Uruguayan diplomatic notes to support and supplement his own protests to Buenos Aires over the aid given Flores. While the *Blancos* of Uruguay wanted war, López vacillated in his actions; in consequence, he partially alienated them from him, without aiding his own relations with Mitre, whose attitude toward Paraguay and López was tempered solely by his need for Urquiza's support.

Encouraged by the obvious coolness between López and the Uruguayan government, Mitre on his part would give López no satisfaction. López, despite rebuffs from Buenos Aires, stood on his dignity in his relations with the strife-torn Uruguayan republic, particularly in connection with what one scholar has termed Uruguay's "overzealous ac-

---

[15] Herrera, *La diplomacia oriental* . . ., II, 382.
[16] Box, 164.

tion" in searching a Paraguayan vessel at Montevideo.[17] The incident itself was smoothed over, yet scars from it remained, and the *Blancos* made no effort to include López in an attempted international mediation of the *Colorado-Blanco* civil war—a move in which the Brazilian emissary, Saraiva, played a considerable part.

Stung by his lack of success in the Uruguayan negotiations, López now took occasion to issue his famous note (August 30, 1864) protesting Brazilian meddling in Uruguay and disclaiming responsibility for the consequences should Brazil invade Uruguay.[18] The "perfect and absolute independence of Uruguay" must be maintained, he declared. At the same time he gave the *Blancos* to understand that Paraguay was not in "disagreement with the Uruguayan state," but "only in disaccord with its present ministry."[19] Thus he encouraged and paved the way for the fall from power of a *Blanco* group and the accession of a die-hard element which knew no compromise in its relations with Brazil. Moreover he "fatally compromised the Blanco government in the eyes of Mitre."[20] The *Blancos* themselves counted on López to support them in the event of an Argentine or Brazilian invasion; consequently, they were obdurate and uncompromising in their foreign relations; but when that attack came, López failed to give them the necessary assistance.

In this same period, too, López made efforts to secure the friendship and support of Urquiza, in which he competed with Mitre. The great *caudillo* of Entre Ríos then entered his function of balance wheel between the two dictators of Paraguay and Argentina. He gave Mitre and López each to understand that he would not oppose permission being given López to cross the thinly populated Misiones region, an area claimed by both Paraguay and Argentina. López seems to have still cherished the belief that the federalists of Argentina would aid him, but his own intransigence served definitely to make Urquiza at least neutral; later his violation of Argentine territory definitely aligned the federalist chieftain against him.

Meanwhile, López was determined that, if Paraguay were to let herself become involved at all in any diplomatic or military move, she was to lead in it. If difficulties should arise and be settled without Paraguayan aid, he felt, "we shall not cut a pretty figure in the eyes of the

[17] *Ibid.*, 170-173; Herrera, II, 532.

[18] Gregorio Benites, *Anales diplomático y militar de la guerra del Paraguay* (2 vols., Asunción, 1906), I, 94-96.

[19] A. Rebaudi, *La declaración de guerra de la república del Paraguay a la República Argentina* . . . (Buenos Aires, 1924), 108-109.

[20] Box, 177-178.

world."[21] The glory of Paraguay and Paraguay's dictator was his prime objective.

Relations between Paraguay and Argentina continued strained through the period of Flores' invasion. Meanwhile, López was actively preparing for war, mobilizing his forces and augmenting them as well as improving their armaments. By September 1864 Paraguay had thirty thousand men in barricks, with ten thousand more immediately available in reserve. "The essential point that emerges from this evidence of the military preparations of Paraguay in 1864 is the fact, much obscured by the later sequence of events, that the general mobilization was at first directed against Argentina and not Brazil."[22] Then, in October, came the Brazilian invasion of Uruguay and the spirited *Blanco* resistance. Had López chosen to go directly to the aid of the *Blanco* government, he would have been acclaimed a hero, a defender of the Plata provinces against the hated Lusitanian neighbor. But, even though his August warning had been ignored, the dictator refused to take immediate cognizance of the snub or to make use of its potentialities. Rather, his efforts were directed toward the inconsequential problem of discovering the authorship of articles in the Buenos Aires press which held him up to personal ridicule.[23]

When news reached Asunción that Brazilian troops crossed into Uruguayan territory, López vacillated for several days. When the Brazilian mail steamer *Marquez de Olinda* arrived at Asunción en route up the river, he still hesitated. The vessel had actually left Asunción before López finally made up his mind and sent the Paraguayan war vessel *Tacuarí* in pursuit. Two days later the *Marquez de Olinda* was brought into Asunción a captive. The Brazilian minister was formally notified that Paraguay, in accordance with her warning of August 30, was closing the river to Brazilian war vessels and merchantmen; the minister quickly demanded his passports—the war was on.[24]

V

Had López now moved directly to the aid of Uruguay, it is quite possible that the *Blanco* government would have withstood the assault against it. Certainly the spirited resistance of Paysandú is indicative of the strength which still remained to the *Blanco* cause. Instead of giving

---

[21] *Ibid.*, 194.
[22] *Ibid.*, 210.
[23] Rebaudi, 112-113.
[24] For a detailed discussion, see Box, 218. See also, Thompson, 25-26.

direct aid to his ally, however, López initiated an invasion of Matto Grosso, where his successes, however complete, could be of no benefit to Uruguay. Only later did he make an effort to drive the Brazilians from Uruguay. Meanwhile, the *Blanco* government, collapsing before the combined onslaught of *Colorado* and Brazilian arms, was succeeded in power by the *Colorado* government of López' enemy Flores.[25]

The Matto Grosso campaign itself was successful, and its plunder in horses and cattle, so it is claimed, served greatly to augment the reserve supplies of Paraguay.[26] To that extent, at least, it was justified, but certainly the exigencies of the situation demanded that at least some aid be given to the *Blancos,* as would have been clear to any statesman or military leader of the caliber López prided himself on possessing. As it was, he permitted Brazil to make great strides in liquidating the Uruguayan troubles undisturbed.

As these events were unfolding themselves, Mitre, the real initiator of the Flores' revolution, maintained a policy of absolute neutrality. To be sure, he could scarcely do otherwise for Argentine public opinion, stimulated by the valiant defense of Paysandú, would tolerate no partiality toward Brazil. Argentine attempts at mediation, however, were coldly rejected by the *Blancos,* who yet trusted in López. Their uncompromising attitude had its effect on Urquiza, whose stand, whatever it might be, would obviously have tremendous bearing on the outcome. Urquiza was in almost constant communication with Mitre, whom he assured that Entre Ríos could be counted upon in an emergency, although he was unwilling to take umbrage at any Paraguayan invasion of the scantily populated Misiones.[27] Then, in January 1865, after the fall of Paysandú, López made formal request for permission to cross Corrientes to attack Brazil—the crowning error of all.[28]

López' move not only came too late to be of any great aid to his Uruguayan allies, but the very idea of making Corrientes the theater of war served to turn Urquiza against López. Now Urquiza pledged himself to back Mitre in the event of violation of Argentine sovereignty by López, even though any sort of support of or aid to the unitarists of Buenos Aires was anathema to the diehards of Urquiza's federalist camp. This *rapprochement* with Urquiza enabled Mitre definitely to reject López' request.

[25] Box, 250-251.
[26] *Ibid.,* 251.
[27] Cf. *ibid.,* 240-249.
[28] Cf. *ibid.,* 254. For the text of the correspondence itself, see Juan Beverina, *La guerra del Paraguay . . .* (7 vols., Buenos Aires, 1921-1934).

López, on his part, had deliberately and blindly antagonized his Argentine neighbor. Fatuously he counted upon the continuation of the old federalist-unitarist antipathies. When the Argentine government refused his request for passage across Corrientes, the Paraguayan dictator forthwith determined upon a proceeding which was to have the most direful consequences. In March 1865 he convoked an extraordinary national congress, which readily ratified the Brazilian war and appointed a special national commission to set forth a highly involved case against Argentina which it submitted to the congress. The body promptly declared war![29]

No word of this startling procedure had been allowed to leak out. Indeed, even as the declaration of war was being made at Asunción, Mitre was vigorously defending the equality of Paraguay's rights as a belligerent and rejecting Brazilian protests at the shipment of munitions to Asunción. "There is a melancholy interest in this proof that the man whom López was accusing of being a disguised ally of Brazil was allowing arms to pass to Paraguay and had resolved to prevent her blockade at the very moment when the tyrant had extracted from a venal congress a declaration of war on Argentina."[30]

Apparently, López' strict secrecy arose from a desire that the expected munition shipment be received without impediment. Only when, seemingly, the munition ship was safe, did López show his hand. Suddenly, without warning, on Good Friday, April 13, 1865, a Paraguayan flotilla appeared before Corrientes and attacked and captured two Argentine gunboats. Troops were landed; the city was taken, and on the following day invasion by land was begun.[31] The munition ship itself, however, eluded him.[32]

No other action on López' part could have come so close to unifying Argentine public opinion against Paraguay and in favor of the historic enemy Brazil. Urquiza, who would gladly have aided López against Brazil alone, wrote Mitre: "Now it falls to our lot to fight once more under the flag which at Caseros united all Argentinians. . . . We go to carry the oxygen of our liberty to a sister people."[33]

Not all the Argentine federalists believed as Urquiza did, however;

---

[29] Cf. Benites, 159-170.

[30] Box, 265-266. Cf., also, *ibid.*, 263-269.

[31] *Partes oficiales y documentos relativos a la guerra del Paraguay* (Buenos Aires, 1871), 3-8; Box, 267-268.

[32] Box, 267.

[33] *Archivo del general Mitre* . . . (28 vols., Buenos Aires, 1911-1914), II, 299.

in fact, some actually aided López, but the prestige of the great *caudillo* patriot of Entre Ríos was still great.[34]

López had made one great mistake after another. His seizure of the *Marquez de Olinda* had been followed by war, yet he made no effort to cross the Misiones and attack Brazil in a vital spot. Instead, the imperial forces were given the time and opportunity to take Paysandú. Meanwhile, too, Urquiza and Mitre were permitted to reach an understanding. Then, at the psychological moment when his great enemy had at last struggled to firm ground and averted the danger of an internal explosion, the Paraguayan dictator belatedly chose to attack Brazil and sent his fatal Corrientes note two weeks before the *Blanco* government fell.

Even now the Paraguayans might have stood on the defensive; Paraguay was all but impregnable except against attack by way of the river, and even there Humaitá stood out to repel any invasion, while, so it developed, Mitre definitely opposed any Brazilian blockade of the river.[35] Instead, however, López attacked Corrientes and forced war against Argentina, as he vainly counted on the aid of the federalists of the provinces.

VI

The general war which followed was one of the bloodiest of all modern history. Yet, as Argentina threw herself into the fray, there was general confidence in the speedy and successful outcome of the war. Three months would suffice to reach Asunción, Mitre promised, and a popular ditty ran:

> "In twenty-four hours, in the barracks,
> In three weeks, in the field,
> In three months, in Asunción."[36]

Actually, it was four years before Asunción was reached.

Time and space do not permit of any extended discussion of the details of the warfare which followed. The campaign "was composed of three great acts," so the famous British explorer Sir Richard F. Burton, a first-hand observer, expressed it. "Act One" was a Paraguayan offensive movement in two columns which followed the Paraná and Uruguay rivers respectively. Within two months both were defeated in detail and the survivors driven back to Paraguay. "Act Two" was

---

[34] *Ibid.*, III, 58.
[35] Rebaudi, 20-21.
[36] Box, 268.

of longer duration, lasting over three years, in which López "vainly attempts to defend the frontiers of the Republic, and gradually retiring northwards, he fights every inch of ground with a prodigious tenacity." Even when Humaitá was finally lost, López doggedly continued. At length, the three-day Battle of Loma Valentina,[37] "the Waterloo of the war," as Burton termed it, put an end to organized, coördinated resistance late in December 1868. "Act Three" was the final stage; in it the dictator was forced to abandon Asunción to the enemy, and for fifteen months, until his death at Cerro Corá on the banks of the River Aquidaban in March 1870, he conducted a steadily losing semi-guerilla warfare.[38]

This war of five years' duration resulted in the all but complete destruction of Paraguay. The continued defeats which marked it may be attributed to the lack of adequate leadership and to the inferiority, in the long run, of Paraguay in manpower and, above all, in resources, a factor aggravated in the extreme by her isolation. So great were the odds against Paraguay that only the stupendous bravery and dogged determination of the Paraguayans sustained by their belief that their alternative was "Victory or Death," prevented an earlier collapse.

The rare bravery of the Paraguayans has become a byword and tradition, even though it is claimed by some that only strictest discipline and fear of the wrath of López sustained the Paraguayan soldier in his unyielding resistance to the ever pressing enemy.[39] No soldier dared flee or offer to surrender, so it is asserted, lest he be shot down in his tracks in conformity to standing orders of the dictator. Apparently such orders were given, but it is incomprehensible that they could have been effective without the willing coöperation of the great bulk of the Paraguayan soldiery. Certainly the Guaraní Indians were thoroughly loyal to López and his cause, and they constituted the vast majority of the population and, therefore, of the army. In one battle, Colonel Thompson, an eyewitness, affirms: "The Paraguayans left 6,000 dead on the field; the allies only took some 350 prisoners, all wounded. This was because the Paraguayans would never surrender, but when wounded, fought on till they were killed."[40] With such losses as these constantly depleting the ranks, it became in time necessary for the military forces

---

[37] Also called Pikisiry.
[38] Burton, xv-xvi.
[39] Koebel, II, 543.
[40] Thompson, 145.

to include males of all ages, from lads in their 'teens to old men and even women.[41]

That López was wasteful of the lives of those under him can scarcely be questioned. His aim was to defeat the enemy, come what might, and in his ego and overweening self-confidence he pursued tactics which were indeed criminally costly in lives. Nor did he have an appreciation of the need for adequate hospital facilities. Due to lack there, many died needlessly.[42]

López himself has been accused of being personally a coward. Washburn declares that he "skulked off" when his troops were defeated.[43] Another account rests on his headlong flight when an enemy shell fell close by.

> "Foreigners in his service are almost if not quite unanimous in declaring him to be a *gallinæ filius albæ* [declared the objectively-minded Burton]; they say that he never once exposed himself in battle; that he . . . shudders at the whistle of a ball, and that he has repeatedly run away, deserting even his family in the hour of danger. Some of those who escaped are so furious that they threaten him with personal violence should they happen to meet him in a propitious place. He certainly never headed a charge, and he has rarely been reported to have fallen a captive."

But, continues Burton, who wrote prior to López' death, "there is no need for the President to act soldier; *L'état c'est lui.* If he falls the cause of Paraguay—and she has a cause—is sheer lost; whilst he lives she has hope."[44]

Possibly no ruler in all Hispanic American history has had so many atrocities laid at his door. The Argentine Rebaudi takes eighty-four pages to present collected accounts of the *Tirano de Sud-América.*[45] Other enemy writers have as systematically blackened his name just as each side in the World War castigated its enemies. Washburn, who as United States minister to Paraguay, had considerable difficulties with him, was unbridled in his writings against him, writings which have been the basis of so much anti-López opinion among North American

---

[41] See Burton, 379-380.
[42] Koebel, II, 544.
[43] Washburn, II, 581.
[44] Burton, 71.
[45] A. Rebaudi, *Un tirano de Sud-América: Francisco Solano López* (Buenos Aires, 1925).

historians.[46] Not until recent years was the pro-López writer given a hearing.

During the first two years of the war atrocity stories made little headway. "Up until that time the Marshal-President had preserved a certain character for moderation, and despite the reports which are always set on foot concerning an enemy, he could not be accused of cruelty."[47] Steady losses, in men and in ground, aroused the dictator. His persecution mania manifested itself in extreme suspiciousness of his subordinates. His exalted ego would not permit him to recognize any fault in himself. As he became more and more embittered, he gave way to fits of passion and became "addicted to port wine and piety; to mass-going and hard drinking."[48] Beset on all sides, he ran amuck. Even though his actions have been greatly exaggerated, it cannot be denied that at times they were little short of those of a madman. He gave way to suspicions of his own family, of his subordinates, of foreigners. All felt the wrath of an irate and at times insane ruler. Especially was it manifested toward the enemy states, who had now entered into a formal alliance against him, a pact by which the three governments, Argentina, Brazil, and Uruguay, obligated themselves to a war to the finish.

This treaty of alliance had been signed on May 1, 1865, and ratification completed the following month.

> "The terms of the Triple Alliance deserve indication. The Preamble declares that events have proved that the peace and security of the three allies is impossible so long as the existing Government of Paraguay is in power. Accordingly . . . the allies declared that since the war was directed against the Government and not the people of Paraguay, they would accept the assistance of all Paraguayans who desire to overthrow that Government. . . . They pledged themselves not to lay down their arms until López had been overthrown; and . . . 'to respect the independence, sovereignty, and territorial integrity of the Republic of Paraguay.' "[49]

But, Paraguay was to be saddled with the whole cost of the war, in the event of her defeat, and "in order to avoid the discussions and wars

---

[46] Burton, who knew Washburn, describes his appearance after his return from Paraguay in 1868: "Physically he was much changed; he had been living in a state of nervous excitement, in an atmosphere of terror and suspicion. . . . Many of his assertions were those of *a man who was hardly responsible for his actions.*" Burton, 410. Box declares: "Washburn's experience of 'diplomacy under difficulties' probably inclined him to what may be called the demoniac interpretation of history. His book is dominated by successive villains and heroes." Box, 9.

[47] Burton, 407.

[48] *Ibid.,* 408.

[49] Box, 270. The complete treaty may be found in *British and Foreign State Papers,* volume LV (London, 1870), 83-87.

to which boundary questions give rise," a settlement of disputed frontiers was provided. In this last there was much of significance, for, under the boundaries set forth, "the two great allies granted each other their fullest claims against Paraguay."[50] It was further provided that the treaty be kept secret until its principal object had been secured.

> "This was natural, since it was evident that were the Paraguayan people to know of the treaty, their fortunes would be irrevocably linked to those of their chief. The treaty was directed as much against the Paraguayan nation as against López. Their determination to destroy him is the measure of the fears of his neighbors: but their fears did not obliterate their territorial ambitions. The publications of the treaty in 1866 by the British Government, whose Minister, Lettsom, in Montevideo had been given a copy in confidence, not only turned neutral public opinion in South America and elsewhere against the allies, but goes far to explain the desperate resistence of Paraguay. The Guaraní people were thereby convinced that their national existence was at stake. López became the embodiment of the national will to live; a will that continued unflagging and heroic for four more ghastly years until it flickered out almost literally with the last man."[51]

Upon the iniquity of this treaty the Paraguayans have subsequently rested most of their case against the allies, and not without reason. Certainly its publication served to weld the Paraguayan people and their ruler into an indissoluble unit. Nor was the treaty a mere idle gesture. Orders to the Brazilian commanders were, so one Brazilian historian attests, that in the event of López asking for a conference, it was to be granted solely if its object was unconditional surrender or else exchange of prisoners.[52]

Following the disclosure of the terms of the secret alliance, López' attitude toward his enemies became one of unreasoning, raving hatred. So great was his desire to besmirch the name of Mitre that two Argentine deserters were flogged till they would say they had been sent by President Mitre to introduce smallpox into the country, and they were then flogged to death.[53] On a later occasion, according to Colonel Thompson, an English engineer in Paraguayan service, it was observed that flags in the allied camp were at half-mast.

---

[50] Box, 272.

[51] *Ibid.*, 272-273.

[52] Joaquim Nabuco, *La guerra del Paraguay* (Paris, 1901), 223. Such was apparently the Brazilian policy. Mitre and Flores, however, actually interviewed López on occasion. Thompson, 123-125.

[53] Thompson, 115.

> "López was in great excitement about this. . . . That morning, too, all the Argentine troops, in parade dress, were marched out, apparently to mass, and López decided that it was Mitre who was dead. To make sure, however, he sent and kidnapped two Argentine sentries that night, who were questioned, but had heard nothing of Mitre's death. They were flogged until they said they knew he was dead. For some time all prisoners and deserters were questioned and flogged till they said Mitre was dead. López was determined he should be dead, and he published his death for some months in his different newspapers. Woe to anyone who should have hinted anything to the contrary! It was, however, the Vice-President of the Argentine Republic, Don Marcos Paz, who died . . . and López knew it after a few days. This was one of his enexplicable tantrums."[54]

Suspicion became rampant with him. When a body of Paraguayan soldiers who had been taken prisoners by the enemy escaped and returned, figuratively with colors flying, to fight for the motherland, they were ordered shot for having previously surrendered.[55]

Francisco Solano had always been suspicious of his brothers, in whom he saw potential rivals. He had steadily kept them under close watch. Now they were imprisoned and eventually shot. When his mother, Doña Juana, came to plead for them, she was flogged by her son's orders.[56] Only the paramour of the dictator, Elisa Lynch herself, escaped the suspicions of the maddened man, but even she was made to keep her place—a step below her lord and master, not alongside him.[57]

In many cases, officers and men who failed against the enemy faced the firing squad. The commander at Humaitá, Colonel Martínez, after holding out in the face of starvation until he and his men were scarcely able to stand, surrendered at length. In revenge, his wife was imprisoned by López and later shot.[58]

Foreign officers with López easily incurred his displeasure. A bitter controversy between the dictator and United States minister Charles A. Washburn finally resulted in the latter being taken off on a United States vessel of war. The exact details of this celebrated case are, however, shrouded in doubt and dispute, due to Washburn's own utter unreliability as a witness.[59]

---

54 *Ibid.*, 242.
55 Koebel, II, 543.
56 Thompson, 324.
57 Koebel, II, 553; Thompson, 326-327.
58 *Ibid.*, 276.
59 See note 46, *supra*.

At length, his forces dissipated and reduced to a mere handful, López and his small body of men, accompanied by Madame Lynch, were fleeing along the banks of the Aquidaban before the closely pressing Brazilians. Overtaken at a place called Cerro Corá, López refused to surrender and was cut down by a Brazilian soldier, March 1, 1870. Thus died the great egotist-dictator, a man of many faults and many bloody crimes, who when his plans went awry, ran amuck; but he was by no means the super-tyrant he has been painted.

With López' death, the war ceased, and well it might, for Paraguay's population, brave, loyal, and patriotic to the end, had been reduced from some eight hundred thousand or more persons in 1864 to fourteen thousand men and one hundred and forty-eight thousand women.[60] Rightly has Paraguay been called the "Niobe among the nations," weeping for her sons.

---

[60] Herrera, *La diplomacia . . . el Mariscal Francisco Solano López,* 31.

CHAPTER THIRTEEN

DIEGO PORTALES, DICTATOR AND ORGANIZER OF CHILE[1]

CHILE, in the century following independence, presents a situation different from that which prevailed among her trans-Andine neighbors. Whereas, in the Plata provinces, the strifes which so harassed the old viceroyalty of the Río de la Plata centered about the question of the degree of control which a central authority might exercise with the further complications arising from the presence of a powerful and imperialistic alien neighbor, Chilean progress was different. Geography made a natural unit of the country; it gave ready access to the various centers of population; and it isolated the whole country from its neighbors. Consequently, neither separatism nor federalism found a place in Chile and the country became a truly unitarist state. Foreign difficulties existed, it is true, but disputes were with neighbors of more or less equal power and resources. Chile's problems then were not regional in their nature; rather, they centered on the degree and nature of the control which the government of the whole country should exercise over the people themselves. Out of the chaos of the initial years of independence, which Bolívar so aptly described as "ploughing the sea," a strong autocratic and oligarchic government was enthroned under the ægis of Portales, and turbulent incipient democracy was crushed. Conservatism was the keynote, and the lasting influence of Portales kept that oligarchy in power through the middle of the century. Even then the liberalism which was espoused by the Chilean rulers who succeeded Manuel Montt did not mean democracy. Not until the 1880's and the rise of Balmaceda did anything approaching popular democracy become involved as a serious issue again.

---

[1] The chief works on the period of Portales are those of two nineteenth-century Chilean historians, Benjamín Vicuña Mackenna, *Introducción a la historia . . . de la administración Montt: D. Portales* (2 vols., Valparaíso, 1863) and Carlos Walker Martínez, *Portales* (Paris, 1879), and the recent invaluable contribution to Chilean historiography by the late Chilean statesman Agustín Edwards, *The dawn: being the history of the birth and consolidation of the Republic of Chile* (London, 1931). The accounts as rendered by Edwards and Vicuña Mackenna have been followed herein. The manuscript work of the late Sidney Grant Thaxter, "Don Diego de Portales, founder of the Republic of Chile," originally written as an M.A. thesis in history at the University of California (1932), has been extensively used for its invaluable references. Acknowledgment is also made of the valuable assistance given in the preparation of this chapter by Mr. James S. Cunningham, Jr., of the University of California.

When finally, in 1818, Chile was definitely freed from Spanish control, Bernardo O'Higgins, natural son of one of the last Spanish viceroys and companion of San Martín, became ruler with the title of "supreme dictator." For a turbulent five years he maintained himself as titular head of the country until, beset on all sides by partisan opposition, he was forced out of office and Ramón Freire came to power. With the advent of Freire in 1823 there began an era of adjustment and of new ideas from which the new nation of Chile was to emerge. The country was torn between rival groups, the *pipiolos* (literally, "novices") or liberals, who were inclined toward a federal form of government, and the *pelucones,* or "bigwigs," so-called from their conservative, antiquated policies, with leanings toward a strong centralism. For seven years friction between these two parties, aided and abetted by the old O'Higginista faction and other minor groups, kept the country in chaotic uproar not unlike that which so characterized the Plata in the same decade. As the Peruvian García Calderón expressed it, "The Chilean people went from liberty to license and from license to barbarism."[2] Presidential changes occurred with kaleidoscopic rapidity until finally, in 1830, the *pelucones* came into power. This new shift brought Diego Portales into political prominence as chief minister of the conservative president, Prieto. Gripping government as a constructive dictator, Portales accomplished notable measures and he made of Chile the first of all Hispanic American nations to achieve stability and any degree of solid republican foundation.

I

Portales was indeed a most curious personality. The Chilean historian Sotomayor Valdés has admirably described him.

> "Portales, when his contradictory qualities are considered as a whole, appears to be an improbable, paradoxical, incredible personage. One may search history in vain for another man in whom there was such a capricious, unexpected, and spontaneous mingling of sagacity and obstinacy, wisdom and absurdity, pride and abnegation, gravity and picaresque humor, moral severity and libertine tendencies, a desire for power and a contempt for wealth, honors, and all the usual fruits of office; an astonishing perspicacity in judging men and a blindness, although infrequent, in respect to certain persons; an inflexibility in persecuting offenders against the State and general kindness in according them his private protection."[3]

[2] Francisco García Calderón, *Latin America: its rise and progress* (New York, 1913), 165.

[3] Ramón Sotomayor Valdés, *Historia de Chile bajo el gobierno del general D. Joaquín Prieto* (4 vols., Santiago, 1900-1903), II, 443-444.

Diego Portales, one of twenty-three children, was born in Santiago de Chile on June 16, 1793. His family was an old and prominent one in colonial Chile; his father and grandfather had each occupied, in turn, the superintendency of the mint at Santiago. The latter had likewise taken an active part in the earlier activities of the wars of independence.[4]

Young Diego's earlier life included rather varied experiences, often diabolic in their nature, which brought him into contact with relatively wide fields of human relationships. In his school days and later youth he appears to have followed only those pursuits which evoked a spontaneous interest in him. Although never a particularly refined individual, it was not that he lacked education. At an early age he was tutored in theology in preparation for the position of chaplain at the Mint and, indeed, was inducted into that sinecure at the age of twelve! For a time he devoted himself to the study of the liberal arts, acquiring a rather thorough command of Latin. He was a founder pupil in the National Institute, from which he in due course received degrees in philosophy and natural law; then he turned to the study of law.

At school young Diego Portales was at least as well known for his adventures and escapades as for his academic superiority. On at least one occasion he persuaded his fellow students to cut classes entirely; again, he broke all the dishes in the kitchen so that no food could be served. On still another, he dressed a mule in the cassock of the rector of the school.

In such fashion, apparently unmarked by any serious efforts, the life of young Diego continued to his twentieth year. Until then he had made no notable progress in his studies, for, as he himself later confessed, he took very little interest in grammar and law, the only type of education at that time. He did, however, show a predilection for amateur drama and theatricals. Likewise, he sang well, for he possessed an excellent voice and a good ear for music. Despite all these cultural contacts he emerged with a tinge of coarseness and jocularity. His schooling had been superficial; he himself was thoroughly a man of the world.

When Diego Portales was twenty-three years of age, he received an appointment as assayer at the Mint, but the life had little attraction for him and within a few months he broke away to enter the world of business. Meanwhile, however, he had entered into marriage with his cousin, Doña Josefa Portales y Larraín.[5]

[4] Edwards, 271.
[5] Vicuña Mackenna, I, 32.

Portales' decision to enter business was seemingly a wise choice. Certainly within a few years his commercial activities brought him enviable wealth and prestige. And, in that environment, he made the contacts which were to draw him into political affairs. His commercial career began in 1821, when, borrowing money from his grandfather, he established himself at Valparaíso as a merchant dealing especially in woollen goods. Later in the same year, he suffered a tragic loss which for a time upset his mental equilibrium and had a decided influence upon his subsequent career: the deaths of his two infant children and, very shortly thereafter, of his wife. Portales had spent months at his wife's bedside and the final shock of her loss so unbalanced him that for a time he became spiritually a misanthrope, almost a mystic, and lapsed into a state of moroseness and cynicism which pervaded his whole being. He sought comfort in religion and for a time attended church daily.[6]

Rather to escape memory than for any other reason, the bereaved youth embarked upon a voyage to Peru. Two years amid the pleasure loving society of the City of Kings brought a startling alteration in Portales, and with it a wholesome mental readjustment. While in Lima he entered into partnership with José Manuel Cea, and soon the firm of Portales, Cea and Company acquired prominence and standing.

Meanwhile, Chile was becoming more and more tangled in a financial mire from which neither executive nor legislative efforts were able to extricate it. Laxity of government and the failure to pay salaries of either civil or military servants caused great dissatisfaction and whetted the spirit of revolt. Meanwhile, also, foreign creditors clamored for the repayment of overdue loans. To meet these demands the Chilean congress authorized a concession for the exclusive privilege of selling certain articles of commerce, notably tobacco and playing cards. The concession itself was awarded by contract to Portales, Cea and Company. Portales, therefore, returned to Chile to manage the monopoly.[7]

Acquisition of the monopoly contract was an important event in the life of Portales, for through it he was brought into politics. Popular dissatisfaction with some of the results of the monopoly resulted eventually in 1826 in the cancellation of the concession by a later congress, which, it happened, was controlled by the *pipiolos,* or liberals. Portales immediately sought to vindicate himself against charges made against

---

[6] *Ibid.,* I, 133 ff.

[7] For the general condition of Chile at this time, see Edwards, 205, and Benjamín Vicuña Mackenna, *Historia jeneral de la República de Chile desde su independencia hasta nuestros días* (5 vols., Santiago, 1866-1882), V, *passim.*

his company and published a detailed account of his transactions. Even though the government liquidating commission which had taken over the concession recognized the validity of most of Portales' contentions, the liberals had gained a powerful enemy.

Heretofore, Portales had been indifferent to politics and political philosophy. Now, however, he learned to hate the liberals. Very soon he threw himself into the political fray. Purchasing a printing press in Valparaíso, he began the publication of a newspaper whose chief function was to attack the liberal régime in general and its administration of the concession in particular. Soon he purchased another larger paper in Santiago, through which he continued his attacks. In self-defense the governing group established newspapers to defend the liberal principles. The tirade of abuse which Portales' pen heaped upon the liberal government was an important factor in convincing the country that the liberal policies had failed, and in 1829 a general reaction set in.[8] As an outstanding leader of the opposition Portales was swept into power on the conservative wave.

Late in 1829 a conservative revolution under the leadership of General Prieto precipitated a period of general anarchy and chaos. Amid rapidly shifting scenes, changes of government were so frequent that one Chilean newspaper was moved to declare in January 1830, "We believe that the day is not far distant when the inquiry of every morning will be 'Who is governor today?' " Now, Portales formally entered political life. When the weak president, Rúiz Tagle, resigned office after a scant six weeks incumbency and was replaced by José Tomás Ovalle, it was Portales who loomed behind Ovalle as the real guiding hand. In fact, the influence of Portales upon Ovalle was so strong that one of his enemies published a set of verses, entitled "El uno y el otro," which concluded with these lines:

"To power the one ascended
By intrigue and by pelf;
Set up by chance or fortune
The other found himself.
The first one is the planner,
The other signs the plan,
José Tomás this other,
Diego, the first man."[9]

---

[8] Vicuña Mackenna's *Portales* includes an extensive appendix of extracts from the writings of Portales. Vicuña Mackenna, *Portales,* I, appendix, *passim.*

[9] *Ibid.,* I, 58-59.

II

On April 6 of that same year, Diego Portales did, indeed, become "the first man" as, assuming the real leadership of the conservative reaction, he became minister of foreign affairs, interior, war, and marine. "The other" continued as president, but from now on Portales was truly the planner.

From this point Portales gradually but thoroughly brought under his control every element of turbulence and opposition until he thoroughly dominated. Meanwhile he proceeded to establish drastic reforms of national institutions.

First of all, however, he embarked upon a policy which aimed at complete destruction of the liberal power. The liberal groups had united behind Freire, the former president, but Freire was no match for the conservatives under the able General Prieto, who defeated them in the Battle of Lircay. Nevertheless, the vanquished were strong enough to obtain rather generous terms in the so-called "Pact of Cuzcuz," only to have Portales reject the agreement entirely. The revolutionists, already disarmed, were left at the mercy of the government, with none of the safeguards supposedly granted them.[10]

Through the brief administration of Ovalle, Portales continued as the Richelieu of Chile. In February 1831 Ovalle resigned on account of ill health, dying a few weeks later. Joaquín Prieto succeeded him, first as provisional, and later as constitutional, president. In the same election which made Prieto president, Portales was named vice-president. It was at this time that the latter displayed one of the unusual quirks in his personality: he began to seek oblivion. Eleven days after the election—before his term was to begin—Portales resigned his newly-acquired office, declaring that the honor was greater than his own past services warranted, that his qualifications were inadequate, and that his business interests were in neglect and required his attention. Congress ignored his arguments and refused to accept the resignation. A month later he renewed his attempt, with the same result, whereupon he declined to take the oath of office. Only in that way was he able to gain his point. Even then he was considered a "minister on leave," as he retired to Valparaíso. He did accept, however, the governorship of the Province of Valparaíso, an office which permitted him to devote the major portion of his time to his own affairs. Even now he could not

[10] Diego Barros Arana, *Historia jeneral de Chile* (16 vols., Santiago, 1889-1902), XV, 590-610, *passim.*

quite divorce himself from national affairs, for Prieto would take no steps of importance without consulting his "minister on leave."[11]

III

The first period of the dictatorship of Diego Portales had seen the death of anarchy and the restoration of order. That accomplished, he had turned to the reorganization of Chile, in which his business experience was of great value to him.

Military reforms of far-reaching importance had been effected under his ministry. To assure order, the national militia had been created, and the police were reorganized. A national military college to train army personnel was established at Santiago.

Other matters, too, were given careful attention by the minister-dictator. Church property and church privileges, lost under the liberal régime, were restored and the new government was assured the support of the clergy, while still dominating the Church.

> "Portales first reformed the army—exile, execution, and demotion were the methods used. He subordinated that body to the will of the civil authorities and excluded all but loyal conservatives from government offices. He restored the Church its property and paved the way for a greater union and coöperation between the Church and the State, not because he was primarily religious, but he knew the value of the Church as a stabilizing agency. . . . He improved the administration of justice. Business prosperity began to return. Relying on a willing aristocracy, an obedient army, and a helpful clergy as the sole vital force of Chile capable of giving to the state a permanent organization adaptable to Chile's needs and conditions he opened the way for the framing of another Constitution."[12]

Actual promulgation of the new constitution did not take place until after Portales' retirement. The congress which undertook the task of drawing it up began its sessions and deliberations during his period and the movement for constitutional reform was begun by him. "Portales was not the material author of the constitution, but he was the inspirer."[13]

The best legal minds of the country had been brought together to draw up the new basic law of the republic. The result was the Constitution of 1833, which continued in force for a century. Under it there was established a strongly centralized governmental system so arranged as

[11] Vicuña Mackenna, I, 67; Walker Martínez, 164-167.
[12] Paul Vanorden Shaw, *Early constitutions of Chile* (New York, 1930), 130-131.
[13] Walker Martínez, 257.

to preserve the country essentially conservative. Thus, an indirectly electéd president, an absolute presidential veto, and property qualifications for officeholders were provided.

When at length the constitution was finally promulgated a national celebration was ordered.

> "A commemorative medal was coined and many official demonstrations of rejoicing were carried out. But the country in general, accustomed by now to the celebrating in pomp of many fugacious constitutions, received the Code of Laws that has lasted longest in the political life of the country with a coldness bordering on distrust."

This constitution "definitely put an end to the era of military dictatorship and of revolutions which had lasted more than a quarter of a century."[14]

A program of international reciprocity and commercial expansion began to materialize during the interim between Portales' two epochs in the ministry, a direct outgrowth of the stabilization of the country which the dictator had effected. Among the efforts in this field was one destined to affect seriously the future tranquillity of Chile: a treaty of commerce attempted with her neighbor and jealous rival, Peru. The rivalry which had already developed between the two countries hindered pacific agreements and eventually led to open warfare.

IV

Before returning to Chile's external relations and Portales' resumption of public office, it is well to examine more closely the man Portales in the privacy of whose personality is to be found the explanation of so much of the activity of the government. The temper of the government was reflected in him.

In contrast to those personages who have made their guiding ambitions so obvious, Portales does not appear to have had any of those high objectives, selfish or otherwise, which obsess the individual until achievement has come. He was a man of few friends. People of his time either admired and feared him, or else they hated him; no one loved him. His most notable defect was a profound haughtiness toward subordinates. His political system was personal. Like many another, he was unable to distinguish the gray which shades between the black of evil and the white of good. To him all men were either good or bad;

---

[14] Edwards, 283-284.

there was no intermediate position. For this reason he had many bitter enemies. Many of them he fearlessly executed or banished, but the latter group continually fomented conspiracy against him. Finally, in 1837, he died a violent death as the culmination of a plot against him.

In government office there was none who showed greater patriotism. However, he sought constantly to escape public office. In no way was he ambitious; on several occasions during his public career he faced congress with an absolute demand that he be permitted to resign and retire, but was never able to give convincing reasons. Apparently he had ulterior motives which he never publicly expressed. One of these seems to have been a resentment at being the cynosure of all eyes.

> "He was irritated by the severity of behavior demanded from statesmen in . . . Santiago where at every corner a chattering housewife or a mischievous gossip-monger examined closely and with a magnifying glass the comings and goings of every well-known person. . . . Portales, a Bohemian, a man of the world, jovial and jocular, felt himself spied upon and was uncomfortable. He wished and contrived to establish a distinct line of demarcation between his public life and his private life. . . . In the intimacy of private life he became transformed. He was ironic, of irregular habits and licentious; and when the mantle of night descended on the capital, the all-powerful minister went gaily and irresponsibly to the houses in which were held the festivities enlivened by harp and guitar."[15]

Portales is described as "a man of rare beauty." He possessed physical proportions which impressed one with their grace and virility. His face was pallid, and though showing signs of dissoluteness, possessed finely-chiseled features: eyes of a beautiful azure blue and delicately formed lips.

Portales was not attracted to the refined or cultured. In speech he commonly used the coarsest of language, which, however, was logical and effective. Three interests absorbed him: "women, clowns, and horses," and above all the first.

There was the dominating passion of Portales—the woman. In this he had a "likeness to Cæsar, the 'first rake of Rome.'" After the death of his wife, Portales never married again. "The sacred state of matrimony was the sacred state of fools," he declared, "notwithstanding that he had been one of the happiest of fools."[16] In his later years he lived

---

[15] *Ibid.*, 270-271.

[16] Vicuña Mackenna, 265-268. Cf., also, the *Epistolario de Portales,* ed. by Ernesto de la Cruz (Santiago, 1930), 17 ff.

with a young Peruvian woman, with whom he was planning marriage when the events of 1837 cut his career short. Subsequently, President Prieto had his three children legitimatized by official decree.[17]

Aside from his amours, another of Portales' interests during his retirement was his three jesters, whom he kept, not only in their ostensible capacity of servants, but as musicians and buffoons for his amusement. Much of his time during his retirement was idled away watching the three pummel each other about or listening to them play.

Portales was not long able to indulge in these personal pastimes which gave him such happiness. He had created numerous political obligations and soon his intense personal loyalty to President Prieto carried him back into the political arena.

V

As the time for a new presidential election came, the country once more found itself in a state of turmoil. The usual military figures sprang up and the liberals strove once more to bring together their cracked and shattered forces. President Prieto was candidate for reëlection, with Rengifo, a conservative of moderate leanings, opposing him. Moved by his loyalty to Prieto, Portales now returned to public office in order more effectively to guide the election campaign. In September 1835 he resumed the portfolios of war and marine, all important in times of domestic crisis; then, when Prieto's reëlection had been assured he added the ministries of the interior and foreign affairs.

Once more Portales was minister-dictator of Chile. In this, his second epoch as ruler of Chile, he was to be even more tyrannical than before. The character of objectives in this new period was, however, different. Previously he had crushed disorder and organized the embryonic republic. Now his attention was centered more on foreign affairs.[18]

To the north of Chile, in Bolivia, the great dictator Andrés Santa Cruz had risen to power and, extending his influence over Peru, had created his Peru-Bolivian Confederation. Now he looked for more worlds to conquer and dreamed of the creation of a great South American federation. The threat against Chile which this activity implied was not lost upon Portales and he welcomed an opportunity to take

[17] Sotomayor Valdés, II, 490-491.

[18] For the international relations of the period, see, especially, Sotomayor Valdés, II, 83-111; Edwards, 307 ff.; and Anson U. Hancock, *History of Chile* (Chicago, 1893), 216-227, *passim.*

action, especially after President Orbegoso of Peru, a tool of Santa Cruz', repudiated the Peru-Chilean commercial treaty.

Meanwhile, Freire, the old liberal chief, had been living in exile in Lima since the Battle of Lircay and Portales' repudiation of the "Pact of Cuzcuz." In the midst of the presidential campaign of 1835, Freire, with Peruvian aid, set forth on an expedition by water to Chile, where he planned "to obstruct the reëlection of President Prieto."[19] Unfortunately for him, however, the crew of the vessel carrying him mutinied and, putting into port, turned the would-be revolutionists over to the government. Portales pushed the prosecution of the offenders with great vigor, but the court-martial refused to authorize a death sentence. Instead, Freire and his cohorts were exiled to Australia. The Chilean dictator angered, sought the impeachment of the offending judges, but failed.

In retaliation for the aid given by Peru to Freire, Portales sent a Chilean war vessel under Garrido northward to Callao to capture the Peruvian fleet. The entire proceedings were carried out with great secrecy: upon pretext of making a friendly visit, Garrido entered the harbor and under cover of night seized the unmanned Peruvian vessels. The following day he delivered a note to the Peruvian government in which it was explained that the seizure was a precautionary measure. Then, under British auspices, a treaty was signed by whose terms Peru agreed to a naval limitation for four months. Garrido, with the Peruvian vessels in company, then sailed back to Chile.

Portales, however, regarded the Peruvian government agreement as a mere play for time on the part of Santa Cruz. Therefore, in a note from President Prieto, hostilities were announced and stringent demands were made upon the Peruvian government. Now the Chilean diplomat Mariano Egaña was granted full plenipotentiary powers and sent as a special envoy to Peru. With him went the Chilean fleet, fully equipped for war.

Meanwhile, Santa Cruz had not been idle, and similar preparations for the now inevitable conflict were being made by the confederation. Consequently, Egaña's efforts at a peaceful settlement upon Chilean terms were met with counter demands; thereupon, the Chilean envoy formally declared a state of war to exist. On December 21, 1836, President Prieto sent a message to congress enumerating the various griev-

[19] Vicuña Mackenna, II, 49.

ances of Chile against Peru, and three days later that body solemnly ratified Egaña's actions.[20]

The congress of Chile, dominated as it was by Portales and his group, gave its whole-hearted approval to the enterprise, but public opinion was by no means entirely in accord with the warlike program of the minister-dictator. The enemies of the government fomented discontent among the masses; conspiracies were the order of the day, and several plots to assassinate Portales were uncovered, most of them within the ranks of the military expedition being prepared against Peru.

Irritated by this opposition and fearless of consequences to his person, Portales brought about the issuance of a series of strong armed and tyrannical decrees. Martial law was proclaimed and a system of summary justice was put into effect, as permanent courts-martial were established in the provinces. A veritable reign of terror was under way. In June 1837 the murder of Portales put an end to the dictatorship. Immediately, he was exalted to a martyr's rank and popular indignation united Chile in carrying out the essentials of the hero-martyr's plans.

Despite repeated threats against his life, Portales personally directed the mobilization of Chilean forces early in 1837. Recruits for the army had to be drafted due to the unpopularity of the movement and to the widespread conspiracies against the government. Prominent among the various conspirators was Colonel Vidaurre, an audacious and ambitious young officer who enjoyed the confidence of Portales. Carefully he and his fellow plotters planned a revolt which was intended to accomplish the overthrow of the government and the advent of Vidaurre's own faction to power.

Meanwhile, Portales himself was planning secretly to accompany the new expedition when it should sail for Peru. On June 2, 1837, he left Valparaíso to review the troops gathered at Quillota, the scene of Vidaurre's projected treachery. Before his departure he was earnestly warned by friends and begged to use greater discretion and to take more care in the protection of his own person. Even though he was at least partially cognizant of Vidaurre's plottings, he counted on his own prestige to overcome opposition.[21]

---

[20] "Speech of the president on the opening of the legislative chamber of Chile, Santiago, June 1, 1835," in *British and foreign state papers* (125 vols., London, 1815-current), XXIII, 278-282.

[21] In the discussion of the assassination of Portales and of its immediate background, Edwards' account has been followed. Edwards, 334-346.

The news of Portales' personal appearance at the seat of incipient revolt caused no little consternation among the conspirators. Vidaurre himself, who was in local command, was taken aback by his chief's cordiality and seeming lack of suspicion when the latter was formally received. As a consequence, Vidaurre vacillated and schemed to throw the public responsibility upon the shoulders of his cohorts, while he himself would make a mock protest at the arrest of Portales, which was by now definitely a part of the plot.

On the day following his arrival, Portales formally reviewed the troops. Meanwhile, it was planned that the revolt should be launched while the review itself was in progress. At the conclusion of the review Portales was suddenly surrounded and made a prisoner along with his staff.

The minister and his official party were now put in irons, and Vidaurre sent letters to prospective revolutionaries throughout the country inviting them to join in the mutiny. Believing Valparaíso to be rebel in sentiment, he sent a regiment to that port to rally the troops there. Meanwhile, however, Admiral Blanco Encalada, commanding the fleet, made plans to defend the city, and the rebels, frightened off, took a new tack: Portales was forced under threat of death to write a letter to the admiral ordering that no resistance be made.[22]

How much more of a hero the great minister-dictator would have been had he refused to acquiesce in the rebel demands! Perhaps, however, he foresaw the reaction which would follow: Blanco Encalada flatly refused to accede to the demands embodied in his chief's letter and countered by calling for the degradation and banishment of the plotters. Vidaurre and his troops, thereupon, retired from the vicinity of Valparaíso. At midnight of June 5 they had reached the Viña del Mar ranch; already desertions had become numerous and the rebels sought to drown their disappointment with liquor. Finally, however, they were forced to make a stand as loyal troops approached. Portales, still a prisoner, was riding in the rear guard, commanded by Captain Florín, a natural son of Vidaurre, when he was suddenly ordered from his carriage and dragged, still in chains, a short distance away. There Florín suddenly gave the order, "Let him have six shots." Vicuña Mackenna describes the scene:

> "Portales faced the soldiers and exclaimed, 'Is it possible, soldiers, that you fire at me?' They withheld the shots at such a sad spectacle, but the irritated Florín twice more repeated the order,

[22] Vicuña Mackenna, II, 310-311.

> and the shots rang out. . . . The body of one of the most extraordinary men who had figured in the political history of Chile and of America wallowed in his own blood in the dust of a public road. . . . Meanwhile, his brutal assassins discharged a pistol in his face and finished him with bayonets."[23]

Portales' body was thereupon robbed, stripped, and horribly mutilated.

VI

The great dictator who had consolidated Chile upon a basis of conservative, aristocratic control and who had demanded, above all, the preservation of law and order, had been brutally slain by a reaction against his own autocratic measures, but with him perished all hope for the revolt's success. Quickly it collapsed amid the indignation of the Chilean people, who, horrified and grief-stricken, gave the late minister a solemn and impressive funeral. The conspirators themselves were promptly and remorselessly hunted down, brought to trial, and executed. The head of Vidaurre was hung upon a gibbet in the plaza of Quillota, scene of the revolt; that of Florín was placed at the spot along the road where its owner had committed his crime. In death, the influence of Portales was even more thorough than in life!

Portales had builded well. Far from demoralizing the campaign against Santa Cruz, the death of the Chilean statesman who had precipitated the war served to spur on the Chilean forces and eventually Santa Cruz was overthrown.

Portales had been hard and unrelenting in his treatment of his enemies. Whatever his means he did give to Chile a lasting internal stability and far greater freedom from internal disorders than was the lot of any other Hispanic American republic. One may not necessarily accept it, but at least it must be conceded that there is some merit in the dictum of a great Chilean historian, Carlos Walker Martínez, who declared: "The error of those who condemn Portales lies in judging with a false criteria his epoch and his acts. That which may be evil now in political procedure may well have been absolutely necessary, prudent, good, in that other time."[24]

---

[23] *Ibid.*, II, 333-334.

[24] Ernesto Quesada, *La época de Rosas* (Buenos Aires, 1898), 317. Quesada devotes an entire chapter to an extended comparison of Portales and Rosas, in whom he sees many similar contributions to their respective country's developments. Cf. *ibid.*, 315-328.

CHAPTER FOURTEEN

MANUEL MONTT, MID-CENTURY AUTOCRAT OF CHILE[1]

THE death of Portales made little change in the course of Chilean development. Portales had established Chile on a conservative basis; for a quarter century after his death the government continued in that mold; in fact, with the exception of a brief period, ultra-conservatism was the keynote.

The war against Santa Cruz and his Peru-Bolivian confederation was continued to a finish. When the first expedition sent against the northern neighbors was a fiasco, a humiliating treaty was concluded on the ground, but the government at home promptly repudiated it. A second expedition, commanded by General Manuel Bulnes, was then sent. Under Bulnes' able generalship, the forces of Santa Cruz were crushed at the decisive Battle of Yungay in January 1838, and the break-up of his confederation was achieved. Portales' objective had been won.

When President Prieto's second term came to an end in 1841, Bulnes loomed as his successor. Not only was he endowed with considerable military prestige, for Yungay had merely capped a long period of service during which he had distinguished himself in the war for independence and later at the Battle of Lircay, but in addition, he was a relative of the retiring president, whose support he readily obtained. His election, therefore, was comparatively easy to effect, as was his reëlection in 1846.

Prominent in the original cabinet of President Bulnes was Manuel Montt, who from this time came to be regarded as "the true representative of the oligarchy of the ultra-conservatives";[2] then, he himself stepped into the presidency—the first and greatest of three Montts to attain to that high office. To a considerable degree during Bulnes' presidency and, above all, during his own incumbency, Montt ruled Chile, a veritable autocrat of the mid-century.

I

Manuel Montt, unlike most of the great political figures of his country, came from an obscure family of the provinces. He himself was born in the little village of Petorca in 1809. In 1821 he came to Santi-

[1] The account of Montt's personal life, as presented herein, is based upon the biography of Luís Galdames, *Manuel Montt* (Santiago, 1904). In addition, Hancock's, *History of Chile* (Chicago, 1893) and Alberto Edwards', *El decenio de Montt* (Santiago, 1932) have been drawn upon heavily.

[2] Agustín Edwards, *My native land* . . . (London, 1928), 150.

ago to attend the National Institute, the only center of instruction in the nascent republic. Now his father was dead and, as one writer puts it, his mother was "unable to give him aid except by caresses and wise counsel."[3] Very soon he attracted the attention of the rector of the Institute, due to his brilliant scholarship which he maintained throughout his entire period of attendance. Shortly after his graduation from the Institute he was made its vice-rector, despite the fact that he was only twenty-three at the time (1832).

For three years Montt served as vice-rector. Then, in 1835, there occurred a student movement against the rector, which occasioned such violence that police were called in to suppress it. Two results came from this juvenile revolt: twenty-six ringleaders were sentenced to stay eight days on their knees in the dining room, and Manuel Montt was appointed to be rector of the Institute, October 1835.[4]

At the time of his appointment, the new rector was only twenty-six years old. Indeed, he was so youthful in his appearance, that it is said when the great Portales visited the Institute, he took him to be one of the gatekeepers when he met him at the door. With some imperiousness, so the story goes, Portales asked where the rector was. Thereupon, rising with dignity to the occasion, Montt replied, "Call one of the servants and have him look."[5] The incident, apocryphal though it may be, was typical of Montt.

As rector and, later, as minister and president, Montt stood firmly for "order and morality and, above all, for discipline and obedience."[6] When the son of the great leader in the war of independence, José Miguel Carrera, became a student at the Institute, Montt became involved in a serious conflict with the lad's mother, who persisted in taking him from the school without regard for and, indeed, in defiance of regulations. The young rector served notice on the lady that school rules were to be obeyed, that henceforth the boy was to leave the Institute only as permitted by the rules. Once again the mother appeared to take the boy away, whereupon Montt flatly declared that if young Carrera should leave he could never return. Still the mother persisted, and Montt ordered the boy dropped from the rolls. In the course of the teapot tempest which followed, as the infuriated mother brought pressure to force reinstatement, Montt threatened to resign if it were

---

[3] Galdames, 13.
[4] *Ibid.*, 23.
[5] *Ibid.*, 36.
[6] *Ibid.*, 31.

granted. If discipline and obedience were not preserved he would not remain.[7]

Manuel Montt continued as rector of the National Institute until 1840, when, during the closing year of Prieto's administration, he became minister of the interior. As rector he bettered the conditions of the faculty and obtained raises in pay for them.

One of Montt's great achievements as rector of the Institute was the reorganization of the curriculum, done in collaboration with the great savant Andrés Bello. "To the initiative of Montt is due also the fact that the classes of the Institute were filled almost entirely by youths of intelligence and promise. Don Antonio Varas, Don Antonio García Reyes, Don José Victorino Lastarria, and Don Agustín Olavarrieta began their academic careers at this time."[8] Even while he was rector, Montt had served as chief officer of the ministry of the interior, a post he occupied at the time of Portales' death, as well as in other capacities. For a time, too, he was deputy in the national congress. Only when he became a member of the cabinet did he retire from his rectorship.

At the age of thirty-one, when most men are just getting their start in life, Manuel Montt became minister of the interior and continued in that capacity, not only through the brief period remaining of Preito's administration but through a good part of President Bulnes' as well. As minister, Montt concerned himself above all with the development of education. In his various efforts to promote educational reforms he ran headlong into conflict with the church, which considered control of education and educational institutions exclusively its prerogative.

Formerly, the religious orders had possessed an almost complete monopoly of the training of teachers, broken only by an occasional private lay school. Under Montt's ministry there was established a national normal school. This was placed under the principalship of Domingo Faustino Sarmiento, the later educator-president of Argentina, who at the time was an exile from Rosas' dictatorship. Likewise, a school of arts was founded.

> "The school . . . was given in charge of a Frenchman, Jariez. The Neapolitan painter, Cicarelli, was also invited to come to Chile at the time the academy of music was founded. Extensive buildings were erected for educational purposes, a naval school was started, a school of agriculture founded, and a department of edu-

---

[7] *Ibid.*, 32-35.

[8] Domingo Amunátegui y Solar, "Don Manuel Montt y el sabio Bello," in *idem.*, *Jesuítas, gobernantes, militares, y escritores* (Santiago, 1934), 176.

> cation created in the government. A Frenchman, Pissis, was given in charge the work of preparing a topographical chart of Chile and making a geological survey."

"These commendable efforts," comments the historian Hancock, "were chiefly due to the zeal of Manuel Montt."[9]

At the end of the year 1842, Montt, as minister, created the National University of Chile, and appointed Andrés Bello its rector. "The greatest eulogy which can be given this institute," declares the Chilean scholar Amunátegui y Solar, "is to record that it has maintained itself on the same high plane for nearly a century and that each year it has rendered more and more important services to our national culture."[10]

The National Institute, Montt's own alma mater, was reformed, a revised curriculum was put into effect, and a new building constructed to house the Institute. Its new rector was Antonio Varas, a close friend of Montt's and subsequently his chief adviser and confidant during his presidency. Between them, further improvement in its curriculum was effected. Later, when he himself was president, Montt brought about the establishment of high schools, or *colegios,* throughout the provinces, and founded a college of mines at Atacama and an astronomical observatory.

II

The second term of Bulnes was marked by considerable vacillation and wavering on the part of the president. In theory only the one party, that of the conservatives, existed, but in actuality that party, which had absorbed most of the old *pipiolos,* the liberals of two decades before, was split into two main divisions, whose leaders were respectively Joaquín Tocornal and Manuel Montt.

> "The first of these personages, who had been the defeated presidential aspirant in 1841, was distinguished by certain ultramontanist tendencies, not yet as clearly accentuated as were those of the clericals of the following decade, but already discernible. The second [Montt], authoritarian and ultraconservative in policy, was a regalist in religion and a liberal when he treated of civil and economic order. . . ."[11]

As yet political lines were none too clearly defined; later, however, the country was to be split politically into several parties or factions, which could achieve success only by alliances one with another. In 1849

[9] Hancock, 228-229.
[10] Amunátegui y Solar, 177.
[11] Alberto Edwards, 11-12.

a more liberal grouping obtained control of congress in the elections of that year. Too, there was developing a definitely liberal, if not radical group, which under the influence of the revolutionary ideas of 1848, organized the *Sociedad de la Igualdad,* or Society of Equality. Through its two leading spirits, Francisco Bilbao and Santiago Acros,[12] it demanded sweeping reforms which aimed not only at the diminution of presidential power but the general democratization of government as well. Forceful measures were taken against this new group. Its Santiago meetings were raided by administration sympathizers and broken up.

> "The conservatives were well aware of their own waning influence with the people, and to hold power again resorted to violent repressions and prepared to elect as Bulnes' successor a president who would make no compromises. That man was Manuel Montt, and he was ably seconded in his presidential candidacy by Don Antonio Varas of the ministry."[13]

The first specific result of the activity of the Society of Equality was the fall of the ministry then in power and its replacement by a cabinet group frankly partisan to the candidacy of Montt. In other words, the aristocratic oligarchy, who had been in control since the advent of Portales to power, decided upon a policy of energetic reaction. When the election of Montt was achieved, it was at great cost to the tranquillity of the state. He himself, as president, represented not so much one man dictatorship, but rather that of a group. And power was maintained chiefly by force.

The Bulnes administration swung, belatedly but strongly, behind the "noble cause" of Montt. Even during the period of the campaign, revolt instigated by the *Sociedad* flared up at San Felipe. Though it was suppressed within forty-eight hours, the rising was taken as an excuse for a proclamation putting part of the country in state of siege for seventy days, shortened later to forty. The *Sociedad* itself was suppressed and many of its members exiled to Peru for a period of time sufficient to isolate them from the campaign.

In the face of such dictatorial tactics, the opposition nevertheless continued its fight. But ardor alone was not enough to win the election, and when the ballots were counted in July 1851, Montt was shown to

---

[12] Arcos was an "echo of 1848." Cf. *Correspondencia de don Antonio Varas sobre elecciones presidenciales y revolución en la provincia de Aconcagua, 1851* (Santiago, 1924), xx.

[13] Hancock, 231.

have one hundred and sixty-two electoral votes to twenty-nine for his opponent, General de la Cruz, a cousin of the president. But De la Cruz and his supporters were unwilling to abide by the result, and on September 7 they launched a revolt at La Serena in the north, followed quickly by a similar movement in the south.

The turn of events impelled the government to take quick action. Extraordinary powers were voted President Bulnes by congress, and Bulnes, severe but patriotic, personally took command of the army against his relative De la Cruz. Three months of fighting ensued, terminated finally by the decisive government victory of Loncomilla in December. That battle, one of the bloodiest in Chilean history, cost the lives of two thousand men, with some fifteen hundred wounded. Eight days later the southern revolutionists made terms, and soon the north, too, was reduced. The entire civil war had taken a toll of over four thousand lives.

III

In the midst of the war Montt took over the reins of government and began a ten-year period of autocracy.

> "Under President Montt the country made considerable material advancement. In May 1851 a new tariff had been adopted by which differential duties on goods were abolished. This measure gave great satisfaction to one class of people, the consumers, if it did not tend to improve the revenues. The new civil code [already prepared by Andrés Bello] was soon given to Chile; tribunals of commerce were organized. . . . Treaties of commerce were concluded with France, with Sardinia, and with the United States, Great Britain and the Argentine Republic. Public libraries were established and schools multiplied. . . . Gas was introduced into the cities, the extensive coal mines of Lota and Coronel were opened, Puerto Montt [to the farther south] was founded, and other colonies of Germans were induced to settle in the southern provinces. A political alliance, for mutual protection against attacks from abroad, was formed with Peru and Ecuador in 1856, Costa Rica soon after joining it."[14]

As a result of the revolutionary attempts of 1851, the new government pushed through a decree in March 1852 depriving persons convicted by court-martial of the right of appeal. During the subsequent rising of 1859 this law was extended to include civil cases as well. Under it many citizens in arms against the government were summarily shot.

---

[14] *Ibid.*, 232-233. Cf., also, Domingo Amunátegui y Solar, *Historia social de Chile* (Santiago, 1932), 278-297, *passim.*

Possibly the most important problem which Montt had to face during his administration, and one that seriously affected the political alignments of the future, was that of the church influence in public life. The question was a dangerous one, and although fundamentally Montt worked for greater state power, he strove desperately for peaceful solutions, even though eventually failing.

Early in the first half of Montt's decade of rule the ultra-conservative senate made known its desire to reëstablish the Jesuit Order. Despite the active disapproval of the president and his able minister Varas, permission for the return of the Jesuits to Chile was granted. Montt opposed the policy, seeking to evade any political and social conflict which might come, and to prevent any increase in the power of the church. Varas led the chamber of deputies in the vote against return, but that body, too, influenced by the active support which the Archbishop of Chile gave the measure, gave its assent and the Jesuit Company was enabled to return. Soon it was engaged in its traditional policy of education, albeit along different lines than those advocated and favored by Montt and Varas.[15]

This conflict with the church was relatively mild, but it paved the way for the later bitter dispute which was to be a principal issue for over a decade.

Most of the Spanish American republics had included in their constitutions the right to regulate church patronage. In the administration of Bulnes, Montt had sought a concordat with the pope conceding this right to Chile, but the attempt failed. Again in 1855 the president and his able assistant revived the idea. But the Papal Court refused to accept their proposal of what was essentially a national church. The concordat which the pope desired would give to the church full appointment of ecclesiastical officers, control over education, and the advance of science and the like. Neither Montt nor Varas would accept this, and both became discouraged over the lack of a possible settlement.

In another social field Montt also gave the law disentailing landed properties. O'Higgins in 1818 had abolished primogeniture, but the law had not been enforced. Again in 1828 this had been decreed, but the Constitution of 1833 restored the former status. The congress under Bulnes had argued extensively on the question but arrived at no solution. The law of 1852 was broadened five years later (1857). Im-

---

[15] See, especially, *ibid.,* 303-310.

portance of this social change lies in the fact that it indirectly prepared the way for democracy in Chile—it was a death blow to aristocracy.[16]

Many progressive features were carried through to a conclusion in the first term of Manuel Montt. Varas, as minister of the interior, established in Santiago such beneficial institutions as a hospital, an insane asylum, and a nonconformist cemetery, and prepared also the national census of 1854. To the administration there must be accorded, too, credit for the commencement of the construction of a penitentiary and the honor of promulgating Andrés Bello's famous Civil Code. Further educational advances are to be noted in the establishment of a school for the deaf and the mute and the importation of famous scholars and teachers.[17]

Economic conditions during this period were excellent. Chilean agriculture, above all, wheat, enjoyed a prosperity augmented by the demands caused by the California gold rush and the similar rush in Australia. In September 1854 there was held in Santiago the first annual exposition of national arts and products, devoted to the fomenting of agriculture and industry.[18]

Financially, the condition of the country was unbelievably good. In the entire period of Montt's presidency there was but one government loan—a seven-million *peso* issue for the purpose of railroad construction. Through Varas' influence a credit organization was established which greatly facilitated Chilean financial progress. An additional measure, and one of political consequence and significance, was the abolition of church tithes, always an important item of church revenue, for which a specific tax was substituted.

After the disturbances of 1851 there was comparative tranquillity in Chile. The elections of 1855, however, presented a new opportunity for disorders. Yet, so strong was the hold of Montt upon Chile that no opposition candidate arose to dispute his reëlection. This did not mean that Montt and his governmental measures were of necessity popular in the country; rather his iron rule was responsible.

The seeming political solidarity of the country was broken by the rise of the important church question. The clerical group broke with Montt and formed a nucleus for future opposition. Their chief grievances rested on the stand Montt and Varas had taken in regard to the return of the Jesuits, and upon their liberal attitude in regard to nonsectarian

[16] *Ibid.*, 310-312.
[17] *Ibid.*, 313-315.
[18] Hancock, 229.

cemeteries; likewise the agreement on tithes had not been exceptionally pleasing to many of the clericals.

In 1856, at the beginning of his second term, Montt made several cabinet changes in an effort to soothe the rising opposition. This move failed to appease the clericals and shortly there developed a serious crisis for which an incident small in itself was responsible. In January 1856 the sacristan of the cathedral protested the government's discharge of a cathedral employee on the ground that the church had exclusive authority over its lay employees. His protest was so vehement that he himself was expelled. Two canons of the cathedral who defended the sacristan were likewise removed by the government. Their case was carried to the supreme court of Chile and when the court ruled in favor of the government, the archbishop, the venerable Valdivieso, defied the government and refused to acquiesce in the court's order. As Montt prepared to expel the recalcitrant archbishop, the latter left for Europe and avoided the issue.

Out of this incident grew formidable church opposition to the government. The Canterbury Society, deriving its name from St. Thomas á Becket, the medieval archbishop of Canterbury who had defied Henry of England, was organized and became the nucleus of the church movement.[19]

Strangely enough the clericals were thrown into alliance with the liberal opposition to the administration. The allied groups soon found themselves with sufficient power in congress to block presidential plans and to formulate an anti-government program of their own. In 1858 came an open rupture between the president and congress, arising out of congressional insistence on the passage of a law permitting the return of political exiles.[20] The struggle of which this was one aspect reached a climax with the refusal of congress to pass the national budget unless certain revisions were made in the cabinet. Thus, what was essentially the issue of later Chilian politics and the basic cause of the bloody civil war against Balmaceda in 1891—the question of parliamentary control over executive acts—was already manifesting itself.[21] Montt himself is said to have seriously considered resigning the presidency rather than acquiesce, but on this occasion a compromise was effected and the particular issue postponed to a later era.

---

[19] Amunátegui y Solar, 319.

[20] Thomas C. Dawson, *The South American republics* (2 vols., New York, 1904), II, 201.

[21] See next chapter.

Even prior to this dispute the administration undertook to effect a political organization of its own, the better to exert its will in congress, and the "National Party," better known as the "Montt-Varistas," was organized under the leadership of the president and his chief minister. This party represented the aristocratic and regalist elements of Chilian society and continued as an important political party long after its co-founders had passed from the scene. Its purpose, a manifesto of December 1857 announced, was to be the election of conservative citizens in opposition to "utopian reformers."[22] The fight was on.

Outside the halls of congress further opposition to the government was forming. Led by the famous Chilian historian, Benjamín Vicuña Mackenna, then at the threshold of his career, a liberal group went so far as to flatly demand the retirement of Montt from office. With liberal propaganda in the press as its chief weapon it conducted a staunch fight against the government.

The government on its part took steps to remove this new menace. A meeting of the radical opposition was forbidden as inimical to public order, and the leaders of the movement were fined and exiled from the country. The periodicals through which the propaganda was being spread were arbitrarily suppressed. Finally, a state of siege for a period of ninety days was proclaimed in the provinces of Santiago, Valparaíso, and Aconcagua. These harsh measures served as a boomerang, for their chief effect was to whip public opinion to a revolutionary pitch.[23]

Thus far Montt had been successful in maintaining his régime. Perhaps the government had now developed too great a confidence in its own strength; certainly it grossly underestimated that of the opposition. Thus, on January 10, 1859, when a revolt broke out in the north under the leadership of the audacious Pedro León Gallo, the movement was belittled by the government and permitted to gain headway. Such an attitude was a serious mistake, for quickly the spirit of insurrection spread from north to south. Thanks to the administration's ability to control the navy and through it the sea, the rising was crushed. Nevertheless, it was a serious blow to the prestige of the president. No government since independence had suffered a revolution so spontaneous and widespread. Only the thoroughgoing repressive measures of the Montt administration had prevented its overthrow.[24]

---

22 Amunátegui y Solar, 323.
23 *Ibid.*, 326-329.
24 *Ibid.*, 329-332.

Following the suppression of the insurrection of 1859, Varas pushed through the congress a new law aimed at the prevention of any recurrence of similar outbreaks. Under this "Law of Civil Responsibility," any person taking up arms against the government was to be held personally responsible for property damages which might be suffered during the period of the revolution.

IV

With the failure of the revolutionary attempt of 1859, the greatest political problem was that of the presidential succession. Varas had obviously been slated to succeed Montt, but any such continuation of the conservative dynasty would require coalition with other political groups. For a time Montt attempted to effect an agreement with other conservative factions, thereby permitting the formation of a party sufficiently strong to maintain its hold upon the government. To conciliate the clericals a new attempt at *rapprochement* with the Papacy was made, but all such moves were abortive in their result. Nevertheless, the Montt-Varista Party proceeded on a policy of vigorous offensive and triumphed at the polls in the next parliamentary elections.

The logical man to continue Montt's policies was, of course, Varas, Montt's own personal choice. But Varas saw clearly that he had no chance to ascend to the presidency unless through the exercise of force, and he declined to be a candidate. Even then his party made valiant efforts to compel his acceptance.[25] Instead, however, a compromise was reached: the moderate or "liberal conservative" José Joaquín Pérez was accepted by the Montt-Varista Party as its choice and, triumphing at the presidential elections of 1861, replaced Montt as president of the Republic of Chile on September 18, 1861.[26] The era of conservative absolutism, inaugurated by Portales in the time of Prieto and continued under Bulnes and Manuel Montt was at an end. Belatedly, the revolution of 1859 had served its purpose, and Montt and the regalists of his following had wisely chosen to step down gracefully. Under Pérez and his immediate successors, Chile continued, still conservative, and not truly liberal until the 1880's.

---

[25] *Ibid.*, 334-336.

[26] Cf. Dawson, II, 202-203. The election itself was unanimous, but soon the Montt-Varistas and their recent bitter opponents, the "reds" of Gallo, were allied against Pérez.

CHAPTER FIFTEEN

BALMACEDA, LIBERAL DICTATOR OF CHILE[1]

THE quarter of a century which followed the administration of President Manuel Montt was one of progress and change in Chile. Externally the country engaged in two foreign wars, as an ally of Peru against the aggression of Spain (1864-1866), and against Peru and Bolivia in the War of the Pacific, 1879 to 1883. The Spanish war had little lasting influence, but the liquidation of problems arising from the War of the Pacific were to affect Chile's external relations for nearly half a century. Its more immediate effects, however, were in the vast increase in the national revenues which came from the nitrates of the newly acquired northern provinces.

Under President Pérez, who served two terms (1861-1871), Chile had internal peace and stability. Pérez was a moderate liberal who managed to keep Chile on an even keel throughout the decade of his presidency. Neither he nor his immediate successors were forceful, dominant individuals. Consequently, congress came more and more to assume extra-constitutional functions. The trend was definitely toward a limitation and curtailment of presidential powers and, in line with this tendency, just at the close of Pérez' administration, the president was restricted to a single consecutive term. Succeeding presidents, Errázuriz, Pinto, and Santa María, each served but one term of five years, instead of the two which had been customary since 1831.

The administration of President Errázuriz saw changes in electoral provisions and procedure which aimed at freer elections and particu-

[1] The chief source of information on Balmaceda is the work of his friend, co-partisan, and literary legatee, Julio Bañados Espinosa, *Balmaceda: su gobierno y la revolución* (2 vols., Paris, 1894). A reply to Bañados, in which many of his more partisan utterances and arguments are combated, was written by the Brazilian historian Joaquim Nabuco in a series of newspaper articles later published in book form in Spanish translation *(Balmaceda,* Valparaíso, 1895). Of especial value for the anti-Balmaceda side is the propaganda pamphlet, *Exposition of the illegal acts of ex-President Balmaceda which caused the civil war in Chile* (Washington, 1891) by Pedro Montt, then congressionalist agent in the United States and later president of Chile. As a collection of documents on the revolution of 1891, the compilation ascribed to Carlos Rojas Arancibia, *Memorándum de la revolución de 1891. Datos para la historia. Recopilados por un ayudante del estado mayor jeneral del ejército de Chile* (Santiago, 1892) is unsurpassed. Sundry pamphlet and other contemporary materials are listed in Aníbal Echeverría y Reyes, *Ensayo bibliográfico sobre la revolución de 1891* (Santiago, 1894).

larly at a diminution of the executive's influence. Capping them was the Reform Law of 1874.

I

Outstanding among the protagonists of free elections was José Manuel Balmaceda, a rising political figure destined to be second only to President Santa María during that President's period in office and, after 1886, president himself. Balmaceda was of a different stamp than his less vigorous immediate predecessors. Like many another liberal reformer he came of a prominent wealthy family. His father had been a staunch supporter of Montt. He himself was born in Santiago in 1841 and educated at the Seminario Conciliar of that city, with the intention of entering the church. His father, however, had obtained for him a post on the staff of former President Montt when the latter went to Lima in 1864 to the so-called "American Congress" on the occasion of the threatened Spanish attack on Peru.[2]

Montt exerted no small influence on Balmaceda, who appears to have modeled his ideas of presidential conduct, but not his own opinions, on the great midcentury autocrat. After returning to Chile he definitely gave up all idea of a sacerdotal career and engaged himself for some time in managing some of his father's estate; meanwhile, he became interested in the reform movement for which the liberals stood and aided it "with money, intelligence, pen, spoken word, and inflexible enthusiasm."[3] He coöperated in the founding of a liberal journal, *La Libertad,* in 1866, but it was another four years before he entered politics as a candidate for office. In 1870, however, when he was elected a deputy to the national congress, he was a full-fledged reformer and before long was a leader in the movement.[4]

When Balmaceda entered congress in 1870 he began a political career which was to make him the outstanding public figure of Chile in his time. "The immense popularity which José Manuel Balmaceda conquered for himself in his parliamentary campaigns from 1870 to 1878 grew unceasingly and paved the way for his entry in the government."[5]

---

[2] Bañados Espinosa, I, 3-8. Shortly before his Peruvian appointment Balmaceda had written a panegyrical pamphlet-biography of Archbishop Valdivieso which was published in the same year. The influence of one of his colleagues (Zenteno) in the course of the Montt mission is said to have been responsible for his turn against the church and conversion to liberalism. See Ricardo Salas Edwards, *Balmaceda y el parlamentarismo en Chile* (2nd ed., Santiago, 1916), 82-83.

[3] Bañados Espinosa, I, 9.

[4] *Ibid.,* I, 10. Cf., also, Salas Edwards, 81-110, for extensive discussion of his political ideas in this period.

[5] Bañados Espinosa, I, 17.

On the eve of the War of the Pacific, Balmaceda was sent to Argentina on a mission of good will in that republic, with whom Chile had unsettled boundary disputes. His dual objective of keeping Argentina neutral in the Pacific conflict and postponing the pending boundary controversy was achieved in a relatively short time, and Balmaceda returned to Chile in 1880.

Arriving in Chile, Balmaceda became a principal advocate of early termination of the war. Soon, too, he threw himself into preparations for the presidential campaign of 1881 in which General Baquedano, military hero of the war, and Domingo Santa María, a leader in the reform movement and choice of President Pinto, loomed as the chief contenders. Both were liberals, although Baquedano had taken no close interest in politics; the conservatives had sullenly all but entirely withdrawn from political activity for the time and had no candidate of their own, but supported the prospective independent candidacy of Baquedano. Balmaceda himself "did not hesitate in giving strong support to the candidacy of Santa María" and is said to have been influential in pursuading Baquedano to withdraw.[6] As a result, Santa María was elected without formal opposition, taking office September 18, 1881.

The government of Domingo Santa María was inaugurated into office amid political calm. The conservatives and the liberal group which had opposed Santa María's election "slept with one eye open." Santa María called into office as "chief of the new ministry (minister of the interior) José Francisco Vergara, soul of the resistance to Baquedano and of the candidacy of the newly-elected, and with him men such as Luís Aldunate and José Manuel Balmaceda, who had been among the most active directors in the last presidential contest."[7] This cabinet was formed to obtain the support of congress rather than to represent the will of the president, for Chilian politics had already developed a system of parliamentary responsibility superficially resembling that of Great Britain.

As minister of foreign relations, Balmaceda negotiated a boundary settlement with Argentina. Likewise, he faced the problems of the still current of War of the Pacific, and he attempted to thwart James G. Blaine's idea of a Pan American Congress which seemed to threaten intervention. Balmaceda's great biographer claims for him the credit of having prevented United States intervention in the war, but actually the

[6] So declares Bañados Espinosa, I, 24. Salas Edwards, on the contrary, asserts that he was a partisan of Baquedano. Cf. Salas Edwards, 44.

[7] Bañados Espinosa, I, 27.

assassination of President Garfield in the United States removed Blaine from office and the United States ceased to take interest.[8]

Under Chile's peculiar election system, a five-year presidential and three-year congressional term, the time for elections for congress came within a few months of Santa María's accession to the presidential office. In the congressional elections of 1882 the conservatives made little or no fight, and the membership of the new congress was divided almost entirely among the several liberal groups.

With the close of the War of the Pacific, Chile saw a tremendous prosperity, as revenues from the newly-acquired provinces swelled the national coffers. These revenues were "put to every sort of use, except the redemption of the paper money." They were applied to pensions for the dependents of war victims, to increases in civil salaries, and to the initiation of a new program of public works.[9] This last, above all, was due largely to the influence of Balmaceda, who continued it during his own presidency.

The most bitterly fought issue of the period was the religious question. In 1883 Santa María proclaimed that the time had come for the realization of religious reforms which had long been the aim of the liberals: secularization of cemeteries, civil marriages and civil registry, and granting of full liberty of conscience. "In the fierce discussion which followed, the eloquent prime minister, Balmaceda, took the lead. Although educated for the priesthood he had developed into an intransigent radical, a passionate advocate of the completest separation of Church and State."[10]

"Despite the sullen resistance of the conservatives and clericals," the reforms were enacted into law. But

> "the women of Chile, the old-fashioned elements of society, and the clergy would not accept the result. The priests refused to perform the marriage ceremony for any one who had been married by civil law, and excommunicated the president and his cabinet. Devout Chilians of all classes would not yield on this point of conscience, and cursed the liberal politicians as betrayers of their God. All other political questions were held in abeyance. Urged by their wives and the priests, the conservatives abandoned the attitude of abstention from politics which they had so long maintained, and went to the polls to do what they could to secure a majority for the

[8] *Ibid.*, I, 27.

[9] Luís Galdames, *Estudio de la historia de Chile* (2nd ed., Santiago, 1911), 436.

[10] Thomas Cleland Dawson, *The South American republics* (2 vols., New York, 1904), II, 214.

repeal of the law. But ladies' entreaties and priests' absolutions availed little against the government's control of the election machinery, and the law remained on the statute books."[11]

As the close of Santa María's term approached, opposition centered on the presidential candidacy of Balmaceda, "the radical, the Anti-Christ, the uncompromising." Balmaceda was the official candidate, but Santa María was unable to rally all the liberal groups to his support. Nevertheless, a majority of the liberals did accept Balmaceda and he was triumphantly elected to the presidency in 1886.

II

The administration of Balmaceda was marked principally by a struggle between the president and congress for ascendancy, aggravated all the more by the bitterness engendered by the religious reforms. For decades the congress had been gradually gathering to itself and asserting powers which tended to make Chile a parliamentary instead of a presidential republic. This was exerted through control of the budget by congress and through time limits on the duration of taxes, and by restrictions on the army and navy so that they could not legally exist without specific annual continuation of congress. Whereas the president himself could not be impeached during his term of office, the congress had required all presidential orders to be countersigned by a cabinet minister, who was impeachable.[12] These and other restrictions were extra-constitutional, but through them congress had made the cabinet responsible to it. On several occasions it had forced a president to dismiss an unacceptable cabinet by refusing to vote appropriations.[13]

Superficially, this was the British parliamentary system, but it differed fundamentally in that it allowed no protection against congressional abuse.[14] Thus, it was not possible for a ministry enjoying popular support to bring about dissolution of congress and to go before the country for approval of its acts. This failure led to much parliamentary confusion, for "it was inevitable that there should occur a struggle between the old institution of public authority, the president, and the newer forces of parliamentary life. The struggle—[which] arose suddenly

[11] *Ibid.*, II, 214-215.

[12] Cf. Montt, 5-6. See, also, Paul S. Reinsch, "Parliamentary government in Chile" in *American Political Science Review* (November, 1909), III, 507-539.

[13] As in Manuel Montt's administration. See chapter 14, supra.

[14] C. de Varigny, "La guerre civile aux Chile," in *Revue des deux mondes* (June 15, 1891), CV, 919.

and was brought to a rapid and complete determination—came about during the term of President Balmaceda."[15]

The government of Balmaceda was one of great political and administrative activity. The president sought, through his selection of cabinet personnel, to "reconcile the great liberal family," to bring together in one united party all the liberal groups. Nevertheless, one cabinet after another went to pieces, and after his first two years in office Balmaceda found himself at odds even with many of the liberals who had supported him.[16]

One of Balmaceda's earliest acts as president was the resumption of relations with the Vatican. A *modus vivendi* was reached, and the "war" between the Chilian government and the church was terminated.[17] Nevertheless, the scars of combat remained; while the acrimony of recent years had gone, Balmaceda was in no sense popular with the conservative clerical element, whom he soon antagonized by his economic policies.

Meanwhile, the great revenues from the saltpeter and nitrate beds permitted the continuation and further development of the extensive program of public works which had had its beginnings in the time of Santa María. By 1887 the national revenues were three times as great as in pre-war years, and still increasing. With the greater finances available Balmaceda envisaged a vast program for Chile.

> "He wished to see the entire territory, from south to north and from east to west, crossed by lines of steel which would assure her defense and transport her products; her principal ports endowed with wharves and breakwaters; and a temple of learning standing out as the greatest ornament of each village of the Republic."[18]

Construction of approximately a thousand kilometers of railroad, as much as all previous governments had done, was inaugurated under Balmaceda. A subsidy was granted for the Trans-Andine line through Uspallata Pass. Some thousands of kilometers of new highways were opened. Bridges and harbor works begun under Santa María were brought to completion; other similar projects were started. Telephonic communication between Valparaíso and Santiago was established. Nearly three thousand kilometers of new telegraph lines were constructed.

---

[15] Cf. Reinsch, III, 519.
[16] Cf. Salas Edwards, 129 ff.
[17] *Ibid.*, 112.
[18] *Ibid.*, 120.

Naval reorganization and the construction of new cruisers and war vessels were effected. Harbor fortifications were improved. Similar military reforms and improvements were put into operation.

"Where the feverish activity of Balmaceda centered most was in the field of public instruction." Higher education, secondary and primary, each received attention. New schools were founded. Government aid to free public instruction was given. New buildings were erected; construction of "more than sixty large primary schools, three normal schools, and a building for the *Dirección-general* of schools, among others" was begun under Balmaceda.[19]

Social institutions, too, fared well. The prison system was organized and coördinated for the first time. Hospitals were aided; over twenty new ones were built and a public health service organized.

Balmaceda represented reform and rehabilitation in Chile. In addition to his great public works program, he attempted to put through further electoral reforms to supplement and extend those of the previous two decades. His projects for economic and social improvement alone had aroused considerable opposition. The conservatives demanded that instead of the increased national income being spent on new undertakings it be used for the redemption of paper money and the repayment of the national debt—even though Chilean bonds were selling well above par.[20]

Chile's government had long been controlled by the upper strata: the great landed proprietors, the capitalists, and the church. Balmaceda attempted to govern without regard to these classes and, as a result, they sought to destroy his power. Balmaceda's own support, made up as it was of diverse liberal elements, rested on foundations which at any moment were in danger of disintegration. On the other hand, the opposition was composed of more compact groups who in the long run would have more cohesion than the president's following. Little by little, it was able to wean away his adherents until some two years after his inauguration Balmaceda found himself in serious difficulties.

The success of the opposition was facilitated by the character of the reforms proposed by Balmaceda, for these struck at the very root of Chilean politics. He proposed that the president be elected by popular vote, that neither the president nor any minister should give an office to any

---

[19] Bañados Espinosa, I, 712. The foregoing account of internal developments is summarized from Bañados Espinosa, I, 702-720. Cf., also, Anson Uriel Hancock, *History of Chile,* 330-331; Theodore Child, "Agricultural Chile," in *Harpers' monthly* (October, 1890), LXXXI, 786, and his "Urban and commercial Chile," in *ibid.* (November, 1890), LXXXI, 901-923; Varigny, CVIII, 409-410.

[20] Chilean 4½% bonds were selling at 107. Salas Edwards, 125.

near relative unless that relative were in every respect qualified to hold it, and, most important of all, that no senators or deputies should have any interest in public contracts. These proposals coincided with his unprecedented campaign on behalf of public works. The projected reforms and the huge expenditures, coupled with Balmaceda's rather arbitrary handling of affairs and patent disregard for the wishes of the politicos, served to crystallize the opposition to him and his administration.

A further group opposing Balmaceda was the foreign interests.

> "By the large foreign element resident in Chile, Balmaceda was regarded with very general aversion, and most especially by the British. He was known to entertain many views by no means consistent with the uninterrupted advancement of foreign interests. He had many times hinted that a period must be put to the extensive grants of concessions which had hitherto been so freely made to European syndicates. The wealth of Tarapacá, he had been heard to say, wealth purchased by Chilian blood in the war with Peru, was flowing in a wide stream to London, and in driblets to Santiago. . . ."[21]

Only the United States minister to Chile, Patrick Egan, showed friendship toward the government during the civil war which was to follow, and he was largely motivated by his intense Hibernian antipathy to any cause favored by British interests.[22]

Before any real effort could be made to put his proposed electoral reforms into effect, however, Balmaceda found himself involved in a most serious constitutional conflict. By 1890 the opposition to Balmaceda and his policies had come to comprise a majority in congress. Nevertheless, the president continued to battle for his program. Since he himself was not eligible for reëlection, he attempted to put up an official

---

[21] Maurice H. Hervey, *Dark days in Chile: an account of the revolution of 1891* (London, 1892), 105. Hervey was special correspondent of the London *Times*. He particularly blames the British nitrate interests as an important factor in bringing about the revolution. See 106-107. The British attitude is somewhat evidenced by the asylum given one congressional leader, the historian Carlos Walker Martínez, in the British legation during a large part of the revolution. "Profiting by an opportunity to place themselves under the French flag," he and two others emerged from the legation and secured passages aboard a French war vessel for Iquique! Hervey, 187. The definitely anti-Balmaceda tone of British diplomatic dispatches is shown in the published British correspondence: Great Britain, Foreign Office, *Correspondence respecting the revolution in Chile* (London, 1892), *passim.*

[22] Cf. United States, Congress, *House executive documents,* 52 cong., 1 sess., XXXIV, no. 91. "Message of the president transmitting the correspondence between the United States and Chile," January 25, 1892, *passim.*

government candidate in much the same fashion as had his predecessors. Reputedly his choice as successor was Enrique Sanfuentes, minister of the interior and head of the cabinet. The congressional tactics, therefore, were to attack the prospective candidate, and accordingly a vote of censure of the Sanfuentes ministry was passed by congress and its resignation demanded.[23]

With this congressional action the issue was joined, and Balmaceda forthwith took the stand that, precedent to the contrary, congress had no constitutional power to force a cabinet out of office. Thus, precedent and the strict letter of the constitution were brought into conflict as congress on is part refused to pass the appropriation bill until a ministry should be appointed in harmony with its own views. For the moment Balmaceda yielded and formed a new ministry under Belisario Prats, whereupon congress voted temporary supplies.

> "Congress and the new ministry now began to seek the removal of objectionable intendentes and other government officers, for the purpose of handicapping the president in the forthcoming elections, particularly if he were scheming for the return of San Fuentes. The president refused to remove anybody, save for a proven indictable offense."[24]

When congress adjourned without having approved the annual supply bill, Balmaceda called it back into extraordinary session; but still the congress continued adamant. Thereupon, the president dismissed the Prats ministry, appointed one in sympathy with him, and prorogued the session, as he was entitled to do under the constitution.

The *Comisión Conservadora* now came to the fore and advised the president to call a new session. This the president and his advisers hesitated to do, lest the storm be renewed, whereupon the *Comisión* stepped in and, acting with very doubtful constitutional authority, itself called congress into session.[25] The deadlock continued until January 1, 1891, at which time the annual appropriations expired and, legally, the government would be without funds with which to carry on. On that date President Balmaceda issued a manifesto in which he set forth his version of the dispute and announced his intention to continue without congress. In this, a lengthy document of seven to eight thousand words, Balmaceda

[23] For an interesting contemporary evaluation of the issues and of their merits, see Hervey, 109-110.

[24] Hancock, 337.

[25] This commission was empowered by the constitution to advise the president on various matters of state. See Article 436 of the Constitution of Chile in Hancock, appendix, 436, for a detail of its powers.

declared it his intention to adhere to his constitutional powers and functions and to stand by the strict letter of the constitution, even though some of its provisions might be considered in many respects a dead letter. He then went on to explain that with the unfairness or the effete provisions of the constitution he had nothing to do, nor had he anything to do with the new theories of parliamentary government until they had been formally embodied in the basic law. "Neither as a Chilian, nor as Chief of the State, nor yet as a man of principles can I accept the political rôle which would impose upon me a parliamentary coalition." He might ordinarily be bound to heed the advice of the *Comisión Conservadora,* he conceded, but of what avail was another extra session of congress which would but spend its time censuring the president and would vote no supplies? He pointed out that new elections would soon take place and the people of Chile could then decide the questions at issue. Meanwhile, he intended to continue the old appropriations and to perform his duty in accordance with his oath of office and his constitutional rights.[26]

On the same day a rump congress met and declared Balmaceda deposed; on January 6, 1891, this body placed the navy under command of Captain Jorge Montt, son of former President Manuel Montt.[27] On the 7th, President Balmaceda declared martial law and Chile was promptly in the throes of civil war.[28]

III

The first step of the congressionalists had been to assure themselves of the support of the navy. Overwhelmingly, the naval officers, who were drawn almost entirely from the old conservative families of the country, embraced the cause of congress, and with them went the rank and file. Only a very few war vessels remained loyal to the government. The army situation was different, however, for most of the troops supported Balmaceda, although there was a fatal lack of capable and qualified leaders.[29]

---

[26] Rojas Arancibia, 7-24.
[27] *Ibid.,* 25-32.
[28] *Ibid.,* 32-33.
[29] The army's loyalty is ascribed by Hancock to the recent increases in pay and promotions and to its jealousy of the fleet. Hancock, 340. Hervey declares that but one general joined the revolt, 81. It would appear that the government had been able to place loyal officers in key positions, removing those suspected of disaffection. Some of these latter appealed to the supreme court, a conservative controlled body, and were sustained in their demands for reinstatement; but meanwhile Balmaceda had assumed dictatorial powers. Hancock, 339.

The congressionalists, through their control of the navy, were able largely to maintain command on the sea, and through it to seize the all-important nitrate port of Iquique and its valuable nitrate revenues. Thus, they not only deprived the government of its principal source of financial support, but acquired for themselves an important means of financing their own cause. Purchases of new modern equipment and munitions were made in the United States and Europe. The government, on its part, was unable to obtain equal supplies.[30]

Through the earlier months of 1891 the civil war was maintained bitterly, with neither side gaining a decided advantage.[31] Iquique had fallen to the fleet after a defense marked by lack of coördination and leadership. Soon the rebels held undisputed possession of the four northern provinces, the nitrate centers. This gave them no inconsiderable advantage. "There they organized a fairly well-ordered government, and, with abundant revenues procured Manlicher rifles, drilled troops and assumed all the outward appearance of seceding states."[32]

The government on its part was unable to obtain from France two new cruisers built for it there but held until the French supreme court could decide upon their release. With them Balmaceda might well coop up the congressionalists in Iquique and crush them there.

> "The cruisers, however, were always reported on the way, but never came. They were in time released by the French court but were unable to obtain crews in European ports, so that they were detained first at one place and then another.
>
> "The fact that they might come, however, may have spurred the revolutionists to their final determination to attack Balmaceda on his own ground, and not wait for him to attack them in the north."[33]

Actually, the difficulties with the warships and other similar troubles were largely the work of active congressional agents in Europe, who harassed and thwarted Balmaceda's own representatives at every turn.[34]

> "By March, public feeling in the south had changed somewhat, and in Santiago and Valparaíso there was not the same general outspoken sympathy for the revolutionary cause as at first. In the

[30] "With a repeating rifle, one congressional soldier became a fair match for three government soldiers armed only with the old-fashioned breechloader." Hancock, 345. Revenues available to the rebels were estimated to aggregate some two million dollars a month. Hervey, 74-75.

[31] The discussions of war operations herein are founded on Hancock's account, 333-371.

[32] *Ibid.*, 347.

[33] *Ibid.*, 347-348.

[34] Cf. *Correspondence on the revolution in Chile, passim.*

> rural districts, the sympathy was generally with Balmaceda. Interest began at this time to be taken in the approaching elections. The old congress would have no existence after May 31st. Senators and deputies must be elected. Soon, too, a new president must be elected, June 25th. President Balmaceda, it was thought, would probably carry the elections for his choice as a successor, he being Don Claudio Vicuña, a country gentleman of vast wealth, and popular enough. This caused some trimming to the winds by many oppositionists in the south, but in the north enthusiasm increased for them and recruiting went on actively."[35]

The new elections resulted as had been expected: the anti-government elements refrained from voting and a congress in sympathy with the president was returned. This congress promptly legalized the president's acts since January and began a discussion of constitutional reform. Shortly, too, presidential elections were held and electors favorable to Vicuña's candidacy were chosen.

Now the problem of the revolutionaries was to bring the war to a close before the president-elect's election could be formally ratified on August 30. Otherwise, they would be at a serious tactical disadvantage. With this in view, the opposition army embarked aboard transports and war vessels for a point some twenty-odd miles north of Valparaíso, where it disembarked, August 20, 1891. At the same time a demonstration was made off Valparaíso.

The congressional army, some eight to ten thousand strong under Colonel Canto moved to cut communications between the capital and Valparaíso and met the Balmaceda forces in battle at Concón. Numerically, the latter were superior, but the congressionalists possessed a strong advantage in the superiority of their equipment. Too, the loyalists lacked adequate generals and there seems to have been dissension among the higher officers. After a bloody battle the government forces were put to flight, and Canto moved rapidly upon Valparaíso. He failed to take that port immediately, but did cut railway communications.

Concón had not marked the destruction of the loyalist army, but it had put the government definitely on the defensive. Now a new engagement on the 28th at Las Cadenas completed the rebel victory. Balmaceda's general was killed and the Balmacedists were routed. Now, indeed, Valparaíso lay at the mercy of the victors. Chaos reigned as they entered the port. Balmacedist leaders fled to the safe asylum of foreign ships in the harbor. Many were taken aboard the United States cruiser

[35] Hancock, 347.

Baltimore; others sought refuge on a German cruiser. Less fortunate ones were shot down without trial.

> "Then followed a scene in the streets of Valparaíso that would make Bacchus blush and put Nero to shame. [So the historian Hancock expresses it.] The rabble turned itself loose and sacked the town without restraint. Incendiarism and ruthless murders followed. Drunken, debauched men and women danced in the streets and were shot at by other drunken men, in wanton sport. By daylight half a thousand corpses were weltering in blood about the streets. Shops and houses were plundered and firemen shot at while trying to extinguish flames."[36]

The Battle of Las Cadenas was over in the morning, "but news of the utter ruin of all his hopes did not reach Balmaceda until half-past seven."

> "It was his wife's saint's day and friends were coming to dine at his house. Characteristically, he did not recall the invitations, and not until the dinner party was over did he arrange to turn over the government of the city to General Baquedano.[37] Then he quietly walked to the Argentine legation and received asylum."[38]

Rioting in Santiago followed that at Valparaíso. "The wild scenes . . . beggared description," declares Hancock, but "the mob confined its energies chiefly to acts of vandalism." The Balmaceda forces themselves offered no further resistance, and arrival of responsible congressional leaders ensured prompt reëstablishment of order, as wholesale arrests of Balmaceda sympathizers were made.[39]

IV

Meanwhile, Balmaceda remained in seclusion in the Argentine legation, with his presence there unknown. Various rumors were afloat, and supposedly he had fled in disguise. Solely the Argentinian minister and a single servant visited him.

At first he did not read the daily newspapers. When he did so, however, and learned of the arrests of many of his friends and supporters, he became convinced that "the series of methodical persecutions was the result of the hatred for him."

> "I am convinced, he said in a letter sent shortly before his death, that the universal persecution is the result of hatred or fear of me. . . . Therefore, being unable to serve my friends and coreligionists,

[36] *Ibid.,* 365.

[37] General Baquedano had maintained a careful neutrality throughout the revolution.

[38] Dawson, II, 225-226.

[39] Many took refuge in the various foreign legations. See *House executive documents,* cited above, 65-68.

> I believe that my own sacrifice is the only thing which will lessen the persecution and the evils, and the only thing which will leave my friends free to return later to a life of work and of political activity."[40]

His constitutional term was about to be concluded. "Above all Balmaceda was determined to resist to the end of his constitutional period."

> "He did not wish, with his ideas of maintenance of public order and of authority received from the people, to abandon his post until the end designated by law. He did not consider himself free or the master of his own will as a citizen, until there had struck in the clock of Time the hour in which the charter and popular will had fixed as the termination of his constitutional period."[41]

Balmaceda's term expired on the 18th of September; now he was no longer president.

> "On the 19th he arose early, dressed himself in staid black clothing, arranged his papers, made his bed, stretched out on it, with his mouth open, took his revolver, placed the muzzle on his left temple, and fired a shot which blew out his brains and killed him instantly."[42]

The triumph of the revolution and the suicide of Balmaceda marked the end of an epoch in the history of Chile.

> "The congressionalists had triumphed; congress was now the devoted instrument of the aristocrats and they proposed to make the most of their success. But one can find little in the political manipulations of the next thirty years that suggests popular government."[43]

---

[40] Bañados Espinosa, II, 643.

[41] *Ibid.*, II, 645.

[42] Galdames, 446. Hervey, writing very shortly afterward, strongly questioned the report of Balmaceda's death, whether suicide or not. Hervey, 302.

[43] Isaac Joslin Cox, "Chile," in *Argentina, Brazil, and Chile since independence*, ed. by A. Curtis Wilgus (Washington, 1935), 360.

III. THE DICTATORS OF PERU, BOLIVIA, AND ECUADOR

By N. ANDREW N. CLEVEN

CHAPTER SIXTEEN

DICTATOR JOSÉ DE SAN MARTÍN

DICTATORSHIP presents features that are not generally pleasing. There is something despicable about dictators. He who decides to arrogate to himself powers, rights, and privileges to dominate can hardly fail to have the seamy side of his character revealed. He who assumes the supreme power in the state is bound to trample upon the rights of the people. The records of dictators reveal the fact that no man can trample upon such rights with immunity. No effort has been made here to make dictatorship attractive. The purpose of these studies is neither to defend nor to condone dictatorship. Nor will it be the purpose to prove that all dictators were in the wrong in assuming dictatorial power, or that all dictatorships have been unmitigated evils. The subject is a highly controversial one and there is bound to be a large difference of opinion about most of the matter presented. There will be no effort to gloss over the mistakes, the errors, and the crimes committed by these dictators. No man, whatever may be his reputation or the renown in which he may be held, will escape criticism. San Martín and Bolívar will be treated as dictators and their dictatorship subjected to severe scrutiny despite the fact that time has dealt with them much more gently than their contemporaries. These two men will be treated as just two more dictators. The immortal Liberator of the South and the equally immortal Liberator of the North will be dealt with as examplars for the less renowned dictators. San Martín, poorly as he will be found to have played the rôle of dictator, will be treated as the first man to begin dictatorship in Peru. He set the style and he wove the pattern of dictatorship for Peru. It was Bolívar, with all his glory and his great fame, who imposed his dictatorship upon Peru, albeit in a much more subtle way, in a much more polished manner than the hero of the South. And that was due rather to the fact that he had become an adept at creating and maintaining dictatorships by the time he came to Peru. Like San Martín he did not want to recognize the painful fact that a political government cannot be superimposed from without with any great likelihood of success. Like San Martín he was guilty of maintaining the rule of foreigners in Peru long after any such rule was needed in that country. They were both guilty of aggravating, as well as introducing, foreignism into Peru. Both of them were foreigners, ruling as foreigners, calling to their aid foreigners as important ministers, and really attempting to foist upon the Peruvian people a rule which made them almost a colonial people—an appendage of Chile in the case of San Martín, and of Colombia in the case of Bolívar. These efforts to foist upon the Peruvian people Utopian schemes for which they were not prepared, retarded rather than aided the progress of the people. They sought to create political entities requiring the centralization of power in the hands of one man in order to perpetuate their own rule. They strove to establish governments out of tune with the larger ideals of their age; and they strove to do so in the hackneyed manner of dictators. San Martín sought to establish a monarchy and Bolívar an aristocracy, both systems demanding a highly centralized form of government.

I

José de San Martín was born February 25, 1778 in Yapeyú, a village in the missions region of Uruguay. Colonel Juan de San Martín, his father, was the governor of the district and remained in that position only a short time after the birth of José.[1] He was a native of the kingdom of León. His mother, Gregoria, was the daughter of Domingo Matorras, and was a Creole. Her parents were both Peninsulars from the north of Spain. His father had achieved fame fighting bandits in the Gran Chaco. Aside from this, José's family was not exceptional. The mother of José was possessed of some beauty and considerable charm. Like most women of her race she lived primarily for her children. She appears to have developed in José a deeply religious nature, a rugged notion of honesty, and a sympathy for the oppressed. His humane and intelligent legislation in behalf of the Indians and the negroes in Peru may be a result of this training. But there is nothing in either parent to show that they possessed great intellectual ability. The academic training of José was also limited. His first eight years could hardly have given him much opportunity for an education of the formal kind. When the family arrived in Madrid in 1786, José was placed in a college for the sons of nobles. He remained there less than three years and did not leave a reputation for intellectual achievements. He did lay the basis for a knowledge in mathematics, but aside from that he was not among those who excelled in scholarship. Nor is there anything

[1] José was the fourth child of five: Manuel Tadeo, Juan Fermín, Justo Rufino, and María Elena. The three brothers were all older than José Francisco. His love for army life was due, it is claimed by Benjamín Vicuña Mackenna, to the love of his brothers for that type of service. He also had the example of his father, who reëntered army service after serving as governor over the *Misiones del Uruguay*.

to show that he had any great desire for learning, although he acquired a knowledge of French and English. José was admitted to service in the Spanish army as a cadet in 1789, and remained in the army until late in 1811.[2] He served in different parts of Spain, in France, in northern Africa, and in Portugal. Until 1808 he had not made much progress, but with the advent of Napoleon in Iberia new opportunities presented themselves and he made some progress. There are those who say that during the twenty-three years of service in the Spanish army he developed habits which had a fatal effect upon his work in Peru, that he was a drug addict and a very heavy drinker, and that he spent no little time in carousing.

The three years prior to his return to America were of much importance to him. He caught some of the zeal for the independence movement, joined the secret revolutionary society, and left Spain for France and England to observe liberal institutions. In London he became a member of the *Logia Lautarina*[3] and became one of its most important

---

[2] A. Rosa in the *Documentos del Archivo de San Martín,* I, gives in the "Antecedentes y títulos de servicios" a list of important dates in the life of San Martín. According to Rosa, San Martín was admitted to the army as a cadet in the regiment of Murcia on July 9, 1789. On June 19, 1793 he was appointed second sublieutenant in the same regiment. On July 28, 1794 he was appointed first sub-lieutenant in the same regiment. On May 8, 1795 he was appointed second lieutenant in the same regiment. On December 28, 1802 he was appointed second adjutant in the battalion of Volunteers of Campo Mayor. On November 2, 1804 he was appointed second captain in the same battalion. In 1808 he came under the influence of the Marquis of Coupigni. He did good service work with him. On January 25, 1810 he was appointed adjutant to General Coupigni. And on June 26, 1811 he was appointed commander of the regiment of Dragons of Sagunto. Rosa also lists important dates in San Martín's career in America. On March 16, 1812 the *Junta* of Buenos Aires made him lieutenant colonel in active service. On December 7, 1812 he was made colonel of Granadiers. On August 27, 1812 he was given permission to marry María de los Remedios Escalada. On December 3, 1813 he was appointed chief of the auxiliary forces for Peru. On December 16, 1813 he was appointed major-general in the same service. On January 10, 1814 he was appointed colonel-major and on January 18, 1814 he was appointed general-in-chief of expedition against Peru. On August 10, 1814 he was appointed governor of Cuyo. On August 1, 1816 he was appointed general-in-chief of the army of the Andes. On June 15, 1817 he was appointed commander-in-chief of the army of Chile. On January 8, 1820 he was appointed captain-general and chief of the army of Chile. On May 6, 1820 he was appointed commander-in-chief of the Liberating Army of Peru. And on September 20, 1822 the Sovereign Congress of Peru voted him a resolution of thanks for his services for Liberty, bestowed upon him the title of Founder of Liberty of Peru, appointed him commander-in-chief of the armies of Peru, and conceded him the right to the honors of the president in all parts of Peru.

[3] The *Logia Lautaro,* or the *Logia Lautarina,* was organized in Paris in 1797 by Francisco de Miranda, bearing the name *Gran Unión Americana,* or the *Sociedad de los Caballeros Racionales.* It was organized upon Masonic principles, with head-

members. He was to have very great respect for these *caballeros racionales* whom he spoke of as the *amigos*. Throughout his whole career in America he was a great lodge man and was very much under its influence in all of his undertakings. It is still a mooted question as to what extent the *amigos* of the *Logia* were responsible for his failure in Peru. That they had a large share in it, no one doubts.[4]

The rôle played by San Martín in Argentina and Chile need not detain one for long. It is of importance only in so far as it bears upon his work in Peru. He devoted most of his time between 1812,[5] when he returned to Argentina, and 1817 to prepare for the invasion of Chile, and the period between 1817 and 1820 to prepare for the liberation of Peru. The great motivating idea during these eight years was the emancipation of Spanish America from the rule of Spain. It was the idea that led him to urge the discontinuance of the policy of getting to Lima by the back door; and to urge the plan to liberate Peru by attacking Spain in Peru from the sea.[6] In the governorship of Cuyo he evolved some of his plans of government, such as the need of a strong executive and a highly centralized government. It is worthy of note that this is his only experience in administration of the civil affairs of state before he established the protectorate in Peru. In Chile he declined to accept the unanimous election to the presidency of that country. Bernardo O'Higgins, chosen for that position, was doubtlessly selected because of his relations with San Martín. It was also done with the sanction of Pueyrredón, the supreme protector of Argentina.

---

quarters in Cadiz, and looking to the *Gran Oriente*, Miranda, in London. Membership was confined to Spanish Americans and to Englishmen vitally interested in the emancipation movement. A *junta* of these men formed the nucleus for the lodge. Gouchon maintains in his *La masonería i la independencia americana* (Valparaiso, 1917) that Madrid and not London was the original home of the *Logia*. Bernardo O'Higgins became a very helpful member, used by Miranda to organize branches in Spain. It was well organized, its rules and regulations definite, the neophite advancing in accordance with his knowledge of its principles and the services in behalf of independence. The nephite promised to give his goods, even his life, to achieve the purpose of the *Logia*. He promised to submit to the sovereigney of the people as the only true source of authority and to work for the establishment of democracy in a republic. He promised to diffuse the principles of the *Logia* and to dedicate his activities to the military and political organization of the new state. He promised to take no important step in any important position without consulting his *amigos* of the *Logia*. He swore not to reveal the secrets of the *Logia* under penalty of death.

[4] The reference to the *amigos* is often made by San Martín.

[5] San Martín landed in Buenos Aires on March 25, 1812.

[6] San Martín suggested this to a political friend in Buenos Aires April 22, 1814. Consult Jorge G. Leguía, *Historia de América* (Lima, 1928), part 2, 204-205.

The expedition to Peru was ready to leave in August 1820. An armed force of about forty-five hundred men constituted the liberating expedition which sailed from Valparaíso on August 20. It was a mixed aggregation of men: Argentines, Chileans, Europeans, and Yankees. There had been some trouble in getting crews to man the ships. The relation of San Martín to these crews offers a display of his less noble side. The whole matter is aggravated by the rôle of the Earl of Dundonald.[7]

The latter had been engaged to prepare a naval force strong enough to drive Spain off the Pacific. The noble Earl possessed naval ability of a very high order. In addition he possessed very high notions of the way in which naval matters should be conducted, and permitted no one to interefere with his rights and powers. Then men of the crews refused to join the expedition until they were assured that their wages would be paid promptly. The Earl felt that their case was a just one and urged San Martín to make them a formal promise to that effect. San Martín declined at first, declaring that the men should be impressed for the crews. The Earl refused this and finally San Martín wrote out a promise, signed by himself and Dundonald, that the wages would be paid promptly and in addition that the men would receive, as soon as Lima had been captured, certain monetary rewards.[8]

The Chilean navy consisted of seven warships and several transports, commanded by Dundonald and Admiral Blanco Encalada, with San Martín as commander of the land forces.[9] On the day the expedition sailed for Peru, O'Higgins issued a decree blockading the coast of Peru. He stated that the army and navy of Chile had sailed "with the lofty design of placing that Territory on an equality with the Independent Towns of America, by freeing them from the infamous Spanish Yoke." From August 25 all the ports and anchorages between Iquique and Guayaquil would be in a state of blockade by the Chilean squadron.

[7] Cochrane, the tenth Earl of Dundonald, was born in 1775 and died in 1860. He was a Scotchman, and came to Chile in 1818 through the activities of José Alvarez, Chilean representative in London. The name usually given to him is Cochrane, but there seems no good reason why he should not be spoken of by the higher title of Dundonald. Much attention will be given to his work in relation to San Martín, and the data found in volume I of his *Narrative of services in the liberation of Chili, Peru, and Brazil from Spanish and Portuguese domination* (2 vols., London, 1859). He gives a picture of San Martín that is not pleasant, but there is little reason to doubt that he has much truth on his side.

[8] Dundonald, *Narrative of services,* I, 77.

[9] The ships were: the *O'Higgins,* the *San Martín,* the *Lautaro,* the *Gulvarano,* the *Hecate,* the *Chacabuco,* and the *Araucano.*

The expedition had not been under way for any length of time when differences arose between San Martín and Dundonald over a landing place. The former preferred Trujillo, but the latter liked Callao, or a place near it. San Martín believed that the north of Peru was ready to declare for independence as soon as the expedition should arrive in Trujillo.[10] Dundonald held that Lima could be easily taken because there were only about three hundred armed men in the whole city. A capture of anything was evidently not included in San Martín's plans. He had come to secure independence for Peru through the pen and not the sword. The Peruvian people were to be educated to the advantages of independence; he was bringing an idea and not a pistol in his kit.[11] For this reason he began a watchful waiting policy from the outset. He chose, accordingly, Pisco, a modest port some two hundred miles south of Lima. The expedition arrived at this place on September 7 and began to land the next day. The patriots had arrived at last. What were the prospects of success? In order to answer that question, a brief account of the conditions in Peru is necessary.

II

Peru had been for more than two centuries Spain's most brilliant, most famous, and most important possession in America. The varied charms, immense riches, and rich Indian heritage had made her the greatest colonial empire in the new world. The viceroyalty had lost, it is true, much of its territory on the creation of the Viceroyalty of Buenos Aires in 1776, when *Alto Perú,* now Bolivia, was detached from it. But there still remained an empire of more than six hundred thousand square miles. The population was not large, however, amounting, according to Vargas, to only about a million people. An incomplete census of 1793 gave the population as 1,076,977 inhabitants, excluding the wild Indians of the *montaña* region. Out of that number 136,311 were Spaniards, 617,700 Indians, 40,377 negro slaves, 241,225 *mestizos,* and 41,404 mulattoes. Lima, Trujillo, Cuzco, and Arequipa were important cities,

---

[10] San Martín had carried on for some years a correspondence with patriots in the north of Peru. He had had his own secret agents in Peru for some years from whom he had come to feel that the Peruvian people would flock *en masse* to the patriot cause with the arrival of the liberating expedition. He had great faith in the zeal and ability of many of their leaders, notably that of the Marqués de Torre Tagle, *Intendente* of Trujillo. It is evident that San Martín placed much faith in the cause of these leaders, and looked for them to take the lead in their own liberation.

[11] Gonzalo Bulnes, *Historia de la espedición libertadora del Perú* (2 vols., Santiago,1887-88).

each dominating a particular region. The first two were in the *costa* region, the other two in the *sierra* region. The most important city was Lima, the viceregal capital, with a population, in 1820, of about 70,000 inhabitants. Of this number 10,000 were Peninsulars, 41,000 negroes (21,000 free and 20,000 slaves), and the remainder Indians and mixed castes.[12] Lima had been, for upwards of two centuries, the heart of the Indies. No city had a greater fame and no other city had a larger number of noble families. The *limeños* were noted for their wealth and their luxurious manner of living. The Peruvian nobility, located in Lima, Trujillo, Huánuco, and Arequipa, was a fair counterpart of that of Spain itself. Basadre states that there were a duke, a grandee of Spain, fifty-eight persons with the title of marquis, forty-five with the title of count and viscount, together with a large number of *caballeros cruzados* and *fijosdalgos*. In no other part of Spanish America was there so powerful a nobility.[13]

All this has its definite bearing upon the rôle of San Martín in Peru. The nobility was the main prop of the colonial régime owing allegiance to the aristocratic, traditionally conservative institutions of the Spanish people. The great majority of the nobles owed their elevation to the graciousness of the monarch. The Peruvian nobility differed, however, from the nobility of other countries. It had large *haciendas* but looked upon manual and industrial labor as degrading. It was not interested in the military and it was not interested in politics. Its power was confined to the salon. The *limeño* nobility was noted for its intellectual and cultural ability. José de la Riva Agüero was a conspicuous member of the nobility and played an important rôle in the political life of the Peruvian people.[14] He was rather an exception, however, for he was interested in politics all his life. The nobility was, as was the French nobility of the middle of the eighteenth century, interested in new

[12] M. Nemesio Vargas, *Historia del Perú independiente* (Lima, 1903), I, 19.

[13] Jorge Basadre, *La iniciación de la república. Contribución al studio de la evolución política y social del Perú* (2 vols., Lima, 1930), I, 1-4.

[14] Riva Agüero y Sánchez Boquete was born in Lima in 1783 and finished his education in Spain. He began a military career but gave it up. He spent much time in France and other parts of Europe studying theories of government and institutional life in general. He began early to support the movement for independence, and was a suspect even before returning to Lima. He secured public employment and used his position in exposing errors and ills in the colonial government. He was a secret agent of *juntas* working for independence and a very active member of the *Logia Lautarina,* which met in his home or in that of Conde de la Vega del Ren. He was especially active in causing desertions from the Spanish military forces even before San Martín arrived in Peru. His career in the dictatorships of San Martín and Bolívar and after can best be treated in its proper place.

thought, nurturing a new and revolutionary spirit. Pedro José Chávez de la Rosa, rector of the *Seminario de San Jerónimo* in Arequipa, and Toribio Rodríguez de Mendoza of the *Convictorio de San Carlos* in Lima, were leaders in educational reforms. They helped to bring on a new era. Javier de Luna Pizarro and Vijil are products of this new movement. The *Carolinos,* the group of young men in the *Colegio de San Carlos* in Lima, did much to bring on a demand for reforms. The press became particularly influential. *La Abeja Republicana, El Correo Mercantil y Político, El Republicano, La Coterra, Los Andes Libres,* and *El Comercio* helped shape public opinion.

The result was that Peru had a more turbulent revolutionary career than any other part of the Indies. The greatest and most dangerous of all the revolutions of the Indies was the revolt of Tupac Amaru II (1780-1781), a social and economic revolt intensified by a resurgent *Indianism.* Nothing in all America compares with the Tupac Amaru revolt in numbers involved, in cruelties inflicted, or in its staggering psychological effects which have not even yet been wholly eradicated from the minds of either the whites or the Indians.[15]

III

San Martín began early the practice of addressing the people through proclamations. He had brought two printing presses with him and had in his service one of the most powerful journalists of his age, the celebrated mulatto Bernardo Monteagudo. On September 8, 1820 he issued several proclamations urging the Peruvians to coöperate with him, promising to continue in the civil administration all who proved loyal to the patriot cause and to respect the titles and privileges of the nobility. He urged the soldiers to desert the cause of Spain and aid in emancipating Peru. He was merely carrying out instructions from the Chilean government. He was empowered to negotiate for recognition of independence for Argentina and Chile as well as Peru. He was to assist the Peruvians to establish a political government, but he was not to infringe upon the rights of the people to determine their own political future.

---

[15] There were also the revolt of Aguilar in 1805 in favor of the restoration of the Inca Empire, the Mateo Silva revolt in 1809 in favor of an independent *junta,* the revolt of Ramón Eduardo Anchoris in which young Riva Agüero took part, and the revolt of Zela in 1811. All these proved to be abortive, but they represent the nature of the discontent in Peru with the colonial régime, and also give evidence of the spirit of the age. Riva Agüero was only one of many who had had his views of life fundamentally changed by travels and studies in the old world. Vargas and Basadre give much light on these activities.

Two excerpts from his proclamations will illustrate the nature of his real mission:[16]

> "Peruvians, here are the engagements under which Chile—before the Supreme Being—and calling all nations to witness as avengers of any violation of the compact, engages to aid you in setting death and toil at defiance. You shall be free and independent. You shall choose your own government and laws, by the spontaneous will of your representatives. No military or civil influence, direct or indirect, shall your brethren use to influence your social dispositions. You shall dismiss the armed force sent to your assistance the moment you judge proper, without regard to our opinion of your danger or security. Never shall any military division occupy the soil of a free people, unless called by your lawful magistrate. Neither by yourselves, nor by our aid, shall party opinions which have preceded your liberty be punished. . . .
>
> "I come to fulfill the expectation of all those who wish to belong to the country which gave them birth, and who desire to be governed by their own laws. On the day when Peru shall freely pronounce as to the form of her institutions, be they whatever they may, *my* functions shall cease. . . ."

The arrival of San Martín caused much concern to the viceregal authorities. On September 14 Viceroy Pezuela invited him to a conference. The conference of Miraflores on September 20 proved a failure because San Martín insisted that he would consider terms of peace only upon the basis of the absolute independence of Peru. San Martín moved to starve out the Spanish. On October 13 he declared in a long proclamation that the viceroy had made peace impossible and that he was determined to drive out the Spaniards.[17] He sent General Arenales with a considerable force into the *sierra* country to help isolate Lima, and Dundonald was to continue to blockade the coast. In the meantime the movement for independence had come to a head in Guayaquil. General Urdaneta began, in the night of October 8-9, the revolution that brought about independence. On October 9 the citizens of the Pearl of the Pacific met in the *Casa de Ayuntamiento* and proclaimed their independence.[18] But a plea for armed aid from San Martín was denied because he feared the effect it would have upon the situation in Colombia. Had he used his combined land and naval forces he might have liberated Ecuador and prevented his own humiliating defeat at the hands of Bolí-

---

16 Dundonald, *Narrative of services,* I, 81-82.

17 Manuel C. Bonilla, *Epopeya de la libertad, 1820-1824* (Lima, 1921), 99-103.

18 Camilio Destruge, *Guayaquil en la campaña libertadora del Perú* (Guayaquil, 1924), 46.

var, for it was over the Guayaquil question that he sustained his greatest defeat in the Peruvian enterprise. Vicuña Mackenna and several others are of the opinion that San Martín made a very serious error in not taking advantage of the Guayaquil situation to gain that city for Peru.[19]

The achievements of Dundonald offset the poor showing made by San Martín. On the night of November 5 Dundonald boldly moved into the bay of Callao and captured the *Esmeralda,* almost before the Spaniards knew what had happened. It was not only one of the most brilliant but also one of the most important feats in the whole period of the wars of emancipation. It destroyed the Spanish naval power on the west coast of South America and meant that supplies could not come to Peru by way of the Pacific.[20] It was the beginning of the end of the war.

San Martín failed to follow up this victory, but continued his watchful waiting policy. The deadly *tercianas* began to exact their toll among the soldiers; more than three thousand men were ill in the hospitals, dying at the rate of thirty a day. The differences between him and Dundonald had become more bitter, and he began to act as if Dundonald were a dangerous rival and treated him as such. The victory of Arenales on December 6 at Cerro de Pasco gave San Martín encouragement, but he failed also to follow that up with any efforts of his own. He moved his headquarters to Huaura and continued to wait. He was awaiting the move of the patriots in Trujillo, urging *Intendente* Torre Tagle to bring about a revolt against Spain.[21] Torre Tagle informed the viceroy that he had a difficult problem keeping the people in check. He called a *cabildo abierto* to discuss the course to be pursued. On December 27 the meeting occurred, and Torre Tagle resigned his office. Independence

[19] Benjamín Vicuña Mackenna, *El Jeneral D. José de San Martín* (2nd ed., Santiago de Chile, 1902), 43-47.

[20] In the course of the capture of the *Esmeralda* by Capt. Coig and his men, Capt. Guise acted in a traitorous manner, disobeying orders to the extent of jeopardizing the success of the whole plan. He cut the chains of the ship against the orders of Dundonald. Had not this been done Lima might have been taken as was Valdivia earlier in the year. Instead of supporting Dundonald in disciplining Guise, he showered honors upon him. The ways of the great San Martín were indeed strange on many an occasion in Peru, and this was one of them. Dundonald's charge that San Martín deliberately ordered Guise to defeat the whole plan for the capture of the *Esmeralda* must, therefore, under the circumstances, be accepted as accurate. Evidently San Martín was determined to prevent Dundonald from getting too much out of the whole expedition.

[21] San Martín had carried on a correspondence with Torre Tagle and on November 20 he wrote him from Supe urging action. Torre Tagle rendered a very great service in the *Intendencia de Trujillo* for the patriot cause and reaped great glory for his acts, as will be seen later.

was declared and a *junta de gobierno* chosen with Torre Tagle as president. Bishop Carrión y Marfil denounced the work of Torre Tagle and the people in the *cabildo abierto*. Torre Tagle made short work out of his opposition, seizing him and other malcontents and shipping them off to Spain. The whole of the north of Peru followed the example of Trujillo.

San Martín now felt it would be a matter of only a few weeks when the whole of Peru would fall into line. And what was to be his rôle? Was he to begin a great military operation, or was he to just sit and wait? Much to the displeasure of most of the patriots, San Martín did nothing. He did move his headquarters to Chincay, but that was all. The year 1820 had been a very unsatisfactory one for the Spanish despite the strange apathy of the commander-in-chief of the liberating army. The Spanish army chiefs decided upon a vigorous campaign, and in a *motín militar* of January 29, 1821 they forced Viceroy Pezuela to resign.[22]

General La Serna became viceroy, but the move was not popular with the people. La Serna appointed General Canterac commander-in-chief of the Spanish forces and General Valdez chief-of-staff. All of these three men were able military commanders and could be depended upon to give the patriots much opposition. But La Serna, like Pezuela, sought to gain time by inducing San Martín to discuss futile peace terms. La Serna was carrying out the most recent instructions from Spain to bring the war to an end by conciliation. Two commissioners were sent to Peru to aid in that work. José Rodríguez Arias died in Panama on his way to Lima, and Manuel Abreu arrived in March 1821. Abreu had a four hours' conference with San Martín on March 25. Abreu suggested a conference between San Martín and La Serna, which, after preliminary steps had been taken, took place on May 23. An armistice of twenty days was agreed to. Efforts to bring about peace were not successful, due, according to García Camba, to the character of Abreu. He holds that Abreu should not have been appointed to such a delicate position for he was wholly unfitted for so difficult a task. He was captain of a frigate, inexperienced in both diplomacy and statescraft, and uncouth. The *limeños* were the last people in the world to be attracted by such a person. Lima was a great cosmopolitan city of culture and

[22] The overthrow of Pezuela, the seventy odd year old viceroy, was done with the dispatch for which *motines militares* are so justly famous. The sympathy of the *limeños* was with the old man and they made no effort to conceal that fact. Since they had no military forces at hand they had to accept the new régime.

social graces, and could not be expected to take a nobody very seriously. García Camba declares that Spain should have sent instead one of its most polished and seasoned men on a mission of such importance. He declares that it was just one more example of the fact that Spain did not know America, and never had known her. It was Spain, rather than America, who won the war for America in America.[23]

The climax of the negotiations came in the conference between San Martín and La Serna at the *hacienda de Punchauca* on May 28. Again San Martín made peace impossible by demanding unconditional independence for Peru. La Serna said that he would have to take that whole question under consideration. San Martín then revealed his plan for the establishment of a Spanish monarchy in independent Peru. A regency was to be appointed with La Serna as president, the armies of the belligerent groups to serve as a single unit under the command of La Serna, or some one appointed by him, and San Martín was to go to Spain to negotiate with the Spanish government. The monarch was to be chosen by the *cortes* of Spain and was to govern in accordance with the constitution adopted by the Peruvian people. The similarity between this plan and that of Iturbide in Mexico is very marked. Did the two men know each other's plans? But the plan of Punchauca failed, and the war continued.

Early in the year 1821, San Martín and his counsellors, chief among whom was the mulatto Monteagudo, issued the *Reglamento Provisional,* for the better government of the liberated portions of Peru. The instrument was to continue in force until "there should be constituted a central authority by the voluntary action of the free people." The four provinces of Trujillo, Huailas, La Costa, and Tarma were each to be called a *presidencia* with a *presidente* at the head. A court, with many of the powers of the Spanish *audiencia,* was established in Trujillo. The financial, civil, and criminal affairs were to be under the *presidente.* Over all was the captain-general, in the person of San Martín, with large powers. Such matters as treason, desertion, or espionage, and any matter which might interfere with the successful prosecution of the war were in his hands. San Martín also took over the powers of the *patrono*

[23] Andrés García Camba, *Memorias del General García Camba para la historia de las armas españolas en el Perú, 1809-1821* (2 vols., Madrid, 1916), I, 578-580. This is one of those excellent publications put out by the *Biblioteca Ayacucho* under the editorship of R. Blanco-Fombona. The introduction, as was to be expected, is very well done. García Camba was well equipped, by reason of his long and conspicuous services, to write this work. His *Memorias* should be translated into English for the larger use to which it could be put.

in ecclesiastical affairs, delegating to the *presidentes* the powers of vice-*patrono*.

The views of San Martín on government had undergone great change, for this government can hardly be said to be either democratic or in accordance with the wishes of the Peruvians for a share in the government. He had not forgotten the fine phrases he had used on his arrival, and in a flamboyant style explained that since he had been entrusted with the problem of restoring a vast part of the American continent, its very existence and its rights, he must use the means which he considered best adapted to attain that great objective. To the people must be given the right to admire the grandeur and the nobility of sacrifice which come through achievement in war; but the great law of necessity must preclude premature reforms desired by a people inexperienced in the fine art of government. In a word, the captain-general was everything—the beginning and the end of all.

The instrument was the work of Monteagudo and Juan García del Río and reveals the dictatorial character of San Martín's rule up to that date. Credit should be given San Martín for having given the people the *reglamento*. He was under no real need of doing so, as far as dictatorships go, or in the light of the philosophy which he was practicing at this time. He showed that he had not wholly succumbed to the artistry of dictators, for dictators are adverse to having their powers delimited even by a *reglamento*.

The failure of the viceregal government to come to terms with the patriots gave it grave concern. Conditions in Lima became daily more and more unsatisfactory. The food supply was running low and desertations increased daily. On June 27 La Serna evacuated Lima, moving into the *sierras*, where food was more plentiful and the chances for a final victory over the patriots was much better than on the coast. But even though the capital was evacuated, San Martín was in no haste to move in. It was not until July 7 that terms for the surrender of Lima were agreed upon, and on the evening of July 10 San Martín tried to enter the city unobserved. In this he failed, and he had to put up with the inconveniences of a public entrance. On July 15 the people in a *cabildo abierto*, called by San Martín, chose July 28 as the day on which to formally proclaim the independence of the country.[24] San Martín was chosen president, but when the delegation came to inform him of

[24] *Colección de leyes . . . de Perú*. The statement of the *cabildo abierto* is an interesting document. More than three hundred of the best people in Lima signed it.

that fact it was astounded at his action. He curtly informed the members that the action of the *cabildo abierto* had been wholly unnecessary. He had already assumed the supreme power of the state. He also wanted them to understand that there was to be no deliberating assembly. He had known too much of congresses in Argentina and Chile to encourage them in Peru.[25] On July 28 independence was duly declared throughout the liberated regions of Peru. In Lima the declaration was made in all the public plazas. San Martín himself performed the act in the *plaza mayor*. On Sunday July 29 a *Te Deum* was chanted; San Martín and the other civil and military authorities attended the services in the cathedral of Lima.

The most important act, for our purposes, was the decree establishing the protectorate over Peru and which made him supreme protector. The following excerpts are of value as explaining his ideology:[26]

> "In undertaking the important enterprise of liberating this Country, I had no other motives than my desire to forward the sacred cause of America, and to promote the happiness of the Peruvian people. . . .
>
> "On my arrival at Pisco, I announced that, owing to the imperious circumstances, I found myself invested with the Supreme Authority, and that I was responsible to the Country for the exercise of it: circumstances have not changed, because Peru has still interior Enemies to combat; and it is consequently necessary that the political and military command should continue in my person.
>
> "I hope, therefore, that, in taking this step, you will do me the justice to believe that I am not actuated by any views or ambition, but for the public good alone. It is sufficiently notorious that I wish only for tranquillity and retirement, after a life so agitated; but I have undertaken a moral responsibility which exacts the sacrifice of my most ardent wish. The experience of 10 years of Revolution in Venezuela, Cundinamarca, Chile, and the United Provinces of Rio de la Plata, have shown me the evils occasioned by unreasonable convocations of Congress while there are Enemies still remaining in the Country. The first step is to secure independence, and afterwards to think of establishing liberty on a solid basis. The scrupulous manner in which I have kept my word, during the course of my public life, gives me a claim to be believed, and I now appeal to it, in declaring solemnly to the People of Peru, that, at the same instant in which your Territory shall be free, I will resign the com-

[25] Dundonald, *Narrative of services,* I. Naturally, Dundonald took much satisfaction in recording these explanations of the relationship between San Martín and the *limeños.* Dundonald had no patience whatever with these dictatorial proceedings.

[26] *British and foreign state papers,* VIII, 1271-73. This document was signed in Lima in the "2nd Year of the Liberty of Peru" by José de San Martín.

mand, to make room for the Government which they may choose to elect. The frankness with which I speak ought to serve as a new guarantee of the sincerity of my intentions.

"I could have so arranged it that Electors, named by the Citizens of the Free Departments, should designate the person who was to govern until the assembling of the Representatives of the Peruvian Nation; but as, on the other hand, the simultaneous and repeated invitation to me, of the great number of Persons of elevated character, and decided influence in this capital, to preside over the Administration of the State, assured me of a popular nomination, and, on the other hand, having already received the assent of the Towns who were under the protection of the liberating Army, I have judged it the most decorous and proper to follow the frank and honourable line of conduct, which ought to tranquillize those Citizens who are jealous of their liberty."

. . . .

"To administer strict justice to all, to recompense virtue and patriotism, and to chastize vice and sedition, wherever they may be found, is the rule that will regulate my actions, whilst I am placed at the head of this nation.

"The installation of a vigorous Government being expedient for the interests of the country, which may preserve it from the evils that might be produced by war, licentiousness and anarchy.

"I declare as follows:—

"1st. That the supreme political and military command of the Free Departments of Peru will from this day be held by me, under the title of 'Protector.'

"2nd. That Don Juan Garcia del Rio is charged with the Department of Minister of State and Foreign Affairs.

"3rd. That Lieutenant Colonel Don Bernardo Monteagudo is charged with the Department of War and Marine and the Auditorship of the Army and Navy.

"4th. That Don Hipolito de Unanue is Secretary of the Treasury.

"5th. That all orders and official communications shall be signed by the responsible Secretaries, and will bear my Rubric, and that the Communications which shall be addressed to me are to come through the Minister to whose Department they relate.

"6th. That the necessary rules for the best system of administration of the public service, will be prepared without delay.

"7th. That the present Decree shall only be in force until the Representatives of the Peruvian Nation shall have met and determined upon the future mode and form of Government."

This decree bears all the earmarks of absolutism, the dictator standing out in bold relief in each sentence of this fateful instrument. García del Río, Monteagudo, and Unánue were appointed *ministros de estado* and the dictatorship began.

Genuine and profound opposition began at once. Foreignism was in charge of the vital elements of the state, for in addition to the supreme protector, who was an Argentine, there were García del Río, a Colombian, and Monteagudo, an Argentine. As if to prepare O'Higgins for reports of opposition to his government, San Martín wrote to him that he had been obliged to assume dictatorial powers because of the anarchy in the capital, explaining that the *amigos* had urged him to take this step.[27]

Dundonald could be expected to voice his opposition to these proceedings in no uncertain terms. It gave him an opportunity to bring the question of the pay of the crews to a head. For eleven months San Martín had stubbornly refused to pay the men in violation of the promise made to the men before leaving Valparaíso. Dundonald was angered because he had not been consulted in the establishment of the protectorate, and took the view that San Martín had acted in violation of the instructions from the Chilean government. He held that he was not bound by the action taken, which he considered was a direct and unwarranted usurpation of power. He was a servant of Chile and not of San Martín and would continue true to his charge. He ordered the flag of Chile to be flown by the navy, and he informed the Peruvian government that he was an officer of Chile and not of Peru. Dundonald was also offended by the manner in which the medals in honor of the declaration of independence had been made. San Martín had taken all the credit to himself and the army and had ignored Dundonald and the navy. The great San Martín should have been the last man in the world to commit such a blunder; and his failure to do so must be taken as another example of the manner in which San Martín handled affairs in Peru. San Martín deteriorated in Peru, a fact emphasized by Vicuña Mackenna.[28]

The interview with San Martín was unsatisfactory,[29] and on August 7 Dundonald wrote his letter condemning the course which he had taken

[27] San Martín to O'Higgins, Lima, August 10, 1821, in Vicuña Mackenna, *El Jeneral D. José de San Martín,* 58-59.

[28] *Ibid.,* 59.

[29] The interview was a stormy one, San Martín displaying, as he did so often in his disputes with Dundonald, the less pleasant side of his character. He declared: "I have only to say that I am Protector of Peru. Chili! Chili! I will not pay a single real to Chili! As to the squadron, you may take it where you please, and do whatever you choose; a couple of schooners are quite enough for me." When Dundonald left, San Martín followed him to the head of the stairs urging him to do what he had done: break with the Chilean government, leave the squadron of Chile to the interests of San Martín, and accept from him the higher title of "First Admiral of Peru." This Dundonald of course declined.

in arbitrarily setting up the protectorate. These excerpts give an idea of the contents:[30]

> "The rocks on which the South American Governments have split have heretofore been bad faith, and consequent temporary expedients. No man has yet risen, save yourself, capable of soaring aloft, and with eagle eye embracing the expanse of the political horizon. But if in your flight, like Icarsus, you trust to waxen wings, your descent may crush the rising liberties of Peru, and involve all South America in anarchy, civil war, and political despotism.
>
> "The real strength of Government is public opinion. . . . What would they say, were it promulgated to the world that he intended not even to remunerate those employed in the navy which contributed to his success.
>
> "See to what a state the Senate had brought the beautiful and fertile province of Chili. . . . I say, therefore, my dear General, that whoever has advised you to commence your Protectorship with devices unworthy of San Martín, is either a thoughtless or a wicked man, whom you should forever banish from your counsels."

The result of the refusal of San Martín to pay the crews of the Chilean squadron had a very painful effect upon him. On September 19 occurred the powerful mutiny in the Chilean navy, as a result of the refusal to pay the sailors. Dundonald and the men knew that San Martín had taken more than five hundred thousand *pesos* to Ancón for safe keeping. He and they went to Ancón and seized the money. Dundonald supervised the use of the money. After all legitimate claims had been paid, he had about two hundred and eighty-five thousand *pesos* left. Out of that sum he paid the crews their wages and also a certain bonus each, and used the remainder for the good of the navy. This mutiny affected San Martín profoundly. Finding Dundonald adamant in his refusal to refund the money, he ordered him to leave Peruvian ports and waters and to return to Chile. Dundonald took his own time in leaving. Strangely enough the Chilean government approved his acts officially.[31] After nearly forty years Dundonald wrote:[32]

> "My own views coincided with them, and I determined that the squadron should be no longer starved nor defrauded. I therefore sailed to Ancón, and personally seized the treasure, before witnesses; respecting all that professed to belong to private individuals, and also the whole of that contained in the Protector's schooner, *Sacra-*

[30] Dundonald, *Narrative of services,* I, 129-132. The letter was written from Callao Roads.

[31] Dundonald, *Narratives of services,* I, 140.

[32] *Ibid.,* I, 163-164, 165-167,

mento, considering it as his private property, though it could not have been other than plunder wrested from the Limeños. . . .

"After a lapse of nearly forty years' anxious consideration, I cannot reproach myself with having done any wrong in the seizure of the money of the Protectoral Government. . . . Years of reflection have only produced the conviction that, were I again placed in similar circumstances, I should adopt precisely the same course."

IV

The legislative measures of San Martín during 1821 were important. On October 8 he issued the *Estatuto Provisional* which was merely a prolongation of the *Reglamento Provisional.* He was now more mature as a dictator, the people did not even have the "first notions of self-government," and he would continue "to exercise the directive power of the state, whose attributions, without being the same, are analogous to that of the legislative and executive power." He would not interfere with the judiciary because the "independence of the judiciary is the one and true safeguard of a people's liberty."[33] He also recognized the debts of Spain for Peru except those which had been used against the movement for American independence. On the subject of the end of the protector's rule, San Martín was vague, declaring:[34]

> "I venture to hope that I shall be able in time to lay down the power which I have taken upon myself, with the consciousness of having faithfully exercised it. If, after having freed Peru from the oppressors, I shall go to seek, in private life, my last felicity, I shall consecrate the rest of my days in contemplating the beneficence of the Great Author of the universe; and in renewing my vows for the continuance of his propitious influence on the lot of my fellow countrymen. . . ."

He ordered the *tributo* abolished and forbade the use of the terms Indians or *naturales* because they were *hijos* of the country and should be called Peruvians.[35] He abolished all the different kinds of personal service known as *mitas, pongos, encomiendas,* and *yanaconazgos* performed by the Indians.[36] He ordered a census taken and established a director general of the census.[37] He abolished punishment by flogging, or *la pena de azotes.*[38] He ordered all dead bodies of persons to be

[33] Graham H. Stuart, *The governmental system of Peru* (Washington, 1925), 4.
[34] *The Annual Register,* 1822.
[35] *Colección de leyes . . . de Perú.* Decree of August 27, 1821.
[36] *Ibid.,* XII. Decree of August 28, 1821.
[37] *Ibid.* Decree of September 12, 1821.
[38] *Ibid.,* XVI. Decree of October 16, 1821.

buried in the pantheon, including monks.[39] He forbade the introduction of obscene books,[40] and declared that ecclesiastical vacancies could be filled only by persons nominated by the protectoral government.[41] This last measure was in keeping with the ecclesiastical policy of San Martín. He had pursued a like policy as governor of Cuyo, brooking no interference either in the management of military or political affairs of the state. The clergy was either for or against the patriot movement, there could be no neutrality, all must serve *la sagrada causa de nuestra rejeneración.* The venerable Archbishop Bartolomé de Las Heras of Lima was expelled because of his support of the Spanish cause. In view of the treatment of the clergy, forcing them to support the patriot cause, it is difficult to follow those who maintain that the clergy did not desire ecclesiastical independence. The Roman Catholic Church fought then, as it had fought before, to regain lost power. It had never been reconciled to the policy of the Spanish government, and looked upon the independence movement as a chance of winning back these lost rights. San Martín was acting only in conformity with the policy of the revolutionary leaders in America to prevent the Roman Catholic Church from getting political power in the new states.

The only military victory of consequence in 1821 was the capture of Callao, all the more important because of the treason to Spain of La Mar, the commander of the *castillos* of Callao. La Mar was an able commander, and his support of the patriot cause was a very important matter.[42] But San Martín failed to make the fall of Callao a means of putting an end to the war. He persisted in the belief that the fall of Lima and Callao meant the end of the war, failing utterly to grasp the idea that the war would have to be fought in the *sierras,* and not on the coast. By the end of the year the army of San Martín was in a very deplorable condition, due to the ravages of disease, pleasures, and inactivity. A conspiracy was organized against San Martín by the discontented elements in the Chilean army. Its leaders were dissatisfied with the men at the head of the government. No Chilean held any position of importance. The men in the confidence of San Martín were

[39] *Ibid.,* XV. Decree of October 25, 1821.
[40] *Ibid.,* XV. Decree of October 31, 1821.
[41] *Ibid.,* XV. Decree of November 6, 1821.
[42] Emilio Gutiérrez de Quintanilla, *Homenaje de le obra de la campaña de Ayacucho al centenario de la libertad sud-americana* (Lima, 1924), 8-11. Quintanilla insists that La Mar was a Peruvian despite the fact that he was born in Guayaquil, because Guayaquil was a part of the Viceroyalty of Peru in 1778 and again in 1806.

Argentines, and the command of military divisions had been given to Argentines. The highest offices in the state were held by an Argentine, a Colombian, and a Peruvian. General Las Heras, one of the ablest of the Chilean generals, knew of the plot but refused to have any part in it, and returned to Chile.[43] Other officers of ability also left the service of San Martín at this time. Bulnes holds that there was a likelihood of a civil war between San Martín and Dundonald, or between Callao and Lima, believing that Dundonald and La Mar were working together to destroy the fortress of Callao, but holding that Dundonald was not guilty of treason. Bulnes praises San Martín highly for his part in the capture of Callao, maintaining that in that affair he showed some of his old-time ability as a great commander.[44] But San Martín permitted the escape of General Canterac, which Bulnes criticizes very severely, for he thereby made Junín and Ayacucho necessary.

Thus by the end of 1821 San Martín was a defeated man. He no longer had the faith of the army. His failure to capture Canterac and his army after the capture of Callao was an error from the effects of which he never recovered.[45] And Vicuña Mackenna adds his view that San Martín *se encierra en una estraña apatía,* permitting the Spaniards freedom to wander about in the *sierras,* prolonging the war to the end of 1824.[46] He had lost his army and his navy, and one by one his ablest friends left. Generals Martínez and Necochea, two very able commanders, went the way of Las Heras. San Martín went back to old Magdalena, the residence of the viceroys, about two leagues from Lima, there to languish away in body and mind. The *limeños* grew tired of their liberators, finding them a very expensive ornament in Lima, especially since the Spanish retained quiet possession of the interior.

The outstanding event of the year 1821 was the crisis in the movement for a monarchy. It came in December, the month of the monarchy, and merits some explanation. The idea of a Spanish American monarchy is an old one. Count Aranda proposed to Charles III that the *Indias occidentales* should be divided into three kingdoms with *infantes* as kings and Charles III as Emperor. The Napoleonic invasion of

---

[43] Las Heras resigned to O'Higgins on September 23, 1821. Las Heras held that he was not bound by the oath which San Martín had exacted of him, for he had no right to exact such an oath.

[44] Bulnes praises especially San Martín's generosity in the capitulation of Callao, citing in full Articles I, II, IV, V, VI, and XII as important examples of this.

[45] Bulnes, *Historia de la espedición libertadora del Perú,* II, 70.

[46] Vicuña Mackenna, *El jeneral D. José de San Martín* (2nd ed., Santiago, 1902), 63.

Iberia revived the idea. *Infanta* Carlota Joaquina, wife of the prince regent of Portugal, then resident in Rio de Janeiro, Brazil, and sister of the exiled Ferdinand VII, asserted her right to govern Spain. The *Carlotinos,* the supporters of her claims, became active in different parts of the Indies. The *porteños* were especially interested and urged the *infanta* to come to Argentina and establish a kingdom.[47] But nothing came of the plan, and the wars of emancipation took their course.

As soon as Argentina had broken with Spain, such leaders as Belgrano, Rivadavia, and others, became active in support of a monarchy for their country.[48] The French, too, were interested, desiring the establishment of a Bourbon monarchy in America. The most spectacular plan was that of Belgrano for a restoration of the Inca empire, with a descendant of the last Inca as emperor, and with Cuzco as the capital. The plan failed to materialize in 1816, but the idea of restoring the Inca empire had many champions, especially among the people in the countries once a part of that empire. Gamarra and Santa Cruz were both greatly interested in the restoration of an empire in which, as *cholos,* they had such a personal interest. Basadre is authority for the statement that the monarchial idea is not dead even yet in Peru, and is not likely to die out for a great many years.

The movement took on new life with the arrival of Le Moyne, the agent of the French ambassador in London, in 1818. He was to consult with Supreme Director Pueyrredón of Argentina for a throne for the Duke of Orleans. At the same time Valentín Gómez strove to induce

---

[47] Even Bartolomé Mitre is of the opinion that had Carlota come in person, at the head of an expedition in 1808, she would have had little difficulty in establishing herself upon a throne there. Consult his *Historia de Belgrano,* I, 235-238.

[48] The English expedition of Popham and Beresford of 1806-1807 was also interested in a monarchy. The interests of Francisco de Miranda in an American monarchy is known to every school boy. Louis Philippe, the Duke of Orleans, was in communication with many South Americans urging establishment of an American monarchy. Belgrano was won to the idea as early as 1806. The plan was to annex Chile to Argentina and to form a kingdom out of the two countries. Carlota's agent, Manuel Baraño, had but small success, however. By 1809 Carlota had also gained a staunch supporter in Liniers. But she was content with sending the Count of Palmella to the *Junta Central de Sevilla* to press her claims to the right to rule Spain, and more especially for the abolition of the Salic Law. Oliveira Lima states that Carlota also had her agents in Chile, Peru, and Mexico. Consult his work on *Don Juan VI del Brazil* and the three works by Carlos A. Villanueva: *Bolívar i el general San Martín, Fernando VII y los nuevos estados,* and *El imperio de los Andes.* Basadre's excellent work on *La iniciación de la república* gives a résumé of the whole monarchial movement in Spanish America.

Baron Desolle to help place the Prince de Luca on an American throne.[49] Both of these plans were based upon the idea that Spain would approve of a monarchy for America. Basadre declares that the failure of the Spanish government to approve the plan was the pride of the Spanish court, the absence of political and diplomatic vision, the confidence in the expedition which it was preparing in Cadiz for America, the nature of the reports of the anarchy that prevailed in Argentina, and the Russian suggestion. The Argentine congress approved the plan for placing the Prince de Luca on the throne of the new American monarchy. This plan, too, failed, despite the support given it by Rondeau, successor to Pueyrredón. And in November 1819 Baron Pasquier, the new chief minister of France, announced that all negotiations had been suspended. Toward the end of 1820 Gómez returned to Argentina. The failure of the movement up to that date may be laid, according to Basadre and Oliveira Lima, to the stubborn opposition of Ferdinand VII, who never gave up the hope of reconquering the Indies. Revolutions in Argentina interfered with the success of the movement. Rondeau gave way to Ramírez. Saavedra, the new governor of Buenos Aires, helped the charges of treason preferred against Rondeau by Ramírez by publishing a pamphlet containing all the documents in the negotiations. By this time, San Martín had already brought to Peru *la primera expedición libertadora; traíale también el más formidable apoyo a la ilusión monarquista.*[50] Thus it was a foreigner who fought the most effective battle for a monarchy in America, and that man was San Martín. It has been noted that he was, in response to invitations from both Pezuela and La Serna, willing to discuss the establishment of a monarchy in an independent Peru. The plan for a monarchy appears to have been presented only obscurely in the conference of Miraflores, but was presented in detail in the celebrated conference of Punchauca.

The monarchial idea was given wide diffusion from the very first by the liberating army in Peru. Monteagudo had made good use of the press. *El Pacificador,* the official paper of the liberating army and edited by Monteagudo, carried several articles by him in favor of a monarchy for Peru. San Martín had taken steps to make the establishment of a monarchy in Peru rather an easy matter. On October 8, 1821 he had decreed the establishment of the *Orden del Sol,*[51] an order to

[49] Baron Desolle was the principal minister of Louis XVIII, and was very anxious to have the plan succeed.

[50] Basadre, *La iniciación de la república,* I, 7.

[51] *Colección de leyes . . . de Perú.*

which men high in the military and civil administration were elected. On November 21 he decreed the division of the *haciendas* of Montalvan and Cuiva, in the valley of the Cañeta, for distribution among the men who had rendered great services since arriving in Peru.[52] On November 24 he decreed that all those who fought against Spain might display the coat of arms of the rank of nobility to which they belonged. To the *consejo de estado* San Martín appointed the Conde del Valle de Oselle, the Marqués de Montemira, the Marqués de Torre Tagle, the Conde de la Vega del Ren, and the Marqués de Torre Velarde.[53] In addition, he had begun to put on the airs of royalty. *Rey José,* as he was called, lived in great style. He set a very expensive table, rode about in great fashion in a *carroza* drawn by six beautiful horses, and cost the state more than thirty thousand *pesos* a year in these trappings.

On December 24 the *consejo de estado* took up, under the presidency of San Martín, the selection of a mission to Europe, and the instructions to be given it. Juan García del Río and Doctor Paroissien were chosen for the mission. They were instructed to consult with the heads of the important countries of Europe on the necessity of establishing a strong government in Peru and to point out the necessity of a strong centralized government, because of the lack of experience in the art of self-government of the people. They were to urge the recognition of the independence of the new state and to show that this independence was to be maintained only through the support of one or two of the great European powers. Great Britain and Russia were thought the best suited for that purpose, the former by reason of her great maritime power, the vastness of her natural resources, and the excellence of her institutions,[54] and the latter because of the power and importance of her political life. The members of the mission were empowered to select a suitable candidate for the throne of the new monarchy. They were to negotiate with the prince of Saxe-Coburg, who was the choice of those at the meeting. In case he should not accept, they were to turn to some prince of the reigning house of Great Britain, preference to be given a

---

[52] The men so honored were: O'Higgins, who received lands to the value of at least five hundred thousand *pesos,* Aldunate, Alvarado, Arenales, Borgoño, Correa (Cirilo), Forster, Guido (Tomás), García del Río, Guise, Las Heras, Heres (Tomás), Lemos, Lazuriaga, Monteagudo, Martínez (Enrique), Miller, Necochea, Paroissien, Sánchez (Santiago), and Dehesa.

[53] The other members were: García del Río, Monteagudo, Unánue, Moreno y Escandón, and de Echagüe.

[54] Ernesto de la Cruz, *La entrevista en Guayaquil* (Santiago de Chile, 1912), 28-31.

member of the Roman Catholic Church. In case none could be induced to accept the throne, they were to turn to other German or Austrian princes, then to Russia, then to France and Portugal, and, if all other efforts failed, then to Spain to give her consent to the selection of the Prince de Luca. If Spain were to consent, she was to be made to understand that under no circumstances would she be allowed to send armed forces to Peru with the prince, and that he would have to take an oath to support the constitution of Peru, an instrument to be made by the Peruvian people themselves. The commissioners were to float a loan for the government of Peru in Europe. On their way to Europe they were to go by way of Chile and Argentina and to urge those governments to support these plans for a monarchy.

These are the main feautres of the famous transaction in the *Sala de Sesiones del Consejo de Estado* in the *heroica y esforzada ciudad de los libres* on the momentous 24th day of December 1821. One may conclude with De la Cruz that, from the evidences presented, San Martín favored a monarchy for Peru.[55] Miller, too, in his *Memoirs,* favored the same idea, although he declares that San Martín did not want the crown for himself.[56] On the other hand, Adolfo Saldias, Argentine minister to Bolivia, denied emphatically that San Martín was a monarchist, that he has anywhere stated that he was a monarchist, or that he tried to establish monarchies in South America. Saldias contends that the document which tells of the proceedings of the *consejo de estado* to send García del Río and Paroissien to Europe did not contain the ideas of San Martín but were the ideas of the *consejo* itself.[57]

The envoys had but little success, failing in Chile and Argentina completely, and in Europe except in the matter of a loan. The loan was floated in London and was for a million pounds sterling. The sovereign congress recalled them towards the end of the year 1822.

The *protectorado* did much more for the establishment of the monarchy than what has already been narrated. Its most important work lay in the effort to educate the people to an appreciation of that idea. The people were to be made to realize that they were unsuited to rule and that a transitional period was necessary to educate them to their duties and obligations in matters of government. Hence they were to be

---

[55] De la Cruz, *La entrevista en Guayaquil,* 34-36.

[56] John Miller, *The memoirs of General Miller.*

[57] De la Cruz, *La entrevista en Guayaquil,* 60-62. De la Cruz is quoting from an address delivered by Saldias in La Paz.

convinced that a constitutional monarchy with a European prince as a ruler was the best form of government for them at the time.

On January 10, 1822 San Martín decreed the creation of the *Sociedad Patriótica,* with Monteagudo as its president, the principal champion of the monarchy. The *sociedad* held several important meetings at which questions dealing with the welfare of the people were discussed. There was by no means a unanimity of opinions as to the best means of promoting that welfare. In the meeting of March 1, 1822 the defense of the monarchical form of government was made by José Ignacio Moreno. He was opposed by Pérez Tudela and Luna Pizarro, two of the most powerful men of the age. In the meeting of March 5 the republicans came determined to defend republicanism. Tudela maintained that while there was a heterogeneity of colors in Peru, there was none in desires and sentiments. *El alma es igual en todos,* for which reason the Indian and the negro should have a right to enjoy liberty which they had ability to defend. Peru was ready for liberty, and needed only a Washington, a Franklin, or a San Martín to enable her to enjoy that liberty. Mariano José de Arce was also an ardent champion of liberty.[58] The *Sociedad Patriótica* had become a means of enlightening the people, but in a manner little pleasing to its founders.[59] The press, too, exercised a powerful influence in shaping public opinion. *El Sol del Perú,* organ of the *Sociedad Patriótica,* did good work. *La Abeja Republicana* gave much space to articles discussing the philosophy of government. *El Republicano, La Cotorra, Los Andes Libres, El Correo Mercantil,* and *Político y Literario* were active. In an earlier issue of *Los Andes Libres* the article by Monteagudo on the *Cuadro político de la revolución,* first published in *El Censor de la Revolución* in Chile, gave expression to his hostile views on liberalism and on the Spaniards.

V

The beginning of the year 1822 saw the beginning of the end of the activities of San Martín in Peru. He had come to the conclusion that the war against Spain could only be brought to an end through the joint efforts of the North and the South. He was determined to have an interview with Bolívar for that purpose. He issued an explanation of his plan in the *Gazeta de Gobierno,* the organ of the protectoral government, in the issue of January 9, 1822. He therein declared that he be-

[58] Consult the interesting work by Raúl Porras Barrenchea on *Mariano José de Arce* (Lima, 1927).

[59] Basadre, *La iniciación de la república,* I, 31-39.

longed to the *causa del continente americano,* that he had assumed supreme power only in order to complete the great work of liberating the whole continent, and that he would go to the Liberator of the North in Guayaquil to discuss with him the best way to attain that objective.

On January 19 he formally decreed the delegation of his powers to Torre Tagle. The latter was to have the title of *supremo delegado* and was to exercise the supreme power in the state until San Martín should decide to again assume that power. On February 8 San Martín embarked on board the *Macedonia* for Guayaquil. At the port of Guanchoco he learned that Bolívar was not at Guayaquil and that he would not arrive in that city for some considerable time. He returned to Callao on March 3 and took up his residence again in the palace of the viceroys at old Magdalena. He resumed his old way of life, but did not resume the supreme power until five months later.

The military situation in Ecuador, as well as in Peru, in this fateful year was of the greatest importance. San Martín sent Santa Cruz with a division of Peruvian troops, at the request of Bolívar, to Ecuador, and arrived on February 19. He immediately placed himself and his famous Division of Numancia under the command of General Sucre. These three men, Santa Cruz, Sucre, and Bolívar, brought about the end of the war in the North. Bolívar won the great Battle of Bomboná on April 7,[60] and Sucre and Santa Cruz won the immortal Battle of Pichincha on May 24. While this great battle has immortalized the name of Sucre, there are those who speak in the highest terms of the great services rendered by Santa Cruz. So much so that it is even called a Peruvian victory. That is the view of Vicuña Mackenna.[61] President Leguía took a like position in causing, during the centennial of the battle in 1924, a testimonial in marble to be made to that effect.[62]

On May 25 Sucre entered Quito and was received by the *quiteños* with much cordiality. On May 29 the *quiteños* in a *cabildo abierto* proclaimed the *Presidencia* of Quito a part of *Gran Colombia.* On June 8 Bolívar issued one of those proclamations for which he is so justly famous, declaring in part.[63]

> "Colombians! All your beauteous fatherland is now free. The victories of Bomboná and Pichincha have completed the work of

[60] This was hardly "a costly and barren victory" as William Spence Robertson would have it. Bolívar thought of it as fully as important as Pichincha.

[61] Vicuña Mackenna, *El jeneral D. José de San Martín,* 67.

[62] Vargas, *Participación de Colombia en la libertad del Perú,* I, 43, footnote 2. The decree was issued on May 15, 1922.

[63] William Spence Robertson, *Rise of the Spanish American republics,* 253-4.

your heroism. From the banks of the Orinoco River to the Peruvian Andes the army of liberation, marching triumphantly, has covered all the territory of Colombia with its protecting arms. . . . Colombians of the South! The blood of your brothers has redeemed you from the horrors of war. . . . The constitution of Colombia is the model of a representative, republican, and strong government. You need not expect to find a better government among the political institutions of the earth, unless it should be this constitution made more perfect. . . . Colombians! Share with me the ocean of joy which floods my heart; and in your own hearts erect altars to the liberating army which has given you glory, peace, and liberty!"

Bolívar and not San Martín was climbing the stairs, the golden stairs, to ever greater and greater heights of glory and fame. San Martín was vegetating in the classic halls of the viceregal palace of old Magdalena, while not only the two upper provinces of Ecuador were slipping through his fingers, but Guayaquil and the Province of Guayas as well. He had already lost in his contest with Bolívar. And the situation in Peru was even less satisfactory. San Martín was, as Bulnes puts it, sitting on a volcano. The Peruvians were heartily tired of foreignism and of the man who had introduced it.

Torre Tagle had soon shown his utter inability to govern. The protectoral palace in Lima became the home of intrigues, the whole taking on an air of an Oriental court. Tomás Guido, successor to Unánue, as *ministro de hacienda,* and who was an Argentine, intrigued against Monteagudo and Monteagudo against him, while García del Río, the Colombian, was intriguing against both. And the less highly placed officers followed their example. Graft and corruption was the order of the day. Each man seemed to have his price. Monteagudo was a bold and able adversary, a second Cardinal Wolsey to a poor specimen of Henry VIII in the person of Torre Tagle. Monteagudo loved luxury and he loved pleasures; in fact he had a passion for them. And above all he loved power. There was something in his negroid makeup that made him cruel and unrelenting in his persecutions of the people whom he did not like. Instead of persecuting the monks as did the ministers of Henry VIII, Monteagudo persecuted the Spaniards. While he was serving both San Martín and Torre Tagle, both of whom favored a conciliatory policy, Monteagudo carried on a relentless policy of persecution against the Spaniards. The Spaniards were, of course, a very powerful class at the time the liberating army arrived in Peru, the number in Lima alone amounting to more than ten thousand. It was Monteagudo's policy to make life unbearable for those Spaniards who did not join the patriot cause.[64]

The most important result of this anti-Spanish policy was the dangerous defeat of Tristán at Ica in May. San Martín had neglected military affairs, leaving the direction of them to underlings. Neither Tristán nor Gamarra was big enough to measure swords with Canterac. In the first place there should have been no engagement at Ica, for every man in Ica was a spy for Canterac. In the second place there was a lamentable lack of coöperation, which was not infrequently the case with many of the patriot officers in Peru. Tristán and Gamarra did not work together, each wanted to be leader. Canterac knew this and made the defeat at Ica a far more important matter than San Martín tried to make it out at the time. He and Torre Tagle had considered Ica as a retreat.[65] The *limeños* gradually calmed their fears, but faith in the ability of San Martín and the government was badly shaken. Ica was a very severe test for San Martín's idealism. There are times when idealism is not enough. Stark realism demands action.

It was at this time that San Martín issued an important proclamation, declaring in part:[66]

> "I will make an ingenious confession to you. It was my intention to go in search of repose after so many years of agitation, but I believed that your independence was not secured. Some trifling danger now presents itself, and so long as there remains the least appearance of it, till you are free you shall not be left by your friend.
>
> "COMPANIONS OF THE UNITED ARMY.
>
> ". . . The campaign of Peru shall finish this year. Your old general assures it. Prepare to conquer."

The defeat of Ica roused San Martín out of his lethargic indifference to a serious concern about the gravity of the situation. He requested the immediate return of Santa Cruz and the Battalion of Numancia. He urged the governments of Chile and Argentina to send troops to Peru, but the request fell upon deaf ears in both countries. San Martín was

---

[64] Bulnes, *Historia de la espedición libertadora del Perú,* II, 438-39. Monteagudo had carried on a like policy, in so far as he was in power to do so in Argentina, and in Chile as well. It is a well-known fact that Monteagudo was a very able lawyer, his training and experience in the celebrated Universidad de San Javier in Chuquisaca prepared him for that profession. Of course, he had mental capabilities that lent themselves to development. He had had varied experiences also in the congress of Argentina of which he was a member. It is due to his influence that the Carrera brothers were executed in Mendoza.

[65] Bulnes, *Historia de la espedición libertadora del Perú,* II, 453.

[66] Dundonald, *Narrative of services,* I, 86.

hardly the man to ask either of them for aid. He had not done much, as they saw in Peru, to give them confidence either in his ability or in the cause in which they were concerned. They were not convinced that he was wholly disinterested in what he was trying to do in Peru. They certainly were not supporting him in his efforts to establish a monarchy. San Martín was a man in the prime of life, he was only forty-four years old, and might, after he had established a monarchy in Peru, turn on them. His contemporaries in these two countries were not looking upon the establishment of a monarchy in America with friendly eyes. A monarchy in America, supported by the European powers, did not appeal to them. There remained Colombia and the great Liberator of the North. But the wily Liberator was not likely to hearken much to a simple request to send troops and money to Peru, unless his larger ideal was served, and served in the manner in which he wanted it served. The fault of most of the historians dealing with Simón Bolívar is that they treat his plans as far too innocent. Bolívar was at this time the arbiter of South America. Before Pichincha he was only the Liberator of the North; after that famous battle he held the destiny of Spanish South America in his hands. San Martín failed utterly to understand this man. It may be that Bolívar was preëminently a pacifist, as Doctor Enrique Finot would have us believe;[67] but his views must not blind us to actual historic facts. While it may be technically true that Bolívar never drew his sword except in defense, we must not be blind to the fact that he was not always above helping to create a situation which meant that his adversary, or opponent, would either have to admit the point at issue, or fight. In the movements for the incorporation of Ecuador and the union of Colombia and Peru, Bolívar was a little more than the *pacifista,* he was the arbiter. It is to the eternal credit of San Martín that he did not force Bolívar to use his armed forces against him, which he would have done had that been really necessary.

The Guayaquil question was of the utmost importance to Bolívar because of the value of the port to the larger economic life of Gran Colombia. He needed an outlet on the Pacific. Between Panama and Trujillo, the only port of any very great consequence is Guayaquil. The richness of the hinterland emphasized the interest which Bolívar and San Martín both had in this Pearl of the Pacific. The fact that the Province of Guayas was the scene of a triangular conflict makes the contest between San Martín and Bolívar all the more important. It is not neces-

[67] Enrique Finot, *Bolívar pacifista* (New York, 1936).

sary to recount the origin of that contest. The thing of importance is the effort put forth by these two men to incorporate the province in their own state. Bolívar invoked the principle of the *uti possidetis juris* of 1810. He contended that the *carta fundamental* of Colombia of 1821 included Guayas; that *una ciudad y un río no pueden constituir una nación;* that Guayaquil had been a dependency of the *Presidencia de Quito;* that it belonged to *Nueva Granada;* and that *Gran Colombia* could not see the incorporation of Guayaquil by any other nation without protest.[68] He informed San Martín that the Guayaquil question would not be solved in the manner that he wanted it solved; that the people of a province could have no right to decide a question which concerned the nation; and that the two northern provinces of Ecuador had already solved the question.[69]

To make sure that the *guayaquileños* would not act in this matter contrary to his wishes, he arrived in Guayaquil on July 11. On his arrival he seized, by a *coup de main,* the reigns of government in Guayaquil. He explained to Santander that while he had not used force, the fear that he might do so caused the *junta* in the city to turn over the government to him. He expressed the hope that the *junta electoral* which would convene in the city on July 28 would decide to join Colombia. In fact it would have to do so, or else he would see to it that it did, adding *en fin,* "Vd. sabe que con modo se hace." It would be difficult to accept this as wholly the work of a *pacifista!* He also declared that he would remain in Guayaquil for a year in order to watch the Spaniards in Peru and to keep the *intrigantes* at bay; and he hoped to make those who did not love Gran Colombia to love her.[70] It is in this state of affairs that San Martín arrived for the famous interview with Bolívar.

Before going into an account of the interview it will be necessary to discuss the movement for a union between *Gran Colombia* and Peru. Bolívar sent Joaquín Mosquera in May 1822 to Peru as his minister in Lima. He was to negotiate a treaty of alliance with Peru, and thereby to solve as many of the outstanding problems between them as possible. He sought to induce Monteagudo to agree to an article by which Peru agreed to the annexation of Guayaquil to *Gran Colombia,* but Montea-

[68] Bolívar to Santander, Cali, January 5, 1822. Lecuna, *Cartas del Libertador* (10 vols., Caracas, 1929-30), III, 6-7.

[69] Bolívar to San Martín, Quito, June 22, 1822. *Ibid.,* III, 50-52.

[70] Bolívar to Santander, Guayaquil, July 22, 1822. Lecuna, *Cartas del Libertador,* III, 53-56.

gudo refused to agree to that point. The question of the future status of the regions of Quijos and Mainas was to be decided by the congress of Peru. Finally on July 6, 1822 the treaty was signed in Lima. The purpose of the treaty, as stated in the preamble, was to secure "forever, to their respective countries, subjects and citizens, the valuable enjoyments of their internal tranquillity, freedom, and national independence." The two countries agreed to "unite, bind, and confederate themselves in peace and war . . . , in order to sustain with their influence . . . , their independence of the Spanish nation, and to all other foreign dominion whatever. . . ." (Art. I). They promised and contracted "a perpetual compact of intimate alliance and firm and constant friendship for the security of their independence and liberty, for their reciprocal and general welfare and their interior tranquillity. . . ." (Art. II). They agreed to settle all differences between them "by those conciliatory and specific means which become two fraternal and confederate nations" (Art. IX). They bound themselves to restore peace and order in case "turbulent and seditious persons, or enemies of those governments legally constituted by the will of the inhabitants, freely, quietly, and peaceably expressed by virtue of the laws" had brought about anarchical conditions (Art. X). In additional articles the two governments expressed the hope that "this league may be general among all the states of America heretofore Spanish." They were to use their good offices to induce the other Spanish American states "to enter into the present compact of union, coalition, and confederation." They were to work for a general assembly of the American states in Panama (Art. III); but [71]

> "the present compact of union, bond, and confederation, shall not in any way interrupt the exercise of the national sovereignty of each one of the contracting parties, either as regards their laws and the establishment and form of their respective governments, or of their relations with other foreign nations. . . ." (Art. VI).

VI

San Martín left a second time on board the *Macedonia* from Callao on July 14, 1822 for Guayaquil. He had not announced his visit, nor had he answered the letter of Bolívar of June 17. He came up the Gulf

[71] *The Annual Register,* LXV, 204-209. Monteagudo in contrast to Mosquera, who was content to state that he was a member of the senate of Gran Colombia, described himself as "counsellor and minister of state and foreign affairs, founder of the order of the Sun, and secretary thereof, decorated with the medal of the liberating army, superintendent-general of the post office, and president of the patriot society." The treaty was ratified by Colombia on July 12, 1822 and signed by Francisco de P. Santander.

of Guayaquil July 25, and was welcomed by Bolívar's aides-de-camp. They expressed the regrets of Bolívar that he had not prepared a proper reception for him, but he had not been informed of the arrival of his distinguished guest. Bolívar also sent him a private note in which he expressed his pleasure in the interview and the hope that it might result in great good for *América meridional*.[72]

The landing and formal greeting between the two great Liberators took place on the morning of July 26.[73] The meeting was cordial, somewhat effusively so on the part of Bolívar, who was given to theatrical demonstrations when he felt that he might dazzle with such conduct. San Martín was in no mood to be demonstratively friendly. Bulnes declares that he was in ill humor over the whole situation. He had come to a bitter realization that Bolívar was certainly not the man he had expected him to be. He realized that he had been outwitted, that Bolívar had not been exactly honest with him in the Guayaquil question, and that little good could come from the interview. He knew that Guayaquil was lost to Peru and was prepared for other disillusionments.[74] De la Cruz expresses much astonishment at the fact that San Martín displayed so little insight into the whole situation. He seemed not to have thought it necessary to keep fully informed of what had taken place in southern Colombia, or about the larger ideals in which Bolívar was so much concerned.

The exact nature of the famous interview still remains a profound mystery. No one knows about any written agreements, or even any action taken during or after the informal interviews. De la Cruz declares that no third party was present during any one of the interviews. All authorities agree that there were three major subjects discussed: the Guayaquil question, the best form of government for the newly created nation-states, and the best way in which to end the war against Spain. Pérez gives his version of the interview, but evidently from second-hand information.[75]

[72] Lecuna, *Cartas del Libertador,* III, 57-58.

[73] One of the most beautiful monuments in all America marks the place where San Martín and Bolívar met.

[74] Bulnes, *Historia de la espedición libertadora del Perú,* II, 468.

[75] J. G. Pérez to Pedro Gual, Guayaquil, July 29, 1822. Lecuna, *Cartas del Libertador,* III, 60-83. The account is very detailed and forms interesting reading. He states that San Martín raised no question about Guayaquil, that he advocated monarchial governments for Spanish America, and that he was willing to aid Bolívar. He felt, also, that the Peruvians would also aid in bringing the war to a speedy end. He states that Bolívar opposed monarchial institutions forcefully and that he did not ask San Martín to aid him in the war. He also states that San Martín did not know the situation in Mexico and did not seem interested!

The conclusion to be drawn appears to be that the importance of this famous interview has been much overrated. Again it is necessary to say that San Martín made a very poor showing in this interview. He failed, as he had done in many other crises in Peru, to grasp what it was all about. He was not even permitted to have a part in ending the war, Bolívar reserving that glory exclusively to himself. San Martín was the one man, above all others, who should have realized that fact. It is the lack of exact and reliable information that on occasion played such dire havoc with him and his plans. He did not know the geography of Peru, or the real sentiment of the Peruvian people. He certainly did not know the machinations and clever maneuverings of Bolívar. He was not even in touch with the conditions in Lima after he left that city. He had to get the latest news from Bolívar. It must have given the shrewd and wily Liberator Bolívar no little satisfaction to have been able, in a rather tense moment in the interview, to inform him that a revolution on July 25 in Lima had forced Torre Tagle to dismiss Monteagudo, his favorite minister, and to send him out of Peru. San Martín had told Bolívar, in answer to a direct question from him, that the *limeños* were satisfied with the protectoral régime. All that the poor great man could say was that if that were true he would give up his power and leave Peru and Argentina for Europe. Assured that the news was accurate, he proceeded to carry out his resolution.

San Martín departed from Guayaquil in a rather hurried fashion, leaving the state ball in his honor, to embark at about midnight July 27-28 for the return trip to Callao. Bolívar afterwards spoke of his sudden departure as a flight, although he spoke of him and himself at the state banquet as the two greatest men in South America. San Martín returned on August 3, and on August 19 he assumed the rôle of supreme dictator. It is very generally admitted that San Martín should not have gone to Guayaquil. Mitre takes that view, and Vicuña Mackenna is even less charitable. The real pathos and tragedy of it all is that he should not have sensed the real nature of the whole situation until it was too late. It may be that San Martín displayed greatness in his decision to leave Peru as soon as the congress had been installed. It may be taken as a sublime act of abnegation and disinterestedness. And it may be taken as the act of a man who knew that he had failed, and that any effort to regain his lost power was useless at the time. As a dictator San Martín was a sorry figure indeed.

VII

The *motín militar* in Lima on July 25 was primarily the work of José de la Riva Agüero, who began to agitate for the dismissal of Monteagudo as soon as San Martín left for Guayaquil. He was still the *presidente* of the *Departamento de Lima* and thus in a position to make his wishes respected. Through the *ayuntamiento* he induced Torre Tagle to dismiss Monteagudo. But dismissal was not enough. The people demanded his arrest, trial, and punishment for his crimes. In order to avoid personal harm to Monteagudo he placed him on board a vessel and sent him away from Peru. Thus ended the rule of the man, who more than any one else, not excepting San Martín himself, was responsible for the enmity of the Peruvians towards the protectoral government. Bulnes declares that the *limeños* were justified in their demands for the removal of Monteagudo, for whom he has nothing but harsh criticism; but he censures the people for the manner in which they got rid of Monteagudo. Riva Agüero set a very bad example in resorting to revolutionary methods to remove a minister. There can be no difference of opinion on that head.[76] Not even San Martín expressed sympathy for Monteagudo, declaring that he had tolerated him too long, and that he ought to have sent him on some diplomatic mission. But Torre Tagle wanted to keep him as minister, and he had agreed to that.[77] Miller declares that Monteagudo deserved his fate.[78]

> "The people had just grounds for insisting upon the removal of Monteagudo. The harsh and uncourteous tone; the oppressive espionage which he had adopted; the cruel manner in which he had banished many highly respectable individuals, together with his suspected views of establishing a monarchical government contrary to the wishes of the people, all served to render him an object of dislike and distrust. The commotion was therefore a natural consequence of his despotic administration, supported so feebly by the weak and desolute Torre Tagle."

It was to be expected that Dundonald should have his views of the fall of Monteagudo. He makes San Martín responsible.[79]

> "Ambitious beyond all bounds, but with a capacity singularly incommensurate with his ambition, he believed that money could accomplish everything. Monteagudo provided this literally by plun-

---

[76] Bulnes, *Historia de la espedición libertadora del Perú,* II, 472.

[77] San Martín to O'Higgins, Lima, August 25, 1822. Vicuña Mackenna, *El jeneral D. José de San Martín,* 84-85.

[78] Miller, *Memoirs of general miller,* I, 335.

[79] Dundonald, *Narrative of services,* I, 222-223.

der and cruelty, whilst San Martín recklessly flung it away in ostentation and bribes. . . . The Minister was permitted to carry on the Government just as he chose; the Protector was meanwhile indulging in the '*otium cum dignitate*' at his country palace near La Legua, his physical powers prostrated by opium and brandy, to which he was a slave, whilst his mental faculties day by day became more torpid from the same debilitating influence. . . . The enormities committed in his name were for the most part not his, but Monteagudo's. . . . Duplicity and cunning were San Martín's great instruments when he was not too indolent to wield them; and while he was wrapped in ease his Minister superadded to these qualities all the cruelty and ferocity which sometimes converts a ruler into a monster, as the Limeños very appropriately designate him. San Martín was not innately cruel, though, as in the execution of the Carreras, he did not hesitate to sacrifice men of far greater patriotism and ability than himself, regarding them as his rivals; but he would not, as Monteagudo did, have endeavoured to tempt me ashore to the house of Torre Tagle, for the purpose of assassinating me; nor, failing in this, would he as Monteagudo also did, have liberated a convict for the express purpose of murdering me on board my own ship. At this distance of time these things may be mentioned, as there can be no delicacy in alluding to Monteagudo, who, having lived the life of a tyrant, died the death of a dog; for having sometime afterwards imprudently returned to the Peruvian capital, he was set upon and killed in the streets by the enraged limeños."

San Martín decreed the reassumption by himself of the powers of supreme protector on August 21, 1822, explaining that he did so not because he wanted power but because he felt that he was under a moral obligation to do so. He had early in January made a rather thorough reorganization of the public administration. He reduced the number of public employees and reduced the salaries of those remaining. He reminded the people, in the preamble to this decree, that it was not the number of employees, or the amount of money paid the employees, that mark a people great. It is, on the contrary, often the cause of their ruin and their debility. An excessive number of public officials has the further disadvantage of withdrawing talent from agriculture and the arts.[80] He also abolished the *pena de horca.*

[80] *Colección de leyes de Perú* (1822), 174. No efforts have been made to make this list complete of decrees issued by San Martín while in Peru. Only some of the more important ones have been given to show that he did much constructive work as dictator, and that he should be given due credit for that work. Nor has any attention been given to the decrees of Torre Tagle as supreme delegate. The decree for the reorganization of the administration also applied to the army and navy.

On January 10, in connection with the establishment of the *Sociedad Patriótica,* he took occasion to state his views on education. Public instruction was the first necessity of human societies, and the government that fails to encourage it was guilty of crime. The object of the *Sociedad* was to encourage a discussion of all questions bearing upon the public good, with no other restriction than that the fundamental laws and the honor of the citizens should be respected. Meetings were to be held every Wednesday and Friday evening and were to be open to the public. On September 14 he prescribed the ceremony for the installation of the congress, and on September 15 he decreed that the normal school built under the supervision of James Thompson, and based upon the Lancastrian system, should be formally opened on September 19.

The congress of Peru began its sessions on September 20 for San Martín.[81] The meetings were held in the *capilla* of the University of San Marcos. The ceremony in which he had a part was extremely brief, much to the surprise of all concerned. He made a brief statement declaring the body duly installed, took off the sash of his high office, and left the hall. He returned to Magdalena and made ready to leave for Chile from Ancón that same day. Guido, his faithful friend and counsellor, states that San Martín appeared greatly relieved after laying down the office of supreme protector. The congress, under the presidency of the celebrated Luna Pizarro, had no intention of permitting San Martín to divest himself of office in such an easy manner. It strove to have him change his mind and remain with them. It sent a commission to Magdalena to request him to accept election as president of Peru, but he declined. The congress then elected him commander-in-chief of the army, but he declined to act as such, although he accepted the title and salary of the office. He reminded the congress of the danger to the cause of independence if he were to remain in Peru. In a special session on the evening of the same day, the congress conferred other honors upon him. He was given the title of *Fundador de la Libertad del Perú,* the

[81] According to Carlos Wiesse the congress had 91 members: 78 were Peruvians 3 Colombians, 5 Ecuadorians *(Quiteños Cuencanos,* and *Guayaquileños),* 1 Bolivian 1 Chilean, and 3 Argentines. As to professions: 28 were lawyers, 26 ecclesiastics 8 medical men, 6 military and naval men, 9 merchants, 6 country gentlemen, 6 public employees, and 3 miners. Wiesse claims that they were an able body of men most of them strongly imbued with the teachings of French philosophers, so that the congress itself resembled the National Convention of France of 1793. Many legislative bodies had met in different parts of Spanish America, but most of them had ended in disorder and anarchy. There were those who predicted a like fate for this sovereign congress, but it had a distinguished career, as congresses of a political nature go.

right to use a tricolored sash, the title of captain-general, and a pension for life. The congress, also, ordered a monument built in his honor. He was to be given the honors of chief of the state for life whenever he was on Peruvian soil. And finally it voted to pay him the salary of supreme protector for life.

Late that evening, September 20, 1822, San Martín mounted a horse and rode to Ancón where he embarked on the *Belgrano,* a Peruvian vessel, and was on his way to Chile before the dawn of the following day. Before leaving he had written this proclamation:[82]

> "I have witnessed the declaration of the independence of the states of Chile and Peru. I hold in my hand the standard which Pizarro brought to enslave the empire of the Incas, and I have ceased to be a public man; thus I am more than rewarded for ten years spent in revolution and warfare. My promises to the countries in which I warred are fulfilled: to make them independent, and leave to their will the election of their governments.
>
> "The presence of a fortunate soldier, however disinterested he may be, is dangerous to newly constituted states. I am also disgusted with hearing that I wish to make myself a sovereign. Nevertheless, I shall always be ready to make the last sacrifice for the liberty of the country, but in the class of a private individual, and in *no other.*
>
> "With respect to my public conduct, my compatriots (as is generally the case) will be divided in their opinions; their children will pronounce the true verdict.
>
> "Peruvians! I leave the national representation established; if you repose implicit confidence in it, you will triumph; if not, anarchy will swallow you up.
>
> "May success preside over your destinies, and may they be crowned with felicity and peace!"

San Martín arrived in Valparaíso on October 12, 1822, "a fugitive from his shortlived splendour, amidst the desolation of despotism."[83] It will suit the purpose, in bringing this account to a close, to use the words of Dundonald, a man who had a large share in calling attention to the weaknesses of the great man. There were many in Chile who urged him to arrest San Martín as soon as he set foot on Chilean soil, but he refused. However, he formally protested to O'Higgins:[84]

---

[82] Miller, *Memoirs of General Miller,* I, 388.

[83] Dundonald, *Narrative of services,* I, 225.

[84] *Ibid.,* I, 227. The letter was addressed to O'Higgins and signed by Cochrane. The concluding sentence was in due legal form: "Given under my hand this 12th day of October, 1822. . . ."

"Don Jose de San Martín, late Commander-in-chief of the Expeditionary forces from Chili for the liberation of Peru, having this day arrived at Valparaiso, and being now within the jurisdiction of the laws of Chili, I lose no time in acquainting you that, if it be the pleasure of the Government to institute an inquiry into the conduct of the said Don Jose de San Martín, I am ready to prove his forcible usurpation of the Supreme Authority of Peru, in violation of the solemn pledge given by his Excellency the Supreme Director of Chili; his attempts to seduce the navy of Chili; his receiving and rewarding deserters from the Chilean Service; his unjustifiably placing the frigates, *Prueba* and *Venganza,* under the flag; with other demonstrations and acts of hostility towards the Republic of Chili."

The Chilean government took no notice of this protest; instead San Martín was given all necessary protection. O'Higgins had, however, to pay for his protection of the distinguished Liberator. The opposition to his rule began from the moment he took charge of the government. General Ramón Freire was ready to make the most of the presence of a traitor to Chile, and sought the help of Dundonald, but the latter declined. Freire took the position that San Martín would have to get out of Chile, and issued a proclamation on November 20, 1822, denouncing San Martín:[85]

"This Province . . . , holds in abhorrence and detestation the tyrant 'Liberator of Peru' who has stained our soil with tears of blood shed for his pretended service. Chacabuco would have terminated the war throughout the Republic, had it not been thought necessary to foster its continuance for the interests of this individual.

"I hold the residence of San Martín in any part of Chile suspicious and dangerous. Let him be off to make some other quarter happy, where he can sell his protection to the ill-fated inhabitants."

The revolution, led by Freire, overthrew O'Higgins and placed Freire in his place at the head of the nation, but not until San Martín had left Chile for Argentina. San Martín found the people of Argentina un-

---

[85] Dundonald, *Narrative of services,* I, 234-236. Dundonald gave his view of the political ills of Spanish South America in a letter to Freire on June 21, 1823, before leaving for his new post in Brazil. He said, in part: "Permit me to add my opinion, that whoever may possess the Supreme authority in Chili—*until after the present generation, educated as it has been under the Spanish colonial yoke, shall have passed away,* will contend with so much error, and so many prejudices, as to be disappointed in his utmost endeavours to pursue steadily the course best calculated to promote the freedom and happiness of the people. I admire the middle and lower classes of Chili, but I have ever found the Senate, the Ministers, and the Convention, actuated by the narrowest policy, which led them to adopt the worst policies. . . ." *Ibid.,* I, 246-248.

friendly and left for Europe. He had become a pathetic figure. He was really a man without a country and without a home. He was literally a fugitive from justice, as Dundonald and Freire termed him, and literally ran away to Europe. "to avoid reprobation in retirement," as Dundonald phrased it. While in Europe, he spent the first few years in an effort to stage a comeback. He declined to return to Peru in the fateful years of 1823 and 1824, when he was invited to return by both Riva Agüero and Bernardo Tagle,[86] because he knew that he would have Bolívar to contend with. He also knew that Riva Agüero and Tagle were really traitors to their country, at least they were in open rebellion against the de facto government. In 1827 he offered his services to La Mar, newly elected president of Peru, and a man for whom he had the greatest admiration; but La Mar declined his offer. In 1829 he returned to Argentina but found the people uninterested in him and his plan, and he returned to Europe. He spent the remainder of his days in Europe, most of the time in France, and on the bounty of a Spanish gentleman much of the time. He carried on an extensive correspondence with former associates in America and in Europe. He had been primarily concerned in America, he declared, with the happiness of the people. The happiness of the people alone mattered, the form of the political government was a minor matter, just so long as the people were happy. After all it was for the people to determine the form of their government; but he was very much opposed to *personalismo* in government, especially to governments ruled in accordance with political constitutions unsuited for the people for which they were made.[87] To which might be replied, in the terms of Sixto García, that San Martín merely liberated certain colonies from the rule of Spain, but did not liberate themselves from themselves. The liberated Spaniards of Peru, especially, remained Spaniards by temperament, by education, and by tradition.

The end came to the man, who has been called the greatest creole of the new world, on August 17, 1850, at three o'clock in the afternoon, in Boulogne sur Mere, France. He was seventy-two years, twenty-three days, and five hours old. As a dictator of Peru he still remains very much of an enigma. The great fame he enjoys as a warrior has been

[86] Torre Tagle changed his name twice. He was made the Marqués de Trujillo by San Martín. The sovereign congress abolished all titles of nobility, and Torre Tagle, or Trujillo, as he than signed himself, took the name of Bernardo Tagle.

[87] Jacinto Sixto García, *San Martín, Bolívar, Gamarra, Santa Cruz, Castilla y las constituciones del Perú* (Lima, 1919), 65.

permitted by his eminent biographers to overshadow his rôle as a dictator. To the writer San Martín remains a pathetically tragic figure as a dictator of Peru, as a man ill equipped by nature, by training, and by political experience to exercise successfully the supreme authority in a state. He should never have essayed the rôle of a dictator with his curious human frailties, his idiosyncracies, and his not unalloted and great ambition.

CHAPTER SEVENTEEN

DICTATOR SIMÓN BOLÍVAR

SIMÓN BOLÍVAR had a rather extensive experience as a dictator. With the possible exception of Santa Cruz, he was a more seasoned adept at that rôle than any of the dictators of Peru, Bolivia, and Ecuador. He was dictator of *Gran Colombia* before he came to be dictator of Peru, and he was dictator of *Gran Colombia* after he left Peru. This discussion, however, will be confined wholly to his career as a dictator of Peru. He was not the immediate successor of San Martín. As a matter of fact, he did not become dictator until almost a whole year after San Martín had laid down his sorry rôle of supreme protector of Peru. In the meantime the Peruvian people established a government of their own. But their efforts to govern themselves were beset with more than the usual perplexities.

On September 21, 1822, the sovereign congress created a multiple executive, known as the *junta gubernativa,* and composed of José de La Mar, Felipe Antonio Alvarado, and Manuel Salazar y Baquijano, the *Conde de Vista Florida.* La Mar was its president. On September 23 the congress decreed that all public authorities should take the oath of allegiance. Vargas declares that a centralized and not a decentralized government was needed at the time. It was not that the triumvirate was incapable, but because it was definitely subordinated to the congress. Vargas also criticizes the choice of the men for the *junta gubernativa,* for the *Conde de Vista Florida* only had had experience in government. Alvarado was chosen because he was a brother of the general-in-chief of Bolívar in order to please the large number of the Bolívar party, while La Mar was chosen because of his friendship with Luna Pizarro and for his social connections. Alvarado had been born in Argentina and La Mar in Ecuador. In the face of a strong desire for a government of Peruvians, the congress made the mistake of raising these two foreigners to the executive, and intensifying the opposition to foreigners. It is well to emphasize the fact that the one really great problem before the Peruvian people between September 7, 1820 and January 27, 1827 was how to rid the country of the rule of the foreigners. The congress had, as early as November 5, 1822, decreed that all vacancies in the army and navy should be filled by Peruvian officers.[1] Other evidences will come to light as the narrative proceeds.

[1] *Colección de leyes de Perú.*

I

The year 1822 did not come to an end without a strengthening of the power of Bolívar in Peru. As early as September 9 he had informed the minister of state and foreign relations of Peru that he felt obliged to state that the condition of affairs in Peru gave *Gran Colombia* the gravest concern. He offered to send four thousand troops to Peru and urged that Argentina and Chile be requested to send troops to Peru.[2] The *junta gubernativa* was in no hurry to reply to this communication. Bolívar had his enemies as well as his friends in the country. Luna Pizarro and many other members of the congress were definitely opposed to Bolívar and his plans. Many of the exiled *guayaquileños,* Olmedo among them, were working hard against him.[3] On November 15 the Colombian government declared that until the Peruvian government had replied to the communication of September 9, no aid would be sent to Peru to end the war with Spain. The intensity of the feeling against Bolívar in the congress is proved by the fact that the congress voted in secret to send emissaries to Colombia to work to prevent the invasion of Peru, as the plans of the Liberator were called.[4]

On October 25 the *junta gubernativa* accepted the offer of Bolívar, paving the way for a convention between the two governments. Juan Paz del Castillo, Colombian minister to Peru, negotiated this instrument. Colombia was to furnish troops on condition that Peru should pay the total cost of the expeditionary forces, to feed, clothe, and equip the troops, the officers to be provided with suitable horses, and the officers and men to be paid regularly on the first of the month. This Colombian Division was to be kept intact and under command of their own Colombian officers.[5]

The year 1823 opened inauspiciously for the opponents of Bolívar in Peru. In the first place, the military situation took on a serious aspect. As early as January 19, 1823 General Valdez inflicted a crushing defeat upon the patriot forces at Tarata. Military reverses are usually a very serious matter, and proved especially so at this time. The *junta gubernativa,* which had never been popular, had to bear the brunt of the defeat at Tarata. Santa Cruz,[6] assisted by Gamarra and La Fuente and

[2] Vargas, *Participación de Colombia en la libertad del Perú, 1824-1924,* I, 69-72.

[3] *Ibid.,* I, 80. Consult also Lorente, *Historia del Perú* (Lima, 1821-27), II, 120.

[4] *Ibid.,* I, 82.

[5] Vargas, *Participación de Colombia en la libertad del Perú,* I, 83-84.

[6] Andrés Santa Cruz, about whom a great deal will be written later, was one of the ablest, the most conspicuous, and the most promising of the younger men of the Peruvian army at this time. He enjoyed great prestige because of his excellent

other military chiefs, led the revolt against the *junta.* The congress was requested to abolish the multiple executive and select a president of Peru instead. The congress refused, and on February 27 the military staged its famous *motín militar* in Miraflores. La Mar was seized and imprisoned, and February 28 the congress abolished the *junta gubernativa,* created a single executive, and elected Riva Agüero president of the Republic.[7]

Riva Agüero was, as has been noted before, one of the most sensationally conspicuous men of his age. He had taken an active part in the affairs of state under the protectorate but had not displayed any marked ability. His great weakness was his great love of power, a weakness that was to be his undoing. He could stand neither prosperity nor adversity; but despite his checkered career, friend and foe alike agree that he was a great patriot, always working, as he saw it, for the welfare of Peru and the Peruvian people.

The election of Riva Agüero did not prove a great victory for the opponents of Bolívar. He was not the man to guide Peru in this critical hour. Many of his appointments to high positions were not well made. On April 8 he raised Santa Cruz to the rank of a general of division and appointed him commander-in-chief of the army. He made Gamarra, Pinto, Miller, and Herrera generals of brigade, and appointed Ramón Herrera minister of war and Gamarra chief-of-staff.

Bolívar concluded that it was time for him to take a more active part in the affairs of Peru. He was still in Guayaquil, but he would not go to Peru until the stage had been properly prepared for him. He urged Santander to secure for him the authorization of the Colombian congress to go to Peru. He believed he had the constitutional power to do so, since Peru would not have to be considered a foreign country and could be treated as *Nueva Granada* and Venezuela had been treated. But he felt that formal authorization from the Colombian congress would be the safest way to proceed.[8] On April 13 he wrote to Riva Agüero that he had been giving a great deal of thought to the grave situation in Peru.

services in the great Battle of Pichincha. He was popular, a wealthy member of the aristocracy, and fearless. His wealth and social position added to his prestige. He had taken a dislike to Sucre, but had a high regard for Bolívar, and was to get preferments at his hands.

[7] Few men had a more varied career than José de la Riva Agüero, and, though we are not dealing with him other than as one of the many accidental "personalities" in this age, he bears careful study.

[8] Bolívar to Santander, Guayaquil, March 29, 1823. Lecuna, *Cartas del Libertador,* III, 150-155.

He stated that he had decided to send Sucre to Peru with the rank of a diplomat to study the conditions in the republic. Sucre was also to have charge of the military interests of Colombia in Peru. He urged Riva Agüero to request the governments of Argentina and Chile to send troops to Peru to end the war, which was, after all, an American war. He concluded by saying that he could not come to Peru without authorization from the congress of Colombia. He had to have some real excuse, otherwise a false interpretation might be put upon his movements, as had been done in the case of three of his colleagues: San Martín, O'Higgins, and Iturbide.[9]

Sucre left Guayaquil April 15 and arrived in Callao early in May. He came to do what he had done in Ecuador, and what he was to do in Bolivia, to prepare the way for Bolívar. There are few who have so faithfully served their superiors as the immaculate Sucre. He came to Lima with great prestige. It was only about a year before that he had made his name and fame immortal at Pichincha. He was a worthy representative of the great Liberator. He was received with great demonstrations of cordiality, and at once set about his task. He was to secure a formal invitation from the congress of Peru to come to end the war in that country. It was for this purpose that he had come to Lima.

President Riva Agüero played a rather innocent game throughout the critical months of the establishment of the Bolivian dictatorship in Peru. He was to repeat the same mistake that San Martín had made. Neither of them sensed fully the danger they were in when dealing with him. Neither of them realized the game that Bolívar was playing, or if they did, they woefully underrated his ability and just as woefully overestimated their own. Riva Agüero underestimated the strength of the Bolívar party in Peru. He began by conciliating those forces by offering to appoint Sucre commander-in-chief of the Peruvian army. Sucre declined to accept the appointment on the ground that he was forbidden to meddle in the political affairs of the country. He made it plain that it was imperative that Bolívar should come in person to Peru to take full control of the government.

Riva Agüero began to realize the precarious situation he was in and sought to stem the feeling towards Bolívar. But it was too late, the congress had already been won over to the cause of Bolívar. As early as May 5, it had decreed a vote of gratitude to Bolívar for what he had already done for the country. On May 14 the congress formally repeated

[9] Lecuna, *Cartas del Libertador,* III, 161-164.

its request to the congress of Colombia to authorize Bolívar to come to Peru. On June 5 the congress of Colombia authorized Bolívar to go to Peru.

Riva Agüero, instead of admitting defeat, sought, through dictatorial methods, to make himself master of Peru. He began by dissolving the congress on the very day that it had voted to invite Bolívar to come to Peru. The congress denied him the right to dissolve a body that had created the very position to which it had elected him. The congress still considered itself as the constituent and the sovereign ruling body in the state. Vargas declares that Riva Agüero had no legal right to dissolve the congress, and that in attempting to do so he was abolishing the very office which he himself was occupying.[10] As was to be expected, Bolívar also held he was without the legal right to dissolve the congress. And in his famous letter of September 4 he reminded Riva Agüero of the fact that it was the *Fundador de la Libertad del Perú* that had convoked the congress, that it had been recognized as a sovereign constituent body by the people, and that he himself was a creature of that body and had sworn to obey it.[11]

II

The Spanish authorities had decided to take advantage of the contest between Riva Agüero and the congress to capture Lima. Sucre, learning of the advance of the Spanish army, ordered Lima evacuated. The government moved to Callao, and Canterac took possession of the capital. The congress, in session in Callao, conferred full military powers upon Sucre on June 21, who took the oath before the congress on the same day. On June 22 it deposed Riva Agüero and ordered him to leave the republic. Sucre, however, permitted him to go to Trujillo instead. Riva Agüero had no intention of submitting to the orders of the congress, and set up his government in Trujillo on July 19. In the meantime the congress had elected Torre Tagle to succeed Riva Agüero. On August 8, the congress declared Riva Agüero guilty of treason and outside the pale of law. And on August 19 the congress decreed that all possible means should be used for his capture.

The Spanish army remained in Lima only about a month. In the meantime Sucre led an expedition into the south of Peru to help Santa Cruz conduct his campaign in that region. On August 25 Santa Cruz met the Spanish forces under Valdez at Zepita. The battle was so close

---

10 Vargas, *Participación de Colombia en la libertad del Perú.*
11 Lecuna, *Cartas del Libertador,* III, 228-230.

that neither commander knew for hours afterwards who had actually won the battle. The victory lay with Santa Cruz, however; and the fame of the battle is preserved in the title of Grand Marshal of Zepita conferred on Santa Cruz. The campaign of 1823 can hardly be said to have brought any glory either for the commanders or for the patriot forces. It had served the purpose of forcing the Spanish royalists away from Lima and into the *sierras.* It had also demonstrated the need of preparing for the final contest in those regions. And it could hardly have failed to arouse in Sucre and Santa Cruz a desire to regain some of the prestige that had been lost in that campaign. It must have convinced Bolívar of the need of preparing for a contest with the seasoned troops of Spain, and that the contest was likely to be more fierce than anything he had so far encountered.

III

The Liberator-President of Colombia had a task before him in Peru, accordingly, worthy the metal of the greatest of leaders. He embarked on the *Chimborazo* at Guayaquil on August 6 and arrived in Callao on September 1. The reception given him was the greatest ever accorded to man in Peru. The stage, it is true, had been well set, although the sincerity and the warmth of the reception should not be minimized. The fame of the great *Libertador* had made him a great figure, the greatest of his age, and in many respects uniquely great. Coupled with this was the realization of the gravity of the situation. If ever a country needed a savior it was Peru. And much as the people might have feared the designs of the *Libertador,* the conscious need of a strong man brought forth their generous acclaim.

President Tagle, the ministers of state, and the army chiefs met Bolívar in Callao and escorted him to the capital. On September 2 the congress met in solemn session to meet him. Vargas declares that this session in honor of Bolívar was the most magnificent and solemn ever held in all of South America.[12] On that day the congress conferred on him full powers to deal with the rump government of Riva Agüero. Before it conferred dictatorial powers upon him, however, the congress wanted to know in what form he wanted the decree to be drawn. The president of the congress wrote to him to that effect. Bolívar replied in one of his most brilliant utterances on September 5. He pointed out that the situation had changed considerably since the Peruvian mission, composed of Olmedo and Sánchez Carrión, had invited him "to come to

[12] Vargas, *Participación de Colombia en la libertad del Perú,* I, 180.

conduct the war and to reëstablish constitutional order." The occupation of the capital by the Spanish forces had greatly altered the whole situation, and he feared that it would be necessary not only to carry on the war but also to reorganize the social order. He had come to look for the enemies of America upon Peruvian soil and would need full authority from the congress to drive those enemies out of the country. He felt that he would need only the full military power of the state, and did not want civil authority, for civil authority of an arbitrary character was distinctly repugnant to him. He reminded the president of the congress of the unique character of his position in Peru. He was offering to the people the greatest civil service that a man had ever offered to any nation. He had come to save the glory and protect the liberty of Peru. To that end he would use his mental faculties to the utmost.[13]

The congress decreed, in the session of September 10, the authority which it believed that Bolívar should have to put his plans into execution. It declared that only dictatorial powers in the hands of this man could bring the war to a close and save the republic. He was, accordingly, given the supreme military power in the state. He was also given complete supreme political power to be used whenever he should judge it necessary to success in the military operations. He was given full power to determine when to use, and when not to use, these dictatorial powers. And finally, he was given full power to act independently of the authority of President Tagle, if he so desired; and was to be assisted by him in every possible manner. He was to have the honors of the chief executive of the state. Bolívar was dictator in everything but in name, and under the cloak of Liberator.[14]

The ceremony of installation was elaborate. On September 13 he formally declared, in the *Salón de Sesiones del Palacio Presidencial* in Lima, that he recognized the national sovereignty and that he would submit to it. On September 14 all the military, civil, and ecclesiastical authorities met in the same place and formally recognized him in his new rôle. After the ceremony a *Te Deum* was chanted in the cathedral in honor of the occasion. On September 15 in the presence of President Tagle and the congress he took the oath of his high office. In a proclamation he promised that the soldiers who had come from the Plata, the Maule, the Magdalena, and the Orinoco would not return to their native countries until they had carried off as trophies the standards of Castilla, or died in the attempt to do so.

[13] Victor E. Ayarzu, *Reseña histórica del senado* (Lima, 1921), 81-82.
[14] Vargas, *Participación de Colombia en la libertad del Perú*. I. 227-8

Among the problems demanding immediate attention was the domestic one. Riva Agüero was in open rebellion against the government and had to be removed. Bolívar wrote to him urging him to join in the war against Spain, but this he declined to do. Both men appealed to the Chilean government. Bolívar sent Juan Salazar to Chile to ask for a loan of money and for men. Riva Agüero did the same. The Chilean government, largely due to the activities of Juan Manuel Egaña, president of the congress of Chile, refused to recognize the government of Tagle and requested Bolívar to dissolve the congress of Peru, to ask for the resignation of Tagle, and to order the election of a new government for Peru. At the same time, it recalled its troops from Peru. Bolívar then turned to Colombia for troops, and six thousand more were sent to Peru, Ecuador having furnished a large number of them.[15] Riva Agüero failed even in getting San Martín to return to aid him. Bolívar was uncertain, for a time, about the support of Santa Cruz, La Fuente, and Gamarra. But he was able to convince them that Riva Agüero was a traitor to the existing order in Peru because of his communications with the Spaniards, and they made short work of Riva Agüero and his faction.

La Fuente, with the valuable aid of Ramón Castilla, went to Trujillo and took the unsuspecting Riva Agüero prisoner on November 25. Tagle ordered Riva Agüero executed on the grounds of treason, but La Fuente refused to carry out the sentence and was supported by Bolívar in that step. Riva Agüero was set free and left later for Europe, and his faction was not able to offer much opposition to Bolívar for some time. Vargas declares that La Fuente and Castilla had rendered Peru a great service by ridding her of a man who had ceased to work for the best interests of his country.[16]

But the affairs of Peru were not progressing to suit Bolívar. The government was not giving the attention that he thought it should to the military situation. He was anxious to have it begin the offensive against the Spaniards by May 1824. He wrote to Santander complaining of the dilatory tactics of the government. He was greatly concerned by the large number of armed men in the service of Spain, more than twelve thousand of them, and of her activities in *Alto Perú*. All of which meant that unprecedented activities were necessary both in Colombia and in Peru.[17]

---

[15] *Ibid.*, I, 261.

[16] *Ibid.*, I, 263.

[17] Lecuna, *Cartas del Libertador,* III, 307-312; written from Trujillo on December 21, 1823.

IV

The year 1824 did not open auspiciously for Bolívar. Colombia and Peru were both slow to act, and the means to carry on war effectively were not forthcoming, despite his strenuous efforts. A powerful reason for all this was the increasing opposition to Bolívar in both countries. The life of a dictator is not a bed of roses, and in the case of Bolívar there was no exception. In a letter to Sucre on January 16, 1824, he gave vent to his pessimism. Like San Martín he was becoming a slave to the Peruvian *La Costa,* complaining of ill health, old age, and the fickle caprice of fortune. He even appears to have had some compunctions of conscience for he likened himself to the rich man who was afraid he would be robbed of his goods, that some one would deprive him of his reputation, "which is the reward and fortune that I have obtained for my immense sacrifice," and that everything caused him alarm. He had asked for his dismissal from the Colombian congress, an act which he felt certain would have the desired effect in both Colombia and Peru. There was a time when he felt eager to do battle with the Spaniards, but he felt so no more. And then, as if to take some comfort out of his situation, he declared that Sucre would experience a similar fate. But Sucre still had youth. "Would that I might be in your position. I would not then tremble for my own fortune. At least I would have my desires, my hopes to caress me." He concluded by doubting the advisability of trying to negotiate with the Spaniards. In any event, he would keep his hands off that business.[18] Berindoaga, Aliaga, and Tagle were all in communication with the enemy. Why not? San Martín had set the example, and Riva Agüero had done so. Peru might be better off as a colony of Spain than of Colombia, under the rule of Ferdinand VII, than of the rule of Dictator Bolívar.

The events of the year 1824 became more favorable to Bolívar as the year grew older. The loss of Callao[19] aroused the congress to action. The rule of Tagle became unbearable with the increased activities of the Spanish. They were gradually closing in on Lima, and were already in possession of the south, the center, and the *sierras.* Canterac was encamped near Jauja, and the great fortress of Callao was in their hands. On February 10 the congress adopted the celebrated degree which made

[18] Lecuna, *Cartas del Libertador,* IV, 24-28.

[19] The *motín militar* of the mulatto Moyano caused the loss of this valuable fortress, although it began as a protest against the failure of the Government to pay its troops in Callao.

Bolívar the absolute Dictator of Peru.[20] It then adjourned to remain adjourned until Bolívar should deem it necessary to call it again into session. Bolívar had reached another rung of the golden ladder of fame. One may agree with General Miller, however, that under the circumstances the act was "of questionable wisdom."[21]

On February 18 Tagle was deposed by the congress, and at once became a most bitter enemy of Bolívar. In a proclamation he denounced Bolívar as the greatest monster that had ever lived, stating that he was the enemy of all good men, that his ambition was insatiable, and that he would destroy Peru. He urged his fellow countrymen to unite as one man against this man, who intended to convert Peru into a desert. Tagle, like Riva Agüero, had a large following, and both groups gave Bolívar grave concern. These men would have deserved greater praise had they worked for the good of their country, and less for themselves, for despite their honied words to the contrary they were both pathetic victims of the *sed de mando*.[22]

Bolívar was determined to surmount all obstacles. He centralized the forces of the administration, reducing the number of employees, cutting the salaries, and entrusting the civil administration to Sánchez Carrión. He raised money by the sale of public property, by contributions, and by seizing the *fundos* of the religious orders and *cofradios*. He abandoned Lima to the Spaniards as the only course open to him, for, unlike San Martín, he realized that military success would have to be achieved in the *sierras*. He moved the capital to Trujillo and gave all his attention to the organization of a great offensive campaign. He believed that old Spain was renewing her efforts for a final drive upon America, and that it was essential to take the offensive.

[20] The decree is a very interesting piece of legislation. The preamble declares that the constitutional régime had failed because it did not provide for the concentration of power in the hands of a man to meet a great crisis. Only dictatorial power deposited in the hands of a man strong enough to wage the war could save the nation. The decree of September 10, 1823 had not given Bolívar enough power. Tagle had failed, even though he had governed according to constitutional principles, because he did not have enough power to meet the crisis. The congress then ordered that the supreme political and military authority should be concentrated in the hands of Bolívar. The use of the full dictatorial powers was to depend upon the exigencies to save the republic. There was to be no interference from President Tagle, and Bolívar was to say when Tagle might exercise his powers as president. The decree also declared that all the articles of the political constitution, and all laws and decrees, which might interfere with the exercise of these dictatorial powers, were to remain automatically inoperative.

[21] Miller, *The memoirs of General Miller*, II, 118.

[22] Vargas, *Participación de Çolombia en la libertad del Perú*, II, 183.

On July 4 he had reached Cerro de Pasco with a powerful army. The topography of the country was an important factor in this campaign. The Andean range divides into three sections in Peru: the western, the central, and the eastern. These ranges come to a point at the *nudo* de Pasco and reopen to form the plain of Bombon and the great valley of the Jauja. The valley lies between the eastern and the western ranges of the Andes. The Spaniards were operating in the Juaja valley, in a region that was really on the top of the world. None of the passes are less than twelve thousand feet above the level of the sea. Many are fully fifteen thousand feet, and the *maseta de Pasco* is more than twelve thousand feet high. An important topographical feature is the celebrated *Lago de Junín.* The whole region between these two Andean ranges is called Huancavelica, more than eleven thousand feet above the level of the sea. In addition to these natural obstacles, there was the danger of being detected by the enemy forces.

On July 9 Bolívar reached the City of Huanacu with his army, and on August 3 he had reached the western shores of the *Lago de Reyes* in the *pampas de Junín.* On August 6 he won the brilliant victory at Junín.[23] The victory opened up a vast field of operations for the patriot army, but not for Bolívar personally. Shortly after the battle he received information from Colombia that the congress had repealed the decree of October 9, 1821, that had given him dictatorial powers. The congress had instead conferred executive powers upon Santander. Bolívar turned over the command of the united liberating army to Sucre, and returned to the coast.[24] Vargas takes the view that Anibal Galindo

---

[23] There is an incident of this battle that reveals the traits of character in both Bolívar and Sucre. Sucre had been ordered by Bolívar to the rear of the army to gather up the stragglers and convalescents. He did the work without a protest, but when the battle was over he wrote a letter to Bolívar complaining bitterly of the menial task he had been ordered to perform. He had been sent to do a piece of work that an adjutant could have done. He, the commander-in-chief of the Colombian army, had been humiliated before the whole army. He concluded with the statement that he saw nothing for him to do but to leave the army and return to Colombia. Bolívar replied that he had not meant to humiliate him or to hurt his feelings, and gave him a lecture on the larger aspects of service. Sucre remained to "fulfill" his brilliant destiny, as will be seen later.

[24] On November 10 Bolívar replied to the letter from Santander, declaring that he was happy over the events that had occurred in Colombia. *La constitución es la reina de sus hijos,* he declared and he would abide by the decision of the congress. It had extricated him from Colombia and released him from all Colombian responsibilities. His reply to the congress was that he wanted it to consider his resignation of the year before as *presidente titular* which was still before the congress. Instead of a vote of thanks which he deserved, the congress had taken away powers which he had never wanted and never requested. He had only the cockade and heart of Colombia and would leave America as soon as the war was over.

is in error in his statement that Bolívar withdrew from the command because his army officers had demanded it. Galindo ignores the cardinal fact that the army was loyal to Bolívar and that the army was well disciplined and its morale excellent. A council of the army chiefs did take place, but for the purpose of petitioning him to retain command of the army. If that were not possible, they wanted him to know that they would continue to give their best services for the success of the common cause.[25]

As soon as Bolívar came back to the coast he began to arrange for even greater operations. On November 8 he suddenly entered Lima to the dismay of Tagle, Berindiaga, Aliaga, and other traitors, who hurriedly left the city. He reorganized the administration, relieving Sánchez Carrión of his office of secretary-general, and restoring the ministry. But the main contest with Spain was still in the future, and no one knew that better than Bolívar. He was still dictator and had full control over the affairs of state, but he judged it wise not to have command of the armed forces. He feared complications with Colombia, and gave orders to Sucre to continue the offensive campaign in the *sierras*.

After playing hide and seek for several weeks, Sucre and La Serna met upon the *pampas de Ayacucho* on December 9, and fought the final battle of the wars of emancipation. It was a setting worthy of the final act. The location has an elevation of more than ten thousand feet above the level of the sea. On the east was the majestic peak of Condorcunca. Sucre had the smaller number of men, but he was the better commander of the two, for he was complete master of the situation, thanks to the splendid plan of the battle. The hero of Ayacucho was General Córdova, who had been the first to approve the plan of La Mar for the great battle.[26] The eagerness of La Serna to begin the battle lost him the victory.[27] Sucre was even greater in victory than in the battle itself. The capitulation signed with La Serna and Canterac showed him noble and generous at the moment of his greatest triumph. He had as prisoners of war: Viceroy La Serna; Generals Canterac, Valdez, Carratala, Monet, and Villalobos; Generals of Brigade Bedoya, Ferraz, Camba,

---

[25] Vargas, *Participación de Colombia en la libertad del Perú,* II, 163-4.

[26] Quintanilla, *Homenaje,* 5-23. He insists that the valor and ability of the Peruvian troops made the victory of Ayacucho possible. As in the case of Pichincha, Ayacucho was a Peruvian victory. Vargas, II, 196-197, has an excellent map showing the routes of the armies in October, November, and December of 1824 in the *sierras*.

[27] The precipitative movement of Rubin de Celis, lost La Serna the battle.

Somorcio, Cacho, Atero, Landazuri, Vigil, Pardo, and Tur; sixteen colonels, sixty-eight lieutenant-colonels, four hundred and eighty-four majors, and minor officials; and more than two thousand troops, seven hundred wounded, and eighteen hundred dead.[28]

The news of the victory of Ayacucho was received throughout Peru with transports of joy. Honors were showered upon the hero of Ayacucho and Pichincha, the two greatest battles of the wars of independence. Sucre was given the title of Grand Marshal of Ayacucho and General Liberator of Peru on December 27, and on Febraury 10, 1825 the congress voted him the sum of two hundred thousand *pesos* as a reward for his services. The genuine satisfaction of Bolívar over Ayacucho is expressed in these two proclamations:[29]

> "Soldiers! You have given liberty to South America, and a quarter of the world is the monument of your glory. Where have you not conquered?
>
> "South America is covered with trophies of your valour; but Ayacucho, like Chimborazo, rears her exalted head above them all.
>
> "Soldiers! Colombia owes to you the glory with which you again cover her. Peru: life, liberty and peace. La Plata and Chile also are your debtor for immense benefits. The good cause, the rights of man, has conquered by your arms in her terrible struggle with the oppressor. Contemplate, then, the blessings you have conferred upon humanity by your heroic sacrifices.
>
> "Soldiers! Receive the limitless gratitude which I bestow upon you in the name of Peru. I pledge myself that you shall be recompensed as you deserve, before you return to your beautiful country. But no. You never can be worthily rewarded. Your services transcend all price.
>
> "Soldiers of Peru! Forever will your country rank you among the first saviours of Peru.
>
> "Soldiers of Colombia! You will live in hundreds of victories until the end of the world."

The other proclamation gives the views of Bolívar on the situation in Peru, which brought him to the republic, and also on some of the things he intended to do for the country.

> *"Peruvians!* The liberating army, commanded by the intrepid and skillful general Sucre, has at once put an end to the war in Peru, and of the American continent, by one of the most glorious victories ever obtained by the arms of the new world. Yes! The

[28] Vargas, *Participación de Colombia en la libertad del Perú,* II, 254.

[29] *Ibid.,* II, 263-265. The translation in *Niles Register,* XXVII, 6-7, 130-131, and in Cleven, *Readings in Hispanic American history,* 455-458.

army has fulfilled the promise I made you on its name to accomplish the liberty of Peru in the course of this year.

"Peruvians! The time has arrived when I must also fufilll the promise I made to you to divest myself of the dictatorship on the day victory would seal your destiny. The congress of Peru will be assembled on the tenth of February (proximo), being the anniversary of the decree by which was confided to me this supreme authority, and which I will then return to the legislative body which honored me with that confidence. These are not empty words.

"Peruvians! Peru has suffered great military disasters. The troops who guarded it occupied the free provinces of the north and carried war against the congress. The navy obeyed no longer the commands of the government. The ex-president, Riva Agüero, by turns a usurper, rebel and traitor, fought against his country and her allies. The auxiliaries of Chile, by their lamentable defection, deprived us of the assistance of their troops. And those of Buenos Aires, having revolted in Callao against their chiefs, delivered that place to the enemy. The president, Tagle, making an appeal to the Spaniards to occupy this capital, achieved the destruction of Peru.

"Discord, misery, discontent and personal interest had spread their bane through every part of the country. Peru seemed to exist no more. All was dissolved! Under these awful circumstances, the congress appointed me a dictator to save the relics of their last hopes.

"The loyalty, the constancy, and the valor of the army of Colombia have performed this wonderful undertaking. The Peruvians, when a civil war was raging, acknowledged the legitimate government, and have rendered immense services to the country, while the troops who protected them, have covered themselves with glory on the fields of Junin and Ayacucho. Factions have disappeared from the soil of Peru. This capital has recovered forever its sweet liberty. Callao is invested, and must be given up by capitulation.

"Peruvians! Peace has succeeded to war; union to discord; order to anarchy; and happiness to misfortune! But never forget, I beseech you, that, for these blessings, you are indebted to the illustrious victors of Ayacucho.

"Peruvians! The day on which your congress will meet will be a day of glory! the day that will consummate the most fervent wishes of my ambition. Do not ask more!"

V

The year has come to a glorious end for Dictator Bolívar. If it had been one of the most trying years of his whole career, it had also been the year in which he had won his greatest victories. On December 21 he decreed that the congress would meet on February 10, 1825. It was not a new body, merely the reconvening of the body that had taken a recess on February 10, 1824, and which had been elected in 1822. There was nothing at the beginning of the year 1825 that indicated that Bolívar intended to divest himself of the dictatorial powers. He was too able a man, and with too much vision, to believe that conditions in Bolivia could be settled between the Battle of Ayacucho and the meeting of the congress. No man knew better the delicate and complicated question of the future of Bolivia than he. Bolivia was not Argentinian and it was not Peruvian. What was to be its future status politically? Four nations had their eyes on this vast inland empire: Argentina, Peru, Colombia, and Brazil. To which of these did Bolívar wish Bolivia to go? To Colombia, of course. And yet there was bound to be a great cry of protest against such a proceeding. The year 1825 will, therefore, be Bolivia's year, and Bolívar is likely to remain dictator long enough to have the future of that country settled.

The situation in Bolivia during the year 1824 and the early part of the year 1825 was a peculiar one. Bolivia, the first to begin the movement for independence in Spanish America,[30] was the last to secure independence. Only Cuba and Panama have come into independent statehood since Bolivia. Her *guerra de quince años* had been a devastating one, the effects upon the political life of which have hardly yet been effaced. The efforts of the *Porteños* to liberate Bolivia had brought on the infamous ravages of Goyeneche. And the strange efforts of General Pedro de Olañeta to save her for Ferdinand VII, brought on the Bolivian invasion of 1825. The defection of Olañeta had caused both Spain and Bolívar great concern. Viceroy La Serna considered him a traitor to Spain, and Bolívar considered him a traitor to the patriot cause. After Ayacucho, therefore, the important problem was Pedro de Olañeta in Bolivia. On December 15, 1824, Bolívar urged Pedro de Olañeta to join the patriot cause.[31] But he refused to desert Ferdinand VII, and would fight for him to the bitter end. Bolívar then sent Sucre with the united liberating army into Bolivia to crush the Olañeta revolution. He entered La Paz February 2, 1825, and began to work for the complete independence of Bolivia. He had met several of the leaders of the independence movement in Bolivia in Puno, Peru, on his way to La Paz. Of these men, the famous Casimiro Olañeta, a nephew of General Olañeta, was one of

[30] It was on May 25, 1809 that the people of the City of Chuquisaca, in a *cabildo abierto,* declared themselves independent of the rule of Spain.

[31] Bolívar to Pedro de Olañeta, Lima, December 15, 1824. Lecuna, *Cartas del Libertador,* IV, 222-224. Bolívar urged him to work for the American cause as the only real cause worthy of support at the time.

the ablest. These leaders convinced him that there was a separate and distinct nationality in Bolivia determined to have a voice in its future political status. They urged him to convene a deliberative assembly of elected deputies from the provinces of Bolivia. He agreed to this, and on his own initiative he issued, February 9, the celebrated decree convoking an assembly for April 19 in Oruro.

As soon as Bolívar learned of the action taken by his lieutenant, he immediately annulled the decree of February 9, and administered a stern rebuke to Sucre. He had acted wholly without orders, having been sent as a military commander serving under Bolívar's orders. He informed him that he had been sent to continue the war against Spain but not to try to set up a new government. He declared that he was still the head of the Peruvian state and that Sucre was in his service. He explained:

> "Neither you, nor I, nor the congress of Peru, nor of Colombia, can break and violate the basis of public law which we have recognized in Spanish America. The basis is that republican governments are being founded within the limits of the former viceroyalties, captaincy generals, or presidencies, like that of Chile. Upper Peru is a dependency of the viceroyalty of Buenos Aires, just as Quito is a contiguous dependency of Bogotá. Although Chile was a dependency of Peru, yet it was in reality separated from Peru some time before the revolution began, just as Guatemala was separated from New Spain. Thus both of these presidencies might rightly become independent of their old viceroyalties; but neither Quito nor Charcas can rightly become independent except by an agreement embodied in a treaty resulting from a war between the parties, or resulting from the deliberations of a congress."

Bolívar concluded by reminding Sucre that the convocation of an assembly was in itself an act of sovereignty. And more than that, the provinces which he had called to exercise sovereign power, would, by that very act, separate themselves from the other provinces of Argentina. Argentina, Peru, and Colombia could certainly not look upon such a proceeding with indifference. He chided Sucre for a lack of moderation. He had assumed the rôle of a San Martín who had, as a military commander, issued an *estatuto provisional*. He instructed him to stick to his task as a military commander to await further orders from him. The congress of Peru was at that very moment considering what powers to give Bolívar in regard to Bolivia. He did not yet know what the decision of the congress would be, and that as soon as a decision was made Bolívar would so inform Sucre. And he concluded by urging him to do nothing that would cause either Colombia or Peru any sacrifice through the liberation of Bolivia.[32]

The receipt of this letter caused consternation among the leaders of Bolivia and gave great grief to Sucre, but he continued the military activities. Failing in his efforts to induce General Olañeta to submit, he defeated him on April 2 in the Battle of Tumusla. Olañeta died from the wounds received in this battle the day after. Scholars are not disposed to give Olañeta much credit for developing a nationality, on the ground that the nationality had been developing all through the colonial period. They contend that the spirit of independence is a heritage of the civil wars between the Pizarro and the Almagro factions.

The establishment of the *real audiencia* of Charcas in 1559 was a recognition of that fact. Geographically, lying between Lima and Buenos Aires, about half way, it was a real entity in itself, a mediterranean land, which continued to develop as such. Its cities of Charcas, Potosí, Cochabamba, La Paz, Tarija, Santa Cruz, and Oruro had become important centers of wealth and culture. The University of San Javier in Charcas had come to be one of the greatest institutions of higher learning in the new world. The establishment in 1776 of the celebrated *Academia Carolina* added great prestige to an already very famous *real audiencia.* With the wealth and culture it was to be expected that a nationality distinctly Bolivian, and differing from anything else in the Indies, would be developed. The separation of the *Presidencia de Charcas* from the Viceroyalty of Peru, and its incorporation with the Viceroyalty of Buenos Aires in 1776 merely tended to accentuate this feeling of nationality. Whatever may be the real facts in this silent process of a nationality, the fact remains that in 1825 there was already a nationality clamoring for expression.. It had also developed a leadership giving articulate expression to its troops and its aspirations.

The interest of Argentina and Peru in Bolivia took concrete form early in the year 1825. On February 8 the congress of Argentina authorized the *poder executivo* to send Juan Antonio Alvarez de Arenales, governor and captain-general of the Province of Salta, to the four provinces of Bolivia to help the people determine their political future. The people were to be allowed to settle that question for themselves.[33] On February 23 the constituent congress of Peru passed a *resolución* pre-

---

[32] Bolívar to Sucre, Lima, February 21, 1825. Lecuna, *Cartas del Libertador,* IV, 263-265.

[33] *Colección oficial de leyes, decretos, ordenes . . . de la república boliviana, años 1825 y 1826* (La Paz), 5.

scribing the manner in which Sucre was to handle the situation in Bolivia. It gave Bolívar permission to take the united liberating army to any part of the country to destroy its enemies. He was authorized to establish provisional governments in the provinces, of a nature most appropriate to the circumstances. In the event that Bolivia was separated from Peru, the government to which Bolivia belonged should indemnify Peru for the cost of emancipation.[34]

On May 9 Argentina formally recognized the independence of the provinces. It sent a delegation to formally thank Bolívar for the services rendered in behalf of the liberty and independence of America, and for the work for law and order which the united liberating army had done in Bolivia. Argentina declared that the provinces of Bolivia had the unquestioned right to determine, for themselves, their political future.[35]

The congress of Peru resumed its sessions on February 10, 1825. Dictator Bolívar gave an account of the use which he had made of his powers during the previous year, and asked to be relieved of his dictatorial functions. It is hardly to be exepected that he was earnest in this matter, or that the congress had any notion of granting his request. His dictatorship was extended for another year, and he set about the realization of several of his pet plans. As early as December 7, 1824 he had issued his celebrated invitation for a congress at Panama. He began to plan for the larger confederation with which idea he had been concerned for several years. *Gran Colombia* was to serve as the nucleus about which a United States of Spanish America, possibly of the Americas, might be built.

In the meantime, he was to make certain that Bolivia would not be lost, but be made into a part of the larger Bolivarian ideal. The creation of Bolivia, which is, after all, the central theme of the year 1825, was not an accident, nor were the interests of Bolívar in that country either as simple or as innocent as they may seem to be on the surface. The creation of this new state, which was to bear his name, was really a very clever stroke of statesmanship. No other power in South America at the time, not even Brazil, was able to do the work as well as Bolívar. There can be no question but that he had in mind the ultimate annexation of Bolivia as well as Peru to *Gran Colombia*. The creation of Bolivia as an independent republic was done to allay any real fear on the part of the other South American states. In time, as will be seen, he

[34] *Ibid.*, 6.
[35] *Ibid.*, 10-11.

sought to have the constitutional régime which he established in Bolivia extended to Peru and to *Gran Colombia.* In order to be able to move about from place to place, unhampered and unincumbered, he decreed on February 24, 1825 the delegation of his powers to a *consejo de gobierno,* composed of La Mar, president, and Sánchez Carrión and Unánue to serve, of course, under his orders. With the establishment of this *consejo,* Bolívar was free to give his attention to Bolivia. And by April 1825 he was ready to undertake a tour of inspection of south Peru and Bolivia.

The tour of inspection which was to keep Bolívar away from Lima for exactly ten months began on April 10, 1825. On May 15 he arrived in Arequipa, remaining there until June 10, when he left for Cuzco. It was while in Arequipa that he decreed the creation of the Bolivian state, as some historians are wont to speak of this act, by approving the act of Sucre on February 9 convoking an *asamblea general* in Oruro for April 15, 1825.[36] This decree was issued on May 16. The acts of the assembly would receive no sanction whatever until the congress of Peru, which was to meet in 1826, had authorized such acts. In the meantime, the provinces were to remain under the immediate authority of Sucre, and to recognize no other central authority than that of Peru until the question had been disposed of by the congress of Peru.[37] On June 3 he decreed that the assembly should meet in Chuquisaca of June 24.

[36] *Ibid.,* 13.

[37] Lecuna, *Cartas del Libertador,* IV, 316-319. On May 15 Bolívar had written a long letter to Sucre from Arequipa, declaring that he approved of the policy which Sucre had inaugurated in Bolivia. It was, after all, no more than right and just that the people should be given a right to choose their own form of government. In order to keep out of the picture Bolívar declared he would not go to Bolivia until the assembly had taken some final action. He would thus be in a better position to deal with Argentina. He ordered Sucre to use great care in keeping the military out of the political activities. The military was to be kept away from the places where elections were held and the troops must be kept at least twenty leagues away from the meeting place of assembly. He would visit Cuzco, Puno, and La Paz, and would remain away from Chuquisaca until after the assembly had taken its action on the future of Bolivia. On May 20 he wrote a long letter to Santander from Arequipa. He took note of the article in the *Morning Chronicle* in which Mollien stated that Bolívar was not well versed in political philosophy, and that his education in general had been very limited. Bolívar declared that while he had not studied the philosophy of Aristotle he had studied Locke, Condillac, Buffon, Dalambert, Helvetius, Montesquieu, Voltaire, Malby, Filangieri, Lalande, Rousseau, Rollin, Berthot *y todos los clásicos de la antigüedad, así filósofos, historiadores, oradores y poetas; y todos los clásicos modernos de España, Francia, Italia y gran parte de los ingleses.* And he concluded with the statement: *Yo multiplico las ideas en muy pocas palabras, aunque sin orden ni concierto.* Lecuna, *Cartas del Libertador,* IV, 333-338.

On June 23 he arrived in Cuzco. He was very much impressed with the ancient capital of the Incas. He gave voice to his sentiments in many letters from this city. In that to Olmedo of June 27, thanking him for a famous poem, and praising the beauty and charm of Cuzco, *el país clásico del sol, de los Incas, de la fábula y de la historia. Aquí el sol verdadero es el oro; los Incas son los vierreyes o perfectos; la fábula es la historia de Garcilaso; la historia la relación de la destrucción de los Indios por Las Casas.* He marvelled at the achievements of the Incas, especially at the fact that they were accomplished without aid from foreign countries. He saw grandeur in the work of Manco Capac because there was more or less of poetry about it.[38]

It was in this classic city of the Incas that Bolívar took certain measures for the good of the Indian people. On July 4 he abolished the title and power of the *caciques.* In the preamble he explained that the constitution of Peru did not recognize inequalities among the citizens, that the hereditary titles had all been abolished, and that the constitution did not recognize the power of the *caciques.*[39]

The second decree of the same date abolished all personal service of the Indians and declared them on a basis equal with that of the other citizens. The constitution of the state declared that all the citizens were equal before the law, and since the Indians had not been recognized as enjoying these rights, he decreed that no citizen would be allowed to demand personal service of the Peruvian Indians, either directly or indirectly, without a contract, freely entered into by them, and for a compensation. All the prefects of the departments, governors, and judges; all ecclesiastical prelates, curates, and their lieutenants; owners of estates, *hacendados,* and owners of mines were forbidden to employ the Indians contrary to their wishes in *faenas, séptimas, mitas, pongueajes,* and in all other domestic and rural labor. He further prohibited the governmental authorities from exacting labor from the Indians for public works, and ordered that all citizens were to do their share of that kind of work. Nor were the Indians to do any service in the army without pay and without their consent.[40]

---

[38] Lecuna, *Cartas del Libertador,* V, 6-8.

[39] *Colección oficial de leyes . . . de la república boliviana,* 30. The old *caciques* were to be treated as citizens of the country, entitled to respect and consideration by the authorities. The powers formerly exercised by them were to be exercised by the local authorities. This bit of legislation, like that of San Martín, and the other bits of legislation by Bolívar for the improvement of the lot of the Indians, was much too idealistic for the Peruvian people. And during the hundred years after independence they have not improved much in their relations with the Indians.

[40] *Colección oficial de leyes . . . de la república boliviana,* 30.

A third decree of that same date dealt with land tenure among the Indians. Again the preamble gave the reasons for the decree: the colonial officials had never divided the lands proportionately, the great majority of the Indians had been deprived of their best lands, and much of the land left in the hands of the Indians had been taken from them illegally by the Spanish. The small amount of land left to the Indians had been detrimental to agriculture and the prosperity of the state. Articles III, IV and V of the decree of Trujillo of April 8, 1824, on the division of the communal lands, were to be in force in Peru. The lands were to be redivided and upon a more equitable basis. This was to be done by persons of honesty and intelligence, appointed by the prefect of the departments.[41] The Indians were to be recognized as having a right to private ownership of lands.

However much one may admire, ideally, the zeal of the Liberator in behalf of the Indians of Peru, the cold fact remains that he was proposing reforms which could not be carried out at the time even by him. That the reforms were essential to real progress can, of course, be admitted; and had he remained in power for a generation or more, he might have enforced many of them; but the very large number of Indians involved and the opposition to be met in an effort to enforce these laws made the problem too great even for a Bolívar to solve. To have given the Indians political equality with the whites, the logical goal of his reform measures, would have brought about a mighty change in the whole life of Peru. But Peru was hardly ready for such a drastic reform.

The interest of the great Liberator in a *confederación americana* has already been referred to. It was natural that this idea should have undergone further development in the sacred city of the Inca empire. Bolívar had now come to the conclusion that such a confederation was possible only if placed under the protection of Great Britain. He was aware of the objections against a formal defensive and offensive alliance with Great Britain, but it was a question of existence. A confederation in league with Great Britain would continue to exist; without such a

[41] In redividing the land three considerations were to be held in mind: the lands belonging to the *caciques* were not to be disturbed, and to the *caciques,* who had no lands, lands were to be given; the Indians who had no land were to be given a mole of land that was rich and fertile; and the land which had been taken away from the Indians in 1814 and given to those who were loyal to the king of Spain was to be returned to the Indians from whom it had been taken. They were to receive also a third as much land in addition to the original amount held by them at the time the lands were taken from them.

relationship the confederation could not exist. He had no desire to be the head of such a confederation and was willing to subordinate himself for the good of America. Under the protection of Great Britain America would go forward in great style. *El senado britanica existe en su mayor vigor, es decir su aristocracia que es de un carácter inmortal, indestructible, tenaz y duro como la platina.* Salvation for America lay in uniting its destinies with those of the British people. Outside of the Britannic constellation, or possibly against it, where would America be? Here was a fine piece of work for the American Congress at Panama to tackle. Great Britain was to be a member of that great body, otherwise all would be lost.[42]

He was also concerned with the situation in Bolivia. It gave him an opportunity to do good. He would establish a government there that was to be a classic example for American governments to follow. The people were already beginning to call him their "Father." He was already the father of three republics and about to be called the father of a fourth. The efforts had been noble and he was satisfied with his work.[43] There were three parties in Bolivia. One favored independence, and it was the largest. Another favored incorporation with Peru, and a third favored incorporation with Argentina. He had no doubt about the outcome, and firmly expected to find the question settled by the time he arrived in Chuquisaca.

Bolívar left Cuzco on July 28 and arrived in Puno on August 5. His reception in Puno was even more friendly than in any other place in which he had been, all of which pleased him greatly. He thoroughly enjoyed such expressions of gratitude; his soul lived on it. It was while in Puno that he again took great interest in the grandeur of the past of these regions. Copacabana and Tiahuanaco both appealed to his poetic instincts and he let his vivid imagination have full sway. He left Puno on August 13 and arrived in La Paz on August 18. Here he was informed that Bolivia had declared its formal independence on August 6, the anniversary of the Battle of Junín, independence from all the nations

---

[42] Bolívar to Santander, Cuzco, June 28, 1825. Lecuna, *Cartas del Libertador,* V, 11-14.

[43] Bolívar to Santander, Cuzco, July 10, 1825. *Ibid.,* V., 26-30. Space does not permit further statements of the views and activities of the Libertador in these mighty natural and cultural forces. He was now in the very heart of Incadom and could be expected to make the most of it. Letters from these places repay careful study. They help reveal another side of his remarkable makeup.

of the new world as well as of the old. The bombastic character of the declaration[44] may be judged from these excerpts:

> "The Lion of Iberia, hurling itself furiously from the pillars of Hercules to the empires of Moctezuma and Atahualpa, has for many centuries torn to pieces the unfortunate body of America, and has fed upon its substance. All the nations of the continent can show the world their deep wound as evidence of the dilaceration they have suffered; but *Alto Perú* has even more enormous ones, and the blood it has shed is the most authentic monument to the ferocity of that monster.
>
> "The world knows that *Alto Perú* has been, on the continent of America, the altar whereon was spilt the first blood of the free, and the land wherein exists the tomb of the last of the tyrants: that Charcas, Potosí, Cochabamba, La Paz, and Santa Cruz have made constant efforts to throw off the peninsular yoke; and that the irretractibility of its vows against the domination of Spain, its heroic opposition, have arrested a thousand times the impetuous marches of the enemy in regions which, without this, would have been enchained, or would save themselves only by the final and most prodigious efforts."

The account of Bolívar in Bolivia would not be complete without some notice of the conduct of the deliberative assembly towards him. The assembly passed, August 11, 1825, a decree which has been called the "deification" of Bolívar, although Sucre came in also for much glory. As evidence of the eternal gratitude to the immortal liberator of Colombia and Peru, to the valiant and virtuous Grand Marshal of Ayacucho, to the liberating army, and to the memory of the dead *Altoperuanos* who created an independent nation, the assembly decreed that this new state should be called the *República de Bolívar.* Bolívar was the good father and protector of the people against the dangers of disorder, anarchy, tyranny, and unjust invasions of every kind. He was to have supreme executive power within its borders and the honors of the protector and president of the Republic. August 6 and July 24 were to be celebrated as civic holidays, the first for the Battle of Junín, the second as the birthday of Bolívar. December 9 was also to be thus celebrated in honor of the Battle of Ayacucho, and Sucre's birthday was also to be celebrated every year. One million *pesos* were to be distributed to the men of the

---

44 *Colección oficial de leyes . . . de la república boliviana,* 14-18. The assembly met in the classic *aula magna* of the *Universidad de San Xavier de Charcas.* It was a suitable place for such an august body and for such a great cause: the *Universidad* was indeed the cradle of their liberties. The document was signed by deputies representing the departments of La Paz, Cochabamba, Charcas, Potosí, and Santa Cruz, forty-eight in all.

united liberating army, the victors of Junín and Ayacucho, as a small premium for their services. And a million *pesos* were set aside for Bolívar. Who would not be a dictator for less reward than this?

Bolívar left La Paz on September 20 and arrived in Oruro on September 24. While here he was planning a constitution for the new state. He felt that the government should be highly centralized, uniting the advantages of those of the United States and Holland, having something of the *gobierno vitalicio* and the liberties of federalism about it.[45] On October 5 Bolívar arrived in the wealthy and powerful city of Potosí, where he was received on a scale of munificence far exceeding anything he had thus far received. General Miller, the Englishman who had played such a large and honorable part in the wars of emancipation, as president of the Department of Potosí, had attended to that. He was entertained in a manner worthy of a monarch. Sagárnaga declares that Rome displayed no more joy at the news of the fall of Carthage, or Thebes at news of the victories of Leuctra and Mantinea, than Potosí did on this memorable day of October 5, 1825, for Bolívar.

One of the most important events in the visit in Potosí was the official reception, the first presidential act of Bolívar in Bolivia, to the Argentine diplomatic mission. The mission, composed of Carlos M. Alvear and José Miguel Díaz Vélez, had come to perform a dual service: to thank Bolívar in the name of the people of Argentina for his great services to the American states in the war for political freedom and liberty; and to urge Bolívar to continue to help the emancipated peoples defend their newly acquired liberties.

Argentina had a right to expect at the hands of the Dictator of Peru a kindly reception. She had given the *Altoperuanos* full liberty to determine their future status. She had a right to expect that Bolívar would aid her in return. She was determined that the Province of Tarija should not be incorporated with Bolivia, and she was fully determined to prevent the Brazilians from enlarging their territories at her expense in Uruguay and Paraguay. She felt that Brazil was an enemy of all Spanish South America, and Bolívar was the man to keep her in check. Bolívar had already forced the Brazilians to recognize his right to Bolivia, and had driven out the Brazilian forces that had invaded Bolivia.[46]

[45] Bolívar to Santander, Oruro, September 25, 1825. Lecuna, *Cartas del Libertador,* V, 94-96.

[46] On March 28, 1825, Sebastián Ramos, governor of the Province of Chiquitos had ceded, on his own authority, the province to Brazil. Sucre would have none of this and sent a force under Francisco López to reconquer Chiquitos from Araujo e Silva, Brazilian commander. He was easily successful, but Sucre was ordered by Bolívar not to carry the war into Brazil.

Alvear and Díaz Vélez had come to negotiate an alliance, offensive and defensive, with Bolívar. The mission was formally received on October 16, but failed to get him to agree to an alliance. He expressed his opinion that any aggressive measures by Brazil against the Spanish American states could not be tolerated, but he declined to take an active part in any war between Argentina and Brazil. Before some definite action had been taken by the America Congress of Panama any alliance would be premature. No doubt the temptation to play a rôle which would have proved greater than any he had thus far played was very great; but he saw no immediate excuse for such a rôle at the time. The Bolivian question was still a rather delicate one, and a neutral policy appealed to him as the wisest course to follow until that question had been solved satisfactorily. Bolívar did agree not to permit Tarija to join Bolivia, much to the consternation and displeasure of the Brazilians. The astuteness of Bolívar lies in his refusal to grant the request of the people of Tarija to join Bolivia. He realized what the Argentine envoys apparently did not, that the people of Tarija would come into the new state despite the objections of Argentina, which happened in 1826.

No account of the visit of Bolívar to Bolivia would be complete without reference to the ascent of the Cerro de Potosí, Bolivia's Mountain of Silver. October 26 was chosen for that event, and proved to be a spectacular one, matched only, if at all, by the visit to the Aventine Hill. The event in Rome was a fervent dedication to a cause, while the visit to the Cerro de Potosí was a celebration of a cause that had triumphed. Bolívar, attended by Sucre, Miller, Alvear, Díaz Vélez, Lanza, Urdininea, Simón Rodríguez, Córdova, Lara, La Mar, O'Leary, Soublette, Silva, Braun, Estenós, Wilson, Ferguson, Lacroix, and the authorities and the *élite* of the city, began the ascent in the morning of that glorious day. Nature was at her best, and the scene from the peak, more than fifteen thousand feet above the level of the sea, was indescribably majestic. The ceremony on the peak was in keeping with the purpose of the occasion. Many women of the city took part. The distinguished and beautiful María Joaquina Costas, assisted by María Téllez, represented Venezuela, Juana Tinajeros represented *Nueva Granada,* Joaquina de la Quintana represented Ecuador, Rita Trigosa represented Peru, and Lucía Ramírez represented Bolivia, and they all paid appropriate honor to the Liberator. Never had the speakers been in better form; and none so more than Bolívar himself. Always the actor in search of the dramatic and the sensational, Bolívar found the Cerro de Potosí a suitable stage for his eloquence and his histrionic ability. With the flags of Bolivia, Peru, Colombia, and Argentina planted on the top of the peak, and waving majestically in the rarified breezes from the four corners of America, Bolívar was in his element. In his *Mi delirio en el Chimborazo* he was not as brilliant as in the address on this occasion.[47]

Bolívar left Potosí on November 1 and arrived in Sucre in November 3. The reception in the classic city of Chuquisaca was in keeping with the traditions of this cultural center of Spanish America. Santa Cruz, as president of the Department of Chuquisaca, had seen to that. After all, there was no city in Spanish America, with the possible exception of Lima, superior to Chuquisaca at the time. The eternal springtime of its climate, the brilliancy of its cultural, social, and political institutions, traditionally the greatest in Spanish America, and the luxurious life of the people made it a most captivating city. Morales declares that the reception given to Bolívar here was the greatest ever given to man in Bolivia. The celebration of the anniversary of Ayacucho was a most brilliant affair.

Bolívar did much to help organize the government of the Republic in Chuquisaca. On December 22 he abolished the *tributo* paid by the Indians, and ordered that all should pay taxes according to their ability to pay. The *tributo* was again levied in 1826 and has been paid by the Indians ever since that date, to the shame of the great Bolivian people. This is a heritage from the colonial period which Bolivia does not seem able to get from under. On December 28 Bolívar established the port of Cobija with the name of La Mar, and on the next day he decreed that the General constituent assembly should begin its sessions on May 25, 1826. On December 30 he delegated the authority he had in Bolivia to Sucre. In the event that Sucre was unable to perform the duties of the office, Santa Cruz was to take his place. On December 31 Bolívar exercised his power over ecclesiastical matters. He decreed the separation of the curates of Sicasica, together with ten others in the Department of La Paz from the Archbishopric of La Plata and incorporating it with the Bishopric of La Paz.[48] This was a rather drastic measure even for

[47] Luís Subieta Sagárnaga, *Bolívar en Potosí* (Potosí, 1925), 84-86. The ceremony is described in great detail by Sagárnaga. Lecuna in the *Cartas del Libertador* reproduces two pictures from the famous artist Tito Salas, one entitled *Mi delirio en el Chimborazo,* volume III, between pages 52-53; the other entitled *Bolívar, Alvear y Sucre en el Cerro de Potosí,* volume V, between 146-147. Both of these give the setting especial attention.

[48] *Colección oficial de leyes . . . de la república boliviana,* 85-88, 96. Bolívar prescribed three kinds of taxes: a personal tax, a property tax, and a tax on the professions, the arts, and the industries. Every man between 18 and 70 years paid a

a dictator to take. As a matter of fact, Bolívar had taken several steps to curb the power of the clergy on this tour. On August 7, he decreed the separation of the provinces of Chucuito and Huancane from the Bishopric of La Paz and ordered them incorporated with the Bishopric of Cuzco. On June 25 he ordered La Fuente to send the Bishop of Cuzco out of the country if he did not issue a certain pastoral letter, and to embargo the goods which the brother of the bishop had in Spain.[49] On November 14 the bishop of La Paz was suspended from his office because he refused to take the oath to the new government.[50] He exiled Friar Andrés de Los Remedios and Friar Manuel del Transito for the murder of Friar Cristoval de la Magdalena, Prefect of the Betlemites, and ordered a school established in the monastery of the Betlemites in Cuzco. He founded a hospital in Cuzco and one in Urubamba, and ordered the monks in the convents in Cuzco to pay for these two hospitals.[51] The clergy opposed these acts but to no avail. Bolívar, like San Martín, would brook no opposition from the ecclesiastical authorities in the affairs of state.

The year 1826 saw Dictator Bolívar wrestling with the question of whether he should continue his dictatorship. He issued a proclamation on January 1 in which he promised that Bolivia should be a free and independent state.[52] On January 3 he left Chuquisaca for a brief visit to Cochabamba. He was so impressed with this city that he wanted it to be the capital of the new state. He went to Tacna and there received a delegation from Arica who petitioned him to incorporate Arica with Bolivia, but this he opposed. This was the second group of people he failed to aid. He may have acted wisely in both instances, but there is a large body of opinion against him, especially in the case of the people of Arica. He committed a great wrong in not permitting the annexation of that port to Bolivia, despite the fact that he had both the Chileans and the Peruvians to conciliate in the matter. It is hard to understand Bolívar's conduct in the four cases: Guayaquil, Bolivia, Tarija, and Arica. He embarked on board the *Chimborazo* at Tacna on February 2 for the return voyage. He arrived in Chorillos on February 7 and in Lima on February 10.

---

tax of 3 *pesos* a year. The soldiers in active service, the monks in monasteries, and the invalids, morally as well as physically, were exempt from this tax. The amount of tax on property and industry was also prescribed.

[49] Lecuna, *Cartas del Libertador,* V, 4-5.

[50] *Colección oficial de leyes . . . de la república boliviana.*

[51] Vargas, *Participación de Colombia en la libertad del Perú.*

[52] *Colección oficial de leyes . . . de la república, boliviana,* 97.

The ten months' tour of inspection had been a great success, although there may be great doubts as to the advisability of retaining dictatorial powers for that length of time. It is the opinion of many historians that he should have laid down his great powers after the Battle of Ayacucho, or at least on February 10, 1826. The war had been won by that time, and there was really no valid reason why he should have the dictatorship. The powerful Spanish party was anxious to have him continue in power and had little difficulty in persuading him to continue his rule. These critics do not, it may be said, pay enough attention to the importance of the Bolivian question. In the mind of Bolívar this was a question of the greatest importance, as has been seen, for he had no desire to leave this great region to the mercies of either Argentina or Brazil. Nor was he disposed to permit the question to cause a war between Peru and Argentina, or between Brazil and Peru, which it might easily have done. In any event, Bolivia was created an independent state and war was averted—an achievement worthy of another year of Bolivian dictatorship. Bolivia had been created, but it was not until May 18 that the *consejo de gobierno* of Peru recognized her as an independent state.[53]

The congress of Peru met on February 10. Bolívar appeared before it and gave an account of his administration of the preceding year. He asked to be relieved of his office, but the congress refused. He stood firm, but allowed the people to believe that he could be induced to continue as dictator. According to Miller, the Peruvians attempted, by almost every means within their power, to induce him to continue in power. The Peruvian women, too, sought to urge him to remain in power. And he remained on. To a group of fair ladies he said:[54]

> "Ladies! silence is the only answer I ought to give to those enchanting expressions, which bind not only the heart but duty. When beauty speaks, what breast can resist it? I have been the soldier of beauty, because liberty is bewitchingly beautiful; she diffuses happiness, and decorates the path of life with flowers."

The feeling towards the great Liberator, however, had undergone a great change. The Peruvians in increasingly large numbers came to questions his honied words and fair promises. What was he really striving to do? What was his objective? The Peruvians feared that he was trying to bring Peru into the Colombian union. He was becoming increasingly autocratic. He was arbitrary and tyrannical. On April 15 he ordered the execution of the sentence of death against Berindoaga,

---

[53] *Colección oficial de leyes . . . de la república boliviana,* 187-188.
[54] Miller, *The memoirs of General Miller,* II, 304.

despite the fact that a very large number of Peruvians besought him to spare his life. Berindoaga was convicted of treason, a very heinous crime in the opinion of Bolívar. He even went so far as to tell those who remonstrated with him that he did not believe much in the conscience of men, or in the law. On August 7 he acted much in the same way in regard to the execution of Aristizabal. The Peruvians became rebellious, revolts broke out in different parts of the country against his rule, but he remained on and did not seem to know when to quit.

Of course, there were reasons why Bolívar wanted to remain on. Most of his great objectives had not yet been achieved. There was the fundamental law which the Bolivians had requested him to write. He was determined to make this law the greatest document of its kind yet produced. He put into it the best that was in him, and with a view to serve his purpose. He was, in other words, not making a constitution merely for Bolivia but for the larger political entity which he had in mind: the *Confederación Americana.* The document was finally ready by May 25 and was sent on to Chuquisaca in the care of Bedford Wilson. It was accompanied by an address to the general constituent assembly.

In view of the fact that much thought has been given of late to Bolívar's views on religion, it is well to note that in the *projecto* for the constitution for Bolivia, he deliberately left out the question of a state church. He explained the omission in these words:[55]

> "Legislators! I shall make mention of an article, which in my conscience I ought to have omitted. No religious creed or profession should be prescribed in a political constitution; for according to the best doctrines concerning fundamental laws, these are the guarantees of civil and political rights; and as religion touches none of these rights, she is, in her nature, not to be defined in the social order, and belongs to intellectual morality. Religion governs man at home, in the cabinet, and in his own bosom, within himself; she alone has a right to examine his most secret conscience. The laws, on the contrary, consider and view the exterior of things; they only govern out of doors, and not within the houses of citizens. Applying these considerations, how can the state rule the consciences of its subjects, watch over the fulfilment of religion, and reward or punish, when the tribunals of all those matters are in heaven, and when God is judge? The inquisition alone could replace these in this world; and is the inquisition, with its incendiary faggots and piles, to return amongst us?

---

[55] Miller, *The memoirs of General Miller,* II, 493-494. A more detailed study will be made of this whole question in the writer's forthcoming work on *The political organization of Bolivia,* to be published by the Carnegie Institution of Washington.

> "Religion is the law of conscience. Every law on this subject annuls religion, as, by imposing necessity upon duty, it would take away the merit of faith, which is the basis of religion. The precepts and sacred dogmas are useful and luminous; they rest on metaphysical evidence; and we ought to profess them; but this is a moral, and not a political duty.
>
> "On the other hand, what are the rights of man with regard to religion in this world? They are in heaven. There is the tribunal which recompenses merit, and renders justice according to the code dictated by the Legislator. As all this belongs to divine jurisdiction, it strikes me, at first sight, as sacrilegious and profane to mix up our ordinances with the commandments of the Lord. It therefore belongs not to the legislator to prescribe religion; for the legislator must impose penalties on the infringment of the laws, to avoid their becoming merely expressions of counsel and advice. When there are neither temporal penalties, nor judges to inflict them, the law ceases to be law.
>
> "The moral development of man is the first intention of the legislator. As far as this development has taken place, man supports his morality by revealed truths, and professes it *de facto,* which is the more efficacious, the more he has acquired it by his own investigation. Besides, fathers of families cannot neglect their religious duties towards their children. The spiritual shepherds are bound to teach the knowledge of heaven; the example of the true disciples of Jesus is the most eloquent lesson of his divine morality; but morality is not commanded, nor is he who commands it the master, nor ought force to be employed in giving counsel. God and his ministers are the authorities of religion, which operates by means exclusively spiritual; but by no manner of means is the national body a religious authority, that body having solely the direction of public power to objects purely temporal."

The project divided Bolivia into the departments of Potosí, Chuquisaca, La Paz, Santa Cruz, Cochabamba, and Oruro, and these into provinces and the provinces into cantons. The form of government was popular and representative, the sovereignty emanating from the people and exercised by the electoral, legislative, executive, and judicial branches of the government. The electoral power was vested in the people, while the legislative power was vested in the tribunes, the senators, and the censors. The first held office for four years, the second for eight, and the third for life. The executive power was vested in a life president, elected by the legislature, a vice-president, and secretary-ministers of state. The president nominated his successor who was elected by the legislature. The president was not responsible for the acts of his administration; that responsibility lay with the vice-president and the ministers. The judicial power was vested in a supreme court, provincial courts, and justices of the peace. The government of the departmental units was highly centralized and under the immediate dependence upon the national government. The municipalities were not given an independent existence, but were administered by the national government. There was a bill of rights which contained the usual civil and political rights. There was also a provision for amending the instrument.[56]

There have been few instruments which have been more severely criticized than this *constitución vitalicia,* as it is called. It has been condemned as a mere camouflage for a monarchy, an unadulterated aristocracy, insuring the government of the country to the politically *élite.* Others have found it an instrument peculiarly well adapted to the people for whom it was drawn. No one knew better than Bolívar the peculiar difficulty of establishing a government of law and order in Spanish America. The life presidency was meant to be, what the monarch is in England, an institution which ensures peace, law, and order in the state.

Bolívar remained in Peru because he could best survive, so he thought, the larger ideals he had in mind. In addition to the constitution for Bolivia, he was working hard on the plan for the *Confederación Americana.* He could not have played the game in Colombia because he was not in power in that country. As a dictator of Peru he was master of the situation, and could speak with authority.

In a letter to Sucre of May 12 he explained in detail the plans he had in mind for this larger union. He declared that the *consejo de gobierno* would recognize the independence of Bolivia and would propose a pact for the union between Peru and Bolivia on the basis of the union of Colombia. The union was to be under a federal form of government and as nearly perfect as possible. But he wanted a larger union, a federation of the three republics: Peru, Colombia, and Bolivia. He outlined, in the large, the constitution which he thought should be drawn up for this larger union. It resembles the *constitución vitalicia* which he was preparing for Bolivia. There was to be a president, a vice-president, and three chambers. The government was to be highly centralized, but federal in character. The vice-president, the three chambers, and the secretaries of state were to govern the *confederación.* Each one of the three republics was to have the same number of secretaries of state. The capital of the *confederación* was to be in Quito or Guayaquil. There were to be one flag, one army, and one nation. He would

[56] Miller, *The Memoirs of General Miller,* II, 496-519.

divide *Gran Colombia* into three states: Venezuela, Cundinamarca, and Quito. The *confederación* was to be called, he thought, *Boliviana.* In any event, Bolivia could not remain outside the *confederación boliviana,* because Argentina or Brazil would seize her. He believed that Chile, Argentina, and Guatemala would join this larger union. Sucre was to work to induce Argentina to accept these principles. And finally, Sucre was not to fear Brazil, because Great Britain was with Spanish South America and would take care of Brazil.[57]

He has undergone a change of heart about the Congress of Panama. Writing to Santander on August 8 he declared that Colombia would have to save herself, neither the *constitución vitalicia* nor the *confederación boliviana* would save her. As for him, he would make no more sacrifices for her, he feared the hordes of *africanos* in Colombia.[58] In a letter to José Antonio Páez of the same date he dealt harshly with the Congress of Panama.[59]

The invitation to this congress had been issued while Bolívar was Dictator of Peru, and so falls within the boundaries of this discussion. The United States, Brazil, Great Britain, and Holland were also invited. The congress did not assemble in Panama until June 22, 1826, and adjourned on July 15. Only Peru, Colombia, Mexico, and Central America attended. Great Britain sent a delegate, as did Bolivia, although the latter did not attend the congress. Holland sent an observer, and the United States appointed two delegates, neither of whom attended the congress. Anderson died on the way, and Sergeant never even left the United States. Inasmuch as Bolívar did not take a personal part in the congress, and since he did not give it the thought and attention that it deserved, there is no need of entering into a discussion of the details of that body. The congress must, however, have a place among the plans of Bolívar while in Peru, because of the larger ideal which prompted it. The conference idea cannot be said to have failed, and the Congress of Panama of 1826 has become the prototype for all subsequent international American gatherings. And for that fact Bolívar deserves great credit.

VI

The dictatorship of Bolívar was drawing to a close, despite these larger ideals. On August 26 the *consejo de gobierno,* under the presidency of Santa Cruz, adopted the *constitución vitalicia.* On August 15

---

[57] Lecuna, *Cartas del Libertador,* V, 289-295.
[58] *Ibid.,* VI., 46-48.
[59] *Ibid.,* VI, 49-52.

Bolívar finally gave the authorities of Peru his answer to their plea to remain among them as dictator. He declined to accept the election as life president which the adoption of the above constitution meant, and he declared that he had been called back to Colombia. And on September 1 he issued the decree which separated him from his supreme powers in Peru. He decreed that Andrés Santa Cruz and the ministers of state were to assume the powers which he was laying down.[60] On September 3, he issued a formal proclamation to the people of Peru, urging them above all else to guard against anarchy. If they had a real horror of anarchy, he felt that they would prosper.[61] He embarked the same day at Callao bound for Guayaquil on board the *Congreso*. The dictatorship of Bolívar in Peru had come to an end. He had reigned in the land for three long years.

Opinion will always differ as to the merits and demerits of the Bolivarian dictatorship in Peru. In many respects he may be said to have founded not only the Republic of Bolivia but that of Peru as well. It was he who finally liberated them both from the rule of Spain, and Peru from the rule of the protectorate. That he was not as innocent in assuming the dictatorship in Peru, as it is sometimes made to appear, need not be taken seriously. No dictatorships really are innocent creations. The thesis has been maintained that Simón Bolívar deliberately sought the rôle of dictator in Peru, and that he sought to perpetuate himself in that rôle as long as it suited his purposes to rule the country. That he performed acts of transcendant importance to the peoples of Peru and Bolivia, as well as to the peoples of the new world, while exercising the dictatorship, cannot be gainsaid. The difficulty lies in determining whether those acts furthered the general welfare of these peoples. Vargas declares, that Bolívar, like Napoleon, the son of democracy, ended up as an autocrat; and that his creations, made at the point of the bayonet, vanished like the mist before the sunshine. It is only truth, he maintains, that can produce lasting results.[62]

Peru may have needed the "strong man" in 1823 and 1824. San Martín had failed to help the people govern themselves. In plain point of fact, he deliberately strove to prevent them from doing so. Therein lies the greatest wrong he committed against the Peruvian people. For Bolívar to have continued that policy, and to have made the rule of the dictator so obnoxious, makes him doubly culpable. These two men, as

[60] Ayarza, *Reseña histórica del senado del Perú* (Lima, 1921), 84-85.
[61] *Ibid.*, 85.
[62] Vargas, *Participación de Colombia en la libertad del Perú*, III, 186.

has been maintained throughout, failed as statesman, delaying the creation of a real democracy for generations, intensifying, rather than reforming, that innate love of unrest with which the people are cursed. The love of revolution, the juggling with the public debts, the mania of public employment, and the overweaning love of a professional career, were all aggravated by these two prototypes of dictators. Vargas holds that the two liberators did not want to create free republics, but wanted to form groups of people who thought as they did and over whom they might rule for the rest of their lives. The main factor was *personalismo.*[63]

The departure of Bolívar did not put an end to the baneful Colombian influence in Peru. The result was the *motín militar* in Lima on January 27, 1827. The situation was saved by the *consejo de gobierno* agreeing to the demands for the abolition of the *constitución vitalicia* and the departure of the Colombian troops from the country. The Constitution of 1823 was substituted for that of 1826. The Colombian troops were embarked at Callao on March 19 and March 21 for Guayaquil. Thus it was that the Republic of Peru actually became an independent sovereign state on January 27, 1827. A strong sentiment was developed against Bolívar, Luna Pizarro returned from exile, and the people turned to the formation of a government of their own, free from the trappings and the pomp and the show of foreign dictators and foreign counsellors. But the age of the dictators did not end with the removal of foreignism. The age had merely begun. It was to continue as long as the crop of *caudillos,* trained in the school of San Martín and Bolívar, lived on.

---

[63] *Ibid.,* III, 253.

CHAPTER EIGHTEEN

DICTATORS GAMARRA, ORBEGOSO, SALAVERRY, AND SANTA CRUZ

I

THE history of Peru from 1828 to 1842 is the history of four men, primarily. These dictators can best be treated as a group, even though Salaverry was out by 1837. Gamarra began and ended the period. Agustín Gamarra was one of Peru's most notorious *caudillos.* He was of humble origin, the son of an Indian woman by Padre Saldivar. Born in Cuzco on August 27, 1785, he was educated in the Franciscan *Colegio* of San Buenaventura. But he preferred the army to the priesthood and early became a soldier in the Spanish army. On January 24, 1821 he joined the patriot cause. San Martín sent him to aid Arenales in the *sierras.* He began revolutionary activities by taking a part in the *motín militar* of 1823 against the *junta gubernativa.* He was rewarded by Riva Agüero with the appointment as chief-of-staff to General Santa Cruz. He took a very prominent part in the celebrated campaign of 1824, serving in Junín and Ayacucho. Sucre earned his undying enmity by failing to promote him after the Battle of Ayacucho. Since La Mar had a large share of honor in that battle, Gamarra classed him with Sucre. Bolívar appointed Gamarra president of the Department of Cuzco, and he lost no time in securing more power. He was a typical *cholo,* and next to Santa Cruz one of the most distinguished *cholos* in Peru. Francisca Zubiaga, the brilliant *cuzcueña* whom he married, was a very powerful political figure. She gave him political support of a very important nature. She was fully as ambitious as her husband and possessed greater political talent than he.[1]

Gamarra began active opposition to President La Mar from the very first, on the ground that he was not a Peruvian. Whatever may be said of Gamarra, he was, as he understood it, a patriotic Peruvian. He was born in Peru and he lived and died for his country. He may have erred, and erred grievously, but he cannot be said to have lacked patriotism in any of the many crises through which he passed. He turned his attention to Bolivia as soon as La Mar was elected. La Mar had one great

---

[1] Doña Francisca made her salon a rendezvous for the political friends of Gamarra. She presided over gatherings in her salon with a grace and a charm that won her undying fame. No history of Peru of that day would be complete without an account of the life and activities of this extraordinary woman.

ambition. He wanted to square accounts with Bolívar for seizing Guayaquil, and for the wrong done to the *guayaquileños* by that act. Gamarra supported him. Gamarra's great interest lay in squaring accounts with Bolívar for the creation of Bolivia. He wanted Bolivia reincorporated with Peru. La Mar gave him permission to take an armed force to the boundary of Bolivia. In 1828 he was ordered to go to Arequipa to aid the Bolivians drive the Colombians out of Bolivia. Gamarra contacted leaders in Bolivia, among whom were Pedro Blanco, José Ballivián, and Casimiro Olañeta. While the details of these intrigues are still shrouded in considerable mystery, the purpose was to force Sucre to resign the presidency of Bolivia and to cause the Colombian troops to leave the country. The conspirators were able to bring about the *motín militar* of April 18 in Chuquisaca. Sucre was badly wounded and appointed a *consejo de ministros* to whom he delegated his powers. General Urdininea, president of the *consejo,* was ill-prepared for the position. Gamarra wrote to Sucre offering to take an army into Bolivia to help him, fearing that Sucre might be assassinated. Sucre had a conference with Gamarra on the banks of the Desaguadero, but declined to accept his offer of military aid. Gamarra crossed the Desaguadero, despite the refusal of Sucre to accept his help; and moved about leisurely, capturing La Paz, Oruro, Potosí, and Chuquisaca. On July 6 he compelled the Bolivian government to sign the Treaty of Piquiza, one of the most infamous treaties of all history. Iturricha declares it to be a résumé of all the perfidies.[2]

The instrument provided that the congress of Bolivia should be called in special session for August 1 to receive the resignation of Sucre, to appoint a provisional government, and to convene a constituent national assembly. This assembly was to abolish the Colombian political institutions and substitute its own in their stead.[3] The congress was duly convened but failed to meet until August 3. In the meantime Sucre prepared to resign, after having read his Farewell Address, but this he was unable to do. He decided that the congress did not wish to begin its session while he was still in Chuquisaca. He resigned his office on August 1 and left Chuquisaca on August 2. The message was read to the congress and his resignation accepted.

Sucre was a victim of circumstances and of ingratitude, suffering for the sins of Bolívar, whose faithful servant he was. Iturricha claims

---

[2] Agustín Iturricha, *Historia de Bolivia bajo la administración del Mariscal Andrés Santa Cruz* (Sucre, 1920), 248.

[3] José María Santivañez, *Vida del General José Ballivián* (New York, 1891), 26.

that Bolívar was one of those men who held that since they have rendered the state a great service they were entitled to exercise the supreme power. He lacked modesty, loved to bask in the sunshine of public popularity, always seeking ovations of the populace. Modesty and disinterestedness were not his forte, refusing to immolate himself for the sacredness of the cause for which he fought. His greatest error lay in his failure to curb militarism, extolling it, placing it at the zenith of his ideals, and making it the instrument by which he achieved power and through which he sought to perpetuate himself in power. Ultimately it brought about the diminution in his glory and relegated him to the rank of a mere militant *caudillo*. Infinitely worse is the fact that he set the example for his subordinates. He was obsessed, as were they, with the love of power. What a heritage he left for his lieutenants, many of whom continued to play the game for another thirty years. Iturricha concludes that Bolívar must take the blame for the whole period of *caudillismo* and *personalismo* in government. What a political leader cannot get in a lawful way, he can get through the use of force of arms, and with no more right than might. Bolívar merely placed the people whom he helped liberate from the thraldom of Spanish absolutism in the thraldom of militant *caudillismo*. He rooted out the fine principles of democracy in his insatiable desire for personal aggrandizement. He made the sword the arbiter of the destinies of nations. He made *extranjerismo* a problem in Bolivia, in the solution of which she undid much she had done and delayed her progress for decades.[3a]

Gamarra remained in Bolivia until after the assembly had begun its sessions. He was opposed to the selection of Santa Cruz and Velasco, and sought to place Blanco in power. He was able to do so, but was to see his puppet removed from power, after having served for five days, and assassinated. The party of Santa Cruz again secured the upper hand, and Bolivia was freed from the baneful influence of Gamarristic intrigues for the time being. Gamarra returned to Bolivia with his troops on October 17, and took up his headquarters in Arequipa. Vargas is of the opinion that Gamarra was the real founder of Bolivia, but admits that he was not actuated by high and noble motives. Gamarra did the work for his own glory and personal advancement. He undertook the invasion of Bolivia in order to discredit the government of La Mar and to have himself elected president of Peru. Despite that fact, Vargas

[3a] Iturricha, *Historia de Bolivia*, 53-55.

maintains that while it was Bolívar who drove the Spanish troops out of Bolivia, it was Gamarra who made Bolivia an independent nation.[4]

Gamarra made much of the fact that he had freed Bolivia of foreignism and made her an independent republic in his proclamation to the Bolivian people of September 26. He declared that her continued existence as an independent nation rested with herself. She might through her new assembly reform the hated *constitución vitalicia.* He added that the inauguration of the new assembly would mark the beginning of the glory and prosperity of the country, stating that the Peruvian army had returned to its own country happy in the thought that it had liberated a friendly and a sister nation. He concluded with the advice, so strange from his lips, that the people should shun revolution, anarchy, and disorder, for in so doing they would make their country great, prosperous, and happy.[5]

In the letter of September 3 from Chuquisaca Gamarra declared that the work of regenerating Bolivia politically had been achieved and with an absolute transformation of its government. She had been elevated from the ranks of a vassal state to one of real freedom. It is worthy of note that Gamarra used the term *Alto Perú,* thereby giving evidence of his great life work, the reincorporation of Bolivia with Peru.[6] On September 4 Casimiro Olañeta replied, declaring that Gamarra had achieved great glory by aiding the Bolivians emancipating themselves from the rule of a foreign country. Bolivia would always be grateful to him for that great service.[7] Olañeta also wrote the Colombian government a note, dated October 11, threatening war upon Colombia should Colombia declare war upon Peru. He declared that the Bolivian people were grateful to Peru for her aid in getting from under the fundamental law, that was *la vergüenza de la especie humana, porque es el pacto de los opresores de los pueblos con cuatro parásitos.* Bolivia refused to live under the rule of Colombia.[8] Vargas declares that Gamarra had undertaken the invasion of Bolivia without authority from the government of Peru, and that it was a revolutionary act for which he deserved the fate of a traitor. On the other hand, the revolution was necessary to crush the bolivarian despotism.[9]

---

[4] Vargas, *Historia del Perú independiente,* IV, 184.
[5] Iturricha, *Historia de Bolivia,* 337.
[6] *Ibid.,* 338-342.
[7] *Ibid.,* 342-345.
[8] Iturricha, *Historia de Bolivia,* 354-355.
[9] Vargas, *Historia del Perú independiente,* IV, 165.

Instead of punishing Gamarra, La Mar sought his aid in the war with Colombia. La Mar laid the whole Colombian coast, between Tumbes and Panama, under a blockade on September 9. Sucre sought to settle the differences between the two countries amicably, but failed. Then came the attempt to assassinate Bolívar on October 25, which also failed through the timely medium of Manuela Saenz. War resulted between the two countries, and despite the efforts of Argentina and Chile the war continued until March 1829 when the Treaty of Girón was signed. The terms of the instrument were humiliating enough for Peru, forcing her to evacuate all the territory occupied by her in Colombia and to reduce her army to 3,000 men, to the appointment of a commission to settle the boundary questions, to respect the independence of each country, and to abstain from interfering with each other's domestic affairs.

The disastrous termination of the war with Colombia merely intensified the rivalry between Gamarra and La Mar. The two men began the contest for control of the state, La Mar seeking the support of Vivanco and Gamarra that of La Fuente and Santa Cruz. La Mar was defeated, arrested on June 7, and exiled shortly thereafter to Costa Rica, where he died in 1830. It was an inglorious ending to the career of one of the greatest heroes of the year 1824, for La Mar ranks with Sucre and Bolívar in the successful campaigns before Junín and Ayacucho. Like them he died in the year 1830, a martyr to a great cause.[10]

Gamarra had achieved the object for which he had been fighting, assuming provisionally the presidency of the country. On August 31, 1829 he was elected president of Peru by the congress, and La Fuente was elected vice-president.[11] They were inaugurated on December 20.

One is concerned with them here only as they strove to lay the basis for future political contests. Gamarra became involved with Santa Cruz of Bolivia. These two great rivals were the rulers of their countries, Santa Cruz having taken office in Bolivia almost seven months before Gamarra took office in Peru. These two men were determined to rule a greater Peru. Of the two, Santa Cruz was by far the abler man, in fact he was the most powerful figure in the two republics. He was making an excellent beginning in Bolivia, laying the foundation of that country on a very solid basis, and displaying statesmanship of the highest order. In short, he was laying the stage on which he was to play, for

---

[10] Of the three men, Sucre died first, having been assassinated on June 4. La Mar died on October 11 and Bolívar on December 17.

[11] Gamarra received fifty-five votes out of sixty-two votes. He was opposed by La Fuente, Bermúdez, Orbegoso, and Reyes.

ten long years, a rôle second in importance only to the *Libertador* himself.

Gamarra feared Santa Cruz. He had been forced to play a secondary rôle to him in the military campaigns of the movement for independence. He realized, as few did, the potential power in Santa Cruz: his great popularity in Peru as well as in Bolivia, his wealth and social position, and his great military ability. He realized also that Santa Cruz could rather easily convince the people of his sincerity; he himself had much more difficulty in doing so. This was one of the great weaknesses of Gamarra and the one obstacle to his larger success: he could not convince the people that he meant well. They took him to be a mere *caudillo,* bent upon obtaining an objective for the mere satisfaction of attaining it.

Santa Cruz had little difficulty in getting the people of Bolivia to support him in his policy towards Gamarra. The gratitude which the people of Bolivia appeared to have felt for him in 1828 was not very deeply rooted. There had never been any very great love between the people of *Alto* and *Bajo* Peru, in the first place, the statements of ardent patriots of Peru to the contrary. One may even go so far as to say that the two peoples had never really been united, the deadly feud between the followers of Pizarro and Almagro having established a chasm between them early in the conquest days. The two peoples developed independently, with two distinct nationalities by the time of emancipation. Gamarra as a loyal *cuzceño* knew that fact full well. Had not his favorite city been a pawn between the Pizarros and the Almagros? The *cuzceños* had long memories, which even a love child like Gamarra could not destroy.

Santa Cruz began at once to show more than the usual interest in Puno and Arequipa. He appeared to Gamarra determined to square accounts with him for the invasion of 1828. The two men had measured wits under Bolívar, Santa Cruz having been president of the Department of Chuquisaca and Gamarra of the Department of Cuzco. Gamarra knew the great ambition of Santa Cruz to take over the leadership when Bolívar should finally lay it down. Besides that fact, Santa Cruz had already been the ruler of Peru, as president of the *consejo de gobierno,* during and immediately following the dictatorship of Bolívar. Gamarra had a good right to fear Santa Cruz.

The discontent in Peru resulted in new political complications. The nature of the rôle Santa Cruz played in fomenting that discontent is still a very much mooted question among historians. There can be no question but that Gamarra strove to prevent Santa Cruz from invading Peru by an offer of an alliance between the two countries. The mission of Mariano Alejo Alvarez had that for its main purpose. In the meantime, Gamarra succeeded in having the boundary differences with Colombia solved satisfactorily. The solution secured him Jaen and Mainas, and served to raise his prestige. The common charge against Santa Cruz is that he employed both money and men in a campaign of propaganda in Peru. There can be no question but that Santa Cruz was laying the stage for an ultimate invasion of Peru.

The *motín militar* of Gregorio Escobedo in Arequipa on August 25 and 26, 1830 brought on a crisis in the relations between Santa Cruz and Gamarra. On September 4 Gamarra left Lima for Arequipa to put down this *motín,* which proved an easy matter. Gamarra moved on to Cuzco. Santa Cruz moved military forces to the Desaguadero as soon as he had learned that Gamarra had reached Cuzco. He was determined to take no chances with Gamarra. Gamarra acted in this crisis in typical *caudillo* fashion. He proposed a friendly alliance with Santa Cruz, and at the same time asking the congress for powers to invade Bolivia. An interview between the two took place on the banks of the Desaguadero on December 15, 16, and 17, but with no other results than a postponement of hostilities. Olañeta had made the demand that Arica should be ceded to Bolivia, which Peru refused.

The death of Bolívar caused a great change to come over both groups. With the passing off the stage of the great disturbing element in Colombia, the danger from that source was removed. *Gran Colombia* fell to pieces almost as soon as the Liberator died—in fact the dissolution had begun before he died. No one of the three countries into which *Gran Colombia* was now divided could cause either Peru or Bolivia much concern. It is true that Flores, the father of independent Ecuador, gave them some concern, but he did not prove a formidable danger. The situation in Argentina was rather serious in 1831, but Santa Cruz succeeded in remaining neutral, although he sought to mediate between the two warring factions. The recognition of the independence of Bolivia by the King of France in June 1831 gave Santa Cruz added prestige. On the other hand the effort of Santa Cruz to secure a more important frontage on the Pacific, gave Gamarra some concern. Few men saw more clearly than Santa Cruz the need of more and better ports for Bolivia. He made Cobija a free port by 1833 in order to encourage the commercial activities of his countrymen. The importance of this move to Gamarra lay not merely in the effort to secure more ports, but rather in the fact that Bolivia was becoming a nation of power in the world of trade. He could always count upon the support of Chile in the event the Bolivians became commercially too powerful.

The plans of Gamarra for a war with Bolivia were destined to failure by the events in Peru itself. The most important of these was the break between Gamarra and La Fuente. When Gamarra went to Arequipa to crush the Escobedo revolt, La Fuente was left in charge of the national administration. He suspended the law prohibiting the importation of flour, and a struggle between them began. Luna Pizarro supported La Fuente, and Riva Agüero was on the side of Gamarra. Doña Francisca also took an active part. La Fuente was deposed and went into exile on April 15, taking refuge on board the *Saint Louis* under command of Sloat.[12] Andrés Reyes took La Fuente's place as president *ad interim,* serving until June 7, when Gamarra reassumed the presidency. The congress remained unfriendly to him, and on June 29 Gamarra again left Lima for the south of Peru. The trouble between Bolivia and Peru was again amicably settled, the Treaty of Tiquina and the Treaty of Arequipa were signed, the latter on November 8. By the latter treaty Gamarra promised to keep the armed forces down to three thousand men, Santa Cruz to one thousand six hundred. It also called for nonintervention in the internal affairs of each, the prohibition of seditious activities of political refugees within the republics, and the recognition of existing boundary lines until a commission had settled the differences over that matter.[13] An additional treaty was signed on January 4, 1832 by which Bolivia was allowed two thousand troops for her army and the right of each state to impose duties on wines, sugars, vinegars, and liquors from Europe. It was not until March 23, 1833 that a treaty of commerce was signed between them.[14]

The relations between Gamarra and Santa Cruz continued menacing, Santa Cruz being accused by Gamarra of aiding La Fuente, who had

[12] Sloat was placed in the embarrassing position, common throughout revolutionary America, of being asked to afford an asylum to men unsuccessful in revlutionary activities. They request such an asylum as a matter of right. Sloat, however, declared that he would not protect La Fuente and would surrender him upon request from the government.

[13] Oscar de Santa Cruz, *Andrés de Santa Cruz,* 383-386. This contains the text of the Treaty of Tiquina and that of Arequipa on pages 387-393.

[14] Casto Rojas, *Historia financiera de Bolivia,* 119-123. Rojas defends the treaty of commerce, although he confuses it with the Treaty of Arequipa, but admitting that there are historians who question its importance. Basadre declares that Cortez and others criticize it, and states that the Treaty of Chuquisaca was printed in *El Conciliador* of March 23, 1833. Consult *La iniciación de la república,* I, 215, note 84.

taken up his residence in Bolivia after his overthrow in 1831. On June 14, 1831 the national assembly of Bolivia had approved all the acts of his dictatorship, conferring the title of *Gran Ciudadano Regenerador de la Patria* and giving him full powers to expel from the republic all persons who should interfere with the constitutional order or who sought to promote disorder. Basadre declares that Santa Cruz sought to emulate his ancestor Inca Manco Capac. In any event Santa Cruz had done a great piece of work in Bolivia, infusing some of the spirit of Manco Capac into the administration of the country. Santa Cruz had also begun to practice Incaic ceremonials. National *fiestas* were held in honor of his wife, elaborate ceremonials for the baptism of his children, and in his own honor.[15] Santa Cruz was laying the basis for a wise, benevolent, and glorious reign, albeit he did it as dictator.

Gamarra and Santa Cruz were moving farther and farther apart. Gamarra was nursing his desire to subjugate Bolivia, despite the fact that the years 1832 and 1833 did not bring forth much for that end. And Santa Cruz nurtured his plan to dominate Peru. Gamarra continued to make enemies within Peru. He was especially unfortunate in the management of the army, persisting in retaining foreign officers despite the great opposition to them. The law of December 12, 1831 giving the president the right to reform the whole army system, gave Gamarra the power to get rid of such officers as Cerdeña, Cortez, Pardo de Zela, Benavides, Necochea, Miller, Plaza, Escudero, and Plasencia, all called *suizos*. *Los suizos* became the butt of attack by the press, and the feeling against them grew more and more intense. On January 1, 1832 Ramón Castilla was arrested because of the part he took in the revolt of that night. Finally the movement against foreign officers in the army became so great that the congress repealed the law of 1831. On March 18, 1833 a plot was discovered to assassinate Gamarra.[16] It was in connection with the anarchic months of 1832 that Vidaurre made his celebrated declaration: *He de reinar el orden. Si fuese preciso, callarán las leyes para mantener las leyes.*

On December 27, 1832 Gamarra resigned the presidency but the congress refused to accept it. The *consejo de estado* presented a series of formal charges against Gamarra for acts committed during the recess of

[15] Basadre, *La iniciación de la república,* I, 216-217.

[16] Felipe Rosel was the leader of this plot. He was executed March 19. He died with the *eclat* which is so often displayed by men of the revolutionary classes about to die. *Rosel marchó al patíbulo como se marcha a una parada* declares Santiago Távara.

the congress. The chamber of deputies discussed these charges, but failed to impeach the president, the vote being twenty-one to thirty-six.[17] The opposition to Gamarra grew in volume. The elections for the national convention were held in accordance with constitutional procedure. Gamarra did not await the convening of the national convention but called a special session of the congress.

In the meantime, Salaverry had appeared upon the scene. He was charged with conspiracy against Gamarra and was ordered exiled. He protested against this act because he had not been tried in accordance with law, and stated that he was innocent of the charge. He published a letter in which he called upon the people to awaken from their lethargy, declaring that tyrants only flourished through the cowardice of the people. All who really wished to be free could be free, the people having the power if they would but use it. Immediately after the appearance of this letter, he was arrested, the government maintaining that he was involved in a conspiracy to assassinate Gamarra. While in prison Salaverry continued to publish articles against the government, and was exiled to Mainas. He began a revolt there and was removed to Cajamarca. Again he continued his revolts, defeating Vidal, who had been sent with a force against him, and won the brilliant victory over Vidal at *Garita de Moche.* Again on November 19 Salaverry defeated Vidal. In these engagements Salaverry had proved himself a very dangerous revolutionary.

The press also took up the attack upon Gamarra. *La Verdad, El Telégrafo de Lima,* and *El Penitente* took part. Doña Francisca was criticized. A form of writing, called the *beata,* became popular. The older established periodicals, like the *Convencional, El Constitucional,* and *El Genio del Rimac,* also took up the questions of the hour. The discussions centered about the nature and the purpose of government. The value of government depended upon the men at the head of it: good men could do great good, evil men great evil. *La Verdad* began the defense of strong government, after the fashion of Moreno and Monteagudo in the *Sociedad Patriótica. El Conciliador, La Oliva de Ayacucho,* and *El Atalaya de Cuzco* took up the defense of strong government. The strong government was a government unrestricted by a constitution, and controlled only by a strong executive. The constitution was attacked because it provided a weak executive, by placing too

[17] The discussions over the charges presented against Gamarra in the chamber of deputies had taken seventeen days and were spirited. But the opponents of the president lacked the necessary votes to bring about the impeachment of that officer.

many restrictions upon his power. The great danger of liberalism lay in the emphasis upon the many rather than upon the few.[18]

The concluding months of Gamarra's administration were marked by defeats for Gamarra. The special session of congress, which he had called, failed because of the lack of a quorum. The national convention met July 6, but failed because of the determined opposition of Gamarra. Gamarra took the position that the national convention had convened illegally, and could have no power to usurp the authority of the national legislature. The national convention began its sessions, however, on September 12, and for some months its time was taken up in conflicts with the chief executive.[19]

The main work before the convention was the drafting of a new political constitution. Luna Pizarro again showed his great ability as a statesman and a parliamentarian. He was the president[20] of the national convention, and under his guidance that body declared itself constituent and proceeded to draft the new fundamental law. In the midst of its labors, the question of a new president for the republic came up, Gamarra's term expiring on December 20. There were four candidates before the convention: Bermúdez (Gamarra's candidate), Niete, Riva Agüero, and Orbegoso. Orbegoso was elected by a vote of forty-seven to thirty-seven, and was inaugurated on December 21.[21] Leave may be taken of Gamarra for the present. With the elevation of Orbegoso to the presidency, he retired to private life to nurse his grudge against his enemies, particularly those who prevented the election of his candidate. Together these two men, Orbegoso and Bermúdez, usher in the next great period in the story.

---

18 Basadre, *La iniciación de la república,* I, 252-260.

19 José Braulio Comporedondo, acting president, in the absence of Gamarra, was opposed to the national convention and impeded its work. The question of the right of certain members to sit in the convention was also a cause of concern. The case of Tellería and Riva Agüero caused trouble. Both were absent from the country at the time of their election, and Comporedondo was unwilling to let them return. When Gamarra reassumed the presidency, November 19, Comporedondo tried to resume his seat in the national convention. This he was refused because he had not submitted to a *residencia,* as acting president of the republic. Finally the convention declared his seat vacant.

20 He had also been president of the sovereign congress of 1822 and of the congress of 1828.

21 Neither Nieto nor Riva Agüro had shown any strength in the convention. Orbegoso owed his election to Luna Pizarro, the powerful deputy from Arequipa. Orbegoso rewarded him by appointment to the Bishopric of Ayacucho. And Santa Cruz later appointed him archbishop of La Plata.

II

Luís José Orbegoso was born August 25, 1795 in Chuquisongo, in the Department of Trujillo. He was the son of Justo de Orbegoso Burutaran y Cortez and the distinguished Doña Francisca Montada, a descendant of the ancient dukes of Olmos. He was to prove one of the most distinguished politicians which the nobility produced, a very great distinction for the nobility continued in power up until the appearance of the "guano bourgeoisie." He was educated in the *Colegio de San Carlos* in Lima; and in 1804 he took up his father's business, the elder Orbegoso having died in that year. On January 19, 1816 he married the celebrated María Josefa Martínez de Pinillos. Orbegoso was one of the most distinguished men of his age, with the character, dignity, and bearing of a man of the old Spanish school. He was physically handsome, personally magnetic, graciously *caballeroso,* humanely a real *caballero:* big-hearted, loyal, and sympathetic. He was truly the *grand seigneur,* to the manner born. Like the members of his class, he did not have an extensive military career. He had the misfortune to come upon the political stage at a time when success was impossible. The woods were, so as to speak, full of pretenders to the dictatorship of the country: Gamarra, La Fuente, Vivanco, Castilla, Echenique, Salaverry, and Santa Cruz. And if more were needed they could be found among the Peruvian exiles in Chile, for Chile was, at this time, a veritable haven for the brood of potential dictators. Among these were Pardo, Beltrán, Arieseuño, Salcedo, Los Negrón, La Puerta, Deustua, Torrico, Escudero, Artaza, González, Taramona, Martínez, Ugarteche, Mariano, Vivero, Lepero, Postigo, Soffía, Mayo, Jiménez, Salmón, Balta, Puertas, and many others.

This rather formidable list of exiles should serve to emphasize a phase of dictatorship which should not be underestimated. The *via dolorosa* is the way of the unfortunate political exile. Proscription and deportation are, next to assassination, favorite means of getting rid of political opponents. The presence of so many exiles in Chile was a matter of grave concern to Peru at this time. Neighboring republics were not infrequently breeding places for revolutions, with baneful results also upon the relations between Peru and her neighbors. The opposition of Chilean leaders was the cause of the fall of Santa Cruz, his implacable enemy in Chile being Diego Portales, ably assisted by Blanco Encalada, Prieto, and Egaña the Younger. The rôle played by these men will be narrated later.

Orbegoso began his administration, as has been noted, on December 21, 1833. Gamarra declared that he would remain out of politics, a statement nobody believed, least of all himself. Dictators are that way. Orbegoso began his work under favorable conditions. The people were heartily weary of Gamarra and the *Gamarristas,* including doña Francisca Zubiaga de Gamarra. Orbegoso's personality appealed powerfully to the better class. He had attained to his high office through legal constitutional means, but above all it was his grand manner and the magnetic charm of his personality that won the people to his side.

He committed, at the very outset, a grave political error in offering Bermúdez a place in his ministry, but Bermúdez declined the offer. Gamarra wanted to continue as the head of the army, a position to which he had been appointed by La Mar. Orbegoso refused to appoint him to that position, and Gamarra and Bermúdez revolted. On January 1, 1834 Orbegoso was to have been assassinated at a performance in his honor in the theatre, but he was informed of the plot and did not attend the performance. On January 4, Bermúdez seized the supreme power of the state, announcing that he had grave doubts as to the legality of the election of Orbegoso. He declared that there would be an election on the first Sunday in February for president and vice-president and that the congress would meet in special session on May 1. Orbegoso had the people on his side and defeated Bermúdez on January 28, and reëntered Lima amid the wildest enthusiasm of the populace. Basadre declares that this enthusiasm amounted to a frenzy, and that for many days Orbegoso was the object of the greatest gratitude and the greatest sympathy. The national convention resumed its sessions on February 6, 1835. Due notice was taken of the events of the revolution, and honors were conferred rather freely upon those it was felt were entitled to them. The city of Callao was given the title of *fiel y generosa* and the *asilo de las leyes y de la libertad.* Orbegoso was made *gran mariscal* and declared to be *benemérito de la Patria en grado heróico y eminente.* And on February 15, 1835 he was given dictatorial powers to enable him to restore order and peace in the republic. He was empowered to seek foreign aid, if that were thought necessary.

The fundamental reason for giving him such large powers was the grave danger to be expected from Gamarra and Bermúdez. Orbegoso used the new powers in a typical dictatorial manner, for he exiled Gamarra, Bermúdez, San Ramón, and Escudero permanently from Peru, and ordered them executed the moment they set foot upon Peruvian soil. He then delegated his supreme powers to Salazar y Baquijano, with the title of supreme delegate. He left immediately for the *sierras,* accompanied by La Fuente, Riva Agüero, Cerdeña, Necochea, and Otero. Miller had gone on ahead in search of Gamarra, and had been joined by Salaverry at Yauli. Orbegoso was fully determined to put down all opposition to his rule in Peru. He had asked the national convention for power to invite the support of Bolivia *para la extirpación de la anarquía.* On April 18 the national convention passed an act authorizing the president of the republic to request such support, but with the distinct understanding that the aid was for *el único y exclusivo objecto de terminar la guerra civil.* Orbegoso kept this law secret for some time.

Santa Cruz had grown constantly more powerful in Bolivia. The country was enjoying peace and prosperity. He was becoming more and more determined to launch his larger ideal. The time appeared ripe for intervention in Peru. He felt that the anarchic conditions there were a great danger to Bolivia. He considered both Gamarra and Salaverry dangerous enemies, for the *caudillos* of Peru had always sought their own personal welfare. Gamarra had taken refuge in Bolivia and might be useful to Santa Cruz. The congress of Bolivia had authorized Santa Cruz in 1833 to prepare to preserve order in Peru. In 1834 he had been requested by Orbegoso to help him restore order there. He denied that Nieto had ever been in his employ, and branded all statements to the contrary false and ridiculous. Gamarra was in favor, according to Santa Cruz, of the Peru-Bolivian Confederation in 1834 on the bases proposed by him. Nieto had done the very thing for which he was accused: breaking up Peru into two states and forming a confederation with Bolivia. Ellespuru had written Santa Cruz on May 23 suggesting the creation of such a union and urging Santa Cruz to assume the headship of the confederation. Santa Cruz declared that the very thing that he was accused of doing, leaders of Peru were proposing.[22]

There were many in Peru who believed that the republic was really a dual state, since North Peru and South Peru were geographically and ethnologically two separate political entities. South Peru and Bolivia have much more in common than do North Peru and South Peru. But the logical division was the threefold one: North Peru, South Peru, and Bolivia. Out of this an ideal confederation might be formed. Luna Pizarro, the celebrated *arequipeño,* had gradually come to the conclusion that a confederation of these three states was the only solution for

[22] Andrés Santa Cruz, *El General Santa-Cruz explica su conducta pública y los móviles de su política en la presidencia de Bolivia y en el protectorado de la confederación peru-boliviana* (Quito, 1840), 65-71.

all countries concerned.[23] On the other hand, Gamarra denied emphatically that he had ever been a party to such an arrangement. He had never changed his mind on the ideal relationship between Peru and Bolivia: a union between the two countries, but with Bolivia in her old place as an integral part of Peru.[24] There is no need of drawing any conclusion except this that both Santa Cruz and Gamarra did not wholly reveal the whole truth about this matter.

Santa Cruz continued to work for his advent into Peru. He appointed Córdova of Arequipa, Bishop of Santa Cruz de la Sierra, and took General Ramón Herrera and Colonel Anaya into the Bolivian army. He sent money to Riva Agüero to enable him to work against La Fuente. He urged Flores of Ecuador to declare war against Peru, sending Colonel Juan Antonio Ayaldeburu to Ecuador for that purpose. Vargas declares that Santa Cruz had tried hard to win La Fuente over to his cause as early as 1832. He had invited La Fuente to come to Bolivia, and La Fuente had lived for some time in Chuquisaca. This did not prove a popular move for either of the men. The people could not understand why so much attention should be given to La Fuente when the two countries were on such bad terms. La Fuente sensed this feeling and he went back to Chile, the favorite rendezvous of Peruvian exiles.

Santa Cruz watched very carefully the turn things were taking in Peru in 1834. In the famous revolution of May 1834, Gamarra, Castilla, Nieto, La Funete, and San Ramón were all fighting Orbegoso.[25] Santa Cruz also watched very carefully the revolutionary activities of Salaverry. Throughout the year 1834 Santa Cruz had also made much use of Guilarte in Peru, learning from him that large armed forces were supporting Gamarra's cause. La Torre, Peruvian minister in Bolivia, who was a supporter of Gamarra, reported faithfully to his colleagues in Peru on the preparations which Santa Cruz was making for eventualities in Peru. La Torre was particularly concerned about the defeat of

---

[23] Basadre, *La iniciación de la república,* I, 277.

[24] Valdivia, *Revolución de Arequipa,* is, according to Basadre, a very good work on this whole period. *La iniciación de la república,* I, 319-320, note 62.

[25] On May 5, 1834 Doña Francisca de Gamarra died in Valparaíso, Chile. It was well for Orbegoso and Santa Cruz that she passed off the stage before they began their efforts to unite the two countries for she might have proved a very formidable opponent to that scheme. The Mariscala Doña Francisca Zubiaga de Gamarra, as Basadre calls her, escaped from Arequipa on May 18, 1834 disguised in the dress of a cleric. She wanted to go to Bolivia, but Santa Cruz denied her permission to enter. She then, in company with Escubedo, embarked on the *Guillermo Rowston* at Islay for Valparaíso. Society turned against her there, even the Peruvians refusing to have much to do with her. *La iniciación de la república,* I, 337.

Orbegoso at Cangallo and Huaylacucho, and the occupation of Tacna by Gamarra and Nieto. On May 18 there was a ray of hope in the opposition of a small force in Arequipa against Gamarra. Orbegoso reëntered Lima May 3 to the great delight of the people.

The year 1834 had also been important in that the new constitution was adopted by the national convention and promulgated as the fundamental law on June 10. Basadre declares that this instrument was meant to be a definite check upon *personalismo,* and was a product of those who opposed Gamarra and Bermúdez. The bill of rights was very important. No Peruvian might be exiled without due process of law, and the domicile was inviolable. *Habeas corpus* was established, recruiting was forbidden except by the regularly constituted authorities, billeting of troops was forbidden except in times of grave danger to the state, forced loans and contributions and taxes not legally levied by the congress were forbidden, the seizure of the supreme power in the state unlawfully was forbidden, and the *residencia* was established for all public functionaries.[26] Immediate reëlection of the president was forbidden and the vice-presidency abolished.

The year 1834 also saw the popularity of Orbegoso waning. The *Señor de los Milagros,* as he was called, had not displayed much ability as a statesman, and had not been able to follow up the victories over the revolutionists. He had been unable to check the orgy of promotions and military appointments by the national convention. He had been unable to pay the officers and men of the army regularly, and that became a great source of real danger to him. He had reduced the salaries of the public employees to about a fourth of their regular figure, and he had thought it necessary to attack the liberty of the press, *El Telégrafo de Lima* becoming the victim because it dared to publish articles against the government.

But the greatest danger to Orbegoso lay in the neighboring republics, especially in Chile and Bolivia. The situation in Chile towards the end of the year was especially critical, not only because of the large number of Peruvian exiles there, but because of the anti-Peruvian policies of its government. Portales, Egaña, and Prieto were bent upon a policy which would destroy Peru's hope of a monopoly of the commerce of the Pacific. The rivalry between Valparaíso and Callao was becoming too strong for the Chileans to accept quietly. To them Valparaíso must

---

[26] Basadre, *La iniciación de la república,* I, 347-348. This document displaced that of 1828, but did not remain very long in force. The dictatorship of Santa Cruz set it aside in 1836 and in 1839 it was replaced by a new constitution.

remain the emporium of the Pacific, permitting no rivalry either from Callao or Guayaquil. The economic phase of the conflict about to begin must certainly not be either ignored or minimized.

The conditions in Bolivia were equally or even more disturbing. The ambitious designs of Santa Cruz were well known to Orbegoso. He sought to conciliate Santa Cruz, and thus postpone the creation of the Peru-Bolivian Confederation. Or if he could not postpone its creation he might at least have a larger share in its creation. But the most important event of the year 1834 was to come from within Peru itself. Riva Agüero and Salaverry both became dangerous to Orbegoso. The latter was to become by far the more dangerous of the two, as will be noted in due time.

III

Felipe Santiago Salaverry was one of Peru's most sensationally remarkable men. And with time he continues to be even more so. He was born in Lima on May 6, 1806, the son of Felipe Santiago de Salaverry and Micaela del Solar Cueva y Estrada. He was educated in private schools, passing the examination in Latin for matriculation in the University of San Marcos as early as 1817. He spent the year 1818-19 in the *Colegio de San Carlos* in Lima. He was a precocious young man, always active and restless, highly imaginative, with a strong and even violent temper.[27] Vargas has very little that is good to say of him. *No tenia un amigo; su trato era peligroso: una distracción, un delito; una ofensa, la muerte,* is his verdict. He was cruel by temperament as well as by condition.[28]

Salaverry entered the patriot army at the age of fourteen, and served with distinction throughout the remainder of the war of emancipation. He was a great friend and admirer of La Mar, for which reason he became an enemy of Gamarra. His revolutionary activities in 1833 have already been noted.[29] In the March 1834 revolution he joined the forces of Orbegoso, and was made general of brigade on June 9. He openly opposed the granting of dictatorial powers to Orbegoso, declaring that a government that resorts to dictatorial powers must fall in the

---

[27] Manuel Bilbao, *Historia de Salaverry* (Buenos Aires, 1867). This book was first written in 1853, and is accounted the best work on this apostle of a new age and a new deal. It is much too lenient on Salaverry and displays much ignorance of the real facts in the life of this dictator.

[28] Vargas, *La historia del Perú independiente,* VII, 90.

[29] His wife, Juana Pérez, daughter of Manuel Pérez and María Feliciana Infantas, was a very brilliant woman, and gave him much support in his military and political work. It was she who secured his release from prison on July 10, 1833.

end. The future of Peru could hardly be expected to be safe through dictatorship.

The year 1835 began disastrously for Orbegoso. The revolt in the Callao garrison on January 1 gave Salaverry his opportunity. He and Nieto crushed that uprising; and Salaverry received the governorship of the *castillos de Callao.* He was no sooner in possession than he began to show signs of ambition. On the evening of February 22 he deported Nieto, and the next day he issued his *pronunciamiento* against Orbegoso. The *consejo de estado* tried to protect the government of Orbegoso but was obliged to leave Lima. Before leaving, however, it had conferred full dictatorial powers upon Orbegoso, which he might use anywhere and without any restrictions whatever. The *consejo* then left for the *sierras* accompanied by Riva Agüero.

On February 25 Salaverry decreed himself *jefe supremo* and took possession of Lima, maintaining that Peru was without a government since Orbegoso was away from the capital. Orbegoso had not governed the people for their good and had merely sought to perpetuate himself in power. An administration was necessary which would free the country from the yoke of bad government. Peru had been independent for ten years, but the people were not free. There had been no real progress in republicanism, the revolution had merely caused a change in rulers, and not in principles. There had only been a *cambio de personas.* The people were not to blame. It was the government that had oppressed them and prevented progress. What was needed? Everything was needed! Democracy must be substituted for monarchy, new codes for the old codes, a new civil procedure to insure the people their civil rights, equality before the law, and a guarantee of public liberty. Prosperity was to come through an increase in the national wealth. The ultimate good of all was of far more importance than the good of only a few, and the ultimate good of the many must mean the greatest degree of happiness for all the people. Names and labels meant nothing. Salaverry declared that he was not guilty of ingratitude in turning against Orbegoso. There was something greater than gratitude, and that was the welfare of the *patria.* Should he serve Orbegoso or the people? He would serve the people, but he had no desire to wage war.[30] The salvation of the country would lie in a new national assembly composed of representatives freely elected by the people.[31]

---

[30] Bilbao holds that Salaverry did not seize power illegally. There was no legally elected power in the state; Orbegoso was a usurper.

[31] Basadre, *La iniciación de la república,* I, 353-354.

A new leader had at last appeared upon the stage of Peru, a man of a different type from the ordinary run of Peruvian dictators. There was nothing new in the ideology of Salaverry. Basadre rightly points out that the ideology in his proclamations was the ideology of the age. The difference lay in the means to be used to attain the ends desired. It was youth who was to regenerate the people, and youth was to provide the leadership. Salaverry was youth personified. He was under thirty, endowed with all that youth boasts: audacious courage, wild-eyed vision, boundless hope, and naïve inexperience. And infinitely more than that, he was gloatingly rejoicing and ever revelling in these possessions.

The seizure of power by Salaverry brought Santa Cruz to Peru. There was no alternative but the use of force to put down the Salaverry dictatorship, the most brazen disregard of legality ever witnessed in that country. The revolt of Salaverry spread rapidly. Gamarra and Santa Cruz sought means to crush it. A union of the two countries was the only solution, the form of the union could be worked out once the new enemy had been removed from the stage.

All the while Gamarra was playing a dual rôle again. He was flirting with Salaverry at the same time that he was playing with Santa Cruz. He was to receive a high position in Peru in return for aid to Salaverry; and he was to receive even a higher position in the new confederation. The confederation was to come about through a division of Peru into two separate States, and these, with Bolivia, to form the new state. With this in view, Gamarra set up a new government in Cuzco, proclaiming himself *presidente* of the *estado del centro del Perú*. Throughout the proclamations which he issued, he assumed the humble rôle of the man who is merely carrying out the orders of the people. He urged the people to support him, promising to make Cuzco the capital of Peru.[32]

[32] This appeal was of importance to the *cuzcueños*. They had never given up hope of having Cuzco made the capital of Peru. It need only be observed, in passing, that few of the cities of Peru were in favor of Lima as the national capital, and that the rivalry between Lima, Cuzco, Trujillo, Arequipa has always been keen. The negotiations, as well as the exact nature of the confederation, were complex in the extreme. Santa Cruz and Gamarra have a different story to tell. Santa Cruz declares that Gamarra urged him to create a confederation of which he should be the head. It was to be composed of the three states in accordance with the plan of Santa Cruz. Santa Cruz thereby definitely disclaims originality for the confederation idea, declaring that the idea was an old one and was supported by many public men, including Gamarra. He also declares that Gamarra agreed with him that a confederation was the best solution of the problems which confronted the two countries. Gamarra emphatically denies that he agreed to the Santa Cruz plan of a confederation. He was in favor of a union of the two countries. He

Santa Cruz, taking alarm at the turn events were taking in Cuzco, began negotiations with Orbegoso. The result was the celebrated Treaty of La Paz of June 15. Bolivia was to send immediately an armed force powerful enough to completely pacify Peru, to be commanded by Santa Cruz or some one acceptable to him. In case Santa Cruz was in command, he was to be commander-in-chief of the armies of both countries. Peru was to bear all the cost of the pacification. As soon as the departments of the south were pacified, Orbegoso was to call an assembly to set up a new state and to enforce the acts of that body. A like reorganization was to take place in the departments of the north as soon as they were pacified. The Bolivian army was to remain in Peru until these objectives had been achieved.[33]

The reaction to these negotiations was pronounced. Salaverry decreed, July 7, the war to the death against the invading Bolivians. He declared that Santa Cruz was not only bent upon crushing his rule but was determined to seize the government of Peru for himself. The Peruvians who should help destroy the Bolivian forces were to be duly rewarded. All those who killed a Bolivian soldier, officer, or chief of the army was to be declared *benemérito de la patria* and exempted from taxation for five years. The same rewards would be given those who refused to give aid to the Bolivians and deprive them of all possible support. Gamarra, who had turned traitor to Salaverry, was to have his armed forces treated in a like manner. The effect upon Gamarra was to drive him out in the open to work against both Santa Cruz and Salaverry, although he leaned more towards Salaverry, with whom he was again to negotiate for a place in his government. Since Santa Cruz has entered upon his rôle in Peru, a brief biographical sketch of his life up to that time may be in order.

IV

The career of Santa Cruz is one of the most remarkable in the history of Latin America, not excepting either San Martín or Bolívar. He was born November 30, 1792,[34] in Huarina, near La Paz. His father was

---

favored the division of Peru into two states and then a union of these three, but under the name and flag of Peru, and under no other conditions whatever. And of course he had not the slightest idea of permitting Santa Cruz to be the head of that union, unless chosen thereto by the people. Gamarra was thus merely reiterating his old pet idea: the reincorporation of Bolivia with Peru.

[33] Santa Cruz, *El General Andrés de Santa-Cruz*, 395-397.

[34] Basadre gives the view that the exact date of his birth is still a mooted question. He gives both 1792 and 1795. On the other hand, Oscar de Santa Cruz gives only the date 1792. There seems little reason for not accepting that year.

José Santa Cruz and his mother María Calahumana, *cacica de Huarina*. The father was Spanish, the mother an Inca princess. The father belonged to the colonial official class, occupying the position of *subdelegado* of Apolobamba in 1810. The mother was a lineal descendant of the last ruling Inca, occupying as such a high position in the socio-political life of the community. It was through his mother that Santa Cruz was able to play a powerful rôle among his competitors. She gave him wealth, social position, and not a little of the fire of the Incaic soul. Her son dreamed of resurrecting the glorious empire of the Incas, and, next to Bolívar, came nearer realizing that dream than any other man.

There was nothing in his formal education that distinguishes him among his contemporaries. It was not of a very intensive character, although he acquired a good style of writing and learned much of the theory and art of government. But his political philosophy was acquired through experience rather than through any wide and intensive study of books on that subject. He chose the army as the most likely career for a young man of his rank, and entered the Spanish service at an early age. He served Spain until he was captured by Arenales in the Battle of Cerro de Pasco, December 6, 1820.

Upon his release he went over, as has been noted, to the patriot ranks. His brilliant career during the wars for independence has also been noted. He was unusually fortunate in his relations with both San Martín and Bolívar. Both of them were greatly taken with him, and gave him preferments which would hardly have come to him but for his wealth and social position. He did not succeed so well with Sucre, for the two men early took a mutual dislike to each other. Both as a prefect and as a president of the *consejo de gobierno* he satisfied Bolívar, for the latter always had a very high regard for this *cholo*. It was Santa Cruz who was able to secure the adoption of the *constitución vitalicia* in Peru, an act which did not enhance his popularity in that country. After his defeat by La Mar for the presidency of Peru he was sent to Chile as Peruvian minister. It was while in Chile that he was elected president of Bolivia (August 12, 1828). He was absent from Bolivia during the fateful months of 1828, as has already been noted.

Santa Cruz had been in no great hurry to return to Bolivia, leaving Valparaíso December 15, 1828, on board the *Aquiles* for Islay. He went to Arequipa, where he remained for several months, awaiting the establishment of peace and order in Bolivia. On March 1, 1829 a commission arrived in Arequipa urging him to come to Bolivia at once. Still he vacillated until the *arequipeños* began to marvel at the manner in which he treated the Bolivians. *La Arequipa Libre,* no doubt voicing the sentiments of other periodicals, even made sport of his indecision, declaring: *Es preciso confesar, que jamás se vió hombre colocado en tan fuerte alternativa. César al pasar el Rubicón no tenía tanta perplejidad.*[35]

But his time had not been spent wholly in idleness. He had organized a secret society, *La Independencia Peruana.* It was said to have been organized on Masonic principles. There were ten members, or *amigos,* who met secretly. The object was to establish and preserve democratic governments. The *gran maestro fundador* was Santa Cruz, who took the name *Hermano Arístides.* The members took a solemn oath of secrecy, the breaking of which was a very, very serious matter: *su pena de que vuestra garganta sea cortada, vuestro cuerpo despedazado y vuestra memoria borrada como infame entre los hombres y en particular entre vuestros hermanos.*

Iturricha declares that Santa Cruz was also hatching great schemes for the future while in Arequipa. He would make himself a great ruler and would perfect the grand ideal which Bolívar was trying to establish. The great Liberator was still living, and, as far as Santa Cruz knew, he was still planning to enlarge *Gran Colombia.* Iturricha maintains that the *protectorado* was conceived in Arequipa, that Santa Cruz made plans for its creation there. The *Independencia Peruana,* founded on April 11, 1829, was a step in the direction of the achievement of that larger ideal.[36] Santa Cruz finally arrived in La Paz on May 19, and on May 24 he took the oath of office as the *presidente* of Bolivia.

The administration of Santa Cruz in Bolivia has already been discussed in certain particulars. The events of that administration, as far as they concern Bolivia alone, have a bearing upon this account only in so far as they affect the dictatorship in Peru. On the very day he took the oath of office, he decreed the classic *ley de olvido,* as it is called. It was a noble effort to conciliate all the different factions of Bolivia. It declared not only a general amnesty, but deliberately drew a veil of oblivion over the past, forbidding all accusations and persecutions of every nature for past events.[37]

For about two years, or up to the meeting of the constituent congress of 1831, Santa Cruz ruled without the benefit of a political constitution.

---

[35] Iturricha, *Historia de Bolivia,* 763.

[36] Unos bolivianos, *Los cinco primeros capítulos del manifiesto de Santa Cruz de 24 de octobre de 1840.*

[37] Santa Cruz, *El General Andrés de Santa-Cruz,* 14-15.

He deliberately refrained from calling the national legislature until the country was calmed and its credit established. Santa Cruz did not have a high regard, at any time, for a government by the people. Their representatives in national congresses are wont, he declared, to make very poor use of their opportunities and of their powers. Too frequently they use their powers despotically, and the oligarchy which is thus established often displays all the evils of which a state may become a victim.

The congress of 1831 met in July and was a body of which Santa Cruz was very proud. It was composed of men of great ability and elevated ideas. These men completed the republican era by giving a political constitution to the country. Before doing so the congress had approved all the administrative acts of the dictator, a favorite practice with all provisional governments in Bolivia. On July 14 it had conferred upon him the title of *gran ciudadano, restaurador de la patria,* and also made him captain-general of the republic.[38] On September 15 it presented him with the medal which had been given to Bolívar.[39] On July 18 it gave him a vote of formal thanks for the services he had rendered the country.[40] It also approved the codes prepared under his direction and ordered them to be called the *Códigos Santa-Cruz.*[41] These codes were the first of their kind in Spanish America, ranking Santa Cruz as among the greatest legislators of his age. He has the great honor of having given to his state the first modernized code of laws for a Spanish American state. Whatever may be the criticism against him for giving his name to the codes, he cannot be deprived of the honor of having conceived such codes and for having made the codes a possibility. On August 14 the general constituent congress elected Santa Cruz constitutional president of Bolivia for a term of four years. He continued to labor for the advancement of the country, encouraging industry and commerce, promoting public improvements, developing education, and pacifying the country.[42]

[38] *Ibid.,* 18, note 1.
[39] *Ibid.,* 19.
[40] *Ibid.,* 21.
[41] *Ibid.,* 18, note 2.
[42] Santa Cruz established the *caja del crédito público* and was able to say that Bolivia was the only country in America without a public foreign debt. He established the University of San Andrés, a College of Medicine, an Academy of Jurisprudence, a College of the Sciences, a Seminary, a new College of the Fine Arts, a Public Library, and a National Institute in La Paz. He established primary schools in many parts of the republic, and was especially interested in the education of the young men in the industrial sciences. He sent many young men to be educated abroad; those in France returned prepared to take up positions in the

Santa Cruz had his critics, as he was bound to have. He believed in efficiency first and democracy afterwards, and progress was possible only through law and order. Those who acted contrary to that fiat were treated roughly, but the marvel is that he did not have to resort to such tactics to any extent. Only his great and growing reputation, his control of the armed forces, and his honesty could carry through the program he had laid out for the country and for himself. He complains bitterly in his *Manifesto* of the lack of appreciation among the people of the work he had done for the welfare of the country. By the middle of the year 1835, when he undertook the pacification of Peru, Santa Cruz was, in many respects, the greatest figure in South American public life. This was the man who attempted the reëstablishment of the great and mighty Inca Empire, the heritage of his mother's people.

The Treaty of La Paz drove Gamarra into the arms of Salaverry. The two men signed a Convention of July 27, 1835, by which the youthful Salaverry promised Gamarra support as ruler of the *Estado Central del Sur*. Gamarra recognized the assembly which Salaverry had convoked as the only legitimate legislative body in Peru. Salaverry also promised to retain in the governmental service all the civil and military functionaries which had served under Gamarra.[43]

Santa Cruz replied by declaring Salaverry outside the pale of law and offering a prize of ten thousand *pesos* for him dead or alive. On July 8 Orbegoso conferred upon Santa Cruz the dictatorial powers which the congress had conferred upon Orbegoso.[44] On July 10 Santa Cruz issued a *declatoria solemne de garantías en favor de la nación peruana,* in which he declared that as *mediador y garante,* which had been conferred upon him, he would carry on the war of pacification in Peru in accordance with the laws of civilized nations. The *potencia mediadora* was a friend of the Peruvian people and would carry out the purpose for which he had been called in the strictest impartiality. In order that this delicate task might be established in the best possible manner he declared that the whole of Peru was under his immediate protection. The *ejército mediador* would maintain the principles of the popular representative system of government, the Roman Catholic religion, and the independence of Peru. He promised to protect deliberating

College of Mining. He was naturally very much interested in the development of the army and succeeded in making it one of the most efficient fighting machines of his age.

[43] Santa Cruz, *El General Andrés de Santa-Cruz,* 461-463.

[44] *Ibid.,* 77-78.

assemblies and to carry out such legislative measures as they might adopt. And if new states, which might be formed, desired to form, with Bolivia, a conferedation, the *ejército mediador* would of course support such an act. In the event such a confederation were formed, a general convention of the confederated states would be called to form a fundamental *pacto federal* for the newly created state. The three states were to be on a basis of the strictest equality, and the army would cause to be respected all the constitutional guarantees. Any Peruvian who should attempt to interfere with the peaceful work of the army would be treated severely.[45] On July 22 the congress of Bolivia, in special session, approved the several acts he had taken in his relation to Peru and authorized him to exercise dictatorial powers until August 6, 1836.[46]

The stage was now set for the pacification of Peru and for the creation of the *Confederación Perú-Boliviana.* There were of course differences of opinion on the legality of all these transactions, in Peru as well as in Bolivia. Vargas contends that Orbegoso had been legally and constitutionally elected president of Peru, and no one questions that the same was true of Santa Cruz. Since the fundamental laws of the two countries granted to the national legislatures the right to confer dictatorial powers upon the chief executive of the nation, there would seem to be no valid grounds for questioning the legality of the proceedings of the two men. Santa Cruz also defended his course upon the larger ideal of the right of a nation to intervene by force of arms if the welfare of the state invaded demanded it. An intervention by Chile in Peru was unjustifiable, but that of Bolivia in Peru, requested by Peru for the purpose of reëstablishing peace and order, was not only justifiable but obligatory. The revolution in Peru was a grave danger to Bolivia, and warranted intervention on the ground of self-defense.[47]

Andrés Martínez, secretary to Salaverry, denied the right of Santa Cruz to intervene in the affairs of Peru.[48] He had not intervened in the affairs of Argentina, where conditions were certainly far more chaotic than in Peru. Why intervene in Peru? *América no es Europa,* and Peru did not need the aid of Santa Cruz; by his acts he was only aggravating the entire situation.[49] The military operations soon settled the

[45] *Ibid.,* 89-90.
[46] *Ibid.,* 92-93.
[47] *Ibid.,* 74-86.
[48] Andrés Martínez, *Contra-exposición que manifiesta la injusticia con que el presidente de Bolivia ha intervenido en los negocios domésticos del Perú.*
[49] Basadre, *La iniciación de la república,* I, 373-374, note 205.

whole question of the right of Santa Cruz to intervene. Santa Cruz met Gamarra on the heights of Yanacocha on August 13 and administered a disastrous defeat. Gamarra escaped. The battle had lasted two and a half hours and netted nine hundred and fifteen prisoners and certain armaments of war.[50] Yanacocha concluded what Santa Cruz termed the first campaign of the pacification expedition. Salaverry removed Gamarra from the presidency of the *consejo de gobierno* in Lima, and on October 19 he ordered Gamarra exiled to Costa Rica. Basadre expresses surprise that Salaverry did not order Gamarra shot, for he deserved that fate at his hands.[51]

Salaverry redoubled his activities upon learning of the defeat of Yanacocha, carrying on with greater fury than ever his order of war to the death. In November began the second campaign of the expedition. Salaverry disembarked at Islay and marched towards Arequipa. The *arequipeños* received him as a usurper and a traitor and refused to give him any aid or support. He abandoned Arequipa for Challapampa. His supporters had also given up Lima.[52] On January 8, 1836 Orbegoso reëntered Lima as a conquering hero. Callao surrendered on January 21, and on January 14 Santa Cruz had declared the men and ships that obeyed Salaverry outside the pale of law.

Fate appeared to have turned against the youth who had raised himself so haughtily and arrogantly to the heights of power, for Santa Cruz, whom he hated so bitterly, was closing in upon him. And on February 7 Salaverry met his Waterloo in the *pueblo de Socabaya.* The defeat was disastrous in the extreme for Salaverry and his cause. He was taken prisoner by Miller together with all his chiefs and officers and more than one thousand five hundred men. Five flags were taken, three of which were sent to La Paz and carried there by José Ballivián. A council of war was organized to try the main officers. Salaverry held that the council had no power to try him, but to no avail. He was condemned to be executed along with his accomplices. February 18, the day of execution, found thousands of people in the *Plaza Mayor* in Arequipa to witness the execution. Salaverry behaved as though he were

[50] Santa Cruz knew how to reward his men. Cerdeña was made grand marshal and Moran general of brigade. Both had rendered brilliant services in the battle. The government of Bolivia awarded gold medals with brilliants for the generals, plain gold medals for the chiefs, and a silver one for the men. The execution of Mariano La Torre took away much of the glory of the victory from Santa Cruz.

[51] Basadre, I, 385.

[52] León and Vivas had played havoc with affairs in Lima on December 28 and 29.

a Messiah and hence a martyr to a great cause; and he wrote a famous protest against his assassination, as he termed his execution.[53]

Those who were shot with him on the same day were General Pablo Fernandini and Colonels Camilo Carrillo, Miguel Rivas, Gregorio Solar, Juan Cárdenas, Manuel Valdivia, Julián Picoaga, and Manuel Moya. Not one of them was thirty-five years of age. Fernandini tried to escape but was killed by the mob, who had little sympathy with any of these leaders. Thus ended the dream of youth in Peru in 1836.

Bilbao has striven to make Salaverry a martyr until the youthful dictator has become a legend among certain people of Peru. On the other hand, a large number criticize him very severely. Basadre declares that Santa Cruz was fully justified in causing his execution, for the personality of Salaverry would always have caused Santa Cruz trouble. Salaverry's dictatorship was the shortest of those dealt with here. Salaverry remains the symbol of youth: fighting at Ayacucho at the age of eighteen, a revolutionary at the age of twenty-six, and a president of Peru at the age of twenty-nine. During all his life he enjoyed all the sweetness of triumph and all the tortures and agonies of failure. He was of the essence of youth with its excessive vivacity, its immense ambition, its rebellion, its temerity, its disdain of age and experience, and its arrogance. Salaverry was born to make revolutions rather than to dominate them. He would begin an enterprise without the least idea of what it would lead to. Men spoke of Gamarra with scorn, of Santa Cruz with odium, of Orbegoso with sneers, but of Salaverry with fear: *el loco Salaverry, el tigre Salaverry,* and like expressions. *Salaverry está en los linderos de la leyenda, pero está también en los linderos de la neurosis,* declares Basadre.[54] The newspapers of the day did not fail to take note of this singular man and his passing. *El Yanacocha* declares on November 18, 1835 that Salaverry was a man of great talent but without wisdom: courageous, scheming, inconsistent, peevish, cruel, indolent, false, and ungrateful. He was irreligious to the point of atheism, corrupt, rapacious, and deceitful; a gambler, prodigal, and at times even avaricious; astute, impudent, vain, boastful, vindicative, and often quixotic. And yet Salaverry could not really be labelled. *Salaverry no tiene modelo: solo se parece a sí mismo,* was the concluding statement of this article.[55]

---

[53] Basadre, *La iniciación de la república,* I, 399-400.
[54] *Ibid.,* I, 402-403.
[55] *Ibid.,* I, 404-405.

The defeat of Salaverry and the restoration of Orbegoso to power in Lima cleared the way for the confederation. The first step was to bring about a division of Peru into two separate states, and was to be accomplished through secessional assemblies. The departments of the south were the first to secede. The assembly of Sicuani, composed of deputies from the departments of Arequipa, Ayacucho, Cuzco, and Puno, was addressed by Santa Cruz on March 17. These excerpts are explanatory:[56]

> "Victory has crowned, at every point, the efforts of the United Army; but in order that the People may enjoy the precious fruits of a lasting peace, it now only remains that you consult the unanimous wishes of your constituents, and that you restrain the impulse of your passions; and of certain injurious prejudices which prevail amongst you; and you will then have it in your power to lay the foundations of reorganization in Peru.
>
> "You can enter upon your duties with feelings of the greatest confidence, free from any compulsion, or apprehension of war, relying on the guarantees by which, in this Treaty, the Government of Bolivia has bound itself, and on the United Army, which will maintain the result of your deliberations."
>
> "You are about to receive a grand problem, namely, whether Peru is in future to be prosperous or to retrograde; the people anxiously await your decision, and desire to know whether their representatives will render them happy or miserable, whether they can rely on the security of their persons and property, or continue ever to be the victims of revolutionary confusion.
>
> "I am an old and faithful friend of Peru; you have summoned me to defend your cause, and, after encountering the perils of war, I have conquered, and thus contributed to confer on you the blessings of peace; you will not refuse to concede to me the right which I possess by these titles, to guard against the difficulties or contentions which have usually prevailed in those Representative Assemblies which have not been regulated by moderation and good feeling, or which have allowed themselves to be influenced by their passions. The measures passed by the Legislative Assemblies, amidst the virulence of party feelings, have always been productive of disastrous results, and, in all probability, they are the primary causes of the anarchy which has consumed the state of Peru. Happily, the Representatives of the Southern Departments, enlightened by the recent misfortunes which they have undergone, and convinced of the indispensable necessity of allowing the people to live in peace, will in all likelihood preserve themselves from these calamities. The qualities required of them give solid grounds for hoping that their meeting will be productive of salutary effects, and that the measures

---

[56] *British and foreign state papers,* XXIV, 770.

which they may pass, inspired by the purest patriotism, will prove that they are worthy of the confidence reposed in them by the people. May Providence encircle this august Assembly with a glory of holy light, and dispel from it the clouds of error; so as to enable its members to see the true interests of their Constituents, to the end that the foundations of a new social reorganization may be laid."

On the same day the assembly decreed the formation of the State of South Peru, ordered its incorporation with the State of North Peru and Bolivia into the Peru-Bolivian Confederation, with Santa Cruz as at its head.[57] A like declaration was made on August 11 by the assembly of Huaura, composed of deputies from the departments of Amazonas, Junín, Libertad, and Lima. The State of North Peru recognized the independence of the State of South Peru. On June 18 the congress of Bolivia, in extra session, approved all the acts of Santa Cruz in the creation of the confederation up to that time. It also extended the dictatorial powers of Santa Cruz to August 6, 1837.[58]

In circulars issued on August 17 and 20, 1836 Santa Cruz declared that the confederation had been duly organized, and that it had been done for the greatest good for all the peoples concerned. He declared, further, that all the American governments should view with satisfaction this effort to preserve peace and order in Peru and Bolivia. The confederation would pursue a friendly policy towards all the foreign powers.[59] And finally on October 28, 1836 Santa Cruz decreed the confederation formally established. The decree, shorn of explanatory statements, reads:[60]

"Considering:

"1. That by Article II of the Declaration of the Independence of the South Peruvian States, dated at Sicuani the 17th of March, 1836, it was pledged to unite itself by bonds of Confederation with the State which is about to be formed in the North, and with Bolivia;

"2. That by the Law of the 22nd of July, 1835, the Republic of Bolivia resolved to confederate itself with the States which might be formed in Peru;

[57] The action was taken in the Sessional Hall in Sicuani, and the document was signed by twenty-three deputies, five from the Department of Arequipa and six from each of the other three departments. The declaration declared that the revolutions of which the whole of Peru had been a victim had arisen because of the union of the north with the south of Peru, and that the only means whereby the general welfare could be served was through a union of these two states with Bolivia in a confederation.

[58] Santa Cruz, *El General Andrés de Santa-Cruz,* 108-109.

[59] *Ibid.,* 478-481.

[60] *British and foreign state papers,* XXIV, 779-780.

"3. That the Assembly of Huaura, upon proclaiming the Independence of the North Peruvian State on the 6th of August, 1836, declared in Article I that it was confederated with the South Peruvian State and with Bolivia;

"4. That by Article IV of the first of the three before-named Instruments, by Article XI of the third, and by the Law of the 19th of June, 1836, passed in Tapacari by the Congress Extraordinary of the Bolivian Republic, I am amply and fully authorized to commence, regulate, and determine everything which concerns the object of the completion of the previously indicated Confederation, and to bring it to perfection;

"5. That by the Congress of Bolivia I am thoroughly empowered to direct the Foreign Affairs of that Republic, and am invested by the Assemblies of Sicuani and Huaura with the whole of the Executive power; and

"6. That it is necessary, in order to satisfy the wishes of the Public, so manifestly pronounced for the Confederation, to hasten the epoch of the new social organization of the three States abovementioned, and to regulate their relations with Foreign Powers;

"I therefore decree:

"Art. I. That the Peru-Bolivian Confederation, composed of the North Peruvian State, of the South Peruvian State, and of the Republic of Bolivia, is hereby established.

"II. That the Congress of Plenipotentiaries charged with the settlement of the basis of the Confederation, shall be composed of three individuals for each of the three above-named States, and shall assemble in the Town of Tacna, on the 24th of January in the ensuing year; to which end my Secretary-General will invite the Government of the Bolivian Republic, and that of the South Peruvian State, to name the Ministers that respectively correspond to each of them.

"III. My Secretary-General shall be the sole channel for all the communications that will have to be expedited or received relative to the Peru-Bolivian Confederation."

Santa Cruz entered Lima August 15, 1836 and took possession of the government of Peru the next day. From the very beginning he experienced opposition to the creation of the confederation. Bolivia had never been enthusiastic about it. The new entity was the creation of a dictator, and despite the fact that there may have been a need for it, the manner in which it was created marked it for failure even before it was formally established.[61] Santa Cruz had learned nothing from his predecessors. San Martín and Bolívar had tried a like experiment and had

[61] Santa Cruz denies that he originated the idea of the confederation, declaring on the other hand he took great pride in nurturing the idea and in bringing about the establishment of the confederation.

failed. Basadre bears evidence to the fact that the assemblies at Sicuani and Huaura had not been free agencies, that the agents of Santa Cruz had carefully supervised their proceedings, and that the army was always in readiness to urge the deputies to do their duty by the idea. Peru and Bolivia may not have been able to govern themselves, but their peoples were not disposed to be mere pawns for a man who strove, so it seemed to them, merely to achieve glory and fame for himself.

Santa Cruz suffered, as did San Martín and Bolívar, from the suspicion of the people as to the real motives of his activities. What was the goal towards which the man was aiming? Was he seeking the welfare of the people, or was he merely working for the love of power, dominion, and prestige? Did he mean to revive the Inca Empire? The people did not forget that he was a *cholo* and was wedded to the traditions of his mother's ancestors. As a *cholo* they believed him possessed of an insatiable ambition. What was the larger game he was playing? Did he know himself? Was he just the opportunist, the mere plaything of destiny? He was thus beset within the confederation itself which might rather easily bring down the whole grandiose idea. Wiesse declares that *santacrusismo* had in it the germs of its own decay. Santa Cruz was too fond of foreigners in his army, a practice which the people of both countries detested. The influence of Bolivia in the domestic affairs of Peru was much too great to hope for the necessary coöperation from the Peruvians. The introduction of the *Códigos de Santa Cruz* into Peru was a distinct mistake for the Peruvians desired to make their own codes. Besides, the codes for Bolivia did not necessarily suit the conditions in Peru. The Peruvians feared, too, should the confederation fall, that their country would remain permanently divided into two separate states, an apprehension which would not down.

The greatest danger to the Peru-Bolivian Confederation was, however, to come from without. While Great Britain, France, and the United States recognized the confederation, the three most powerful states in South America refused to do so. They took the position that the confederation was a menace to the future greatness of South America. They took a hostile attitude towards the confederation from the very beginning, arguing that Santa Cruz was a menace to America. Brazil was in no position to do much because of the troubles within the empire itself, and the weakness of the regency of Dom Pedro *Segundo*. The situation in Argentina and Chile was different. Both of these two countries emerged by 1836 from under revolutionary activities. The former was under the control of the magnificent Nero of America, Juan

Manuel de Rosas. He could be counted upon as brooking no rival in the shape of the confederation. The strong man in Chile was Diego Portales, who had acquired a political philosophy exceedingly dangerous to all national competitors. He had been born in Santiago de Chile on January 26, 1793, and had developed into one of the most sinister, as well as one of the most powerful figures of his age. He was lacking in culture, unprincipled, without any social background, and utterly lacking in religion. He believed that to govern one must oppress, must cause the people to fear the government, and that the government need not itself follow the strict meaning of the law. He believed in might as the only principle for a State to follow. He was arbitrary, unscrupulous, an enemy of counsel, and with no respect for generosity. The state must be powerful and must brook no rivals. Chile must have, above all else, according to Portales, a powerful navy, a navy superior to any other power on the Pacific coast of South America, in order to achieve and retain the hegemony of Pacific South America. General Prieto, president of Chile, was of the same opinion as Portales. To such men Santa Cruz was a distinct challenge, a man whom they hated with an intensity that was as genuine as it was fierce. It is not that Chile was imperialistic, but she had to have more territory. Besides Chile had profited by the brief rule of Salaverry, who had granted her exceptionally advantageous commercial concessions. It will be Chile who will give to Santa Cruz his greatest problems.

Santa Cruz set about bravely to solve the many problems that presented themselves to him on his arrival in Lima. He took up the administrative reforms which were badly needed. The army was also in need of reform. Santa Cruz introduced many of the practices in the Bolivian management of the army. The term of service was to be for six years for the infantry, eight years for the cavalry and the artillery, and twelve years for the musicians. A Supreme Tribunal of Military Justice was established, and regulations drawn up for the formation of the national guard. And a plan was evolved for granting lands to the soldiers who had served their terms in the army. The Bolivian civil and criminal codes were introduced, as has been seen, and other reforms made in the judiciary. The educational system was improved, and means were taken for improving the care of orphans and for the public health. Of great importance, too, were the economic reforms. The ships of all countries, including those of Spain, were admitted to all the ports of Peru. The postal system, the customs collections, and navigation were also improved. The concession to William Wheelright is an example. There were also improvements in the departmental, provincial, and municipal administration. The visitor-general of the treasury was created with full power to investigate the revenue system of the country. Interior revenue officers were abolished, the monetary system improved, and the lottery established in all the capitals of the State of South Peru.[62]

Perhaps the most important economic measure was the negotiation of treaties of commerce with foreign powers. One of the first countries to enter into a treaty of this kind was our own country. Samuel Larned, the *chargé d'affaires* of the United States, signed a treaty of commerce and navigation on November 30, 1836 with the confederation in Lima. Certain articles of this treaty were important. Article II provided the favored nation treatment in commercial matters. Article X established religious freedom for our nationals in the confederation. Article XVI defined the blockade, and Article XVII solved satisfactorily the vexatious question of search of vessels at sea. On June 5, 1837 Great Britain entered into a similar treaty with the confederation, except that Santa Cruz promised to coöperate in the abolition of the negro slave trade. On November 20, 1836 a treaty of commerce and friendship was signed with Ecuador.[63]

The differences between Chile and Santa Cruz came to a head over the abrogation of the treaty with Chile of January 20, 1835. Chile refused to permit him to abrogate the treaty and began hostilities on August 21, 1836, with an attack upon the *Aquiles* in Callao. Despite the efforts of Santa Cruz to settle the differences in a friendly way, Chile declared war on December 28. Peruvian exiles in Chile, including Gamarra, La Fuente, Nieto, Ramón Castilla, and many others, who violently opposed the confederation, aided Chile. They provided false information unknowingly but fomented the war which Vargas brands as a disgraceful, infamous, and dishonorable war. Despite the fact that the war was unpopular in Chile, the congress gave President Prieto dictatorial powers to prosecute it on December 24. Vargas severely criticizes Olañeta, Santa Cruz's envoy, accusing him of playing a double rôle, using the opportunity to further his own personal interests. He desired to get rid of Santa Cruz and wanted the war with Chile for that purpose. Olañeta had already left enough evidences of his disloyalties, *sus antecedentes* were against him.[64] Chile and the federation both sent

---

62 Basadre, *La iniciación de la república,* I, 421-427.
63 Santa Cruz, *El General Andrés de Santa-Cruz,* 401-404.
64 Vargas, *Historia del Perú independiente,* VIII, 123.

their manifestos and counter manifestos broadcast throughout America on the causes of the war and the responsibility of beginning it.

The efforts to bring the war to an end through mediation and arbitration failed, Chile declaring she was unalterably opposed to intervention of a foreign power in a family quarrel.[65] The assassination of Portales on June 16, 1837 brought hope of peace, Santa Cruz announcing on July 22 that the Divine Providence had made peace possible by removing the instigator of the war. But Chile remained obdurate, demanding the dissolution of the confederation as a price of peace, because Santa Cruz had become a danger on account of his attack upon the sovereignty of Peru. Basadre declares that Chile was hardly honest in her position. Chile had not protested the formation of other confederations, not even against the plan of Bolívar to annex both Peru and Bolivia to *Gran Colombia.* Chile wanted war.[66] The efforts to end the war having failed, Chile proceeded to prepare for the invasion of Peru. The expedition of three thousand man was placed under command of the distinguished Admiral Blanco Encalada.

Before going further into an account of the war, the work of perfecting the political structure of the confederation should be dealt with. The Assembly of Tacna was not held on January 24, 1837, as the decree of October 28, 1836 had ordered, but on May 1. Santa Cruz appointed the nine deputies to this assembly. He should have had them chosen by the people which would have prevented considerable opposition to his whole scheme.[67] The assembly adopted the *pacto fundamental de la confederación Perú-Boliviana* on May 1, 1837, in Tacna.

---

[65] The reply bore the date of February 24, 1837. On February 15 Ecuador had proposed mediation, naming Juan José Flores and José Joaquín Olmedo as mediators. Santa Cruz appointed Juan García del Rio. Chile declined mediation on May 12, and the scheme failed.

[66] Basadre, *La iniciación de la república,* II, 7-141. This whole volume is devoted to the relations between Chile and Santa Cruz. Basadre denies that Santa Cruz was involved in the assassination of Portales on the ground that there is not enough evidence to prove his guilt. Vidaurre, Riva Agüero, Méndez, Olañeta, Vicuña Mackenna, Bulnes, Vargas, and Wiesse hold to the same view. Of course Santa Cruz was aware of the *motín* at Quillota on January 3, 1837, holding that the revolt had made the expedition against the confederation impossible.

[67] The *ministros plenipotenciarios* chosen were: for the State of North Peru: Tomás Diegues, bishop of Trujillo, Manuel Tellería, and Francisco Quiroz; for the State of South Peru: José Sebastián de Goyeneche y Barreda, bishop of Arequipa, Juan José Larrea, and Pedro José Flórez; and for Bolivia: José María (Mendizábal), archbishop of La Plata, Pedro Buitrago, and Miguel María de Aguirre.

The essential features of the *pacto* were: the statement, in the preamble, that the confederation was the best means of preserving internal and external security for the three component states; that the three states were to enjoy perfect equality and that citizenship was common to all three; that the protectoral government was to be composed of the legislative, executive, and judicial branches; that each was to pay the foreign debt acquired before the establishment of the confederation; that each state should provide at least one major port for commerce with foreign nations; that each state should retain its own monetary system, its own coat of arms, and its own flag; that the confederation was to have its own flag; that the *pacto* could be amended; and that there was to be a general diet of thirty-three members, eleven from each department.[68]

The *ministros plenipotenciarios,* as the members of the Assembly of Tacna were called, considered the *pacto* a *tratado.* The *pacto* was not very well received. The State of South Peru and the State of North Peru did ratify the instrument, but Bolivia refused to do so. The Bolivian congress, in extra session of June 1, 1838, in Cochabamba, adopted the bases which it wanted for a constitution of the confederation. Santa Cruz insisted that Bolivia did not, by refusing to ratify the *Pacto de Tacna,* repudiate the confederation, or refuse to continue as a member of it. The congress which refused to ratify the *pacto* approved all the acts of Santa Cruz's administration and formally declared its adhesion to the confederation. He declared that the *pacto* was not the confederation any more than the constitution of Bolivia was the state of Bolivia. It was a question merely of agreeing upon an instrument that would be acceptable to all three states. The *proclama del congreso boliviano a la nación* of September 12, 1837, made that plain.[69] The fact remains, however, that Santa Cruz had acted too arbitrarily and that his own people had given him a very serious admonition. It was to remind

---

[68] The legislature was bicameral, with a senate and a chamber of deputies. The senate was to have fifteen members, three from each state; the chamber to have twenty-one, or seven from each state. The senators were appointive, the deputies elective. The executive was to be called supreme protector, elected for ten-year periods, without restrictions upon number of terms this officer might serve. Of course Santa Cruz was the first supreme protector. He had large powers. There was a *consejo de ministros* appointed by him. The judiciary was complicated, but emphasis was placed upon the right of each state to its own judiciary. At the outset, and during the course of the war, Santa Cruz was to exercise the functions of the supreme protector, and was not compelled to call a session of the congress to choose his successor until six months after the war was over.

[69] Santa Cruz, *El General Adrés de Santa-Cruz,* 148-150.

him that he was becoming the dictator who insists that things must be done his way, or not at all.

The outstanding events of the dictatorship of Santa Cruz from the adoption of the *Pacto de Tacna* until the end of that dictatorship were his wars with Chile and Argentina. The instructions to Blanco Encalada for the expedition against Santa Cruz were explicit. He was to revindicate the rights of Chile and remove Santa Cruz from Bolivia as well as from Peru. Chile was also to aid Argentina take the Department of Tarija away from Bolivia. In lieu of this department Bolivia was to receive the Department of Arequipa with a suitable port on the Pacific. And finally there was to be an alliance between Chile and Peru.[70]

The expedition left Valparaíso September 15 and arrived in Arica on September 24. Gamarra and Castilla accompanied the expedition. They advised Blanco not to go to Arequipa but to Puno, on the ground that Puno was less able to defend itself since the troops were on the eastern front fighting Argentina,[71] but Blanco disregarded the advice and went to Arequipa, arriving in that city October 12. The Chileans acted highhandedly, calling a *cabildo abierto,* which was attended by only a very few people, and proclaiming Antonio Gutiérrez de la Fuente provisional *jefe supremo* of Peru. The great majority of the *arequipeños* was opposed to the Chileans, a fact which the Peruvian advisors to Blanco had ignored. They had erred, also, in their estimate of the volume of opposition to Santa Cruz in Peru and in Bolivia. In addition to these facts, Blanco did not seem to possess the ability to rouse himself to exercise the energy the situation demanded. His army, too, was in a very poor condition, as compared with the army of Santa Cruz. Blanco was in no position to fight Santa Cruz, who had one of the best equipped and disciplined armies of any man at the time, in Chile or in any other country in America. Santa Cruz made use of the press to urge upon the people to unite in the scandalous war against them. *El Eco del Protectorado,* the most powerful paper of the day, and *El Eco del Norte,* carried appeals to the people. Orbegoso, Niete, Cerdeña, Ballivián, Brown, and Herrera, also, issued proclamations urging the people to fight Chile. On November 5 Santa Cruz concentrated his army at Uzuña, but Blanco did not dare to risk a battle, and sued for peace. On December 17 the

[70] Basadre, *La iniciación de la república,* II, 154-155. The expedition consisted of the *Libertad,* the *Aquiles,* the *Monteagudo,* the *Valparaíso,* the *Arequipeño,* the *Orbegoso,* the *Santa Cruz,* and the *Peruviana,* as well as sixteen transports, carrying more than three thousand troops.

[71] Argentina had declared war on Santa Cruz on May 19, 1837.

famous Treaty of Paucarpata was signed,[72] and hostilities ceased for the time. The terms of the treaty are interesting, but, as the treaty was never ratified by Chile, they are of mere academic interest.[73]

Santa Cruz is universally criticized for the leniency of the terms of this capitulation. He is universally condemned for the leniency shown towards Chile in the salvation of her armed forces in Peru. He should have crushed them since he had them in a position where he could have done so, and in a position of their own choice. He could have crippled his powerful opponent at the time to such an extent as to make it impossible for him to have waged war against the confederation for a decade or more. But instead, through a false notion of generosity, he allowed them all to escape, believing that the Chileans would repay him for such generosity. He certainly did not understand the spirit of the Chileans at the time, and their determination to keep Peru and Bolivia from becoming their competitors. And all authorities without a single exception declare that this generosity of the protector caused the fall of the confederation. The Chilean government repudiated the Treaty of Paucarpata on December 18, 1837, and immediately began the preparation for the invasion of Peru on a far greater scale than before. But before going into that phase of the war with Chile, it is necessary to turn to the war with Argentina.

Juan Manuel de Rosas, the dictator of Argentina, was, above all else, a great patriot, jealously guarding every foot of Argentine territory and

---

[72] Negotiations began on November 8. On November 14 an interview took place between Santa Cruz and Blanco at San Lucas de Paucarpata. The treaty was signed by Manuel Blanco Encalada, Ramón Herrera, Anselmo Quiros, Antonio José de Irisarry, and Juan Gualberto Valdivia for Chile and by Andrés Santa Cruz and Manuel de la Cruz Méndez for the confederation. The titles given by Santa Cruz were elaborate. He was *Gran Ciudadano, Restaurador, Capitán General y Presidente de Bolivia, Supremo Protector de la Confederación Perú-Boliviana, Gran Mariscal, Pacificador del Perú, General de Brigada de Colombia, Condecorado con las medallas de Libertadores de Quito y de Pichincha, con la del Libertador Simón Bolívar y con la de Cobija, Gran Oficial de la Legión de Honor de Francia, Fundador y Jefe Supremo de la Legión de Honor Boliviana y la Nacional del Perú*, etc., etc. This array of titles explains not only the positions the man occupied but also his pride and vanity.

[73] There was to be perpetual peace and amity between the two countries, all differences of the past to be forgotten, each one reiterating the innocent statement that neither one had harbored evil intentions towards the other. Chile would return the *Santa Cruz, Arequipeño* and the *Peruviana* and withdraw her troops from Quilca. Chile would settle all outstanding differences amicably, forswear use of the principle of intervention, and solve all differences that might arise by arbitration and conciliation. Peru would not punish any of the Peruvians who had had a part in the war, and finally, the government of Great Britain was to be requested to aid in the execution of this treaty.

desirous of regaining lost territory. He believed that Argentina had been deprived of territory by Bolívar and was bent on retaking the Department of Tarija. Rosas, whom Santa Cruz called *el tirano más feroz y brutal, que se ha conocido en los anales de la historia americana,* saw in Santa Cruz a grave danger to the future peace and safety of his country, and had little difficulty in trumping up a cause for a war against him. He alleged that Santa Cruz was harboring exiles from Argentina and would have to be punished for that protection. The alliance proposed by Chile was wrecked because Rosas had demanded territory both from Bolivia and Peru, as well as the payment by them of the whole cost of the war. Rosas declared that Santa Cruz' invasion of Peru was a crime against all the republics of America and against the classic rights of man, and he would fight until Santa Cruz was out of Peru. Basadre claims that Rosas had no just cause for war against Santa Cruz. He also believes that it was fortunate for Santa Cruz that Ecuador remained neutral since she was in a position to have caused Santa Cruz considerable trouble.[74] The war between Rosas and Santa Cruz was of brief duration, the Battle of Montenegro, June 24, 1837, forcing Rosas to sue for peace. It was a war from which Rosas gained no fame and which contributed to his own downfall.

The second Chilean campaign against Santa Cruz began late in 1837. The main purpose of the campaign was *la destrucción del Protectorado de Santa Cruz,* according to Gonzalo Bulnes,[75] and to avenge the humiliations of the Peace of Paucarpata. On January 8, 1838 Manuel Bulnes was appointed *jeneral en jefe del nuevo ejército restaurador del Perú,* but it was not until July 10 that the expedition began. Gamarra was again a member of the advisors of the Chileans. La Fuente, too, lost no time in supporting the Chileans. These two men declared that Santa Cruz was losing power, that Orbegoso had turned against him, and that Santa Cruz would not be able to hold out against Chile. Orbegoso had reassumed supreme power in the north, and would coöperate with the Chileans. To complicate matters in Peru Vivanco and Pardo began a plan for the restoration of the independence of Peru without the aid of either Gamarra or La Fuente. But Chile made her bargain with Gamarra by which he was to be restored to power in Peru.

The second expedition was much larger than the first, consisting of about fifty-four hundred men. José María de la Cruz was the chief-of-staff to Bulnes, and Gamarra, La Fuente, Castilla, Vivanco, Pardo, and

[74] Basadre, *La iniciación de la república,* II, 183-189.
[75] Gonzalo Bulnes, *Historia de la campaña del Perú en 1838.*

Martínez were only a part of the expedition. The instructions to Bulnes ordered him to destroy Santa Cruz and restore to Chile, Peru, and Bolivia their full rights. He was to aid in reëstablishing Peruvian independence, but was to abstain scrupulously from taking any part in the civil wars, and under no circumstances to permit his men to be placed under any command but that of himself. And he was to take no Peruvian property under any pretext whatsoever. The expedition landed at Ancón on August 6.

The situation in Peru had changed greatly between May and the time of the arrival of the Chilean expedition. The people had begun to turn against Santa Cruz with avidity. Orbegoso and Nieto had turned against him and began a definite movement for the restoration of Peruvian independence.[76] On July 24 Trujillo pronounced against Santa Cruz, Chancay on July 25, Lambayeque on the 26th, Huacho and Santa on the 25th, San Pedro de Chavín, Collapingos, and Santiago de Cabana on the 27th, Piura on the 28th, Huantar, Huasco, Llamellin, San Luís, and Huari on the 29th, and Lima and Sihuas on the 30th. But there was opposition to both Niete and Orebgoso. Otero and Morán were against them and forced them to leave Lima to their forces. Niete and Orbegoso then took their forces to the *sierras.*

The story of Peru again becomes a story of *personalismo,* not of patriotism, except in so far as it may serve the purpose of a *caudillo.* San Martín had his *partidarios,* Bolívar his, and Riva Agüero his. La Fuente, Gamarra, Santa Cruz, and Orbegoso had theirs. Basadre finds that the Peruvian nationalism had been best exemplified, up to that time, in Riva Agüero, but holds that the *nacionalismo riva-agüerino* was too much tied up with *españolismo* and class spirit. The purest nationalism had been that of Luna Pizarro.[77]

[76] Nieto was a powerful figure at this time. He had been born in Ilo in 1803, entered the Spanish service early, and joined the patriot forces in 1822. He served in the battles of Torata and Moquegua in 1823 and in Junín and Ayacucho in 1824, serving with great distinction in the last battle as adjutant to La Mar. He fought in the war against Colombia in 1828-1829, distinguishing himself in the Battle of Tarqui. In 1833 he pronounced in favor of a union between Peru and Bolivia. Salaverry exiled him. He returned and his Peruvianism forced him to turn against Santa Cruz in 1835 and go to Chile. He again went over to Santa Cruz when the Chileans declared war against Santa Cruz, declaring that he would fight any enemy of Peru. With the victory over the Chileans, he again turned against Santa Cruz as an enemy of Peru. Nieto took his army from Trujillo across the deserts of Casma and Huarmey to a place near Lima. Orbegoso ordered him to take up a position at Chancay, where he arrived at the time the second expedition left Valparaíso. On July 29 the *cabildo abierto* in Lima ordered him to enter the city with his army, which he did.

[77] Basadre, *La iniciación de la república,* II, 245-247.

The Garrido mission, sent to interview Orbegoso by Bulnes, failed because Orbegoso had again decided to support Santa Cruz. He had taken this decision because he wanted to save the Peruvian people from another triumph of *gamarrismo*. The Chileans and the Peruvians prepared for battle. On August 21 the Peruvians won the Battle of Guía. Bulnes lost, declares Basadre, because of the *anarquismo de la raza. . . . Los hombres de 1829 parecen los mismos en 1838, 1879, y 1880.* There were the same conditions in each: revolution among the enemy, the false hope of winning without organization, the unnecessary attention to details and ignoring the larger phase of the action, war among the chiefs of the army, the disorganization in the moment of decisive action, the failure to use the necessary elements and factors at hand, the eagerness to blame the failure upon somebody else, and *el consuelo de la derrota mediante la locuacidad: ¡qué familiares, qué genuinos resultan! En fondo, el anarquismo de la raza.*[78]

And the result to the Peruvians? The occupation of Lima by the Chileans! On August 24, 1838, Gamarra again became provisional president of Peru, taking the oath of office on August 26. Trujillo still stood in favor of the restoration. La Fuente was there. On September 27 Vidal was elected president of the Department of Huaylas. Thus by the end of September, 1838, Peru had eight presidents: Orbegoso of the State of North Peru, Gamarra of the resurrected republic, Santa Cruz, protector of the confederation, Riva Agüero against Orbegoso in the State of North Peru, Pío Tristán of the State of South Peru, Nieto also of the State of North Peru, and Vidal, as before mentioned, of the Department of Huaylas. The news of this situation must have been rather galling to San Martín in exile in France!

On November 8 Gamarra and Bulnes decided to evacuate Lima at the approach of Santa Cruz, and on November 10 Santa Cruz reëntered Lima to the frantic delight of the people. He was the recipient of the same degree of genuine enthusiasm as that which was accorded San Martín in 1821, Bolívar in 1824, Luna Pizarro in 1827, and Orbegoso in 1834. Orbegoso joined Santa Cruz, but he was not received in a manner acceptable to his pride, and he boarded the *Andromede* in Callao on December 4 and left for Guayaquil. And that marks the end of Dictator Gamarra as a political figure in Peru. He spent several years in Guayaquil and returned to Trujillo where he died in 1847.

---

[78] *Ibid.*, II, 275.

It may be said of Orbegoso, with much truth, that he was an accident, really a creature of circumstance. He came as a protest against *gamarrismo.* In order to save himself from Gamarra, Bermúdez, and Salaverry, he begged Santa Cruz to help him. When Santa Cruz had created the confederation, Orbegoso felt that he had committed an unpardonable crime against the Peruvian people, and turned against Santa Cruz. And when the Chilean invasions came, he again turned to Santa Cruz in the hope that Peru might be saved. Finding that he was no longer able to play the rôle he desired, like San Martín, he exiled himself from his native land. But unlike him he returned to die in his beloved Trujillo. No man was more genuinely *trujilleño* than Luís José Orbegoso. But Orbegoso had transgressed his *dharma,* to use a Hindu term, and suffered the consequences.[79] Orbegoso was the second of these four dictators to pass off the stage of Peru. The third will soon be disposed of.

The war with Chile continued. On November 16 Bulnes, La Fuente, and Vidal took up headquarters at Huaylas. Santa Cruz strove to establish a front from Chancay to Cerro de Pasco. Bulnes mapped out a very different plan of action. On January 5, 1839 the two armies met at the *puente de Buin.* The army of Santa Cruz was caught in a very heavy rainstorm and was badly defeated. Santa Cruz failed here, as he had at Zepita, to gauge the real importance of Buin, and with the most disastrous results. On January 7 Bulnes issued his famous proclamation from Yungay, declaring that he would win, and thus cause to disappear *la detestada confederación.*[80]

On January 20 occurred the famous Battle of Yungay, a veritable Waterloo for Santa Cruz and for all that he stood. The heir to the grandeur and the glory of the Incas had fallen on the altar of dictatorship. There are many versions of the Battle of Yungay. Santa Cruz claims that the battle was lost for him through the flight of Colonel Guilarte with seven hundred men at the crucial point in the battle.[81] The losses of the Peruvians and Bolivians were heavy: two generals and more than fourteen hundred troops. The Chileans lost about thirteen hundred men, but Bulnes declares that the Chileans captured three generals, nine colonels, one hundred and fifty officers, seven hundred

---

[79] *Ibid.,* II, 324-328.

[80] Bulnes, *Historia de la campaña del Perú en 1838,* 372-373.

[81] The Chileans took all the glory for the victory. A national military march was composed in its honor, an honor not given to other victories, such as Tacna, Arica, Miraflores, and Chorillos.

prisoners, seven flags, all the artillery with twenty-five hundred guns, and much army material. Santa Cruz, and some of the chiefs and about a hundred men, escaped, riding posthaste towards Lima. There had been something providential about the great victory of the Chileans at Yungay, something spontaneous, something inexplicable.[82]

In the palace of Riva Agüero Santa Cruz broke down and wept like a child while relating the story of the defeat. On February 20 he resigned as president of Bolivia and as protector of the confederation. Basadre finds that Santa Cruz displayed, in this hour of defeat, none of the elements of greatness. He considered himself as a Bolivian and the Peruvians as foreigners, resigning as a defeated administrator, as a bureaucrat, formulating phrases in a purely formalistic manner. He arrived in Islay on February 22 and was received by Crompton, English consul. On February 23 demands were made upon Crompton for the surrender of Santa Cruz. Crompton refused, called in fifty men from the *Sammarang* and helped him board that vessel. On board the same ship were Riva Agüero, Cerdeña, García del Río, Irrisari, Miller, and Rivero. Santa Cruz left his country for a perpetual exile, never being permitted to return to Bolivia.

The causes for the fall of Santa Cruz are many. The rôle of a dictator is, at best, a very precarious one. The fault was largely his own, lacking the ability necessary to be a successful dictator. He lacked the greater qualities of leadership, its fiery enthusiasm, and great insight. He was a good administrator but a poor strategist. And still the real cause of his fall lay outside of himself and in the condition of the times. The greatest obstacle to the success of his grandiose idea was the rising tide of nationalism and democracy. Add to this the real fear and suspicion the people had of him. *¿Adonde vamos? ¿Por qué?* became more than idle questions. These questions were even more important to the other peoples of America than to the Peruvians and the Bolivians. They feared this *cholo* of Bolivia. One may agree with Basadre that Santa Cruz did not understand the *kairos* of his time. Eternal greatness is the victim of time. No human being can control the *kairos*. If a man has genius he will sense, through intuition, the true course of time. He will vision the future and help unravel the course of events through obedience and not through an effort to dominate or command it. In a word, man is but the servant of the *kairos* of his age, and achieves success, glory, and fame only as he puts himself in tune with that *kairos*. Hence

[82] Basadre, *La iniciación de la república,* II, 369-371.

Santa Cruz was not great in the sense that Bismarck, Napoleon, Lenin, Washington, Lincoln, Juárez, Bolívar, and Portales were great. Basadre concludes that Santa Cruz was, at least in Peru, *sólo la aproximación de un hombre grande.*

The enmity towards Santa Cruz in the countries in which he had played his rôle took various forms. Even before he went into exile, much of his work was undone in both Peru and Bolivia. Orbegoso was declared outside the pale of law, Gamarra decreed that honors should be paid to Salaverry and all those who were assassinated on February 18, 1836 in the *plaza* of Arequipa, and all who died in the battles of Yanacocha and Socabaya. In Bolivia his property was seized and confiscated, and on November 2, 1839 the constituent congress of Bolivia declared him a traitor to Bolivia, unworthy the name Bolivian; his name struck off the civil and military lists of the republic, and he was declared outside the pale of law.[83] While these acts may seem unduly harsh, they are neither new nor unusually harsh. It is the way of life among the people of these three republics, where politics is a profession and statescraft is at a premium. Expatriation, confiscation of property of the fallen leaders, and persecution of them and often of their families are a part of the game.

To make sure that Santa Cruz should never be able to return, Bolivia, through the leadership of José Ballivián, induced Peru and Chile to enter into a convention by which they bound themselves to keep him out of their countries. In October 1845 the *artículos acordados entre los gobiernos de Bolivia, de Chile y de Perú relativamente a Don Andrés Santa Cruz* were signed by representatives of those three governments. Santa Cruz was to remain in Europe for six years. Most of his property was restored to him and he was paid an annual salary for his expenses while in exile.[84] Ecuador had indignantly refused to be a party to such an abuse of the rights of governments. Santa Cruz left for his exile towards the end of 1845 on an English vessel by way of the Straits of Magellan.

The career of Santa Cruz between 1845 and 1865 was not without interest. He was one of those who toyed with the idea of European invasion of Spanish America for the purpose of establishing peace and order in its countries. Mixed up with that was the idea of establishing mon-

[83] *Colección de Leyes . . . de Perú.* Consult also the *Redactor del Congreso de Bolivia* for 1839.

[84] José M. Aponte, *La batalla de Ingavi: recuerdos históricos* (La Paz, 1911), 269-272. The treaty is given in full in this work.

archies in Spanish America as the best means of maintaining peace and order in the Spanish new world. In 1855 Santa Cruz came to Argentina, going inland as far as Salta, to take part in the presidential campaign in Bolivia of that year. On February 14, 1855 he had published a manifesto to the Bolivian people urging them to support his candidacy. The election went against Santa Cruz, Córdova and Linares both receiving a larger number of votes than he. He returned to Europe and served his country at different times as its diplomatic representatives before European governments. He lived most of the time in France, a friend and counsellor of Napoleon III. On September 23, 1865 Santa Cruz died in Versailles, his mortal remains still resting in the great house of Louis XIV, according to Aponte.[85] Dictators come and go in Spanish America. Some of them, such as Santa Cruz, rose to great heights and then toppled off—almost into oblivion. The third dictator of the four had fallen. Now to dispose of the fourth and last.

V

Gamarra reëntered Lima on February 24, 1839, and on July 10, 1840 he was elected constitutional president of the republic. It soon became evident that he did not mean to restore peace and order between Bolivia and Peru. It meant that Gamarra desired to dominate Bolivia and make her an integral part of Peru. He set about preparing to invade Bolivia. On January 11, 1841 the *consejo de estado* gave him dictatorial powers to put down rebellion in Peru, and on July 6 of the same year he was given dictatorial powers to go into Bolivia to prevent the reëstablishment there of the power of Santa Cruz. The Bolivians took alarm at the extraordinary interest Gamarra was taking in their domestic affairs, and decided to unite to meet any effort he might make to dominate their country. José Ballivián gave the leaders in both countries concern. Neither Gamarra nor Velasco had treated him as he felt he should have been treated. Aponte believes that José Ballivián desired to make an alliance with Gamarra in order to help him wrest power from Velasco. Gamarra declined to treat with him, declaring him a traitor, outside the pale of law, and a public enemy. Gamarra began his invasion of Bolivia on July 12, 1841. Velasco turned to Ballivián for aid in this national

[85] Aponte, *La batalla de Ingavi,* 293-295. Aponte declares that Santa Cruz was undoubtedly one of the greatest men of South America. His *pan peruanismo* meant the reunion of the two Perus. He loved Cuzco, Arequipa, Puno, and La Paz. In fact he loved the whole of the *altoplano* of which he was a child. Aponte also declares that Juan de Aroma praises Santa Cruz highly in his *Páginas diplomáticas del Perú,* as does José de la Riva Agüero y Osma in his *La historia en el Perú.*

crisis. The two men agreed to work together to fight Gamarra, Ballivián becoming commander-in-chief of the Bolivian army.

On November 18, 1841 the two armies met in battle on the famous *pampa* of Ingavi. The battle, which lasted less than an hour, was one of the most brilliant in South American history. Ballivián had less than four thousand men, Gamarra more than five thousand. Not only were the Peruvians disastrously defeated, but Gamarra was killed in the battle. When found he was dressed in the beautiful uniform of a *generalísimo* of the Peruvian army. Ramón Castilla, the chief-of-staff of the Peruvian army, was the only man from Peru to get any glory out of that momentous contest. He was wounded and was taken prisoner, along with twenty-four army chiefs, one hundred and fifty officials, and more than three thousand troops. The Bolivians lost only five hundred men.

On the afternoon of the battle, Ballivián issued a brilliant proclamation, taking due notice of the passing of the *caudillo par excellence* of Peru, Agustín Gamarra.[86] Gamarra passed off the stage of dictators with at least the saving grace of having died on the battlefield. And yet there seems but little in his whole life to commend! Between 1828 and 1842, and longer, he was the evil genius of the Peruvian people. He is the best example of that brood of dictators, and would-be dictators, that were hatched in the days when the two giants strutted about on their sacred soil. About the only noble thing about him was that he passed off the scene, thus ridding the world of another dictator.

---

[86] Aponte, *La batalla de Ingavi,* 161-164. The Peruvians took due note of his passing. On December 13, 1841 elaborate services were held in his memory. Later a beautiful mausoleum was built for his remains in Lima. Aponte believes that his remains are still a part of the soil of the *pampa* de Ingavi, and that the remains in the beautiful mausoleum in Lima are those of Juan Pedro Garavita.

CHAPTER NINETEEN

DICTATOR MARIANO MELGAREJO

THE dictator of dictators of Bolivia was Mariano Melgarejo. No one among the many dictators of that country has such an unsavory reputation as this notoriously famous son of Tarata. Among the dictators of South America he is ranked with Juan Manuel de Rosas, and with Melgarejo's contemporary, Francisco Solano López. These three men have come to occupy, in the minds of scholars as well as the populace, a class by themselves. And yet all of the three left an imperishable impression of doing good by being bad. Rosas left a people united into a distinct nationality, although it was whipped into a definite reality in opposition to the Nero of the new world. López left a people, in the very depths of penury, thoroughly determined and able to recreate an unconquerable nation. And Melgarejo left a people more thoroughly knit together into a nationality than they had ever been before. All three countries were saved from foreign absorption and undue mutilation. It is true, that of the three, Melgarejo was compelled to sacrifice more of the national territory than either of the other two. But he saved Bolivia from mutilation by choosing the lesser of two evils. Melgarejo stands preëminently at the head of the long list of dictators of Bolivia, and the *sexenio* of his rule remains the acme of dictatorship in that unfortunate country.

I

Mariano Melgarejo was born on April 13, 1820 in the Department of Cochabamba, a natural son of Lorenzo Valencia by Ignacio Melgarejo. According to d'Arlach Mariano was the natural son of a Spaniard by a *Quechua* Indian woman.[1] This love child, this bastard, was the victim of ignorance and vicious affection. His mother loved him with a love that knew no bounds, but failed to give the training that a child and a young boy should have. This is the criticism of both friend and foe; but, of course, the whole life of Melgarejo is still, as it has been ever since his rise to power, a subject of the most pronounced differences of opinion. He has his friends and he has his innumerable enemies. Friend and foe are alike, however, of the opinion that Mariano had in him the making of a real gentleman: a potential scholar, a very great

[1] Tomás O'Connor d'Arlach, *El General Melgarejo: hechos y dichos de este hombre célebre* (La Paz, 1913), viii.

warrior, and an ever greater statesman. He was spoiled by too much motherly affection, by association with the people of his mother, and by the stigma that attaches to bastardy. As a child of passion he also became a slave of passion, and absolute slave of strong drink and of women. The sins of his parents, if one may be so old-fashioned as to point to that fact, were indeed visited upon him. The lure of excitement, the insatiable desire for adventure, and the love of the lure of the Bohemian world made him a willing slave. The greatest of his crimes were committed under the blind influence of liquor and passion: the acts of moments of orgies fit only for the brothel. The opinion is well-nigh universal that Melgarejo possessed a very gracious and charmnig personality. He was generous, compassionate, sympathetic, and chivalrous to a fault when sober. He had much in him of the true poet: the troubadour and the *minnesinger*. The magnetism of his personality was almost irresistible, his power over both men and women was almost unbelievable.[2]

Young Mariano ran away from home at the age of nine, and shortly afterwards he entered the army. The only formal education he received was in the barracks; his audacity and valor gained him both promotion and fame relatively early. He loved the rôle of the revolutionary and began to play it while still quite young. He was restless, ceaselessly active, and unduly fond of conflict. He did brilliant work in the Battle of Montenegro and in Ingavi. He was a great admirer of José Ballivián and became his staunch supporter against Velasco; but he turned against Ballivián in disgust over the tyrannical acts of the dictator. He was very much opposed to Belzu and was marked for death by that dictator. In fact he was seized in the Cochabamba revolution against Belzu, and was condemned to be shot. The people of Cochabamba interceded for him, and he was pardoned, much to the disgust of those who declared that Belzu had made a mistake.

The *coup de main* of March 27, 1865 was a rather tragic sequel to the pardoning act in Cochabamba. On the other hand, it was this *coup de main,* one of the greatest feats in history, which established Melgarejo in power for five long years. Guzmán justly declares that Melgarejo did not just spring into power from a clear sky, and that the tyranny of Achá invited relief from that tyranny. Melgarejo had become the hero of the army and was the incarnation of all that was vicious in Bolivarian militarism of his day. He was the heir to the predominating lust for power which inhered in the military system. Melgarejo came to the

[2] Ramón Sotomayor Valdés, *La legación en Bolivia* (Santiago de Chile, 1912).

rescue, strange as it may seem, of the great principles of the Constitution of 1861. Achá was opposed to that democratic fundamental law and sought to set it aside. Guzmán declares that Achá and his followers invited revolution, and Melgarejo saw his time had come.[3]

The revolution of December 1864 was the result. Melgarejo secured possession of the presidential palace in Cochabamba on December 28, and the next day he proclaimed himself provisional president of Bolivia. In the decree he explained that he had taken this solemn step merely to put an end to the intolerable tyranny of the rule of Achá and the interest of Bolivia. It was the sacred duty of all good Bolivians to come to the rescue of their country.[4] Mariano Donato Muñoz, whom Melgarejo had made his secretary-general, explained, in a circular of the same date, that Melgarejo knew, as a good citizen, the duty before him. As a soldier he knew how to use the army for the lofty mission of saving his country.[5] And Melgarejo, following his practice of being good to his soldiers, turned the presidential palace of Cochabamba over to them to be looted. They spared nothing, not even the public documents or the private property of Achá. His army was with him and enabled him to rule the country for six years. He levied a contribution upon the City of Cochabamba for almost seven hundred thousand *pesos.* This was a way of rewarding his soldiers and running the government.

The opposition to the rule of Melgarejo was keen from the very beginning, so that he was kept busy putting down revolutions in several parts of the republic. He moved the national government about from place to place, as Santa Cruz and Belzu had done before him.[6] He was little influenced by these revolutions, usually making his rule a little more tyrannical after each revolution.

The nature of Melgarejo's government may be judged, in a large measure, by the measures adopted. On January 3, 1865 he suppressed

---

[3] Alcibíades Guzmán, *Libertad ó despotismo en Bolivia. El antimelgarejismo después de Melgarejo. Controversia histórica sobre política y derecho constitucional* (La Paz, 1916), 179-180.

[4] *Colección de leyes . . . de Bolivia.*

[5] *Ibid.*

[6] He left his government from Cochabamba on January 13, 1865, and was in La Paz on January 22. Then to Caracolla, Oruro, La Paz, Oruro, Potosí, Sucre, Cochabamba, Potosí, and Sucre. In 1866 to Cotocoro, Viacha, La Paz, Laja, La Paz, Villa de Aroma, Cochabamba, Ciudad Melgarejo, Villa de la Victoria, and La Paz. In 1867 he was able to remain quiet as far as revolutions were concerned. In 1868 he was again on the move from Potosí to Sucre, Potosí, Sucre, Potosí, and La Paz. In 1869 from Melgarejo City to Cochabamba to La Paz. The next year was also a quiet year. And in January 1871 occurred the revolution which ended his hateful dictatorship.

the municipal council of Cochabamba, and on January 30 made that decree applicable for the whole of the country. These municipal councils had failed, he declared, to perform the duties for which they had been created. On January 13 he abolished the *consejo de estado* as an obstacle to the proper administration of the state. On April 28 he established a professorship in all the academies of the republic. On April 29 he ordered that the priests should reside in their benefices, and on May 4 he ordered that the higher ecclesiastical dignitaries should visit their districts at least once a year. On the same day he ordered that synods should meet annually, and on October 2 he ordered that all dead human bodies should be buried in regularly constituted cemeteries. On October 29 he proclaimed neutrality in the Hispano-Chilean conflict. On December 6 he decreed that all who opposed his government would be considered as traitors to the country, the accused to be given an oral trial and condemned to be shot. He further declared that all the people would have to help the government to the best of their ability, those refusing to do so were to be treated as traitors to the country and punished accordingly. All who should take part in revolutions were to have their property confiscated, and all who should spread false reports about the government, and all authors of newspaper articles, were to be considered as traitors to the country and treated accordingly. And all municipalities, revolting against the national government, were to be declared in a state of siege, and separated from all the other parts of tne republic. He added that he meant to pacify the country and preferred to do so without resort to the use of force, but if it were necessary to use force to do so he would do that. In any event the country would have to adjust itself to his rule, or take the consequences. In the preamble to this celebrated decree, he explained that his policy of leniency and generosity had been misunderstood, that his government had been accepted by a majority of the people and by many foreign powers. The people might rest assured, he declared, that he would do his duty by preserving order and by putting down revolutions.[7]

On January 24, 1866 he issued a call for the meeting of the national assembly on August 6, and on February 10 he issued regulations for the national elections. The national assembly was to scrutinize the ballots cast and to draft a new political constitution. On March 20, he issued orders compelling the Indians to show proof of the ownership of

[7] *Colección de leyes . . . de Bolivia.* These measures are all to be found in this work for the years concerned. This *Colección* differs from that of Peru in that it is arranged by years, not by subjects.

the lands they held, or surrender them to the government. The surrendered lands might then be sold by the government. On April 16 he decreed that the *sayañas,* Indian lands in Yungas, were to be sold. On April 20 he decreed the abrogation of the decree of January 24, calling a meeting of the national assembly. On June 11 he decreed the signing of the Treaty of Alliance with Chile and Peru of April 11, the purpose of the treaty being to aid them in fighting Spain in case she should attempt to invade their territories. On September 5 he created the new Department of Tarata. On September 13 he decreed that September 18, Chilean Independence Day, was to be celebrated as a national holiday. On January 1, 1867 he divided the Department of La Paz into two departments: that of La Paz and that of Mejillones. On January 24 he decreed the ratification of the Treaty of Limits with Chile, signed on August 10, 1866. On February 24 he gained a signal victory, the *corte supremo* ruling on that day that the dictatorship of Melgarejo was legal.

But the *corte supremo* was not satisfied with this decision alone and proceeded to make the place of the principle of dictatorship even more explicit. On September 27, 1867 the *corte supremo* ruled that the Constitution of 1861, which was still in operation, although the country was ruled by a dictator, did not prevent the national government from taking action against the prefects of the republic.

The national assembly met on August 6, 1868 at the order of Melgarejo. On August 7 it declared itself constituent and decreed a general amnesty. On August 11 it proclaimed Melgarejo provisional president of Bolivia, and on September 26 it approved all the administrative acts of the dictatorship from December 28, 1864 to August 6, 1868. The national assembly also passed a decree expressing confidence in the national government, and commending Melgarejo for having established order and for having served the *causa americana* in such an admirable manner. The assembly also promulgated a new constitution; and on September 7 it passed an act regulating the national elections. On October 8 the assembly passed an act establishing a *consejo municipal* in the capital of every department and province and in some cantons in the republic. On the same day it approved the budget for the year 1868-1869. But on December 21 Melgarejo issued a decree suspending the constitutional guarantees and granting himself dictatorial powers. And on February 3, 1869 he issued the *supremo decreto* suspending the Constitution of 1868 and assuming the dictatorship. He explained, in the preamble to that decree, that the conditions of the republic demanded such action in view of the activities of demagogues and party leaders.

On November 10 he issued the *supremo decreto* conferring supreme power upon the *consejo de ministros* during his absence from the capital.

II

Before concluding the account of Melgarejo's dictatorship, it may be well to give the testimony of our diplomatic agents in Bolivia during this period. Writing to Seward from Cochabamba on January 24, 1865 Hall declared that Melgarejo had forced Achá to surrender, adding: "The revolution was exclusively the work of about five hundred soldiers, for the most part without officers. The people of the country have nothing to do with it."[8] In his dispatch of March 6, 1865 from Cochabamba, Hall explained to Seward why he had not recognized the government of Melgarejo:[9]

> "The Provisional President entered La Paz, not only without opposition, but with considerable popular demonstrations in his favor; and the country has submitted to his rule, which is purely military and despotic, without any legal or constitutional restraint.
>
> "Were the Provisional Government now here, I should regard it as my duty to call officially on the President and the Secretary of Foreign Affairs, and thus recognize it as the *de facto* Government of the country. But now, it is at La Paz, whence it will proceed to Oruro at an early day. From Oruro, it is reported, it will proceed to Sucre and Potosí. But its sojourn at Oruro and its movements elsewhere will depend upon military and revolutionary exigencies. . . . Should any matter of official business require it, I shall promptly seek the Government wherever it is to be found."

Hall stated, in his dispatch to Seward of April 9, 1865, from Cochabamba, that Belzu had returned to Bolivia and had taken up arms against Melgarejo. Belzu had been forced to take refuge in the presidential palace in La Paz, where he was besieged and forced to surrender to Melgarejo, and shot to death. He declared that the defeat and death of Belzu was a good thing for Bolivia. If Belzu had won, *desperados* and persons from the lowest orders would have plundered Cochabamba. Hall was much concerned about the question of his relations to the Melgarejo government. He finally takes the position that he must await instructions from the Washington government, explaining his position to Muñoz of May 11, 1865 in a note to him.[10]

---

[8] Department of Senate, Despatches, Bolivia, volume III.
[9] *Ibid.*, volume III.
[10] *Ibid.*, volume II.

"Even had I possessed such authority, however, before proceeding to exercise it, it would have been my duty to await the decision of the people of Bolivia upon the new state of affairs thus suddenly presented for their consideration and action. It would have been exceedingly disrespectful to them in me to anticipate *their* judgment upon the proceedings of the 28th of December, and to take it upon myself to decide in advance that they would ratify those proceedings and accept the new Government provisionally organized as their Government—as *their* trusted agent to transact *their* business with Foreign Powers. I repeat, that, had it been within my competency (which it was not) to resume the exercise of my diplomatic functions after their interruption and suspension by the occurrences of the 28th of December, the respect I entertain for the people of Bolivia and the consideration they are so eminently entitled to at my hands, would have preëmptorily required of me to await their recognition of the new Government, before presuming myself, as the representative of a Foreign Power, to recognize it as *theirs*."

The Spanish Question was given by Hall in the dispatch to Seward of March 31, 1866, from Cochabamba, as the cause for not holding a presidential election in that year. But despite that fact Melgarejo ought to be recognized by the United States.[11]

"Melgarejo's Government is as firmly established as has been that of any of his predecessors in office. For thirty years there has been no *accession* to the Presidency in this country by election. All Melgarejo's predecessors came into power originally by military violence—all save the three first Presidents of Bolivia, Bolívar, Sucre, and Velasco. Velasco was overthrown by Santa Cruz before he had been in office one year. It is utterly vain to hope for, at present, a constitutional Government in Bolivia. Were a President elected tomorrow by a majority of the popular votes—however great that majority—he could not maintain his position six months, without a military force at his command, superior to that which any of the numerous aspirants for the Presidency could organize against him. . . . I do not believe, for a moment, that Melgarejo out of the way, there would be any other than a military Government established. I believe—I have no doubt whatever—that if he were to die, the country would be immediately plunged into civil war by some three or four, or five or six rival aspirants for the Presidency."

Finally on July 16, 1866 Hall recognized the Melgarejo government as the *de facto* government of Bolivia. On September 24, 1865 Hall complained in a despatch to Seward from Cochabamba that Melgarejo marched his government from place to place in the republic to put down revolution against his government, explaining,[12]

[11] *Ibid.*, volume II.
[12] *Ibid.*, volume II.

"Since the first of January last, with the view of strengthening and confirming his rule, he has, with his army of one thousand men, more or less, marched—

"From Cochabamba to Oruro, 36 leagues.
Oruro to La Paz, 49 leagues.
La Paz back to Oruro, 49 leagues.
Oruro back to La Paz, 49 leagues.
La Paz back to Oruro, 49 leagues.
Oruro to Potosi, 63 leagues.
Potosi to Sucre, 32 leagues.
Sucre to Cochabamba, 75 leagues.
Cochabamba to Oruro, 36 leagues.
Oruro back to Cochabamba, 36 leagues.
Cochabamba to Sucre, 75 leagues.
Sucre to Potosi, 32 leagues.
Potosi back to Sucre, 32 leagues.

"Total leagues 613.

"Each one of the above-named Cities has thrown off the authority of the Provisional President after his departure from it, with his army. . . ."

But Melgarejo had triumphed against the Constitutionalists, his opponents.

"There is now no force in arms in this country against Melgarejo. By his courage and energy, the superior discipline of his troops, and his artillery, he has triumphed over all opposition. It is most confidently believed by gentlemen of intelligence here, who are very far from being friendly to Melgarejo, that the success of the Constitutionalists (so called) would not have resulted in the pacification of the country. On the contrary, it is believed that they would have quarrelled and fought among themselves immediately, had they succeeded in putting down Melgarejo—there having been among them five or six aspirants for the Presidency. We can expect for a long time to come no other established Government than Melgarejo's."

And on April 16, 1866 Hall declared in a despatch from Cochabamba to Seward:[13]

"Entire quiet continues to prevail throughout the country. Since their total defeat in January by Gen. Melgarejo, his opponents have abandoned the idea of a further struggle with him; at least for the present. There is no force in arms against his Government in any part of the Republic, so far as I can learn. He has just caused the publication of a general amnesty, and it is believed, that all of the opposition who have fled from their homes will speedily return to them.

[13] *Ibid.*, volume II.

He has made common cause with Chile and Peru against Spain, and, through their Ministers in Bolivia, established the most friendly relations with these Republics, I can see no prospect, whatever, of an armed opposition to his rule, which would have the slightest chance of success. Such opposition will doubtless arise, sooner or later, as it has done with *every one* of his Presidential predecessors, with one exception; but *when* it will arise it is impossible to foresee. His authority may exist, unimpaired, for years, as did that of his Dictatorial predecessors, Santa Cruz, Ballivian, and Belzu; or he may fall within a shorter period, as did Cordova and Linares. Each of these Presidential personages came into power by election. General Sucre became President by the revolution against Spain. He was driven out of office in 1828, and General Blanco became President for a few days, when he was assassinated, to be succeeded by General Santa Cruz. A revolution in 1839 expelled Santa Cruz, and elevated General Velasco to the Chair of State, and a new revolution in 1841 demanded the return of Santa Cruz. That General being unable, however, to enter the country, General Ballivian was proclaimed President by the army, and maintained himself at the head of affairs until December 1847, when General Velasco again became Chief Magistrate of the Republic. After only a year's continuance in office he has been expelled again by the recent revolution, which has probably created Belzu his successor.

" . . . He is the President of the Army, and owes his elevation entirely to the military portion of the community. . . .

" . . . He has decided that the seat of Government is not permanent, but shall be regarded as existing wherever the administration happens to reside for the time being. . . ."

Caldwell, successor to Hall, who arrived in La Paz on October 22, 1868, was even more impressed with Melgarejo than Hall had been. In a despatch to Seward from La Paz of February 8, 1869 Caldwell stated that there had been a revolution against Melgarejo and that an attempt had been made upon his life on February 3, 1869. Melgarejo then assumed dictatorial powers. Caldwell declared:[14]

"I think I may say . . . that the President has the good of the country at heart; and is intent upon doing the best that can be done, to prevent anarchy and confusion, and to secure peace and prosperity to Bolivia.

" . . . He lives in the affection of his soldiers and the masses of the People, and defies the hatred and rage of his enemies, and treats them as enemies of the country. . . .

" . . . The overthrow of the Constitution [that of 1828] is but a pretext; the real desire is to gratify the desire for the personal

[14] *Ibid.*, volume III.

political preference and for indiscriminate rapine and slaughter during the Revolution."

Markbrett, successor to Caldwell, declared in a despatch from Cochabamba to Fish of November 8, 1869 that Agustín Morales had failed in his revolution against Melgarejo, but added that he felt that Morales was a most dangerous rival of Melgarejo.[15] Markbrett was a keen observer and a faithful informant for the state department. In a dispatch from Cochabamba to Fish of April 9, 1870 he stated that the right of suffrage had been extended to all who could read and write, except the clergy and the military. These two latter groups were excluded from the exercise of all public political functions, but the military in active service were included in the class of those who might acquire the franchise through intelligence tests. Markbrett was also impressed with the pan-Americanism of Melgarejo, calling attention to the fact that Bolivia gave citizenship rights to all American born who declared their intention of making Bolivia their permanent homes. He also gave an example of the tolerant liberalism of some of the higher clergy of Bolivia at the time. In a dispatch from Cochabamba to Fish of April 28, 1870 he declared that Rodríguez, the newly appointed bishop of Santa Cruz, was a very liberal man in his theological views. Bishop Rodríguez had been consecrated on April 27, 1870. He had come in person to Markbrett to invite him

---

[15] *Ibid.*, volume III. In a despatch of November 25, 1869 Markbrett stated that Henry Meiggs had loaned four million *soles* to the Bolivian government, that he was to receive eight per cent interest a year on the loan, and had been given the *guano* deposits of Mejillones and the imports levied at Arica as security. In return Meiggs was to pay six *soles* a ton of two hundred and forty pounds.

In a despatch of February 8, 1870 Markbrett stated that Juan de la Cruz Benavente had been appointed Bolivian representative to the Peace Conference of Washington. The statement of the titles and honors of Melgarejo are interesting: He was Well Deserver of his Country, in a high and eminent degree, Provisional President of the Republic, Citizen of Bolivia, Conserver of the Public Order and Peace, Grand Cross of the Imperial Order of the Cross-Bearer of Brazil, General of Division of Chile, etc., etc., etc. The honors which Melgarejo had received from Brazil and Chile are of more academic importance, for they mark the reward for services to those countries in solving boundary questions with them—and incidentally turning over to them a goodly bit of the national territory of Bolivia.

In a despatch to Fish of December 25, 1869, Markbrett stated that his predecessor, Caldwell, had decided to accept the invitation of Melgarejo to be his minister to the United States. The government of the United States declined to receive Caldwell as Bolivian minister to the United States, Fish believing that this did not comport with the practice of our country in such matters; "as inexpedient to receive a citizen of the United States as a resident diplomatic agent of a foreign power," is the way he phrased it.

to be one of the three *padrones,* or godfathers. To the reply that Markbrett was a Protestant, the bishop had replied that he[16]

> "was no bigot; that we were all marching under the same holy banner of Christ; that protestants were as good as Catholics; and that at the next session of the Bolivian Congress he would give me proof of his sincerity by advocating a law establishing religious liberty throughout the Republic. . . . I have reported that matter for the only reason that you may perceive that liberal and enlightened views are progressing in this country."

The end of the Melgarejo régime was approaching. Markbrett declared in a dispatch to Fish of June 30, 1870 from La Paz, that the sinister rule of this tyrant could not go on much longer.[17]

> "One thing is certain, however, that this state of affairs cannot possibly last much longer. Everybody is sick and disgusted with this misrule. The opposition to Melgarejo although silent, is intense; and his own men, owing to the many bitter humiliations and indignities to which they are constantly subjected will forsake him at the first safe opportunity that may offer."

The Congress of Bolivia met in regular session on August 6, 1870 in Oruro. In his Message to that body Melgarejo declared, among other things:[18]

> "How happy will this country be on the day when her sons shall think only of dedicating their strong arms and the inspirations of their genius to labor and industry, instead of wasting their powers upon internal dissentions and dark machinations of one party against another.
>
> "It is sad to have to confess that although nobody seems to be willing to contribute to the national treasury yet all wish to live from it. The office seeking mania which forms so marked a contrast to the labor loving spirit which exists in other countries—transforming them into blooming states—is to our country the great incubus which prevents its rapid development."

Markbrett also stated that the *diezmos* had been abolished throughout Bolivia and that the Holy See had agreed to its abolition. He also stated that Bolivia had been represented in the Vatican Council of 1869-1870 by Archbishop Pedro de Puch and Bishop Calixto Claviko of La Paz. The government of Bolivia had paid their expenses.

---

[16] Despatches, Bolivia, volume III.
[17] *Ibid.,* volume IV.
[18] *Ibid.,* volume IV.

III

There can be little excuse for attempting to explain Melgarejo either as a man or as a dictator. He belongs to that group whom Ramón Mejias describes in his *La locura en la historia* as men who are fit subjects for the psychologist and the sociologist rather than the historian. Melgarejo was simply an intemperate soldier, who was altogether too often the slave of women and strong drinks, one of Lombroso's *enfermos de sociedad*. He was one of those human beings who act as they do because of certain maladjustments of their cerebral makeup, as Gall and Lavater would put it. *Melgarejismo* has about it the symptoms and peculiarities of a social disease. It implies, in the first place, a people submissive to resistance, a people willing to endure wrongs and ills rather than to fight for right and justice. *Melgarejismo* implies a willingness to submit to persecutions, deportations, espionage, and delations, rather than fight to make such wrongs and crimes impossible. The tools of *melgarejismo* are not the *puñal* and the *veneno,* but adulations towards the *mandatario*. *Melgarejismo* must be sanguinary and anarchic so that the people may duly appreciate the few liberties and protections which the *caudillo* dictator graciously permits them to enjoy.

Melgarejo played the game of the dictator. He had about him, at all times, four *rifleros,* men armed to the teeth, doing their deadly work without fear or favor. He had his faithful henchmen, and a subservient press. *La Situación* in La Paz and *La Actualidad* in Sucre saw only the good side of Melgarejo. He was a leader personifying all that was noble, good, generous, loyal, and patriotic. He was the first citizen of America, *El Gran Capitán de los Siglos.* He had cut off the head of the hydra of revolution and given the country peace and prosperity. He had caused liberalism to flourish in Bolivia during his *sexenio;* and when he ceased to rule a great cloud of obscurity passed over his country.

Of course, there were good things about Melgarejo. His Americanism, which sought to remove all the boundaries between the states and make all America one great family, had something of the grandiose about it. It is, of course, difficult to say how much of that idea was his own, and how much of it was the idea of his secretary-general, Muñoz. It may well be that all the foreign and domestic policies of Melgarejo were those of Mariano Justo Muñoz, the man who served him throughout his entire dictatorship. But when he fell he was treated as dictators are treated in Bolivia. The constituent assembly nullified all the acts of his administration.[19] This was, in fact, merely approving the *supremo decreto* of the provisional government of Morales of July 15, 1871.[20]

Mariano Melgarejo had gone the way of dictators. He had been able to escape death at the hands of infuriated Indians. The end was in keeping with his life. And on November 23, 1871 he was assassinated by the husband of his daughter, General José Sánchez, in Lima. In giving an account of this tragic end, Markbrett declared, in a dispatch to Fish of December 16, 1871 from Cochabamba:[21]

---

19 The act was passed on August 9, 1871.

20 See Corral, *Memoria del secretario jeneral de estado que presente a la asamblea constituente de 1871* (Sucre, June 24, 1871), 16-24. This is an unbound document. The Meiggs and the Church contracts are dealt with in considerable detail. Corral gives other means used by Melgarejo to raise money. He cites these: the loan by La Chambre y Compañía for one million *pesos,* that of Armand y Compañía de Burdeos for two hundred and fifty thousand *pesos,* that of Concha y Toro for ten thousand *bolivianos,* that of Meiggs for four million *pesos fuertes,* that of George E. Church for ten million pounds sterling, that of Clement Torreti for buying up all the *moneda feble of Bolivia* (sum not specified), various contracts for *guano* by Pedro López Gama, and that of A. D. Piper for colonization purposes. Then there were the sales of the Indian lands between 1865 and 1870, amounting to one million three hundred thousand *bolivianos.*

21 Despatches, Bolivia, volume IV. The private life of Melgarejo was one series of debaucheries after he had left the woman whom he had married when quite young. This woman was Rosa Rojas, a member of a very respectable family in Cochabamba. She was much too good for him. He soon tired of her and chose for his mistress a beautiful young woman of La Paz, Juana Sánchez, by name. While he was always unfaithful, as far as women were concerned, he loved this woman to distraction. Like the mistresses of public men, Juana Sánchez played an interesting rôle. It was her business, in the first place, to try to keep her lover. This meant the ability to know her man, to cater to his every mood and whim. There were times when she urged him to get rid of his opponents in a very cruel manner. On the other hand she was also able to induce him not to commit certain crimes which he might otherwise have committed. Juana Sánchez is accordingly a woman about whom there is a great deal of difference of opinion. Her enemies charge her with responsibility for all that was mean, brutal, and savage in him. His mad love for her and her charms, it is claimed, made him a perfect slave of her wiles, ambitions, and caprices. On the other hand her defenders claim that whatever was good, noble, and generous in Melgarejo was due to her great influence over him. Melgarejo had two daughters by a woman named Ignacia Beizaga, a native of Cochabamba. José Aurelio Sánchez, the man who murdered Melgarejo, and the man whom Melgarejo had raised to high position in the army, married Melgarjo's daughter Valentina, one of the two daughters by Ignacia Beizaga. And the son of Sánchez and Valentina, Severo, married Rosaura Sánchez. The affair in Lima was claimed to have been due to the effort of Juana Sánchez to break off all relations with Melgarejo. There is also the view that trouble really came to a climax over the control of certain property which Melgarejo did not want Juana Sánchez to have and which she was determined to retain possession of. Whatever may be the real cause of the murder, the fact appears to be that Melgarejo was killed by her brother in an effort to prevent him from getting into the room where Juana Sánchez was. There was no sympathy for Melgarejo, as Markbrett brought

"His was a reckless and desperate career. By a bold stroke in this city on the 28th of December 1864—which unfortunately for the country—succeeded—he usurped the Presidency of this Republic. His Government, which lasted over six years, was the most arbitrary and tyrannical with which Bolivia has been cursed. His private life was scandalous beyond belief; and on the whole I think the world lost nothing by his death. His assassination has caused a profound sensation throughout the country but has excited little sympathy."

---

out in his despatch. He came to the end which such a life might be expected to bring about. It is obvious, without any further details, that a man living such a life could hardly be expected to bring into the government affairs that honesty and sincerity which good government demands. For in addition to despotism, *per se,* there was the attack upon the public treasury to meet the financial demands of his family and friends. Melgarejo was able to rule because he enabled his in-laws and friends to use public money. One hastens to remark, of course, in this connection, that there is nothing unusual about this raid upon the public treasury by a public official and his cohorts. Nor will it be historically accurate to say that Melgarejo was any worse than many of his predecessors or successors in the presidential chair of Bolivia. One merely emphasizes the fact that Melgarejo also engaged in raids upon the public treasury in addition to the many other errors and crimes committed during the *sexenio* period in which he was in power in Bolivia. One certainly does not mean to say that Melgarejo was the only public official in Bolivia who had a mistress. Such a statement would betray an ignorance utterly unpardonable in one who lays any claim to a knowledge of the social life of Bolivia. One may merely call attention to the ability of Juana Sánchez as a mistress in a very critical period of the political history of Bolivia; and to place her alongside the mistresses of history. Juana Sánchez deserves a place alongside that of Madame Lynch of Paraguay, a contemporary of Juana Sánchez. See Tomás O'Connor d' Arlach, *Rozas, Francia y Melgarejo* (La Paz, 1914).

CHAPTER TWENTY

DICTATOR JUAN JOSÉ FLORES

ECUADOR has also had a large crop of dictators, and is, like Peru and Bolivia, a creature of dictatorship. Like them she is greatly indebted to Bolívar, as well as to San Martín, for emancipation from the rule of Spain. One need not here go again into any phase of the movement for independence in Ecuador except as it concerns Juan José Flores. The account of the dictatorship of Flores will be more easily understood in the light of its geographic setting. In point of size, the country is much smaller than either of the other two, less than half as large, in fact. But like them she has always had, geographically, a distinct existence. Her past is fully as brilliant as either of the other two, her tradition lacking none of the features of either. Her leading cities, like those of Peru and Bolivia, were great cultural centers during the colonial period. Vying with Chuquisaca and Lima, as centers of learning in the Indies, Quito early was called *La Luz de América.* Like Peru and Bolivia, Ecuador's population is predominating Indian, and like most, too, her future will be tied up with the faith of the Indian. Moisés Sáenz' studies show that the white rule of the Indian has not been wholly one of unmixed blessing to either group, and that the future will demand a more intelligent attention to Indianism than in the past, if real progress is to be made.[1]

The country is divided into the cis-Andine, the inter-Andine, and the trans-Andine regions, each with its own peculiar physiographic and climatic features. The first two of these have been of the most importance to its people thus far, but the trans-Andine region is likely to be of the utmost importance in the future. The inter-Andine region has been the great cultural center of the country, with Quito, Ambato, and Cuenca as bases. Topographically, this region possesses an aspect of majesty and grandeur. "Nowhere in the world can there be found such an assemblage of snow-clad peaks, several of which are active volcanoes." There are twenty-one of these snow-capped peaks grouped around these central plains almost within sight of one another. Cotopaxi, Antisana, Pichincha, and, above all, Chimborazo are among the great peaks of the world. There are two hydraulic systems, one flowing into the Atlantic and the other into the Pacific. The Napo, the Tigre, the Mira, the Esmeraldas,

[1] Moisés Sáenz, *Sobre el indio peruano y incorporación al medio nacional* (Mexico, 1933).

and the Guayas are all important rivers. The Guayas, with the great Gulf of Guayaquil, is of the very greatest importance economically to the Ecuadorian people. This river is the main feature of the cis-Andine region and is a most important part of the famous *costa* country.

No account of the inhabitants of the country would be complete without an emphasis upon regionalism. Regionalism has played a rôle no less important in Ecuador than in Peru and Bolivia. The *costeños* of Ecuador, like the *costeños* of the other two countries, are a people apart. The *guayaquileños* are particularly noted for their *costeño* characteristics. No whit less distinct are the people of the *sierras*. The *quiteños* are peculiarly an upland people. It would be difficult to find two groups of people of the same race who are so different from one another as the *guayaquileños* and the *quiteños*. There is no effort here to make it appear that regionalism is the only factor in the revolutionary activities of the people of Ecuador during the two dictatorships which are to be dealt with. It is the purpose, however, to emphasize the very powerful effect of regionalism upon personalism during those periods. Both Flores the Elder and García Moreno were *costeños,* albeit from the two opposite coastal regions, one from the Caribbean Sea and the other from the Gulf of Guayaquil. Regionalism, or sectionalism, may be said to have been more important in the history of Ecuador than the ethnological factor in shaping the political, social, and economic life of the Ecuadorian people.

I

Juan José Flores was born in Puerto Cabello in 1800. He was thus a Venezuelan like Miranda, Bolívar, and Sucre. He is not known to have received much of a formal education, but took up life in the Spanish army at an early age. No one became more thoroughly a child of the army than he, not even excepting Belzu and Melgarejo. La Gouhir believes that Flores has been too harshly criticized and that his work for Ecuador has been greatly underestimated. Flores was imposed upon Ecuador by the conditions of the times and more especially by the army; and he did what the people wanted him to do.[2] It is La Gouhir's opinion that Flores was one of the most prominent figures of America in 1830. In the wars of emancipation he played an important rôle, becoming early a most trusted lieutenant of the great Liberator. In fact he became one of the most intimate aides of Bolívar, fighting in all more than twenty-three battles. He was a lieutenant-colonel at the age of twenty, a colonel

[2] J. L. R. [José La Gouhir y Rodas], *Historia del Ecuador* (Quito, 1920).

at twenty-two, a general of brigade at twenty-six, and a general of division at the age of twenty-nine. In the Battle of Carabobo he was mayor chief-of-staff in the army of the West, and in the Battle of Cuenca he was chief-of-staff to Bolívar. The defeat at Pasto caused him to retire from the army service to live in Popayán. He was appointed second in command to General Solom, and in 1824 he succeeded to the command of the army of which Solom had been chief. He brought the war in Ecuador to an end by his triumphs at Sucuimbo and Pasto. He was then appointed to the command of the armies in Ecuador, quelled the *motín militar* in Quito and in Guayaquil, and fought valiantly in defence of Ecuador against the Peruvians in 1829. In the war against Peru he won, with Sucre, the immortal Battle of Tarqui.

It was in this battle that he gained the undying gratitude of Bolívar.[3] Bolívar also spoke highly of him as a political administrator.[4] After establishing order at Guayaquil, Bolívar declared that *cada día descubre nuevos medios de reforma.*[5] On May 14, 1828 he wrote to Flores thanking him for the kind sentiments expressed by him, declaring that they were the *más elocuente y la más bella entre miles que se han hecho en Colombia,* and *que doy a Vd. la enhorabuena.*[6] Bolívar refused to believe that Flores had anything to do with the assassination of Sucre;[7] and when Ecuador broke away from *Gran Colombia* and his friend Flores had become president of the country, Bolívar still had faith in him.[8] It was to Flores he wrote the gloomy letter from Barranquilla, on November 9, 1830, about the uselessness of their work in America, and urged him to avenge the assassination of Sucre.[9] On the same day he also wrote to him that if the Ecuadorian people desired independence they should be given what they wanted. They were a sovereign people and had a right to decide their own destiny.[10] But Bolívar had detected the change in Flores and so informed Rafael Urdaneta on December 7, 1830.[11] And that was the end of Bolívar.

El Rey de la Noche, as Flores was called, was free to continue his ambitious climb towards glory, fame, and death. Sucre and Bolívar

[3] Lecuna, *Cartas del Libertador,* VIII, 257.
[4] Bolívar to Flores, Bogotá, September 12, 1827 in *ibid.,* VII., 19.
[5] *Ibid.,* VII, 80.
[6] *Ibid.,* VII, 272-273.
[7] Bolívar to J. F. Madrid, July 24, 1830 in *ibid.,* IX, 284.
[8] Bolívar to Montilla, November 8, 1830 in *ibid.,* IX, 374-375.
[9] Lacuna, *Cartas del Libertador,* IX, 377.
[10] *Ibid.,* IX, 378.
[11] *Ibid.,* IX, 406. The letter was written from Santa Marta.

were both out of the way. The Pacific coast republics of South America were now in the hands of Andrés Santa Cruz and Juan José Flores, both of whom remained the favorites of Bolívar to the end of that man's life. Both considered themselves the heirs to the Bolivian mantle of leadership, and both were to become, for a considerable length of time, the two most powerful men of their age.

II

The people of Ecuador, as has been seen, were prepared for the break with *Gran Colombia* before Bolívar died. As early as May 12, 1830 Ramón Miño went to Flores to inform him that the Ecuadorians wanted independence from *Gran Colombia,* and asked him to call a *cabildo abierto* in Quito to consider that grave question. On May 13, 1830 an assembly of the *quiteños* met in such a *cabildo* and declared the country independent.[12] They chose Flores civil and military chief of the republic. On May 31, 1830 Flores decreed the assembly of the constituent assembly in Riobamba. On August 10 the assembly began its sessions. Flores was continued as the supreme head of the state, to remain in power until a constitution had been adopted. The only serious problem in connection with the drafting of the fundamental law was that dealing with the basis of representation in the national legislature. Regionalism was a powerful factor and forced the adoption of the plan for equal representation for all the departments, rather than proportional representation. After the adoption of the constitution the assembly elected Flores President of the republic by a vote of nineteen to one. Olmedo was elected vice-president. On September 22 Flores and Olmedo were inaugurated, and the Flores régime had begun. Flores chose José Felix Valdivieso, minister secretary of state, and Antonio Martínez Pallares, minister of war. On September 24 the assembly voted honors to Bolívar, proclaiming him Father of the Country and Protector of South Colombia.

Ecuador had become an independent nation but was in none too healthy a condition. There were many who felt that the whole affair had been unfair to Bolívar. General Rafael Urdaneta became the leader of this group, and began a revolution in favor of the preservation of the Colombian union on November 28. On December 2 revolutionists of

---

[12] The meeting was held in the *aula* of the University of Quito, after the fashion of the Bolivians in 1825. José Joaquín Olmedo, the Poet of Victory, and Vicente Ramón Roca, two of Ecuador's most distinguished citizens, were members of the assembly. José Fernández Salvador was president of the body.

Cuenca joined the Urdaneta forces, and those of Quito joined a few days later. Urdaneta acted rather harshly with the *guayaquileños,* ordering part of the City of Guayaquil burned because they had not paid the whole levy of fifty thousand dollars made by him upon them. This fire took place on December 23, 1830 and was just another of the acts for which Urdaneta was noted. He had ordered Saragura burned for a like cause. Cevallos declares that Urdaneta carried on a ruinous revolution, playing havoc with the political institutions of the country. The news of the death of Bolívar was fatal to the Urdaneta revolution and he was easily defeated. With him went into exile some twenty-five army chiefs, including two generals and eight colonels. In all, forty-four officers fell with Urdaneta. This was a very good thing for the country for none of them were of much use to Ecuador.

The suppression of the Urdaneta revolution was only one of the problems that had to be solved by the new state. The constitution was ill-suited to the needs of the country, the finances were in a chaotic condition, the army was much too large, and the number of foreigners in the service of the republic was much too large. The most important of these problems was that of how to rid the country of foreignism, because Ecuador, like Peru and Bolivia, had a very large number of foreigners in its service. The army had a large number of foreign troops as well as foreign officers. Both groups had joined the army largely for the purpose of adventure and advancement, and could be counted upon to stir up trouble in order to have something to do. Cevallos declares that most of the foreign officers were immoral and could easily be preyed upon by discontented elements. The whole situation was aggravated by the fact that Flores himself was a foreigner and in favor of foreign officers. The problem of the Ecuadorian people was thus even more important than that confronting the Bolivian people immediately following the establishment of independence, but even more important because of the larger number of foreigners in Ecuador. The Colombian influence was of course even greater than in Bolivia, and the danger from Mosquera of Colombia and Páez of Venezuela was not to be minimized.

The chief interest of Flores lay in the acquisition of Cauca and Popayán. Cevallos defends his action in incorporating these, because Cauca was independent of Colombia and Popayán was a part of Quito. The congress of Ecuador, invoking the *uti possidetis juris* of 1810, declared that these two regions belonged to Ecuador, and formally annexed them in 1831. Colombia would not accept this action; trouble began between the two countries, and Pasto was again taken over by

Colombia. In the same year Flores took formal possession of the Galápagos Islands, causing them to be explored and settlements made in them. While the deposits of *guano* were not the cause for the settlement of those islands, *guano* had already been discovered and its importance noted even as early as 1824. The territorial aspirations of Flores gave the people of Ecuador grave concern. They were interested in the large army which he considered necessary for his work. The finances of the republic did not warrant the maintenance of such a large force and the opposition grew against it. They opposed the appointment of García del Río as minister of *hacienda* in 1831, on the score that he was a foreigner. Cevallos declares that the trouble with the government of Flores was that he had no system, no principles, and that he was merely ruling a group of separate departments. He feels that Flores made a great mistake in keeping the people in the dark about his real policies, and the people were thus getting tired of his rule.[13]

In 1832 Flores was becoming distinctly unpopular throughout the republic. He was charged with a desire to make Ecuador ultimately a part of either of the two other former members of *Gran Colombia.* He was himself a Venezuelan and was thought to work in the interest of Páez. García del Río was also held to favor subordinating Ecuador to Colombia, his native land. In addition to these grievances, the people found others. They felt that Flores had been too good to his exceptionally large family, at the expense of the state. They also believed that he had been a party to the assassination of Sucre, and opposed the manner in which he treated General Matheu, whom he had exiled. Flores had roused the feeling of the better classes by his crude criticism of certain respectable families in Quito because of certain customs and manner of life among them. There was still much about even the most powerful *quiteño* families that was colonial, but it was hardly to be expected that Flores could do much good by ridicule.

The opposition became more articulate in 1833, one of the most significant years in the history of Ecuador. The newspapers became active in opposition to the *sistema floreana. El Republicano* of Quito and *El Hombre Libre* of Guayaquil were both active in airing the wrongs and errors of the administration. Of even greater importance was the work of the *Quiteño Libre.* This organization owed much to the genius of Francisco Hall,[14] who had come to Colombia in search of adventure

[13] Pedro Fermín Cevallos, *Resumen de la historia del Ecuador desde su origen hasta 1845* (Guayaquil, 1886), V, 64-7.

[14] Hall was an Englishman, and suffered martyrdom for his views in his adopted country.

under the great Liberator. He had won immortal fame in the Battle of Pichincha and had remained in Ecuador. He was a great student of the newer social, political, and economic ideas of his age, especially those of Jeremy Bentham. He became a rabid republican and turned against Bolívar when he assumed dictatorial powers. He was a bitter enemy of Flores, and gathered about him many of the young men of Quito in an effort to get rid of Flores. They organized the celebrated society called *El Quiteño Libre* in 1833, and began the issue of *El Quiteño Libre,* which soon became a very powerful organ against the whole *sistema floreana.* At the same time one of Ecuador's most celebrated sons, Rocafuerte,[15] a *guayaquileño,* began active opposition to Flores. He returned from his very extensive sojourn abroad in 1833, a great personality, and began to exercise a powerful influence upon his fellow countrymen. He became especially interested in *El Quiteño Libre,* published for the first time on May 12, 1833.[16] The paper was received with enthusiasm, but lasted only four months. Flores had his own newspapers: *La Gazeta del Gobierno del Ecuador, El Amigo del Orden, El Nueve de Octubre, El Trece de Febrero,* and *El Investidaro.* The society *El Quiteño Libre* also published *Las Facultades Extraordinarias,* which also exercised a large influence.

Among the most important events of the year 1833 were those in which the congress had a part. It began its sessions on September 10 and became at once a center of great controversies. It wrestled for some time over the question of whether Rocafuerte, who had been elected from Pichincha, was a citizen of Ecuador, but it decided that since he had never been naturalized a Mexican citizen he was legally entitled to his seat in the congress. He began at once to cause the Flores forces much trouble. He was especially bitter in his attacks on García del Río, whom he had had for an enemy for many years. Rocafuerte failed because the congress gave Flores dictatorial powers, a step which Rocafuerte fought bitterly.

Flores began at once to use his new powers to get rid of his opponents through deportation.[17] Rocafuerte, Moncaya, Ascasubi, and Muñis were

[15] Few men have had a more varied career than Rocafuerte, comparable, if at all, only to Miranda. He travelled in Spain, France, England, the United States, Cuba, and Mexico championing democracy. His services in Mexico were especially interesting. His work in Ecuador will be related later.

[16] For the objects of this paper see Cevallos, *Resumen de la historia del Ecuador,* V, 124.

[17] Decrees were issued, after the fashion of the kings of France, ordering the expulsion of all whom the government decided should be expelled. All was of course declared done in the interest of peace and order. This Florian concept of conserving himself in power naturally defeated the very ends for which he was working.

among those exiled. Revolution was the only possible result of such high-handed proceedings. Rocafuerte returned to Guayaquil and had little difficulty in getting the support of its people, and the famous October revolution was the result. On October 18 Flores left Quito for Guayaquil. On the next day the revolution broke out in Quito. On November 24 Flores defeated the *guayaquileños,* but he did not remain victor very long.

The year 1834 was a continuation of the year 1833. The contest between Flores and Rocafuerte came to an end through a compromise, the two signing the treaty of July 19, 1834 whereby Flores agreed not to oppose the election of Rocafuerte to the presidency. The congress met in Quito on January 7, 1835 under the name of the national convention. On April 20 Rocafuerte entered Quito. The convention, called by Rocafuerte, began its sessions in Ambato on June 22. Olmedo was its president and made a powerful address in which he urged a democratic procedure, and respect for the majesty of the people and for democratic institutions. Rocafuerte was elected provisional president. The convention voted thanks to Flores, pronouncing him the *primer ciudadano del Ecuador.*[18] Flores was also appointed commander-in-chief of the army with all the rights and powers which usually belonged to the office of captain-general. But Flores did not long remain inactive. He was elected senator from two provinces, and was a conspicuous member during the special session of the congress, attacking two ministers so forcefully that they were removed by Rocafuerte on January 9, 1837, six days after the congress began its sessions.

Rocafuerte served out his constitutional term although not without much dissatisfaction. On January 15, 1839 the congress began its regular session and elected Flores president by a vote of twenty-nine out of thirty-eight votes cast. Flores was inaugurated on the same day, and began his duties in the midst of very general satisfaction. He was able to make the people feel that he meant what he promised. He had but one aim, and that was the welfare of the nation, whatever that might mean. He would appoint to office only those who were fitted by merit, aptitude, and honesty for the position. The *amigos del país* was organized to aid him in this work. For about eight months Ecuador enjoyed peace and prosperity. Several acts of the government were of importance: the opening of the port of San Lorenzo, the reduction of the *dias de fiestas,* and the admission of foreigners as teachers in the schools

[18] Cevallos, *Resumen de la historia del Ecuador,* V, 279.

of the republic. The treaty with Spain was ratified on February 15, 1840, whereby Ecuador was recognized as an independent nation. The presence of Santa Cruz as an exile had no influence upon the affairs of the republic, although Flores was interested in the revival of the Peru-Bolivian confederation. On the other hand Flores was greatly interested in the ecclesiastical policy pursued by Mosquera, and the civil war in Colombia over the suppression of the convents in 1839 was followed with the keenest attention in Ecuador. In no South American country was the Roman Catholic Church more powerful than in Ecuador.

In 1841 Flores had difficulties with the special session of congress, with the result that Flores dissolved the congress. He went to war with Colombia over Pasto and was again defeated. It was one of the most inglorious wars fought by Flores. The opposition against the dictator became more and more pronounced. The congress was called in special session on January 15, 1843. In his lengthy message to that body Flores spoke of Ecuador as an isthmus of snow between two seas of fire, referring to the policy of Peru and Colombia towards his country.[19] The congress drew up a new political constitution which it promulgated on March 31, 1843. Cevallos brands this congress a scandalous one, and Rocafuerte fought against it and the dictatorial tactics of Flores. The ecclesiastical authorities were especially opposed to it, but were forced to submit; Flores thereby hastened his own fall from power by the acts against them.

But the act which caused more concern, and which brought about a revolution, was the passage by the congress of the law imposing a tax of three *pesos* upon every male citizen over the age of eighteen years. This law, passed on June 5, 1843, was to relieve the burdens upon the Indians, who had been paying the hated *tributo* for more than three centuries. So fierce was the opposition against the Law of the Three *Pesos* that revolution broke out a few days after the passage of the act. The cry *Mueron los tres pesos* caused Flores to have the act repealed, and the revolters gave up the fight. The year 1844 passed peacefully, Cevallos declaring: *El año de 1844, a Dios gracias, se vencio en sosegada paz.*[20]

The *período floreano* was, however, drawing to its close. The powerful Rocafuerte took over the leadership of the opposition and began the famous March revolution of 1845. He won an easy victory over Flores

[19] *Ibid.,* V, 428.
[20] *Ibid.,* V, 488.

and General Itamendi. Rocafuerte gave way to the *grito* of the enemies of Flores that Flores must be driven from public life, and on June 17 he signed the famous convention with Flores. The latter agreed to leave his country for Europe and to remain away until the political institutions of Ecuador had been reformed. The convention is one of the most important in the whole history of Spanish America, and the conduct of Flores one of the finest examples ever set by any *caudillo* in America, according to Cevallos.[21]

The *Grito de 6 de Marzo de 1845* meant that the national cause had triumphed and that *Floreanismo* had lost its grip upon the vitals of the Ecuadorian people. The revolution of March 1845 brought about the real independence of Ecuador, for with Flores went also the baneful foreign counsellors of the national government. Cevallos considers the defeat of Flores of the utmost importance to Ecuador, for the people began to live after his fall. This is the larger significance of the defeat of *floreanismo,* as he sees it.[22] La Gouhir contends that Flores desired to perpetuate himself in power, after the fashion of Bolívar, and that that was the main purpose of the *constitución floreana.*[23] He finds that while the year 1844 was outwardly peaceful, inwardly Ecuador was a seething volcano, ready to explode or erupt at the least notice. Flores had become the great *tirano* and had to be driven out of Ecuador at all costs. Flores had displayed in his government of Ecuador the worst that the military, the foreigners, and the speculators possessed. His tyranny and insatiable ambition had made Flores a dismal figure at last, and deservedly so.

But Flores was not to be disposed of in such an easy manner. He had no sooner reached Spain than he began a scheme for the reduction of Ecuador, perhaps for the reduction, ultimately, of the whole of Spanish America. Queen Regent Cristina gave him assistance with the idea of regaining the lost possessions of America. The interest of Spain and Europe in America between 1845 and 1870 is known to every school boy, and need not be considered here, except to place these activities of Flores in their proper setting. It may be the most charitable thing to say of Flores that he merely desired to reëstablish himself in Ecuador and had no part in the larger and more sinister movement. Be the facts what they may, on October 12, 1846 the news arrived in Ecuador that

[21] *Ibid.,* V, 497.
[22] *Ibid.,* V, 490.
[23] Important features of this instrument were those that made the term of the deputies eight years, the senators twelve years, and created a powerful presidency.

Flores was fitting out an expedition against Spanish America. His agents were busy in London, Paris, and Madrid, with Ricardo Wright working in Ireland and England securing support for him. The plan was to take the ships to the Canaries from whence the expedition to America was to start. But the diplomatic remonstrances with the British government had the effect of inducing it to prohibit the preparations for the expedition in British possessions on the ground that such action was illegal. The ships were embargoed by orders from Lord Palmerston and offered for sale.[24] This brought to an end an inglorious undertaking.

The alarm caused in Spanish America by this *floreano* fiasco was very great. Nothing had so powerfully revived the fear of Spain. The *peligro español* took on the fear of an *invasión europea.* In all parts of Spanish America the cry went up against the *reconquista godo-floreana.* The press took up the cry and began to demand that an American congress ought to be called to deal with dangers of this kind. The result was a great outburst of patriotism and internationalism, with much discussion of fraternal unions and confederations.[25] There was an increase in land and sea armaments in the American republics, and a congress of the Americas met in Lima in 1847-1848. García Moreno took an active part in the movement for the American congress, using the powerful paper *La Nación* for the expression of his views. He was a brilliant journalist and urged the formation of a *confederación de estas repúblicas hermanas* and a *congreso de sus plenipotenciarios.* And on February 8, 1848, at the celebrated *congreso* of Lima, the *confederación del Pacífico* was created by this *congreso.* This was a veritable defensive league against all and every power that might attempt to invade these republics.

Our diplomatic agents in Ecuador were keen observers of events and personalities in this period. The following excerpts are of interest. Van Allan wrote to Clayton, February 1, 1850, from Quito:[26]

> "Juan Jose Flores was of humble, Indian origin. When very young he was the servant in the employment of a Spanish officer, who was engaged at the time, in the protracted resistance against the struggles of Spanish America for independence. This master was taken prisoner in action, and young Flores, after some time, was found a private soldier in the ranks of the army of the Patriots.

[24] The ships were the *Glenelg,* the *Monarch,* and the *Neptune.* Palmerston made his statement on November 23, 1846. Gouhir, *Historia de la república del Ecuador,* 354.

[25] *Ibid.,* 355-356.

[26] Department of State, Despatches, Ecuador, volume II.

His courage, ambition and perseverance were marked by his successive stages of advancement, until he received from Bolivar a General's Commission. He was then appointed Intendant in the province of Quito. But, he was of a restless, unquiet spirit, and soon began to betray uneasiness in this subordinate sphere, and at length, he boldly aspired to independent authority, though at the risk of breaking up the Republic of Colombia. His ardent ambition was impaired by no difficulties, and any sacrifice which it required, he was not merely willing, but eager to make. His measures were generally chosen with an astounding degree of ingenuity and skill, and he had a profound knowledge of men, and of motives. His persuasion was irresistible, and the fascination of his presence and manners was great. He brought over the army to his designs, and, thus strengthened and emboldened, declared the independence of the province of Quito. In this emergency, Gen. Sucre was dispatched to Bolivar to supersede him in his government, but, on the way thither, he was assassinated, and some hesitate not to ascribe the deed to the instigation of Flores himself. Bolivar was about to send a force to Quito, to reduce it to quiet and subordination, but before the necessary arrangements were completed, he died, and Flores, being thus unembarrassed by the only man, whom he had occasion really to fear, found himself comparatively secure, whatever might be his plans. His great purpose of the division of the Republic, he now fully accomplished, in conjunction with Gen. Paez of Venezuela, and he was elected the first President of the Ecuador, whilst his coadjutor likewise became the President of Venezuela.

"Subsequently, Flores was elected for two years, and, when they had passed, Congress not having been organized, owing to disputed seats, he held office in violation of the Constitution, for two years longer. When the next Congress met, the Constitution was amended and Gen. Flores was elected for eight years, two only of which elapsed, when a revolution of a violent character broke out against the President, and he capitulated. By the terms, it was agreed, that there should be paid him, annually, the sum of twenty thousand dollars, and that his private fortune should be secured to his family provided that he would retire from the country. He did so, but these conditions have never been fulfilled on the part of the Ecuador, and hence have arisen the attempts of Gen. Flores to regain his position, since he has never by word or deed, renounced his constitutional right to the Presidency, but only the practical exercise of the office.

"After thus finding the party in power of another to their expressed stipulation, Gen. Flores repaired to Europe, with a determination to promote his interest in some way. Such were his skill and address, that he succeeded in procuring from Queen Cristina, of Spain, a loan of two millions of dollars, to further his designs. It is regarded as in the highest degree marvellous, that Cristina, well known as exceedingly penurious, should have aided so largely a design, about the accomplishment of which there must have been much uncertainty. It is stated, on good authority, that Cristina entered into the plans of Gen. Flores, for the sake of providing for her children by Munoz, to whom it was proposed to give, at length, three crowns, those of New Granada, Ecuador and Peru. Flores collected together 6,000 men, with whom he intended making the endeavor to reestablish his authority. Only two hundred of this number were soldiers. The rest were mostly artisans. An agent of his was engaged in fitting out several vessels in the port of London. . . .

"From what I have learned, he governed the country with great skill and energy. He made many valuable improvements. He courted the members of the old established families, and drew them generally to his support. His well nigh irresistible passion often changed an enemy into a fast and valuable friend. That, in a country exposed to constant political convulsions, he, for so long a time, held the reins of power, is owing, as much as to any single cause, to his winning and captivating address. His success in Europe may be attributed to the same cause. His reverses have, undoubtedly, much disciplined and enlarged his mind, and his greater acquaintance with men and with the world, has, unquestionably, given him a deeper insight into the theory and practice of Government. His mind is one of surprising acuteness and readiness of apprehension. He is a constant observer and quick thinker. He would probably, now, be the best Governor of the State in South America. It should be added that he has not the reputation of a sanguinary man, which fact is, in these countries, a singularity. He has always preferred to gain men over to his side by flattery and artful policy, than to inflict on them summary vengeance. His attempt upon the Republic was not, as has been represented, an effort to usurp dominion, or to continue in office longer than his allotted period, but, primarily, at least, to secure the prerogatives which he had been lawfully chosen to exercise, and which he was forced, temporarily, to suspend, not by the people, generally, but by an interested and jealous faction."

Van Allan gave his views on the cause and nature of the frequent revolutions in South America in a dispatch to Clayton from Quito of May 9, 1850.[27]

"In South America, every man of great ambition is unwilling to wait, until the constitutional course of events may bring him to station and influence, but he seeks power by taking the lead in rebellion against the existing Government. Liberty, in these countries, is generally the cry of those who wish to rally to a party to resist and crush the established authority. Constitutions are made and unmade. Change follows change, and the prosperity of the

[27] *Ibid.*, volume II,

country is not advanced and rebellious subjects are as restless and uneasy as ever. There is no definite public purpose professed by revolutions. Each actor strives only for his own ascendency, and not for the triumph of any principle or measure. Lives are thrown away, wealth is squandered, government is interrupted, and the industry of the people paralized, either without an object, or for one of mere selfish character. Very many persons here think it highly disreputable, by a course of dilligent labor, to promote their own welfare and that of their country, who, nevertheless, experience no feeling of shame at their endeavor to keep the international and foreign relations of the Republic in constant embarrassment and disturbance. . . . They are moved solely by a desire of private plunder and individual profit."

The dispatch to Clayton by Van Allan from Quito of June 1, 1850 also contains a paragraph of interest on Flores:[28]

"It is not surprising that, in such a condition of things, hopes for the return of General Flores, after having been secretly entertained in the hearts of many, should now be whispered, and that elements, which during his presidency were united, and afterwards separated, should now again be drawing together. The enemies of Flores either are, or pretend to be, in a state of great alarm at his expected return. At assemblages of his friends, his health is drunk with significance. Such an occupation of the public mind, both inimical and friendly, with the name of the Ex-president is full of meaning. From what I have seen and heard, and from what I am able to conjecture on reasonable grounds, it would not be a strange thing, if six months hence should find Flores exercising dictatorial authority in the Ecuador. I shall say nothing of the right of this man's claims, but of one thing I am fully persuaded, that he is the only man fit for the crisis. . . ."

Cushing, successor to Van Allan, had a very different view of the whole matter. In a dispatch to Clay from Guayaquil of February 29, 1852 he declared:[29]

"He is a native of Venezuela of humble origin. His public career began very early in life and he was continually in the public service either military or civil stations until he left the Country in 1845. He conspired against his friend and patron General Bolivar and was mainly instrumental in dissolving the Colombian Confederacy. The division took place in 1830 and from that time until he left the Country he was continually President of Ecuador either by election or usurpation, with the exception of four years—the presidential term of Rocafuerte. During all this time he did nothing for the

[28] *Ibid.*, volume II.
[29] *Ibid.*, volume II.

Country but used the public revenues for the benefit of himself and his favorites. He has not left a single monument to his patriotism—nothing to show that he cared for the general welfare. He erected for himself a splendid mansion in Quito at an expense of eighty thousand dollars in which his family still resides. He gave another house worth seven or eight thousand dollars to a strolling actress. He owns three estates between Guayaquil and Quito either of which is equal in extent to one of our largest Counties and would be considered princely under a stable Government. He also owns valuable gold mines. None of his property came to him by descent or marriage; he acquired the whole of it while in the public service upon salaries not sufficient to support a man of his expensive habits. After the expiration of Rocafuerte's term Genl. Flores was reëlected President for two years—then he held the office two years longer in violation of the Constitution. And then to mitigate the odium at home and abroad in consequence of his bold and palpable usurpations, he constituted a Junta at Quito which he denominated a Convention, consisting of members virtually chosen by himself. This Junta adopted a new Constitution dictated by him and elected him President for a term of eight years. The proceedings of that Junta did not pacify the disaffected citizens of Ecuador but rather increased the opposition to General Flores. A revolution and civil war ensued which resulted in his capitulation upon the terms agreed to between him and the Provisional Government constituted by the leaders of the revolution. He agreed to submit and leave the country for two years on condition that they would pay him twenty thousand dollars in money to support him during his absence—continue to pay him an annual salary equal to that of Commander in Chief of the Army—pay to the military officers who served under him regular pensions according to their rank—protect his private property, etc. The twenty thousand dollars were paid to him and he went to Europe. Before the two years expired, in concert with the Queen of Spain he was fitting out an expedition to invade and subjugate this Country. This project was frustrated by the Government of Great Britain. The agreement in respect to his salary has not been complied with, and I believe the opinion is general in Ecuador that a nation cannot be bound by any such agreement with a usurper and traitor."

Cushing declared in a dispatch to Webster from Guayaquil on June 1, 1852 that "the people of Ecuador are utterly opposed to the return of General Flores and I think there is no reasonable probability of his success unless he is sustained by some Government more powerful than that of Peru." And on August 1, 1852, in a dispatch to Webster from Guayaquil, he declared that the expedition had been a definite failure:[30]

[30] *Ibid.*, volume II.

"I have the honor to inform you that the wretched Expedition of Genl. Flores is broken up and dispersed. Though secretly encouraged and aided by the Government of Peru; though favored here and in Lima by the diplomatic representatives of some of the most powerful Governments of Europe—though tolerated as a lawful belligerent by all the squadrons of the Pacific in despite of these most conclusive proofs that it was 'under the acknowledged authority deriving protection from the flag or command of any Government'; and that it was organized and conducted in flagrant violation of the rules of civilized warfare—Yet the curse of an overseeing Providence rested upon it. . . ."

There is much more to this phase of the life of Juan José Flores, for the whole had its distinct international angles, as Cushing insinuates above; but there is little excuse for prolonging the account of the dictatorship of Flores in order to complete the larger story of the *expedición floreana.* Juan José Flores never returned to assume the supreme power in Ecuador. He came back during the dictatorship of Gabriel García Moreno, but as a subordinate to him, and not as the ruler of the state, even behind the throne. García Moreno could be counted upon to permit no such exercise of power as long as he was on the scene. One may take leave of the Father of Ecuador as a peaceful and law-abiding citizen, willing to serve his country in a subordinate position to the best of his ability. He passed off the stage in 1864 in a natural manner, mourned by thousands of Ecuadorians who had, in course of time, forgotten some of his crimes as a dictator. The good that he had done, and there was much of that, was credited to him.

IV. THE DICTATORS OF COLOMBIA AND VENEZUELA

By J. FRED RIPPY

CHAPTER TWENTY-ONE

THE DICTATORS OF COLOMBIA

I

ALTHOUGH Colombia was for more than ninety years, and especially during the period from 1855 to 1903, one of the most turbulent nations of Spanish America, its political life has not been characterized by either numerous or long-term dictators. Apparently its people have preferred disorders to dictatorships; at any rate they have been intolerant toward military despotism. The autocratic rule of General Rafael Urdaneta lasted only eight months—September 1830 to May 1831—and that of José María Melo merely a little more than seven—April 17 to December 4, 1854. General Tomás Cipriano de Mosquera's eight years of government were divided into four different periods; the dictatorship of Rafael Reyes lasted only half a decade; and although Rafael Núñez was dominant for at least twelve years, he governed through numerous substitutes, and he was a journalist and a scholar, not a general. Moreover, the reader has already observed that dictatorial tendencies along with declining health caused the impairment of Bolívar's influence and brought to an end his eleven-year domination in Great Colombia. His actual dictatorship was endured for only a little more than two years after the close of the war for independence.

Since 1830, Colombia has, therefore, had only three men worth serious consideration as dictators: Mosquera, Núñez, and Reyes. And the methods of these were not completely and constantly dictatorial. It ought to be added, however, that many of the presidents exercised discretionary powers under the constitution, and that not a few of them attempted, often with success, both to impose their successors and to determine the personnel of congress through electoral interference.

Despite their faults, these three men, all of pure Spanish blood, rank high among Spanish American leaders. Two of them possessed tremendous physical energy, and were only a little less dexterous with the pen than with the sword. The third, Núñez, as already intimated, was a gifted writer.

It is not difficult for the historian to present a satisfactory explanation of Colombia's political turbulence. This seems to be found, as suggested in part by Bolívar, in physical environment, racial composition, colonial heritage, and the prolonged and expensive struggle for independence from Spain.

The chief physical features of Colombia are its three chains of minutely dissected mountains, its baffling jungle, and its difficult rivers flowing for the most part through steaming tropics. The bearing of these topographical impediments upon the achievement of national unity and tranquillity is not difficult to detect.

Hardly more than twenty per cent of the population of the country in 1830 consisted of pure whites, who were probably less numerous than the negroes and mulattoes and were outnumbered three to one by the Indians and *mestizos*. Primitive viewpoints were dominant among almost two-thirds of the citizens of the young republic. No organic unity existed, and scarcely any community of interests and ideals. If homogeneous nations have great difficulty in agreeing upon goals and policies, the problem must have been far more baffling in Colombia.

Then there was the dead weight of the political heritage from the colonial period: a class system; intellectual repression; a poor, illiterate, and superstitious population; a wealthy, powerful, and intolerant clergy; and little experience in self-government, with what little there was centering around the town councils and thus tending to magnify local loyalties. Moreover, the centers of population had been left in almost complete isolation—separated by mountain and jungle—because the mother country had failed to construct a system of roads and to improve the rivers and ports.

Finally, the long war for independence and its aftermath were influential factors. Colombia made a large contribution to that war both in money and in men. As the present writer has remarked on another occasion,

> "Its government borrowed more than sixteen million dollars from England, requisitioned large amounts from its own population, and lost more than two hundred thousand men on the battlefields of northern South America. In 1838 Colombia's portion of the debt occasioned by the struggle for independence was nearly fifty-two million *pesos*. Due to the terrible devastations of the war, the population of Colombia proper was less by a hundred thousand in 1825 than it had been in 1809. Thus when the long struggle came to an end, the Colombians found themselves almost exhausted physically and economically, without experience in political affairs, and lacking in civic leadership. The war produced an abundant crop of generals whose ambitions were destined to disturb the tranquillity of

the new nation, but it brought forth few political leaders to guide the ship of state."[1]

Although political contests in Colombia were frequently motivated by the desire of the leaders, and especially the army officers, for power and for the privilege of distributing the contents of the treasury, substantial issues and idealistic aspirations were by no means lacking. More frequently than the inhabitants of any other country of Spanish America perhaps, the Colombians quarreled and fought over ideals and convictions. One group favored centralism, another championed federalism. Some demanded universal manhood suffrage; the abolition of the death penalty; unlimited freedom of religion, speech, and the press; the disestablishment of the Roman Catholic Church or the curtailment of its functions, wealth, and power; and the encouragement of immigration of whatever faith. Others favored a limited suffrage, an established religion, a privileged and wealthy clergy, numerous restraints on popular liberty, and the exclusion of foreigners with unorthodox beliefs. Some insisted upon a large, well-paid, and highly-privileged army, while others held opposite convictions. A passionate, politically inexperienced, and intolerant people could not adjust these conflicting interests and ideals by means of the ballot or compromise. They resorted to firearms and the sword. Men abandoned family and fortune with the ardor of Spanish crusaders, laid waste the country, and decided incompatible issues upon the field of combat. Between 1830 and 1903 Colombia was harrowed by ten revolutions involving most of the national domain and seventy uprisings confined to more limited areas. Until recently, most of its chief executives, whether national or local, were generals who had received their training in the war for independence or in subsequent civil wars.[2]

II

Tomás Cipriano de Mosquera, the first important dictator of Colombia proper, was a member of one of South America's most distinguished families. His earliest American ancestor was a *conquistador,* a captain in the army of Gonzalo Pizarro, and later governor of the Province of Popayán. His uncle served as a member of the Spanish Regency and signed the Constitution of Cádiz (1812). His father was a man of wealth, learning, and social distinction. His mother, an Arboleda, be-

---

[1] A. Curtis Wilgus, ed., *The Caribbean area* (Washington, 1934), 396.

[2] For a fuller survey of the national history of the republic, see the author's "Modern Colombia," in Wilgus, *The Caribbean area,* 392-414, and authorities therein cited.

longed to a family which produced scholars, poets, diplomats, and statesmen. One of his brothers held many prominent offices, including those of president and vice-president; another had a long career in the diplomatic service; a third was an eminent archbishop; and a cousin was an outstanding politician for many years. Born in the town of Popayán on September 26, 1798, Tomás Cipriano had by no means completed his formal education when the movement for independence began. At the early age of fifteen he joined the patriot forces, and although too young to take a major part in this epochal conflict, he nevertheless became aide-de-camp of Bolívar, and was promoted to the rank of brigadier general before he reached thirty. The Liberator also appointed him intendant of Guayaquil and governor of the provinces of Barbacoas and Cauca.

During this early period of his life he suffered two misfortunes: he was severely wounded in battle; and he was defeated by the insurgent commander José María Obando, who revolted against the Bolívar dictatorship late in 1828. He never fully recovered from either. His left jawbone, which was shattered by a bullet from the enemy, was replaced by a piece of silver plate that seriously affected his enunciation and greatly impaired his oratorical powers. His burning resentment toward Obando later led to a duel, was partially responsible for a civil war, and resulted in many undignified efforts to exact vengeance.

The retirement of Bolívar, to whom Don Tomás was ardently devoted, left the young army officer in an embarrassing position. His brother Joaquín, who had joined the opposition to the Liberator, became the first president of Colombia proper; and, being a civilian, was not disposed to grant the militarists all the favors they were demanding. Moreover, Popayán was now in the hands of Generals Obando and José Hilario López, who were both Don Tomás' enemies. It was clear that these and other military leaders were planning to revolt against his distinguished kinsmen and inaugurate a régime more favorable to the interests of the veterans of the war against the Spaniards. Tomás Mosquera could not well oppose his companions of the battlefield, nor could he bring himself to take up arms against his own brother. He decided that it would be best for him to make an extensive tour of Europe!

After an absence of nearly four years, he returned to his native land and served two or three terms in congress. He then became secretary of war, and before many months had passed, found himself confronting a formidable revolution. The outstanding leader of the uprising, which soon involved almost the entire nation, was none other than his enemy José María Obando, with whom he had recently fought a duel. Mosquera resigned his cabinet position and went forth to the field of conflict. In April 1841 he restored his military reputation by winning a decisive victory at Tescua, in the province of Santander. He reported the encounter as if he had been the entire army: "On the field of battle I have triumphed completely. . . . The country is saved! It could not have been different. It was April 1, and during the combat I wielded the same sword with which the Liberator won the victory at Junín."[3] He was highly elated, and in the midst of his enthusiasm he shot several prisoners. Such summary vengeance was already becoming a habit.

He hoped the people would call him to the presidency, but the victorious party had developed more popular generals, one of whom was Mosquera's son-in-law (the husband of his only daughter), Pedro Alcántara Herrán, likewise one of the young brigadier generals of Bolívar. Herrán became president on May 2, 1841. Don Tomás might indeed have received the second prize, but he rejected the idea of the vice-presidency with disdain.[4]

Soon afterward he became a roving plenipotentiary to the neighboring republics of the south, where he negotiated treaties and agreements with Chile, Bolivia, and Peru. His main purpose, the extradition of Obando, he failed to achieve. While in Valparaíso, however, he managed to publish (1843) a two-volume diatribe in answer to the alleged defamatory charges of his enemy. The title which Mosquera gave his work was: *A critical examination of the libel . . . published in Lima by the fugitive criminal José María Obando.*[5]

Mosquera still had his mind firmly fixed on the highest office in Colombia. As the summer of 1844 approached, he was haughtily awaiting a call to the presidential mansion. He declared that if his name failed to appear among the candidates he would bid good-by to his native land forever. "He who may not govern the republic," he said, "ought not to save it a second time."[6] He did not hesitate to suggest his availability in numerous letters to his friends, and his name finally appeared in the lists. He was confronted by two strong opponents, but he won the prize after a difficult contest. He was supported by most of the militarists and a large part of the clergy, although several members of

---

[3] Gustavo Arboleda, *Historia contemporánea de Colombia* (6 vols., Bogotá, 1918-1935), I, 477.

[4] Raimundo Rivas, *Cuatro figuras colombianas* (Bogotá, 1933), 4-28, gives an interesting sketch of Mosquera's career down to 1845.

[5] *Examen crítico del libelo publicado . . . en Lima por el reo profugo José María Obando.*

[6] Rivas, 26.

his family, including his brother the archbishop, had serious misgivings regarding Don Tomás' character. They feared he might disgrace them along with their country. The archbishop remarked that his ambitious kinsman was quick-tempered, frivolous, vain, and imprudent; he thought, moreover, that there was little hope of reform.[7]

With Mosquera's first administration as a whole they must have been most agreeably surprised. He gave the nation one of the best governments it was to have in many a day. He built roads and highways, subsidized steamboat navigation on the Magdalena, negotiated the famous treaty of 1846 with the United States, gave encouragement to the building of a railway across Panama, introduced salutary reforms in the monetary system and government finance, stimulated education, science, and the arts, and began the construction of a new national Capitol. Moreover, he showed unwonted respect for personal rights, permitting freedom of the press in spite of the fact that he was bitterly attacked by many of the newspapers.[8] It is true that the members of congress usually bowed to his will, but this compliance was motivated by hope of reward rather than fear of punishment. The constitution under which he governed permitted the lawmakers to hold administrative positions also! Perhaps Mosquera's major weakness as an administrator was his disposition to confer public office upon relatives and intimate friends without sufficient regard for their qualifications.[9]

When his four-year term came to an end on March 31, 1849 he graciously transmitted his authority to his successor, who not only belonged to the opposition party, but was a personal enemy named José Hilario López! In general, he had managed to hold himself in restraint. He was not yet a tyrant, nor even a dictator. He made a better chief executive than anyone had expected.[10]

At the close of his administration he and General Herrán set up a commission business with a central office in New York City and various

---

[7] Arboleda, II, 181.

[8] Toward the end of his term he recommended that this freedom be curtailed, but the senate refused to comply.

[9] The minister of the United States in Colombia later reported that Mosquera, during his first administration, turned his wife out of the national palace and installed another woman (Allan A. Burton to W. H. Seward, no. 300, January 4, 1867, Despatches, Colombia, vol. 25). Rivas says that Mosquera became so angry because of the attacks of journalists that he was on the point of having his enemies summarily shot and then committing suicide; but that a prominent friend managed to restore his equilibrium by suggesting that the republic had a monument in store for him provided he learned to dominate his passions (Rivas, 29).

[10] A detailed discussion of Mosquera's first administration is presented by Arboleda, II, 196-451.

branches on both the Atlantic and the Pacific coasts of Colombia. For almost three years he lived in the United States, where, besides devoting himself to matters of commerce, he found time to publish a small work on the geography of New Granada[11] as well as his memoirs of Bolívar[12] —and then his business enterprise collapsed, with serious losses to all concerned.[13]

The attempt of General José María Melo, another ambitious soldier of the independence period, to set up a dictatorship furnished Mosquera an opportunity to return to public life in May 1854. He landed on the Caribbean coast as the furious champion of the constitutional order. The executive whom Melo had overthrown was Don Tomás' old enemy Obando, but that mattered little. Mosquera had forgiven José María early in 1849, or at any rate had permitted him to come home from his long exile; and it was believed in some quarters, moreover, that Obando had connived in this scheme to establish a dictatorship.

Coöperating with Herrán and López, Mosquera began the bloody struggle to depose Melo. He had command of the Army of the North; López lead the Army of the South; and Herrán was commander-in-chief of all the constitutional forces. After Melo was at length driven from power in December 1854, Mosquera was eager to execute some of the leaders of the *coup d' état,* but his compatriots restrained him, and the insurgents were merely confined in unsanitary prisons instead. Vice-presidents were set up to complete Obando's term, which was to end on March 31, 1857. At that time Mosquera hoped he would have another chance at the presidency. Meanwhile, he would have to be satisfied with a seat first in the house and then in the senate.

Mosquera was so eager for a second term that he was willing to be the candidate of either party. And when both rejected him, he set up a political organization of his own, which he called the moderate or national party. He was defeated despite all of his efforts, but he managed to secure the presidency of a congress which gave Colombia a new constitution, a fundamental law copied largely from that of the United States. Don Tomás had become a federalist.

In 1859 he was elected president of the State of Cauca, and within a year he was leading a revolution against the federal government, which was then headed by Mariano Ospina, scholar, journalist, and a liberal

[11] *Memoria sobre la geografía, física y política, de la Nueva Granada* (New York, 1852). An English translation by Theodore Dwight was published the following year.

[12] *Memorias sobre la vida del libertador Simón Bolívar* (New York, 1853).

[13] Rivas, 32; Allan A. Burton's letter, cited above, note 9.

of long standing. And at last Mosquera and his old enemy Obando were fighting under the same banner! Although Mosquera had formerly been a conservative, he was now a champion of the most advanced principles of the radical decalogue, including state rights. In July 1861, he drove Ospina from power and seized Bogotá, celebrating his triumph by shooting a few more prisoners of war.

He began forthwith a desperate attack upon the Roman Catholic Church—mainly, it was rumored, because the clergy had refused to support his candidacy during the previous presidential campaign. He expelled the Jesuits, exiled certain members of the secular hierarchy, suppressed the convents, confiscated property held in mortmain, and asserted the right of the national government to exercise rigid supervision in all ecclesiastical matters. In 1863 he called another constitutional convention, which soon promulgated a new fundamental charter providing an extreme federal system of government and ratifying his statutory provisions against the Roman Catholic organization. Almost every personal liberty was guaranteed in the new constitution, but the term of the chief executive was limited to two years, largely because the legislators feared Mosquera's autocratic power. In fact, while choosing him for the first president under the new régime, the convention stipulated that he should relinquish the office on April 1, 1864.

Now that the country was again under his control, he devoted his attention seriously to another project which had been revolving in his mind for two years or more.[14] It was nothing less than the restoration of *La Gran Colombia* under the federal system which he had learned to admire while in the United States. In a short time he was at war with Ecuador and victorious at the Battle of Cuaspud. He had triumphed over an enemy superior in numbers under the command of Juan José Flores, another of Bolívar's brigadier generals; and he was proud as a peacock. Flores was no match for him on the battlefield; Don Tomás admitted that. And what is more, the Liberator had discovered it long ago. For with intimate knowledge of the talents of both, had Bolívar not given Mosquera his sword and Flores his coffee service? For some reason, however, Mosquera abandoned his grand plan of confederation. Perhaps he did so only temporarily until he could obtain more adequate resources. At the end of his term he went to Europe as a roving minister to Holland, Prussia, Spain, and England, where he negotiated a British loan and was given the unique thirty-fourth degree in masonry!

[14] He confided his plan to the American minister early in 1861 (George W. Jones to the Secretary of State, no. 45, March 16, 1861, Despatches from Colombia, 1861).

How he loved sonorous titles! "Grand General of the Union, General-in-Chief of the Colombian Guard, Member of the Order of Liberators of Cundinamarca, Member of the Order of Liberators of South Colombia and Peru, and decorated with the medals of Barbacoas and Tescua as well as with the cross of Cuaspud."

Back in Colombia, he was elected president for another two years. Taking charge of the government in April 1866, he was soon in the midst of a bitter conflict with the conservatives and the clergy. Some of the members of congress refused to comply with his demands, and he began to govern without any "nice regard for the constitution and the laws." He was acting on impulse and passion. He bore down upon his adversaries like a whirlwind. He proceeded as if he had but a day to carry out his policies.[15] He began to talk and act like a monarch, stressing forms and ceremonies and boasting of his blood relationship to the queen of the French. His vanity was beginning to assume the most odious forms. Was he in his dotage? Was he mad? British diplomats thought so.[16] He was at last proving himself to be the tyrant which those who knew him intimately had long expected him to become. The radicals now joined the conservatives in attacking him; and near the end of April 1867, he declared martial law, dismissed congress, had some of his opponents imprisoned, and openly proclaimed himself the supreme chief of the nation.

His dictatorship was not long tolerated. On May 23 a group of army officers and politicians executed a *coup d'état,* seized the aged chief executive, and hurried him off to prison to await trial for his political excesses. In November the senate convicted him on several counts and sent him into exile. Before the end of the year he published his defense;[17] and during his sojourn in Lima he found time to publish another book. For a man in his dotage he was exhibiting unwonted stamina! He was no doubt suffering from megalomania, but he was not crazy! The title of his latest book was *Cosmogonía.*[18] In the land of the Incas he had ascended into the realm of metaphysics.

But he soon came back to earth—and to his native land. In 1869, after his two-year term of ostracism had expired, he was once more a candidate for the presidency. Defeated, he ran for the presidency of the

[15] Burton to Seward, no. 280, November 2, 1866, Despatches from Colombia, vol. 25.

[16] Robert Bunch to Edmund Hammond, September 12, 1866, London, Public Records Office, Foreign Office, 55 (Colombia), vol. 188B.

[17] *Defensa del Gran General Tomás C. Mosquera* (Bogotá, 1867).

[18] *Cosmogony.* The book was published at Lima in 1868.

sovereign State of Cauca, to which post he was elected in 1871. After holding this office for two years he appeared once more in the national senate. And in 1876 and 1877 he unsheathed his sword in another civil war. He fought in behalf of the constitutional authorities, and on the winning side. When peace was restored he returned to the beautiful Cauca Valley and settled down on his *hacienda,* where death overtook him at the age of eighty (October 7, 1878).[19]

Such was Colombia's most picturesque and energetic dictator. His temperament was neither wholly liberal nor entirely conservative. Although sternly autocratic, with incurable tendencies toward personal government, he was not afraid of change, and one may discover liberal impulses in his essentially fickle nature. Bold, tenacious, tireless, and often cruel, he was not without patriotism, and he was seldom known to shrink from personal danger. The victim of terrible fits of anger, he was also tender-hearted, often shedding copious tears; but self-love was superior to every other passion. He was fond of noise and pomp; he coveted glory and adulation. His character cannot withstand microscopic examination. He belonged to that class of ambitious men whom nature failed to provide with moral scruples. Endowed with a remarkably strong and handsome physique, he lacked the corresponding qualities of character and mind. He did not possess that moral grandeur which comes from a clear orientation and firm devotion to principles. Like Julius Cæsar, whom he is said to have resembled physically, he was capable of the grandest and the pettiest of actions. In Colombian history he played two rôles which were diametrically opposed. He became president in 1845 in a strictly legal manner, usually kept himself under control, and governed for four years in conformity with his oath. In 1861 he fought his way to power and attempted to rule like an absolute monarch. A moderate conservative during his first administration, he became an autocratic innovator in later years. Such a transformation was not the work of magic, for fundamentally he was always the same restless, volcanic man, with fervent imagination and scant education, who sought to hide his essential ignorance and superficiality behind an imposing front.[20]

---

[19] The brief accounts of his later career will be found in Rivas, 31-35, and in José María Henao y Gerardo Arrubla, *Historia de Colombia* (Bogotá, 1926), 646, *passim.* Mosquera also wrote of this revolution: *Ojeada sobre la situación política y militar de Colombia* (Bogotá, 1877).

[20] One of the best sketches of his character was written by Núñez, "El Gran General Mosquera," in *La reforma política en Colombia* (Bogotá, 1885), 597-604. See also Rivas, 56-64, and Henao y Arrubla, 616-617. José María Quijano Wallis,

III

Rafael Núñez was in many respects a very different man from Mosquera. He was a poet, a social philosopher, and a lawyer. He derived no prestige from family connections or from service under the Liberator. Nor was his power based upon achievements on the battlefield: in all of his life he participated in only one military action—the siege of Cartagena in 1840. His dominance was achieved by personal attraction and the sheer force of intellectual power and shrewdness. A radical in his youth and early manhood, he either changed his views because of honest conviction or had the astuteness to observe the trend of the times. At a period when Colombians were weary of a liberalism and an extreme federalism that had brought license and chaos, he announced himself as the champion of moderation, nationalism, and domestic order, and soon plunged headlong into the widening current of reaction. With the backing of clergy, conservative politicians, and militarists, he set up a dictatorship. Like García Moreno of Ecuador, he became a theocratic Cæsar.[21]

The son of an army officer who, in a land where generals were amazingly numerous, seems never to have risen higher than a colonel, Rafael was born in Cartagena on September 28, 1825. He was educated in a small college of that city and at San Bartolomé in Bogatá. He entered the political arena and began to publish poetry before he was twenty-two; and at the age of twenty-seven, after holding minor government positions both in his native city and on the Isthmus of Panama, he became rector of his *alma mater* in Cartagena. Early in 1853 he entered the national congress, where he took a prominent part in framing the constitution of that year. Thereafter he was either a member of that legislative body, or acting chief executive of the Province of Panama or Cartagena, or serving in some national cabinet post continually until 1863, when he entered the consular service and sailed for Europe by way of the United States. He remained in Europe for thirteen years, observ-

in his *Memorias* (Grottafarrata, 1919), 54-68, *passim,* presents a laudatory account of Mosquera's career. Estanislao Gómez Barrientos, in his *Don Mariano Ospina y su época* (2 vols., Medellin, 1913-1915), *passim,* is rather hostile. A contemporary American diplomat accused Mosquera of graft and shocking personal immorality (Burton and Seward, nos. 295 and 300, January 4 and February 7, 1867, Despatches from Colombia, vol. 25). The legislation of his period may be consulted in *Codificación nacional,* XI-XIII, XIX, XXIII.

[21] *Cf.* Cornelio Hispano [Ismael López], *Cesarismo teocrático* (San José, Costa Rica, 1922).

ing, studying, and writing articles for the newspapers of Colombia—articles later assembled in a book published in Bogotá in 1874.[22]

During all this period he was a liberal; in fact, during most of these early years he was even a radical, a free thinker, and a skeptic. He later claimed, however, that he left Colombia in 1863 because he was disgusted with the extreme views of the ardent liberals who had controlled the destiny of Colombia almost uninterruptedly since they came to power under José Hilario López in 1849.[23]

Nevertheless, Núñez was one of the candidates of the Liberal Party for the presidency in 1875, and after his defeat he did not join the conservatives immediately; he organized a moderate group of his own, which was called the Independent Party, and became governor of the sovereign State of Bolívar. The next year a revolution was launched by the conservatives, who hoped to secure radical aid, but failed in their expectations, and were suppressed after a bloody war. They had invited Núñez to join the uprising, but he had refused, remarking that he did not care to embark in a ship that was bound to founder.[24]

In 1878 he took his seat once more in the national congress, and was elected president of that body. One of the duties of this office was that of administering the oath to the new president of Colombia, General Julián Trujillo. Núñez seized the occasion to make an eloquent speech and promulgate one of his favorite political slogans. "We have arrived at the point where we are confronted by this dilemma," he said, "fundamental administrative regeneration of catastrophe."[25] Thereafter *regeneration* became his constant battle cry.

For some time, however, there were abundant doubts with respect both to his aims and his political sympathies. In 1879 he was elected president mainly by the votes of the independent liberals, although he received the support of a few conservatives and radicals. On April 8, 1880, shortly before he reached fifty-five, he took charge of his high office. In his inaugural address he painted a dark picture of conditions in Colombia, made a plea for tolerance, spoke of the necessity of building railroads, stimulating education, agriculture, and industry, and maintaining peace and order.[26] The radicals made a vigorous effort to recover his allegiance, but failed. Since the constitution limited him to a

---

[22] *Ensayo sobre crítica social.*

[23] Máximo Nieto, *Recuedros de la regeneración* (Bogotá, 1924), 331-332.

[24] *Ibid.*, 27.

[25] Henao y Arrubla, 690.

[26] Rafael Núñez, *La reforma política en Colombia* (Bogotá, 1885), 19-24, for this address.

term of two years without the privilege of immediate reëlection, he surrendered his power on March 31, 1882; but not until he had dictated his successor and secured the office of first designate for himself.

During the course of his administration he had entered into secret communications with some of the conservatives, who now began to think of him as their candidate for 1883. After he returned to Cartagena, these conservative friends continued their work until they finally persuaded the directorate of their party to accept him. Since he was already the candidate of the independents, this conservative ratification insured his election. The radical majority in congress, however, chose a general of their party as first designate, and a revolution seemed imminent. Moreover, conditions were made worse by the failure of the president-elect to arrive on April 1, 1884 and take the oath of office.

The cause of this delay remains a mystery. Perhaps Núñez was afraid of assassination, for he had been receiving menacing letters for some time. Perhaps he feared that his assumption of authority would precipitate a civil war, and hesitated before taking such a momentous step. Perhaps it was because his new wife, whom he had recently married before he obtained a divorce from his former spouse, was difficult to persuade to go along with him and brave the criticism of the haughty ladies of Bogotá. Whatever the reason, his conservative and independent supporters became very restless and made secret plans for raising troops in the states adjacent to the capital.[27] It was August before he arrived at the seat of government and assumed his duties as chief executive.

"One epoch of our history has passed," he said in his inaugural address,

> "and we ought to consecrate our united and loyal efforts to the task of facilitating the peaceful arrival of another which must succeed it. The Hispanic-American republics . . . are entering one by one into a period of stability . . . after years of discord and war. We must undertake a similar evolution under the auspices of a policy truly liberal, incompatible with all intolerance and as free from the dogmatism of those who believe too much as from that of those who believe too little. As an irrevocable member of Colombian liberalism, I shall spare no pains on my part to bring together its scattered forces, for I consider it synonymous with morality and justice in action. . . . May Divine Providence grant us all sufficient virtue and foresight not to ignore the clamor of the people, to the end that we may restore the prestige of our free institutions, make them na-

[27] For the political machinations of this critical period see Nieto, 51-128.

> tional in practice, and turn resolutely away from the tortuous and dangerous path which . . . has brought us to the brink of a terrible abyss."[28]

It was his final appeal to the radicals to return to the fold of moderate liberalism. Already he was on the point of throwing himself into the arms of the conservatives. As an apparent demonstration of his good faith he gave cabinet positions to three well-known radicals, and sent two more of them to Santander to settle electoral difficulties in that state.

But the radicals were too suspicious and exasperated to listen. Whether justified in their view at this particular time or not, they considered Don Rafael a traitor. Sporadic uprisings soon began to occur, and before the end of the year 1884 almost the whole country was in revolt. In suppressing the insurgents, Núñez had to depend almost entirely upon the support of the conservatives, for a number of the independent liberal generals betrayed him. By the time the civil war terminated he was completely in the hands of the Conservative Party. He announced to his victorious troops that the Constitution of 1863 had ceased to exist. He was now ready to undertake drastic reforms.

What formerly he had discussed in vague terms he now announced in unmistakable language. The meaning of regeneration was clarified. He called together a convention of hand-picked conservatives in November 1885, and laid before them his views.

> "Enervating particularism should be replaced by vigorous generality. The codes which establish and define the law ought to be national; and likewise the public administration charged with the duty of making them effective. . . . Religious sentiments should be invoked as an aid to social culture; the system of education ought to be based primarily upon the Divine teaching of Christianity, for this is the *alma mater* of the world's civilization. If we aspire to be free, it is necessary that we commence by being just. The sphere of action of each individual therefore has a necessary limit in the field of action of others and in the common interest. The press, for the same reason, should be a torch and not a firebrand, a tonic and not a poison: it ought to be a messenger of truth and not of error and calumny. . . . Religious tolerance does not exclude the recognition of the obvious fact that Catholic beliefs are predominant in Columbia. . . .
>
> "Civil wars have not only sown our fields with dead bodies, but have prevented the natural growth of our agriculture and our industry. Trade languishes for the same reason, and because fiscal poverty and the lack of foreign credit have left us in a paralyzed state owing to the absence of railways. . . ."

[28] Henao y Arrubla, 695.

He then went on to remark that while most of the nations of Spanish America had suffered similar tribulations and some of them were, in fact, still in the painful cycle of transition, none had traveled so far as Colombia along the path of chimeras. None of their legislators had established absolute freedom of the press, free trade in arms and munitions, immunity for political crimes, and complete sovereignty of the various sections which constituted the national domain. Nor had any of them deliberately tried to destroy the religious faith of their people. Yet Colombians had done all of this and more. They had, in short, made of liberty a stupid ideal similar to the bloody idols of barbarous tribes; and by their extravagance they had submerged the people in chaos and moral depression. He hoped that his compatriots might now be regenerated without passing under the galling dictatorship of a Rosas, a Santa Anna, or a Carrera.[29]

As a matter of fact, the Colombians were at that very moment on the verge of being subjected to the dictatorship of a political philosopher supported by a conservative clergy and an expensive army and police. And that philosopher was none other than Rafael Núñez. A centralized constitution was promulgated in 1886; the states were reduced to provinces; and the Roman Catholic Church was restored to all of its ancient privileges and given an annual government subsidy besides. Agreements signed with the pope in 1887 and afterward, left Colombia more completely in the power of Roman Catholicism than any other nation in the world.[30]

Had he gone farther than he intended? Was he still a liberal at heart? Had the revolt of the radical liberals in 1885 driven him into the camp of a reactionary group with whom he did not agree, but from whom he was unable to extricate himself because he did not have the moral courage either to defy them or resign from the presidency? Many Colombians thought so at the time, and still think so. They assert that as late as August 1884 he was a sincere liberal whose program was merely one of administrative reform: improvement in the national and local administrations, religious toleration, and effective suffrage. They say that he was, like Bolívar, one of Colombia's frustrated statesmen.[31]

[29] This address is printed in Manuel Antonio Pombo and José Joaquín Guerra, *Constituciones de Colombia* (Bogotá, 1911), II, 1183-1188.

[30] A good analysis of these agreements may be found in J. Lloyd Mecham, *Church and state in Latin America* (Chapel Hill, 1934), 156-165.

[31] Rivas, 161-190; Cornelio Hispano, 47; Julio H. Palacio, *Núñez: recuerdos y memorias* (Barranquilla, n. d.), 68-69.

Although there is evidence which tends to justify their contentions, evidence equally convincing tends to support a different conclusion. He did try to placate the liberals in August 1884, but he may have been merely playing for time until the conservative forces could be organized. He also refused to sign the Constitution in 1886, shifting this duty to a substitute who was left in charge of the executive power; but his refusal may not have been caused by the conviction that this fundamental charter had gone too far. He may have been displeased because it was not reactionary enough.

One of his intimates unconsciously presents evidence of autocratic and reactionary tendencies on the part of Núñez in 1886 and 1887. At that time the champion of regeneration, recalling the words of the Liberator, remarked that he too may have been plowing the sea. The new constitution was not sufficiently centralized; the legislature had been left too powerful and would meet too frequently; the council of state might impair the strength of the executive; radicalism might yet gain a foothold in the provinces; members of the national parliament, lacking the moral stamina to resist the clamor of the sections, would continue to play politics. He also delivered a tirade against the press and the system of state education, remarking that the journalists should be curbed, and that the schools should inculcate respect for religion, law, and authority, as well as love of virtue and humanity. Moreover, he vaguely revealed the fact that he was toying with the idea of dictatorship, asking himself whether he would be able to resist the storm of indignation which his assumption of supreme power would arouse, and recalling the unhappy experience of Bolívar, Urdaneta, Melo, and Mosquera.[32]

He soon resolved his Hamlet-like doubts and erected an autocracy upon a military and ecclesiastical foundation. The clergy took charge of the schools, entered once more into politics, and became the most effective propagandists for the new régime. The army saw to it that none but friends were admitted to the polls. Freedom of conscience, freedom of teaching, and freedom of the press ceased to exist. The president sentenced without trial any and all who could by the greatest stretch of the imagination be considered as having fomented sedition or even hostility to the dictator. Members of the opposition, his former friends and supporters, were no more than aliens in their native country. "There is neither constitution nor law in the land," wrote a diplomat from the United States in 1888, "save the uncontrolled will of President Núñez.

---

[32] Nieto, 283-346.

All the safeguards of personal rights and constitutional limitations of executive authority . . . are utterly disregarded. All departments of the government . . . are under the absolute control of the president."[33]

The dictator did not rule from Bogotá, however. He disliked both its climate and its society. There was a tendency to ostracize his second wife, Soledad Román de Núñez; and perhaps he was afraid of assassination.[34] He governed instead from his small country estate, Cabrero, just outside of the old walls of Cartagena—governed with the aid of his wife and through puppets in the palace of San Carlos in the national capital.[35]

And what were the achievements of his long rule? They were the Constitution of 1886; the restoration of the wealth and privileges of the clergy; an era of peace without liberty; a few internal improvements; a backward and very inadequately supported educational system; millions of *pesos* of depreciated currency; inevitable petty graft on the part of distant agents; a low credit-rating abroad; and sycophancy, adulation, and monuments.[36]

Regeneration or catstrophe! No, neither; but a good deal of repression and stagnation under the name of regeneration—and after his death (September 18, 1894) the deluge: years of revolution and another dictator. Whether Núñez was a frustrated idealist or a deliberate despot, the result was the same for Colombia. The real dilemma which the nation faced in 1886 was the dilemma confronted by the majority of the states of Spanish America during almost the whole of their national existence; it was the dilemma of chaos or the mailed fist.

---

[33] John G. Walker to Thomas F. Bayard, no. 109, May 7, 1888, Despatches from Colombia, vol. 41. See also Dabney H. Maury to the Secretary of State, no. 134, August 1, 1888, vol. 42; and Jacob Sleeper to the Secretary of State, no. 72, September 25, 1894, vol. 52. *Cf.* J. M. Quijano Wallis, 156-158, 519-520, 538-539.

[34] Señora Núñez had not occupied San Carlos during the first administration of her husband. On October 10, 1880 (no. 216, Despatches from Colombia, vol. 34) Ernest Dichman wrote the Secretary of State that the Colombian president had gone to the coast to be near his young wife whom he had married without the formality of obtaining a divorce from his previous wife. He then remarked that if this second wife had occupied the presidential mansion at Bogotá, she would have been left in disagreeable isolation. Palacio, 70-71, says that Núñez lived alone in the palace of San Carlos during his first administration. He also adds that the Regenerator indulged in amorous excesses during his younger days.

This second wife must have been a rather remarkable woman. For her character and her influence upon Núñez, see Nieto, 127 ff.; Palacio, 7-8, *passim;* and Daniel Lamaitre, *Soledad Román de Núñez* (Bogotá, 1927).

[35] Palacio, 22-23; and Jacob Sleeper, letter cited in note 33 above.

[36] Marco Fidel Suárez, *Rafael Núñez* (Bogotá, 1894), and Carlos Calderón Reyes, *Núñez y la regeneración* (Sevilla, 1895), are two very laudatory accounts of his work.

IV

Rafael Reyes, Colombia's third outstanding dictator, was scarcely less colorful than Tomás de Mosquera, whom he resembled in many ways. He possessed similar pride and egotism; the same restless, active, impatient temperament; the same liberal impulses latent in a disposition prevailingly conservative; and equally amazing reserves of physical strength. Like Mosquera also, he was fond of the pen as well as of the sword, received only a superficial formal education, possessed great courage, and achieved distinction largely by virtue of his dynamic energy and his military prowess. Reyes was, however, somewhat less egotistical, not so much given to fits of passion, and perhaps superior in administrative ability, even if the comparison be limited to Mosquera's first term when Don Tomás was at his best. In personal appearance there was no similarity. Reyes was much larger and less handsome.

Born in Santa Rosa de Viterbo, Province of Boyacá, on October 24, 1850, he lost his father at an early age, and was forced to begin work by the time he was twelve. He managed, however, to acquire the rudiments of an education in the schools of his native province before going away to Popayán in order to engage in commerce with his elder brother Elías. From that city he soon went out into the wilds in search of quinine and other forest products; and he was scarcely twenty-four when he and his brothers Enrique and Nestor embarked on an adventure as daring as any ever attempted by the *conquistadores*. It was nothing less than the exploration and occupation of the vast region along the Putumayo River in the heart of the South American jungle. Leaving Elías behind to look after the firm and storehouses, they went to Pasto, and then set out across the mountains to the southeast in search of a navigable tributary of the Amazon. They were on foot, and accompanied by a few *peons* who transported their luggage. After weeks of incredible hardships in which they lost four of the baggage-carriers, they finally reached the Putumayo, where they found some friendly Indians who furnished them a canoe and six of their braves to accompany them on their voyage. Two days of rowing brought them to a point which they considered the termination of potential steam navigation to the northwest, and they named the spot Sofía in honor of Rafael's young wife. This ceremony completed, they continued down stream for six hundred miles until they approached a region inhabited by cannibals. Here the Indian aides refused to go farther; but the Reyes brothers, undaunted, let them depart and managed to secure the help of the more dangerous savages. Another six hundred miles carried them to the mouth of the Putumayo and to the broad Amazon, where they took passage on a small steamer which made a monthly voyage between Iquitos and Pará. They finally reached the latter city some six months after their departure from Pasto; and Rafael, now reduced almost to a skeleton by intense heat, insect pests, and lack of proper food, proceeded to Rio de Janeiro.

There he had a long interview with Dom Pedro II, who showed him every courtesy. After a sojourn of two months in the Brazilian capital, he returned to Pará, where he bought a small steamer, hired a crew, laid in provisions, and started up the Amazon. He continued on this mighty river to its juncture with the Putumayo, and thence up that stream until eventually he reached Sofía again. He had discovered a convenient water route from the jungles of Colombia to the Atlantic Ocean. He had also found an area rich in rubber, quinine, sarsaparilla, cacao, vegetable ivory, and precious woods.

This, however, was no more than the beginning of his arduous adventures. With the exception of brief intervals at home with his family or when he accompanied Dom Pedro to the Philadelphia Centennial celebration in 1876, he remained in the region for ten years, exploring half a dozen tributaries of the upper Amazon, collecting merchandise, founding colonies, and suppressing the slave trade. His brother Enrique died of malignant fever; his brother Nestor was eaten by the cannibals; but Rafael brought out the body of the one and the bones of the other, and returned to look after his colonies and the collection of medicinal plants and rubber.

In spite of all his exertions, his grand enterprise was destined to collapse. A fall in the price of quinine and the dread diseases of the tropics, which wiped out his settlements, caused the firm of Reyes Brothers and Company to crash, and in 1885 his commercial and patriotic enterprise was abandoned. He had arrived in Cali near the end of the previous year a ruined and discouraged man.[37]

But another door of adventure opened in the nick of time. Already the revolution against Núñez had begun, and without hesitation Reyes joined the forces of the government. He moved like a whirlwind across southwestern Colombia defeating and scattering the enemy in almost every engagement. Then, boarding a frail bark with a few hundred soldiers, he set out for Panama, and suppressed the insurgents there. Afterward he rushed to Cartagena, relieved that city, and advanced forth-

[37] Rafael Reyes, *Escritos varios* (Bogotá, 1920), 23-24, 453-475, 583-589.

with up the steaming Magdalena. On October 18, 1885, already wearing the epaulets of a general, he commanded the grand parade of the victorious armies in Bogotá. A *Te Deum* was sung in the Cathedral, followed by a benediction pronounced by the archbishop—the first of its kind in twenty-five years. An eyewitness noted that young Reyes was all vivacity, all action. He was only thirty-five.[38]

Now one of the popular heroes of the conservative reaction, he was elected by the State of Cauca to the constitutional convention. As a member of this assembly, he was less extreme than most of his collaborators. He presented a moderate constitution of his own, revealed solicitude for the prestige of his adopted state, made an appeal for religious toleration, and raised his voice in favor of maintaining universal manhood suffrage. In time of war the humble workers of Colombia were conscripted without asking whether they could read or write. Why should they be subjected now to a literacy test which would deprive them of the right to participate in governing the country they had fought to save and would be expected to defend? On the whole, his exertions in this convention were vain.[39]

During the next decade he occupied a seat in congress or served in cabinet or diplomatic positions; and in 1895 he confronted another liberal revolt. If he had been a whirlwind ten years before, he was now a veritable hurricane. In less than three months the uprising was suppressed. He was almost uniformly victorious, and the outstanding leader of the government troops.[40]

Hoping now to be the next president of Colombia, he announced his candidacy in 1897; but the majority of the conservatives preferred a civilian for that high office, and he retired from the campaign before the election was held. In 1898 he was chosen as designate for the executive power, but this subordinate position had little attraction for him. He entered the diplomatic service instead, not only holding various posts in Europe, but going as head of the Colombian delegation to the Pan-American conference which met in Mexico City late in 1901, where he attracted much attention by his pro-Spanish pronouncements and because of the paper which he read on his tropical explorations.[41]

---

[38] *Ibid.*, 101, 571-574, *passim;* Nieto, 240-246; Henao y Arrubla, 723-724, 727.

[39] *Antecedentes de la constitución de Colombia de 1886* (Bogotá, 1913), 75-77, *passim;* Henao y Arrubla, 731; Pombo y Guerra, II, 1194-1254.

[40] Henao y Arrubla, 752-753, 764; Reyes, 115, 121, *passim.*

[41] Reyes, 51-53, 451-475; J. Fred Rippy, *Latin America in world politics* (New York, 1931), 245-246, and authorities cited.

Late in 1903 he was back in Bogotá, urging the ratification of the Hay-Herrán Treaty conceding to the United States government the right to construct a canal across the Isthmus of Panama. The treaty was rejected, the Panamanians revolted in November, and Reyes was dispatched to suppress the insurgents. He hurried to Cartagena, where he embarked with a few hundred soldiers to save the isthmus a second time. But the war vessels of the United States would not permit him to land, and he proceeded forthwith to Washington as head of a diplomatic mission. Here his efforts were equally futile, but he returned to his native country with the hope that Colombia would one day receive compensation for its losses.[42] As the grim Reaper approached him nearly twenty years later this hope was on the point of being attained.

A few days after his return from the United States he announced his candidacy for chief executive a second time, and after a close contest in which the liberals refrained from voting, he was victorious over another warrior, the candidate of the extreme conservatives. On August 7, 1904, he took charge of the government. Then almost fifty-four, he was growing bald and stout. With his tall figure, massive frame, and heavy mustache trained in Teutonic fashion, he resembled a general in the Kaiser's armies.

As president, he faced a difficult task. A three years' war, following closely upon the uprising of 1895 and ending only in November 1902, had laid waste the country, depleted its finances, and left a heritage of misery and bitterness. The majority of congress was against him and apparently determined to oppose his policies; and matters were brought to a crisis by Reyes' torrential impatience. He had moved as a cyclone in 1895, and he proposed to govern in the same way. A frank admirer of Porfirio Díaz, whose work he had just observed in Mexico, he was now disposed to follow the Mexican model. Most of the measures he recommended bore the seal of *urgent,* and he governed with little respect for the constitution which he had helped to frame in 1886. He obeyed what he called the "supreme law of necessity"—which was no law at all!

Within a few weeks he had a collision with congress, mainly because its members refused to accept his recommendations regarding the budget. Whereupon he not only declared its sessions closed, but imprisoned some of its members and banished others. A few days later he received news, or pretended to receive news, that there was danger of an invasion from Venezuela and a revolt in the border provinces of Colombia. He

---

[42] Reyes, 3-4, 476-491.

speedily declared martial law and assumed plenary powers; and making use of his enlarged authority, he proceeded to issue legislative decrees regarding education, the press, and many other matters, as well as with respect to financial affairs. Finally, on February 1, 1905, he issued a call for a national assembly to be composed of three deputies from each of the nine administrative departments into which the national territory was divided. These twenty-seven men were to be selected by committees presided over by the governors of the respective administrative divisions. They were to be chosen without respect for party affiliations, and the assembly was to meet on March 15. It was not to have power to initiate anything; its duty was to approve and ratify!

The new body of lawmakers—composed of liberals as well as of conservatives from both divisions of that party, but selected no doubt with careful attention to their pliability—met at the appointed time, and adjusted their speed to the tempo of the impatient executive. There was little oratory except during the opening ceremonies. By April 30 they had ratified all of Reyes' legislative decrees, made ten fundamental changes in the constitution, and put the stamp of their approval on seventy-four laws besides. They were thus functioning in both a legislative and a constituent capacity. These duties finished, they were dismissed.

Before the end of the year 1905 Reyes called them together once more in order to have them ratify other measures he had thought of since April. But on this occasion they proved less amenable, and he soon dismissed them. He was now thoroughly determined that these twenty-seven gentlemen should not meet again until he had effected some changes in personnel. On April 1, 1907, after such changes had been duly made, he called his friends, supporters, and puppets together for a third time. During this session there was not quite so much work to do, but they placed their stamp on forty laws and two constitutional amendments before disbanding on June 15, 1907. In July and August 1908, they met for another thirty days and ratified twenty-eight laws as well as three modifications in the constitution. And on February 22, 1909, they assembled for their fifth and last time, passing not only a number of statutes but approving five further changes in the fundamental charter.

Truly this was efficiency! Reyes' slogans were *restoration and harmony; peace, work, and progress.* Rising at four o'clock himself—at any rate his friends declared that he did—he expected others to be equally diligent. He was putting into practice the old English proverb:

"Those who reach the heights, are those who work while their companions sleep."[43]

But the trend of all this activity was clear. He was making himself dictator of Colombia, and the people and politicians were becoming more and more restless as he curtailed the freedom of the press, ignored the members of congress, dismissed the vice-president and the national council of government, postponed elections, placed his pliant agents in the courts, and lengthened his term from six to ten years. They expected him sooner or later to return to the Bolívar idea of life tenure with power to designate his successor; and suspicions of graft were not lacking. As early as the end of the year 1905 a conspiracy to overthrow him was discovered in Bogotá, and on February 10, 1906 he barely escaped assassination. He built railways and highways, beautified the capital, opened night schools for laborers, gave more attention than most of his predecessors to the system of education in general, placed the finances of the nation on a sounder basis, sought to stimulate agriculture and industry, and resumed the services on the national debt. But nothing, not even the adulation of the clergy nor his numerous voyages to almost all sections of the country, could win his political enemies or reconcile the people to his dictatorial policies. They would not tolerate even a benevolent despot.

Matters reached a crisis early in 1909 when he attempted to have his puppet assembly ratify a treaty with the United States regarding Panama. The students and populace of the capital raised an outcry, which he found it difficult to ignore. He vacillated: he turned over his authority to the first designate for a day—merely long enough for the unpopular treaty to be withdrawn from the assembly; he declared a state of siege in Bogotá, only to raise it three days later, dismiss his marionettes, and promise to call a regular session of congress on July 20. Meantime, it is likely that he was making a careful investigation with respect to the loyalty of the generals in all parts of the country. On June 4 he left the national capital and hurried down to the Magdalena. On July 13 he wrote out his resignation at Santa Marta, and a few days later he sailed for Europe and voluntary exile.[44]

---

[43] Reyes, v, 89.

[44] Baldomero Sanin Cano, in his *Administración Reyes* (1904-1909), published at Lausanne in 1909, gives a very laudatory account of Reyes' work. More critical accounts will be found in Henao y Arrubla, 763-761, and in Pombo y Guerra, II, 1258-1296. For the legislation of the period see *Leyes de Colombia,* (Bogotá, 1905-1910).

He spent the next ten years in travel in various parts of the world. He visited not only the European countries, but northern Africa, the Near East, the United States, and most of the nations of Hispanic America. He also found time to publish three books.[45] And then, late in 1919, he returned home to settle down, engage in real estate speculation, receive the adulation of his friends, welcome a visit of a Bourbon prince, write an occasional article for the newspaper or a note or two to the Colombian president, and publish another book in which he assembled a miscellany relating to all phases of his long and interesting career. The last item in the volume consisted of moral advice to his sons and grandsons. It was dated July 1920.[46] A year later he was dead. Colombia has had no more dictators since he left the palace of San Carlos in the summer of 1909.

---

[45] These works were: *Viaje a España y Portugal* (Madrid, 1912); *The two Americas* (New York, 1914); and *Notas de un viaje de Bogotá a la Patagonia y Tierra del Fuego* (Bogotá, 1917).

[46] The book, cited previously, was entitled *Escritos varios.* A balanced biography of Reyes has not yet been written. The sketch by R. Cuervo Márquez, *Colombia y su regeneración* (Caracas, 1907), is no less eulogistic than that of Sanin Cano.

CHAPTER TWENTY-TWO

THE DICTATORS OF VENEZUELA

I

PARADOXICAL as it may seem, Venezuela has been even more turbulent than Colombia and at the same time has had a much larger number of dictators. From this fact, perhaps, it may be argued that despots provoke revolts as well as suppress them. Between 1830 and 1935 the country was dominated by at least eight dictators: José Antonio Páez, José Tadeo and José Gregorio Monagas, Juan Crisóstomo Falcón, Antonio Guzmán Blanco, Joaquín Crespo, Cipriano Castro, and Juan Vicente Gómez. And yet the period of political disorder in Venezuela lasted longer than in Colombia, extending to some extent into the third decade of the present century, although, as in the case of Colombia, the era of greatest turbulence, with the possible exception of the first two decades after the initiation of the independence movement, embraced the latter half of the nineteenth century. Moreover, Venezuelan political history differed from that of Colombia in at least two other respects: the national government of Venezuela was frequently overthrown by insurrection while that of Colombia was deposed but rarely; and civilian chief executives made a large contribution to Colombian political life while they made almost none to that of Venezuela. With reference to the dictators of the two countries, it is interesting to observe that those of Venezuela were mostly mix-bloods whereas those of Colombia were of pure Spanish descent.

In attempting to explain the political history of Venezuela one must resort, as in the case of Colombia, to physical environment, racial composition, heritage from the mother country, and the protracted struggle for independence. If these factors fail to illuminate the subject, the historian will hardly know where to turn in search of light.

The topographical handicaps of Venezuela are somewhat less severe than those of Colombia. Although there are three mountainous regions, two of these, the Andes and the coast range, are closely connected and lie along the border of the national domain, while the third, the Guiana Highlands, which constitute almost half of the area of the country, has been of little importance because of the scarcity of its inhabitants. The *llanos,* which stretch between these two elevated regions, are likewise sparsely inhabited, but the plainsmen have been a turbulent and influential element in Venezuelan history. Since early colonial times the bulk of the population has been concentrated in the western and northern highlands, with the basin of Lake Maracaibo becoming more important since the last years of the nineteenth century. This topography and concentration of settlements would have made the preservation of order and the maintenance of national unity comparatively easy if it had not been for the lack of good roads, the want of unity in the colonial administration, and the nature of the *llanos,* to which insurgents could flee from the arm of the national government, and from which revolutionary bands organized with more or less impunity could find a ready approach to the capital.

The people of Venezuela, however, would appear not to be adapted to the smooth functioning of a democratic republic. Of the eight hundred thousand people living in the country in 1810 less than a fourth were pure whites, almost a sixth were pure Indians, sixty-two thousand were negro slaves, and more than half were either African freedmen or mixtures of the three races. Since that period the percentage of mix-bloods has tended to increase at the expense of the other elements. In contemporary Venezuela it is not unlikely that the African strain is almost as large as the Indian, while not more than ten or fifteen per cent of the population is of pure Caucasian descent.

The Spanish government, which had preserved the native tribes and permitted the introduction of the Africans, had not succeeded in educating any considerable number of either of these two races or of the various types of mix-bloods which resulted from their cross-breeding with each other or with the whites. Indeed, not a few of the whites themselves were illiterate at the close of the colonial period. These primitive and mixed inhabitants had taken little or no part in the political affairs of the colony. Accustomed to the domination of landlords, local Spanish officials, and churchmen, they were disposed to follow their leaders blindly. They were ready to enlist in the army of any militarist who appealed to their simple fancy or offered them opportunity for plunder and adventure. And frequently they were compelled to enlist!

And there was still another factor in the colonial heritage which contributed to the disorders of the national period. A unified political administration was not set up until shortly before the end of the colonial epoch. The ultimate territorial limits of the colony were not established until 1777; the *audiencia* was not set up until 1786; the ecclesiastical jurisdiction was not consolidated until 1803; and uniformity of fiscal administration was not achieved even at the close of the colonial period. The country was thus divided into confusing and overlapping jurisdictions and the spirit of localism and regionalism was stimulated. Federalism would therefore become popular and national unity would be difficult to attain, especially since Spain built few good roads.

Finally, it is doubtful whether any major division of South America contributed so largely to the struggle for independence or suffered so severely from its losses as did Venezuela. In that country were born the first generals of the revolution, and Venezuelans directed the decisive battles of the epic contest for freedom in all northern South America. The nation produced seven commanding generals and furnished the first presidents of the five republics created in the area. Yet almost as many battles were fought on Venezuelan soil during the period as in half of the other republics combined. Nearly three hundred thousand Venezuelans fell on the battlefields of the revolution, or perished in the terrible earthquake of 1812, or died of disease and famine. The population of the country was less by at least a hundred thousand in 1825 than it was in 1810, and it had not reached a million even in 1839. The public debt contracted during the war amounted to more than nineteen million dollars; the losses in property are not known, although it is probable that half of the national wealth was destroyed. The nation was thoroughly exhausted; the shackles of militarism were firmly fastened upon the people. The generals developed during the period would dominate the country for almost forty years, and when they passed from the stage another generation of ambitious generals and still another would arise to take their place. Civilian administrations would be infrequent, ineffective, and ephemeral.

Political principles were largely without salutary influence, while parties were unstable and lacking in differentiating criteria. Many passionate slogans were proclaimed—the holy constitution, the immaculate confederation, the wicked goths, the cruel tyrants, freedom, popular sovereignty, the sacred right of insurrection—to arouse the multitudes, but the leaders who announced such maxims usually forgot to apply them after they had fought their way to power.

II

The *llanos* require especial emphasis, for, as already intimated, the plainsmen were influential in Venezuelan history during the first century in particular. They first crushed the independence movement and then contributed largely to its success. Páez and Crespo were sons of the great plains; the Monagas dynasty drew its wealth and prestige from the great stock ranches; Falcón and Guzmán Blanco, though living elsewhere, based their ascendancy in part upon the plainsmen: Gómez, while drawing the sinews of his power from the oil wells, managed to exact tribute from the *llanero* ranchmen. And many an insurgent used the plains as a base for his operations.

The plains of Venezuela stretch for more than six hundred miles from the delta of the Orinoco to the northeastern range of the Andes; and from the mountains which border the Caribbean coast to the rivers Orinoco, Apure, and Arauca, they extend for a distance of some two hundred miles. They are an area of rivers and lagoons, and of level grasslands broken here and there by clumps of trees, with strips of thick forest along the waterways. They hold, as it were, an intermediate position between prairie and desert, varying toward the one or the other according to the season of the year. During the dry season—from October to April—no rain falls for weeks or even months. The *llanos* become parched, the rivers shrink, the smaller streams and the little lakes dry up entirely, and the plains become a veritable land of death. Thousands of animals perish from thirst or starvation. Then comes the season of rainfall, and the landscape becomes green as the withered grasses drink up the welcome gift of the rain gods. Soon the swollen streams begin to overflow their banks in the lower levels, and before the rains cease thousands of square miles of lowlands are flooded. The livestock and wild animals seek refuge on the low tablelands which stand out above the floods, but there is not room and food for all. The climate is hot the year round and there are numerous insects, reptiles, and wild beasts: mosquitoes, sandflies, vampire bats, ticks, poisonous snakes, boas, alligators, crocodiles, electric eels, sharp-toothed *caribes* (fierce fish), and jaguars.

While the *llanos* are similar in many ways to the *pampas* of Argentina, it will be observed that there are marked differences in rainfall and temperature, and consequently in fauna and flora. The *pampas* are an ideal region for the livestock industry, and some of the area is well adapted to agriculture; the *llanos* suffer from the handicaps of heat, flood, drouth, insect pests, carniverous beasts, and deadly reptiles. The vast plains of Venezuela probably must forever remain in the pastoral stage, and the livestock industry must develop amidst numerous hazards.

The nomadic Indians who roamed over this region before the coming of the Europeans, varied in disposition from the dull and gentle people who dwelt in the center and west to the shrewd and fierce Caribs of the southeast. During the seventeenth and eighteenth centuries they were subjected first to the sway of the Catholic missionaries, supported by the

Spanish soldiers, and then, to some extent, to the civil officials of the colonial régime. The whites, who gradually migrated to the region, settled mainly in the villages and began forthwith to produce a race of *mestizos.* Although a few negro slaves were introduced, the Africans were never numerous on the plains; and while agriculture was probably crudely developed in a few places, particularly near the villages, the main occupation of the region was the tending of livestock introduced from the mother country. The herds of cattle increased rapidly, and horses appear to have managed to thrive despite the hazards, at least until the middle of the nineteenth century. Since that time they have not flourished. In the course of the colonial period the Indians were largely absorbed, and a pastoral civilization was developed. The grazing lands passed into the hands of men who lived in the near-by towns or in the more pleasant highlands farther to the east and north. The work on the ranches was done by the primitive and mixed races whose position in society was little better than that of the European serfs. The population of the great plains of Venezuela was between three and four hundred thousand about the time the long struggle for independence from Spain began. The cattle numbered four million or more, and there were probably two or three hundred thousand head of horses.[1]

Although the inhabitants of these plains had long been compelled to defend themselves against bands of robbers and Caribs, they did not receive their first experience in actual warfare until 1812. In that year a modern Attila assumed leadership among them and led them to victory over the patriots.

This warrior, a native of Spain, an atrocious ruffian, half pirate and half smuggler, first appeared in the *llanos* in 1809 when he was sent by

[1] On the geography and racial composition of Venezuela see F. Depons, *Travels in South America* (2 vols., London, 1807); Agustin Codazzi, *Resumen de la geografía de Venezuela* (Paris, 1841); Clarence F. Jones, *South America* (New York, 1930), 608-661; Chester Lloyd Jones, *Caribbean backgrounds and prospects* (New York, 1931), 30-31, *passim.*

On its history during the colonial period and the wars for independence, consult Rafael María Baralt, *Resumen de la historia de Venezuela desde el descubrimiento hasta 1797* (Paris, 1841); Rafael Baralt and Ramón Díaz *Resumen de la historia de Venezuela desde 1797 hasta 1830* (Paris, 1841); José Gil Fortoul, *Historia constitucional de Venezuela* (3 vols., Caracas, 1930), vol. I.

Ramón Páez, the son of José Antonio Páz, gives a fairly good account of life on the plains in his *Wild scenes in South America* (New York, 1862). Since this author was very much under the influence of Sarmiento's *Facundo,* however, one must read his sketches with caution or else one will receive the impression of too great similarity between the *llanos* and the *pampas.*

the Spanish colonial officials as a sort of exiled criminal to the town of Calabozo. His name was José Tomás Boves. Fearless, rash, astute, and hungry for power; sadistic, Satanic, and relentless, this red-headed, fair-skinned, blue-eyed Spaniard visited the various villages and ranches of the plains and soon gained an ascendancy over the inhabitants of the region.

In 1812 he began to organize a royal army. The *llaneros* flocked around him by the hundreds, and looked upon him as a demigod of war. Within a few months he had collected a horde of cavalry.

> "Wild-eyed, lithe as panthers, torsos over-developed and legs under-developed by constant riding, living on meat almost unsalted, caring not whether they fought for or against the King of Spain provided they could rob and kill, thousands of these centaurs, armed with long, sharp lances, suddenly burst out of their native llanos with . . . Boves . . . at their head, and swarmed like sanguinary locusts against that part of Venezuela held by Bolívar and his comrades."

Crouching low, pressing bare knees against the lean flanks of their mounts, uttering hideous yells, brandishing lances dripping with blood, riding close together, wave upon wave, and supported by the cruel infantry of another Spaniard named Tomás Morales, these savage horsemen completely crushed and scattered the patriot armies in less than two years. In December 1814, however, Boves was slain.[2]

III

The allegiance of the *llaneros* was soon transferred to another leader, a man who was equally bold and far more fascinating—imperious and implacable, but seldom cruel, a patriot and not a royalist. In fact, as Bolívar and his dispirited followers were retreating before the wild horsemen of the plains, José Antonio Páez, a worthier leader, was rising under the very eyes of Boves. For Páez, who was born on the northern edge of the *llanos* in 1790, had begun his exploits among the cowboys of Apure as early as 1807, and was a cavalry leader of some distinction by 1814.

Between the latter date and 1821, when his fierce plainsmen turned the columns of the Spaniards at Carabobo, his reputation had grown until his influence in Venezuela was inferior only to that of Bolívar himself. By 1826 his prestige had risen still higher; by the end of 1829 he was dominant; and from then until 1846 he was the arbiter of Vene-

[2] T. Y. Ybarra, *Bolívar, the passionate warrior* (New York, 1929), 91-100. The quotation is from page 93.

zuela's political destiny. Although his methods were not entirely dictatorial, excepting the period from 1861 to 1863—since he usually showed much respect for the law and the lawmakers, and nearly always permitted freedom of the press—he must be listed as the first dictator of the Venezuelan nation.[3]

About him was a touch of the mythological. The son of humble parents and a younger member of a numerous family of children, he was sent to school for a few months in his eighth year and then put to work with his relatives. At the age of seventeen he left the scenes of his childhood and went forth to carve out his destiny. He journeyed southward until he reached the valley of the distant Apure, where he obtained employment as a cattle *peon* on first one ranch and then another. For more than two years he worked at this arduous task and as a cattle salesman. Thereafter he became a ranchman on his own account. And shortly before the end of the year 1810, now scarcely twenty, he became interested in the struggle for independence and enlisted in the patriot army. Imprisoned in the town of Barinas for a few weeks in 1813, he managed to escape and flee to the Apure. Before the end of the following year he was organizing a band of horsemen far to the south in the plains of the Meta and the Casanare, beyond the borders of Venezuela. His daring raids against the royalists and the Spaniards during the four years following attracted the attention of Bolívar, who had finally decided to make the great plains the base of his operations after several vain attempts to liberate northern South America. For the next three years José Antonio was one of the Liberator's most successful and daring young officers. No enterprise was too dangerous for him to attempt. At the head of his brave horsemen he moved across the plains with the speed of a prairie fire. The decisive patriot victory at Carabobo, where he commanded two regiments of infantry and some fifteen of cavalry, was attributed by Bolívar to Páez' superb leadership and indomitable courage. One may imagine this cowboy chief, as a Venezuelan has remarked, "charging beside Agamemnon into the ranks of the Trojans; riding beside Hector, brandishing his spear in the faces of the Greeks; seated beside Ulysses, craftily devising stratagems for the discomfiture of adversaries."[4] History reveals few men more resourceful in guerrilla warfare.

[3] Francisco de Miranda and Bolívar were dictators for brief periods before independence was won, and Venezuela was a part of Great Colombia at the time of Bolívar's later dictatorship.

[4] Ybarra, 147-148. In these and the following pages, Ybarra, although perhaps too eulogistic, gives a vivid account of the early career of Páez. R. B. Cunning-

Soon after the Battle of Carabobo, the Liberator departed for Ecuador and Peru, leaving Páez in supreme command in Venezuela. He was now only thirty-one, and his long career had just begun. Twice he would be constitutional president of Venezuela; twice he would practically choose his successor; and after a period of exile, his partisans would frankly raise him to a dictatorship at the age of seventy-one!

What were the bases of his power? In order to answer this question it will be necessary to be reminded of the character of the Venezuelan people, and especially the plainsmen, and to examine the physical and psychological traits of the man.

What type of men did he dominate during the earlier stages of his career? It may not be amiss to observe them once more. In the main, they were Indians and *mestizos,* with a scattered representation of negroes, mulattoes, and Indo-Africans *(zambos)* besides. Such people had seldom known any other life than one of subjection to some stronger personality. The prestige of the group who dominated them was derived from wealth, official position, or the color of the skin. The first masters and guides of the negroes and mulattoes were the planters and the clergy. And the first rulers of the Indians and the offspring of their miscegenation with the other races were the padres, the planters, the ranchmen, and the local civil authorities. Among all of these primitive and mixed races dependence and servilism had become habitual. For them, a leader was nothing short of a psychological necessity. Moreover, they were desperately poor, and in the ranks of Páez they expected to find better food and raiment as well as opportunity for plunder and adventure. And finally, the ancestors of both Indians and negroes were so accustomed to warfare and depredation that their descendants may have been driven by an irresistible inner impulse.

In the great *llanero* they found a sympathetic leader, a man who drew them to him by an overwhelming personal magnetism. He was a *rubio,* with massive chest, magnificent head, a wealth of wavy chestnut hair, and large vivacious eyes. He was strong, and skillful in the management of horses and cattle—a talent for which they had the maximum of appreciation. He was brave and generous. In the midst of danger and suffering he would never abandon them. He was democratic and approachable, fond of joking and dancing, sufficiently talented in music to play the guitar and sing the cowboy songs of the region. The humble plains-

hame Graham, likewise laudatory, presents an interesting, though often slightly inaccurate, story of the *llanero's* early life in his *José Antonio Páez* (Philadelphia, n. d.). No good biography of this remarkable man has been written.

men became his people, cheerful slaves of his will, prompt to follow him anywhere.[5] It was as a cowboy chieftain that he rode into power.

The white oligarchy then set out to win him. They found him modest and respectful in the presence of gentlemen of wealth and learning, ready to heed their advice and to govern mainly in their interest. He was a useful man; he could restrain the restless masses and make the aristocracy secure. As early as 1826 they took him in, and he soon became one of them. The confiscated property of the royalists had already made him a man of wealth. Within a few years he would become a man of culture. Almost forgotten were the negro slaves, the black freedmen, and the Indian and the *mestizo* laborers. Suffrage was hedged about by property and literacy tests; the slaves were to be emancipated by a very gradual process involving a long period of apprenticeship and compensation for the masters. As for the rest, he respected the liberty of the press, established a few schools, constructed a few public works, set up an ephemeral bank, sought to stimulate industry, immigration, and foreign commerce, suppressed five revolutions between 1830 and 1846, and displayed honesty in the management of the public funds. His government was stern, but seldom cruel. Until 1846 he dominated Venezuelan political life. Although he was actual chief executive for only eight years during the period, no president was elected whom he did not favor.

His sway might have continued indefinitely if the oligarchy had not split into two factions, with one group appealing to the lower classes. In 1846 Antonio Leocadio Guzmán, a sort of demagogue who was restive under Páez' dominance, set out to win the presidency. The great *llanero* declared for José Tadeo Monagas, and Monagas was elected. On two occasions this chief of the independence period had revolted against the authority of Páez, but subsequently he had helped the *llanero* to suppress a rebellion, and Páez thought he could be trusted. The new executive, however, soon revealed dictatorial and ruthless tendencies; and within less than a year after Monagas took charge of the government in 1847, Páez began a revolt against his despotic régime.

The uprising was unsuccessful, and the *llanero* was captured and imprisoned. After several months of miserable confinement, he was finally released and sent into exile (1850). He went to the United States, where he was accorded an enthusiastic reception, and where he remained, living for the most part in New York, until in 1858 he was called back

[5] This view is based in part upon Pedro Manuel Arcaya, *Estudios sobre personajes y hechos de la historia venezolana* (Caracas, 1911), 33-42. But Arcaya must be followed with circumspection; he is an apologist for dictatorships in Spanish America.

to Venezuela by a friendly government which had overthrown the Monagas brothers—José Tadeo and José Gregorio. Finding conditions in his native land more unfavorable to him and more chaotic than he had hoped, he sailed once again for New York. But after a little more than a year, he received another Macedonian call from his friends. Proceeding once more to Venezuela, he took command of the national army in April 1861, and in the following September overthrew the government and proclaimed himself dictator.

Páez really had no constructive policies to carry out. He was merely the agent of a desperate reaction against federalism and other reforms advocated by Juan C. Falcón, A. L. Guzmán, Antonio Guzmán Blanco, and their followers. His dictatorship did not last long. He curtailed the freedom of the press and sought to curry favor with the clergy by signing a concordat with the Holy See. He also ordered the laws to be codified, reorganized the courts, and made some effort to stimulate agriculture and stockraising. But the majority of his countrymen were hostile to his government. In June 1863 he was overthrown by Falcón.[6]

He then departed a third time for the classic land of liberty. In 1867 he began the publication of his autobiography in New York, and he sailed for Buenos Aires the following year as an agent for some North American cattle buyers. In Argentina he was lionized as the lone survivor of the glorious war for independence, and was given the rank and pay of a general in the Argentine army. He was then able to enjoy some of the comforts of life and to engage in further travel. After a visit to several of the republics of South America, he returned again to New York, where he died in June 18, 1873, at the beginning of his eighty-fourth year.[7] He is now one of Venezuela's national heroes.[8]

---

[6] The best account of Páez' political career will be found in Gil Fortoul, II, *passim.* Cunninghame Graham, though always interesting, is rather unreliable. The legislation of the period may be consulted in *Recopilación de leyes y decretos de Venezuela* (54 vols., Caracas, 1890ff.), I, IV, *passim.*

[7] For the years of exile see Cunninghame Graham, 293-308; Adolfo P. Carranza, *El General Páez* (Buenos Aires, 1924); and Páez' *Autobiografía del general José Antonio Páez* (3rd ed., 2 vols., New York, 1878), II, 479-488. Although not always reliable, this is in many respects an excellent autobiography. The activities of the *llanero* while in the United States present an interesting topic for investigation. The following works indicate that he carried on some propaganda in his behalf: Thomas Williams, *Monagas and Páez* (New York, 1850); Simón Camacho, *La vuelta del general José Antonio Páez a Venezuela, 1858* (New York, 1858). During his second exile he wrote a book on Napoleon I: *Máximas de Napoleón sobre el arte de guerra* (New York, 1865).

[8] His remains lie in the Pantheon at Caracas. The unveiling of a statue to him in the national capital in 1905 furnished the occasion for two orations on his career:

V

Antonio Guzmán Blanco was one of the most able, progressive, vain, and corrupt leaders that any Spanish American nation ever produced. He was unquestionably a gifted administrator and not without talent as a warrior, but he was ambitious also for fame as a scholar and man of letters; and covetousness, pride, and passion for flattery and glory were his besetting sins. At times he acted like a man with ardent humanitarian impulses; but it is probable that even in these instances he was motivated by an egotistic desire for the praise of his contemporaries and the plaudits of posterity.

The son of the unstable, ambitious, and petulant Antonio Leocadio Guzmán, he was born in Caracas in February 1829. Although somewhat frail in youth, he was given the best education his native land had to offer. Deeply devoted to his father, who was an able journalist and at times a demagogue, Antonio, when a youth of only eighteen, saw his parent condemned to perpetual banishment, and followed him into exile. But a sudden turn of fortune—José Tadeo Monagas' decision to take the so-called liberals into camp—soon brought the agitator back to Caracas, where he occupied a cabinet post and later became vice-president; and in a short time the son was given an opportunity for observation in a foreign land. For the next nine years he held various positions in the Venezuelan consular and diplomatic service in the United States, including those of consul in Philadelphia and New York and secretary of the Venezuelan legation in Washington.

His sojourn was interrupted by the revolution of March 1858 and the overthrow of the Monagas family, events which cost him his position. While in the United States he became familiar with the works of John C. Calhoun and others, and became an admirer—who knows him sin-

---

Eduardo Blanco, *Ante la estatua de Páez en el acta de ser inaugurada* (Caracas, 1905); and Tomás Michelena, *Resumen de la vida militar y política del ciudadano esclarecido general José Antonio Páez* (Caracas, 1905).

With the exception of H. F. Blow, who was shocked at the treachery of the *llanero* in assuming a dictatorship (Blow to Seward, November 7, 1861, Despatches from Venezuela, vol. 12), diplomats from the United States referred to Páez in terms of highest respect. One of them said that he was a disinterested patriot who had ruled his country with prudence, tact, and moderation, and who deserved to be called the Washington of Venezuela (B. G. Shields to James A. Buchanan, no. 47, January 7, 1848, vol. 4). Another was deeply touched as the venerable statesman set sail for the United States in 1863. "God grant," he said, "that . . . in such a land his rest may be peaceful as his course has been eventful and honorable." (E. D. Culver to Seward, no. 30, August 11, 1863, vol. 13.)

cere?—of a federal system of government soon to be severely tested.[9] He returned home only to be imprisoned by the old oligarchy which was shortly to elevate Páez to a dictatorship; and after a few weeks he was expelled from the country, along with his father and many others. In the Island of St. Thomas he met another exile, Juan C. Falcón, who was soon to become the romantic leader of the hosts of federation and democracy, and the first of Venezuela's democratic Cæsars, just as Páez and José Tadeo Monagas were its first oligarchic Cæsars. Falcón was already saturated with the social idealism and romanticism of Victor Hugo and Lamartine, whose works he had read industriously;[10] and the Guzmáns now added another slogan to his vocabulary. It was the slogan of federalism, immaculate and sacred.[11] The younger Guzmán, having barely reached the age of thirty, joined Falcón's revolution, which turned out to be a bloody civil war that lasted four years.

At the beginning of June 1863, after the dictatorship of Páez had been overthrown, a constituent assembly elected Falcón president of Venezuela, and Antonio Guzmán Blanco vice-president, "without being disqualified by virtue of such election from holding in the meantime any other public charge."[12] He was sent forthwith to London where he negotiated a loan on terms quite unfavorable for the republic.[13]

Returning to Venezuela, he served as acting president from November

[9] Guzmán Blanco later published a source-book on the subject: *Derecho federal: colección de escritos de los mas afamados publicistas de los Estados Unidos del Norte* (4 vols., Caracas, 1879).

[10] On Falcón, whose career cannot be discussed here, see Jacinto Regino Pachano, *Biografía del Mariscal Juan C. Falcón* (Paris, 1876), and Julio Alberto Díaz, *Mariscal Juan Crisóstomo Falcón* (Caracas, 1928).

[11] Pierson, following the recent writers of Venezuela, suggests that federation was *merely* a slogan. He quotes the following statement reported to have been made by the elder Guzmán in Congress in 1867: "I do not know whence is derived the idea that the people of Venezuela have a love for federation when they do not know what the word means. This idea came from me and from others when we said to ourselves: supposing that every revolution needs a banner, now that the convention of Valencia has not wanted to baptize the Constitution with the name federal, let us invoke that idea, because Señores, if our opponents had said Federation, we would have said Centralism." (W. W. Pierson, "Political problems in Venezuela," in Wilgus, ed., *The Caribbean area,* 422.) I have not been able to find the original, although the Venezuelan historians have often referred to the matter. The statement seems to have been made at a very inappropriate moment, since Falcón's power was being seriously threatened in 1867.

[12] *Recopilación de leyes y decretos de Venezuela,* IV, 263.

[13] Pedro Manuel Arcaya, *Venezuela y su actual régimen* (Washington, 1935), 145-146. Fausto Teodora de Aldrey and Rafael Hernández Gutiérrez, in their *Rasgos biográficos . . . del general Guzmán Blanco* (Caracas, 1876), 88-135, present a long defense of this loan transaction.

5, 1864 to July 24, 1865, and from October 3 of the latter year until the end of April 1866. And between these two periods in the Yellow House he held two cabinet posts! He then set out for Europe a second time with the view of refunding and consolidating the entire national debt.[14]

Early in 1867, after a severe attack of cholera while in Paris, he came back to Caracas and married Ana Teresa Ibarra, a beauty of the Venezuelan capital and a member of one of its leading families. He then retired to private life, but his tranquillity was soon interrupted by the outbreak of an insurrection. Falcón placed him in charge of the government troops, and the revolutionists were speedily suppressed. Probably sensing that there was more trouble ahead, however, Guzmán Blanco set out on a third voyage to Europe. During his absence Falcón was overthrown by the old Monagas clan, and the leader of the confederation movement was once more sent into exile.

Don Antonio ventured nevertheless to return to Venezuela in 1868. In fact, he was bold enough not only to inaugurate secret plans for the overthrow of José Ruperto Monagas, the son of the old José Tadeo, but to attack the government openly in the press. In August of the following year, either with the view of testing his popularity and making the final plans for an insurrection, or—as some of his friends say—for the purpose of trying to effect a reconciliation of all factions, Guzmán Blanco gave a grand ball. The affair ended in a riot. A mob attacked his house, broke up the dance, and set him flying to the legation of the United States to avoid assassination. His father took refuge in that of Brazil. A few days later they both left in great haste for Curaçao.

There, Venezuelan expatriates gathered around him, while José Ignacio Pulido and other federalist chiefs carried on spasmodic revolutionary operations in the various states of the republic. At the opportune moment Don Antonio landed on the coast and assumed command, and on April 27, 1870 he finally took Caracas after a bloody battle. He began immediately a dictatorship which was not successfully challenged for eighteen years.[15]

Such was his rapid and sensational rise to power: acting president at the age of thirty-five, dictator at forty-one! He was immensely proud of the record, and as soon as he suppressed the remnants of the Mona-

---

[14] Aldrey and Gutiérrez, 141-186. For the legislation of the period, see *Recopilación de leyes y decretos,* IV, 388, *passim.*

[15] Aldrey y Gutiérrez, 185-191, *passim;* James R. Patridge to Hamilton Fish, no. 17, August 22, 1869; no. 59, January 25, 1870; no. 87, July 20, 1870, Despatches from Colombia, vols. 18 and 19.

gas sympathizers, he had some of his friends publish a laudatory account of his life in a Caracas newspaper.[16]

He was fond of representing himself as a man of destiny upon whom an unseen power had imposed one patriotic and benevolent task after another. On one occasion he declared that since childhood, destiny had compelled him to depart from the path of his inclinations repeatedly. As a child he had lived on the edge of a beautiful field, and all of his tastes led him to prefer the independent life of a country gentleman; but his father decided that he must have an education. He soon developed a fondness for literature, and decided to devote his life to *belles lettres*. His father insisted, however, that he prepare himself for a profession, and he chose that of medicine, only to find the strain of laboratory and morgue too much for his delicate nerves. He then studied law and received his degree, but discovered that the practice of jurisprudence required too much trickery and injustice. Another turn of the wheel of fortune sent him into exile and the foreign service of Venezuela. Tired of this kind of labor, he returned home with the hope of settling down to a quiet life on his estate; but within eight days he was imprisoned, and after two months of confinement, was sent into exile. Stopping at St. Thomas on his way to the United States, he met General Falcón, and was persuaded that it was his duty to assist in liberating his country from the tyrannical oligarchy. For four long years he confronted the perils and suffered the hardships of a sanguinary civil war. With Falcón in charge of the government and the holy federation established at last, he supposed that he would now be free to retire to private life or travel abroad. But once more fate willed otherwise, and he was compelled to aid Falcón in his large administrative tasks. Having given this further service to his fatherland, he now turned his thoughts once more to the joys of private life, only to have his repose disturbed by the overthrow of his chief's successor, the insults and persecutions of his enemies, and finally the outrage of August 14, 1869, for which the Monagas clan was undoubtedly responsible. He felt that he must vindicate his honor and save his country, and once again he went forth to the field of battle. Within seventy days from the beginning of his great campaign, he swept the enemy from power. He then sent his emissaries to Martinique in search of Falcón, whom he desired to restore to the national palace, but when these agents reached the island they found that the venerable chieftain was dead, and, therefore, General Guzmán Blanco, much against his

[16] This first appeared as articles in *La opinión nacional* in 1872 and 1873.

will, had to continue at the head of the victorious hosts. The Septennium over, he took his family to Europe in search of peace and rest, but scarcely two years passed before an ignorant and corrupt soldier tried to perpetuate himself in power, and the man of destiny had to return and save Venezuela for the third time.[17]

In view of Guzmán Blanco's patent thirst for power and glory,[18] this pretended diffidence seems absurd. But it is only one illustration of the many hollow pretenses and inconsistencies of his long rule. Both he and his press preached the sacred principles of liberalism; and then he proceeded to violate them all. He was forever recalling how his father was defeated for the presidency in 1846 by means of scandalous electoral frauds; and yet elections were a mere farce during his entire régime. Articles appeared daily in his controlled newspapers praising the noble campaigns made by the senior Guzmán against the governments of 1840 and 1846; but the despotic son would not permit the journalists to publish the slightest criticism of his acts. He represented himself to be the ardent champion of state rights; but every state executive was his appointee and tool, and he refused to permit the slightest local autonomy. He extolled the virtues of peace and order; and yet his vanity with reference to his military record led to an interminable stream of articles and books recounting his strategy and heroism, thus keeping alive the very martial spirit which he should have attempted to abate. Posing as a sincere friend of the masses, he continued to subject them to compulsory recruitment.[19]

His vanity was extravagant and ridiculous. He distributed medals with a free hand, careful always to have his name inscribed upon them. He sought every degree known to the world of learning, and obtained most of them, honorary and otherwise, except the degree of Doctor of Divinity. He addressed every literary and scientific society in the land, and was a member of them all. Owing to wounded pride and anger because an archbishop refused to have a *Te Deum* sung in his honor, rather than to any firm convictions of liberalism, he made a devastating attack on the Roman Catholic Church, expelling its ministers, suppress-

---

[17] Antonio Guzmán Blanco, *Discurso inaugural* (Caracas, 1883), 8-14. This is an address given before the Venezuelan Academy of Language and Literature on July 27, 1883.

[18] One of the books published at his instigation, no doubt, was entitled: *Glorias del ilustre americano, regenerador, y pacificador de Venezuela, General Guzmán Blanco* (Caracas, 1875).

[19] Arcaya, 21-24; Aldrey and Gutiérrez, *passim;* and *Glorias del ilustre americano, passim.*

ing its convents, secularizing its schools and cemeteries, establishing civil marriage and civil registration of births and deaths, reducing its ministers to abject servility, and making the institution an object of contempt in Venezuela. He compelled the author of every book to point out on the title page that his work was published during the administration of Guzmán Blanco. He had numerous streets, bridges, roads, aqueducts, schools, parks, and public buildings named in his honor. He ordered oil portraits of himself hung in all government buildings and in some of the churches. He erected statues to practically every political and military personage of Venezuela, excepting José Antonio Páez, and had his own name inscribed somewhere on the pedestals. He even had numerous statues and allegorical figures erected to himself. He is said to have appeared in a painting as a grown man among those who gathered about the deathbed of Bolívar, although Don Antonio was less than two years old when the Liberator died! In another painting he was represented as St. Paul, with Mark on one side and John on the other, and Matthew and Luke in the background! He presented full-length portraits of himself to numerous friends, who were expected to hang them conspicuously in their dwellings; and many an artist was employed to paint his beautiful wife. He erected the national Pantheon for the ashes of Venezuela's illustrious dead, and was careful to have his name carved on its portals. He built extravagant palaces in town and country, gave elaborate banquets, and served the best of dishes, wines, and cigars. Numerous medals granted by every European government that wished to flatter him covered his chest. The decorations and gold braid on his uniform were as luxuriant as the beard that covered his chin.[20]

And yet, despite all this extravagance and his ready disposition to augment his private fortune at public expense, his long rule was signalized by solid achievements. These may be summarized under three headings: peace, education, and material progress.

Although he spilled much blood in his struggle for power, few revolutions occurred after he consolidated his government in 1872. And all these he speedily suppressed. For anarchy he substituted order.

One of his first decrees after taking charge of the government dealt with education, which became thereafter the subject of his constant

[20] This amazing record of extravagance is described by William Eleroy Curtis, in his *Venezuela. A land where it's always summer* (New York, 1896), 100-118, *passim.* It is for the most part confirmed in *Recopilación de leyes y decretos de Venezuela,* V- XIV. Mary Watters' volume, *A history of the church in Venezuela* (Chapel Hill, 1933), 183-213, contains an excellent account of the dictator's relations with the church.

solicitude. Primary education was made free and compulsory, and nearly seventeen hundred schools of this type were built; secondary schools were established in all the leading towns; technical institutes were constructed in several cities; and institutions of higher learning received greater subsidies than ever before. He also encouraged various learned societies and codified the laws. In all branches of knowledge with no direct bearing on political issues, there was progress.[21]

In the material realm many improvements occurred. He built roads and bridges, improved the docks, encouraged navigation, beautified the towns, gave considerable attention to sanitation, and either completed, initiated, or planned nearly all of the railways which the country was to have prior to 1913.[22] He reorganized finances, restored the national credit, greatly reduced the national debt, in spite of new loans floated in Europe, and encouraged mining, agriculture, and the pastoral industries. Although he was careful to provide for a comfortable old age, and often gave profitable concessions to friends and relatives, and although he spent an inordinate amount on statues and monuments, the country enjoyed unwonted prosperity under his government, which was in many ways better than any that Venezuela had known since the early days of the republic.[23]

Into the other side of the balance must be placed the degrading and debasing effects of his tyranny. The dispatches of the diplomats of the United States in Venezuela frequently describe his system of government and his personal traits.

In August 1870, one of them wrote that the dungeons of La Guayra and the prisons of the capital were crowded with men whose only crime was opposition to Guzmán Blanco. "The number of these unfortunates," it was added, "is daily increasing from new arrests, under any or without pretext, by any of his officers or subalterns; and is daily diminished

---

[21] See *Recopilación de leyes y decretos,* V, 89-98, for the compulsory school law, which was dated June 27, 1870. The number of primary and secondary schools and the sums devoted to their support appear in the various annual budgets, which are printed in the same work, V-XIV, *passim.* Other important legislation of the period will also be found in these volumes.

[22] W. Rodney Long, *Railways of South America* (pt. 2, Washington, 1927), 341-381.

[23] An impartial biography of Guzmán Blanco has not been written. José Güell y Mercador's, *Guzmán Blanco y su tiempo* (Caracas, 1883) is somewhat less eulogistic than the sketch by Aldrey and Gutiérrez, already cited. Manuel Landaeta Rosales' *Hoja de servicios del general Antonio Guzmán Blanco* (Caracas, 1899) is a sort of funeral oration. Francisco González Guinán's account of the period *(Historia contemporánea de Venezuela,* vols. IX-XI) is not impartial. He held several high posts under Guzmán Blanco's dictatorship.

by the constant deaths from the pestilence engendered by filth, insufficient food, crowd, and neglect."[24]

Three years later another remarked that the government was "intensely personal and arbitrary." Guzmán Blanco, he said, was ambitious, energetic, capricious, and exceedingly vain. Moreover, he judged him to be "wholly destitute of earnest and profound convictions." "He allows no man in his cabinet nor among his personal confidents to have an individual opinion. He insists on deciding the most trivial questions himself, and gives personal attention to the smallest details, not allowing his cabinet officers the slightest discretion."[25]

A third diplomat described at length the statues and the marble tablets set up to commemorate his achievements, while a fourth pointed out how he continued to rule from some European metropolis with other men theoretically at the head of the government, a remark which evoked from the venerable clerk of the state department the following comment: "Venezuela is a pocket-borough of Guzmán Blanco's. He cannot serve two consecutive terms, so every two years he goes to Europe, leaving [behind] a perfectly irresponsible president-puppet, whose wires he pulls from Paris."[26]

And a former secretary of the American legation in Venezuela not only spoke of the "inordinate vanity of the man which prompted him to erect statues to himself in every conceivable place," but recalled the dictator's remark that there were only two illustrious Americans: himself and George Washington! He also accused Don Antõnio of dishonesty in the management of government finances, declaring that the Venezuelan had "succeeded in acquiring a vast amount of property" during his dictatorship.[27]

[24] Partridge to Fish, no. 88, August 8, 1870, Despatches from Venezuela, vol. 19.

[25] William A. Pile to *idem, Confidential,* August 7, 1873, vol. 21. In an earlier report Minister Pile estimated the population of Venezuela at this time as follows: whites, 350,000; negroes, 150,000; Indians, 300,000; mixed, 500,000; total, 1,300,000. He said that the party of Guzmán Blanco was composed of "a small minority of the educated white population and a large majority of the colored and mixed races," whose notions of republican government were "crude and ill-defined." He thought the masses of Venezuela were not prepared for the exercise of popular government *(idem* to *idem,* no. 9, October 30, 1871, vol. 19).

[26] W. L. Scruggs to James G. Blaine, no. 47, October 29, 1889, vol. 39; Charles S. Scott to Bayard, no. 236, May 23, 1886, vol. 38. The quotation is from A. A. Adee's marginal note.

[27] A. W. Barrett, in the New York *Herald,* January 6, 1890. On September 4, 1879 Minister Jehu Baker (letter to Secretary Evarts, no. 161, Despatches from Venezuela, vol. 25) spoke of the dictator's "unscrupulous greed and . . . insufferable arrogance." Baker said that Guzmán Blanco's rule was an autocracy upheld by military force.

Perhaps one may venture to conclude this discussion of Guzmán Blanco and his work with a caricature written by a literary artist. The portrayal dealt with an imaginary dictator named Losada, but Don Antonio must have been the suggestive prototype.

With a mighty effort Losada shook the republic

> "nearly free from the shackles of ignorance and sloth. . . . He established schools and hospitals, built roads, bridges, railroads, and palaces, and bestowed generous subsidies upon the arts and sciences. . . . Other presidents had been rapacious without reason. Losada amassed enormous wealth, but his people had their share of the benefits.
>
> "The joint in his armor was his insatiate passion for monuments and tokens commemorating his glory. In every town he caused to be erected statues of himself bearing legends in praise of his greatness. In the walls of every public edifice tablets were fixed reciting his splendor and the gratitude of his subjects. His statuettes and portraits were scattered throughout the land in every house and hut. One of the sycophants in his court painted him as St. John, with a halo and a train of attendants in full uniform. . . . He ordered from a French sculptor a marble group including himself with Napoleon, Alexander the Great, and one or two others whom he deemed worthy of the honor.
>
> "He ransacked Europe for decorations. . . . On state occasions his breast was covered from shoulder with crosses, stars, golden roses, medals, and ribbons."

And now he wishes a portrait executed by a New York artist.

> "He wants himself in the center of the canvas, of course. He is to be painted as Jupiter sitting on Olympus, with the clouds at his feet. At one side of him stands George Washington, in full regimentals, with his hand on the president's shoulder. An angel with outstretched wings hovers overhead, and is placing a laurel wreath" [on the dictator's brow]. "In the background are cannon, more angels, and soldiers."

Losada is a "dictator clear down to his finger ends. He is a kind of combination of Julius Cæsar, Lucifer, and Chauncey Depew in Sepia."[28]

Ingenious, virile, and versatile as he was, Guzmán Blanco had some difficulty with his puppets. Francisco Linares Alcántara, selected for the rôle in 1877, died the following year; and the dictator had to return from Paris in order to clear away the chaos and the generals. Joaquín Crespo, who became the marionette in 1885, rendered due homage during his two-year term, but later revolted. And although Hermógenes

---

[28] O. Henry, *Cabbages and kings* (New York, 1913), 234-235, 243, 245-246.

López, who took charge of affairs in August 1887, displayed proper respect for his chief, Doctor Juan Pablo Rojas Paúl, who was imposed as the dummy in 1888, soon revealed a will and ideas of his own. He favored a civil régime, and permitted freedom of the press as well as some liberty in elections. He also had the remains of Páez brought home from the United States and safely deposited in the Pantheon—the remains of the stern old *llanero* who was once the bitter enemy of the Guzmáns.

Guzmán Blanco—living in his fine mansion on the Champs Elysées, with his eldest daughter now the wife of the Duke de Morny[29]—was furious. But so charmed was he by the society of Paris that he lingered there a while longer. And then it was too late. Pent up resentment against him broke out in a fury. One of his statues had been dragged down during the anarchy in 1879; but now, on October 26, 1889, almost every monument and tablet and portrait was demolished throughout the country, and his properties were attacked besides.[30] He considered chartering a fleet and returning home, but was restrained by sober second thoughts. Too many of his generals were unfaithful, the people were too enraged, and he was too old and broken in health to "venture upon the high seas like another Napoleon returning from Elba."[31] He remained in Paris—remained and pined for the palms, the blue mountains, and the tropical skies. And there, oppressed by profound nostalgia, he died on July 30, 1899, at the age of threescore and ten.[32]

VI

With General Cipriano Castro, who seized the government on October 23, 1899, the dictatorship in Venezuela reached its nadir. Nobody has discussed Castro with impartiality. His friends and flatterers have rep-

---

[29] Curtis, 107.

[30] Scruggs to Blaine, despatch cited in note 26. Curtis, 135-150, describes the events of 1888-1889 in detail. The statues, monuments, portraits, and tablets were torn down in Caracas on October 26, 1889.

[31] Barrett, in the New York *Herald,* January 6, 1890.

[32] Arcaya, 25. Arcaya erroneously states, however, that Guzmán Blanco died in 1898. In 1894 the ex-dictator published a book entitled, *En defensa de la causa liberal* (Paris, 1894). It was an answer to L. Level de Goda's *Historia contemporánea de Venezuela, política y militar* (Barcelona, 1893), and to Domingo Antonio Olavarría's *Estudios histórico-políticos* (Valencia, 1894); but it also contained a very laudatory account of Falcón's military achievements. Olavarría's work is rather hostile toward the party of Guzmán Blanco and his rule. In 1883 the dictator had published in Caracas a monograph on Bolívar *(El libertador de la América del Sur;* also a London edition, 1885). While Guzmán Blanco was in exile, R. F. Seijas issued a brief biography of him entitled *El presidente* (Madrid, 1891).

resented him as an Olympic hero; his enemies have denounced him as a Satanic villain. Perhaps the view of his enemies is nearer the truth. He combined the traits of P. T. Barnum, Boss Tweed, and Nero. For almost nine years he maintained himself in power by means of bribery, military force, extravagant propaganda, and a persistent defiance of foreign governments which tended to arouse the national spirit of the Venezuelans.

He was born on October 14, 1858 in a highland valley of the Andes, in the Venezuelan Province of Táchira. He received little or no formal education, and began work on a cattle ranch at an early age. He first entered politics in 1884, and became governor of Táchira in 1888 during the administration of Rojas Paúl. When the latter, in accord with Venezuelan custom, dictated his successor in 1890, in the person of Doctor Raimundo Andueza Palacio, Castro became deputy to the national congress. He cast his lot with the civilian presidents.

In a short time he was called upon to defend his chief. General Joaquín Crespo, who had for two years been one of the puppets of Guzmán Blanco, resented the imposition of Palacio, and began a revolt against him in 1892 when he attempted to prlong his term. Crespo was soon joined by a number of other restive generals, and Castro was placed in command of the government troops in his native provine. Unsuccessful in his first military operations, he was forced to flee to Colombia. Crespo overthrew Palacio, governed the country for another six years, and then placed General Ignacio Andrade in charge in 1898. This led to further revolts and the death of Crespo in a battle on his native plains. Observing the situation closely from Colombia, where for almost seven years he had been engaged in the cattle business, Castro decided it was about time for him to reënter politics. The brave old *llanero* was dead, some of the army chiefs seemed ready to abandon General Andrade, and the occasion looked propitious. Crossing the border with a little band of soldiers on May 23, 1899, he easily advanced toward Caracas. Treachery and the aid of other generals, José Ignacio Pulido, José Manuel Hernández, and Juan Vicente Gómez among them, soon gave him possession of the national capital.[33]

[33] Arcaya, 51-56; *Recopilación de leyes y decretos,* XXII, 622-623; Esteban Roldán Oliarte, *El general Juan Vicente Gómez* (Mexico, 1933), 15-31; *Enciclopedia universal ilustrada europeo-americana* (Madrid, n. d.), under "Castro, Cipriano." The early life of Castro is obscure. So far as the present writer knows, no reputable biographer has ever dealt with him. For the colorful career of Joaquín Cespo, consult León Lameda and Manuel Landaeta Rosales, *Historia militar y*

His troubles, however, were by no means over. His enemies, though scattered, still kept up the fight, and some of his friends, Hernández in particular, became jealous and abandoned him. Perhaps he was only saved by the strong arm of Gómez and the pressure of foreign governments whose attempts to coerce him made him for a time a national hero. Bidding defiance to Germany, England, and Italy, whose joint coercive action against Venezuela was limited by the Monroe Doctrine and the attitude of the United States, and collecting tribute from foreign investors or transferring their concessions to natives, he erected about himself a bulwark of patriotic sentiment. The blockade by the three European countries was soon lifted, and by 1903 the insurgents were suppressed. With unscrupulous astuteness he continued to play the rôle of dictator, tyrant, Boxer, and Redeemer until a serious malady compelled him to depart for Europe in November 1908 for surgical attention.[34]

His political career was hazardous and stormy throughout, and doubtless because of the realization that he was engaged in a desperate enterprise, he pursued a course that was as completely selfish as it was ruthless. He was determined to rule as long as he could and at the same time amass a fortune against the day when he would have to take up his residence in a foreign land. Few men have been less influenced by moral restraints. He imprisoned his opponents or forced them to flee, he governed Venezuela as if it were his private estate, and he acted like a man who had only a few years to live and no fear of a judgment day. He was one of the most irresponsible tyrants that Spanish America ever produced.

Poor in his youth—perhaps even a barefoot *peon*—he now gave himself freely to wine, women, and luxury. He surrounded himself with gorgeous draperies, beautiful rugs, portraits, and statuary. He ate like a gourmand, drank like a toper, and lived like a libertine. His champagne was especially bottled for him, and he smoked the most expensive Havana cigars. He levied tribute from many an enterprise, became the

---

política del general Joaquín Crespo (2 vols., Caracas, 1897), and Manuel Modesto Gallegos, *Generales Antonio Guzmán Blanco y Joaquín Crespo* (Caracas, 1934).

[34] For Castro's relations with the European countries and the United States see Chester Lloyd Jones, *The Caribbean since 1900* (New York, 1936), 208-277; J. Fred Rippy, *Latin America in world politics* (New York, 1931), 182-199; and Tito V. Lisoni, *La política exterior del general Cipriano Castro* (Santiago de Chile, 1908).

owner of several ranches, built palaces in town and by the seashore, and deposited large sums of money in foreign banks.[35]

Meantime, his controlled press was delirious in its adulation. Castro merely assumed the title of Supreme Chief of the Liberal Revolutionary Restoration, but the newspapers employed every extravagant term that the genius of sycophants could invent: renowned and invincible *caudillo;* savior of the country and defender of its sovereignty and integrity; the founder of peace; the Moses of the republic; the first democrat of America; the formidable athlete whose hand was upholding the rights of the world; magistrate, administrator, warrior, and the hope of Venezuela. All these phrases were written in his honor as he danced his way across the nation in the spring of 1905 in preparation for a longer lease on power. The press reported his progress under the daily caption of "The Apotheosis of the Hero," and one writer, having exhausted his originality, recalled his history of North America, and declared that Castro was first in war, first in peace, and first in the hearts of Venezuelans. Even as the voice of Jesus raised Lazarus from the tomb, so Castro spoke to the corpse of Venezuela and called it back to life.[36] Surely servilism and debasement could go no further!

If all of this seems incredible, let one examine the more sober reports of the contemporary diplomats of the United States in Venezuela. Although their despatches were somewhat prejudiced, especially in the later years, perhaps they are as impartial witnesses as the historian can find.

"General Castro," said one of these diplomats on November 7, 1899, "is a very small, dark man who seems to have a considerable admixture of Indian blood. . . . He talks well and with facility, and appears to be a man who reaches decisions quickly. I think he means well."[37]

"General Castro," wrote another on October 5, 1901, "claims the right to send persons who are offensive to him to jail, and . . . he keeps them there without giving them the right to be heard. I have been told that he now has between 400 and 500 of his enemies in his Caracas Bastile,

---

[35] *The Outlook* LXXX (May 20, 1905), 167-172; New York *Times,* December 6, 8, 12, and 14, 1924; George W. Crichfield, *American supremacy* (2 vols., New York, 1908), I, 254-257. Crichfield was violently prejudiced, and there was much propaganda against Castro in the United States; but the present writer believes that the statements in these paragraphs are essentially accurate. For the various monopolies which he established, see *Recopilación de leyes y decretos,* XXVII, 325-327, *passim,* XXVIII, 126, 128, 132, 133, 139, *passim.*

[36] *Viaje del general Cipriano Castro . . . en abril y mayo de 1905* (Caracas, 1905), 20-21, 27, *passim.*

[37] Francis B. Loomis to John Hay, no. 340, Despatches from Venezuela, vol. 50.

and many others in durance very vile at Maracaibo." He then referred to the dictator's financial transactions. "The general opinion," wrote the American minister, "is that he is putting away a large sum of money against the rainy day when he will have to retire from power."[38]

Six weeks later the same writer reported:

> "He is a very determined, obstinate man; a sincere believer in himself. . . . His enemies, and they are legion, plan and plot with astonishing assiduity. . . . His policy has been . . . to cut down expenses in every possible way so as to have a neat little private fortune at his disposal. On the whole he is playing his part quite as skillfully and subtly as his *alter ego* the Sultan of Turkey could play it.
>
> " . . . His most trustworthy soldiers he keeps at Caracas, and he is so afraid that they may be induced to desert him that after nightfall no one is allowed to pass along . . . the sidewalk abutting the houses where they are quartered. Sentinels stand at the doors, and order all passers-by to cross over to the other side."[39]

Subsequent reports deal with the formidable revolution of Manuel Antonio Matos, the wealthy brother-in-law of the deceased Guzmán Blanco. For a brief period in 1902 it appeared that Castro's dictatorial days were numbered; but by the spring of 1903 all the insurrectionists were suppressed. On March 21, 1903 Castro went through the farce of offering his resignation. It was merely a gesture made for political effect, "with the previous knowledge and consent of Congress."[40]

On September 12, 1904 Minister Norman Hutchinson reported that Castro had initiated a policy of establishing monopolies. Government favorites were given the exclusive right to butcher and sell beef throughout the country. The sale of matches and alcohol was also monopolized.[41]

A few days later Hutchinson wrote that Castro had undertaken a national journey in search of support for himself and his so-called reforms. Commenting on the popularity of the dictator and his personal traits, Hutchinson said:

> "In so far as I can make out, General Castro is far from popular in Caracas, is regarded in an uncertain light in the provinces, but

[38] Herbert W. Bowen to *idem,* no. 28, October 5, 1901, vol. 54. See also New York *Times,* December 14, 1924.

[39] *Idem* to *idem,* no. 344, November 16, 1901.

[40] *Idem* to *idem,* no. 46, November 30, 1901, no. 97, May 8, 1902, and no. 103, June 14, 1902. See also *idem* to *idem,* no. 117, August 10, 1902, and William Russell to *idem,* telegrams of March 21 and 24, 1903, vol. 55.

[41] To Hay, no. 322, vol. 57.

has considerable power with his friends, and with many who fear him, and whom he has had in prison.

"The army . . . seems to be on his side. He has treated it better than it has ever been treated before, especially the rank and file, and he takes good care who his officers are.

"The Legislature, the Courts, his Cabinet, and the Press, all seem to do as he wills. The Press is particularly ridiculous in its daily and persistent epics to his greatness. . . .

"Personally he is a very vain man, a result of having pushed himself upon the national pedestal. He speaks at great length and with ease, and often says worthy things, but is not trusted for desiring to do them. He is notoriously unfaithful to his wife, who has had sufficient spirit to shoot at him once. . . . He is particularly fond of dancing at all times, and consequently all entertainments in his honor take the form of dances. . . ."[42]

Near the end of October 1904, Hutchinson gave further details of Castro's conceit and the debasement of his flatterers. "He believes he got rid of the [allied] fleet by his diplomacy," wrote Hutchinson. "The newspapers are comparing him to Alexander the Great, Napoleon, and Washington."[43]

As Castro began another tour of Venezuela in April 1905, the minister thought the dictator was preparing to leave the country. He reported in some detail as follows:

"Venezuelan President with much baggage left here today overland for San Fernando, on the Apure River, where his fleet will meet him. His wife and sisters leave as soon as possible for Trinidad and Europe. He will await favorable news before returning. He has ordered his gold to be taken to New York and Europe. . . . Gómez now acting president.[44]

"I have the honor to inform you that my French and Brazilian colleagues have just told me that they also have learned that President Castro is sending his gold to New York and Europe. His friend, Rendiles, has already deposited about $2,000,000 for him in a New York bank; and his friends, Jalvis and Contreras, will take about $1,000,000 to Curaçao this week, and will go with it from there to New York. . . . All this gold was stolen from the Custom house by President Castro. . . . The wife and the sisters of President Castro leave here tomorrow for Trinidad, and will leave for Europe unless better news comes from the States."[45]

---

[42] To Hay, no. 323, September 16, 1904.
[43] To *idem,* no. 348, October 29, 1904.
[44] Bowen to Hay, telegram of April 12, 1905, vol. 58.
[45] *Idem* to *idem,* no. 406, April 16, 1905.

But Castro did not go abroad. He merely made a journey of forty days through the republic, leaving Gómez in charge of the government to read the letters and articles of sychopants and learn how popular his rival was. Meantime, a servile congress decreed that May 23 should be a national holiday, and Castro's head appeared on some new stamps. In the following June he was elected president for six years more. The honor was conferred by electors, "who were chosen by the Congress, and the vote was unanimous, as General Castro was the only candidate."[46]

He could now proceed with his monopolies and concessions. One favorite was given a monopoly of the manufacture of glass throughout the republic, and another was granted the exclusive right to establish flour mills. A third was given the sole right to raise sugar cane and textile plants in the State of Carabobo, while a fourth received the exclusive privilege "to explore certain portions of the sea and to exploit whatever he finds, except fish."[47]

And congress continued to grovel. In August 1905 it ordered the erection of a triumphal arch to commemorate the national restoration. The date of May 23, 1899 should be inscribed in letters of gold on its front. The left supporting column should bear this inscription: "The patriotic energy of General Cipriano Castro, chief of the Liberal Revolutionary Restoration and President of the Republic, saved the honor of the latter on December 9, 1902." This was the day when he refused to submit to the ultimatums of Germany and England. The right column would have quotations from Bolívar and Castro carved on its base.[48]

May 23, 1906 was a great holiday. Abject flattery filled the press and rolled from a thousand tongues. But this was not enough. Gómez appeared to be gaining in popularity. Tired and in ill health, or else pretending that he was, Castro had turned over the government temporarily to Gómez early in April; and now as the great holiday celebrations were in progress he issued a proclamation in which he stated that he intended to retire completely from public life. At the next session of congress he would present his resignation. But he was not in earnest; he was merely soliciting popular acclaim.[49]

---

[46] Hutchinson to Hay, May 14 and June 7, 1905.

[47] *Idem* to *idem*, no. 442, June 25, 1905; *idem* to *idem*, nos. 453 and 454, July 22, 1905, vol. 59.

[48] William Russell to Elihu Root, no. 8, August 25, 1905. See also *Recopilación de leyes y decretos*, XXVIII, 178-179.

[49] *Idem* to *idem*, telegrams of April 10 and May 24, and letter of May 27, 1906, vol. 60.

Once more the plan worked. Two delegates from each state and territory were named to meet in Caracas on June 12, and then proceed to Valencia, where Castro was residing, in order to present him the proclamations of the people urging him to desist from his purpose and return to power. They met in due time and acted their part, and even Gómez issued a flattering address to the people in Castro's behalf. The dictator then informed the delegation that he would take charge of the government on July 5.[50]

Late in 1908 he became ill again—perhaps really ill this time—suffering from an acute infection of the kidneys. On November 23 he turned over the government once more to Gómez,[51] and a day later he left for Europe, where he intended to undergo an operation. He would find it most difficult to return to his native land.

For fifteen years he was almost a man without a country. His operation, if he had one, was apparently successful; but his movements are still somewhat shrouded. The Venezuelan press was under the thumb of Gómez, and colored the news to suit his convenience; reports in the newspapers in the United States were probably not entirely reliable. Such news accounts as are available indicate that Castro was restless, homesick for his native land, and that he longed to return to power. Early in 1909 he attempted to get back into Venezuela, and was said to have been intercepted by war vessels of the United States, England, and France. In July 1911 he tried again, and it was rumored that he actually landed on Venezuelan soil. Late in 1912 he arrived in the port of New York, where he was prevented from landing by the immigration authorities, but after a brief detention he was allowed to enter. According to reports, he was present at the inauguration of Woodrow Wilson, but departed for Europe a few days later. Near the end of July 1913 it was rumored that he had taken the Venezuelan town of Coro. Early in 1914 he was said to be in Trinidad; in July 1915 he was deported from the Danish West Indies; in the summer of 1916 he spent some time in New York, but early in August he and his wife sailed for Puerto Rico. It was said that they had been living for some time in the Barbadoes, but now they established a permanent residence in San Juan. In August 1917 he visited Cuba and Mexico; in the following September he was in New York again; and late in October he was reported to be in Trinidad.

---

[50] *Idem* to *idem*, no. 83, June 10, and no. 84, June 24, 1906.

[51] *Recopilación de leyes y decretos*, XXXI, 77.

Thereafter his name appeared very rarely in the newspapers of the United States. Perhaps he was living quietly with his relatives in his San Juan home. Early in December 1920 he and his wife arrived in Cuba, en route for the United States. Late in July 1924 there was rumor of an attempt to assassinate him in San Juan. On the fourth of the following December he died. The end was said to have come in a shabby little house on an obscure street in the Puerto Rican capital, his death being caused by a hemorrhage of the stomach. A feature article in the New York *Times* recalled his unique career, his lack of education, his cattle rustling on the Colombian frontier, his rise from obscure poverty to the rank of a multimillionaire. "Such," said the journalist, "was the Andean cattle thief who put his country in his pocket and drank champagne as he laughed at the foreign officers."[52]

VII

Juan Vicente Gómez, with all of his faults, proved to be a better head of the Venezuelan nation than might have been expected of a man brought up in the corrupt and tyrannical school of Castro. Although avaricious, despotic, and doubtless cruel, he and his associates appear to have managed the material interests of the country as well or better than they were administered during almost any other period in the history of the republic. For length of dictatorial rule he holds the record in South America, and, except for Porfirio Díaz of Mexico, in all Spanish America.

It is impossible at this time to present a thorough and balanced estimate of the man and his work. More was written concerning him while he was still alive than about most other living men in history; but very few wrote with impartiality, and none with a thorough mastery of the

[52] New York *Times,* December 14, 1924. The account of Castro's activities during his exile is taken largely from the reports in this newspaper. The reader will find Ramón Tello Mendoza's *Documentos del general Cipriano Castro* (6 vols., Caracas, 1903-1908) an interesting supplement to the *Recopilación de leyes y decretos de Venezuela,* XXII-XXXI, which contains much of the legislation of the period. From these sources it will be observed that Castro's dictatorship was not completely barren. He devoted considerable sums to education and public works, although the military organization and the public officials absorbed the major part of the budget. He also kept up the payments on the foreign contract debt and some of the foreign damage claims after 1905, although he continued to have trouble over the cancellation of concessions held by the French, the Dutch, the English, and citizens of the United States. See Council of the Corporation of Foreign Bondholders, *Annual Report* (London, 1906-1908), vols. 33-35, *passim,* under "Venezuela."

facts, which indeed are not yet available.[53] Subsidized journalists and friends represented him to be the greatest of all Venezuelan statesmen, with the sole exception of Bolívar. Others portrayed him as the worst tyrant Spanish America had ever produced, but many of these were the unfortunate friends of Castro or professional revolutionists.

The fourth in what came to be a large family of children, Juan Vicente was born of humble Indian, or largely Indian, parents in the frontier State of Táchira on July 24, 1857.[54] The death of his father threw upon him at an early age heavy domestic responsibilities. With no formal education and with scarcely the ability to read and write, he set to work with the crops and the cattle. If reports are true, he had unusual ability to accumulate wealth, for when he joined Castro in support of the Andueza Palacio government in 1892, he was said to be a man of large means. He spent seven years of exile near Cúcuta, Colombia, where he acquired a ranch named Argentina and reëstablished his fortune.

Joining Castro in the revolution of 1899, he came into office with him, serving first as governor of the Federal District and then as civil and military chief of Táchira. At the end of March 1901 he became vice-president of the nation, an office which he held continuously until November 23, 1908. During this period he also acted as president on two or three occasions, but his greatest achievements were on the battlefield, for he was largely responsible for the suppression of the revolutions against Castro, with whose troubled fortunes he was closely associated for nine years.[55]

Castro's departure for Europe in November 1908, left the government in Gómez' hands, but friends of the absent dictator were set over his erstwhile subordinate to observe his movements. An alleged conspiracy, the report of the appearance of hostile Dutch war vessels, and a favor-

[53] The best sources now accessible are: *Recopilación de leyes y decretos de Venezuela,* XXXI-LVIII; Luís Correa, *El general Juan Vicente Gómez; documentos para la historia de su gobierno* (3 vols., Caracas, 1925); and the annual reports of the Council of the Corporation of Foreign Bondholders (London, 1908-1935), vols. 35-62, which reveal the confidence of foreign investors in his government.

[54] There is some disagreement regarding the year of his birth, but 1857 seems to be correct.

[55] The best accounts of his early career will be found in Roldán Oliarte, 23-67; in Manuel Landaeta Rosales, *Rasgos biográficos del general Juan Vicente Gómez* (Caracas, 1909); in Victoriano Márquez Bustillos, *Semblanza del general Juan Vicente Gómez* (Caracas, 1919); and in Eleazar López Contreras, *Cualidades militares del general Juan Vicente Gómez* (Caracas, 1917). All of these authors, however, are too eulogistic.

able agitation by the populace of Caracas—spontaneous or induced—furnished good reason or pretext for a declaration of martial law and the seizure of power in his own name on December 19, 1908.[56] He was the dictator of Venezuela for the next twenty-seven years, although others acted as head of the civil government on two occasions.

In spite of a good deal of sham connected with his rule, his dictatorship was characterized by greater frankness than the average in Spanish America. The six constitutions adopted during his long dominance guaranteed practically all of the personal liberties, but neither the ballot, nor the press, nor political discussion was free. The fundamental charters also continued the federal system, but the state elections were a farce, and the state executives were the mere henchman of the supreme chief whose sovereign will strictly defined the limits of local autonomy. Nevertheless, it is true that each of these six constitutions frankly and progressively concentrated greater authority in the hands of Gómez, so that his dictatorship could finally be described as legal.

This admission, however, should not be allowed to convey the impression that he was bound by any law that he felt disposed to violate. His dictatorship was legal merely in the sense that it was erected upon a legal basis laid out in constitutional provisions. It was not legal in any other sense, for he was not strictly subject to any statute which conflicted with his desires. He was never legally married, but he was the father of an incredible number of children. The legal restrictions and rules of procedure which hedged about the administration of justice meant little when the parties concerned were personal enemies or the owners of property or concessions coveted by him or his coadjutors. He is accused of having sent thousands to prison, to exile, or to forced labor on the highways and other public works without the semblance of a legal trial. Most of these charges not even his friends and sycophants have denied. They have admitted that he was arbitrary, patriarchal, and polygamous, and that he was owner of immense properties—of hotels and industries as well as farms and ranches. For the word cruelty they substituted the word relentless or stern, while declaring that his procedure obeyed reasons of state, a conception freely employed by the benevolent despots of an earlier age in Europe. In short, they frankly

[56] On these events consult R. Bracamonte, *El general Gómez y el XIX de deciembre* (Caracas, 1916); and *Conjuración contra la vida de general Juan Vicente Gómez* (Caracas, 1911).

agreed that he was a dictator, but justified the system, which they represented as being progressive and patriotic.[57]

It must be admitted that his long rule was signalized by certain achievements. It is an undeniable fact that he kept the peace. The few revolts that occurred during the period were of minor importance and brief duration. He also maintained harmonious relations with foreign nations, introduced something of order and system into the management of economic and fiscal affairs, paid off the foreign debt, gave the country a strong financial position, and made Venezuela an attractive country for foreign investment. He likewise spent large sums on public works, sanitation, science, history of the colonial and early national periods, literature, philosophy, and all the arts. But the sums spent for education were not commensurate with other expenditures, and higher education was disproportionately emphasized; and although he applied some stimulants to agriculture, stockraising, and industry, the material advancement of the nation might have been greater if he had released these enterprises from the impediments of monopoly and special privilege.

In many respects he was favored by fortune. He came upon the scene at an opportune moment. He enjoyed all the advantages which resulted from rising prices, the accumulation of surplus capital in the United States, the discovery of petroleum in Venezuela, new methods of transportation, and new inventions in military science. Airplanes, high-speed automobiles, good roads, and modern equipment made possible the organization and rapid movement of a scientific army against which insurgents with their inferior supplies and old-time guerrilla methods of warfare were ineffective.

Moreover, one may raise the question whether the administrative

---

[57] The attacks on Gómez were numerous and delirious, too numerous to list in detail. The following are typical: Manuel Flores Cabrera, *Siniestro recuento* (Santo Domingo, 1914); Diego Córdoba, *Venezuela agonizante; Viva la revolución!* (Mérida, Yucatán, 1926); José Rafael Pocaterra, *Gómez, the shame of America* (Paris, 1929); César Gonzales Ruano, *El terror en América* (Madrid, 1930); L. Garza, *Gómez, tirano tropical* (Orense, Spain, 1933). Most of them deal with torture and other cruelties to which prisoners were subjected. The ablest works written in his defense were: Laureano, Vallenilla Lanz, *Cesarismo democrático* (Caracas, 1919) and *Críticas de sinceridad y exactitud* (Caracas, 1921); Pedro Manuel Arcaya, *Estudios sobre personajes y hechos de la historia venezolana* (Caracas, 1911) and *Venezuela y su actual régimen,* already cited; Nemesio García Naranjo, *Venezuela and its ruler* (New York, 1927); Esteben Roldán Oliarte, *El general Juan Vicente Gómez* (Mexico, 1933); and Cyrus Norman Clark, *Venezuela and her progressive ruler* (Caracas, 1929) and *Venezuela under General Juan Vicente Gómez* (Caracas, 1933).

ability that characterized his régime was his own or that of keen young men who gathered around him and gave their services in return for high remuneration. Perhaps Gómez did little more than organize the army and maintain peace while foreign investors developed the country's resources largely on their own terms[58] and bright young men administered the government, praised the dictator, and participated in a sort of cultural revival confined to the favored few. Indeed, Gómez, like Páez, unconsciously may have permitted himself to be used as the agent of an élite oligarchy, content to forget his kinsmen of Indian and *mestizo* lineage and leave them in their misery[59] while he engaged in his rural avocations, indulged in his amorous extravagance, and enjoyed the prestige of position and wealth.

At any rate he was not a glutton, a drunkard, or an international nuisance, nor even an imposter or a charlatan. Unlike most dictators, he had little fondness for pomp, ceremony, or personal luxuries. He always shunned formality, seldom made a speech, and in many respects was simple and moderate in his tastes.[60] In short, he had sufficient virtues to make him respectable and competent, and to draw around him some of the most gifted men of the country, who associated themselves with his rule, obeyed him, probably often guided and used him, and developed a political philosophy to justify his system. For the first time since the days of Maximilian, perhaps, Spanish-American writers renounced the democratic republic; and they renounced it not in the interest of monarchy, but in favor of dictatorship, which they christened "Democratic Cæsarism."

In the main, this new philosophy was the work of Laureano Vallenilla Lanz and Pedro Manuel Arcaya. And they developed their new theory with cleverness and plausibility. They linked it with the careers of two of Venezuela's outstanding national heroes, Bolívar and Páez,

[58] The national revenues were less in 1918 than in 1909 (*Codificación de leyes y decretos,* XXXII, 321, XLI, 292-293). It was in 1918 that oil development began on a large scale. See also *Law on Hydrocarbons . . . of July 18, 1925* (Caracas, [1925]).

[59] Labor laws were passed in 1928 and following; but they were none too progressive, and perhaps were not rigidly enforced. At any rate this is the view of personal observers. For the legislation see Geneva Labor Office, *Legislación social de América latina* (Geneva, 1929), II, 537ff.; and "Labor Legislation in Venezuela," in U. S. Bureau of Labor Statistics, *Bulletin,* no. 459.

[60] Chester Lloyd Jones' "Gómez of Venezuela," in *World Affairs,* vol. 99 (June, 1936), 89-93, is a good sketch of the dictator in English. Lothrop Stoddard's articles: "Gómez is Venezuela," in *World's Work,* vol. 59 (December, 1930), 66-68, and "When Gómez was Venezuela," in *Current History,* vol. 43 (February, 1936), are perhaps too enthusiastic.

emphasizing the political utterances of the one and the personal prowess of the other; and they sought to give their philosophy a scientific aspect by basing it upon sociological and psychological assumptions regarding the Venezuelan people.

They recalled that Bolívar had serious doubts with respect to the capacity of the Venezuelans to operate a democratic system of government, and that he was compelled to assume a dictatorship. They were fervent in their praise of his model Constitution of 1826 as well as of his realistic insistance upon the adaptation of governments to the people to be governed. And they concluded that Democratic Cæsarism was the only real, and as yet the only possible, government for Venezuela.

They described the phenomenal rise of Páez in terms which justified the dictatorial system. Vallenilla Lanz called him the "necessary gendarme," and Arcaya maintained that his career furnished the key to the understanding of the whole of Venezuelan national history. By virtue of his prestige, of his irresistible faculty of suggestion, the great *llanero* became the acknowledged chief of the Venezuelans, the *caudillo* whom they loved and obeyed; they were his people, ready to follow him to the death in any enterprise. He stirred in them inherited ancestral drives: atavistic instincts for war and the psychological craving for a leader and guide, whom they found personified in him. In this connection Arcaya asserted: "In the ladder of our evolution, a few rungs back, that is to say, a few generations back, we find the Indian of our forests and the Negro of the African plains. The one and the other lived under the régime of absolute chiefs, and at times they venerated their *caciques* or kings as gods." Thus there was embedded in the depths of the popular soul a submission complex—innate servilism and the love for a chief. And the conditions which explained the career of Páez were still in existence in Venezuela, where the urge to war and submission to a leader continued to be an inexorable drive. The cohesive force that maintained the social organization in tact was not that abstract thing called the law, but the lively sentiment of affection or fear of men for a man.

Failing to recognize this fact, the idealists of Venezuela had tried to attach legal fetters to their born leaders. Inspired by abstract political theories and nourished artificially by the metaphysical rhetoric of the time, they believed that it was "possible to establish . . . a true democracy after the style and manner of Switzerland and the United States." Since they had never observed their own country closely, they could not see that the influence of Páez and other *caudillos* was not based upon the civilian groups about them. The theorists could not understand that the strength of such men was drawn from a prestige derived from the satisfaction of an intense psychological yearning, because this subject was not explained in any of their books. Believing in the progress of the people in political customs, confident of the innate goodness of men, imagining that the masses were capable of exercising all political powers, they did not suspect the savage that was asleep in the popular soul, prompt to awaken with the noise of angry and tumultuous discussion. They insisted on parties, political agitation, and numerous elections; and revolutions and anarchy were the result.

Such were the views of these two writers.[61] Their latest elaboration was presented by Arcaya in 1935, shortly before Gómez died. In a work published by Arcaya at that time, he denounced "democratic mysticism" at length, ascribing all of Venezuela's political evils largely to its influence, and surveying the national history of the country to illustrate his thesis.

In none of the political struggles of Venezuela, he declared, was any transcendental political or social question agitated. All was reduced to the proposition of overthrowing the men who governed and substituting others for them. And the ambitions of military chiefs had been far less important than the "puerile enthusiasms" of the masses, intense mental excitement, and the influence of ideas that authorized the right of insurrection. "All our evils are rooted," he said, "in the fatal circumstance that when we freed ourselves from Spain, the world was dominated by the absurd mysticism which lighted the flame of the French Revolution."

> "This was a medley of false concepts. It was supposed to be possible to regulate the political life of all peoples by means of Social Compacts, or written constitutions inspired by reason and philosophy. The citizen would necessarily desire the common welfare, which involved his own, and there was no better formula for giving expression to this aspiration than that of suffrage. . . . Thus the people, by a majority vote if unanimity should be unattainable, would elect as their governors virtuous persons with correct orientation. With the view of preventing these from succumbing to the temptation to abuse their authority, there should be set up the counterpoise of a legislative power, likewise elected by the people, who doubtless would also select as their representa-

[61] See Arcaya's *Estudios sobre personajes y hechos de la historia de Venezuela* 33-47, and Vallenilla Lanz's *Cesarismo democrático* (Caracas, 1919), 189-263.

tives enlightened and virtuous citizens; and, besides, there would be a judicial power, composed of honest men versed in the law who would punish every transgression against the wise statutes enacted by the legislature.

"The erroneous nature of this concept no one is now able to deny in good faith. The basis of the system is the supposed wisdom and conscience of the voters. But if they were all wise and just men, as they must be for a democracy to be a reality, there would be no need for the system itself, . . . that is to say, it would not be necessary to govern anyone. The wise and just men would come together from time to time, in assemblies better inspired than those of the Olympic gods, in order to decide what was convenient for the life of the community; and no coercion of any sort would be needed, since each member of society would do voluntarily whatever was required.

"But in no part of the world is the majority, or even an important minority, composed of such eminent men animated . . . by the spirit of public service. Nor is it certain that the voter will wish to take the trouble to find them, or have the disposition to prefer those who are found. In casting his ballot, he will always be actuated by purely personal considerations. . . ."

Arcaya insisted that, in reality, all governments were monarchies or oligarchies or dictatorships, and rejoiced that the world was coming to prefer dictators. There had been a time, he said, when he supposed this system was required only in particular circumstances such as existed in Venezuela and in a few other countries of Spanish America. This had been his view twenty-six years before, but subsequently his ideas had been "purified" by observation:

"What I imagined to be a peculiar phenomenon of Venezuela . . . the desire of a people to be ruled by a chief or Conductor whom they loved and respected, a desire which I attributed to our ethnic heritage, that I now look upon as a normal aspiration which has always been felt, in the depths of the soul, by all the peoples of the earth, and which in our day is being frankly expressed everywhere.

"It appeared to me then that this desire, this tendency of ours, had impeded in my country the practice of ideal democracy, whose realization I believed entirely possible among peoples with a different ancestral psychology.

"Such an ingenious supposition has not withstood . . . the spectacle of reality nor a more extensive study of history. I have followed with eager attention the process by which democratic mysticism has been vanishing from the modern mind. . . ."[62]

---

[62] *Venezuela y su actual régimen,* 8, 70-72, *passim.*

Thus the western world seems to be returning politically to the point where it stood more than a century ago. Democratic republics are scarcely more numerous now than they were then; despots strut and fret upon many a stage, and the champions of a political system from which so much was expected are again on the defensive. It is time to scrutinize these new systems, and to reëxamine those great dynamic ideas which form the political basis of an era that appears to be passing. For men should at least pause for sober contemplation before plunging into this new régime. It were better to "bear the ills we have than fly to others that we know not of."

V. THE DICTATORS OF BRAZIL

By ALAN K. MANCHESTER

CHAPTER TWENTY-THREE

CONSTITUTIONAL DICTATORSHIP IN BRAZIL

IF DICTATORSHIP implies the seizure of power either under the guise of legality or by the forceable ejection of the group in office, the concentration of all functions of the state in the hands of the "leader," and the perpetuation of that control for an indefinite period, Brazil has not produced dictators. Portuguese America has not conformed to the pattern of European dictatorship so carefully formulated by Max Lerner[1] and may not, therefore, be listed among those states in which either fascist or proletarian dictatorship has taken root.

There is no example in Brazil of the laborious building of a movement toward the concentration of power in the hands of a man or of a group by the creation of an ideology favorable to despotism, no anti-liberal, anti-equality, anti-parliamentary propaganda built on the paralysis of the democratic state at moments of crisis. There has been no nationalistic cult demanding the annihilation of class, or sectional, or economic, or religious loyalties; no appeal for the abolition of chaotic tolerance induced by the legal guarantees of bills of personal rights in favor of order maintained by militant force. Nor has the myth of a cultural renaissance been preached. No such ideology creating hatreds and loyalties from deep-seated prejudices has prepared the path for a dictator in Brazil.

Nor has there appeared the legendary, romanticized figure of the "leader" heading an efficient party organization developed in the form of a pyramid with its base resting on the local unit in town and hamlet and its apex merging in the dictator himself. No private army has forced submission to the ideology of the movement or the will of the head of the party; no huge administrative organization paralleling the governmental agencies has been created; no *imperium in imperio* maintaining itself by terrorism has seduced the regular police, the army and the magistrates of the nation. No dramatic thrust at power has placed such a "leader" in control nor has such a dictatorial party been able to entrench itself in the governmental agencies of the country.

Nor, moreover, has Brazil conformed to the pattern of Spanish American dictatorship formulated by Professor J. Fred Rippy.[2] Un-

---

[1] "The pattern of dictatorship," in *Dictatorship in the modern world,* edited by Guy Stanton Ford (Minneapolis, 1935), 1-23.

[2] "Dictatorships in Spanish America" in *ibid.,* 49-80.

like the Spanish American countries, Brazil achieved its independence without long and expensive wars. No abrupt break with the colonial heritage marked the beginning of the national period; financial resources and administrative agents were available to initiate the new régime, which in most respects closely resembled the old. Brazil escaped the anarchy of "atomic, imperious wills operating in a medium where the strong man was admired for his virility and liberty worshipped as a fetish," where men despite the idealism of constitution-writers viewed the government as an instrument to be captured and used for the benefit of the leader and his followers. In Hispanic American countries, crises of internal disorder aggravated by the threat of foreign invasion and conquest produced a chaos which invited the seizure of power by the man on horseback with his brilliant uniform and seductive slogans. The inability of these Hispanic American states to create a workable substitute for the governmental systems of the colonial régime, resulting from lack of training in and traditions of self-government, produced a state of anarchy which demanded a strong executive unhampered by popular restraints, while the democratic forms set up by idealists who had ill-digested the principles of the French Revolution and the American constitution presented an opportunity for the man who was willing to gamble his life for power. This "anarchistic equalitarianism" which permitted a man of iron will and direct action, regardless of the class of society from which he sprang, to seize the reins of government, arrogate to himself all functions of the state, and perpetuate himself in power has not been characteristic of Brazil.

If, on the other hand, dictatorship implies the preëminence of the national executive not alone over the other branches of the national government but over state and municipal administration as well, then Brazil has been governed by dictators since the cry of independence was raised on the banks of the Ypiranga. In general, opposition to the will of the executive has been stamped out in the national legislative body, in the judiciary, and in individual provinces or states. The press has been restrained, and at times intimidation, or even terror, has been utilized to bolster the power of the man by whose will the state was ordered. Government services have been purged of those who refused to fit into the organization which culminated in the national executive; and submission to authority, entrenchment of powerful economic interests, privileged classes, gaudy trappings, and intolerance—attributes of dictatorship—have characterized Brazilian governments.

Neither the effective technique developed by European dictators during the past two decades nor the more flamboyant and simpler method of direct force employed by Spanish Americans has been necessary in Brazil. The concentration of power in the hands of the executive has been a direct and natural reflection of social and political conditions characteristic of the nation. Democratic institutions have not broken down as in Europe because democracy has never existed; nor has it been possible to overthrow the supremacy of the legislative branch since only partially in theory and never in practice has the sovereign power resided in the elected representatives of the people. To be a dictator, the national executive, whether he was called emperor or president, has had only to exercise powers granted to him by the constitution and to act in accordance with the dictates of social and economic conditions which have precluded the effective functioning of democratic institutions. At times the executive has transcended the powers vested in him, but such occasions have been rare; in general the head of the state has been the dictator of its destinies.

This situation is the natural result of the transition from the colonial régime to independence. Whereas in the United States our starting point was thirteen sovereign states, which under the pressure of necessity relinquished specific powers and delegated them to a national government, Brazilians began with an all-powerful central government which has conferred rights on the smaller units of the nation, while retaining for itself those key powers essential to the maintainance of its own position. The trend in each country has been from opposite poles in a contrary direction. Neither in breaking away from the centralized control maintained by Portugal nor in the transition to a republic did Brazil swing to the opposite extreme of governmental practice, even in theory. There is, therefore, a continuity in the development of Portuguese America which perpetuated the centralized absolutism of the executive under constitutional forms. This is true with reference both to the empire and to the republic. In both instances the organization of the government granted the preponderance of power to the executive, and under both régimes social and economic conditions have precluded the creation of a type of electorate capable of developing effective democratic institutions.

I

When the young Pedro, looking up from the despatches which reached him by special messenger on the margins of the little stream called Ypiranga, proclaimed the independence of Brazil to the expectant group of horsemen gathered around him, Brazilian society had already crystallized along lines which were to determine the political trend of the nation, decisively for the next half century, and to a lesser degree even to the present. By that date a native Brazilian aristocracy—the element which after ten years of struggle was to assume the dominant rôle in the social and political life of the country—had emerged.

The roots of that aristocracy go far back into the colonial period during which society developed into four main classes: the royal administrative officials sent out from Portugal, the stable colonist who based his economic position on the possession of land, the mercantile element in the towns, and the mass of laborers, overwhelmingly agricultural, both slave and free. Colonial-born, bred in a society that looked back on achievements in which the mother country had little or no share, and cherishing an ancestry which in many instances could be traced for over two centuries, the landowning group constituted a class antagonistic to the element which was more immediately continental Portuguese by origin or tradition. The large landowner established his family socially as well as financially and arrogated to himself absolute power over slaves, dependents, renters, share-croppers, mechanics, overseers, members of his own family—over all who existed on his possessions. In the north and along the coast of São Vicente, the *senhor de engenho* enjoyed the distinction which titles granted in Portugal; the ranch owner of Pernambuco or Bahia, of São Paulo or Rio Grande to the south ruled over his vast tracts of land as a feudal lord over his vassals or serfs. Largely self-sufficient on his plantation, this native aristocrat asserted an independence of royal authority which resulted in a passive but often effective resistance or in open opposition through the medium of the municipal councils.

This native aristocracy forced newcomers into a position of social inferiority by obliging them to enter the despised field of commerce. The mercantile life of the colony was largely in the hands of a Portuguese element which dreamed of returning home after the accumulation of wealth or, by an occasional shift of interest, of climbing into the native aristocracy by the purchase of land and the acquisition of the right to vote in the elections for the town councils. This element was greatly augmented in numbers and importance by the influx of Portuguese who fled to the colony when the Court was moved to Rio de Janeiro.[3]

[3] Alan K. Manchester, "The rise of the Brazilian aristocracy" in *The Hispanic American Historical Review, XI* (1931), 145-168.

Thus in 1822 there existed in Brazil two antagonistic classes dependent for their economic welfare on the colony itself: a landowning native aristocracy and a mercantile Portuguese element. Opposed to both were the loyalists dependent for their positions on the royal will. The great mass of slave and free laborers were inarticulate pawns, inconsequential as active participants in the shaping of the political or social destinies of the nation.

By winning the impressionable young Pedro to their side when the Portuguese *côrtes* attempted to reëstablish the colonial status of the co-kingdom of Brazil, the native aristocracy and the commercial element were influential in precipitating independence and in expelling the loyalist element. And yet, as these loyalists were expelled or silenced and the possibility waned of reconquest by a military force from Portugal, these two groups developed a cleavage which was to prove significant in shaping the political organization of the new nation.[4]

The major part of the native aristocracy envisioned a constitutional monarchy with the powers of the sovereign effectively limited by an assembly; an ineffectual minority proposed a republic which would entirely do away with the hereditary executive. In either case a large degree of autonomy would be granted to the several provinces. Decentralization would be substituted for the royal absolutism which during the colonial régime had concentrated in itself all functions of the state and had asserted direct supervision over all affairs of the provinces, even to the municipal councils. Thus would these feudal lords guarantee their social and economic position through the exercise of preëminent political power.

The Portuguese element opposed this shift of the center of political gravity from an absolutist head either to an assembly in which the native aristocracy would predominate or to the individual provinces where the local oligarchies would become to all intent and purposes so many sovereign powers. That element favored an absolute monarchy under Dom Pedro, with a government entirely independent of the Lisbon court but with the crowns united in one family. To this absolutist group belonged the mercantile class profiting by the direct trade with the outside world permitted under the open-door policy inaugurated in 1808, the Portuguese officeholders thrown out in 1821 by the decrees of the *côrtes* which suppressed the Brazilian courts and governmental

[4] Manoel de Oliveira Lima, *O movimento da independencia, 1821-1822* (São Paulo, 1922), 149, 180-183.

departments instituted during the residence of Dom João in Rio, and some native Brazilians who, while they admitted the advantages of self-government, questioned whether under conditions existing in Brazil this type of government could be put into practice.

As the success of the revolt against the *côrtes* became apparent, the divergence between the constitutionalists and the absolutists grew so acute that it superseded independence as the paramount political issue of the nation. By relying largely on the former, Dom Pedro resisted the aggression of the *côrtes* and established his authority throughout the empire; yet the tradition of his family, his own arbitrary nature, and the anarchy which the disintegrating factors of decentralization had sown throughout Spanish America inclined him toward absolutism.[5]

The issue reached a crisis with the convening of the constituent assembly in April 1823, a body which in reality represented almost exclusively those social and economic elements of the population of the empire from which the constitutionalists and absolutists drew support. The royalist administrative officials of the old régime had been expelled or converted to the absolutist group and the great bulk of the population comprising the lower classes remained inarticulate. In the assembly the constitutionalists exercised an effective majority control.

As the constitution took shape, the fundamental viewpoint of the majority became obvious. Since, in its opinion, the sovereign power resided in the people, to the representatives of the people, meeting in the assembly, was delegated ultimate authority. From that body the emperor would receive his powers and would become, if not the creature, at least the coördinate equal of the assembly; under no circumstances was he to become its master. The point of view was of vital importance to the assembly, to Dom Pedro, and to the future development of the empire. If it won the upper hand, the fundamental basis of the political organization of the new nation would differ radically from that upon which the colonial administration had rested. Were it to be put into practice, the legislative branch of the new government, controlled by the feudal landowner, and not the executive, whether emperor or president, would become the decisive factor and the door opened to decentralization and the possibility of anarchic dictatorship characteristic of Spanish American republics. For the moment the practical question was this: should the constitution be derived from

[5] Alan K. Manchester, "The paradoxical Pedro, First Emperor of Brazil," in *The Hispanic American Historical Review, XII* (1932), 176-197.

the people through the assembly or from the traditional absolutism of Portugal through Dom Pedro?

Less than a month after the assembly began its sessions,[6] Muniz Tavares, a deputy, proposed that the emperor be required to expel from Brazil all Portuguese-born suspected of hostility to independence. Later the *Sentinella* and the *Tamoyo,* constitutionalist papers under the control of deputies sitting in the assembly, attacked all Portuguese-born in the service of Brazil; two Portuguese officers in the army severely chastised the supposed author of a particularly obnoxious article; the troops, largely Portuguese, demanded the punishment of the Brazilian deputies responsible for the papers; and the assembly began an investigation into the whole affair. Confronted with the necessity of choosing sides, Dom Pedro moved the troops to a site near the palace and ordered the assembly to dissolve without having finished the constitution. Evicted by the army, the deputies ended their sessions on November 12.[7]

The emperor then appointed ten men, five of whom had belonged to the assembly, with power to prepare a constitution based on the original work of that body but modified and amplified to safeguard his prerogatives. In December the final draft was finished; it was approved by several town councils; and without submitting it to a representative body, Dom Pedro proclaimed the new constitution in force on March 25, 1824. Thus in theory the constitution was derived not from the people through delegated representatives but from the traditional absolutism of the crown through the emperor: theoretically the ultimate authority resided in the head of the state who of his own will conferred upon a restricted group in the empire the right to participate to a limited extent in the government of the nation.

Practice followed theory in this case. Constitutions in Latin America have proven in the main to be scraps of paper on which are written the ideals of enthusiastic political theorists. This Constitution of 1824, however, served as the instrument under which Brazil was governed for sixty-five years and influenced the framing of the constitution of

---

[6] The record of the proceedings of the constituent assembly may be found in Brazil, *Annaes do parlamento brazileiro: assembléa constituinte, 1823* (6 vols., Rio de Janeiro, 1874).

[7] A. M. V. de Drummond, "Annotações de A. M. V. de Drummond á sua biographia" in *Annaes da Bibliotheca Nacional,* XIII, pt. 3, 1-149; Manoel de Oliveira Lima, *O movimento da independencia, passim;* R. O. de Langgaard Menezes, "A constituinte de 1823" in *Revista do Instituto Historico e Geographico Brasileiro,* special volume VI, pt. 3, 63-84.

the republic. Often violated by the headstrong Pedro who promulgated it, modified by the Additional Act of 1834 which in turn was reinterpreted by various acts in 1841, it was scrupulously observed by the second Pedro. As a document which reflects actual practice it is significant both from the standpoint of its origin and as a reflection of the power vested in the head of the state.

Under the constitution,[8] the provinces were little more than administrative subdivisions of the empire, without political or economic autonomy. Representatives to the national assembly were chosen by indirect election, the senators being selected by the emperor for life from a triple list submitted by the provinces. Provincial councils were restricted to debate only, on matters strictly pertaining to local affairs; they had no legislative, no financial, and no administrative powers; and the resolutions on matters of local interest were submitted to the national assembly for enactment into law. Moreover, all decisions of municipal councils had to be submitted first to the provincial councils and then to the national authorities. The real power of each province centered in the president, appointed by the emperor and subject to removal at his will. It was he, the creature of the emperor, who controlled not only the province but the municipalities within the province and who through his position managed the electoral process leading to province or national office. The right to levy taxes and vote expenditures, whether applicable to the provinces or to the nation, was vested in the national government. The emperor could dissolve the national assembly at will, sanction or veto bills, appoint and dismiss the ministry irrespective of the majority opinion of the assembly, and pardon criminals or reduce sentences imposed on them. On him was conferred a Moderative Power which was defined as the "key to the whole political organization, intrusted exclusively to the emperor as supreme chief and first representative of the nation, that he" might "incessantly watch over the maintenance of the independence, equilibrium, and harmony of the rest of the political powers." Despite the creation of the provincial and national assemblies, the Constitution of 1824 continued the strict centralization characteristic of the colonial régime.

Dom Pedro thus elected to side with the absolutists, arraying against himself the stirring power of the native Brazilian aristocracy which had been so largely instrumental in precipitating independence. That he meant to practice what he preached in his constitution was evident

[8] The constitution is easily accessible in H. G. James, *The constitutional system of Brazil* (Washington, 1923), 237-252.

even before the final draft was proclaimed. The Andradas, through whom the native aristocracy had won access to the emperor, were exiled to France when the constituent assembly was dissolved. He suppressed by energetic measures the revolutionary movement which, originating in Pernambuco in protest against the dissolution of the assembly and spreading to three adjacent provinces toward the north, had set up the independent "Confederation of the Equator" with a constitution based on that of the Republic of Columbia. He delayed convoking the national assembly stipulated in his constitution; presidents of provinces were permitted to rule as despotically as the old colonial governors and captains-general; and public functionaries and officials of the army and navy were allowed to act as a privileged class which could maltreat citizens with impunity. Courts responsible to Dom Pedro refused redress, and the liberty of the press was extinguished.[9] In form Brazil was a constitutional empire; in reality it was an empire ruled by a dictator who in practice exceeded even those large powers retained by him in the constitution formulated under his direction.

The opposition of the constitutionalists was deepened by the emperor's foreign policy. When his father, Dom João VI, died in Lisbon early in 1826, Dom Pedro assumed the title of King of Portugal despite the keen antipathy felt by the Brazilians for such a union considered dangerous to the independence of Brazil. After issuing decrees to be executed in Lisbon and after promulgating a constitution for Portugal, he abdicated in favor of his eight year old daughter, Maria da Gloria. Rightly or wrongly, the Brazilian constitutionalists were convinced that it was the intention of the emperor and the absolutist Portuguese party to unite once more the two branches of the house of Bragança under one head and to recolonize Brazil.

His policy in regard to the demands of Great Britain aroused even greater resentment. Recognition by England of Brazilian independence was imperative due to the peculiar relationship existing between Great Britain and Portugal. Until recognition was obtained from London, Portugal could refuse to acknowledge the independence of the empire; nor could any other European power be induced to take the step until Dom Pedro had settled with Lisbon and London. The price demanded by England was twofold: the guarantee by the new state of the continuance of the traditional British preëminence in the economic life of Brazil, and the abolition of the slave trade. Agreement to the first stipu-

[9] John Armitage, *History of Brazil* (2 vols., London, 1836), I, 200 ff.

lation would have been obtained from an assembly only after a severe struggle; consent to the second could not have been won under any condition. The slave trade treaty completely alienated the land aristocracy which believed in the slave trade as the only available source of agricultural labor. It was only by exercising absolute power that Dom Pedro was able to purchase recognition of the independence of the new empire.[10]

The third phase of his foreign policy, the war with Buenos Aires over the *Banda Oriental* by which the emperor hoped to extend the boundaries of Brazil to the River Plate, resulted in a fiasco. Despite the fact that he took the field personally to encourage enlistment and restore the morale of the troops, the war remained unpopular, and he failed to achieve success.

Independence of Brazil from Portugal had been won, but independence of the Brazilians from the domination of the Portuguese absolutist element in Brazil was still only an aspiration in 1830. There was no place in the government for the constitutionalist; the native aristocracy was still as completely under Portuguese dominance as during the colonial régime. In the provinces of Minas Geraes, Bahia, Pernambuco, São Paulo, and Rio de Janeiro resentment threatened the disintegration of the empire. In the City of Rio de Janeiro, rioting between the Portuguese element and Brazilians, cheering the constitution, liberty, and the freedom of the press, forced the issue. For a time Dom Pedro vacillated between the two groups, but on April 6, 1831 he swung to the side of the absolutists and appointed a ministry of his favorites, all of whom were unpopular with the Brazilian element. On the same day the small republican group began a revolution which the constitutionalists immediately utilized as a means by which they might overthrow the power of the absolutists who surrounded the emperor. At two o'clock on the morning of the seventh Dom Pedro on his own initiative wrote out his abdication in favor of his five-year-old son.[11] Later he sailed for Europe to spend the last three years of his life in a successful crusade against the reactionary element in Portugal where his brother Dom Miguel had usurped the throne.

Thus the native Brazilian aristocracy, which for ten years had been fighting to impose constitutional restraints on the power of the head of

---

[10] Manoel de Oliveira Lima, *O reconhecimento do imperio* (Rio de Janeiro, 1901), *passim;* Alan K. Manchester, *British preëminence in Brazil* (Chapel Hill, 1933), 54-108, 186-219.

[11] Armitage, *History of Brazil,* II, 107-143.

the state, unexpectedly rid the nation entirely of the man who since independence had dictated the affairs of the nation. He was gone, but the extreme centralist system which he had established remained: would the Brazilian element, which at last had come into the control of the government, sweep aside the fundamental basis on which the empire had been built, substituting for it either a federal republic or a monarchy stringently restricted by a predominant legislative body and local autonomy of the provinces? The opportunity was obvious, but divergence of opinion prevented effective action.

There were three main factions which contended for supremacy while rioting and disorder spread through the provinces: the moderate liberals who desired that reforms be effected through the legally constituted agencies then in operation by the personnel actually in office; the radicals who, distrusting the chamber of deputies elected under the old régime and the senate composed of life members selected by Dom Pedro, wished to frame an entirely new constitution through a specially elected constituent assembly; and the reactionaries who worked to restore the old régime by securing the return of Dom Pedro as regent. A small but vociferous group advocated a republic.[12]

The moderate liberals, into whose lap the government fell so unexpectedly as a result of the revolution of April 7, held on in power until 1837. Confronted with deplorable economic conditions in the country at large, as well as in government finances, and faced with disorder that attained revolutionary proportions[13] in Ceará (1831-32), Pernambuco (1832-35), Pará (1831-33 and 1835-37), Bahia (1837-38), and Rio Grande do Sul (1835-45), the liberals were driven to exercise the powers vested in the executive head of the nation by the Constitution of 1824. To strengthen their position and combat disorder and anarchy, Evaristo da Veiga organized a club, its membership of public officials such as the regents, the ministers of state, senators, deputies, and the lower ranks of functionaries, and merchants, bankers, lawyers, physicians, and industrialists offering effective opposition to the decentralist, federal clubs founded by the radicals.[14] To a regency of three elected by plurality vote of the assembly was assigned the task of exercising the somewhat restricted functions of the emperor during his minority.

[12] Max Fleiuss, *Historia administrativa do Brasil* (São Paulo, 1925), 155-156.

[13] Gonzaga Duque Estrada, *Revoluções brazileiras* (2d ed., Rio de Janeiro, 1905), *passim*.

[14] Aureliano Leal, *Historia constitucional do Brazil* (Rio de Janeiro, 1915), 88ff.; Osvaldo Orico, *Evaristo da Veiga e sua epoca* (Rio de Janeiro, 1933), 36-77.

To suppress disorder, Father Diogo Antonio Feijó was appointed minister of justice by the regents who signed a contract by which he obtained a free hand in the punishment of disorderly elements, in the dismissal of refractory public officials, and in the maintenance of a newspaper responsible solely to himself. An unorthodox priest in whom radical philosophy struggled with an imperious will and love of order, Feijó took vigorous steps to establish the authority of the central government. The old militia largely responsible to the municipal authorities was replaced by a national guard more directly under the control of the regency. Disorder was suppressed with an iron hand; imprisonment, dismissal, or even banishment was meted out to citizen, government functionary, or military official who evidenced insubordination. Thus was checked the tide of disintegration which threatened the empire after the abdication of Pedro I.

It was not until three years after they assumed control that the liberals succeeded in modifying the constitution. By the *Acto Addicional* of 1834, which was considered an amendment to the Constitution of 1824, a single regent was substituted for the triumvirate. At the same time the council of state responsible to the emperor was abolished and greater autonomy granted to the provinces. The old provincial councils with action limited to discussion and proposal were replaced by provincial legislatures with power, among others, to control public instruction, to raise and spend money for municipal and provincial purposes provided such legislation did not interfere with the general revenues of the central government, to regulate the police forces, and to rule on proposals made by the municipal councils. The appointment of the presidents of the provinces was still left in the hands of the emperor, however.[15]

Feijó, who was elected regent in 1835, suppressed[16] the major portion of the disorders in the north, but the revolt in Rio Grande do Sul which broke out the year he assumed the regency resisted his efforts and took on a republican and separatist aspect.[17] The anarchy characteristic of the period of very mild liberalism inaugurated at the abdication of Dom Pedro incited a union between reactionaries and a portion of the

[15] Leal, *Historia constitucional,* 11-51.

[16] Orico, *Evaristo da Veiga,* 62-80. An excellent short sketch of Feijó's life is available in the article by Washington Luis in Eugenio Egas, *Diogo Antonio Feijó* (São Paulo, 1913), 76-111.

[17] Tristão de Alencar Araripe, "Guerra civil do Rio Grande do Sul" in *Revista do Instituto Historico e Geographico Brasileiro,* XLIII, pt. 2; XLV, pt. 2; XLVI, pt. 2; XLVII, pt. 2.

moderate liberals who favored a return to the strict centralization of the first empire. For a time Feijó held on against the majority group in the chamber, but in 1837 he resigned in favor of the conservatives. Confronted in their turn with the growing seriousness of the revolt in the south and a new outbreak in the north (Maranhão, 1838-41), the conservatives determined to wipe out the decentralist trend. They were aided in achieving their objective by the proclamation of the majority of Dom Pedro on July 23, 1840, a step in which both liberals and conservatives united. Their most effective work, however, was achieved through the less dramatic method of the reinterpretation of the *Acto Addicional* by legislative enactment.[18]

For almost ten years the door had remained open to a complete remodeling of the basic organization of the Brazilian nation. With the constitutional dictator unceremoniously evicted and the absolutist Portuguese element brought to heel, the native aristocracy was in a position to shift the center of political gravity from the personal head of the state to the elected representatives of the landowning class, and from the abundance of its power concede autonomy to the provinces. That it did not do so was due in part to the fact that it was into the hands of the moderates, chosen for office under the electoral pressure of the absolutist Pedro, that the machinery of government fell in 1831;[19] it was due, also, in part to the fact that widespread disorder and chronic revolutions forced the group in possession of the national government to resort to the dictatorial powers retained by Dom Pedro for the personal head of the state. To the Brazilians charged with the management of the nation, the Constitution of 1824 was a handy instrument, to be tampered with only in a mild and deliberate fashion.

The real issue throughout the period, therefore, centered not in how to formulate a new constitution which would embody the aspirations of the native aristocracy of 1823, but in whether the Brazilians in national office could hold the state together by exercising the dictatorial powers conceded by the old instrument of government. It was a critical period by no means terminated by the declaration of the majority of the emperor. But largely through the efforts of Evaristo da Veiga, who by his clubs, his oratory, and his newspapers kept alive the idea of monarchy, and the imperious determination of Antonio Feijó who as minister of

[18] For a survey of the nine years of Pedro's minority see the somewhat impassioned but interesting monograph by J. M. Pereira da Silva entitled *Historia do Brazil durante a menoridade de D. Pedro II* (2d ed., Rio de Janeiro, 1888).

[19] Opposition to radical reforms was particularly strong in the senate (Leal, *Historia constitucional,* 13-46, 93).

justice and regent checked disorder and subjected the military to the civil authorities, the state was turned over to the new emperor still intact with the dictatorial prerogatives of the head of the state only slightly modified.

In 1840 Dom Pedro II was still too young to exercise personal rule. Eight more critical years were to pass before he assumed the direction of the affairs of the nation, years of serious disorder and revolution. But the swing of the pendulum toward liberalism had reached its extreme with the *Acto Addicional* of 1834; the reactionary conservatives who three years later forced the resignation of Feijó were determined to reëstablish the authoritative centralist régime of the first empire. To amcomplish their objective they had first to nullify the liberalizing measures of the period from 1831 to 1837 and then to force the rebellious sections of the nation into submission.

The first objective was achieved largely through the enactment of three laws. The first, passed two months before the regency terminated through the proclamation of Pedro's majority, reinterpreted the *Acto Addicional* by revoking the objectionable powers granted by that act to the provinces. The second, passed on November 23, 1841, created anew the council of state abolished by the *Acto Addicional.* By the new law the councillors held office for life but the emperor at will could retire them from active service. They were to render opinions to the emperor on matters requested by him; and in theory they were subject to trial before the senate for counsels rendered contrary to the constitution and the interests of the state. The third act,[20] passed December 3 of the same year, reorganized the criminal code in such a way as to place the judiciary more directly under the control of the emperor. Two months later the sections of the act dealing with the police were amplified still further. In each province there were to be appointed either by the emperor or by the presidents, who were subject to the emperor's appointment, a chief of police for the whole province and as many local chiefs as were necessary. In addition to the regular duties, these officials were charged with the specific obligations of preventing secret and illegal gatherings of any kind, formerly a matter under the jurisdiction of the local justice of the peace; of guaranteeing public safety and tranquillity

[20] Fleiuss, *Historia administrativa,* 208-211. The text of the Constitution of 1824, of the *Acto Addicional,* of the law of May 12, 1840, of the law of November 23, 1841, and of the Constitution of 1891 may be found, if the *Collecção das leis (e decisões) do Brasil* (Rio de Janeiro, 1844-) are not available, in the special volume of the *Revista do Instituto Historico e Geographico Brasileiro* entitled *Diccionario Historico, Geographico e Ethnographico do Brasil,* pt. 1, 304-328.

—no small task in view of the epidemic of revolutions incited by the reactionary measures of the government in Rio; and of supervising the municipal councils, hotbeds of decentralist activity.

The frankly centralist policy in the ascendency in Rio de Janeiro provoked resentment in the provinces. In 1842 Minas Geraes and São Paulo protested by an appeal to force,[21] the movement in Rio Grande do Sul continued, and in 1848 a final, despairing effort in favor of local autonomy broke out in Pernambuco. The protests were futile in the face of the growing sentiment in favor of the centralists who stood for order and public tranquillity, and, more pertinent, in the face of the effective measures taken by the coterie of ministers and councillors surrounding the young emperor. By 1848 the nation was pacified, and Pedro, now twenty-three years of age, began his more than thirty years of "personal rule."

Thus was bridged the gap between the dictatorial rule of the first Pedro who instituted a system in which the ultimate authority resided in the personal head of the state and the assumption of that power by the second Pedro. Despite the drastic efforts of the liberal constitutionalists and, to a lesser extent, of the radical republicans, little or no modification in the original organization of the state had been achieved during the seventeen intervening years, and the second Pedro inherited a system essentially the same as that over which the first emperor presided. To wield dictatorial power he had only to exercise prerogatives stipulated in the constitution.

Did Dom Pedro II exercise the dictatorial powers which he inherited? Did he under the authority of the moderative power set up a veiled and irresponsible despotism? Was the empire, as Rojas Paúl, president of Venezuela, called it, "the only republic which existed in America" or, as Bartolomé Mitre of Argentina styled it, "the crowned democracy of America"? Was the parliamentary form with its ministries dependent on a majority in the chamber of deputies, its equilibrium between the two great parties, the conservatives and liberals, its prime minister responsible for the selection of his colleagues, and its roster of great orators and statesmen only the stage on which actors moved at the command of the emperor? Was the empire in reality a constitutional dictatorship?

Critics of the empire answer in a very positive affirmative. Defenders deprecate the issue by reference to the virtues of the emperor, his un-

---

[21] José Antonio Marinho, *Historia do movimento . . . de Minas Geraes* (Rio de Janeiro, 1844), *passim;* João Baptista de Moraes, "A revolução de 1842" in *Revista do Instituto Historico e Geographico de S. Paulo,* XII (1907), 441-617.

doubted patriotism, his unselfish devotion to duty, his loyalty to the nation rather than to a faction, and his vigilance which guaranteed the smooth functioning of the machinery of government. In the minds of critic and defender lurks the evil connotation of the term despot and dictator, a connotation which beclouds the issue with an unfortunate emotional reaction. Whether the exercise of preëminent power by the personal head of the state is or is not morally justifiable depends on the political philosophy of the prosecutor or advocate. The problem is not pertinent to this study.

The response manifested by Dom Pedro II to the situation which he encountered during the twoscore years following his assumption of power was dictated in part by the social organization of the empire. Regardless of his personal inclinations his attitude toward the functions of his office was shaped in large part by the type of population upon which the parliamentary system actually rested in Brazil.

Illiteracy eliminated the bulk of the population of the empire from intelligent participation in the political machine,[22] and property qualifications in the constitution limited the electorate to a select group. In 1844 there were in Rio de Janeiro sixteen public schools, sixteen private primary schools for girls, and eighteen private primary schools for boys for a total population of approximately two hundred thousand. As late as 1869 there were in the whole empire 3,516 public primary schools with 115,735 pupils of both sexes. In that year, of the nearly eight and one-half million inhabitants, slightly over one million nine hundred thousand were of school age (six to fifteen years). Thus, in that year there was one public school for each 2,394 free inhabitants, or one for every 541 children of school age. With the primitive housing, the widely scattered population, and the lack of transportation facilities, the system was woefully inadequate, even after granting allowance for the work of the private schools.

Secondary and professional school training was almost as inadequate from the standpoint of universal education. As late as 1887 the three principal secondary schools preparing students for the professional courses, located in São Paulo, Recife, and Rio de Janeiro, counted a total

---

[22] The Constitution of 1824 did not debar illiterates from voting if they met the qualifications of citizenship, residence, age, property, etc. When the republican constitution imposed a literacy test, special provision was made for those unable to read who had qualified as voters under the empire (A. Tavares de Lyra, "Regimen eleitoral" in *Revista do Instituto Historico e Geographico Brasileiro,* special volume, *Diccionario Historico, Geographico e Ethnographico do Brasil,* pt. 1, 334-336).

of eleven hundred, while in the 292 secondary schools throughout the empire considerably fewer than eleven thousand students were enrolled. The military and commercial schools founded by Dom João VI in 1809 continued to function, while the law schools located in the cities of São Paulo and Olinda attracted the most promising sons of the leading families.[23] Schools of medicine, of mines, of fine arts, of music, and eventually a normal school (1880) were promoted. Seminaries offered preparation for priests or monastic acolytes.

In reality the system was fairly adequate for the land aristocracy, but totally inadequate for the rank and file of the free citizens of the nation. The compulsory education law of 1851, by which a heavy fine was imposed on parents who refused to send to school children of more than seven years of age, remained a dead letter.[24] Free public school education, the basis upon which an active electorate is built, remained an ideal throughout Pedro's reign.

The property qualifications of the Constitution of 1824 further restricted the electorate. All men over twenty-five (twenty-one if married) who received a net annual income of one hundred *milreis* from property, industry, commerce, or employment could vote in the parochial church meetings for the electors. Any citizen qualified to vote in this primary election might serve as an elector provided his net annual income was not less than two hundred *milreis*. These electors voted for the national deputies and senators and for the members of the provisional councils (later the provincial legislatures). Any citizen permitted to be an elector was eligible to be elected a national deputy provided his net annual income was not less than four hundred *milreis* and provided also that he professed the religion of the state. The property requirement for the life senatorship was a net annual income of at least eight hundred *milreis*.

The educational situation and the property qualifications of the constitution reflected the social life of the first half century of the empire. When Pedro II assumed personal power, Brazilian society was divided into two main classes: on the one hand were the landowners and slaveholders, and on the other, the mass of slaves and free labor. Between these two classes there was an incipient bourgeoisie element made up of the mercantile interests, still mostly foreign. An indeterminate number

[23] Fleiuss, *Historia administrativa,* 198-200.

[24] Agenor de Roure, "O ensino publico" in *Revista do Instituto Historico e Geographico Brasileiro,* special volume, *Contribuições para a biographia de D. Pedro II,* pt. 1, 627-661. The law of 1851 also stipulated that there should be at least one public school in each parish.

of small farmers, many of them colored freedmen, existed, but they were dependent on the large landowner. Some of this group were renters; some were forced either by written contract or by necessity to use the sugar mill or roads or personal services of the plantation owner; in most cases they were only slightly less dependent on the large landowner than were the laborers on the plantation.

Of the approximately seven million estimated population of the middle of the century slightly over two million were whites, one million one hundred thousand were free colored, over three million were negro slaves, and the rest were Indians. Misagenation was common. The bulk of the population lived on the coast with the exception of Minas Geraes where gold and diamond mines had attracted a virile, restless type of settler during the eighteenth century. With the decline of the mines this relatively dense population (the province was estimated to have well over a million inhabitants at the middle of the century) was turning to agriculture.

The increase in coffee production made São Paulo the most prosperous province in the empire during the decade of the fifties. To the south stretched limitless forests which yielded at last to the plains of Rio Grande do Sul where the vigorous *gaucho* ruled his ranches as the head of the clan. In Pernambuco economic and social life was geared to the production of sugar. Here, especially, the plantation owners lived like feudal lords. They constituted a homogeneous class, ruling over their estates and over the small towns as medieval barons. Descended from some of the best blood of Portugal, these Pernambuco landowners cherished the oldest cultural tradition of the empire. Bahia, its rival, was more prosperous due to a greater diversity of production, for in addition to sugar, tobacco and cotton were cultivated extensively.

To the west of Minas, Bahia, and Pernambuco lay the *sertão,* the region of mystery and fear, where no policing enforced the law, where taxes were never collected, and where Dom Pedro was only a name. To dispose of his cotton and hides the *sertanejo* of Bahia spent fifteen to twenty days to bring his picturesque caravan of a dozen or so mules or horses to the coast. With him came his wife perched on the bags strapped to the sides of one of the mules; on another chattered a monkey and on still another rode a vivid, vociferous macaw. To the north and west the equally primitive, but more sluggish life of Maranhão and the Amazon Valley offered less opportunity for an intelligent electorate.

The most populous province of the empire was that of Rio de Janeiro with its million and a half inhabitants. Foreign settlements of Swiss and Germans prospered frôm their corn and potatoes, their butter and cream cheese. Sugar along the coast and coffee in the interior offered an opportunity to the landowning class. In the City of Rio de Janeiro was concentrated the manufacturing activity of the empire. Of the estimated seventy-two factories in the country, fifty-two were in the city and province of Rio de Janeiro, ten in Bahia, four in Pernambuco, two in Maranhão, and one each in São Paulo, Minas, Paraná, and Rio Grande do Sul. These factories produced hats, candles, soap, beer, cigars, coarse cotton cloth, and porcelain. The labor was foreign for the most part, although free negroes and mulattoes were often employed.[25]

The significant feature of this survey of the economic life of the empire is the plantation. It was a self-sustaining unit both economically and socially. A coffee estate cultivated cane, cotton, and mandioc; it had its droves of cattle and its hives of bees; its grapes for wine and its black or brown beans. On it lived the owner and his family, his overseers, sometimes a chaplain and a tutor, shepherds, carpenters, masons, smiths, and slaves of the hoe and sickle. Under the shadow of the great planters gathered a heterogeneous community comparable to the *bravi*, the guitarrists, the friars, and the bullfighters of the eighteenth century Portuguese noble. The power of the great landowner was feudalistic and patriarchal. A house prisoner, the Brazilian lady was nevertheless mistress of the plantation, buying from itinerant peddlers and managing the intricate functioning of the large establishment.

The son of a planter was sent away at an early age, nine or ten, to prepare for a professional school. In the *collegio* he studied Latin grammar, rhetoric, French classics, sacred history, geography, writing, and music. At fifteen or sixteen he entered the professional school of the family's choice: the ablest was sent to the law schools of São Paulo or Olinda; another went to a medical school; a third entered a military school; the fourth a seminary. If there was a stupid son who could not succeed in a profession, he was put in business, an occupation frowned upon by gentlemen.

The choice profession was the law which fitted a man to serve not only as a magistrate but as a member of the assembly, perhaps even of the ministry or imperial council. It likewise opened the door to the diplomatic service. After a pre-law course in Latin, geometry, rational and moral philosophy, and other subjects, the student entered the five-year law course during which he studied the philosophy of law, public law,

---

[25] Gilberto Freyre, "Social life in Brazil in the middle of the nineteeth century" in *The Hispanic American Historical Review,* V (1922), 600-605.

analysis of the imperial constitution, Roman law, diplomacy, ecclesiastical, civil, mercantile, and marine law, political economy, and the theory and practice of general law. It was not until the last generation of the empire that any considerable number of the sons of the comfortably rich merchant class began to attend the professional schools.

It is obvious from this hurried description[26] of the economic and social basis of the life of the empire at the middle of the century that the "Brazilian people," to which such constant reference was made in the political discussions of the time, was a figment of the wishful thinking of political theorists. Neither the small farmers, nor the free agricultural laborers, the factory workers, the overseers, the *sertanejos,* the cowboys, the house servants and hangers-on, the wandering pedlers and the Indians, constituted the "Brazilian people" capable of exercising the functions of a constitutional parliamentary régime. The "Brazilian people," as a matter of fact, was restricted to the three or four hundred thousand persons belonging to the large landowning, slaveholding families. From them came the lawyers, the physicians, the engineers, the diplomats, the high officials of the government, and the directors of the multifarious enterprises of the nation. It was these persons who knew how to read, who had some ideas about the world, and who could comprehend within the limits of their education and personal philosophy what a parliamentary system entailed—it was these families who constituted the real electorate of Brazil under the empire. And it was only these out of the seven or eight millions of population of the empire who could serve intelligently as the electorate.[27]

The manner in which elections were conducted[28] vitiated at the outset the functioning of a parliamentary system. The somewhat laconic provisions for the election of deputies and senators contained in the constitution proclaimed by Dom Pedro I and amplified by the decree of March 26, 1824, resulted in practices characterized by disorder and coercion rather than by a free and impartial expression of opinion by the voters.

On the day of election the chairman of the electoral assembly (a magistrate with jurisdiction in the community) proposed to the mass of people assembled in the church the names of four citizens, two to serve as secre-

---

[26] This description was taken in large part from Freyre's article, cited above, 597-630.

[27] Gilberto Amado, "As Instituições Politicas e o Meio Social no Brasil" in *A margem da historia da Republica* (a collection of essays by Carneiro Leão, Celso Vieira, and others), 66-74.

[28] Tavares de Lyra, "Regimen eleitoral," 334-336.

taries, two as tellers. These four citizens were approved or rejected by acclamation. Together with the chairman and the curate these four citizens constituted the election committee. To this committee the regulations granted unlimited power. It accepted or rejected votes as it saw fit. There was no roll call, no fixed time either to initiate or terminate the voting, no registered list of eligible voters. The chairman was instructed to enquire of the "bystanders" if anyone present was aware of any fraud or collusion the object of which was to bring about the election of specific individuals. In case of denunciation, the accused was deprived of the privilege of voting in the election then being held, an effective means by which opposition votes might be counted out. In the committee also was vested the duty of determining the number of electors to be chosen for the parish in accordance with the provisions of the law, a stipulation which permitted the exercise of wide latitude by the committee members in fixing the number of firesides in the community, the basis on which the ratio of electors was determined. To secure a committee favorable to one of the contending factions meant victory for that faction in the election.

In the primary elections, therefore, the result was decided by turbulence, violence, and force. The group which failed to win the initial contest over the committee lost the election—the usual procedure was for the losing faction to denounce the coercion practiced by the victors and withdraw from the church. That party won which possessed not the most votes but the most clubs.

Victory in the primary elections did not necessarily guarantee victory in the secondary elections. Frequently, the electors, meeting as the electoral college, merely signed the official ballot in blank and sent it to the president of the province to be filled in, the president, it will be remembered, being subject to appointment by the emperor. Many times, moreover, during the reactionary period of centralization following 1837, the ministers of the empire refused to recognize the validity of the election of a member of the opposition and ordered the presidents of provinces to proceed to a new election. Thus, during the first two decades, were chosen the deputies to the lower house of the national assembly, and thus were prepared the triple lists of senators for the selection of the emperor.

A description of electoral practices appears in the statement made to the emperor by the ministry in May 1842. Pressure was brought to bear, so the statement declares, on public employees, soldiers, sailors, municipal officials, and citizens of all classes to force them to vote irrespective of their inclinations. Armed mobs under orders of ruffians invaded the churches where elections were being held, threw out the committee in charge, installed one of their own selection, and saw to it that electors designated by their backers were chosen. Votes were cast by hundreds, signed with the names of children, foreigners, inhabitants of other parishes, or fictitious persons, and the subservient committee accepted or rejected ballots at will. In districts where the legal total of electors did not excede one hundred, more than a thousand were often named.

In the effort to remedy the evils of the system various reforms were passed during the period of the empire.[29] In 1842 an attempt was made to eliminate the abuses practiced at the primary elections. A committee composed of the justice of the peace, the curate, and the local chief of police were to determine prior to the elections the eligibility both of the voters and the electors; the election committee was henceforth to be selected by sixteen citizens chosen by lot from eligible voters and its discretionary powers limited to ascertaining the identity of the voter, not his eligibility—measures which tended to eliminate mob action in favor of elections controlled more directly by the local aristocracy. The part assigned to the local chief of police, who was dependent for his job on the province chief, who in turn owed his position either to the president of the province or directly to the emperor, assured the central authority in Rio de Janeiro of direct influence in local elections.

Due to vigorous protests against the interference of the police in determining the qualifications of voters, the duty of determining eligibility was entrusted, in 1846, to a committee composed of electors presided over by the justice of the peace, with the right of appeal to the municipal judge and the district court of appeals. In 1855 the assembly, on questionable constitutional grounds, ruled ineligible for election either to the provincial legislature or to the national assembly high government officials exercising jurisdiction in the district where the election was held. These officials included the presidents of the provinces and their ministers, army commanders, federal or provincial treasury inspectors, chiefs of police—from provincial to local—and the higher magistrates. The same law divided the provinces into districts from which one deputy to the national chamber was to be elected, a provision modified five years later by enlarging the districts to include three deputies.

In 1875 a further attempt to tinker with the system in the effort to get "free elections" by qualified voters only, tightened the regulations

[29] For a résumé of these reforms see Tavares de Lyra, "Regimen eleitoral," 336-342.

governing the preparation of eligibility lists. Six years later the entire scheme was rephrased by the famous *Lei Saraiva* (January 9, 1881). This final attempt at electoral reform under the empire was an honest effort to correct abuses: it established direct election with a property qualification of two hundred *milreis* net income; it set rigid and detailed provisions to guarantee the integrity of the qualification and election boards; it attempted to guarantee secret ballot; and it carefully specified the details governing the actual conduct of the election. It was, as Tavares de Lyra says, "undoubtedly a magnificent law," had it worked! It did not, for the fundamental problem did not lie in the machinery by which elections were held.[30]

In the final analysis, regardless of election laws, the social and economic organization of the empire precluded a free expression of opinion by the masses of "Brazilian people" through the use of the ballot. Unless the plantation owner could control elections through his influence in the community, the choice of electors would fall to a local strong arm leader *(mandão)* at the head of a band of ruffians. If on the other hand the feudalistic landowner was left unhampered by the central government in the elections to the national assembly, the separatist trends resulting in the chaos of the regency period would destroy the effectiveness of the Rio government and embarrass the personal head of the state in the exercise of prerogatives granted to him by the constitution. Depending largely on the appointive powers which subjected to his will the administrative and police officials of the provinces, Dom Pedro through his ministers wielded decisive influence in the choice of deputies to the lower house, and by the additional safeguard arising from his use of the pencil in scratching names from the triple list of candidates for senatorial vacancies, he doubly assured himself of a satisfactory upper chamber.

In the face of conditions which rendered impossible the proper functioning of the electorate as the real basis of parliamentary government, Dom Pedro adopted a compromise course of action: the forms of the parliamentary system were maintained but the ultimate authority in the choice of ministers, the selection of the members of the assembly, the control of the judiciary and police, and the determination of policies were retained in the personal head of the state. In the words of Joaquim Nabuco "ministers, councillors of state, even the opposition were attentive to his wishes, his preferences, his disapproval." Of the preëminent rôle played by the emperor in the national government there could be no doubt, in the opinion of Affonso Celso. Through powers vested in him

[30] Tavares de Lyra, "Regimen eleitoral," 342.

by the constitution and under the compulsion of social and economic conditions Dom Pedro "reigned, governed, and administered" the empire.[31]

That he played his rôle well is equally certain. The calibre of men who served in his council of state and his ministries, the unquestioned ability of those selected for the senate, and the generally high level maintained in the election of the deputies testify to his good judgment and the smooth functioning of the system under his personal direction for thirty years is a tribute to his ability. Toward the end of his rule, no ministry existed without a majority in the lower house, although the emperor was forced at times to dissolve the assembly in order to obtain the desired majority through a controlled election; a minister who disagreed with the president of the ministry or who was defeated in an election resigned his office; and under the careful eye of the emperor the two parties, the liberals and conservatives, rotated in power.

At the height of his career Dom Pedro desired a ministry which would do the executive work for him, men who would listen and conform but who were not necessarily servile agents. He exercised a kind of censorship and general superintendency. In the conflict of factions and the grouping into clans characteristic of the politics of the empire, he remained an impartial agent, the supreme arbiter who never yielded his prerogative as the court of ultimate appeal. The success of his enormous influence lay in its obscurity. Freedom of the press and of speech, and freedom of action by the assembly and ministers were assured on condition that the final approval or rejection should remain in his hands. By his restraint and wisdom he checked the excesses of public agents and factional spirit. Under the forms of a constitutional monarchy he was in reality absolute ruler of the empire.[32]

II

In 1889 Dom Pedro was deposed and the Constitution of 1824 was discarded. A republic replaced the empire. On the basis of the trend, which culminated in the revolution, the new order should have seen the preëminent position of the personal head of the state restricted and the dictatorial powers, exercised since the independence of Brazil by the

---

[31] F. J. Oliveira Vianna, *O occaso do imperio* (São Paulo, 1925), 29-41, 52-62; Affonso Celso, *Oito annos de parlamento. Poder pessoal de D. Pedro II* (São Paulo, 1929 ?), 185-208; Joaquim Nabuco, *Um estadista do imperio* (Rio de Janeiro, n. d.), I, 347-349.

[32] Tavares de Lyra, "Regimen eleitoral," 284-285; Clovis Bevilaqua, "Centralização crescente," *idem,* 313-324.

executive, curtailed in favor of the delegated representatives of the nation chosen by the body of citizens in a free and unhampered election. But did the new régime modify the basis on which the government of the country had rested? Was the preëminent position of the executive curtailed, even by the constitution? Did constitutional dictatorship cease under the republic? Or was the old system perpetuated under new forms? Were social and economic conditions modified to such an extent that the executive could relinquish his paramount position? Was it, in short, possible for the president of the republic to exercise dictatorial powers without overstepping the authority vested in him by the new régime? The answer to these questions depends in part on the causes of the collapse of the empire and in part on the turn which events took during and immediately following the crisis in November 1889. In the final analysis the problem goes back to essentially the same factors which prevented the satisfactory development of the absolutist empire into a truly parliamentary form of government.

During the last twenty years of Dom Pedro's reign a crescendo of protest arose against the rôle played by the emperor in the government of the nation. About 1868 there appeared two fairly well defined parties: a new liberal group favoring a thorough remodeling of the constitution, and an extreme radical group preaching a republic. The former advocated the abolition of the moderative power, an elective senate with restricted term of office, popular election of presidents of provinces, abolition of the national guard, direct and universal suffrage, elective police, emancipation of the slaves, a judicial system independent of the executive and subject to the legislative branch, and responsibility of the ministers to the assembly. The empire should be retained—but on the model of the English system. Behind the movement were able leaders such as Silveira Martins, Rangel Pestana, Nabuco de Araujo, Theophilo Ottoni, and Zacharias de Góes. Success would bring decentralization, the curtailment of the power of the executive, and the transfer of ultimate authority from the personal head of the state to the elected representatives of the people.

The second group came into existence as a definite party in 1871 by the publication of a manifesto[33] in the Rio newspaper *A Republica* and by a convention held in Itú two years later. Some of the advocates of the new liberal group, such as Rangel Pestana and Theophilo Ottoni,

[33] A copy of the manifesto is available in *Revista do Instituto Historico e Geographico Brasileiro*, special volume, *Contribuições para a biographia de D Pedro II*, pt. 1, 554-563, note.

switched to the republican camp, small in numbers but able in propaganda which appealed to the imagination rather than to reason. Except in the provinces of São Paulo and Rio Grande do Sul the party failed to take root, but participation in the movement by such men as the publicist Quintino Bocayuva, the jurist Lafayette Rodrigues Pereira, the Jacobine Aristides Lobo, and the future presidents of the republic, Campos Salles and Prudente de Moraes, gave it a certain importance. The impetus acquired by the manifesto and the convention failed to carry the movement far, however, and it did not become a significant factor in the political life of the nation until the events of 1888 and 1889 raised it to unexpected prominence. The paper *A Republica* barely lasted four years.[34]

These protests were evidences of a trend which was undermining the empire and threatening its collapse. The empire had rested on four principal pillars, the landowning aristocracy, the clergy, the professional classes, and the army. By 1889 these elements had become apathetic or actively hostile in their attitude toward the monarchy, and the empire in reality was little more than a form. That an uprising engendered almost overnight in Rio de Janeiro could sweep it into the discard is ample evidence of this shift in the attitude of the former supporters of the empire.

The land aristocracy, the traditional ruling class which had played such a prominent rôle in the government of the nation since independence, was alienated through the emancipation of the slaves without compensation to the owners.[35] Approximately 720,000 slaves with an estimated value of something over two hundred million dollars were liberated on May 13, 1888, with the emphatic approval of Princess Isabella, acting regent for Dom Pedro who was in Europe. Within a month after the passage of the bill several of the municipalities of the provinces of Rio de Janeiro, São Paulo, and Minas Geraes directly petitioned the national assembly demanding indemnity for liberated slaves and the calling of a constituent assembly to discuss the problem of the future government of Brazil. Many planters joined the republicans or stood by quiescent when the crisis came a year later.

The clergy were alienated by the liberal trend manifested during the

[34] A. O. Viveiras de Castro, "A idéa republicana" in *Revista do Instituto Historico e Geographico Brasileiro,* special volume, *Contribuições para a biographia de D. Pedro* II, pt. 1, 549-579.

[35] Osorio Duque Estrada, *A abolição, 1831-1888* (Rio de Janeiro, 1918), *passim;* Percy A. Martin, "Slavery and abolition in Brazil" in *The Hispanic American Historical Review,* XIII (1933), 151-196.

latter half of the century and by an unfortunate incident which embittered the relations of church and state. The bishop of Olinda, who reflected the vigorous ultramontane policy of the Vatican after 1870, precipitated a crisis by issuing orders directly contrary to the laws of the empire. He commanded without the sanction of the state that the Pernambuco units of a semireligious, semistate organization known as the *Irmandade* should expel all members who were masons. When instructed by the government to rescind the order, the bishop refused, stating that he declined to abide by the constitution since he recognized no authority higher than the church. By the clever diplomacy of Baron Penedo, Pope Pius IX overruled the bishop. The Rio government, instead of being content with the victory, forced the trial of the refractory bishop together with the bishop of Pará who had supported him and obtained a conviction and sentence of four years of imprisonment at hard labor. Dom Pedro commuted the hard labor, and after two years granted pardon to both bishops, who had acquired the status of martyrs in church circles. The vigorous attitude of the state toward the church drove the ultramontane clergy into opposition to the monarchy.[36]

The support of the third pillar, the professional classes and particularly the lawyers who constituted the most influential element in the group, was lost through the antimonarchial propaganda instituted by the new liberals and the republicans. The crescendo of protest, already referred to, seriously damaged the prestige of the empire. The attacks of the republicans, futile and sporadic until 1888, took on a note of menace when planters lent their support after the emancipation of the slaves. Republican newspapers sprang up almost overnight, until by 1889 there were more than fourscore of them. Ex-ministers who had left the restraining hand of the emperor, added their voices to the chorus of disapproval. Eusebio de Queiroz, Ferreira Vianna, José de Alencar, and other influential members of the government, directed scathing attacks at the emperor and the dictatorship which he practiced under parliamentary form. Silveira Martins, senator from Rio Grande do Sul, insisted on the floor of the assembly that "the government is bad; the system is bad. We are living under a disguised absolutism; it is necessary to end it." The conviction grew among the intellectuals that the

[36] A. O. Viveiros de Castro, "Questão religiosa" in *Revista do Instituto Historico e Geographico Brasileiro,* special volume, *Contribuições para a biographia de D. Pedro II,* pt. 1, 477-534.

golden days of the empire were over and that a radical change was necessary.[37]

That change would have been highly improbable, however, had the last pillar of the empire remained firm in its allegiance to the emperor. The antagonism of the army effected the revolution to which the other elements either adhered or gave their tacit consent. To the action of the army after the revolution is due in large part also the frustration of the ideals of the republicans and the continuance of the constitutional dictatorship, none the less effective although under new forms.

Throughout the period of the second empire, militarism had played a subordinate part in the government. Of the fifty-four ministers of war under Dom Pedro II only eighteen were officers; as a class, army officers during the last thirty years of the empire did not constitute a decisive element in the society and administration of the country. It is true that the army rendered good service in foreign wars, particularly in the Paraguayan War, but the higher officers acquired new ideas along with their medals. Floriano Peixoto, then major in the expeditionary force which ran the younger López to earth, wrote to Cunha Mattos, "that is the kind of man we need in Brazil." In another letter he expressed the opinion that during the war he had seen the solution to the class war in Brazil: as a liberal, he affirms, he could not desire a government by the sword, but no one could doubt in the face of the example which he had witnessed that it was the sword by which the blood of society was to be purified.[38] In 1886 General Deodoro da Fonseca wrote to the civilian minister of war stoutly asserting that only the army realized what discipline meant and only the army practiced it. If fate should decree the debasement of the military class, he continued, and he should become merely the commanding officer of a national guard, he would break his sword and seek the post of a deputy in the assembly where he also "could insult whom his caprice should prompt."[39]

The army was recruited from voluntary or forced enlistment, sources which drew men from the lowest rung of society, those whose point of view approximated the attitude of the slave for the master. Empire or republic, military dictatorship or democracy, meant little to them; they

[37] Percy A. Martin, "Causes of the collapse of the Brazilian empire" in *The Hispanic American Historical Review,* IV (1921), 4-48.

[38] Quoted by Fleiuss, *Historia administrativa,* 411. Fleiuss cites verbatim many documents and letters bearing on the revolution of 1889 and the early months of the republic in *ibid.,* 411-489.

[39] Deodoro to Cotegipe (minister of war), November 14, 1886 (the letter is given verbatim by Fleiuss, *Historia administrativa,* note 416-418).

followed the orders of the overseer in gold braid and trappings. The vital point in the relations between the civil government and the military lay in the attitude assumed by the handful of higher officers.

During the middle eighties that group developed a sharp class consciousness at odds with the civil government over an issue which evolved into a test of strength between the civilians of the legislature and military officers and their sympathizers. In the opinion of the latter group, members of the army were subject to military discipline only when on duty or in action. Since no law debarred army officers from participating in politics, the favorite occupation of the Brazilian, a number of officers had won election to the lower house or had been appointed to life membership in the senate. A minority, this element in the assembly sided with the army and openly attacked the members of the cabinet, including the minister of war. Some of this group insisted on the right to express their views through the press or in public gatherings, despite the express prohibition through ministerial decree forbidding the publication of articles in the press by officers without prior consent of the minister of war.

The clash between the military and the government was initiated by a vigorous attack in the *Jornal do Commercio* written by Lieutenant-Colonel Senna Madureira against an innocuous bill proposed by Senator Paranaguá. Other incidents followed until Cunha Mattos, accused by a deputy of conduct unbecoming an officer in the Paraguayan War, in defiance of the law forbidding such action, replied by an acrimonious attack on the deputy. He was censured and punished with a nominal imprisonment of eight hours in the headquarters of the general staff. The Viscount of Pelotas, a hero of the Paraguayan War, rose to his defense on the floor of the senate, insisting that regardless of the law, a soldier wounded in his military honor had the imprescriptible right to avenge himself, and that he himself would so proceed whether or not there was a law to prevent him. Additional cases of a similar nature followed.

These and like incidents occurring in the six years following 1883 have been magnified by advocates of the revolt of 1889 to prove that the army was the victim of intolerable injustice and persecution by the imperial government. After a careful study of the question Professor Percy A. Martin was convinced that the grievances of the army were either "frivolous or based on palpable misunderstanding." That the imperial government treated the army with neglect is possible, but that the neglect was studied or prompted by animus is unsupported by evidence.[40] Friv-

[40] "Causes of the Collapse of the Brazilian Empire," 26-39.

olous the grievances might have been, but they became ominous when the most popular official in the entire army, Deodoro da Fonseca, openly sided with the officers against the minister of war.

A situation that was fast becoming grave was rendered more serious by the machinations of Benjamin Constant, an officer assigned as professor of mathematics to the military school in Rio de Janeiro, an adherent of the positivist theories of Comte, and an ardent republican. He was a vigorous, daring, stern-willed individual, who shortly after the proclamation of the republic advocated a frank dictatorship with the ministers of the provisional government as mere secretaries to the dictator. Through his dynamic personality he won the loyalty of the young officers and cadets of the military school and gained the support of the powerful Military Club to which many of the leading officers located in Rio belonged. Largely through his efforts, the antagonism to the government created among the higher officers of the army was crystallized and directed into action and Deodoro da Fonseca won over to a plot to overthrow the old order.

Until November 11, 1889, only one civilian, Ruy Barbosa, editor of the *Diario de Noticias,* had been acquainted with the plans. At a meeting held in Deodoro's house on the evening of that day other civilian republicans such as Quintino Bocayuva and Aristides Lobo were present. The group laid definite plans for the overthrow of the empire "as a measure of urgent necessity for the salvation of the country and the only possible means of restoring the army." Two days later Floriano Peixoto, adjutant-general of the army, joined the conspiracy. The revolt occurred on the fifteenth, the emperor resigned the next day, and the republic was proclaimed. To the action of Deodoro da Fonseca and Floriano Peixoto is due the success of the armed insubordination which forced the resignation of the ministry and settled the military question to the satisfaction of the army. To the vigorous influence of Benjamin Constant exerted on Deodoro after the events of the morning of the fifteenth is due in large part the final decision to oust Dom Pedro and set up the republic.[41]

The revolution was the work of a small fraction of the army, precipitated by the skillful direction of a limited number of active republicans, both civilian and military. The republic certainly was not the product of a widespread demand. A situation of minor importance served as the

[41] For contrasting accounts of the revolution see: Christiano B. Ottoni, *O advento da republica no Brasil* (Rio de Janeiro, 1890), and Affonso Celso, Visconde de Ouro Preto, *Advento da dictadura militar no Brasil* (Paris, 1891).

incident which by virtue of the slow crumbling of the foundations on which the stability of the empire rested, was able to destroy the old order and initiate the new.[42] From the point of view of this study the significant factor in the transition was the rôle played by the army. Three days after the revolt, Aristides Lobo, minister of the interior under the provisional government, confessed that the revolt had been the work exclusively of the military; the collaboration of the civilian element, he conceded, was almost nonexistent. As masters of the situation, would the military leaders establish a republic differing in theory and practice from the dictatorial rule of the empire or would they continue the centralized system with preëminent power in the hands of the executive?

III

Under the circumstances the answer for the immediate future was obvious. A military dictatorship was the normal result of the situation.[43] Deodoro, whose contempt for the civilian politician was the product of limited intelligence and a total want of political acumen, was provisional head of the government. With him were associated the far more intelligent Floriano Peixoto, who believed in the efficacy of the sword as a purge for the ills of society, and the determined theorist Benjamin Constant, who frankly advocated a military dictatorship. As the sole agents by which the new régime had been achieved, the army strutted its superiority over the other classes of society.

For fifteen months Brazil lived under a military dictatorship. Army officers replaced civilians in governmental positions; the pay of privates and officers was raised and the number of higher officials vastly increased; legal rights of civilians were ignored by the new holders of office who resembled the royal agents of colonial days in their arbitrary and contemptuous administration; and the members of the provisional government doubled their own salaries and created innumerable posts for favorites. Freedom of the press and of speech was suppressed. Although the majority of Deodoro's first ministry under the provisional government were civilians, the real authority lay in the hands of the military whose control extended throughout the provinces.

It was under these conditions that the new instrument of government was formulated. A constituent assembly, composed of republicans hand-

---

[42] A very detailed account of the republican movement to the end of the constituent assembly was written by Felisbello F. de O. Freire, *Historia constitucional da republica dos E. U. do Brasil* (3 vols., Rio de Janeiro, 1894-95).

[43] Ruy Barbosa, *Dictadura e republica* (Rio de Janeiro, 1932), *passim.*

picked under the efficient direction of the provisional government, was scheduled to convene on November 15, 1890. Prior to that date, a project of a constitution was formulated by a commission of five members appointed shortly after the revolution. Using three separate documents prepared by individual members, the committee drew up a proposal which was submitted to Deodoro for approval. Dissatisfied with the result but using the proposal as a basis of action, Deodoro, in collaboration with his ministry and particularly with Ruy Barbosa, formulated the draft which was promulgated in June 1890 as the project to be submitted to the assembly.[44] This body ratified the document with minor changes.[45]

Thus was repeated with slight differences the method used by Dom Pedro I to secure a constitution considered satisfactory by the small coterie surrounding the personal head of the state. The instrument was the product not of a body of Brazilians representing the various elements constituting the society of the nation but of a small group acting under a military dictatorship. The idealistic civilian, Ruy Barbosa, with his devotion to the constitution of the United States, exerted no little influence in shaping the document, but the presence of a dictatorial point of view is evident in the provisions guaranteeing the preëminent position of the federal government. Once again the Brazilian nation received a constitution from above, handed down to it by the administrative masters of the country.

The formulation of state constitutions followed a parallel course. For more than a year the states remained under the governors appointed by and solely responsible to the provisional government in Rio de Janeiro. It was not until after it had issued the draft to be submitted to the national constituent assembly that the provisional government ordered the governors to promulgate constitutions to be submitted to constituent assemblies of their respective states. Beginning in October 1890, the heads of the various states decreed constitutions which were approved by the special assemblies called for the purpose. These had scarcely been put into operation, however, when the coup which deposed Deodoro and installed Floriano Peixoto in power caused their annulment and forced the adoption of new ones the following year. The individual states, therefore, enjoyed no constitutional status of any kind until after the federal

[44] Fleiuss, *Historia administrativa,* 451-452.

[45] James, *Constitutional system,* 9-11; Brazil, *Annaes do Congresso Constituinte da Republica* (3 vols., Rio de Janeiro 1924-26).

government was definitely organized and set into operation under the new régime.[46]

In the eyes of a citizen of the United States, whose point of view is derived from the actual functioning of government under our constitution, the document promulgated by Deodoro and ratified by the constituent assembly apparently instituted a régime which precluded the exercise of dictatorial power either under the forms of a parliamentary system or under the guise of a federal distribution of powers. It decentralized the government by guaranteeing the local autonomy of the states, specified powers being reserved for the federal government and general powers being vested in the states. The check and balance system was adopted with specific powers delegated to the legislative, executive, and judicial branches; a long bill of rights safeguarded the liberties of the individual; and universal manhood suffrage restricted only by a literacy test based the whole structure on the Brazilian people. Presumably the ultimate authority resided in the citizens of the nation acting through their delegated representatives.[47]

A closer scrutiny dispels that illusion.[48] In reality the federal government wielded the preponderant power and in the federal government itself the executive enacted the decisive rôle. Implied powers were granted specifically to the federal government despite an attempt in the constituent assembly to insert a contrary provision. By assigning to the national assembly the function of legislating on civil, criminal, and commercial law, the constitution definitely established the principle of unified legislation, or in other words, the principle that substantive law was a concern of the national government. It was equally specific in affirming that in all questions of conflict between the rights and powers of the states and those of the federal government the ultimate authority resided in the latter. Moreover, the constitution might be amended by congress itself without any ratification by the states and regardless of proposals or suggestions by state legislatures.

The most conclusive evidence of the preponderance of the federal government, however, lies in the right granted to it by the constitution to intervene in the affairs of the states and the authorization to suspend the guarantees of personal liberty by the declaration of a state of siege. The

[46] James, *Constitutional system,* 11-12.

[47] A copy of the constitution is available in James, *Constitutional system,* 221-236.

[48] Probably the most authoritative set of commentaries on disputed points arising from varied interpretations of the republican constitution is to be found in João Barbalho Uchôa Cavalcanti, *Constituição federal brasileira. Commentarios* (Rio de Janeiro, 1902).

national government was empowered to intervene in affairs pertinent to the states in order to repel foreign invasion or invasion of one state by another, to maintain the republican form, to reëstablish order upon request of the state government, and to insure the execution of federal laws and judgments. In terminology this grant of power closely resembled that of the similar provision in our constitution; in practice, it proved incomparably more important. Whereas in theory all branches of the national government were to collaborate in declaring for intervention, in reality the power devolved upon the president who as commander-in-chief of the armed forces and chief executive of the nation was charged with the maintenance of internal security and order, and was authorized to declare a state of siege in the recess of congress.

The duty to maintain the republican form of government was interpreted to mean not alone the outward forms, for intervention was held to be justifiable when the regular functioning of those forms broke down. Thus, when in the opinion of the national government, which as a matter of fact meant in the opinion of the president, a state government ceased to function adequately, or federal laws and judgments were flouted, or public tranquillity was disturbed, the national government could step in and run that state until such time as it considered expedient to withdraw. Such intervention has occurred frequently since the founding of the republic.

A significant illustration[49] of the use of the power of intervention by the president occurred in 1921. In that year the national election was bitterly contested between Arthur Bernardes, the machine candidate, and Nilo Peçanha, senator from the State of Rio de Janeiro, who was backed by disgruntled elements throughout the nation but especially by the military class. Bernardes was declared elected over the protest of the Peçanha faction. In the election for state officers in Rio de Janeiro both parties claimed the victory. The case, which was particularly acute since the dominant party in the state supported Peçanha, was brought before the federal supreme court through an application by one of the rival parties for a writ of *habeas corpus*. According to the Brazilian interpretation *habeas corpus* may be used, as in this country, to force the appearance in court of a person held in custody or it may be used in the sense of a *quo warranto* writ to secure an ouster from office or to place in office the party legally elected to it.

The supreme court granted the writ on December 27, and under the protection of an order from the president of the republic the petitioners

[49] James, *Constitutional system,* 138-140.

assumed office on the thirty-first, the day on which the national congress adjourned. At the same time the opposition party went through the forms of installation before the rival legislature and set up a parallel government. The party protected by the writ protested to the supreme court, which inquired of the federal district judge in the state whether the writ had been fulfilled. The latter asserted that the order of the supreme court had been carried out and that the petitioners had been placed in office. The president of the republic then declared that the state government had ceased to function properly, and appointed a federal intervenor to take over the government of the state until order and tranquillity might be restored. When Peçanha's faction appealed to the supreme court in protest against intervention, that body ruled that since its order had been fulfilled and since it was not responsible for the disturbances and duality of government subsequent to the installation of the petitioners the matter was closed as far as the court was concerned. Thus by powers granted to the federal government through the constitution the chief executive of the nation was able to intervene effectively in local state politics.

An equally powerful weapon was granted to the central government in authorizing it to declare a state of siege.[50] By Article XXXIV the assembly might suspend the constitutional guarantees in one or more points of the national territory for a definite period of time in case of emergency arising from foreign invasion or from grave internal commotion. If congress was not in session, the executive was empowered to declare the state of siege, and once invoked, the measure was wielded by the president. In practice it was the executive who determined when "internal commotion" reached the emergency stage. Becoming operative immediately upon issuance, it might last for one or two days or for several months, with extension upon the expiration of the period set. Until 1898 it was held to include members of congress, and by the phraseology of the constitution it might suspend all constitutional guarantees including those of property. In practice, however, it came to refer to the individual guarantees listed under the bill of rights. A decree might list specific rights to be suspended; in such cases the most common practice abrogated immunity from arrest and freedom of the press. It is obvious that this power, which has been invoked many times, placed an effective weapon in the hands of the federal government, and when utilized in conjunction with the right to intervene contained possibilities of domination by the central authorities in the political affairs of the states.

[50] *Ibid.*, 155-171.

Thus it was that by utilizing powers granted by the constitution, the federal government held the whip hand over the states. In the central government itself the executive enacted the decisive rôle. This preponderance of the president resulted from powers vested in him by the constitution and from his position as the political boss of the party in power. He was accorded all the powers assigned to the president by our constitution with additional spheres of action arising from practices peculiar to the Brazilian point of view. In addition to the familiar duty of issuing decrees and regulations for the execution of laws passed by the congress, he was charged with extensive legislative powers delegated to him by the assembly, particularly in matters of finance where broad latitude was left him in the expenditure of funds. The appointive power, even to department heads and consuls, was made exclusively an executive matter, a provision which placed a decisive political weapon in the hands of the president. It was upon his recommendation that the assembly authorized intervention and declared a state of siege; it was he who executed both decrees; and it was in his power to evoke both measures during the recess of the assembly.

The constitutional powers of the president were reinforced by his position as political boss of the faction in power, a position which he held for the four years of his term of office. By an understanding between the heads of the states, until recently between the controlling political forces of Minas Geraes and São Paulo, the next candidate for the national presidency was agreed upon; a caucus consisting largely of the members of congress, who were the creatures of the state administrations, ratified the nomination; an election supervised by the nominators voted the candidate into office; and a congress which ratified the selection passed on the legality of the result. Once in office the president held the whip hand through his power of patronage and his possession of the controlling voice in the use of the weapons of intervention and state of siege. Thus an oligarchy perpetuated itself from term to term, and a dictator acting on the basis of constitutional grants of power and with the consent and coöperation of the controlling factions in the states directed the destinies of the nation. With the exception of Floriano Peixoto, whose case was exceptional, no executive, whether an irresponsible militarist or a civilian autocrat, has held office beyond the legal term; and yet every president has wielded powers of a dictatorial nature.

The system rested on the control of the states by the local executives. Like the national president, the state executive possessed practically unrestricted patronage privileges, exercised extensive legislative functions through the ordinance power, acted as head of the state militarized police, in some cases veritable armies, and controlled the significant unit on which the scheme rested, namely, the municipal governments. The control over municipal affairs was guaranteed by the general practice of vesting in the state president, or his subservient assembly, power to pass on the validity of local elections, to supervise finances, and to suspend or annul the resolutions or acts of the municipal authorities. As a general rule also the prefects were appointed by the central state authority.[51]

The base on which this centralized, republican structure rested, therefore, was not the electorate. That body was as incapable of intelligent functioning as under the empire.[52] As in the time of Dom Pedro, repeated attempts to reform the law in the hope of establishing an effective electorate by tinkering with the machinery proved fruitless. In the words of Tavares de Lyra, the electoral laws were perfect; the defect lay in the setting in which they were supposed to function. Resistance to the intolerance, the exclusiveness, the abuses, the omnipotence of the group in control of the machinery was useless.[53] With an illiteracy rate of nearly eighty per cent for the nation at large and no effective public opinion to serve as a check on the action of the machine, the electorate became the slave to the political masters of the states and nation.

In reality the base on which the republic rested was a small army turned out by the professional schools. These lawyers, physicians, engineers, descendants of the old land aristocracy, or sons of slaves, of mulattoes, or of half-breeds, turned to public office rather than to their profession for a living. Positions without too much work were created for them; it was on them that the state executives depended to guarantee satisfactory election results. The party voters, in addition to these members of the machine, were the multitudinous hangers-on who held small government jobs, either state or federal, merchants dependent for favors on those in power, employees subject to pressure from the employer, dependent artisans, and the friends of the local political chiefs.[54] By force or fraud this body, until the last election numbering less than a million voters, was utilized by the machine to maintain permanence in office.

---

[51] *Ibid.*, 174-195.

[52] Oliveira Vianna, "O idealismo da constituição" in *Á margem da historia da republica,* 137-143.

[53] Tavares de Lyra, "Regimen eleitoral," 346-347.

[54] Gilberto Amado, "As instituições politicas e o meio social no Brasil," 72-75; Oliveira Vianna, "O idealismo da constituição," 143-158; A. Carneiro Leão, "Os deveres das novas gerações Brasileiras" in *Á margem da historia da depublica,* 17-22.

Thus the revolution of 1889 inaugurated an oligarchical dictatorship which derived its existence both from constitutional provisions and from the political system engendered by the social and economic conditions characteristic of the Brazilian nation. Whereas under the empire the entire machine was under the permanent control of one man who, in Dom Pedro II's case, happened to be an exceptionally enlightened individual, under the republic an oligarchy was forced to seize and hold the machine under the forms of universal manhood suffrage and to settle every four years the vexing problem of a successor for the dictatorial chair. That oligarchy was composed of a cultured aristocracy of wealth, still based in the main on the possession of land but open also to the newer industrial and merchant magnates.[55] It was this element which has furnished the stabilizing influence in the social and political development of Brazil since independence; and it has been from and by this element that the dictatorial executives of the republic have been chosen. Almost without exception they have been men of culture, of unimpeachable social and professional standing, and of long experience in politics.

In the selection of the official candidates—all of them without exception have won the election—the pendulum has swung between the military and the civilian. The military executives, such as Deodoro da Fonseca and Floriano Peixoto, have tended to expand the normally preponderant powers of their office in defiance of the civilian machine, whereas the civilian executives, such as Prudente de Moraes Barros and Campos Salles, have held in the main to the sphere of action permitted by the constitution and practices of Brazilian politics. The first term was filled by the two militarists, Deodoro da Fonseca, who precipitated a revolt which forced his resignation when he dissolved the assembly and proclaimed an undisguised dictatorship, and Floriano Peixoto, who crushed rebellions with an iron hand and held the new-born republic together by a despotic rule of terror. From 1894 until 1910 civilians were elected. In 1910 Marshal Hermes da Fonseca, nephew of Deodoro and representative of the army which was striving once more to gain political supremacy, won over the opposition candidate, Ruy Barbosa, put forward by the machines of Minas Geraes, São Paulo, and Bahia. The civilian element regained control in 1914, however, through the election

[55] For the rise of the industrial and commercial element see the chapters on industry (XIX) by Getulio das Neves and F. T. de Sousa Reis, and on commerce (XX) by Ramalho Ortigão in *Revista do Instituto Historico e Geographico Brasileiro,* special volume, *Diccionario Historico, Geographico e Ethnographico do Brasil,* pt. 1. Alberto de Faria's biography of Mauá is equally helpful.

of Wenceslau Braz of Minas Geraes, and has maintained its position ever since despite an attempted coup by the army in 1922 by which it hoped to install Marshal Hermes da Fonseca as provisional chief and an uprising in São Paulo two years later backed by the same element. With the exception of two terms, therefore, civilians have served as presidents of the republic.

In recent years there has arisen a question of more fundamental importance than the conflict between the military and civilian elements for control of the dictatorial chair of the presidency. It is particularly significant since it touches a vital point in the system inaugurated in 1889. Due to the wealth, population, and economic importance of Minas Geraes and São Paulo the choice of official candidates by the oligarchy alternated, with two exceptions until 1930, between those two states. The growing importance of other states, particularly of Rio Grande do Sul, has complicated the problem of selecting the man who is to succeed to the vitally important position of chief executive and national political boss. The successful effort of Washington Luis, a native of São Paulo, to break precedent and force the election of Julio Prestes, a fellow Paulista, as his successor precipitated the formidable revolution of 1930. In October of that year, a month prior to the inauguration of Julio Prestes, Washington Luis was deposed and the defeated candidate from Rio Grande do Sul, Getulio Vargas, was installed as provisional chief of the national government with full dictatorial powers.

The situation of 1889 was repeated. Vargas dissolved the national congress, state legislatures, and municipal councils, ruling the nation from top to bottom through his personal representatives, many of them young military officers. Civilians have predominated in his cabinet, however, and the military element has been subordinated to his leadership. A new constitution was promulgated in 1934 and Vargas was elected president.[56] It is too soon after the event to evaluate the revolution and the new constitution as they affect the problem under discussion in this study. It is obvious, nevertheless, that the Minas Geraes-São Paulo hegemony has been challenged successfully and it is equally obvious that the choice of a successor to the chief executive will constitute a more difficult problem for solution by the ruling oligarchy of the republic.

---

[56] Percy A. Martin in *Argentina, Brazil, and Chile since Independence* (Washington, 1935), chapter on contemporary Brazil, 263-276.

IV

In Brazil it has not been necessary for one man after seizing the central executive position to arrogate to himself extraordinary powers. Any one who occupied that post, whether as emperor or president, exercised prerogatives which assured him the decisive voice in national and state politics. These prerogatives were derived from constitutional provisions and from the social and political organization of Brazil. By virtue of the fact that there was no abrupt break, no violent swing of the pendulum to the opposite extreme when independence was won, the tradition of colonial centralization of power in the personal head of the state continued into the empire. Limitations on the power of that head of the state were imposed largely by himself or with his consent. When the republic replaced the empire, the new system, again shaped largely by centralist autocrats and handed down to the nation by the executive masters of the country, continued the fundamental preëminence of the national executive.

From the inception of independence to the Constitution of 1934 there has been a slow trend away from the absolutism of one man, upon whose will no restrictions or limitations were placed, toward a constitutional dictatorship in which an influential member of an oligarchy was granted extensive powers for a short period of time. A significant feature of that trend has been the ever widening base on which the system has rested. From the close corporation of Portuguese surrounding the first Pedro the base expanded to take in the Brazilian land aristocracy under the second Pedro. With the republic the newer aristocracy of wealth based on industry and commerce was admitted. Whether the new constitution has broadened the base still further is a moot point; apparently the provisions of the document point in that direction, but whether practice will follow that lead time alone will reveal.

The constitutions of 1824 and 1891 established governmental systems which operated because they formulated régimes suited in the main to the social and political development of the country. As long as the aristocracy, based on the possession of land during the empire but drawn also from commercial and industrial classes under the republic, supported the systems set up by these documents, they endured. When a sufficiently large portion of that aristocracy of wealth turned against them, a new régime was inaugurated. The stabilizing factor in the situation has been this aristocracy which, relatively small in number, has in reality constituted an oligarchy decisive in its influence since the first move toward independence. It has been this oligarchy which has prevented the seizure of power by an outsider, which served as the chief pillar on which the empire rested, and which under the republic has selected from its midst the man who was to constitute the keystone of the arch.

Brazil, therefore, has had dictators; but they have been dictators who acted under the authority of constitutional provision and with the consent of the significant element in the social organization of the nation. When, as in the case of Dom Pedro I or Marshal Deodoro da Fonseca or even Washington Luis, the dictator in the opinion of the oligarchy exceeded the limit of his powers, he was deposed. Floriano Peixoto, a possible exception to this statement, voluntarily retired at the expiration of his term and turned over the government to the choice of the civilian aristocracy. The history of dictators and dictatorships in Brazil centers, therefore, not so much on the individuals who have wielded the preëminent powers of the personal head of the government, important and significant as they are, but rather on the social and political development of the country which has made this constitutional dictatorship the logical form of government for the nation.

VI. APPENDIX

JUAN MANUEL DE ROSAS AND THE CHURCH

By Almon R. Wright

I

A FEW miles to the west of Buenos Aires lay a military encampment in the decade of the 1840's which was maintained by the Argentine dictator, Juan Manuel de Rosas. To this place were brought his foes when they unfortunately fell into the hands of his dreaded spies. Here they were condemned, executed, and buried. This field of blood, paradoxically as it may seem, was known as *Los Santos Lugares,* the sacred places. It derived its name from the fact that a Franciscan chapel and house were here located. On the same site were the representatives of Rosas' agency of terror and the representatives of the missionary zeal of the Catholic Church. Perhaps it is needless to add that this Franciscan establishment was quite subordinate to the military and political purposes of the dictator. At a later date an observer would have found that *Los Santos Lugares* was a cemetery with a church in the midst. Approaching closer he would have noticed an inscription bearing the name of Rosas as founder of the church and also a plaque depicting a man dying in the service of the "illustrious General Rosas."[1]

In the second quarter of the last century, Argentina was a primitive frontier country. The dictator was a typical product of his age: self-reliant, poorly educated, and a man of action. His religion was that of a frontier people, for his Catholicism was much affected by a natural love of pomp and show and by an innate superstition.[2] If one may believe that a basis of fact lies behind some of the anecdotes concerning him, one may conclude that he did not regard the clergy always with the respect, or the sacraments always with the reverence, which one might expect. One anecdote purports to show the dictator as enjoying a practical joke at the expense of his chaplain. The latter seems to have suffered intensely from innumerable corns on his foot. Few were the days when he could walk. On one of his visits to Rosas he is said to have given a doleful report of his condition. As he reached the door to go, an attendant, on Rosas' orders and to his great enjoyment, tramped on the poor man's foot. On another occasion, we are told, Rosas ordered elaborate

[1] Frederico Barbará, *Rosas* (Buenos Aires, 1933), 116.

[2] See the first chapter of Carlos Ibarguren, *Juan Manuel de Rosas; su vida, su tiempo, su drama* (Buenos Aires, 1930).

preparations to be made for the baptism of a negro servant. The order discomforted the latter and mystified the members of the dictator's household, to his delight. At the appointed moment the chaplain baptized not in the name of the Father, Son, and Holy Spirit, but in the name of the Sacred Cross of the Federation, and the negro, instead of being given the customary saint's name, was to be called Juan Manuel de la Patria Federal.[3]

For solving the difficult problems of harmonizing the power of the state with the authority of the church, Rosas had little preparation. He had little knowledge of the political philosophy underlying those questions. He was ignorant of the attempts of the Spanish crown to control the colonial church from the sixteenth to the nineteenth century. Nor could he fully appreciate the altered status of the relations between the state and the church resulting from the Argentine revolution and the establishment of independence. But upon reaching supreme power he inherited a problem which was the outcome of a long historical development. One can review here only in brief outline the background of Rosas' relations with the Church.[4]

II

From the time of Ferdinand and Isabella the Spanish royal house developed a large body of regulations by which the viceroys sought to control the colonial church. These royal representatives had the authority and the obligation to choose ecclesiastical officers, provide for the salvation of the souls of the Indians, and supervise the conduct of the clergy. The Spanish Crown was solicitous to safeguard the jurisdiction of the royal courts, to restrict the authority of the ecclesiastical tribunals, and to circumscribe the use of the weapons of excommunication and inquisition. In more purely economic matters the Spanish Crown was ever vigilant to maintain civil power over the ecclesiastical. In 1501 Pope Alexander VI granted to Ferdinand and Isabella the privilege and the responsibility of administering the tithes. They promulgated a schedule by which the tax was levied upon the products of agriculture and industry, and upon the property of nearly all classes of the population. They and their successors arranged for the distribution of the proceeds of this revenue either directly by royal decree or indirectly by passing upon the charters of rules and regulations with which all the

[3] Barbará, 98-100, 37-38.

[4] From the writer's "Church and state in the Province of La Plata to 1861," unpublished thesis in the library of the University of Illinois, 25-162.

cathedral churches were founded. In many ways the government assisted in strengthening the church. It subsidized the members of the regular clergy extensively in the sixteenth century. When the revenues from the tithes were inadequate, it made up the deficiency. When earthquakes destroyed old cathedrals or when an expanding frontier necessitated new churches, it contributed generously.

With the overthrow of the political authority of Spain over the provinces of La Plata, the revolutionists were immediately confronted with the problem of defining the ecclesiastical authority. Were the new governments of the independent state to assume the powers and the financial responsibilities which Spain claimed and accepted? Their answer was in the affirmative, to the effect that the political and economic control by the mother country over the colonial church was a sovereign power which the independent state inherited. But what was the viewpoint of the church? To the pope, that authority was exercised as a concession from the Holy See not as a sovereign power, or as a right resulting from the agreement of equal parties. Since the papacy did not immediately recognize the independence of Argentina, it did not sanction the intervention of the new governments in church matters. Unwilling to antagonize the papacy by extreme measures, the revolutionists preferred to leave unexercised certain ecclesiastical powers. For illustration, the offices of bishop, when they became vacant, were left unfilled.

The lack of spiritual leadership from the pope or from the bishops had a demoralizing effect. Hence in the 1820's Bernardino Rivadavia instituted a "Civil Constitution of the Clergy" after the French prototype. He appears to have hoped to remedy the degraded condition of the clergy and to bind the church of Buenos Aires more closely to the government of the province. Among his reforms were the abolition of the tithes, the reduction in the number of church officers, monasteries, and convents, and the confiscation of some of the property of the regular orders. He championed the cause of toleration. He sought to substitute salaries and unemployment doles from the state for the old tithe system.

III

The Rivadavian plan of reform aroused bitter hostility among the clergy and among the fanatically religious laymen. But Rivadavia had political enemies, also; among them was Rosas. The dictator considered him to be an adherent of the cause of a powerful central government, a "savage unitarian." Therefore, his religious changes were also to be opposed. But there was much in Rivadavia's "Civil Constitution of the Clergy" which harmonized with Rosas' own views. As the former sought to strengthen the arm of the government at the expense of the church, so, also, Rosas weakened every force which might offer opposition to his own tyranny. As Rivadavia followed a strong nationalist policy in his relations with the papacy and with Europe, so, also, Rosas pursued belligerently a nationalist policy against his European enemies. In many questions concerning the church, however, the dictator was unwilling to go as far as his predecessor.

One problem, the significance of which was readily grasped by Rosas and one which those familiar with the political practices in the United States will understand, was the matter of patronage. The right to nominate, and thereby in reality to choose, ecclesiastical officeholders was claimed by the Spanish monarchs from time immemorial. The papacy acquiesced in the nomination of the candidates by the state, but insisted that the conferring of the spiritual authority lay with the Holy See or its representatives. The Argentine state claimed this right which Spain had held, but when Rosas came into power the pope had not yet recognized the claim. One of the ministers of government, Manuel José García, formulated a long treatise justifying the claim by presenting opinions of learned men and a review of precedents. This discussion, which was called *Memorial composed of the precedents established concerning the provision of the apostolic vicar and the bishop of this church by the high pope,* has standing as one of the fundamental discourses by which the government may conduct its relations with the church.[5]

The author of this ponderous work wisely wrote a brief summary of the political theory contained therein. Because of the frequent reference which is made to this *Memorial* one may properly examine some of the fourteen points which constitute the summary. To begin with, the author upheld the view that, with the collapse of the Spanish Empire and the establishment of independent states, the sovereign powers of the mother country descended upon the new nations. In Argentina, however, except for those powers delegated to the federal government, each province assumed sovereignty. According to García's third point the patronage and the maintenance of the church were most important attributes of that sovereignty. Therefore, civil officers only might nominate or present to the pope the candidates for archbishops, bishops, and the other ecclesiastical dignitaries. Employing the word "patronage" to

[5] *Registro oficial de la Repúblic Argentina* (Buenos Aires, 1879-1884), II, 315 (hereafter cited as R. O.); Hector Esquivel, *Régimen eclesiástico argentino* (Buenos Aires, 1928), 175.

cover matters other than church officers, García argued that, for the same reasons, to the government belonged the authority to grant or deny the validity of papal documents with the exception of those referring to penance. To it should be referred questions concerning the boundaries of dioceses, and the alteration of the charters upon which the churches were founded. In another point García declared that no ecclesiastical officer might take an oath of consecration to his religious duties without a reservation safeguarding the rights of the Argentine nation. His fourteenth point contained the assertion that until an agreement providing for a reciprocal acknowledgment of the sovereignty of the state and the rights of the church was reached, relations with the papacy would be considered as suspended.[6]

It is an interesting fact that the period of Rosas' influence witnessed the production not only of the famous treatise above described but also a second equally famous explanation by a better known author. It is improbable that Rosas had the understanding or patience to appreciate the *Memorial.* His native cunning guided him in seizing the essence of power. He seldom felt the need to justify his acts. But at the close of his reign, realizing perhaps that some of his failures were due to an incomplete knowledge, he received from the eminent lawyer, Velez Sarsfield, the *Treatise on the public ecclesiastical law.* The viewpoint of Velez Sarsfield was similar to that of García but his treatment of the subject was more direct and simple.[7]

Rosas seems to have had one guiding principle in his relations with the church: that he was the champion of the Catholic faith, and therefore, his enemies were the enemies of God.[8] Those whom he called "savage unitarians" were atheists attacking the faith "which is that which engenders Christian and civic virtues, which constitutes the base of the happiness of states."[9] One would hardly expect him to permit atheists, his political emenies, to hold ecclesiastical office. Loyalty to the federal cause, that is, personal loyalty to Rosas, is repeatedly mentioned in the official records of these appointments as the most essential qualification.[10]

---

[6] *R. O.*, II, 316, 318-19.

[7] Velez Sarsfield to Rosas, April 6 and May 2, 1850, in Adolfo Saldias, *Papeles de Rozas* (La Plata, 1904), II, 30-31, 38; Esquivel, 192.

[8] Andrés Lamas, *Apuntes históricos sobre las agresiones del dictator . . .* (Montevideo, 1849), as quoted in Ernesto Quesada, *Época de Rosas, su verdadero carácter histórico* (Buenos Aires, 1898), page xxxi.

[9] As quoted in Ibarguren, 326.

[10] *R. O.*, II, 346, 367, 406.

In messages to the provincial legislature on December 27, 1840 the general rule was affirmed that vacancies in the ecclesiastical council of Buenos Aires were filled by those distinguished "for their virtue and adherence to the sacred cause of the Federation."[11]

To what extent the clergy suffered at the hands of Rosas' secret agents will probably never be satisfactorily settled. The fact that he made many appointments to the ecclesiastical senate at Buenos Aires suggests that the many deaths of members of that body may have resulted from his methods of violence.[12] Evidence is lacking to prove that these fatalities were due to the *mazorca,* but it seems probable that some of the clergy met the fate of thousands of victims of that organization. The opposition of the ecclesiastical senate of Buenos Aires to Rosas' tool in the person of Mariano Medrano undoubtedly displeased the dictator, but he seems to have kept some of the offices in that body vacant for a particular purpose.[13] In return for the accumulated tasks placed upon the remaining members due to these vacancies, Rosas openly announced that an additional compensation would be given.[14]

IV

The successful candidates for church offices found that not only was an acceptable political record essential, but that a promise of continued support of the dictator's position was necessary. By a decree of October 18, 1839 the bishop of Cuyo was required to swear

> "that he would coöperate through sermons, lectures, confessions, doctrines, conversations, and councils so that men and women of all classes and conditions, whatever they may be, and even slaves of both sexes, and children of all classes, may use the red federal emblem of our Confederation, the men on the left side on the breast in front of the heart and the ladies and other women of all classes, little and great, on the head on the left side."[15]

In pursuance of this decree, the apostolic vicar was required to send a circular to the parish priests to be read by them to their congregations. According to the injunction in this document those who disobeyed were

[11] Heraclio Mabragaña, *Los Mensajes. Historia del desenvolvimiento de la nación argentina, redactada cronologicamente por sus gobernantes, 1810-1910* (Buenos Aires, 1910), II, 7.

[12] Balcarce to the Legislature, May 31, 1833, *Ibid.,* I, 273; *R. O.,* II, 406, 286.

[13] Rosas to the Legislature, December 27, 1837, Mabragaña, I, 356; *R. O.,* II, 286, 298.

[14] Rosas to the Legislature, December 27, 1837, Mabragaña, I, 356; *R. O.,* II, 388.

[15] *R. O.,* II, 404-05.

first to be warned and on a second offense were to be deprived of spiritual comforts. The edict was to be enforced jointly by the police and the clergy![16] Thus Rosas sought in the enforcement of his decrees to strengthen the police power of his agents by resorting to threats of depriving his subjects of the blessings of their church.

The dictator not only added new duties of a propagandist character to the work of the clergy, but he also sought to control the conduct of the church service. In 1833 the apostolic vicar complied with the request that he establish the practice of imploring divine guidance for the preservation of the republic, the happiness of its people and the direction of its rulers.[17] The minister of government, Balcarce, acknowledged before the provincial legislature that the clergy had coöperated in this request.[18] In the following year Medrano gave another example of his good will, or better his subservience, to the dictator. He required the observance of an order, given the force of law and probably inspired by the government, by which church services were to be limited in time. Long diffuse sermons were not conducive to increasing the devotion of the masses. Moral discussions were to be shortened, and the subjects expounded from the pulpits were to be theological in character.[19] The government also ratified another order of the apostolic vicar which in minute fashion prescribed the manner of clothing for the different classes of the clergy and for the different occasions.[20]

The subservience of the clergy to the dictatorship of Rosas was strikingly displayed in church feasts and processions. Pictures of the "Illustrious Restorer of the Laws" and of his wife, the "Encarnation of Ezcurra," were carried to the cathedral in a magnificent procession headed by no other than the apostolic vicar, Medrano, and accompanied by the élite of Buenos Aires society.[21] A French observer noted that Rosas "induced the entire population to adore his own portrait; he had incense burned before that portrait in the churches . . . and he desired that discourses should be addressed to himself in public ceremonies. . . ."[22] He commanded that the celebration of holidays, such

[16] Esquivel, 186-87.
[17] *R. O.*, II, 307.
[18] Balcarce to the Legislature, May 31, 1833, Mabragaña, I, 273.
[19] *R. O.*, II, 337.
[20] *R. O.*, II, 357.
[21] Esquivel, 188.
[22] As quoted by W. S. Robertson, "Foreign estimates of the Argentine dictator, Juan Manuel Rosas," in *The Hispanic American Historical Review,* X (May, 1930), 131.

as the anniversary of Argentine independence, be carried out with appropriate ceremonies in the churches.[23] When he returned from Indian wars on the frontier in 1836, Rosas prescribed in detail the commemorative ceremonies to be held in the cathedral.[24]

Religious holidays had disadvantages, for on such days the business of the communities ceased. In the person of the minister, García de Zúniga, the state took measures to decrease the number of such occasions. He pointed out that the commerce, industry, and agriculture of the capital city and of the provinces were seriously crippled by the one hundred and fifty feast days. The coastal trade was especially hampered, for frequently the one or two days in the week, when the weather permitted these traders to go to sea, were religious holidays.[25] Medrano concurred in these views noting that the feast days were abused, and that they were marked by neglect of religious duties and by an excessive number of crimes. He ordered, subject to the pope's approval, a reduction in the number of such days.[26] Two years later Medrano addressed the faithful to the effect that the pope had ratified the provisional curtailment and called upon them in the name of the Holy See to observe the new calendar.[27] The reform was restricted, however, to the diocese of Buenos Aires, and years later Medrano attempted to bring further relief.[28]

One of the best known institutions of the church is the Index, which in its broad sense means the attempt of the ecclesiastical authorities to safeguard their people from injurious reading and reflection. Of necessity Rosas established a censorship to protect his subjects from the writings of his detractors.[29] But his restriction of the press was extended from political to religious subject matter. On July 1, 1831 a decree was issued by which the apostolic vicar was made responsible for issuing official manuals of doctrine and schedules of prayer, subject, however, to the approval of the government. Later in the same year another decree was promulgated which contained an account of alleged abuses of

[23] Antonio Zinny, *La Gaceta Mercantil de Buenos Aires 1823-1852, resumen de su contenido con relación a la parte americana y con especialidad a la historia de la república argentina* (Buenos Aires, 1912), II, 372, 379, 381, 386.

[24] Barbará, 124.

[25] *R. O.*, II, 303.

[26] Balcarce to the Legislature, May 31, 1833, Mabragaña, I, 273; *R. O.*, II, 303.

[27] *R. O.*, II, 339.

[28] Rosas to the Legislature, December 27, 1847 and December 27, 1848, Mabragaña, II, 179, 236; *R. O.*, II, 451.

[29] Rosas to the Legislature, May 7, 1832 and December 27, 1837, Mabragaña, I, 263, 359.

the Rivadavian régime and a prohibition of the circulation of books, pictures, engravings, and sculptured works which attacked the truth of the state religion and the divinity of Christ.[30] Such an elastic provision might easily have been so interpreted and enforced as to mean the end of the religious toleration for which Rivadavia worked. But it does not appear to have been employed in that way. In 1833 all ministers of a faith other than Catholic were required to present certificates from the proper authorities of their homelands to show evidence of good character and the purposes of immigration.[31] Protestant missionaries were thus permitted to live in Argentina although their activities might be considerably circumscribed.

Although marriage was considered to be a matter exclusively in the hands of the church, Rosas' government enacted a number of laws on that subject. These also reveal an unexpected liberality to non-Catholic residents. Early in 1833 the case of a marriage between a Catholic and a Protestant attracted the attention of the provisional legislature at Buenos Aires, and from this consideration came a general law on the subject. This comprehensive decree required the appearance of both parties to a marriage, if both were non-Catholic, before a chamber of justice. If their certificates of good character were found to be satisfactory, the judge was authorized to grant a license. The law prescribed that registers be kept for such marriages between two foreigners both being Catholic, and for deaths of non-Catholic residents.[32] Foreigners who belonged to recognized Protestant churches and who possessed the necessary consular certificates were permitted by another decree to publish the banns from the pulpits of their chapels on three successive Sundays.[33] These regulations show that Rosas was intolerant not so much of religious differences as of political opposition, which he characterized as hostility to the cause of the confederation and of God.

From the time when Argentine separation from Spain was effected, the position of the ecclesiastical courts and the scope of their jurisdiction were ill defined. In the colonial period, friction between the civil and the ecclesiastical courts was constant. When Rosas rose to preëminence, one of the desirable objects to be attained was a clarification of the jurisdiction of the state and the church in this field. In purely spiritual matters the apostolic vicar and Rosas' ministers agreed that final adjudica-

30 *R. O.*, II, 283, 284.
31 *R. O.*, II, 315.
32 *R. O.*, II, 307, 315.
33 *R. O.*, II, 319.

tion should be made in the Platean provinces.[34] This did not mean that the right to appeal cases in the ecclesiastical courts was abolished. According to a law of 1834 it was agreed that an appeal might be carried from the bishop's court to another ecclesiastic nominated by that bishop and ratified by the government. A further consideration of a case was afforded in the provision for a decision by the diocesan prelate and two members of the clerical senate proposed by the bishop and agreed to by the government.[35] These regulations were to remain the law in the diocese of Buenos Aires only in theory. No definition could be made of that which was purely spiritual, and no satisfactory distinction could be made between the civil and ecclesiastical spheres. For many years after the time of Rosas no real organization of church courts was effected, and no real agreement on their scope of authority was reached.

The dictator is usually given credit for personal honesty in so far as deriving financial gain from his position is concerned. But Rosas struggled repeatedly with monetary difficulties which necessitated curtailing expenditures wherever possible. One of these reductions affected those members of the clergy whom Rivadavia pensioned when their clerical posts were abolished. Rosas' government opened to these beneficiaries of the dole new positions, particularly rural curacies in distant Patagonia.[36]

Several issues of paper money during the rule of Rosas materially reduced the fixed obligations of the government. But this type of inflation rendered difficult the position of the honest clergy. Medrano noted that the depreciated currency brought about differences in the buying power of the fees, which the clergy asked for their religious services, from one parish to another. Some priests were detrimentally affected, but others took advantage of the situation to make exorbitant demands.[37] A commission of five ecclesiastics was named by the apostolic vicar and the government to work out a uniform schedule of fees. Their task was completed and given the status of law on February 1, 1832. The clergy was permitted to ask a sum of from twelve to forty *pesos* for interments, depending upon the age and social status of the deceased. The officiating priest was allowed three-fourths of this fee, the remainder being allocated to the parish church.[38] The framers of the law took note of the fre-

[34] *R. O.*, II, 290.
[35] Velez Sarsfield, 140.
[36] *R. O.*, II, 277.
[37] *R. O.*, II, 298-99.
[38] Rosas to the Legislature, December 27, 1838, Mabragaña, I, 391; *R. O.*, II, 299.

quency with which parties to a marriage dispensed with the nuptial mass and of the disorders and misunderstandings which proceeded from this indifference to a sacrament of the church. Civil and ecclesiastical authorities joined in attempting to remedy this situation by fixing the marriage fee at from sixteen to thirty *pesos,* four-fifths of which was to be retained by the priest. To require a fee for baptism might impose the burden of eternal damnation upon some poor native who lacked three *pesos.* Although the law established this amount as rightfully belonging to the priest for the baptism sacrament, he was cautioned to be charitable to those overburdened by the economic miseries of this life.[39]

V

In one policy, particularly, Rosas reversed the plans of his predecessor, Rivadavia. His favor to the regular orders of the clergy is emphasized by those who look upon his régime as wholly reactionary. One of his decrees ordained the reëstablishment of a Dominican monastery, thereby "repairing the injury inflicted by the unjust and violent suppression" of 1822. Padre Inchaurregui was directed to request from his superior in the order a number of monks who would be faithful to the national cause of the confederation.[40] Some years later the dictator announced to the legislature that the convent of Recollect friars was being reëstablished. This monastery, likewise, had been suppressed two decades earlier and had fallen into ruins.[41] Within a Franciscan monastery a feud broke out between two factions. According to one version the quarrel concerned the alleged scandalous conduct of certain members and resulted in mutual threats of violence. The guardian of the monastery appealed to Rosas for advice and help. The latter accomodatingly decreed the imprisonment of the culprits until arrangements for their deportation were made.[42]

In 1836 six members of the Jesuit Order, which had been outlawed in the Platean provinces for nearly seventy years, were welcomed in Argentina by the civil authorities and by the populace. Rosas, "considering that the occasion had arrived for supporting the reëstablishment in this province of the said company so respected among us for their imponderable services," granted them their former college for a lodging.

---

[39] *R. O.,* II, 299.

[40] *R. O.,* II, 355-56; Rosas to the Legislature, December 31, 1835, Mabragaña, I, 295.

[41] Rosas to the Legislature, December 27, 1838 and December 27, 1844, Mabragaña, I, 389, II, 77.

[42] Barbará, 94; *R. O.,* II, 393.

In this place they might live, according to the dictator's edict, observing their rules, welcoming their fellows from Europe, and establishing halls of learning.[43] Glad to have an excuse for his neglect of education, Rosas granted the Jesuits authority to teach Latin, Greek, mathematics, rhetoric, and law. He instructed the city architect to help them find suitable quarters, and he commanded the rector of the University of Buenos Aires to place at their disposal furniture and equipment. Another decree of the same day, December 7, 1836, conferred a monthly subsidy of four hundred and fifty *pesos* upon the new organization.[44] The educational and missionary activities of the Jesuits grew rapidly. In his annual message to the legislature in December 1837, Rosas announced that their students numbered three hundred. A year later he approved their proposal to establish missions in the *pampas*.[45] Their religious activities in the capital expanded as shown by the fact that the government gave them possession of the church of San Ignacio de Loyola. To make such arrangements Rosas arbitrarily changed parish boundaries regardless of the wishes of the priests and their parishioners.[46]

It must have been a keen disappointment to the dictator to discover that these ecclesiastics upon whom he showered so many blessings turned out to be "savage unitarians." He informed the legislature that the order had not fulfilled the hopes of the confederation and that it was hostile to the political principles of the nation.[47] Then he began and continued with persistence a campaign against them. The governor of Córdoba was informed of their alleged sedition, and when that province proceeded actively against them Rosas sent his commendation. The provinces of San Juan and Catamarca also were praised for their swift action against the Jesuits.[48] Although disloyalty was given as the crime of the order, the tyrant is said to have attempted to place the image of himself and his wife in the church of San Ignacio. The Jesuits declined to permit such sacrilege. Thereupon, Rosas expelled them on the pretext of conspiring to aid the French blockade of the Argentine coast which was proclaimed in 1838.[49]

---

[43] *R. O.*, II, 364; Rosas to the Legislature, January 1, 1837, Mabragaña, I, 316.
[44] *R. O.*, II, 366.
[45] Mabragaña, I, 357, 389.
[46] *Ibid.*, I, 389; *R. O.*, II, 393.
[47] Rosas to the Legislature, December 27, 1841, Mabragaña, II, 28.
[48] Rosas to the Legislature, December 27, 1847 and December 27, 1848, *ibid.*, II, 176, 222, 225, 227, 228.
[49] Esquivel, 189.

In connection with the French action against the dictator, the substance of an alleged decree may be of interest. In no official publication does this law appear, and hence its authenticity may be doubted, but yet it is by no means disproved. Under date of July 31, 1839, the government is said to have affirmed that since

> "this people . . . placed under the protection of the French Saint Martin, bishop of Tours, has not been successful up to the present in freeing itself from the periodic fevers . . . droughts and epidemics . . . without our patron on his part ever having made any effective and perceptible effort to free us from this horrible calamity . . . [and since] for the invasions of our frontier Indians and civil and foreign wars . . . our French patron has been tranquil in the sky without affording us the least protection as was his duty.
>
> "For these considerations it is granted and decreed: Article I: The French unitarian who has been until today patron of this city, Saint Martin, bishop of Tours . . . is separated forever from his position of patron of Buenos Aires."[50]

While Rosas may never have dictated such a law it is characteristic of the man.

The financial exigencies of the Rosas régime did not permit him to afford the aid to educational projects which Rivadavia hoped to carry out, although a decree of 1834 authorized the reopening of the College of Ecclesiastical Studies which the latter founded in 1822.[51] In 1832 the dictator sanguinely noted the continued progress of the University of Buenos Aires.[52] Three years later, the government sanctioned only such subjects as were "useful and necessary to the public cause." These included medicine, mathematics, and jurisprudence. On December 27, 1838 Rosas announced the entire withdrawal of financial support for that university.[53] Educational facilities for younger students also suffered. In December 1835 Rosas announced that the course of study for the boys' school at Buenos Aires had been altered "for the benefit of the people and the treasury." Three years later all government financial support for this institution was withdrawn.[54] It is not surprising under these circumstances that he was willing for religious organizations to assume educational responsibilities.

The Argentine treasury did not permit the dictator to subsidize the

---

[50] Barbará, 19-22.

[51] *R. O.*, II, 319.

[52] Mabragaña, I, 261.

[53] Rosas to the Legislature, December 31, 1835 and December 27, 1838, *ibid.*, I, 295, 390.

[54] *Ibid.*

building and repair of churches and cathedrals. In 1834 plans were drawn and a site chosen for a bishop's palace in the capital city, and in the following year authorization was granted for the repair of the cathedral. In neither plan was any help from the treasury guaranteed.[55] Some funds were obtained by giving public entertainments, the proceeds being applied to the expenses of repair. A play is said to have been produced in the theatre at Buenos Aires honoring the dictator, and at the same time providing money for the work on the cathedral.[56] In his messages to the legislature, Rosas repeatedly announced that progress was being made in various building plans, and with evident satisfaction added that no public funds were being used.[57]

VI

The régime of Rosas witnessed, after considerable diplomatic fencing, the establishment of formal relations between the Argentine state and the papacy. At a time when diplomatic connections between the Holy See and Spain were suspended, Pope Pius VII determined to send Juan Muzi as apostolic vicar to Chile.[58] On his way to Santiago in January 1824, Muzi visited Buenos Aires, but the Rivadavian government had no official communications with him. On his return from Chile, the papal representative established his residence at Montevideo from December 4, 1824 to February 6, 1825. Ignoring any claims or rights of the government at Buenos Aires, Muzi designated Mariano Medrano as governor of the diocese of Buenos Aires and as apostolic vicar.[59] This appointment was not recognized by the civil authorities.

On October 8, 1829, the provisional government of the Province of Buenos Aires addressed the pope on the need for a diocesan bishop, for a larger number of priests, and concerning the insufficient means for sustaining parish organizations. The government suggested two candidates for the position of bishop *in partibus infidelium,* Diego Estanislao Zavaleta and Mariano Medrano.[60] In this plea the previous designation of the second of the two candidates by the apostolic vicar was completely ignored. Pope Pius VIII had approved the nomination of Medrano by

---

[55] *R. O.,* II, 327, 346.

[56] Ricardo Levene, *Lecciones de historia argentina* (Buenos Aires, 1919), II, 367n.

[57] Rosas to the Legislature, May 7, 1832, December 31, 1835 and December 27, 1837, Mabragaña, I, 261, 295, 356.

[58] Frances H. Hendricks, *Church and state in Chile before 1891,* unpublished thesis in the library of the University of Illinois, 104ff.

[59] Esquivel, 166-70.

[60] *R. O.,* II, 277-78.

Muzi previously made, and in his reply to this appeal he expressed his pleasure that "the election of the person whom we have considered worthy of such a pious and sacred ministry has been in conformity with the desires later expressed by Your Excellency."[61] On May 10, 1830, the pope issued a rescript in which the Platean ecclesiastic was formally named apostolic delegate and bishop of Aulon.[62] In this interchange of communications the Argentine government is revealed as anxious to maintain its right to present to the pope candidates for high office, while the papacy is shown to be just as insistent in ignoring any such right on the part of the Platean state. Canon law required that Medrano be consecrated either by the pope or by his representative. He journeyed to Rio de Janeiro where the papal nuncio conducted the ceremony.[63] Upon his return, he found that the ecclesiastical council of the diocese of Buenos Aires refused to permit him to take possession of the office. A new minister of government, a tool of Rosas and an enemy of that body, brushed aside the objections as invalid, and in 1831 issued a formal decree acknowledging Medrano's appointment.[64] But the question was not fully settled. When the bulls of Pope Gergory XVI instituting Medrano as the first bishop of Buenos Aires arrived in 1832, the minister, who was to consider them, was Manuel José García, author of the *Memorial* above described. His solution of the problem was to grant a conditional exequatur upon the bulls accepting Medrano "as if he had been nominated and presented formally." But he refused to approve certain papal assertions directed against the national patronage.[65] By diplomatic evasions the papacy and the government of Rosas succeeded in agreeing upon a bishop for Buenos Aires. A *modus vivendi* was established which was to be repeatedly employed for a century to come.

The dictator's personal attention to the diplomatic negotiations with the papacy was probably not great. He seems to have left the task of formulating legal evasions to others. His primary aim was to perpetuate his own power. For this end he sought to fill ecclesiastical offices and make the priesthood an agency for his own propaganda. With this object in view he fostered elaborate religious ceremonies and established a rigid censorship. He aided the religious orders and welcomed the Jesuits, for this policy was popular with the masses. Finally his ministers adopted a clever course with regard to the papacy. The establish-

61 As quoted in Esquivel, 172.
62 *R. O.*, II, 278.
63 Zinny, I, 285.
64 *R. O.*, II, 284, 282.
65 *R. O.*, II, 321.

ment of relations with the Holy See restored to the Argentine people their religious father whom they had never repudiated. On the other hand, by attaching conditions to the resumption of relations with the papacy the growing nationalist sentiment of Argentinians was not injured. It is a tribute to Rosas' political acumen that during the more than twenty years of his rule he did not, as some modern dictators have done, violate the powerful religious sentiments of his people.

INDEX

Prepared by Raul d'Eça